KU-199-880

ENCOUNTERING THE EVERYDAY

Also by Michael Hviid Jacobsen:

The Contemporary Goffman (ed., 2009)
Public Sociology (ed., 2008)
The Sociology of Zygmunt Bauman (ed. with P. Poder, 2008)
Bauman Beyond Postmodernity (with S. Marshman and K. Tester, 2007)
Bauman Before Postmodernity (with K. Tester, 2005)
Erving Goffman (with S. Kristiansen, 2002)
The Transformation of Modernity (ed. with M. Carleheden, 2001)

Encountering the Everyday

An Introduction to the Sociologies of the Unnoticed

Michael Hviid Jacobsen

Associate Professor of Sociology, Aalborg University

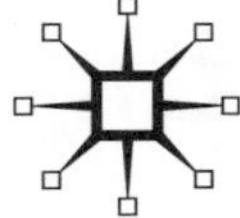

First published 2009 by
PALGRAVE MACMILLAN
Houndmills, Basingstoke, Hampshire RG21 6XS and
175 Fifth Avenue, New York, N.Y. 10010
Companies and representatives throughout the world

PALGRAVE MACMILLAN is the global academic imprint of the Palgrave Macmillan division of St. Martin's Press, LLC and of Palgrave Macmillan Ltd. Macmillan® is a registered trademark in the United States, United Kingdom and other countries. Palgrave is a registered trademark in the European Union and other countries.

ISBN-13: 978-0-230-20122-4 hardback
ISBN-10: 0-230-20122-9 hardback
ISBN-13: 978-0-230-20123-1 paperback
ISBN-10: 0-230-20123-7 paperback

This book is printed on paper suitable for recycling and made from fully managed and sustained forest sources. Logging, pulping and manufacturing processes are expected to conform to the environmental regulations of the country of origin.

A catalogue record for this book is available from the British Library.

A catalog record for this book is available from the Library of Congress.

10 9 8 7 6 5 4 3 2 1
18 17 16 15 14 13 12 11 10 09

Printed and bound in China

To Camilla
whose well-being consumes my thoughts every day

Contents

List of Contributors

Ann-Dorte Christensen (b. 1954) is Professor at the Department of Sociology, Social Work and Organisation, Aalborg University, Denmark. Current fields of research are everyday life, gender studies, social movements, global/local citizenship and belonging and political narratives. Among her publications in English are *Equal Democracies? Gender and Politics in the Nordic Countries* (co-author, 1999), 'The Danish gender models: between movement politics and representative politics' (2004), 'Young women's attitudes towards feminism and gender equality' (2008) and 'Gender, class and family: men and gender equality in a Danish context' (with Jørgen Elm Larsen, 2008).

Norman K. Denzin (b. 1941) is Distinguished Professor of Communications and Research Professor of Communications, Cinema Studies, Sociology, Criticism and Interpretive Theory at the Sociology Department, University of Illinois, United States. His academic interests include interpretive theory, performance studies, qualitative research methodology and the study of media, culture and society. He is the author, co-author or co-editor of over 50 books and 200 professional articles and chapters. His publications include *The Cinematic Society* (1995), *Interpretive Ethnography* (1996), *Interpretive Interactionism* (2001), *Reading Race* (2002), *Performance Ethnography* (2003), *Flags in the Window* (2007), *Searching for Yellowstone* (2008) and he is co-editor of the *Handbook of Qualitative Research.*

Michael E. Gardiner (b. 1961) is Professor at the Department of Sociology, University of Western Ontario, Canada. His research interests focus especially on dialogical social theory, ethics, everyday life and utopianism. Publications include *The Dialogics of Critique: M. M. Bakhtin and the Theory of Ideology* (1992), *Critiques of Everyday Life* (2000), *Mikhail Bakhtin: Masters of Modern Social Thought* (4 vols, 2003), *Bakhtin and the Human Sciences: No Last Words* (edited with Michael M. Bell, 1998) and *Rethinking Everyday Life: And Nothing Turned Itself Inside Out*, a special double issue of *Cultural Studies* (edited with Gregory J. Seigworth, 2004).

Stephen Hester (b. 1947) is Professor of Sociology, Bangor University, United

Kingdom. His interests are in ethnomethodology, conversation analysis and membership categorization analysis. Previous publications include *Deviance in Classrooms* (with David Hargeaves and Frank Mellor, 1975), *A Sociology of Crime* (with Peter Eglin, 1992), *Local Educational Order* (co-edited with David Francis, 2000), *Language, Interaction and National Identity* (co-edited with William Housley, 2002), *The Montreal Massacre: A Story of Membership Categorization Analysis* (with Peter Eglin, 2003), *An Invitation to Ethnomethodology* (with David Francis, 2004), *Orders of Ordinary Action* (co-edited with David Francis, 2007), and *Descriptions of 'Deviance'* (forthcoming).

David Inglis (b. 1973) is Professor of Sociology at the University of Aberdeen, United Kingdom. He writes in the areas of social theory and the sociology of culture. He has particular research interests in the history of social thought, the sociology of aesthetics and the cultural sociology of globalization and globality. He is editor of the journal *Cultural Sociology* and has published a number of books including *Culture and Everyday Life* (2005) and *Confronting Culture: Sociological Vistas* (2003).

Michael Hviid Jacobsen (b. 1971) is Associate Professor, PhD and Director of Studies of Sociology at the Department of Sociology, Social Work and Organisation, Aalborg University, Denmark. For several years he has written on everyday life sociology and conducted studies especially of death and dying with an everyday life perspective. Publications in English include *The Transformation of Modernity* (edited with Mikael Carleheden, 2001), *Erving Goffman* (with Søren Kristiansen, 2002), *Bauman Before Postmodernity* (with Keith Tester, 2005), *Bauman Beyond Postmodernity* (with Sophia Marshman and Keith Tester, 2007), *The Sociology of Zygmunt Bauman* (edited with Poul Poder, 2008) and *The Contemporary Goffman* (edited, 2009).

Anja Jørgensen (b. 1969) is PhD and Associate Professor at the Department of Sociology, Social Work and Organisation, Aalborg University, Denmark. Her research interests are local communities in transition and in terms of theory she is inspired by the Chicago School. Her publications include *De fattige og udstødte i Aalborg by* (1998), *Filantropi, selvhjælp og interesseorganisering* (co-editor, 2001), *Når kvarteret opdager sig selv* (2006), *Håndværk og Horisonter* (co-editor, 2007) and *Betingelser for fællesskab* (with Anne-Kirstine Mølholt, 2007).

Joseph A. Kotarba (b. 1947) is Professor of Sociology at the University of Houston, Texas, United States. His two major areas of study are the sociology of health and the sociology of culture. He is currently examining the social dimensions of occupational illness and injury, specifically among professional athletes and the social meanings of Latino music in America. Publications include *The Social Meanings of Chronic Pain* (1983), *The Existential Self and Society* (edited with Andrea Fontana, 1984), *Postmodern Existential Sociology* (edited with John M. Johnson, 2002), *Growing Old with Rock 'n' Roll* (2008) and *Understanding Society through Music* (edited with Phillip Vannini, 2008).

Søren Kristiansen (b. 1971) is Associate Professor, PhD and Head of Department at the Department of Sociology, Social Work and Organisation, Aalborg University, Denmark. His main research interests are social problems, gambling, research ethics and computer assisted qualitative data analysis. His publications include *Deltagende observation* (with Hanne Katrine Krogstrup, 1998), *Farligt feltarbejde* (with Michael Hviid Jacobsen, 2001), *Erving Goffman* (with Michael Hviid Jacobsen, 2002), *Hverdagslivet* (edited with Michael Hviid Jacobsen, 2005) and *Kvalitativ dataanalyse og software* (2005).

Søren Overgaard (b. 1973) has a PhD in Philosophy and is RCUK Academic Fellow and Lecturer at the University of Hull, United Kingdom. He has two main research areas: the philosophy of mind, broadly construed, and philosophical method. He is the author of *Husserl and Heidegger on Being in the World* (2004) and *Wittgenstein and Other Minds: Rethinking Subjectivity and Intersubjectivity with Wittgenstein, Levinas and Husserl* (2007), and co-editor of *Subjectivity and Transcendence* (with Arne Grøn and Iben Damgaard, 2007).

Poul Poder (b. 1965) is PhD and Assistant Professor of Sociology as the University of Copenhagen, Denmark. His general research interests include social theory, sociology of emotion and organisations and power. His PhD thesis is entitled *Feelings of Power and the Power of Feelings: Handling Emotion in Organisational Change* (2004). More recent publications include 'Relatively liquid inter-personal relationships in flexible work life' (2007), *The Sociology of Zygmunt Bauman* (edited with Michael Hviid Jacobsen, 2008) and 'The political regulation of anger in organizations' (2008).

Robert C. Prus (b. 1946) is Professor at the Department of Sociology, University of Waterloo, Canada. A symbolic interactionist, pragmatist ethnographer and social theorist, he is currently tracing the developmental flows of pragmatist thought from the classical Greek era to the present time. Publications include *Road Hustler* (with C. R. D. Sharper, 1977), *Hookers, Rounders and Desk Clerks* (with Styllianoss Irini, 1980), *Making Sales* (1989), *Pursuing Customers* (1989), *Symbolic Interaction and Ethnographic Research* (1996), *Subcultural Mosaics and Intersubjective Realities* (1997), *Beyond the Power Mystique* (1999) and *The Deviant Mystique* (with Scott Grills, 2003).

Antony J. Puddephatt (b. 1975) is an Assistant Professor in the Department of Sociology at Lakehead University, Canada. His research interests include sociological theory, particularly the social thought of George Herbert Mead, the sociology of science and technology and ethnographic research methods. His publications include articles in *Social Epistemology, Symbolic Interaction, Sociological Focus, Studies in Symbolic Interaction, American Sociologist, Qualitative Sociology Review* and *Sociological Quarterly.*

Derek Schilling (b. 1969) is Associate Professor of French and Cinema Studies at Rutgers University, United States. His publications include a monograph on literary aesthetics, memory and the sociology of everydayness in the work of Georges Perec (*Mémoires du quotidien: les lieux de Perec*, 2006) and a comprehensive study of film-maker Eric Rohmer (*Eric Rohmer*, 2007). His current research focuses on interwar literary representations of the Paris suburbs in relation to the discourse of modern town planning.

Dennis Smith (b. 1945) is Professor of Sociology, Head of the Department of Social Sciences at Loughborough University, United Kingdom, and editor of *Current Sociology.* He has researched and written on historical sociology, the development of cities and social theory. He has written several articles, chapters and books including *Conflict and Compromise: Class Formation in English Society 1830–1914* (1982), *Barrington Moore: Violence, Morality and Social Change* (1983), *The Chicago School* (1988), *Capitalist Democracy on Trial: The Transatlantic Debate from Tocqueville to the Present* (1990), *The Rise of Historical Sociology* (1991), *Zygmunt Bauman: Prophet of Postmodernity* (1999), *Norbert Elias and Modern Social Theory* (2000) and *Globalization: The Hidden Agenda* (2006).

Paul ten Have (b. 1937) was, until his retirement in 2002, Associate Professor of Sociology at the Department of Sociology and Anthropology of the University of Amsterdam, the Netherlands. He has written numerous articles and several books on qualitative research, ethnomethodology and conversation analysis. Recent publications include *Understanding Qualitative Research and Ethnomethodology* (2004), 'On the interactive constitution of medical encounters' (2006) and *Doing Conversation Analysis: A Practical Guide*, 2nd edn (2007).

Phillip Vannini (b. 1974) is Assistant Professor of Communication and Culture at Royal Roads University in Victoria, BC, Canada. He is editor of *Body/Embodiment: Symbolic Interactionism and the Sociology of the Body* (2006), *Material Culture and Technology in Everyday Life: Ethnographic Approaches* (forthcoming), *Authenticity in Self, Culture and Society* (forthcoming), and co-author of *Music in the Sociological Imagination* (2008). His articles on social semiotic themes have appeared in such journals as *Symbolic Interaction, Studies in Symbolic Interaction, Social Psychology Quarterly, Sociological Focus, Qualitative Inquiry* and *Critical Discourse Studies.*

Dennis D. Waskul (b. 1969) is Assistant Professor of Sociology at Minnesota State University, Mankato, United States. He is author of *Self-Games and Body-Play* (2003), editor of *net.seXXX* (2004) and co-editor of *Body/Embodiment* (2006). He has published numerous articles and book chapters in areas of sexualities, sociology of the body, sociology of the senses, computer-mediated communications and fantasy role-playing games. He has also held numerous executive positions in the Society for the Study of Symbolic Interaction and is currently an associate editor for the journal *Symbolic Interaction.*

Dan Zahavi (b. 1967) is Professor of Philosophy and Director of the Center for Subjectivity Research, University of Copenhagen, Denmark. He is mainly working on themes related to self, self-experience and social cognition. Publications include *Intentionalität und Konstitution* (1992), *Self-Awareness and Alterity* (1999), *Husserl and Transcendental Intersubjectivity* (2001), *Husser's Phenomenology* (2003), *Subjectivity and Selfhood* (2005), *Phänomenologie für Einsteiger* (2007) and The *Phenomenological Mind* (with Shaun Gallagher, 2008).

Acknowledgements

Once, Umberto Eco, in his wonderful *How to Travel with a Salmon and Other Essays*, stated: 'It can sometimes happen that a scholar, his task completed, discovers that he has no one to thank. Never mind. He will invent some debts. Research without indebtedness is suspect, and somebody must always, somehow, be thanked.' No debts or acknowledgements, however, had to be artificially conjured up or invented in connection to the completion of this book. Many people were involved in the process and many people deserve my unreserved gratitude.

First of all, thanks to all the authors whose invaluable contributions illustrate a genuine, ongoing and die-hard concern with all the exciting facets –even the most infinitesimal and unnoticed – of everyday life. My thanks also go to my friend and colleague for many years, Søren Kristiansen, who several years ago joined me on the journey of charting the map of everyday life. I also wish to extend my gratitude to Emily Salz at Palgrave Macmillan for taking a keen and sincere interest in this book from start to finish and for recognizing the importance of the project. And thanks to the many wonderful and insightful students from the Sociology Program at Aalborg University whose continuous interest in and curiosity regarding everyday life sparked me to write this book in the first place. Finally, on a more personal note, my unreserved thanks to Ann and Nicklas for accepting that our everyday life was sometimes postponed or diluted during the process of completing this book. The waiting is now over.

Michael Hviid Jacobsen
Aalborg University, Denmark

Introduction

The Everyday: An Introduction to an Introduction

Michael Hviid Jacobsen

> The task is not so much to see what no one yet has seen, but to think what nobody yet has thought about that which everyone sees.
>
> Arthur Schopenhauer, *The World as Will and Representation*

> We want to be the poets of our life, first of all in the smallest and most commonplace matters.
>
> Friedrich Nietzsche, *The Gay Science*

Encountering the unnoticed

One of my local banks recently advertised at bus stops around the city with the bold and colourful message: *The everyday is the most important!* Despite the unquestionable monetary motives behind this advertisement, I must agree – everyday life *is* important to most if not all of us, as bank customers but equally as ordinary participants in, as well as sociological investigators of, everyday life. To me and my fellow contributors in this book, everyday life is indeed deserving of special sociological attention exactly because it provides us with an important entry into or prism through which more comprehensive, general and foundational aspects of modern social life can be studied. Everyday life constitutes one of the most obvious arenas for researching and accessing a multitude of phenomena, processes and problems of social life because it is 'just there', it is accessible and it is something with which we are all familiar. However, whether it is *the* most important aspect of social life, as boldly proclaimed by the banking company, I will leave to the reader's discretion to decide.

The importance and obviousness of everyday life notwithstanding, it is a difficult domain – also for sociologists – to grapple with and grasp. Thus, Alvin W. Gouldner accurately described how everyday life 'is the pedestrian and mundane life that is so commonly recurrent that its participants scarcely notice it. EDL [everyday life] is the seen-but-unnoticed life' (1975: 422). Another of the greats of sociology, Harold Garfinkel (1967: 41), remarked how people continuously uphold and 'furnish a background of seen but unnoticed features' of everyday life, whereby everyday life is made understandable, meaningful and safe. Everyday life is indeed something that is 'just there', something unnoticed and something we hardly ever – unless nosy and obnoxious sociologists persist to pressurize us – think about or contemplate. Everyday life belongs to the largely neglected realm of the familiar, taken-for-granted, common sense and trivial – in short, the unnoticed. Hence the subtitle of this book: *An Introduction to the Sociologies of the Unnoticed*.

The intention of this book is ambitious: to make the unnoticed noticed, to sociologists as well as to everybody else. This, however, is easier said than done. Maurice Blanchot hit the nail on the head concerning the inherent difficulties associated with comprehending and approaching everyday life as an area or object of social research when insisting that 'whatever its other aspects, the everyday has this essential trait: it allows no hold. It escapes' (1987: 14). Despite such difficulties, everyday life, at least in sociology, has not entirely escaped attention, although its fates and fortunes have fluctuated considerably, to which I return more substantially later. Suffice to establish initially, the vast bulk of books devoted to and published on everyday life within sociology appeared in a pioneering period from the late 1960s to the early 1980s (for some of the most prominent examples, see, for example, Birenbaum and Sagarin 1973; Douglas 1970a; Douglas et al. 1980; McCall and Simmons 1966; Morris 1977; Strauss 1969; Truzzi 1968 and Weigert 1981). After this early period of rapid expansion and unprecedented attention, everyday life gradually moved into the wings, or perhaps rather attempted to consolidate its newly gained foothold in sociology, before in recent years making a triumphant and glorious reappearance.

For many years, however, everyday life was not seen as a legitimate scientific or career-improving concern of sociologists – it was trivial, banal and ordinary (in the worst sense of these terms) – and henceforth it was regarded, at best with shrugs of the shoulders, or at worst with ill-concealed contempt and suspicion. Consequently, very few sociologists consciously made a career out of investigating the everyday. However, in their personal meditations on everyday life, Andrew Metcalfe and Ann Game (2002) as well as Thomas Moore (1996) aptly illustrated how the everyday is, in fact, far from trivial and tedious. In their poetic description, they showed the all-embracing human experiences such as wonder, grace and joy, but also sorrow, despair and sacrifice, as part and parcel of our everyday worlds. They also show, however, how everyday life can be and increasingly is eroded and how a re-enchantment and rediscovery of the everyday is of paramount importance, in sociology and elsewhere. In short, everyday life embodies and evokes ambivalence, not just in how it is lived and experienced by 'ordinary' people, but also in the way it is approached by sociologists. Therefore, it makes us wonder why the everyday was almost routinely neglected, overlooked or scorned by many factions of conventional sociology.

One major reason for the neglect of the everyday world as a field worthy of scientific status and relevance in its own right should, according to David A. Karp and William A. Yoels, presumably be attributed to the pronounced desire among many sociologists to imitate the natural sciences and their predilection for precise measurement of variables and the testing of hypotheses. In this respect, the world of everyday life proved a difficult testing ground and a phenomenon almost impossible to quantify. Another probable reason for the neglect of everyday life among sociologists can be ascribed to their long-standing preference for investigating areas and issues with obvious social policy implications, 'which might persuade the public that sociologists have something to say about "important" issues' (Karp and Yoels 1993: 26). Everyday life, in this respect, has been regarded as a non-institutional, non-political and therefore also non-important topic to study. Everyday life, due to its supposedly unscientific, pre-scientific and rather common sense nature, has therefore for a long period of time been seen as inferior to more rigorous research into 'hardcore' scientific matters such as formal institutions, voting behaviour, class mobility, structural change, social and economic inequality and political movements (see Douglas 1970b).

From a specifically Danish perspective, yet with wider implications, Torben Berg Sørensen once provided a possible, and credible, answer to why and how the 'big-scale sociology' (that is, Marxism, structuralism and functionalism) had succeeded in monopolizing the discipline at the expense of 'small-scale sociology' (that is, everyday life sociologies):

> In most countries, big-scale sociology remains the most prominent. In this respect, Denmark is no exception to the rule – the already sparse attention dedicated to sociology as such in Denmark is almost exclusively oriented towards big-scale sociology, which has been concerned with the living conditions of different groups in society and with inequality, with the relationship between economic, social and political development and other 'big' issues, whereas small-scale sociology has almost been overlooked and forgotten.
>
> (Berg Sørensen 1991: 9)

Berg Sørensen termed this tendency 'the macro illusion'. And true, for many years this scenario was indeed the case, in Denmark, where this introduction was written, as well as elsewhere. However, in recent years, as we shall see throughout this book, everyday life sociology, or 'small-scale' sociology as Berg

Sørensen somewhat inaccurately calls it, has received renewed attention, and once again tops the research agendas of ever-new generations of sociologists eager to explore the unnoticed aspects of social life. Moreover, this book will also show how everyday life and quotidian existence has, in fact, been a recurring and ubiquitous, yet often unnoticed, presence in many sociological theories, traditions and perspectives all along.

The revival of the everyday

As this book will show, despite historical fluctuations, the everyday has been – and increasingly become – part and parcel of sociology for at least the last 100 years. Actually, the very first sociology department in the world, established in 1892 at the University of Chicago, developed and sustained a special attention to the everyday experiences of people living in the new urban megalopolises sprouting all over the American continent at the threshold of the 20th century. Despite the work of these early inspirational Chicagoans, the everyday remained virtually absent from and was neglected in most sociology textbooks, courses and academic journals for the better part of the first half of the 20th century. The everyday as a topic deserving sociological attention required years of maturation until, from the late 1960s onwards, it began to attract more widespread attention and recognition in sociology. As Michel de Certeau observed in the preface to his *The Practice of Everyday Life* on the change of perspective that increasingly began to privilege the everyday:

> The floodlights have moved away from the actors who possess proper names and social blazons, turning first toward the chorus of secondary characters, then settling on the mass of the audience. The increasingly sociological and anthropological perspective of inquiry privileges the anonymous and the everyday in which zoom lenses cut out metonymic details – parts taken for the whole.
>
> (de Certeau 1988: v)

By privileging and emphasizing everyday life in sociology, by eschewing many of the abstractions and academic circumbendibus associated with previously dominant positivist, functionalist and structuralist positions, a new and refreshing perspective on society and social organization gradually began to emerge and, as Alf Lüdtke asserted, in the 'studies of the everyday toil and festive joys of men and women, the young and the old, individuals [began to] emerge as actors on the social stage' (1995: 4). With the rise of various everyday life sociologies in the latter part of the 20th century, a shift in the focus of sociology from the so-called 'orthodox consensus' and its privileging of quantitative methods and macro-oriented research agendas to more micro-oriented and creative areas and methods of research was well underway. Perhaps – at least from a broader sociological perspective – the rise of everyday life sociologies in the United States in the 1960s and 1970s is of paramount importance in this change of perspective because it inspired many later developments elsewhere, especially in Europe. Of the atmosphere of this embryonic coming to life of North American everyday life sociologies in the late 1960s, it has been observed:

> It emerged in an atmosphere, especially in California, of eclectic synthesis and excitement about the creation and synthesis of new ideas. Everyday life was also nurtured and shaped by the surrounding background of California's secularism, heterogeneous beliefs and pluralistic subcultures, fostering an atmosphere of innovation, divergence and freedom. From Berkeley, use of the everyday life perspective spread to other departments of the University of California system, where compatible thinkers were located .... While a unified concept remained, no movement developed to press for the identification and recognition of all this work under the everyday life rubric. As a result, individual practitioners chose freely from among the various theories, used and combined them as they saw fit, and made their own decisions as to whether they wanted to affiliate themselves with the everyday life label.
>
> (Adler, Adler and Fontana 1987: 221–2)

These heydays of everyday life sociologies throughout the 1960s and 1970s saw an explosion of interest in mundane topics, and in detailed empirical studies of various sections and especially subcultures, counter-cultures or deviant groups within society with an everyday life perspective. In this wave of pioneering excitement about the 'discovery' of the world of the everyday, some even went as far as describing everyday life as the very foundation and *raison d'être* of sociology, thereby perhaps – although in a topsy-turvy manner – committing a fallacy as grievous as that described above as 'the macro illusion'. Jack D. Douglas, at least in principle, came dangerously close to committing what could be termed 'the everyday illusion' when he courageously and programmatically proclaimed:

> All of sociology necessarily begins with the understanding of everyday life, and all of sociology is directed either to increasing our understanding of everyday life or, more practically, to improving our everyday lives .... Sociology, like all disciplines that purport to be theoretical and applied sciences of human action, necessarily begins and ends with the understanding of everyday life.
>
> (Douglas 1970b: 3)

Obviously, such excitement, support and unreserved privileging of the everyday must be seen against a social-scientific canvas on which everyday life had been seen, at best, as an irrelevant pastime, and at worst, as an embarrassment and inferior preoccupation for 'real' scientists – a phenomenon whose annoying presence and mentioning merely added to the, at the time, rapidly expanding 'inferiority complex' among many sociologists (Machlup 1956).

This emerging interest in the everyday, at least in the United States, also struck a chord and found common ground with the flourishing sociological radicalism at the time (Crook 1998: 523). With the coming of the 1980s, in which sociology in many places found itself 'in the doldrums' (Collins 1986), with the waning of student radicalism, with sociology politically disfavoured and with an increased focus on more macro-oriented topics, the interest in everyday life sociology did perhaps not disappear, but the inspirational novelty and intensity from the heyday gradually wore off. At the same time, however, the everyday tradition became increasingly diversified, and the relative consensus from the 1960s and 1970s dissolved into a variety of distinct perspectives and competing positions (see Adler et al. 1987). During the latter part of the 1990s, however, the everyday once again regained momentum, perhaps as a corollary of the renewed interest in qualitative sociology, and although there is no necessary or naturally given connection between everyday life sociology and qualitative methods, a discernible affinity between everyday life approaches and a preference for qualitative methodology has persisted throughout the years. Perhaps conducting qualitative research is, in itself, an everyday activity, so that scholars with a propensity to work with qualitative methods use the vicissitudes and experiences of their own everyday lives to carry out research and vice versa? (See Glassner and Hertz 1999.) Unsurprisingly, the interest in everyday life and the interest in qualitative sociology have continued to mutually reinforce each other throughout the years.

What has happened since the turn of the millennium is that the interest in the everyday, so prominent especially on the American continent in the late 1960s and early 1970s, has now been rediscovered by new generations of sociologists. Thus, in recent years, a revival of and renewed interest in the everyday in sociology and related disciplines can be witnessed – a revival accompanied by torrents of new literature containing innovative theoretical treatment, conceptual development, groundbreaking empirical investigation and a return to and rereading of many of the classical texts from the heyday of everyday life sociology.

Whereas the mushrooming of everyday life sociologies in the late 1960s coincided with a general proliferation of sub-divisions and many other new areas of research in sociology, today it seems as if the everyday has finally been established as a field of research in its own right, and the last few years have shown a heretofore unseen outpouring of sociology books dedicated specifically to everyday life (see, for example, Bennett and Watson 2002a; Gardiner 2000; Highmore 2002a, 2002b; Moran 2005; Roberts 2006; Sheringham 2006).[1] As a consequence of this renewed interest, Michael E. Gardiner observed (or perhaps even warned) how 'the trickle of new scholarly work that marked a renewal of interest in "everyday life", which began in earnest some six or eight years ago (at least in the Anglo-American world), now threatens to turn into a flood' (2008).

The reasons for this recent remarkable revival are many, and may be sought outside as well as inside the confines of sociology itself. One possible explanation, locating the answer in external social conditions and changes, would claim that, due to unprecedented amounts of leisure time and equally unprecedented economic prosperity today, people increasingly take an interest in designing and living out their everyday lives in ways unavailable to previous generations – an interest mirrored in and accentuated by sociologists' writings and analyses. Another explanation, looking at the theoretical interior of sociology itself, would claim that the discipline in recent years has experienced something of an epistemic rupture – evident in the extensive interest in topics such as individualization, life politics, reflexivity and identity – and thereby has increasingly been colonized by more micro-oriented perspectives such as, for example, everyday life sociologies. Many more possible and plausible explanations could be offered, but the 'right' answer probably contains a combination of these different explanations. Such explanations notwithstanding, everyday life sociologies today flourish in an unprecedented fashion, and this becomes evident when scanning the amount of journal articles published, the content of title catalogues from publishing houses and the topics of international conferences and seminars, not to mention the interest taken by students in their reports and projects in everyday life theories and themes.[2]

However, despite recent renewed attention from scholars and academics, everyday life is in fact as old as society itself, and theorizing about or contemplating the everyday can be traced as far back as debates between ancient Greek philosophers and dramatists, in which Plato's contempt for the humdrum 'upside-down existence' of the cave dwellers was matched by Euripides's valorisation of the underworld of everyday life (see Gouldner 1975).[3] Moreover, a prolonged interest in writing and elaborating on the everyday, although not as an object of scientific scrutiny or curiosity in itself, can be discerned from medieval Christianity to Enlightenment philosophy (Felski 1999–2000).

Although everyday life is as old as human society and has existed in all known cultures and societies:

> everyday life is a relatively recent invention. The concept does not make its

> first appearance in social thought until the 1920s, while its emergence as a recognized area of inquiry in sociology is limited largely to the period after the Second World War.
>
> (Bennett and Watson 2002b: x)

Tony Bennett and Diane Watson continue by stating how the concept of the everyday at first found its way into Western social thought especially through the work of Georg Lukács and later Georg Simmel, who inspired scholars on the American and European continents alike to undertake investigations of the multiplicity of mundane aspects of social life – in Lukács's own case ranging from elucidation of the commodification of everyday life to class struggles in capitalist society, and in Simmel's case from the mental life of metropolitan inhabitants to the sociology of the meal. So whereas everyday life sociology was for many years primarily associated with North American sociology, its breeding ground was in fact Continental European social thought in the first half of the 20th century. In the decades following the 1960s and 1970s American revival of everyday life sociology, the everyday began to find its way back into many European social research contexts. Thus, separate chapters in this book deal with how everyday life perspectives, as part of the more widespread revival of everyday life sociology, developed in a specifically Scandinavian context, in a German/Continental European context and in a French context.

Due to this overwhelming popularity of and expansion in writings and theories dealing with the everyday throughout the last decades, everyday life has turned into a central concern of many sociologists or schools of thought. This made Norbert Elias comment on the potential fate of the everyday when it increasingly becomes appropriated by sociologists:

> Not so long ago, the concept of everyday life could be used in an ordinary, everyday way. One could talk in all innocence of 'the way things happen in everyday life' without pausing to wonder what 'everyday life' might actually mean. But now the concept of the everyday has become anything but everyday: it is loaded with the freight of theoretical reflection, and in this form it has become a key concept for a number of schools of contemporary sociology.
>
> (Elias 1998: 166–7)

Alvin W. Gouldner even went as far as claiming that 'the everyday' was in fact, already at the outset, an academic construction and invention because 'EDL [everyday life], after all, is not an ordinary concept but an extraordinary one; the concept of EDL was not concerted by "ordinary" men but by "extraordinary" men: intellectuals' (1975: 418). In a similar vein, Rita Felski mused how 'the everyday ceases to be everyday when it is subject to critical scrutiny' (1999–2000: 215). Thus, despite its mundane connotations, everyday life is in fact something that is abstracted, objectified, exoticized and made measurable and extraordinary because it has increasingly become part and parcel of the conceptual and theoretical toolbox of academic disciplines, including sociology. And this is exactly what this book is all about – how a variety of everyday life sociologies make the everyday an object of scientific scrutiny and a realm of study (see also Jacobsen and Kristiansen 2005). But what is this everyday life that has attracted so much renewed attention from sociologists?

What is 'the everyday'?

As shown above, the concept of everyday is – or has become – anything but everyday. Although we tend to use it almost indiscriminately, the everyday is indeed a complex and fuzzy phenomenon loaded with meaning, while at the same time it seems deceivingly trivial and tangible. In fact, 'the everyday' is almost overloaded with meaning. Moreover, exactly because we tend to take the everyday for granted, because we refrain from reflecting upon it unless asked by an inquisitive sociologist, it is difficult, if often not downright impossible, to articulate what we actually mean by 'the everyday'.

There is widespread agreement among sociologists that everyday life is indeed difficult to capture, delimit and define, and that 'the everyday' therefore continues to occupy an uncertain ontological position within the social sciences. Rita Felski therefore admitted how 'those who use the term ["everyday life"] are often reluctant to explain exactly what it means .... Everyday life is rarely taken under the microscope and scrutinized as a concept ... . As a term, everyday life remains strangely amorphous' (1999–2000: 15–17). Norbert Elias also remarked how the concept of 'the everyday', as it is used by sociologists today, 'is anything but homogeneous. It shimmers with many colours, has numerous meanings with a whole spectrum of undertones' (1998: 167). Similarly, Harold Garfinkel, during the heyday of everyday life sociologies, stated that:

> although sociologists take socially structured scenes of everyday life as a point of departure they rarely see, as a task of sociological inquiry in its own right, the general questions of how any such world is possible. Instead, the possibility of the everyday world is either settled by theoretical representation or merely assumed.
>
> (Garfinkel 1967: 36)

Following in the footsteps of Alfred Schutz, as did Garfinkel, many other scholars have subsequently observed how the concept, category or experience of the everyday is in fact problematic (see, for example, Heller 1986; Smith 1987; Koev 2002). From time to time, it may prove problematic for people living everyday life, but it is also problematic for sociologists trying to approach and grasp the entity of the everyday. Mike Featherstone observed how the difficulties of defining and delimiting the everyday are because 'everyday life is the life-world which provides the ultimate ground from which spring all our conceptualizations, definitions and narratives'. At the same time, the everyday also 'appears to be a residual category into which can be jettisoned all the irritating bits and pieces which do not fit into orderly thought' (Featherstone 1992: 160). In this way, the everyday escapes rigid classification because it is so enormously encompassing, yet at the same time it remains wide open to theoretical interpretation and construction, because we can attribute all the fragments not fitting elsewhere to everyday life. Despite its problematic and complex status, there are, however, many ways to attempt to arrest or capture the everyday. We can look at its semantics, its definitions, its antonyms, its theoretical/typological conceptualizations and so on. Let us try out some of these options.

Looking at everyday life semantically, it may be said to consist of two basic elements, two words – the 'everyday' and 'life' – and thus everyday life is first and foremost something that is *lived* on a *daily* basis; one could say that everyday life is *lived out*. Everyday life is also something – a part of reality – that is *carved out* by people creating or constructing life in everyday environments. Likewise, the everyday as phenomenon is carved out also by the sociologist, and therefore sociologists of everyday life are interested in where it is lived, how it is lived, why it is lived, with whom it is lived, when it is lived, and so on – all those obnoxious questions that only those who take something seriously can pose.

Another way to approach the problematic concept of the everyday is by looking at its synonyms, the 'grammar' of the everyday, as it were (see Sandywell 2004: 161–6). Frequently evoked synonyms – some more appropriate than others – for everyday life are 'daily life', the 'mundane world', 'prosaic existence', 'private life', 'ordinary life', 'quotidian life', 'the salient', 'the life-world', and Harold Garfinkel (1988) poetically proposed the term 'immortal ordinary society', but all these synonyms, like the everyday concept itself, in themselves entail as much confusion as clarification. Perhaps formal and abstract definitions of the 'everyday' are more useful? As Kolyo Koev asserted, 'there may be different definitions of everyday life: broader or narrower, with a higher or lower level of abstraction, each of the constituting an element of a possible more comprehensive theory of everyday life. And each of the having its validity' (2002: 57).

Examples of such valid formal definitions are by Danish sociologist Birte Bech-Jørgensen, who defined everyday life as 'the life which we live, sustain and renew, recreate and transform every day' (1994: 17). Maurice Blanchot elaborated and specified further by claiming that 'in its first approximation, the everyday is what we are first of all, and most often: at work, at leisure, awake, asleep, in the street, in private existence. The everyday, then, is ourselves, ordinarily' (1987: 12). Henri Lefebvre stated that 'the everyday is therefore the most universal and the most unique condition, the most social and the most individuated, the most obvious and the best hidden' (1987: 9). And Guy Debord went as far as claiming that the everyday 'is the measure of all things' (in Felski 1999–2000: 15).

Although all such definitions or approximations take us some way in explicating what the 'everyday' means, they are, however, somewhat programmatic and seem to conceal as much as they reveal. As yet an alternative route to illuminating what can be meant by 'the everyday', it is sometimes – through antonyms – more fruitful to contrast it with that which is not 'everyday'. Norbert Elias stated that, in order to comprehend and capture the everyday, we need to look at that which is *not* regarded as everyday. He provided a useful inventory of notions of the 'non-everyday' in order to enhance and focus our understanding of the everyday by suggesting the following antithetical activities or domains to everyday life:

- The everyday *as opposed to* holiday (feast day).
- Everyday = routine *as opposed to* extraordinary areas of society not subject to routine.
- Everyday = the working day (especially for the working class) *as opposed to* the bourgeois sphere, that is, people living on profits and in luxury, without really working.
- Everyday = the life of the masses *as opposed to* the life of the privileged and powerful (kings, princes and princesses, presidents, members of government, party leaders, members of parliament, business leaders, and so on).
- Everyday = the sphere of mundane events *as opposed to* everything regarded by traditional political historiography as the only relevant or 'great' events in history, that is, the centre stage in history.
- Everyday = private life (family, love, children) *as opposed to* public or occupational life.
- Everyday = the sphere of natural, spontaneous, unreflecting, genuine experience and thinking *as opposed to* the sphere of reflective, artificial, unspontaneous, especially scientific experience and thinking.
- Everyday (everyday consciousness) = ideological, naïve, superficial and false experience and thinking *as opposed to* correct, genuine and true experience and thinking (Elias 1998: 171).

As this list illustrates, the everyday is primarily opposed to times, places, events or experiences that are deemed non-everyday. In a similar fashion to Elias, Mike Featherstone (1992) contrasted everyday life with 'heroic life', with the latter emphasizing extraordinary experiences and events such as courageous struggles, quests for pride, glory and fame and pursuits of wealth, property and earthly love. Although this distinction between everyday life and heroic life – as well as other antonyms – may hold some promise, chapters in this book will show, however, that some everyday life sociologies in fact pay heed and homage to struggles, combats and more extraordinary enterprises as central aspects of everyday life (for example, the sociology of the absurd), the everyday life as heroic.[4]

Having looked at semantics, definitions and antonyms, in our quest for clarification, we are left with theoretical/typological conceptualizations. Mike Featherstone attempted to arrest the fleeting and fuzzy everyday life by proposing the following frequently recurring features of everyday life, and hence also of everyday life theories aimed at investigating and analysing the everyday:

- An emphasis on what happens every day, the routine, repetitive taken-for-granted experiences, beliefs and practices.
- An emphasis on the sphere of reproduction and maintenance, the pre-institutional zone of basic activities, predominantly carried out by women.
- An emphasis on the present providing a non-reflexive sense of immersion in the immediacy of current experiences and activities.
- An emphasis on the non-individual embodied sense of being together in spontaneous common activities outside, or in the interstices, of the official institutional domains.
- An emphasis on heterogeneous knowledge over rationality and the linearity of writing (Featherstone 1992: 161).

All these five features, as well as many more, as this book will show, are indeed present in most descriptions and theories of everyday life, but such a focus also leaves out other and perhaps equally important aspects of everyday life.[5]

According to another everyday life theorist, Andrew J. Weigert, the everyday consists of three interrelated levels of human existence and biography:

- the daily routines of our patterns of thoughts, words and deeds
- the social structures and social beliefs that normalize and legitimate some actions and routines and deem others abnormal and illegitimate
- the underlying assumptions and basic principles of any human life (Weigert 1981: 297–8).

According to Weigert, these three levels all constitute the junctions of individual and structure, self and society, and therefore this is where the everyday should be located. Added to these levels, however, I think we need to add a fourth level – the substance of this book – namely the theorization of the everyday as carried out by academics and scholars, the abstraction of the everyday, as it were. We shall return briefly to the varieties of this theorization below.

As should be obvious from the above, what makes everyday life – as compared with, but also equivalent to, so many other phenomena of interest to sociologists – so difficult to define, describe and delimit is the fact that the everyday is *not* one thing. In fact, as Weigert (1981: 35) stated, everyday life is not simply a 'thing'. Everyday life is far more complex and encompassing than to be boiled down to semantics, one-line definitions, synonyms, antonyms and sketchy typological conceptualizations. Everyday life is, as mentioned, problematic, difficult to capture, because – in the wonderful words of Georg Simmel – it is always *in statu nascendi*, something constantly evolving, emerging and coalescing at the same time as it is always not yet. In his analysis of the 'forms of sociation' and interactions between people, well before the concept of 'the everyday' was first coined within sociology, Simmel named this problematic scientific determination of the myriad of micro-processes that constitute a large proportion of everyday life as 'the problem of sociology':

> What renders the scientific determination of such obscure social forms difficult is ... the fact that as a rule they are not yet established as stable, supraindividual structures, but exhibit society, as it were, *in statu nascendi*. They do so not, of course, in the sense that they are the very first beginnings ... but in the sense that they originate each day and each hour .... We are dealing here with microscopic-molecular processes, so to speak .... That people look at one another and are jealous of one another; that they exchange letters or have dinner together; that apart from all tangible interests they strike one another as pleasant or unpleasant ... that people dress and adorn themselves for each other – these are a few casually chosen illustrations from the whole range of relations that play between one person and another.
>
> (Simmel 1908/1959: 326–8)

According to Simmel, such 'relations that play between one person and another' constitute everyday life and crystallize society, in its *statu nascendi*, as we know, comprehend and perceive it. This makes it difficult – but also worthwhile and indeed imperative – to try to capture everyday life.

As should be obvious from the selections of ideas, thoughts and concepts represented above, there are almost as many understandings and dimensions of everyday life as there are theorists trying to capture it. Let me, however, try to summarize what, at least according to many household theories, everyday life has been and can be described as:

- a place/space/location/domain
- a temporal dimension
- an attitude/mentality/state of consciousness
- specific artefacts/implements/tools
- an approach/orientation/perspective (theoretical and/or methodological)
- an academic abstraction/conglomeration (for example, the domain and interest of everyday life sociologies)
- perhaps most important of all, an experience (equally the experience of everyday people and everyday life sociologists) or rather 'an emporium of experiences'.

Let me elaborate briefly on what is meant by each of these aspects in most, or at least many, everyday life sociologies. First, the home often constitutes the primary realm of the everyday, and although the everyday can also be brought outside the home and into other social domains and regions, the home and the activities unfolding there are seen as everyday life *par excellence*.

Second, everyday life refers to the rhythms and repetitions taking place on a daily basis – 'day after day' (Felski 1999–2000: 18–22) – and, in fact, as the concept every*day* shows, sociologists often, although not exclusively, deal with *daily* and not *nightly* rhythms and repetitions when studying every*day* life.

Third, people in everyday life are frequently described as displaying a 'natural attitude', an unreflexive, pretheoretical and practical mentality, by which they tend to take things for granted and refrain from theorizing or scrutinizing that which is of no immediate concern or importance (Zimmerman and Pollner 1970).

Fourth, the everyday is made possible through all the technologies, props and objects that are brought into use by people in their daily doings and which are seen as serving a purpose in their everyday lives.

Fifth, the everyday requires a special way of looking at, approaching, investigating, understanding or dealing with the world of everyday life on behalf of students or scholars of society, which is often contrasted with other less everyday approaches and perspectives that do not look at everyday life as such (see Queiroz 1989).[6]

Sixth, in continuation of the previous point, everyday life is objectified, purified and abstracted through analyses by, for example, sociologists who thereby construct it as an object, a 'thing' or 'theme' to be studied; the sociological construction of everyday life, as one could call it. In this way, 'the everyday' in sociological terminology is also a reduction of a multitude of experiences, events and actions into one coherent and unified corpus.

Seventh, it is the experience of all of the above and, I shall contend, our most fundamental and pristine perception of and entry point into the world. This experience is both *Erfahrung* and *Erlebnis,* in Walter Benjamin's subtle distinction, simultaneously something instantaneous, immediate and simply lived-through as well as something that can be accumulated, reflected upon, critically evaluated and communicated (Highmore 2002b: 67). As such an emporium of experiences, the everyday is the beginning of everything.

As is evident from these seven points above, which may not even be exhaustive, what makes everyday life so difficult to capture is that it is or seems to be *everywhere*. As an emporium of experiences, everyday life is *universally available*, although it is not necessarily the same type of everyday life experienced by different people at different times and different places. It is also *ineradicable* (despite claims of a relentless 'colonization of the life-world by the system', as Jürgen Habermas famously theorizes), and it is therefore also *inescapable*. Thus, as experience, we cannot escape the everyday – 'there simply is no avoiding the essential process of everyday life' (Weigert 1981: 298) – because the everyday equals what phenomenologists call the 'paramount reality', a reality we always eventually return to, and 'among the multiple realities there is one that presents itself as the reality *par excellence* – this is the reality of everyday life, the paramount reality. Tension of consciousness is highest in everyday life, impossible to ignore' (Berger and Luckmann 1966: 21). And indeed, everyday life as this paramount reality is not ignored – at least not any more – by sociologists.

Sociologies of everyday life

Just as the everyday in itself is complex and indeed almost impossible to define and delimit, so the ideas and theories on the everyday cover a vast and heterogeneous territory. Initially, some clarification of the concept of 'everyday life sociology' is therefore needed. First, it is incorrect to speak of everyday life sociology in the singular. Although it is easy to indulge in this bad habit, it is, as this book will seek to illustrate, best thought and spoken of in the plural. There is a multitude of perspectives on, approaches to and theories of everyday life – which are sometimes at odds with each other – and in these sociologies of everyday life, everyday life is the focus and object of analysis, hence sociologies *of* everyday life or everyday life *sociologies*.

Second, it is incorrect to regard everyday life sociologies as a specialized sub-branch within sociology, equal to, for example, political sociology or economic sociology. Although everyday life sociologies throughout their short but turbulent history have often been ranked among those sub-sociologies such as educational sociology, sociology of death and dying, sociology of religion, urban sociology, sociology of childhood, sociology of health and illness, and so on, each dealing almost exclusively with a substantive area of society, such a classification is misleading. Because everyday life is everywhere, everyday life sociologies cover a much vaster terrain than merely one substantive domain of social life, and everyday life thinking is therefore part and parcel of many if not all of these other sub-divisions in sociology.

In fact, everyday life provides a wonderful microcosm for studying most aspects of social life, including politics, economics, death and dying, childhood, religion, education, urbanism, health and illness. Naturally, everyday life sociologies encompass various and different ways of approaching such substantive fields of research, which in turn makes it problematic to speak of everyday life sociology (in the singular) as a uniform monolith. As Kolyo Koev mused:

> Is it worthwhile using a *totalizing* concept of 'everyday life', or does it make more sense adhering to the 'pragmatic' point of view that every sociological study is, one way or the other, a study of everyday life, no matter how defined?
>
> (Koev 2002: 56, original emphasis)

My answer is 'yes', and this book therefore rejects any such totalizing aspirations when it comes to understanding everyday life in its entirety, as well as any monopolizing aspirations when it comes to defining or delimiting everyday life sociologies. Since everyday life is everywhere, we shall need the entire template of theoretical reflection and understanding to capture it.

Once we have clarified or approximated the scientific status of everyday life sociologies, one question inevitably arises: What is it that everyday life sociologies do? Jack D. Douglas once formally defined the purpose of the sociology of everyday life (although misleadingly mentioned in the singular) as 'a sociological orientation concerned with the experiencing, observing, understanding, describing, analysing and communicating about people interacting in concrete situations' (1980: 1). And indeed, although some sociologies of everyday life are not specifically involved in looking at people interacting in concrete situations, Douglas's definition highlights how everyday life sociologies are engaged in experiencing, observing, understanding, describing, analysing and communicating insights on and insights obtained from everyday life. But we can be more specific than this.

First of all, everyday life sociologies naturally *investigate* everyday life – they take everyday life activities, objects, states of mind, understandings and so on, in all their wonderful variety, as the starting point of analysis. Secondly, and perhaps more importantly, they also *question* everyday life. As Ben Highmore stated, 'To question everyday life and to allow everyday life to question our understanding of the world is to specifically invite a theoretical articulation of everyday life' (2002a: 3). Therefore, everyday life sociologies are interested in theoretically (and conceptually) investigating, describing, dissecting, analysing and communicating about everyday life.[7] If everyday life sociologies did not aspire to reach such a theoretical/conceptual level, they would be nothing more than mere everyday consciousness inseparable from the ideas and thoughts entertained by ordinary non-sociological members of society. Highmore continues by stating that 'everyday life invites a kind of theorising that throws our most cherished *theoretical* values and practices into crisis' (2002a: 3, original emphasis). everyday life sociologies indeed approach the world by taking a *critical* theoretical stance on everyday life – by making everyday life as it is lived by people a *theoretical problem*.

Because of this theoretical outlook of everyday life sociologies. it is important to emphasize that – despite or perhaps rather because of their at times seemingly everyday character – they do not start from scratch. All everyday life sociologies contain a certain amount of theoretical and philosophical substance on how to understand, approach, investigate, describe, analyse and communicate everyday life. Agnes Heller revealed how, 'irrespective of their particular theoretical or philosophical provenance and inspiration, all sociologies of everyday life operate strictly under the guidance of a philosophical paradigm' (1986: 150). They ask philosophical or theoretical questions such as: What is everyday life? How, and by what, is it constituted? What are the stocks of knowledge and actions sustaining it? What are the problems of living it? and so on.

Heller, however, went on to claim that:

> although all paradigms of the sociology of everyday life are, in the last instance, philosophical in character, not all philosophical paradigms can be used for such a purpose. Certain paradigms must be phased out precisely because it is everyday life that is under consideration, others because everyday life is under *sociological* consideration.
>
> (Heller 1986: 151, original emphasis)

These philosophical paradigms most often associated with, and guiding, everyday life *sociologies* are phenomenology, interactionism, existentialism, pragmatism and hermeneutics. Sometimes, as a few chapters in this book will illustrate, Marxism, structuralism, cultural studies or critical theory have also proved particularly useful and powerful when describing and analysing more structural or hidden aspects of everyday life. Without these theoretical and philosophical foundations and aspirations, everyday life sociologies would be nothing more than a trivial and uncritical recounting and rehashing of people's own quotidian activities.

However, Heller's observation that not all philosophical paradigms are suitable in buttressing an interest in the everyday is indeed important. She claims that purely subjective paradigms of the constitution of the world (such as orthodox Kantianism) do not lend themselves to the understanding and study of everyday life because it is, first and foremost, an intersubjective sphere. Everyday life is not 'my' property – it belongs to 'us'; everyday life is constituted by extensive networks of social communication, meaning and interaction. Heller also insists that paradigms that define everyday life as a realm of total alienation or reification (according to her such as the work of Martin Heidegger and Theodor W. Adorno) cannot be used in a *sociological* appreciation of everyday life (but must remain a purely philosophical exercise) because such positions, with their abstract theoretical constructs claiming that everyday life is thoroughly fetishized or inauthentic, cannot be operationalized or translated into operational concepts in actual empirical research with the practitioners of, or participants in, everyday life.

In purely philosophical positions on everyday life there exists, as it were, a one-way communication *from* the philosopher *to* the participants living everyday life, which makes empirical research redundant or irrelevant, whereas the relationship between the sociologist of everyday life and the 'members'[8] of everyday life is a two-way street – everyday life sociologists take seriously, through a theoretical lens and without necessarily validating, the actions, accounts, meanings, feelings and experiences of people in their own right. Consequently, as yet another central feature of most sociologies of everyday life, Jack D. Douglas stated that sociologists of everyday life do not moralize when accounting for what people do, why, when or how. According to him, everyday life is – or should be – allowed to speak for itself without the imposition of morality or alien meanings: 'Sociologists of everyday life do not begin by imposing their own meanings on their observations. They do not say "I think premarital intercourse is immoral because ...". They are concerned with finding what the members perceive, think and feel' (1980: 2).[9]

Based on the above, it is my contention that everyday life sociologies serve, at least, two important purposes at the same time. On the one hand, their aim is – primarily via theoretical means – to transcend common-sense perceptions and our taking everyday life for granted, and to cultivate and invite a scientifically based and sometimes critical perspective on the everyday world as it is lived (what could be termed *defamiliarization* – making the familiar appear strange).

On the other hand, however, they also seek to make everyday life tolerable, understandable and liveable to people so they can live secure, meaningful and unalienated everyday lives (what could be called *refamiliarization* – making the strange less strange). This is a synchronous task, the purpose of which is to elucidate everyday life as a sphere in which countervailing tendencies struggle – the familiar and the unfamiliar, the taken for granted and the as yet unnoticed. Therefore, the main reason why the sociologies of everyday life – like so many other sociologies – are needed is exactly because they make the unintelligible intelligible. According to Ben Highmore, 'everyday life is not simply the name given to a reality readily available for scrutiny; it is also the name for aspects of life that lie hidden', and therefore it is the task of everyday life sociologists 'to make the invisible visible (Highmore 2002a: 1–2). Similarly, Zygmunt Bauman and Tim May eloquently explained the role and *raison d'être* of sociology in general, which could easily be extended to account for the distinctive hallmark of everyday life sociology:

> It may open up new and previously unsuspected possibilities of living one's life with other with more self-awareness, more comprehension of our surroundings in terms of greater self and social knowledge and perhaps also with more freedom and control. To all of those who think that living [everyday] life in a more conscious way is worth the effort, [everyday life] sociology is a welcome guide.
>
> (Bauman and May 2001: 10, my additions)

As mentioned, there are many everyday life sociologies available that may assist people in living life in a more conscious way, and it is indeed difficult, if not downright impossible to provide an exhaustive inventory of them all, although not from lack of trying. For example, the first comprehensive introduction – with something of a North American bias – contained chapters on symbolic interactionism, Erving Goffman's dramaturgical perspective, labelling theory, phenomenology and ethnomethodology, and existentialism (Douglas et al. 1980). Later, Andrew J. Weigert (1981) suggested four major different paths or tracks in everyday life sociology: Erving Goffman's dramaturgy, Harold Garfinkel's ethnomethodology, the phenomenological tradition associated with Alfred Schutz, Peter L. Berger and Thomas Luckmann, and finally Henri Lefebvre's critical everyday life perspective.

From a more Europeanized perspective, Laura Bovone (1989) attempted to differentiate between the principal everyday life perspectives: the neo-Marxist stream (Jürgen Habermas and Agnes Heller), the phenomenological approach (Schutz, Berger and Luckmann), North American microsociology (Goffman, Garfinkel and the ethnomethodological movement), and the French anthropological everyday life sociology (most notably associated with the works of Michel Maffesoli and the Centre d'études sur l'actuel et le quotidien).

Although these attempts all provide useful overviews of some of the most prominent everyday life sociologies, their accounts are, however, far from exhaustive or complete – and neither is the overview provided in this book. Ever new developments – as well as nationally or regionally embedded preferences and perspectives – make it impossible to present anything but a motley collection or potpourri of possible and prevalent everyday life sociologies. In this book the most prominent and time-honoured traditions will be presented, supplemented by some of the more overlooked and obscure, and yet equally important, everyday life sociologies.

Before providing a peephole into the possible future of this myriad of everyday life sociologies, allow me briefly to recount and puncture some oft-heard myths about sociological theories of everyday life. First, everyday life sociologies are, from time to time, criticized for dealing with the apparent cosiness and consensus of everyday life without taking a closer and more critical look at the 'real' problems of society. And indeed, everyday life studies often, and naturally, emphasize everyday events and experiences. Jack D. Douglas once accurately described how 'most of our everyday lives are lived in roughly the same way we cook something' (1980: 15). As we all know, cooking requires the mastery of an equal amount of routine and reflexivity. Moreover, we need certain recipes (Alfred Schutz's term) in order to master the art of cooking. The same goes for living and analysing everyday life – routine, reflexivity and (socially and culturally available) recipes are all integral parts of everyday living. But just like cooking, everyday life can go wrong and the meal can be spoiled. Many everyday life sociologies, abundantly and vividly, exactly show how the everyday world is far from always a cosy place of consensus and peaceful coexistence. It is – or quite often turns into – a place of pressures, tensions, problems, conflicts and disagreements. In short, *everyday life is ambivalent,* and several chapters in this book show how living everyday existence is quite often problematic for people.

Second, everyday life sociologies are sometimes accused of taking an interest in what are regarded as the conventional, tedious and trivial matters of human existence. Allow me to correct this view: sociologies of everyday life can equally focus on the mundane and ordinary activities as on the more extraordinary and exotic: for example, that which takes place in subcultural environments, hidden settings and obscure communities.

Some of the most fascinating everyday life sociology to date was in fact reported in Marcello Truzzi's classic *Sociology and Everyday Life* (1968). In this early collection of everyday life studies, we learned about such diverse topics as erotic hierarchies, the tipping culture in American society, the social significance of card playing, the role and status of the executioner, Beatlemania fan culture, the social role of the dwarf, the sociology of sleep, sexual modesty in a nudist camp, draftee behaviour in the cold war army, prospects for religious cults, members of the flying saucerians, apprenticeships in prostitution, the social meaning of Santa Claus, the decline of the American circus, rape, bicycling, mafia gang culture and death (Truzzi 1968).[10] Perhaps some of this sounds excessively obscure and exotic but all these detailed studies deal with different experiences of the everyday.

Compared with the 1960s, perhaps we have throughout the years grown increasingly accustomed to, and become satiated with, such descriptive micro studies and the often somewhat alternative topics they touch upon. But what these everyday studies, along with many others, show and continue to show is *the power of the unnoticed* and the unobserved. As a more recent example, Joe Moran, in his wonderful *Queuing for Beginners: The Story of Daily Life from Breakfast to Bedtime* (2007), reveals how the apparently most tedious and trivial matters of everyday life contain hidden meanings and hints of broader cultural, social and historical importance and relevance.

Third, and perhaps most severely, everyday life sociologies have also – as a direct consequence of the former two critical points – been subjected to claims or accusations of micro-reductionism. And perhaps this is not without valid reason. In one of the oft-quoted introductions to everyday life sociology, Patricia A. Adler, Peter Adler and Andrea Fontana start out from the premise that 'everyday life sociology comprises a broad spectrum of *micro perspectives*' (Adler et al. 1987: 217, my emphasis). Stephen Crook also observed how initially, 'in its heyday, "everyday life" served as a rubric through which to assert the sociological significance of the structures and practices of *micro-social settings* from streets of lounge rooms and bars to backyards' (Crook 1998: 539, my emphasis). These observations, however, can and should be contested.

Actually, initially when the 'everyday' first appeared in any systematic manner in sociology, it was far from exclusively micro-oriented (think of the works of Georg Lukács or Georg Simmel): that is, being focused on the micro in itself, *sui generis*. Rather, the specifically micro-oriented perspective of everyday life sociology should be traced back to the American continent in the late 1950s and early 1960s, as an opposition to the deterministic, over-socialized, mono-causal and 'absolutist' traditions of both positivism and critical sociology (Adler et al. 1987: 218). Thus, Laura Bovone insisted that the growing interest in the everyday throughout the 1960s should 'be linked to the crisis of totalizing classical sociologies, such as those of positivism, Marxism and functionalism, and, hence, of their claims to organize rationally the various aspects of social behaviour into macromodels and macrosystems' (1989: 42).

Take a closer look at many of the sociology books or journal articles published in the 1950s and 1960s – quite often macro perspectives reigned sovereign. Instead, most sociologies of everyday life somehow seek to link human reproduction with social reproduction; they connect the micro and macro, agency and structure, because that is what takes place in everyday life. As Agnes Heller insists, 'everyday life is all those activities which characterize individual reproduction taken together, which in turn create possibilities for social reproduction' (1984: 21). In this way, everyday life – and with it everyday life sociologies – is securely located at the intersection of individual and society. It seeks, in C. Wright Mills's (1959) terminology, to make individual and biographical 'private troubles' meaningful and intelligible through linking them to and seeing them through wider 'public issues'.

Ben Highmore (2002a: 5) proposed how everyday life brings together different 'tendencies' that cut across conventional boundaries of sociality, such as agency–structure, micro–macro, resistance–power, particular–general and experiences/feelings–institutions/discourses. To privilege only one side of the dashed pairs is perhaps – as part of sociology's tendency artificially to compartmentalize the world into either macro or micro – inevitable, but it is also to miss a central feature of everyday life as a domain that centripalizes as much as it centrifugalizes, combines as much as it fragments, unites as much as it divides.

Thus, the sociologies of everyday life are far from merely or exclusively micro-oriented endeavours. As Tony Bennett and Diana Watson asserted:

> The sociology of everyday life enjoys a distinctive place within sociology as an area of inquiry in which the study of the forms of social behaviour and social interaction that takes place within everyday social settings and the analysis of more general social processes and relationships meet and intermesh.
>
> (Bennett and Watson 2002b: ix)

As many chapters in this book also illustrate, the world of everyday life is not isolated from, immune to or essentially different from what occurs in surrounding society, in the macro-level structures, cultural domains and meso-level institutions. Although a fundamental feature of everyday life is unquestionably human co-present interaction, this everyday 'interaction order' (Goffman 1983) cannot meaningfully be separated from more comprehensive and encompassing structural presences and developments. And the opposite is indisputably also the case: macro-level structures, cultural domains and meso level institutions are not impervious to changes and occurrences in the world of everyday life. In fact, everyday life – consisting of momentary and situational human encounters – may be considered as constituting the very cradle of modern society, the micro-hotbed of modern social macro-order (see, for example, Collins 1981; Jacobsen and Jensen 2009).

everyday life encounters may even be said to constitute the bricks and mortar of society as we know, perceive and encounter it:

> Features of co-present interaction make it fundamental to social order, both local and global. The immediacy and inherent indexicality of all human existence means that the fine, fleeting, yet essentially social moments of

> everyday life anchor and articulate the modern macro-order. Through the trust, commitment and detailed understandings made possible in situations of co-presence the essential space-time distantiation of modern society is achieved .... The infusion of everyday life, including production and consumption as well as cultural forms, with temporally and spatially distant events marks the modern world.
>
> (Boden and Molotch 1994: 277)

In short, everyday life is everywhere and cuts across everything. As Sue Hemmings, Elizabeth B. Silva and Kenneth Thompson succinctly observed on this world of everyday life that the sociologies of everyday life tirelessly try to keep abreast and track of:

> Everyday life is like the air we breathe or the ground on which we build: it is the foundation of social life. In learning to make strange the taken-for-granted realities within which we live our lives, we take a major step towards adopting a sociological imagination and towards the analysis of the traditional sociological concerns of social order and social change.
>
> (Hemmings et al. 2002: 302)

The future of everyday life sociologies

Now that we have described the rise and fall, the revival and subsequent proliferation and gradual recognition of everyday life in sociology, and attempted to illustrate and narrow down the enormously varied utility of the concept of 'the everyday' within the discipline and the concomitant development of sub-disciplines dealing with everyday life, it could be interesting to ponder the future of everyday life sociology. Although Danish multi-artist Robert Storm Petersen once aphoristically warned that 'it is difficult to prognosticate, especially about the future', I shall briefly venture into discussing possible scenarios for the present and future status of everyday life in sociology.

I am well aware that everyday life sociologies throughout the years have taken many unexpected and unforeseen twists and turns. The most accurate description of the current status of everyday life in sociology is perhaps to say that it finds itself at a crossroads between continued expansion, proliferation and refinement on the one hand, and a return to the neglect, disparagement and suspicion surrounding everyday life sociology from years gone by on the other. And perhaps everyday life sociologies are endemically standing at a crossroads. Thus, two decades ago, it was observed by other sociologists trying to diagnose, prognosticate and predict the future of everyday life sociology how:

> everyday life sociology is at a crossroads. It has a rich heritage of making valuable theoretical, epistemological and substantive contributions to social science. It also has continuing potential to fill lacunae in empirical knowledge and conceptual understanding of the everyday world. It has a secure foothold in the discipline as an established alternative approach. Everyday life sociology is routinely published by university presses, its own journals, and to a lesser degree, by mainstream journals. Last, some of its subfields have lost their cultlike isolation and become increasingly integrated into the discipline.
>
> (Adler et al. 1987: 230)

Compared with the situation at the time this diagnosis was offered, perhaps everyday life sociology can no longer pride itself on proposing an 'alternative approach' to the study of society. Today, everyday life has become an accepted household phenomenon and tolerated member of sociology. Therefore, despite the continued under-representation of everyday life sociology in most mainstream and high-rated international journals, which is – although perhaps to a lesser extent than two decades ago – still the case, then all should apparently be well and a glorious future awaiting everyday life sociology seems secured.

However, these authors also warned how there might be a fly in the ointment when stating as their final assessment of the future of everyday life sociology:

> Several dangers lie ahead. First, the field must continue to advance new perspectives on substantive, epistemological and theoretical issues rather than merely applying existing ones. Second, with the imminent retirement of many of its founders, leadership must emerge from within its ranks. Third, there is a near absence of research centres with the critical mass of faculty necessary to train the next generation of everyday life sociologists. Without this regenerative capacity, everyday life may have a limited future and faces a bankruptcy that threatens not only itself but the insight it brings to the entire discipline.
>
> (Adler et al. 1987: 230)

My diagnosis is, however, less reserved and more open to positive prospects than to dangers. Let me dwell briefly on the three points mentioned above. First, everyday life sociology has constantly been able to reinvent and redirect itself by adapting to and incorporating ever new insights – substantive, epistemological and theoretical – thereby mirroring the changes taking place in lived everyday life. Nothing seems to suggest that everyday life sociology should have lost this ability, or lacks the energy to continue down this track.

There are even signs that everyday life sociology in years to come might even expand its domain. Because the designs, technologies and consumption items so characteristic of everyday life in contemporary advanced capitalism – think of cellphones, iPods and laptop computers just to mention a few examples – have become an increasingly important and integral part of people's lives, everyday life sociology has begun to capture the attention of scholars working within research areas – often insensitive to sociological insights – concerned with everyday design, technologies and consumption (see, for example, Haddon 2004; Oxlade 1994; Shove et al. 2007; Vinck 2003). And this is only the top of the iceberg.

Thus, because the conditions of and circumstances for everyday living continuously change, so do the theories and approaches devoted to the analyses of the everyday, and several chapters in this book illustrate how everyday life sociology in recent years has gradually 'spilled over' into and itself been inspired by a variety of neighbouring disciplines.

Second, the transition from the pioneering period of the foundational figures in the heydays of everyday life sociology throughout the 1960s and 1970s to the present day has not been either easy or smooth. There might even have been something of a generational gap aggravated by the general situation of sociology throughout the 1980s and 1990s. But it seems as if there has been, and continues to be, a rich underwood of younger scholars willing to pick up the gauntlet of the erstwhile practitioners of everyday life sociology, and revitalize their ideas and discover previously uncharted territory.

Finally, everyday life sociology may still suffer from a lack of highly profiled research centres, a lack of organized faculty of a 'critical mass' at universities and a lack of financial funding, but perhaps its ultimate strength and vibrancy is exactly due to its continuous non-institutionalized, non-officialized and non-formalized status in sociology. I leave this proposition open to interpretation.

My conviction is that today, perhaps more than ever before, we need everyday life sociology because it continues to ask those questions and provide those answers that most other branches of sociology seem to neglect or overlook. Everyday life needs sociology, and although our sociological knowledge of everyday life is always a step or two behind the lived everyday life of people, sociological insights might shed light on everyday life in a way making it easier – or even better – to be lived.

But sociology also needs everyday life, and Kolyo Koev (2002: 61) accurately characterized everyday life as 'the constant disturber of sociological comfort'. As such a disturber of sociological comfort, of sociological doxa, sociology needs everyday life just as much as everyday life needs sociology. Obviously, everyday life will continue to exist even if sociology – although at its own expense – should suddenly decide to forget all about everyday life. But our understanding of and engagement with everyday life will be greatly enhanced if sociology continues to take a genuine interest in it.

The structure, content and 'spirit' of the book

Everyday life, as shown above, is – although it may seem familiar and easily comprehensible – an enormously complex, multi-faceted and encompassing phenomenon. The purpose of this book is simultaneously to illustrate and reduce this complexity by providing a theoretical overview over the vast territory covered by a variety of everyday life sociologies. The intention is to introduce readers to the everyday by way of a historically structured odyssey through varieties of theoretical traditions, conceptual developments and empirical examples of how everyday life sociologies, from each powerful perspective and through each original lens, have approached, exposed and explained the everyday.

The book provides the first comprehensive and updated introduction to everyday life sociologies for many years. The contributors all present the theoretical and methodological groundwork, developments and perspectives of distinct everyday life traditions, and relate these to and exemplify them through actual research. The book can either be read from start to finish as a chronological, although not exhaustive, introduction to the history of everyday life sociologies, or each chapter can be read in its own right.

The book is divided into three overall sections, somewhat chronologically organized. The first initially captures the early foundational groundwork for establishing everyday life sociology throughout the first part of the 20th century. The second section is devoted to the later offspring from the mid-century which provided many comments on, corrections to or further developments of the foundational period, and the third and final section is reserved for chapters dealing with more recent developments and combinations within or innovations in and expansions of the everyday perspective. This section shows how everyday life sociology continues to expand by interweaving with ever-new themes, topics and disciplines, and by incorporating insights from the 'bountiful prodigality of human experience' (Zygmunt Bauman's succinct expression). This division of the book does not insist, however, that those traditions described throughout the earlier sections are today outdated or of little relevance to contemporary theorizing. These traditions and approaches are indeed still very much alive and kicking in everyday life sociology, either in their own right or as foundational prerequisites for subsequent developments and refinements.

Part I: Foundation

The first section, presenting the foundational traditions, tracks or trajectories, in turn deals with Chicago sociology, American pragmatism, phenomenological sociology, symbolic interactionism, existential sociology and critical everyday life sociologies.

In Chapter 1 on Chicago sociology by *Anja Jørgensen* and *Dennis Smith*, we encounter the embryonic beginnings of sociology on the American continent and the kick-off to everyday life sociology as such. The authors initially describe the novel experience of the metropolitan urban setting that inspired and constituted the empirical domain for the pioneering Chicago sociologists, especially in the first quarter of the 20th century. Moreover, they focus on and list the founding and central figures of the so-called 'Chicago School' of sociology, such as Albion W. Small, William I. Thomas, Jane Addams, Robert E. Park and Louis Wirth. Subsequently, they move on to show how Chicago sociology, far from constituting a monolithic and internally coherent structure, contains a variety of different trajectories: human ecology, social (dis)organization, social psychology and action research/social work. Jørgensen and Smith end the chapter by concluding on the significance of the Chicago School for their successors in everyday life sociology. Both methodically and theoretically, these early pioneers used everyday life as a point of departure for understanding internal differences between social and ethnic groups, and especially how these different social and ethnic groups handled the new circumstances, conditions and possibilities that were produced by the modern urban environment.

Chapter 2 by *Robert C. Prus* and *Antony J. Puddephatt* picks up the torch from the first chapter by looking into American pragmatism as an early inspirational precursor for many later developments in everyday life sociology. In fact, pragmatism – as a philosophical perspective on social life, knowledge, human action and practice – became evident in a variety of especially American contributions to everyday life studies because of its privileging of practical knowledge and its focus on the importance of meaning, social processes and social relationships as foundations for knowledge. Prus and Puddephatt initially trace the roots of the pragmatist perspective in Western social thought, and illustrate how pragmatism offers a third alternative option to knowledge alongside empiricists and rationalists. Next they describe the ideas of key pragmatists from the late 19th century onwards – Charles S. Peirce, William James, Ferdinand Schiller and John Dewey – and show the continued relevance of pragmatist ideas for later everyday life sociologists through such themes and understandings as the self, symbols, mind, reflexivity, meaning, intersubjectivity, interaction, interpretation, community, roles and sympathetic introspection. All of these concepts and themes have remained household phenomena in everyday life sociology, and the chapter shows how pragmatism remains one of the most important – yet quite often overlooked – philosophical premises for everyday life theorizing and investigation in sociology.

In Chapter 3 by *Søren Overgaard* and *Dan Zahavi* we encounter another of the philosophical underpinnings of everyday life sociology as well as one of the most classic substantial contributions, phenomenological sociology. With its focus on subjectivity, intersubjectivity, sociality, life-world and experience, phenomenology has continued to inform many subsequent developments in everyday life sociology, and alongside symbolic interactionism (the topic of Chapter 4), it undoubtedly remains one of the most central approaches to everyday life. In this chapter, Overgaard and Zahavi initially outline the phenomenological movement by looking at the Continental European philosophers Edmund Husserl and Martin Heidegger from the threshold of the 20th century onwards. Key concerns in these early phenomenological studies are intentionality, consciousness and being, and later developments from Emmanuel Lévinas and Maurice Merleau-Ponty included a focus on ethics, the body and human perception. The authors then move from the realm of philosophy to the domain of sociology, by looking into the spillover effect of these early phenomenological formulations and ideas on phenomenological everyday life sociology throughout the 20th century. By way of doing this they delineate the perspectives of Alfred Schutz, Peter L. Berger, Thomas Luckmann and finally the ethnomethodological movement (the topic of Chapter 9). The chapter concludes with a discussion of the criticisms raised against phenomenological sociology.

Chapter 4 is written by *Dennis D. Waskul* and deals with one of the quintessential perspectives on or approaches to everyday life within sociology, symbolic interactionism. To many, especially on the American continent, symbolic interactionism is almost synonymous with everyday life sociology. However, as this chapter shows, it offers only one rather specific perspective on how to understand, conceptualize and investigate everyday life. A core characteristic of symbolic interactionism is a concern with what people 'do', and thus human action and interaction – coupled with a focus especially on symbolically meaningful expressions as means of communication – constitute the cornerstones of the approach. In the chapter, Waskul initially shows – by way of a very mundane example of the meaning of 'a kiss' – how symbolic interactionism is concerned with the symbolic significance of such an apparently physical action. Following this, the author outlines the conceptual apparatus of symbolic interactionism, especially Herbert Blumer's contribution, which is oriented towards understanding and describing the active processes by which people craft social worlds, create meaning, accomplish self, define situations and engage in cooperative, situated and structured joint action. Waskul also provides an overview of intellectual forerunners (for example, Charles Horton Cooley and George Herbert Mead) and successors to symbolic interactionist thinking, and concludes the chapter with a view on the variations and bifurcations within symbolic interactionism, and by predicting possible futures for symbolic interactionist everyday life sociology.

Existential sociology is the topic of Chapter 5 by *Joseph A. Kotarba*, who in the chapter provides an intriguing introduction to existential social thought as a fertile perspective on self, society, human existence and last but not least everyday life. He starts out by describing how existentialism is both style and substance – a way of approaching the world as well as an analytical framework for comprehending how the self confronts society. In the chapter, Kotarba explains how existentialists reject all-encompassing universal theories and instead – due to their individualistic ethos – prefer to look at the multi-faceted and multitudinous aspects of everyday life and the human encounter with the world as it is experienced, in all its forms, by people in different circumstances. A key feature of existential thought is that everyday life is dramatic, by which is meant that people in everyday life situations are forced to perform their everyday lives and selves on stages perhaps of their own choosing, but stages on which they are nevertheless bound to encounter confrontations and limitations. Throughout the chapter, the author outlines the major achievements and features of existential sociology by looking at the intellectual forerunners of existentialism, its focus on freedom, agency and human emotions, the priority of the self and the impact of postmodern social thought on the existentialist project. Kotarba concludes the chapter by way of a series of studies that emanate from a common existential perspective on everyday life.

The final chapter in this section on foundations, Chapter 6, is authored by *Michael E. Gardiner* and looks at the more critical roots of everyday life thinking, which has, in general, often been looked upon as relatively consensual and conservative. The critical perspective described by Gardiner comes in many different guises, but is primarily a German and Marxist-oriented endeavour looking at the conflicts, struggles and problems of modern everyday life as it is lived out in the shadow of a capitalist economic system. Throughout the chapter Gardiner accessibly invites the reader into the complex yet important ideas and concepts of a variety of critical social thinkers, from Karl Marx and Friedrich Engels via Georg Simmel and Georg Lukács to transitional figures such as Walter Benjamin. Common to these otherwise somewhat different perspectives is a deep-seated concern with what Gardiner poignantly terms 'everyday utopianism' as a perspective on how to transcend the limitations of modern everyday life. Because they all adhere, in varying degrees, to a dialectical and ambivalent understanding of the nature of society, this everyday utopianism is concerned with escaping and transforming the routinized, reified, rationalized, ideological and debased character of everyday living. Moreover each of the theoretical perspectives depicts and describes everyday life in the transformational period from premodern to modern society and through a keen eye on such important themes as politics, economics, religion, urbanism and commodification.

All in all, the chapters included in this first section centre around the classical roots and foundational perspectives and traditions of early everyday life sociology, and the philosophical ideas and theoretical notions that inspired them, as well as suggested their unmistakable impact on later developments and empirical applications.

Part II: Fermentation

The second section dealing with the period of fermentation contains chapters on French sociologies of the quotidian, Erving Goffman, ethnomethodology, conversation analysis and the sociology of the absurd, all of which climbed to prominence in the decades immediately following the Second World War on the European and American continents alike and reached a peak during the 1960s and 1970s.

In Chapter 7 by *Derek Schilling*, we are introduced to the specifically French variant of everyday life sociology, or the 'sociology of the quotidian' as it is often termed, which is a sociological perspective incorporating a variety of influences and positions ranging from structuralist Marxism and materialist dialectics to critical anthropology. Contrary to many other everyday life perspectives, an unmistakable political preoccupation and critical mentality remains an integral part of this particular perspective. Throughout the chapter, Schilling presents the important ideas of central figures of and developments within this French everyday life perspective, including the work of Henri Lefebvre, cause commune, Michel de Certeau and Michel Maffesoli. A core concern throughout much of the French-flavoured tradition is a dialectical perspective, which looks at how social structures infringe upon and restrict human autonomy, and how alienation and subjugation are widespread human experiences in modern everyday life. But it also testifies to the possibility of resistance through everyday strategies and tactics as ways of overcoming what Lefebvre termed 'the pseudo-everyday', an artificially constructed everyday life by modern capitalist consumerism. Although mystification and a masking of 'reality' are part and parcel of everyday life, it is also inside this self-same everyday life that the seeds of resistance reside. Thus, as was also the case with Chapter 6 from the previous section on critical everyday life theories, this chapter describes the inherent struggles and conflicts characteristic of contemporary everyday life, colonized by consumerism and capitalism, and their resolution through a diverse range of alternative actions such as, for example, spontaneity, revolutionary politics, consciousness-raising, creativity, interstitial activities and hedonistic pleasure.

Chapter 8 by *Søren Kristiansen* is devoted to the pioneering perspective on the so-called 'interaction order' as advanced by Erving Goffman. Whereas all the other chapters included in this book deal with collective paradigms, perspectives, traditions or schools of thought, the originality and novelty of Goffman's perspective on everyday life – methodologically and conceptually – warrant a chapter of its own. A trademark of Goffman's sociology was his situational and episodic view of social order, and central to his situational sociology was a concern with uncovering the unnoticed and infinitesimal yet utterly important rituals, strategies and games that constitute everyday encounters. These different everyday meetings and interactions in turn constitute a specific 'interaction order' which Goffman regarded as an analytical domain in its own right. Throughout the chapter, Kristiansen shows how the different metaphors methodically and analytically employed by Goffman – metaphors of theatre, ritual and strategic interaction – underpin an understanding of everyday life as multi-faceted and polymorphous, but an everyday life that can be captured through different conceptual lenses. Moreover, the author illustrates how Goffman's sociology – sometimes referred to as phenomenological, dramaturgical or symbolic interactionist – contains an interesting perspective on the human self as performance and dramatic effect. The chapter concludes with a listing of some empirical applications of Goffman's perspective on everyday life.

Ethnomethodology constitutes the topic of Chapter 9 by *Stephen Hester*. Ethnomethodology is a tradition that borrows several ideas from Erving Goffman but which also extends, develops and carries his ideas much further. Whereas Goffman, and most other sociologists, take the existence of some sort of social order (also in everyday life) for granted, the task of the ethnomethodologists is exactly to problematize this taken-for-grantedness and show how everyday life and social order is, in fact, something that is accomplished. Thus, in this chapter the reader is invited into the wonderful world of the taken-for-granted and common-sense but nevertheless important 'ethnomethods' that people continuously use and draw upon in everyday situations. Ethnomethodology's ambition – as Hester explains – is to detect and describe how members experience and actively accomplish the often unnoticed everyday life through a variety of procedures and actions. Throughout the chapter, Hester initially identifies ethnomethodology's phenomena, presents its terminology and vocabulary, describes the diversity of its programme, outlines its analytic procedures and preferred methods, provides empirical examples. Towards the end he substantially considers especially two exemplary classic studies in order to illustrate how ethnomethodology can assist us in understanding everyday life. These classic studies – Harold Garfinkel's 'breaching experiments' and Harvey Sacks's 'membership categorization analysis' – are particularly helpful in highlighting how everyday social order is practically achieved and accomplished.

The ethnomethodological perspective is also present in Chapter 10 by *Paul ten*

Have who focuses specifically on the branch of ethnomethodology labelled 'conversation analysis'. The main concern in conversation analysis is with talk – how people verbally communicate with each other in everyday or institutional encounters. Originally developed by students of Harold Garfinkel, conversation analysis has today received widespread recognition as a perspective or analytical strategy in its own right. Like ethnomethodology, conversation analysis is concerned with understanding social order, however with an emphasis on verbally constructed, maintained and accomplished social order. The objective of conversation analysis is thus to specify the ways in which participants moment-by-moment organize their talking together. Initially in the chapter, ten Have traces the historical background of conversation analysis or 'talk-in-interaction' as it was later called, its early formulations and later developments, and distinguishes between 'pure' and 'applied' conversation analysis. Subsequently, he presents some of the basic notions and tenets of the analytical strategy of the perspective: for example, sequence organization and repair, turn-taking and properties. Throughout the chapter, ten Have – by way of concrete examples of the procedures involved in conversational analysis – illustrates how conversation analysis is actually carried out, using transcripts from conversational sessions such as telephone calls and face-to-face conversation. In the chapter it becomes evident that conversation analysis is a useful appliance from the methodical and theoretical toolbox of everyday life sociology.

The concluding chapter of the section is Chapter 11 by *Michael Hviid Jacobsen*, who introduces perhaps the smallest and most overlooked of everyday life sociologies, the sociology of the absurd. Notwithstanding such neglect, this overlooked and apparently forgotten perspective on everyday life offers a fertile view on the conflicting nature of everyday life through a situational and episodic lens in which absurdity – the idea that life has no inherent or objective meaning – dominates. A hybrid between Weberian sociology, existentialism, dramaturgy, symbolic interactionism, ethnomethodology and a variety of other theoretical sources, the sociology of the absurd is presented and discussed and the author initially traces the intellectual ancestry of the absurdist approach. Hviid Jacobsen then shows how the sociology of the absurd provides everyday life sociology with an impressive, insightful and useful array of concepts and typologies for use in actual empirical social research. Moreover, he illustrates how an absurdist perspective may be used as a somewhat distanced yet involved and appropriate methodological stance when investigating everyday life phenomena. The chapter concludes with a recapitulation of some of the main criticisms raised against absurdist sociology, and a reappraisal of the sociology of the absurd as an alternative approach to analysing, understanding and investigating central aspects of modern, pluralist and complex everyday life.

The chapters in this section all describe central developments of everyday life sociology from the mid-20th century, which especially emerged and culminated in the tumultuous decades of the 1960s and 1970s. Common to these otherwise rather different perspectives and positions is their ambition to delineate and capture the myriad of everyday experiences, ranging from interactional etiquettes and dramatic self-presentations to class struggles, tactics and strategies. Moreover, they tend to privilege a creative perspective of human agency, and advance a relentless critique of structuralist or functionalist ideas of social order.

Part III: Dissemination

Finally, the section on the disseminated and proliferating everyday life perspective deals with Scandinavian everyday life sociologies, the sociology of emotions, social semiotics, cultural studies and everyday life, and finally interpretive interactionism. Although the seeds of these traditions, approaches and perspectives were perhaps sown quite some time ago, all of these perspectives have all gained foothold in the sociological imagination of new generations of students and scholars of everyday life, especially throughout the last couple of decades.

The section begins with Chapter 12 by *Ann-Dorte Christensen* on Scandinavian everyday life sociologies. Similar to the chapter beginning the second section of the book, this chapter also deals with a rather local and regional everyday life tradition. Often overlooked – perhaps because of language barriers – in wider parts of international everyday life sociology, the specifically Scandinavian perspective on everyday life offers many fruitful insights on the life-world to be adopted elsewhere. Initially, Christiansen shows how the history of everyday life sociology in Scandinavia can be traced back to mid-18th-century studies of countryside folk culture, but especially how it was from the late 1960s onwards that a sustained everyday life sociology – 'the new everyday life' – was established. Moreover, she describes different everyday life perspectives from Danish and Norwegian national contexts, and illustrates how actual empirical research, a focus on the home as the institutional setting of every life and a concern with gender have continuously prevailed. As Christensen shows throughout the chapter, Scandinavian everyday life sociology both builds upon and expands more conventional everyday life traditions, perhaps most prominently phenomenology. She also hints at some of the areas in which the Scandinavian perspective may be 'exported' to wider contexts and supplement conventional everyday life sociologies, such as its preoccupation with gender, its life-mode analyses, its concern with everyday life under the auspices of welfare state policies and ethnic minority problems.

Chapter 13 by *Poul Poder* concerns itself with a perspective that in recent years has attracted increasing attention among sociologists, namely the sociology of emotions. In this chapter we are treated to a generous introduction to the theoretical positions and analytical potentials of different variants of the sociology of emotions. Poder's chapter is instrumental in elucidating the importance of emotions in everyday exchange and social intercourse. The chapter begins with a definition of emotions and an overview of a variety of theoretical perspectives on emotions, ranging from dramaturgical and cultural, via exchange and symbolic interactionist perspectives, to structural and evolutionary positions. Contrary to purely physiological understandings, Poder makes it clear that to sociologists, social context and intersubjective meaning are important features in the shaping and understanding of emotions and feelings in everyday life. Following this, he introduces and discusses primarily three sociologically potent perspectives: Arlie R. Hochschild's theory of 'feeling rules', 'display rules' and 'emotion management', Candace Clark's theory of emotions as part of a 'socio-emotional economy' of exchange, and Randall Collins's theory of 'interaction ritual chains' and 'emotional energies'. Despite their different focus and background assumptions, these theoretical templates all convincingly agree on how a focus on emotions and feelings is essential to understanding a variety of social contexts, situations and events.

In Chapter 14 by *Phillip Vannini* we encounter an everyday world full of things, of 'stuff'. The topic of the chapter is the perspective of social semiotics, and throughout the chapter the reader is invited to consider how their everyday encounters and everyday experiences are, to a large extent, made possible and filtered through stuff such as computers, television, credit cards, mobile phones and clothing items. Social semiotics is a perspective concerned with the interpretive and critical study of the resources, the stuff, we use in everyday life to construct meaning, and it concerns itself with the meanings of signification. Moreover, social semiotics activates different modes of expressing meaning through all the senses: the visual, the tactile, the aural, the gustatory, and even the olfactory, either alone or in combination. Initially Vannini provides a historical overview of the development of social semiotics, then he accessibly demonstrates how social semiotics offers invaluable theoretical understandings and ideas. Social semiotics as an everyday life approach also provides a research strategy, and Vannini points out how social semiotics is especially useful when applied to specific and concrete problems, for example through collecting, documenting and cataloguing the resources people use in everyday life. The chapter concludes with some illuminating research findings from recent semiotic studies of the unnoticed stuff of everyday life.

Cultural studies can equally be seen as a challenge to, an extension of or an opposition to everyday life sociology. In Chapter 15 by *David Inglis* it becomes obvious, however, that cultural studies and everyday life sociology to a certain extent share common ground and may mutually inspire and stimulate each other. Although the cultural studies tradition has been keen to establish itself as a distinct orientation, its unmistakable interest in everyday matters makes it an unavoidable resource and source of inspiration for everyday life sociologists. In this chapter, Inglis distinguishes between different strains and developments within cultural studies, and recaptures their important contributions. Common to these different strains is their ambition to identify and to tap into what they see as the hidden social and cultural energies of everyday activities, and to rescue them from the condescension of those who see little value in such quotidian activities. Moreover, cultural studies may assist the everyday life sociologist in appreciating the polyphony of forms of resilience and resistance to power in everyday settings. Throughout the chapter, the author, by way of examples from youth culture, working-class culture and popular culture, illustrates how a cultural studies perspective may invigorate everyday life sociology with a critically cultural and often even explicitly politicized edge.

The book is concluded by Chapter 16 by *Norman K. Denzin*, who introduces the increasingly publicized perspective of interpretive interactionism. As part of a postmodern, critical and existential perspective on everyday life, interpretive interactionism incorporates insights from a diversified range of intellectual sources of inspiration. Initially, the heritage and groundwork of interpretive interactionism is outlined, with its emphasis on existential, interactional and biographical texts; ideographic and emic approaches; naturalistic strategies of research; interpretive evaluation of individuals' experiences; asking 'how' questions instead of 'why' questions; and a concern with gender, power, emotion, affect and knowledge. Denzin then shows how so-called 'epiphanies' – turning-points, ruptures and transformational experiences – constitute a central but often overlooked component of people's everyday lives. He illustrates these epiphanies, and their internal variations, with extracts from biographical texts, interview material and so-called 'mystories'. Moreover, central to interpretive interactionism is a focus on the perceived tension (and its overcoming) between society and biography, social structure and the individual, as C. Wright Mills classically championed in his 'sociological imagination'. With the coming of the late post-modern period' the everyday lives of people become increasingly mediated, commoditized and visually experienced, and the author shows how this new late postmodern condition offers problems but also potentials for everyday life sociology and everyday living.

The chapters included in this third and final section all testify to the fact that everyday life sociology does not stand still. It evolves continuously, although perhaps slowly, incorporates ever-new perspectives, combines with other traditions and positions, proposes new agendas and is always on the lookout for uncharted territories, undiscovered themes and novel experiences. As such, it tries, energetically and insistently, to keep track of and keep up with the many twists and turns of human everyday life.

Despite their diverging thematic, theoretical, methodological and substantial focus and different preferences, propositions, predilections and perspectives, the chapters included in this book all aspire to capture everyday life sociologically and the aforementioned 'emporium of experience' by which it is characterized. The 'spirit' of this book is therefore that since the everyday is a complex, multi-faceted and polymorphous phenomenon, we need all the insights, methods, theories, concepts and analytical strategies offered and developed by a variety of sociological perspectives and traditions. Thus, the everyday can be captured and comprehended by an endless array of equally stimulating – but essentially different and competing – theoretical approaches and perspectives.

Therefore, this book – privileging or prioritizing no perspective – is against the monopolization of the everyday by a 'right' or 'correct' version of researching or understanding the everyday. While recognizing that matters of 'appropriateness', personal 'persuasion' or 'pragmatic' considerations may eventually and necessarily guide the sociologist of everyday life in actual research, the richness and extensive nature of the everyday requires, in principle as well as practice, open-mindedness and humility. Another important feature of the 'spirit' of this book is the insistence that although everyday life may easily be lived and practiced without recourse to theoretical insights or sociological wisdom, in order to *understand* the largely unnoticed aspects of everyday living, theoretical perspectives and frameworks provide inevitable tools. Since understanding is and remains a key concern of sociology, this book aspires to aid this task of understanding. At the end of the (every)day, if the book turns out also to assist in *improving* everyday life, its expectations have been satisfied a thousandfold.

As the many chapters of this book show, the everyday is, and continues to be, an important and indeed inescapable part of the lives and experiences of people and sociologists alike – inescapable because important and important because inescapable – and as Andrew J. Weigert asserted, 'the quest for an adequate interpretation and understanding of everyday life is a never-ending and limitless task' (1981: 298). Thus, the sociological quest for exploring and understanding everyday life is and remains a never-ending, perhaps even utopian, task, and this book merely attempts to assist readers in taking part in this task. This book, although written for fellow sociologists and other students of society in related disciplines, is dedicated to Michel de Certeau's 'ordinary man', to the 'common hero, an ubiquitous character, walking in countless thousands on the streets' (de Certeau 1988: v).

Notes

1. This could be interpreted as the natural consequence of the gradual appropriation of the everyday by the cultural studies tradition in which often abstract analyses, theoretical verbosity and academic wording take precedence over more mundane and unpretentious descriptions, although some everyday life sociologies – perhaps particularly ethnomethodology – are also guilty of the charge of describing and analysing everyday life through a choice of words and terminology that remain anything but everyday.
2. Special issues of academic journals dedicated exclusively to everyday life are, however, few and far between (as notable evidence of these exceptions, see *Current Sociology*, 37(1) 1989 and *Cultural Studies,* 18(2/3) 2004).
3. Alf Lüdtke's edited volume *The History of Everyday Life* (1995) highlights some of the key contributors and some of the major achievements in early theorizing about everyday life, especially in Europe and particularly in Germany.
4. Another illuminating antonym to 'the everyday' was proposed by Jack D. Douglas, who differentiated between the 'everyday' and the 'anyday', where the former refers to that which in fact takes place every day, whereas the latter refers to those phenomena or experiences that 'a person can encounter at almost any time and any place within the normally expected boundaries of everyday discourse, insofar as the persons involved are intimate enough' (Truzzi 1968: 1; see also Douglas 1967).
5. However, studies of everyday life – at least to some extent – do not only emphasize features of irrationality and unreflexivity in describing everyday life. In fact, different traditions and approaches, such as perhaps most prominently ethnomethodology and phenomenology, explicitly stress reflexivity and an understanding of rationality as 'rules of the game' as fundamental and intrinsic aspects of living everyday life (see, for example, Garfinkel 1967: 262–83).
6. Michel Maffesoli identified three basic tenets or aspects of everyday life as perspective or approach. First, the researcher of everyday life is necessarily involved in their object of inquiry and cannot be totally abstracted from it – the researcher is, in short, *participant*. Second, the researcher of everyday life takes account of the resurgence, both in social practices and in our analyses of them, of *experience*. Third, the theme of the everyday demands a *conceptual audacity* aimed at breaking the closure of economic-political logic underlying so many sociological analyses (Maffesoli 1989).
7. From this, however, there does not follow a preferred or privileged perspective on the relationship between theory and data, deduction and induction. everyday life sociologies cover the entire continuum, stretching from abstract theoretical elaboration at the one pole, via all possible hybrid positions to concrete empirical investigation at the other, and as the chapters in this book will show, valid and valuable understandings and analyses of everyday life can be advanced and promoted from any epistemological, theoretical or methodological position.
8. The specific use of the term 'members', which is a term with strong ethnomethodological and interactionist connotations, is far from invoked by all everyday life sociologies, By using 'members' as a term describing the people inhabiting and living everyday life, a view of humans as active, creative and reflexive is explicitly assumed – a view in which everyday life is an accomplishment or outcome of the actions and interactions of these members. In her excavation of and excursion into so-called 'creative sociologies', Monica B. Morris justified this neologism for everyday life sociology by asserting that:

   > the basic assumption underlying the 'creative' approaches in sociology are: that

> human beings are not merely acted *upon* by social facts or social forces; that they are constantly shaping and 'creating' their own social worlds in interaction with others; and that special methods are required for the study and understanding of these uniquely human processes.
>
> (Morris 1977: 8)

Not all everyday life sociologies, however, subscribe to such an activist and creative image of human beings.

9. Despite this supposed neutrality, what has also been characterized as 'ethnomethodological indifference', everyday life evokes strong emotions among practitioners of sociology. As Rita Felski observed in a discussion of the importance of everyday life sociology to feminist theory, everyday life 'is rarely viewed with neutrality .... Everyday life has long been subject to intense and conflicting emotional investments' (1999–2000: 16, 30). True, some protagonists of everyday life sociology have stressed the superiority of mundane everyday matters over more macro-oriented topics, while antagonists have also been known to claim the opposite. Moreover, some everyday life sociologists have come close to regarding everyday life as a more authentic, more accurate and more genuine arena for investigating society than, for example, studying formal institutions. Despite sectarian sensibilities among certain everyday life camps, most sociologists conducting everyday life research have developed positions and perspectives in which the everyday is taken seriously while avoiding the dangers of conflating sociology with everyday common sense.
10. In another inspirational volume also edited by Marcello Truzzi, *Sociology for Pleasure*, we encounter equally varied analyses of a multitude of ordinary and extraordinary aspects of everyday life, for example the sociology of the telephone, the poker game, the waiting line, graffiti, *Playboy Magazine*, transsexuality, autoeroticism, gambling, breast fetish, skin colour alteration, bullfights and baseball games, and an incisive analysis of the everyday life unfolding inside the 'ivory towers' of academia itself (Truzzi 1974). All of these studies point to the fact that everyday life is a domain in which the ordinary and the extraordinary overlap considerably and coexist.

Bibliography

Adler, Patricia A., Peter Adler and Andrea Fontana (1987) 'Everyday life sociology.' *Annual Review of Sociology*, 13: 217–35.

Bauman, Zygmunt and Tim May (2001) *Thinking Sociologically*, 2nd edition. Oxford: Blackwell.

Bech-Jørgensen, Birte (1994) *Når hver dag bliver til hverdag*. Copenhagen: Akademisk Forlag.

Bennett, Tony and Diane Watson (eds) (2002a) *Understanding Everyday Life*. Oxford: Blackwell.

Bennett, Tony and Diane Watson (2002b) 'Understanding everyday life: introduction', in Tony Bennett and Diane Watson (eds), *Understanding Everyday Life*. Oxford: Blackwell.

Berg Sørensen, Torben (1991) *Sociologien i hverdagen – indføring i nyere gruppesociologi*. Århus: Forlaget Gestus.

Berger, Peter L. and Thomas Luckmann (1966) *The Social Construction of Reality: A Treatise in the Sociology of Knowledge*. New York: Anchor.

Birenbaum, Arnold and Edward Sagarin (1973) *People in Places: The Sociology of the Familiar*. London: Nelson.

Blanchot, Maurice (1987) 'Everyday speech'. *Yale French Studies*, 73: 12–20.

Boden, Deirdre and Harvey L. Molotch (1994) 'The compulsion of proximity', in Roger Griedland and Deirdre Boden (eds), *NowHere: Space, Time and Modernity*. Berkeley, CA: University of California Press.

Bovone, Laura (1989) 'Theories of everyday life: search for meaning or a negation of meaning?' *Current Sociology*, 37(1): 41–60.

Collins, Randall (1981) 'On the micro-foundations of macro-sociology.' *American Journal of Sociology*, 86: 984–1015.

Collins, Randall (1986) 'Is 1980s sociology in the doldrums?' *American Journal of Sociology*, 91: 1336–55.

Crook, Stephen (1998) 'Minotaurs and other monsters: "everyday life" in recent social theory.' *Sociology*, 32(3): 523–40.

De Certeau, Michel (1988) *The Practice of Everyday Life*. Berkeley, CA: University of California Press.

Douglas, Jack. D. (1967) *The Social Meanings of Suicide*. Princeton, NJ: Princeton University Press.

Douglas, Jack D. (ed.) (1970a) *Understanding Everyday Life: Toward the Reconstruction of Sociological Knowledge*. London: Routledge & Kegan Paul.

Douglas, Jack D. (1970b) 'Understanding everyday Life', in Jack D. Douglas (ed.), *Understanding Everyday Life: Toward the Reconstruction of Sociological Knowledge*. London: Routledge & Kegan Paul.

Douglas, Jack D. (1980) 'Introduction to the sociologies of everyday life', in Jack D. Douglas, Patricia A. Adler, Peter Adler, Andrea Fontana, C. Robert Freeman and Joseph A. Kotarba, *Introduction to the Sociologies of Everyday Life*. Boston, MA: Allyn & Bacon.

Douglas, Jack D., Patricia A. Adler, Peter Adler, Andrea Fontana, C. Robert Freeman and Joseph A. Kotarba (1980) *Introduction to the Sociologies of Everyday Life*. Boston, MA: Allyn & Bacon.

Elias, Norbert (1998) 'On the concept of everyday life', in Johan Goudsblom and Stephen Mennell (eds). *The Norbert Elias Reader*. Oxford: Blackwell.

Featherstone, Mike (1992) 'The heroic life and everyday life.' *Theory, Culture and Society*, 9: 159–82.

Felski, Rita (1999–2000) 'The invention of everyday life.' *New Formations*, 39: 15–31.

Gardiner, Michael E. (2000) *Critiques of Everyday Life: An Introduction*. London: Routledge.

Gardiner, Michael E. (2008) 'Review essay of: John Roberts: *Philosophizing the Everyday: Revolutionary Praxis and the Fate of Cultural Theory*, and Michael Sheringham: *Everyday Life: Theories and Practices from Surrealism to the Present*'. *Space and Culture* (forthcoming).

Garfinkel, Harold (1988) 'Evidence for locally produced, naturally accountable phenomena of order, logic, reason, meaning, method etc. in and as of the essential quiddity of immortal ordinary society (I of IV): An announcement of studies'. *Sociological Theory*, 6: 103–9.

Garfinkel, Harold (1967) *Studies in Ethnomethodology*. Cambridge: Polity Press.

Glassner, Barry and Rosanna Hertz (eds) (1999) *Qualitative Sociology as Everyday Life*. Thousand Oaks, CA: Sage.

Goffman, Erving (1983) 'The interaction order.' *American Sociological Review*, 48: 1–17.

Gouldner, Alvin W. (1975) 'Sociology and the everyday life', in Lewis A. Coser (ed.), *The Idea of Social Structure*. New York: Free Press.

Haddon, Leslie (2004) *The Invisible Future: The Seamless Integration of Technology into Everyday Life*. New York: McGraw-Hill.

Heller, Agnes (1984) *Everyday Life*. London: Routledge & Kegan Paul.

Heller, Agnes (1986) 'The sociology of everyday life', in Ulf Himmelstrand (ed.), *The Social Reproduction of Organization and Culture*. London: Sage.

Hemmings, Sue, Elizabeth B. Silva and Kenneth Thompson (2002) 'Accounting for the everyday', in Tony Bennett and Diane Watson (eds), *Understanding Everyday Life*. Oxford: Blackwell.

Highmore, Ben (ed.) (2002a) *The Everyday Life Reader*. London: Routledge.

Highmore, Ben (2002b) *Everyday Life and Cultural Theory: An Introduction*. London: Routledge.

Jacobsen, Michael Hviid and Ole B. Jensen (2009) *Sic parvis magna – den mikrosociologiske fantasi*. Aalborg: Aalborg University Press (forthcoming).

Jacobsen, Michael Hviid and Søren Kristiansen (eds) (2005) *Hverdagslivet – sociologier om det upåagtede*. Copenhagen: Hans Reitzels Forlag.

Karp, David A. and William A. Yoels (1993) *Sociology and Everyday Life*. Itasca, Ill.: F. E. Peacock.

Koev, Kolyo (2002) 'Sociology and everyday life: problemizing the relationship.' *Sociological Problems*, special issue available at: http://www.ceeol.com/aspx/getdocument.aspx?logid=5andid=b287370b-8ee1-11d6-a01b-0020eda6408d.

Lefebvre, Henri (1987) 'The everyday and everydayness.' *Yale French Studies*, 73: 7–11.

Lüdtke, Alf (ed.) (1995) *The History of Everyday Life*. Princeton, NJ: Princeton University Press.

Machlup, Fritz (1956) 'The inferiority complex in the social sciences', in Mary Sennholz (ed.), *On Freedom and Free Enterprise: Essays in Honor of Ludwig von Mises*. Princeton, NJ: Van Nordstrand.

Maffesoli, Michel (1989) 'Editorial preface: the everyday perspective.' *Current Sociology*, 37(1): v–vi.

McCall, George J. and Jerry L. Simmons (1966) *Identities and Interactions*. New York: Free Press.

Metcalfe, Andrew and Ann Game (2002) *The Mystery of Everyday Life*. Annandale, VA: Federation Press.

Mills, Charles Wright (1959) *The Sociological Imagination*. New York: Oxford University Press.

Moore, Thomas (1996) *The Re-Enchantment of Everyday Life*. New York: Harper-Collins.

Moran, Joe (2005) *Reading the Everyday*. London: Routledge.

Moran, Joe (2007) *Queuing for Beginners: The Story of Daily Life from Breakfast to Bedtime*. London: Profile.

Morris, Monica B. (1977) *An Excursion into Creative Sociology*. Oxford: Blackwell.

Oxlade, Chris (1994) *Everyday Things*. Danbury, CT: Franklin Watts.

Queiroz, Jean Manuel de (1989) 'The sociology of everyday life as a perspective.' *Current Sociology*, 37 (1): 31–40.

Roberts, John (2006) *Philosophizing the Everyday: Revolutionary Praxis and the Fate of Cultural Theory*. Ann Arbor, MI: Pluto Press.

Sandywell, Barry (2004) 'The myth of everyday life: toward a heterology of the ordinary.' *Cultural Studies*, 18 (2/3):160–80.

Sheringham, Michael (2006) *Everyday Life: Theories and Practices from Surrealism to the Present*. Oxford: Oxford University Press.

Shove, Elizabeth, Matthew Watson, Jack Ingram and Martin Handford (2007) *The Design of Everyday Life*. Oxford: Berg.

Simmel, Georg (1908/1959) 'The problem of sociology', in Kurt H. Wolff (ed.), *Georg Simmel,*

1958–1918: A Collection of Essays. Columbus, OH: Ohio State Press.
Smith, Dorothy E. (1987) *The Everyday World as Problematic: A Feminist Sociology*. Milton Keynes: Open University Press.
Strauss, Anselm L. (1969) *Mirrors and Masks: The Search for Identity*. London: Martin Robertson.
Truzzi, Marcello (ed.) (1968) *Sociology and Everyday Life*. Englewood Cliffs, NJ: Prentice-Hall.
Truzzi, Marcello (ed.) (1974) *Sociology for Pleasure*. Englewood Cliffs, NJ: Prentice-Hall.
Vinck, Dominique (ed.) (2003) *Everyday Engineering: An Ethnography of Design and Innovation*. Cambridge, MA: MIT Press.
Weigert, Andrew J. (1981) *Sociology of Everyday Life*. New York: Longman.
Zimmerman, Don E. and Melvin Pollner (1970) 'The everyday world as a phenomenon', in Jack D. Douglas (ed.), *Understanding Everyday Life: Toward the Reconstruction of Sociological Knowledge*. London: Routledge & Kegan Paul.

Part I
Foundation

CONTENTS

CHAPTER 1

The Chicago School of Sociology

Survival in the Urban Jungle

ANJA JØRGENSEN AND DENNIS SMITH

Noticing the unnoticed

The sociological ideas that came from Chicago, and the debates surrounding them, are a central part of the repertoire available to anyone seriously interested in exploring how modern society – and perhaps especially the everyday life of modern society – works: in other words, the largely unnoticed routines, structures and assumptions that shape our everyday social existence. We take for granted the speed, complexity, diversity and anonymity of modern urban life. Individuals adapt to those conditions without a conscious effort of thought. However, it was not always like this. Chicago was a dramatic example of the large modern business and manufacturing city, relentlessly imposing and impersonal. It posed the challenge of survival under conditions that we all now take for granted but which shocked people profoundly when they first appeared. The modern city was deeply disturbing. Chicago in particular became the object of intense sociological attention, focusing on the often-unnoticed aspects of urban everyday life.

Chicago sociology provides an interesting perspective on everyday life because these new conditions constituted a catalyst in the development of a wide range of lifestyles and ways of behaving that Chicago sociologists used as a point of departure for their research. Based upon a mixture of anthropological field study, life story and mapping techniques, they used everyday life as an empirical base for understanding larger social phenomena, social processes and social actions characteristic of modernity. Their objectives were to understand social life in the urban environment, approaching the city as being synonymous with modernity, by mixing an empirical orientation with theoretical pragmatism, and being preoccupied with human experience, and finally driven by social and political circumstances. In this chapter, we initially briefly outline the socio-historical background of the development of Chicago sociology and discuss the founders and most prominent figures of the so-called 'Chicago School'. Finally, we propose four trajectories along which the varied contributions of Chicago sociology to everyday life research developed.

The growth of the City of Chicago and sociology in Chicago

Chicago began as a frontier settlement.[1] By the 1850s it was a major entrepôt and processor of grain and livestock, a railroad and shipping terminal and a magnet for incoming Irish, Poles, Swedes, Danes and Germans. Thirty years later, by the 1880s, the city had grown in size more than 15-fold, drawing in immigrants from southern Europe and the south. It had become the fourth biggest city in the country. Table 1.1 illustrates the rapid growth in population of Chicago at 30-year intervals, 1850–1940.

Another three decades brought spawning suburbs, imposing architecture, great civic parks and growing racial tension, culminating in a massive riot in 1919. By 1940, Chicago, long established as the nation's second city, was highly segregated, notorious for gang crime, ridden with political corruption and dominated by an increasingly well-organized Democratic Party machine.

The University of Chicago was established in 1892 as part of a sustained bid for respectability and influence which also led to the great Columbian Exposition (or Chicago World Fair) the following year. It was at the University of Chicago, that the world's first sociology department was established. Albion W. Small (1854–1926) was the sociology department's founding professor. One of its main self-imposed tasks was to map the urban jungle and make sense of the

Table 1.1 Rapid growth in the population of Chicago at 30-year intervals (1850–1940)

Year	Population size	Ranking within United States
1850	29,963	24th
1880	503,185	4th
1910	2,185,283	2nd
1940	3,396,962	2nd

Source: adapted from Gibson (1998).

pathways people wove through it. Sociology as a practical, empirical science was only just emerging from the more abstract and metaphysical realm of social philosophy. Meanwhile, social philosophy, which continued to influence sociology, was in its turn struggling to detach itself from the grip of religious orthodoxy. Christianity remained a powerful force, but the blows struck by Charles Darwin's theory of evolution shattered many spiritual certainties.

The early Chicago sociologists drew upon the very 'American' approach of pragmatism, which said that the best test of a concept's or theory's truth or validity is whether it helps someone with a problem to think their way through to a practical solution. Educationist John Dewey (1859–1952) and philosopher George Herbert Mead (1863–1931), both of the University of Chicago, were adherents of this approach. Both also helped in the practical work of Hull House, a settlement that worked closely with immigrant communities in Chicago, especially women.[2] Another powerful influence was German philosophy and social science. For example, some Chicago sociologists drew upon the work of Georg Simmel (1858–1918), who analysed the condition of the restless urbanite no longer supported or hemmed in by strong communal values. Robert E. Park (1864–1944), perhaps the best-known of the Chicago sociologists, was a great admirer of Simmel.

Among the Chicago sociologists, there were at least four main responses to the modern city and the capitalist market driving so many of its processes. One response was optimism, the response that says: 'How promising! Things are going well in our cities even if that is not always obvious on the surface. Basically, everything is in place to enable us to build a good society in which people can be comfortable and live productive and satisfying lives. We just have to work hard to help make this happen.' Louis Wirth (1897–1952) was one of the Chicago sociologists subscribing to this view, despite some ambivalence, as we shall see later.

Another approach comes from outrage. It says: 'How unjust! People are not being treated in the way that their humanity requires. Nor is society organized to give everyone a fair chance to live the comfortable, productive and satisfying lives to which they have a right. We must make the existence of this injustice clear to everybody.' Albion W. Small, as mentioned the first head of the Chicago sociology department, began as a determined optimist about modern America but became progressively more disillusioned and outraged.

A third approach responded to life in the city by saying: 'How complex! We need to engage our capacity for empathy but at the same time step back a little. We must use our powers of objective observation to convey as accurately as possible the challenges and dilemmas facing people in different situations as they adjust to modern urban society.' William I. Thomas (1863–1947) spent most of his career trying to combine as effectively as he could the twin missions of exposing injustice and conveying the complexity of social life.

A fourth approach says: 'How interesting! When you look beyond the passions aroused by particular struggles between individuals and groups you can see patterns that are invisible to those most directly involved. It is a fascinating challenge to bring to light these unnoticed trends and processes, to see the similarities that lie behind the fascinating mix of diverse ethnic, cultural and socio-economic groups that jostle with each other in cities.' Robert E. Park was guided by the two responses 'how complex' and 'how interesting' throughout his career as a sociologist.

To summarize: between 1892 and the end of the First World War, the Chicago School of sociology, as it later became known, began to establish the traditions of thought and work that made it famous. Those were the days of Small, Thomas and, at Hull House, the radical feminist Jane Addams (1860–1935).[3] During the 1920s and the early 1930s, the Chicago School was dominant in American sociology, intellectually and institutionally. During that period, Park reigned alongside Ernest W. Burgess (1886–1966).[4] By the end of the Second World War, however, the Chicago School had lost its institutional dominance in the face of the challenge coming from sociology departments in places like Columbia and Harvard.

Let us trace the changing ways in which Chicago sociology noticed the unnoticed by looking at the writings and contributions of the following individuals: Albion W. Small, William I. Thomas, Jane Addams, Robert E. Park and Louis Wirth. We shall conclude by briefly reviewing four different research traditions or trajectories that came out of the Chicago School: human ecology, social (dis)organization, social psychology and action research.

	Optimism ('How promising!')		
Curiosity ('How interesting!')	**Louis Wirth**	**Albion W. Small**	**Outrage** ('How unjust!')
	Robert E. Park	**William I. Thomas**	
	Sensitivity to ambiguity and contradiction ('How complex!')		

Figure 1.1 Responses of Chicago sociologists to capitalism and the modern city

Albion W. Small

In Albion W. Small's view, before sociologists could make their full contribution to society, they would have to strengthen sociology itself. Small wanted to build up sociology as a discipline with at least as much credibility as economics (see Small 1905). He wanted sociology to have theoretical rigour and political clout. It should also have the practical tools to discover the knowledge policy makers and administrators needed to pursue those interests. Small wanted to produce not dreamers but practical researchers. That meant hard fighting within the University of Chicago itself. For example, Small challenged the claim of academic economists to have a monopoly over teaching statistics.[5]

Within two years of his appointment at Chicago, Small had written a textbook with the help of George E. Vincent, the department's first graduate student. This book, *An Introduction to the Study of Society*, was put before undergraduates as a 'laboratory guide' (Small and Vincent 1894: 15). The laboratory was, in effect, the city of Chicago. Over two decades before the era of Park and Burgess, Small and Vincent emphasized themes that became closely associated with the Chicago School. For example, the increase in residential segregation on lines of national, ethnic or religious background and economic circumstances; the part played by public opinion; the need for more effective involvement by professionals and educated citizens in the politics and administration of the city; and the project of organizing systematic empirical research at ground level, so to speak, covering as many aspects of the city's development as possible.

Small wanted sociologists to construct a 'natural history' of Chicago, looking in detail at how its population was distributed and grouped, the forms of conflict that arose, and the 'defects and failures of institutions and activities ... especially faults of municipal government'. He was especially impressed by the work underway at Hull House, where 'sociological maps' were being produced. Small wanted more such maps to be made that would 'show by colours (a) the distribution of nationalities; (b) the average weekly wages; (c) the location of churches, schools, jails, police stations, saloons, gambling houses, brothels, etc.' (Small and Vincent 1894: 195–6). Small spent almost his entire career at Chicago making the case for sociology and fighting to build up his discipline within the university. His colleague, William I. Thomas, provided one of the first major examples of what an empirical sociologist with theoretical insight could produce.

William I. Thomas

The Polish Peasant in Europe and America (originally published in 1918–20) is William I. Thomas's masterpiece, written with Polish philosopher Florian W.

Znaniecki (1882–1958). This is an ambitious book with a challenging intellectual agenda. It shines a spotlight on the hidden structures and processes that channelled demographic flows across the Atlantic and shaped and reshaped the inner lives of the migrants themselves. Consider the range of themes that are covered: a comparison between change processes occurring in Poland and the United States during the late 19th and early 20th centuries; an analysis of the way transformations at the level of social organization and the level of the personality intersect and interact; with respect to each society, examination of specific institutions and practices such as the family, marriage, social class system, cultural environment, economic life and religion, relating them to broader societal developments placed in a historical and comparative context; suggestions about potential strategies for dealing with different aspects of social and personal disorganization; systematic speculations about possible patterns of future development in Polish and American society; and finally, a checklist of theoretical and practical issues requiring investigation through comparative research.

The task for sociologists, say Thomas and Znaniecki, is to examine social organization; that is, the way human behaviour is regulated by rules embedded in institutions. Social psychology conducts parallel studies of individual organization, which means personal rule-following by specific men and women expressed in terms of their consistently applied attitudes and values. If attitudes shift and support for institutional rules is weakened or withdrawn, the likely result is social disorganization. As long as at least some individuals remain 'organized' at a personal level, there is scope for innovators to emerge from amongst this group, people who can lead the way towards a new, more stable, form of social organization.

In practice, processes of disorganization and reorganization are underway constantly. In Poland, for example, the rural peasant family and the old-style peasant village were both in decay by the late 19th century. However, in that society peasant leadership was so dynamic that the gap was filled by a multitude of cooperative enterprises such as agricultural associations, which were not just economic but also social, engaging the active interest of all concerned. Things were different for Polish immigrants in America. Polish-American associations were set up but they turned out to be too narrow and parochial to bind the Polish community together. As Thomas and Znaniecki observed, it was left in a state of social disorganization:

> How could the resulting delinquency, immorality, family break-up and demoralization be dealt with, in Chicago and elsewhere? Enter the social technician who could intervene actively in practical situations by suggesting 'thorough schemes and plans of action' which would help individuals

> to develop 'the ability to control their own activities by conscious reflection.
>
> (Thomas and Znaniecki 1918–20/1927: 72)

Thomas worked hard to develop the social technician's role, as he saw it, through his involvement in the reform activities organized by Hull House. He was prominent in the work of the Juvenile Protective Association, the Immigrants' Protective League and the Chicago Vice Commission, set up in 1910. These involvements allowed him to obtain a large amount of case-study material, including life histories, which he regarded as an especially useful kind of empirical evidence.

Thomas's practical involvement in reform work was closely intertwined with his scholarly writing. For example, in works such as *Sex and Society* (1907), he examined the part played by gender in the workings of social personality and social organization. In particular, he argued that women had been victims of subjection throughout the ages. At the time this was a 'dangerous' opinion. When he made the same point in a lecture on women, one of his enemies denounced his words in a letter to the university president as a 'vicious attack upon the social system of America'.[6]

Thomas analysed these materials with an approach to human action that reflected the deep influence by pragmatism, although he always denied being greatly influenced by John Dewey, his co-worker at Hull House. Thomas's approach emphasized the interplay of four key factors. One was the part played by the pursuit of control of a person's environment as a means to improve survival chances. Control was achieved through a second factor, the application of attention to the world, looking for opportunities to manipulate it. Once control has been acquired, conscious control can relax into regular habit, the third factor. Finally, habit is always liable to be disrupted by a situation of crisis that revives and focuses attention and the search for control. These crisis situations are occasions when 'social technicians' are often especially useful.

Unfortunately, no social technician was on hand to alleviate Thomas's unhappy situation when he encountered his own crisis in 1918, shortly before the publication of *The Polish Peasant*. The FBI arrested him at a Chicago hotel where he was sojourning with the wife of an army officer who was serving in France. There was a court case, and although Thomas was not convicted of any charge, the publicity ruined his hopes of continuing his academic career in Chicago. Ironically, the target of the prosecution may not have been Thomas himself, but his wife Harriet, who was, like Jane Addams of Hull House, an active campaigner in the peace movement opposing US military involvement in the war in Europe.

Jane Addams

Jane Addams combined action research with social work. Her main base was Hull House, a settlement established in 1889 by herself and Ellen Gates Star (1859–1940) which had very close connections with the Department of Sociology at the University of Chicago (see Deegan 1988).[7] The residents of Hull House were mainly female (Levin and Trost 1996: 138). Settlements of this kind were typically set up to give middle-class students and graduates contact with people in slum areas. The settlement movement started in London, England, where a group of students connected to the church established Toynbee Hall in the East End of London. The intention was that Christian students would stay in the settlement and help poor people improve their way of life. More specifically, the encounter between residents/students and the underprivileged from the poor areas of Chicago would strengthen the poor personally, culturally and in literary culture, while at the same time giving students from better-off families an in-depth and direct knowledge of how life was experienced in the poor areas (Jørgensen 1999: 7ff).

At Hull House an extensive research programme was carried out to map the scale, magnitude and character of social problems in the poor areas in Chicago (Deegan 1995: 335). This research took the form of 'action research', and had a clear political aim: to change the situation of the underprivileged. Addams made a distinction between research that would contribute to improvements in society, and research that would contribute to the development of sociology (Hull House 1895/1970). Addams, her fellow researchers and other persons close to Hull House especially emphasized the first of these in their own work. Martin Bulmer puts it this way:

> In Chicago … Hull-House became not just an independent social agency but a centre at which reformers, politicians and academics discussed social problems in depth. In Chicago, some of the earliest local surveys were carried out by members of the settlement house movement, many of whom were middle-class women college graduates, for whom social welfare was one of the few socially acceptable forms of work open.
>
> (Bulmer 1984: 23)

The anthology *Hull House Maps and Papers* (1895/1970), edited by Jane Addams, contains contributions from residents, mainly touching on the problem of poverty. Their research agenda and techniques became a model for subsequent Chicago sociologists (Deegan 1995: 55), taking as a starting point the geographical location and distribution of the phenomena being studied, a precursor of the mapping technique later taken up and refined by human ecologists such as

Park and Burgess. The Hull House anthology dealt with, for example, disease and social conditions, exploitation of labour, ghettoes and immigrants, social relief organizations, work and creativity, and also the condition of women in Chicago.

Through the efforts of Addams, Hull House was connected to many national and international political associations and pressure groups, through which research results could be distributed and transformed into action (Sibley 1995: 164ff). She took an active part in several feminist movements including the Woman's Peace Party (Sibley 1995: 165), involvements that marginalized her within sociology circles and in society (Deegan 1995: 336). Addams's political commitments made many in the outside world increasingly suspicious of her. Indeed, at the beginning of the First World War members of the Department of Sociology at the University of Chicago cut off relations with Hull House (Deegan 1995: 335; Sibley 1995: 166ff). Commentators, such as Irene Levin and Jan Trost (1996), Mary Jo Deegan (1995) and David Sibley (1995), argued that the Department of Sociology was quite pleased to be rid of the women associated with Hull House.

Robert E. Park

Robert E. Park believed the city could most fruitfully be understood as a concentrated and extreme version of processes within society as a whole. He opposed the construction of urban and rural areas as two divided worlds. According to Park, modern industrialized society has an influence on social processes and relations, no matter whether the geographic context is urban or rural. In the city, however, these effects occur more quickly and affect a larger number of individuals.

Park's reaction to urban conditions was a combination of his great curiosity about the new phenomena and problems that sprang up in the city, and his awareness that the city distils the essence of the complex social relations of modernity. He was preoccupied by the fact that the social geography of the modern city developed in accordance with fixed patterns so that different groups of society were not distributed evenly over urban space. This interest led him to the development of human ecology. Park wanted sociology through empirical research to form the basis of public discussion, debate and politics as a crucial part of modern democratic society. In his view, sociologists had to leave the library and 'get the seat of their pants dirty in real research' (quoted in Lindner 1996: 81).

Together with Roderick McKenzie and Burgess, Park published the anthology *The City* in 1925. This anthology developed the approach of human ecology, which is concerned with understanding and explaining the regularities of urban processes and the social life that develops within them (Park, Burgess and McKenzie 1925). In his article 'The city: suggestions for the investigation of human behaviour in the city environment' (1915), Park focused on mobility and segregation as the main causes for the impersonality of city life. Like Simmel, Park saw urban culture as distinct and different from small communities in rural areas. However, there are many highly nuanced moral environments in the cities, making it difficult to maintain the idea of one single urban culture. Although there are probably certain circumstances which characterize urban life and urban culture as a whole, over time, every single individual in the city discovers 'the moral climate in which his peculiar nature obtains the stimulation that bring his innate qualities to full and free expression' (Park 1915: 608).

Human ecology was a human analogy to the ecology of plants. The Danish phytogeographer Eugenius Warming (1841–1924) and his dissertation *Oecology of Plants – An Introduction to the Study of Plant Communities* (1895/1909) inspired Park, Burgess and McKenzie to draw upon scientific work about plants and their ability to create communities. They developed human ecology on the basis of Warming's research among the hydrofyt, xerofyt, halofyt and mesofyt communities. The main points in Warming's work were that each species lives in harmony with its natural conditions; if these natural conditions change, some species can be forced to move or be destroyed if they do not manage to accommodate; species are not distributed evenly throughout their growing zone; the species are in constantly conflict about territory (they try to force their way into each other's territory in order to change the equilibrium); and the species will settle down in places where they can protect themselves from competition and where they can contribute to the community. Park and his colleagues drew upon these ideas when formulating the well-known concentric circle-model of the city of Chicago, as illustrated in Figure 1.2.

The model helps explain that newcomers start their life in the city of Chicago in the zone in transition II and then work their way out to zones III, IV or V. Thus, every person belongs to a certain community and a certain geographical area in the city. Processes of sorting and shifting occur among the different elements of population and different zones of transition until people find the places where they most effectively can protect themselves from competition and contribute to the community (Park et al. 1925).

Apart from demographic segregation and physical expansion, human ecology also grasped phenomena such as social interaction and processes of social change. Human ecology made it possible to contain these aspects in one single coherent understanding, whereby social interaction and social change are seen as processes that develop in accordance with certain patterns from one order to another. According to Park, social action should be understood as a

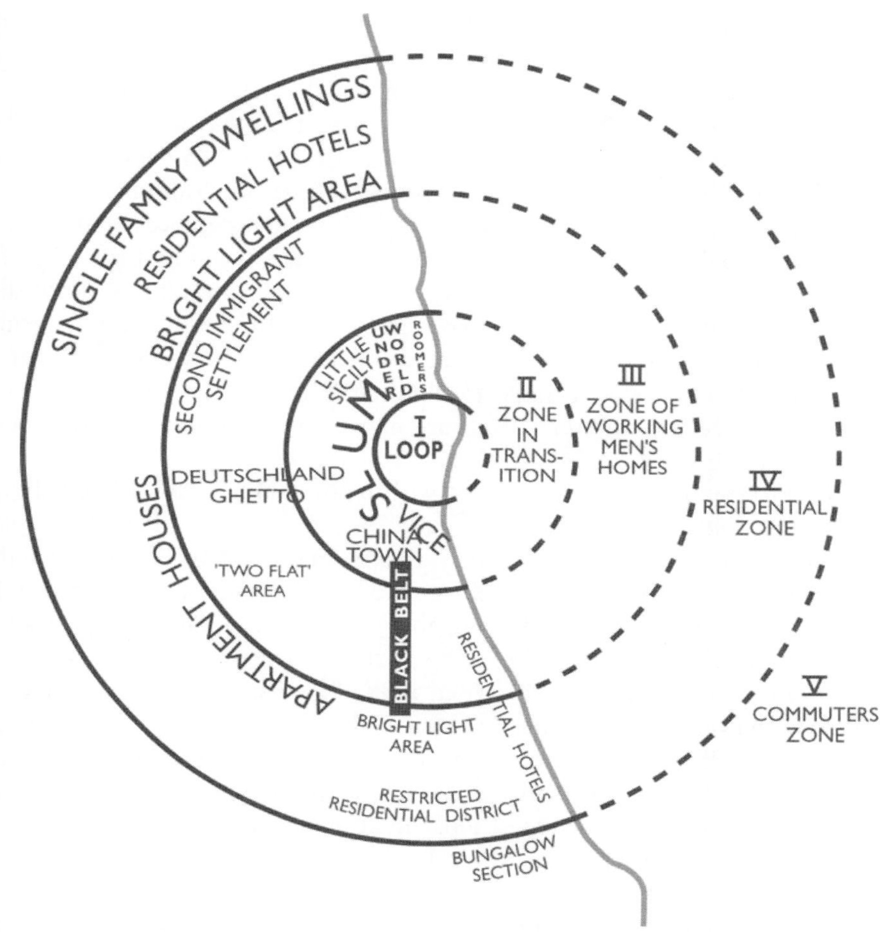

Figure 1.2 The Burgess model of the expansion of the big city and the different urban districts

Source: Park, Burgess and McKenzie (1925: 54).

process occurring in different phases such as competition, conflict and assimilation or absorption, each representing different forms of interaction and different stages in an evolutionary process (Park and Burgess 1921: 785). Competition and conflict belong to the basic level, whereas adaptation and assimilation occur at a higher level, where society has acquired more structure and become a political and moral community. The argument is that social interaction grows from a primitive or natural order, where the important thing is to survive, and develops until a superstructure with common morality, norms and values has been established. In this way, competition and conflicts provide a basis for a more refined community, a society with political and/or moral community, as Park and Burgess have it.

Park and Burgess were opposed to others who tried to draw analogies between nature and the social world, such as for example Adam Smith in *The Wealth of Nations* (1776/2007). While Smith had his point of departure in the idea of 'the survival of the fittest' (that is, 'every man for himself'), Park and Burgess, on the contrary, argued that society is about competitive collaboration, so that individuals are at the same time both in competition and in collaboration with each other within the political and moral community (Park and Burgess 1921: 558). Competition between individuals undergoes a transformation from the basic level of existential competition to a social level where competition consists of a struggle to obtain the necessaries of life (Gaziano 1996: 881). These two different levels are named the symbiotic and the social level, respectively.

How was research to be carried out within this human ecology paradigm? 'Go into the district', 'get the feeling' and 'become acquainted with people': Park's instructions, as reported by his students, may seem trivial at first sight. These instructions do not have much in common with the sophisticated techniques and refined approaches we know today from methodological discussions on field studies. However, they should be understood against the background of the 'sociology of the library' (Lindner 1996: 82). Park, who often took his students with him to different places in Chicago to observe people, insisted that field studies were at least as important as visiting the library and looking for information in archives. He himself characterized his typical instructions to a researcher as expressing 'the art of looking at events as evidence of things in progress, the full significance of which he does not seek to assess' (Park 1955: 110; Lindner 1996: 81).

Park recommended anthropological field studies in the city and the specific method the Chicago sociologists named 'mapping'. According to him, the modern (or civilized) human being lives in the city where the social life can be studied as if it was a laboratory (Park 1952: 73). The anthropological approach, modern/civilized men and women, and the city were, in Park's view, aspects of the same subject. According to him, the sociologist should study people in their normal and natural neighbourhood environments, in contrast to laboratory experiments in which the researcher artificially isolates individuals in order to observe individual reactions. This is because sociology focuses on relations and interactions between individuals, groups, institutions, and so on:

> Because of the opportunity it offers, particularly to the exceptional and abnormal types of man, a great city tends to spread out and lay bare to the

> public view in a massive manner all characters and traits which are ordinarily obscured and suppressed in smaller communities. The city, in short, shows the good and evil in human nature in excess. It is this fact, perhaps, more than any other which justifies the view that would make of the city a laboratory or clinic in which human nature and social processes may be most conveniently and profitably studied.
>
> (Park 1915: 612)

The diverse new relationships and ways of life that flourish in the city when people are released from traditional norms are best studied in-depth with the aid of anthropological methods. Burgess and Thomas as well as Park's contemporaries and students such as Frederic Thrasher, Harvey W. Zorbaugh, Nels Anderson and Donald R. Cressey were all inspired by anthropology. They used a combination of different methods when they carried out their fieldwork in the city of Chicago. Thus, observation methods were widely used in many empirical studies. Park believed it was necessary for the researcher to have direct contact with his field to get the right feeling of the current complex of problems.

This method of carrying out observations has little to do with what we today call field observations, based as it is on a number of more formalized techniques and guidelines. While there are hardly any explicit reflections about method in the works of the early Chicago sociologists, this was not because they did not think about what they did and what consequences it had for their research. Rather, this absence has to be seen in the light of the fact that field studies in sociological contexts were very new and different, and also that for example Park was extremely busy counterbalancing and opposing what he called 'library sociology'. In short, the Chicago sociologists were more interested in developing a new form of field-oriented sociology in actual research practice than in drawing up formal procedures and rules. The following quotation from Park to his students has been noted by Howard S. Becker (b. 1928), a later exponent of Chicago sociology:

> You have been told to go grubbing in the library, thereby accumulating a mass of notes and a liberal coating of grime. You have been told to choose problems wherever you can find musty stacks of routine records based on trivial schedules prepared by tired bureaucrats and filled out by reluctant applicants for aid or fussy do-gooders or indifferent clerks. That is called 'getting the hands dirty in real research'. Those who thus counsel you are wise and honourable; the reasons they offer are of great value. But one thing more is needful: first hand observation. Go and sit in the lounges of the luxury hotels and on the doorstep of the flophouses; sit on the Gold Coast

> setters and on the slum shake-downs; sit in Orchestra Hall and in the Star and Garter Burlesk. In short, gentlemen, go get the seat of your pants dirty in real research.
>
> (quoted in Lindner 1996: 81ff)

For this reason, Park's 'method' has sometimes been characterized as a kind of advanced journalism. 'Super journalism', 'reporters in depth', 'super reporters' and also 'engaged journalism' are merely some of the labels that have been attached to this special method of Park. He was known to go for many walks in Chicago, and obviously this was an important source of inspiration and influence for him, but he never finished and published in book form any major empirical field study. Park primarily wrote articles about different empirical problems and phenomena, as well as a number of articles that shed light on concepts and theories. His sociological approach was mainly influential through his tutorial sessions with students and his discussions with colleagues.

Park's fascination with and inspiration by journalism were far from incidental, and were a result of his own experiences in that occupation. After he received his education (in engineering, psychology, history and philosophy), he worked over a 20-year period as a journalist at different daily papers in Minneapolis, Detroit, Denver and New York, and as a press agent for the black civil rights campaigner Booker T. Washington (Lindner 1996: 33). Park wanted to take the commitment and spirit that reigned in journalism to the university environment. Within the press world it was more important to discover new tendencies and problems, presenting these impressions in a way that readers found interesting and relevant, than it was to produce dense and difficult scientific treatises on theory or methods. However, it is important not to misunderstand Park in this respect: he did indeed believe that journalism could have a stimulating effect on sociology, but he did not believe that sociology was identical to journalism.

The preference that Chicago sociologists such as Park had for empirical studies has subsequently been criticized as being subordinated to the idea that true knowledge and understanding are only achievable through first-hand observations (see, for example, Downes and Rock 1998). However, Park's approach was much more subtle and complex than this implies. He certainly thought that journalism combined certain working methods (specifically the use of observation and interviews) with a daring spirit, and that this combination could indeed inform contemporary sociology. However, it was a special spirit or method of work that he wanted to see imported from journalism, not its lack of interest in theoretical matters. Park, however, was keen to ensure that sociological research should have a basis (human ecology) that was not dominated by the need to conform to the dictates of a specific theory. In particular, the researcher had to be very careful to ensure that a preoccupation with current theory and existing scientific knowledge did not overshadow the field study and its potential for producing new insights. In Park's view, in fieldwork it is important to strike a balance between familiarizing yourself with the case or phenomenon under study and maintaining sufficient detachment to ensure objectivity. Furthermore, scientific research had to be carried out without prejudices and without too many presumptions about the likely findings (Lindner 1996: 101).

Louis Wirth

Louis Wirth, born in Germany, was a first-generation American and a second-generation Chicago sociologist. Wirth came to the United States in 1911 when he was 14 years old, although he did not take American citizenship until 13 years later. He was first a doctoral student then, from 1931, a teacher at the University of Chicago where he remained until his death in 1952. Wirth's intellectual career was shaped by his dual heritage, both European and American. From Germany and Central Europe he drew upon writers such as Georg Simmel and Karl Mannheim (1893–1947) with their sensitivity to the themes of fragmentation and alienation in urban life. From his Chicago teachers, especially Park, Wirth learned the pleasure of exploring the dense anthropological and cultural texture of specific human communities in the city, revelling in their complexity. This approach was strongly evident in his first major work, *The Ghetto* (1928/1998).

Take, for example, Wirth's description of the regular market in the district of Maxwell Street, Milwaukee Avenue and Division Street in Chicago. He noticed that local Jewish traders had a strong preference for that area. Why? Because in the 1920s it was a 'Polish' area and Poles from all over the city came there to do their shopping. There is an irony in this. In Poland, anti-Semitic feelings had a long history, often leading to acts of violence. But here, in the Chicago markets, the two sides seek each other out. They have contempt for each other but they 'know' each other and understand each other's business methods. They can haggle at length and enjoy little victories by bargaining the other down. These observations made this part of the book a kind of postscript to *The Polish Peasant*, in which Thomas and Znaniecki as mentioned above had looked at the European origins of Chicago's Poles. Wirth complemented this by looking at how Jews from Europe, including Poland, had settled into Chicago life.

Typically, newly arrived Jews in America recreated the ghetto, maintaining a separation between themselves and non-Jews. Within the ghetto, old European divisions amongst different groups of Jews persisted. Over time, many Jews in Chicago began to assimilate with mainstream society, especially on the north and south sides of the city. Paradoxically, as more Jews moved out of the old ghetto on the west side of Chicago, new ghettoes were recreated in more prosperous districts, and as a result, 'ghettoized' personalities persisted. This failure to escape the ghetto horrified Wirth. In his view, the ghetto was 'shallow in content and out of touch with the world ... the product of sectarianism and isolation, of prejudices and taboos ... a closed community'. In fact, 'not until the Jew gets out of the ghetto, does he live a really full life' (Wirth 1928/1998: 225–6).

So Wirth did not romanticize the local Jewish community. In fact, his comments did not just apply to Jews but to all those trapped by poverty, ignorance or conservatism in their little local 'villages'. But where are escapees from the ghetto, Jewish or non-Jewish, to go? And will they be better off? To these questions Wirth had two answers, one pessimistic, one optimistic.

Especially during the 1930s, Wirth was intensely aware of living in an anomic society experiencing a near-catastrophic 'disintegration in culture and group solidarity' such that 'much of life's activity loses its sense and meaning' (Wirth 1936: xxv). In his paper 'Urbanism as a way of life' (originally published in 1938),[8] he argued that ecological processes in the city were detaching people from 'organic nature' (Wirth 1938: 46). They became locked into an impersonal world of 'secondary' relationships where utility and efficiency were paramount while kinship, neighbourhood and old ethnic solidarities were breaking down. Human ties became 'impersonal, superficial, transitory and segmental' (Wirth 1938: 54), and human exchanges were conducted in 'a spirit of competition, aggrandisement and mutual exploitation' (Wirth 1938: 56). At best, men and women were likely to become insecure, irritable and liable to extreme mood swings. At worst, they face 'personal disorganization, mental breakdown, suicide, delinquency, crime, corruption and disorder' (Wirth 1938: 61). This was Wirth's gloomy and pessimistic perspective on urban living.

So, at least on the face of it, during the 1930s Wirth was not able to invest confidence in either the local urban community or the big city as a potential framework for providing a satisfying and meaningful human existence. However, by the late 1940s he had a more positive and optimistic response to this issue. It was the task of intellectuals such as Wirth himself to take the lead in shaping a new urban culture based on open communication and a positive spirit of mutual tolerance, compromise and cooperation between groups. That meant influencing public opinion by getting into the public arena: it was not possible any more for 'saints to sit in their ivory towers while burly sinners rule the world' (Wirth 1948: 15). So Wirth got into the public arena. He advised the National Resources Planning Board (1935–43), and then, in 1944, became

Director of Planning for the Illinois Post-War Planning Commission. He very actively campaigned for the establishment of public planning bodies at the level of the metropolitan region, dealing with matters such as housing, health, transport and education. In this way, Wirth put into practice the strategy of taking useful knowledge and strategies developed within social science departments into the public realm of government and politics.

Wirth had the same taste for dealing with empirical complexity that both Thomas and Park had injected into the Chicago School. He was less detached than Park but he did not follow Thomas's tactic of, so to speak, getting down into the bear pit and fighting alongside those who had been unjustly treated. Instead he preferred to reach upwards towards the heights of power and try to change the rules by which resources were distributed and applied. He was a planner rather than an agitator. Furthermore, he was an optimistic planner, and reinjected into the Chicago School the strong confidence in the future of the United States that had been Small's hallmark when he first became head of Chicago's Department of Sociology over half a century before.

The four trajectories of the Chicago School

We conclude this chapter by observing that there have been many attempts to divide and classify the Chicago school into different periods, just as many efforts have been made to subdivide the school into different scientific clusters and approaches (see, for example, Abbott 1999; Andersson 2003; Bulmer 1984; Carey 1975; Fine 1995; Hannerz 1980; Kurtz 1984; Lindner 1996; Smith 1988). Andrew Abbott (1999), for instance, argues that there were three trajectories: *a human ecological trajectory*, *a trajectory of social (dis)organizing* and *a social psychological trajectory*. Perhaps it is more reasonable and accurate to include a fourth trajectory, one based on the *action research and social work* that developed close to the student settlement Hull House in Chicago. By summarizing these approaches below, we shall review the ground we have just covered from a different perspective before concluding on the continued relevance to everyday life sociology of the Chicago School.

The human ecological trajectory

Focused on the relations between the spatial and the social. This trajectory was inspired by biology; in the theoretical and conceptual development biological metaphors were used and biological analogies were drawn. This trajectory is mainly represented by Robert E. Park, Ernest W. Burgess and Roderick McKenzie, who jointly published the book *The City* in 1925. The book was an attempt to formulate the human ecology as a theoretical background for studies of the relations between the social and the city as locality.

Park defined human ecology 'as an organization that springs up from the competition that is linked to the struggle to survive' (in Gaziano 1996: 886). The human ecological perspective is seen as a natural stage of evolution (civilization process), where the first stage constitutes an unconscious community marked with competition between individuals. From this grow more refined sorts of communities: economic, political, organizational and moral, which are all based on communication rather than competition, and which replace each other successively and rebuild on the remains from the former period. At each level there are also different forms of interactions, starting with competition at the basic level and continuing with conflict at the economic level, adjustment at the political level and finally incorporation or assimilation at the moral level. Competition occurs in such a way that the biological balance is undermined in the course of time. In order to get to a new balance a process of stabilization takes place (termed succession) that entails a spatial or geographical dispersal (Park 1952: 229; Burgess 1925/1967: 51).

As has been argued, on this point Park and Burgess differ from other authors who have tried to make analogies between the natural and the social world, for example Adam Smith in his *The Wealth of Nations* (1776/2007). The golden age of the human ecological trajectory was from about 1921 to about 1932. Emanuel Gaziano (1996) has argued that the approach of using plant biology as a metaphor for the development of society began as early as about 1910 at the University of Chicago. This was four years before Park was appointed at the university and about 15 years prior to the publication of *The City: Suggestions for Investigations of Human Behaviour in the Urban Environment* by Park, Burgess and McKenzie (1925).

First published in 1895, Eugenius Warming's treatise *Plantesamfund: Grundtræk af den økologiske Plantegeografi* was translated into English in 1909. The English version, entitled *Oecology of Plants – An Introduction to the Study of Plant Communities*, was welcomed all over the world. In Chicago, according to Gaziano (1996: 878), there was very close contact between biologists and sociologists. Gaziano argues that *ecology* was used explicitly as a term in sociology for the first time in *The City* from 1925. When Park wrote the article entitled 'Suggestions for investigations of human behaviour in the urban environment' (the first chapter in *The City*, also by Park, was entitled in a similar way), he did not use the biological terms but these were added to the edition from 1925. There are various articles about different biological subjects from plant community to community of ants and animal behaviour in the *Introduction to the Science of Sociology* from 1921 by Park and Burgess.[9]

The trajectory of social (dis)organizing

Robert E. Park's students in particular contributed a variety of empirical studies: for example, of immigrants (Thomas and Znaniecki 1918–20/1927), homeless people and tramps (Anderson 1923/1998), life in the ghettos (Wirth 1928/1998), 'taxi-dance halls' (Cressey 1932), specific areas of Chicago (Zorbaugh 1929/1976), criminal gangs (Whyte 1943/1993) and criminals (Shaw 1930/1966). Chicago was the main research site for many anthropological field studies. Although many of these studies were based on the human ecological approach, other theoretical aspects were also introduced.

Louis Wirth based his way of thinking on the trajectory of social (dis)organizing, but he was not especially interested in human ecology. He was, among others, inspired by Georg Simmel, and his works can be regarded as a further development of the analysis that Simmel made in his essay about the big cities and the mental life that was published in 1903. William I. Thomas is another of the principal characters of this trajectory. As has been discussed, together with Florian Znaniecki, he wrote *The Polish Peasant in Europe and America* with its analysis of the culture and social organizing of immigrants. This thorough analysis of the Polish immigrants' life within the social and cultural conditions they experienced in America is one of the first studies of immigrants' culture and social organizing; in this work, for the first time, 'the life story' method was employed.

These studies of social organizing and disorganizing showed how people experienced life and how societal changes at the macro level became noticeable at the micro level. These studies were intended to elucidate the complexity of social problems without giving instructions about how these social problems could be solved or should be mitigated. In other words, while many of these studies appealed indirectly to social reformers, they entrusted to others the task of organizing and implementing the reform work. They analysed the complexity of the relevant social situations and often displayed their injustice, but did not provide specific guidance for action.

The social psychological trajectory

The main focus here was on the relationship between individual consciousness and the group/society, mainly represented by George Herbert Mead and John Dewey, but later sociologists like Erving Goffman (1922–1982), Howard S. Becker (b. 1928), Herbert Blumer (1900–1987) and William I. Thomas were also of pivotal significance. To take one example, Thomas and Znaniecki contributed to this social psychological trajectory with their conceptual work on attitudes and desires (Abbott 1999: 6). According to Thomas and Znaniecki, relations between the individual and the social had to be examined in the light of objective elements (social values) as well as subjective characteristics (attitudes). It is action (or activity) that connects the individual with the objective elements.

The individual is shaped, besides social values, by four basic desires: the desire for new experiences, the desire for security, the desire for attention and also the wish for recognition or acknowledgement. These desires are of differing importance to each individual and are closely connected with their temperament or attitude. When an individual with their basic desires interacts with the group, a process takes place that transforms their temperament into a social personality. Thomas and Znaniecki defined social psychology as the science that examines attitudes in the light of social culture and examines values especially those that regulates the rules of social behaviour (Bulmer 1984: 56ff). For Thomas and Znaniecki, social theory united social psychology and sociology (Bulmer 1984).

Action research and social work

Finally, turning to the sociological work of the women in Hull House, this can be regarded, on one side, as an extension of the positions of John Dewey, George Herbert Mead and William I. Thomas (Deegan 1995: 336),[10] and on the other side, as a new kind of sociology, in which committed practitioners combined home and work in a new kind of intellectual and practical community. In this they carried out research, conducted political and theoretical discussions in public, and carried out specific social work for the poor in Chicago, such as is the case in the work of Jane Addams at Hull House (Deegan 1995: 336).

Mary Jo Deegan states that the research carried out at Hull House can be characterized as 'cultural feminism' and 'critical pragmatism'. According to Deegan, while cultural feminism placed feminine values at the centre, critical pragmatism was focused upon the requirement to produce progressive, free and independent knowledge about everyday life problems (Deegan 1995: 336). Deegan labels the combination of these two approaches as 'feministic pragmatism', and she considers it to have been unique at that time, providing a means with the help of feminine values to try and resolve or alleviate the problems of everyday life (Deegan 1995: 336).

The workers at Hull House moved beyond the dominant attitudes of their contemporaries at the University of Chicago – which were, as has been seen, a mixture of curiosity, awareness of complexity, outrage at injustice and optimism about the possibilities for melioration – to a new and more challenging approach: that is, social and political action. It is ironic that this fourth stream of Chicago sociology, the one that sought to change society as well as study it, an approach that was pioneered by a corps of daring and amazing women, should be the one that was afterwards neglected, downgraded and ignored not only by contemporaries but also, until recently, by the historians of the Chicago School.

All four trajectories deal with and touch upon the world of everyday life in each their different way and they therefore also in different ways contribute with invaluable insights into the world of everyday life.

As we have tried to demonstrate throughout this chapter, the Chicago School is compound and diverse in many ways. However, one of the common features in this tradition has continuously been a focus on the everyday life based on studies of the very diverse population of the city of Chicago. By observing, interviewing and mapping different social and ethnic groups in their so called 'natural environments', Chicago sociologists used everyday life as a point of departure for understanding internal differences between these groups, and especially how these different social and ethnic groups handled the new circumstances, conditions and possibilities that were produced by the modern urban environment. By using the everyday life perspective it was possible to learn more about lifestyles and sub-cultures that were previously unknown, and at the same time focus on life conditions – often very unequal – which left some groups in underprivileged positions while others enjoyed highly privileged situations of life.

Following the foundational period of the Chicago School from the late 19th to the early 20th century, which has constituted the focal point of this chapter, sociologists trained at the University of Chicago continued to develop and refine the different perspectives. Later sociologists such as Erving Goffman, Herbert Blumer, Everett C. Hughes and Howard S. Becker are some of the prominent successors and heirs to this tradition.

Notes

1. On the development of the city of Chicago, see Mayer and Wade (1969). See also http://www.encyclopaedia.Chicagohistory.org/pages/700025.html.
2. On Dewey, see Ryan (1995) and Westbrook (1991). On Mead, see Cook (1993) and Joas (1985). On Hull House, see Bryan and Davis (1991), Hull House (1895/1970) and Addams (1910).
3. On Small, see Christakes (1978) and Dibble (1975). On Thomas, see Janowitz (1966) and Volkart (1951). On Addams, see Linn (2000).
4. On Park, see Matthews (1977). On Burgess, see Bogue (1974).
5. For details, see http://www.brocku.ca/MeadProject/Small/Small_1894_letter.html.
6. Quoted in Matthews (1977: 102).
7. Mead and Thomas from the Department of Sociology played a significant mentoring role for a large part of the scientific work that was carried out in Hull House (Deegan 1995: 335).

8. Originally from Wirth (1938). Citations are to the version republished in Hatt and Reiss (1957: 46–63).
9. Human ecology developed into different directions, hence it includes the direction of Park, Burgess and McKenzie, in which the ecological ideas are used as metaphors and analogies, and in a more fundamentalist direction that in a determinist way interprets all aspects of social and cultural life as a result of natural selection – a position that among others W. C. Allee presents in his article 'Co-operation among animals', published in the *American Journal of Sociology* in 1931 (Gaziano 1996: 884). In many studies that are based on the human ecology way of thinking, an explicit review of human ecology has not been formulated; terms like 'natural development', 'natural history' and 'natural process' remain indications that the human ecology constitutes the theoretical basis.
10. The pragmatic inspiration was derived from, among others, Dewey, Mead and Thomas.

Bibliography

Abbott, Andrew (1999) *Department and Discipline – Chicago Sociology at One Hundred*. Chicago, IL: University of Chicago Press.

Addams, Jane (1910) *Twenty Years at Hull House*. New York: Macmillan.

Anderson, Nels (1923/1998) *On Hobos and Homelessness*. Chicago, IL: University of Chicago Press.

Andersson, Oscar (2003) *Chicagoskolan – institutionaliseringen, idétraditionen och vetenskaben*. Lund: Sociologiska Institutionen, Lunds Universitet.

Bogue, Douglas J. (ed.) (1974) *The Basic Writings of Ernest W. Burgess*. Chicago, IL: University of Chicago Press.

Bryan, Mary L. and Allen F. Davis (eds) (1991) *100 Years at Hull-House*. Indianapolis, IN: Indiana University Press.

Bulmer, Martin (1984) *The Chicago School of Sociology: Institutionalization, Diversity and the Rise of Sociological Research*. Chicago, IL: University of Chicago Press.

Burgess, Ernest W. (1925/1967) 'Introduction to a research project', in Robert E. Park, Ernest W. Burgess and Roderick McKenzie, *The City – Suggestions for Investigation of Human Behavior in the Urban Environment*. Chicago, IL: University of Chicago Press.

Carey, James T. (1975) *Sociology and Public Affairs: The Chicago School*. Beverly Hills, CA: Sage.

Christakes, George (1978) *Albion W. Small*. Boston, MA: Twayne.

Cook, Gary A. (1993) *George Herbert Mead: The Making of a Social Pragmatist*. Chicago, IL: University of Illinois Press.

Cressey, Paul G. (1932) *The Taxi-Dance Hall*. Chicago, IL: University of Chicago Press.

Deegan, Mary Jo (1988) *Jane Addams and the Men of the Chicago School 1892–1918*. New Brunswick, NJ: Transaction.

Deegan, Mary Jo (1995) 'The second sex and the Chicago School', in Gary Alan Fine (ed.), *A Second Chicago School?* Chicago, IL: University of Chicago Press.

Dibble, Vernon K. (1975) *The Legacy of Albion Small*. Chicago, IL: University of Chicago Press.

Downes, David and Paul Rock (1998) *Understanding Deviance – A Guide to the Sociology of Crime and Rule Breaking*. Oxford: Oxford University Press.

Fine, Gary Alan (1995) *A Second Chicago School? – The Development of a Postwar American Sociology*. Chicago, IL: University of Chicago Press.

Gaziano, Emanuel (1996) 'Ecological metaphors as scientific boundary work: innovation and authority in interwar sociology and biology.' *American Journal of Sociology*, 101 (4): 874–907.

Gibson, Campbell (1998) *Population of the 100 Largest Cities and Other Urban Places in the United States: 1790 to 1990*. Washington, DC: US Bureau of the Census/Population Division.

Hannerz, Ulf (1980) *Exploring the City: Inquiries Toward an Urban Anthropology*. New York: Columbia University Press.

Hatt, Paul K. and Albert J. Reiss (1957) *Cities and Society: The Revised Reader in Urban Sociology*. Glencoe, IL: Free Press.

Hull House (1895/1970) *Hull House Maps and Papers by Residents of Hull House, A Social Settlement: A Presentation of Nationalities and Wages in a Congested District of Chicago , Together with Comments and Essays on Problems Growing out of the Social Conditions*. New York: Crowell.

Janowitz, Morris (ed.) (1966) *W. I. Thomas on Social Organization and Social Personality: Selected Papers*. Chicago, IL: University of Chicago Press.

Joas, Hans (1985) *G. H. Mead: A Contemporary Re-Examination of His Thought*. Cambridge, MA: MIT Press.

Jørgensen, Anja (1999) *Kristeligt Studenter Settlement – fra privat filantropi til offentligt støttet socialt arbejde*. Aalborg: ALFUFF.

Kurtz, Lester R. (1984) *Evaluating Chicago Sociology: A Guide to the Literature, With an Annotated Bibliography*. Chicago, IL: University of Chicago Press.

Levin, Irene and Jan Trost (1996) *Å forstå hverdagen*. Otta: Tano & Aschehoug.

Lindner, Rolf (1996) *The Reportage of Urban Culture – Robert Park and the Chicago School*. Cambridge: Cambridge University Press.

Linn, James W. (2000) *Jane Addams: A Biography*. Champaign, IL: University of Illinois Press.

Mannheim, Karl (1936) *Ideology and Utopia* (translated with an introduction by Louis Wirth). London: Routledge.

Matthews, Fred H. (1977) *Quest for an American Sociology: Robert E. Park and the Chicago School*. Montreal: McGill-Queen's University Press.

Mayer, Harold M. and Richard C. Wade (1969) *Chicago: Growth of a Metropolis*. Chicago, IL: University of Chicago Press.

Park, Robert E. (1915) 'The city: suggestions for the investigation of human behavior in the city environment.' *American Journal of Sociology*, 20 (5): 577–612.

Park, Robert E. (1952) *Human Communities – The City and Human Ecology* (Vol. II of the Collected Papers of Robert E. Park). Glencoe, IL: Free Press.

Park, Robert E. (1955) *Society* (Vol. III of the Collected Papers of Robert E. Park). Glencoe, IL: Free Press.

Park, Robert E. and Ernest W. Burgess (1921) *Introduction to the Science of Sociology*. Chicago, IL: University of Chicago Press.

Park, Robert E., Ernest W. Burgess and Roderick McKenzie (1925) *The City – Suggestions for Investigation of Human Behavior in the Urban Environment*. Chicago, IL: University of Chicago Press.

Ryan, Alan (1995) *John Dewey and the High Tide of American Liberalism*. New York: W. W. Norton.

Shaw, Clifford R. (1930/1966) *The Jack Roller – A Delinquent Boy's Own Story*. Chicago, IL: University of Chicago Press.

Sibley, David (1995) *Geographies of Exclusion*. London: Routledge.

Small, Albion W. (1905) *General Sociology: An Exposition of the Main Development in Sociological Theory from Spencer to Ratzenhofer*. Chicago, IL: University of Chicago Press.

Small, Albion W. and George E. Vincent (1894) *An Introduction to the Study of Society*. New York: American Book Company.

Smith, Adam (1776/2007) *The Wealth of Nations*. Petersfield: Harriman House.

Smith, Dennis (1988) *The Chicago School – A Liberal Critique of Capitalism*. New York: St. Martin's Press.

Thomas, William I. (1907) *Sex and Society: Studies in the Social Psychology of Sex*. Chicago, IL: University of Chicago Press.

Thomas, William I. and Florian Znaniecki (1918–20/1927) *The Polish Peasant in Europe and America*, Vols I–II. New York: Alfred A. Knopf.

Volkart, Edmund H. (ed.) (1951) *Social Behavior and Personality: Contributions of W. I. Thomas to Theory and Social Research*. New York: Social Science Research Council.

Warming, Eugenius (1985/1909) *Oecology of Plants – An Introduction to the Study of Plant Communities*. Oxford: Clarendon Press.

Westbrook, Robert B. (1991) *John Dewey and American Democracy*. Ithaca, NY: Cornell University Press.

Whyte, William Foote (1943/1993) *Street Corner Society – The Social Structure of an Italian Slum*. Chicago, IL: University of Chicago Press.

Wirth, Louis (1928/1998) *The Ghetto*. New Brunswick, NJ: Transaction.

Wirth, Louis (1936) 'Preface', in Karl Mannheim: *Ideology and Utopia*. London: Routledge.

Wirth, Louis (1938) 'Urbanism as a way of life.' *American Journal of Sociology*, 44 (1): 1–24.

Wirth, Louis (1948) 'Consensus and mass communication.' *American Sociological Review*, 13 (1): 1–15.

Zorbaugh, Harvey W. (1929/1976) *The Gold Coast and the Slum: A Sociological Study of Chicago's Near North Side*. Chicago, IL: University of Chicago Press.

CHAPTER 2

American Pragmatism

Examining Everyday Life 'in the Making'[1]

ROBERT C. PRUS AND ANTONY J. PUDDEPHATT

Introduction

Although often disregarded by those in the social sciences and the humanities, pragmatism is essential for a more adequate understanding of community life and the human condition more generally. Not only does pragmatist theory attend to the nature of human knowing and acting, it also addresses the very foundations of reality, including people's relationships to one another, the material environments in which they live and act, and the broader cosmos in which they find themselves. Indeed, pragmatist social theory is concerned with the very things that give meaning to everyday life as it is realized in practice.

In part, a disregard for pragmatist social thought among social scientists seems predicated on three common misconceptions. The first is that pragmatist social thought is a recent, uniquely American, democratic invention that lacks the conceptual sophistication and potency of classical European social theory. The second misconception is that pragmatism is an individualist, subjectivist approach that cannot deal with community life on a broader base and lacks the capacity to deal with matters of power and conflict as well as more molar social processes. The third misconception is that pragmatism is primarily a philosophical standpoint and cannot be used to study the world out there in more sustained empirical terms. As we shall indicate, those adopting these viewpoints are not only badly mistaken in their assumptions, they also appear to have become mired in philosophical viewpoints that substantially misrepresent human group life as it takes place on a day-to-day basis. Quite directly, it is only through pragmatist-informed scholarship that we, as social scientists, will be able to achieve more accurate, authentic representations of everyday life as a humanly engaged process.

In what follows, we shall do three things. First, we briefly locate the roots of pragmatist social theory amidst the longstanding debates between the empiricists (also materialists, objectivists and positivists) and the idealists (also rationalists, subjectivists) that have characterized Western social thought since the classical Greek era. Next, we discuss the key ideas in American pragmatism, attending to the works of Charles Sanders Peirce, William James, Ferdinand Schiller, John Dewey and George Herbert Mead. Then we address the empirical features of pragmatist social thought as these have been developed by Charles Horton Cooley, Herbert Blumer and other scholars working in what has become known as Chicago-style symbolic interactionism.

The pragmatist divide: the intellectual legacy

> There is absolutely nothing new in the pragmatic method. Socrates was an adept at it. Aristotle used it methodically. Locke, Berkeley and Hume made momentous contributions to truth by its means. Shadworth Hodgson keeps insisting that realities are only what they are 'known-as'. But forerunners of pragmatism used it in fragments: they were preluders only. Not until in our time has it generalized itself, become conscious of a universal mission .... A pragmatist turns his back resolutely and once for all upon a lot of inveterate habits dear to professional philosophers. He turns away from abstraction and insufficiency, from verbal solutions, from bad a priori reasons, from fixed principles, closed systems, and pretended absolutes and origins. He turns towards concreteness and adequacy, towards facts, towards action, and towards power .... It means the open air and possibilities of nature, as against dogma, artificiality and the pretence of finality in truth.
>
> (James 1907: 30–1)

Following William James's acknowledgement of some fundamental aspects of pragmatist thought in early Greek philosophy, we shall briefly address some of the roots of Western social thought before focusing more directly on American pragmatism.

If we take the classical Greek era (circa 700–300 BCE) as a reference point, we can distinguish empiricism, idealism and pragmatism as three broad but consequential intellectual emphases. While there is considerable variation in each of these three broad categories, these approaches represent longstanding intellectual tensions in the history of Western social thought. Most common are debates between the empiricist and materialist philosophers on the one hand (for whom reality is defined by the physical nature of the external world), and idealists on the other (for whom reality is based on thought or spiritual consciousness). However, amidst these polarities, we can also find extended discussions of human knowing and acting in the work of the early Greeks, which largely resemble contemporary constructionist, relativist and pragmatist formulations.

Beyond the contributions to the broader study of knowing and acting by numerous other Greek authors (for example, Herodotus, 485–425 BCE; Thucydides, 460–400 BCE; and Isocrates, 436–438 BCE), we find a great many pragmatist themes discussed in the work of Plato (427–347 BCE). Thus, Plato discusses the 'problematics of knowing' at length in *Sophist*, *Philibus*, *Parmenides* and *Theaetetus*. Somewhat relatedly, he provides extended considerations of language (*Cratylus*), self-knowledge (*Charmides*), love (*Symposium*), friendship (*Lysis*) and courage (*Laches*), amongst other matters of knowing and acting. Those who examine *Republic* and *Laws* will also find that Plato provides many comparative observations of diverse Greek life-worlds and people's viewpoints, thoughts, practices and interchanges as he engages in extended deliberations regarding the viability of various policies and other strategic ventures for managing community life (Plato 1997). However, Plato's pragmatist considerations of human knowing and acting are often overlooked amidst the various idealist, theological and sceptic positions that his speakers sometimes assume. Notably as well, it is Plato's student, Aristotle (384–322 BCE), who more explicitly and consistently considered what people do in practice, how they manage their activities on a day-to-day basis, and the implications of adopting particular lines of action over others. Thus, although Aristotle is often viewed more exclusively as an objectivist, his attentiveness to human knowing and acting assumes a much different, strikingly pragmatist quality.

Adopting a distinctively secular position that is attentive to the biological nature of the human condition, Aristotle not only broke with the idealism and mind-body dualism that is often associated with Plato, but he also focused much more centrally on purposive activity and the associated matters of speech, deliberation, agency and community interchange (see especially *Nicomachean Ethics*, *Politics*, *Rhetoric*, *Rhetoric to Alexander* and *Poetics*). Maintaining these emphases, along with an insistence on the unity of body, activity and mind, Aristotle articulated many of the conceptual features of what is now known as 'pragmatist thought' (see Prus 2003, 2004, 2007a).

Tracing the flows of pragmatist thought from the Greeks to the present, Robert Prus has encountered a series of 'Aristotelian-inspired' pragmatist revivals over the intervening centuries. Albeit in uneven pockets of activity, various scholars in the fields of rhetoric, philosophy, religion, politics and poetics have from time to time directly built on Aristotle's works or on that of others who had earlier, often indirectly, done so.

American pragmatist theory: emergent formulations

Whereas a closer examination of the scholarly works of the American pragmatists indicates only limited familiarity with classical Greek scholarship, the more fundamental concepts that Charles Sanders Peirce, William James, John Dewey and George Herbert Mead share with Aristotle are noteworthy. By emphasizing activity, speech, intentionality, reflectivity, interchange, community, process, and an insistence on the unity of mind, body and activity, the American pragmatists were able to launch a concerted attack on empiricist and idealist philosophies, and develop an exceptionally viable analytic framework to study knowledge and action within community life.[2]

Attending to everyday life as something 'in the making', pragmatists are concerned with the emergent, processual, interconstituted relationship between 'knowing' and 'doing' that takes place as people engage the world around them. Therefore, all instances of speech, knowledge and social life are envisioned as products of activity. However, even with these overarching emphases, readers may be cautioned that, like the problematic, emergent, and situated conceptions of reality it addresses, American pragmatism has had a notably uneven developmental flow, with numerous internal debates about the nature of pragmatism and its implications for the study of human knowing and acting.

Still (and differences aside), because they envision human knowing as integrally linked to activity (and process), the pragmatists do not accept the claim that reality exists as a pre-given, transcendental state (idealism) which can be discovered independently through rational dialogue, nor do they accept the claim that reality emanates exclusively from the objective nature of the external world (as presumed by the empiricists). For the pragmatists, reality is continually reconstituted within the problem-solving adjustments of people as they collectively act (and react) toward the challenges posed by their physical and social environments. As such, any conceptions of empirical phenomena, along with notions of truth, justice, law or the gods, can only achieve viability as minded reference points insofar as these notions are shared in a community context. As such, language is a necessary medium for all knowledge. Built on a shared base of meaning, it is language that allows people to compare, assess, act toward and reconstitute definitions of reality on an ongoing basis. Indeed, abstract, reflective thought would not be possible at all without language, since it is only in language that the concepts and ideas generated within the community are located.

Denoting interim stances, viewpoints or methods for considering and acting toward things, knowledge is always something in the making. Like other activities, knowledge is subject to continuities and modifications (that is, extension, revision and rejection) as people attend to, consider, anticipate, test out and make use of concepts over time. Mindful of the virtually unlimited array of contexts in which people find themselves in everyday life, the pragmatist position is relativist, pluralist and developmental in its emphasis. As a result, knowledge is simultaneously a product of the past, an enabling device in the present, and an ever-emergent set of comprehensions toward the future. Meanings emerge and are transformed as people engage things in specific instances, and as they make indications to themselves and others through the course of activity.

Outsiders frequently allege that pragmatism is anti-scientific. These claims are mistaken. Indeed, many of the emphases of pragmatist philosophy were inspired by the rise of modern science as well as the evolutionary theory of Charles Darwin (see Mead 1930, 1936). Further, science can be seen as a sustained realm of pragmatist methodology in practice, as often was suggested through explicit examples given by Peirce, Dewey and Mead, among others.[3] The pragmatist argument, thus, is *not* against science as a purposive, meaning-making and instrumental human undertaking, but it is against those (for example, empiricists and idealists) who fail to recognize or refuse to acknowledge the emergent, socially constituted *and* enacted foundations of all manners of knowledge and action in science as well as in everyday life.

In what follows, consideration is first given to the writings of Charles Sanders Peirce, William James, Ferdinand Schiller, John Dewey and George Herbert Mead. Subsequently, attention is given to Charles Horton Cooley, early Chicago sociology, and the symbolic interactionist tradition associated with Herbert Blumer. Some may be surprised to see Cooley and Blumer referenced so centrally in a discussion of pragmatism, but it should be observed that these scholars were responsible not only for giving pragmatism a more direct and sustained visibility in the social sciences, but also for more fully realizing the pragmatist agenda of assessing things in practice – including pragmatist philosophy – through direct, first-hand examinations of human group life in the making.

Charles Sanders Peirce

Often credited as the 'founder' of pragmatism, Charles Sanders Peirce (1839–1914) is considered by some to be the greatest of American philosophers because of his extended fluency with philosophy, logic, mathematics and science (Smith 1966). Still, Peirce's involvements in pragmatism were rather circuitous. Thus, Peirce (1978–1906/1934: 5.12) observes that in the early 1870s he and a group of young men (including William James) met to discuss metaphysics and related matters. While defining the style of their thought as 'distinctively British', Peirce notes that his own debate with the philosophy of Immanuel Kant (1724–1804) was extended by others whose backgrounds were more diverse. Here, Peirce references Alexander Bain's definition of belief as 'that upon which a man is prepared to act', which constitutes the premise of which pragmatism is little more than a corollary.

Fundamentally, Peirce argued that knowledge is neither a product of the ideal forms carried in our heads nor of the reality of the presumed percept of experience. Rather, Peirce founded reality in the practical effects we imagine of objects, which are generated in the process of experience. In this way, Peirce asks how people construct knowledge of phenomena for intentioned use in concrete circumstances. Peirce's formulation of this pragmatist maxim is as follows:

> In order to ascertain the meaning of an intellectual conception one should consider what practical consequences that might conceivably result by necessity from the truth of that conception; and the sum of these consequences will constitute the entire meaning of the conception.[4]
>
> (Peirce 1878–1906/1934: 5.9)

The core of Peirce's theory of knowledge is disarmingly simple, yet has been long-held as a result of, first, the exhaustiveness and flexibility of the definition; second, the emphasis on the process of experience through action that is necessary to build anticipations and beliefs resulting in various practical consequences; and third, the naturalistic conception of how knowledge is actually constructed in real time contexts and specific situations, over and above the ideal thought experiments in regards to knowledge, found in the classical epistemology of traditional philosophy.

Indeed, Peirce's pragmatism is situated in opposition to idealist, rationalist and empiricist modes of philosophy. Peirce distanced himself from the idealism of Socrates and Plato, who argued that symbols or forms exist prior to human experience. Inspired to some extent by the naturalist philosophy of Aristotle, Peirce envisioned knowledge as an outgrowth of people's practical encounters with things in material environments of activity. Thus, 'pragmatism' was coined on the basis of the Greek word *pragma*, meaning activity or that which is practical. As such, belief for Peirce always referred to modes of conduct, and the practical consequences that would result from it being true. Hence, beliefs and thoughts can only be distinguished by the resultant action that would accompany it. Thus, pragmatism is at root a philosophy of action; wherein mind, ideas and reality are tested and re-tested every day; not through some abstract formula of verification, but through their survival in everyday contexts of instrumental activity.

For Peirce, thought emerges as a way to categorize and represent responses to environmental stimuli (Scheffler 1974). Once positive results of various actions are symbolized as useful, individuals are able to use these responses to enable lines of action that would result in some kind of psychological satisfaction, which is the underlying motivator for accruing patterned, signified beliefs. Since individuals experience frustration at not being allowed to act in a way that they wish, thought enables new conceptions of conduct to be introduced in a way to allow previously blocked action to go on unabated. This leads to patterns of action that are then verified to the subject through successful repetition, and ultimately lead to new habits of conduct that are judged to be efficacious. This is the basic starting point to how people learn. It is this basic assumption about knowledge that allows all complex, scientific and social activities to form and take shape. The basic doctrine of pragmatism can be extended to capture the most abstract, speculative and detached theoretical ideas generated in everyday life, as all imply some sort of practical *conduct*. Thus, statements are only meaningfully distinct if they lead to different consequences through action.

Peirce was consumed with the question of how knowledge in the form of universals is constructed, and invoked the concepts of 'firstness', 'secondness' and 'thirdness' as a way to try to explain it. Firstness refers to an independent reality (spontaneous nature), while secondness implies a relation between different aspects of this reality, leading to thirdness, which enters the level of symbolic mediation (the foundation for scientific laws). Thus, we can only be fully conscious of the third level of awareness, which is a symbolic construct, in formulating shared knowledge claims.

As such, Peirce is well known for his development of semiotics, which refers simply to a 'theory of signs'. Here, Peirce addresses the distinctions between a sign, its object or reference point, and a logical referent or some meaning or theory of connection between the sign and that to which it refers. Since all knowledge of reality is based on our construction and adjudication of signs, then people's conceptions of being are always linked to language, and hence, the human community. In the following quotation, Peirce establishes the symbolic or sign-based nature of humanly experienced reality. Since reality can only be developed through our reliance on signs, objects are brought into existence through the use of linguistically-enabled concepts:

> We do not obtain the conception of Being, in the sense implied in the copula, by observing that all the things which we can think of have something in common, for there is no such thing to be observed. We get it by reflecting upon signs – words or thoughts; we observe that different predicates may be attached to the same subject, and that each makes some

> conception applicable to the subject; then we imagine that a subject has something true of it – and that we call Being. The conception of being is, therefore, a conception about a sign.
>
> (Peirce 1878–1906/1934: 5.294)

Although Peirce spent comparatively little time talking about the role of the community in constructing claims about reality, it is clear that he was not a psychological reductionist. Since all notions of reality must be built upon signs, which are codified into symbolic packages of language to be shared with others, our notions of reality cannot be developed and sustained on any long-term basis in isolation from others. Thus, it should be acknowledged that Peirce explicitly located human conceptions of reality within ongoing community interchange. It is only here that competing claims to reality in the form of laws can be tested, scrutinized, argued over and collectively adopted for shorter or more sustained periods.

This emphasis on the community is important in Peirce's development of pragmatism as a general refutation against the rationalist philosophy developed by René Descartes (1596–1650). Descartes argued that the individual thinker could ascertain reality by simply throwing all knowledge into doubt, and then, using reason alone, building up a stable sense of reality through a cumulative process of monological thought. Peirce argued against this line, in that, first, throwing everything into doubt was not possible in the first place, in that we always carry biases and attitudes along with us guiding inquiry; and second, the real can never be ascertained by a sole individual; rather, the real must be founded in the intersubjective agreement forged by a community. Thus, our own senses and lines of logic can often fail us, and must be checked by others. If some notion of reality holds not only for one individual's perspective, but for several, then reality can be temporarily assured as a result of its presumed independence from any one investigator's opinion, logic and sensory apparatus:

> The real, then, is that which, sooner or later, information and reasoning would finally result in, and which is therefore independent of the vagaries of me and you. Thus, the very origin of the conception of reality shows that this conception essentially involves the notion of a 'community', without definite limits, and capable of a definite increase of knowledge. And so those two series of cognition – the real and the unreal – consist of those which, at a time sufficiently future, the community will always continue to re-affirm; and of those which, under the same conditions, will ever after be denied .... There is nothing, then, to prevent our knowing outward things as they really are, and it is most likely that we do thus know them in numberless cases, although we can never be absolutely certain of doing so in any special case.
>
> (Peirce 1878–1906/1934: 5.311)

It is in this sense that Peirce tends to be more of an 'objectivist' than the other pragmatist philosophers considered here. Growing up with a keen interest in the sciences and the logic of experimentation, Peirce was a firm believer in the ability to get at a reality that is independent of human perspectives (Murphy 1990). Still, he contended that it is only through the critical scrutiny of the surrounding social collective that traces of this independent status of reality, recognized in the form of collectively shared signs, can be born.

William James

Sociologists tend to dismiss William James (1842–1910), probably as a result of his reputation as a 'psychologist' and his over-attentiveness to religious spirituality as a realm of human lived experience. However, James is much more central to the development of sociologically styled pragmatism than is often assumed. Thus, whereas the symbolic interactionists tend to align themselves much more fundamentally with John Dewey and George Herbert Mead, James has a great deal to offer contemporary sociological conceptions of knowledge and action, and also developed insightful critiques of rationalist and empiricist thought.[5]

While James had studied in Germany with Wilhelm Wundt (1832–1920) and likely would have been exposed to Wundt's *Ethics*, we have found little evidence that he took much direct inspiration from the German scholars. James may have developed a generalized receptivity to pragmatism during his studies in Germany, but he did not engage with this topic until considerably later in his career. Also, James (1907: 6) identified Charles Sanders Peirce and especially Ferdinand Canning Scott Schiller as the central sources inspiring his own version of pragmatism.[6]

James (1898/1967) extended the naturalistic basis of Peirce's pragmatism, considering more closely the psychological and physiological components of how people develop knowledge in the practical activity of solving problems. James's interests in psychology provided the starting point of the assumptions surrounding an organic, cognate and self-directed inquirer, leading to an epistemology that differs remarkably with most traditional metaphysical systems of thought. Like Peirce, James sought meanings for things in their practical effects, and truth in the resultant action that could be realized based on the execution of a thought or belief toward some sort of purposive action. Thus, knowledge was never derived in some neutral and unimpassioned fashion, but emerged through the conviction and purpose of an actor determined to bring about some goal. Mead here acknowledged the groundwork laid by James for the extension of the pragmatist tradition:

> Knowledge predicates conduct, and conduct sets the process within which it must be understood .... For James the act is a living physiological affair, and must be placed in the struggle for existence ... Efficacy [of knowledge] can be determined not by its agreement with a pre-existent reality but by its solution of the difficulty within which the act finds itself. Here we have the soil from which pragmatism sprung.
>
> (Mead 1930: 223–4)

Thus it was James, perhaps more than any of the other pragmatists, who urged that the study of knowledge ought to be conducted in a way that is attuned to how it is actually accomplished, by minded, physiological organisms engaging in purposeful goals within concrete environments of action. To try to consider how people approach learning and study abstractly (as is done in traditional philosophical accounts), apart from these living, breathing processes by which all organisms must generate knowledge, is inaccurate and idealistic at best. James pushed the need to study knowledge acquisition as a full-blown naturalistic process.

Also following Peirce, James equated truth with the psychological satisfaction of being able to engage in a line of conduct that was previously blocked. James realized that thought serves first and foremost an instrumental purpose, used to consider new lines of action in the world. If a particular line of action is desired, yet frustrated, the individual feels a subjective pang of irritation, motivating a solution to the problem. By internally playing out different lines of conduct that would allow this frustrated action to be realized, the actor chooses a particular action to bring about the most positive result. If the idea is successfully executed in order to meet a desired goal, a feeling of relief and satisfaction arises.

Since James stressed positive outcomes and psychological satisfaction as the primary criterion for validating knowledge, he is sometimes dismissed as subjectivist. Certainly the truth of a claim must do more than simply satisfy an actor's appetite to solve a particular problem. And, whether that problem is solved (and the knowledge efficacious) must hang on more than whether the individual believes that it is satisfactory. This is not entirely fair, since a closer look at James's *The Meaning of Truth* (1909) points out three major criteria that go beyond mere psychological satisfaction for judging that which is pragmatically true. First, there is to be a close connection of the belief or claim with the particular situation at hand. Second, the new idea should be compatible with what is already known about the matter under consideration. Third, the new idea must contribute to an action that brings about a result that is intended and judged beneficial and satisfactory by those in the setting.

With these matters in mind, it should be stressed that James also attended to the ever-shifting fluidity of the environment in which people live, act and think. James emphasized that truth is a matter that is continually reformulated through the process of inquiry and action on the part of human communities. For James, considering truth in an absolutist sense was nothing more than a tidy but ultimately useless conception. We cannot make some sort of fictitious comparison to an imagined reality from the view of God. If our view of reality is only the sum total of practical effects (for example, sensations, actions) that would result from that statement of reality being true, then we cannot expand a notion of truth beyond the bounds of testable experience. This is why James's position is so important – it was a turn against how truth *should be justified* understood to how it is *actually justified* within the practices of self-interested, emotional, purpose-driven and habit-forming individuals in social collectives.

Ferdinand Canning Scott Schiller

> The saying of Protagoras is like the views we have mentioned; he said that man is the measure of all things, meaning simply that that which seems to each man assuredly is. If this is so, it follows that the same thing both is and is not, and is bad and good, and that the contents of all other opposite statements are true, because often a particular thing appears beautiful to some and ugly to others, and that which appears to each man is the measure. This difficulty may be solved by considering the source of the opinion. It seems to have arisen in some cases from the doctrine of the natural philosophers, and in others from the fact that all men have not the same views about the same things, but a particular thing appears pleasant to some and the contrary of pleasant to others.
>
> (Aristotle, *Metaphysics*, Book XI, 6, 1062b; here quoted from Aristotle 1984)

Although his work is scarcely known in the social sciences, the British scholar Ferdinand Canning Scott Schiller (1864–1937) was not only intricately involved in the development of American pragmatism – according to James (1907) – and was a very important source of inspiration for James's formulations of pragmatist thought, but also provided (1907) a particularly coherent and extended early statement on pragmatism.

Like James (as well as many contemporary interpretivists), Schiller lacked a strong conception of intersubjectivity compared with Dewey and (particularly) Mead. Nevertheless, he (1907; see especially chapters 1, 2 and 5–9) clarified a number of important pragmatist issues regarding human knowing as a problematic and relativist phenomenon.

Whereas his familiarity with the works of Aristotle seemed notably limited, Schiller explicitly located the pragmatist debate in classical Greek scholarship. Thus, in developing his *Studies of Humanism* (1907), Schiller built extensively on the Greek sophist Protagoras (circa 490–420 BCE) in challenging Platonist idealism as well as the related idealism/rationalism of Kant and others who emphasized the disparities between true (or objective, external) reality and the allegedly flawed, subjectivist modes human knowing.

Building on the relativist philosophy of Protagoras, Schiller not only developed an extended pragmatist rationale for rejecting the depersonalized and dehumanized notions of truth with which Plato and Kant, amongst others, had worked, he also addressed the ambiguous, processual and adjustive nature of human knowing within the lived environment at some length. Still, because, first, he defined his approach as 'humanist' rather than explicitly 'pragmatist'; second, he concentrated on more individualized sources of knowing in the later chapters of his text; and third, he resided in England rather than the United States, most of those commenting on American pragmatism have missed his contributions to this intellectual venture as well as the more obvious linkages he provides between classical Greek and contemporary pragmatist thought.

John Dewey

Like William James, John Dewey (1859–1952) was a prolific author, yet his work was characterized by a variety of tensions and much of his work had a more diffuse flow. While it is easy to become lost in the massive set of materials that Dewey (1910/1975, 1922/2002, 1929/1958, 1934) developed, there is no question that many contemporary sociological conceptions of self, meaning and the production of knowledge are indebted to his philosophy.[7] Mead, for example, would derive important aspects in much of his social psychology and his view of meaning through his association with Dewey. As with the other pragmatists, *activity* is the core of Dewey's approach to the study of meaning and the development of knowledge within human communities (Biesta and Burbules 2003: 31–5).

Perhaps the best starting point to understand Dewey's thought is his influential article 'The reflex-arc concept in psychology' (1896). In this paper, Dewey criticized behaviourist psychology for its over-emphasis on a stimulus–response conception of thought and action. Dewey argued that stimulus–response models are an over-simplified way of considering how organisms act. He claims that organisms do not merely respond passively to stimuli as they are prompted by various elements of the environment. Rather, organisms actively, selectively adjust to what is in the environment in the process of meeting tensions associated with survival and comfort. This 'selection process' changes the entire range of stimuli that the organism encounters, and hence brings about an entirely different matrix of responses. These responses are not necessarily instinctually determined, but could be based on learning and the development of habits. It is this interchange of living organisms and their environments that divides them qualitatively from inanimate phenomena. In sum, we cannot consider living organisms as simply reactive to external stimuli like billiard balls, since even simple organisms such as cells and plants selectively engage or adjust themselves to their environments in purposeful ways.

The capacity of human beings to choose more complex lines of action is allowed by their special ability to symbolize and represent forms of conduct internally to themselves and others before acting. As animals that are capable of reflective, symbolic thought in the selection of environmental resources, humans are ever more grossly misrepresented by a stimulus–response model. Indeed, the capacity of intelligent conduct greatly increases when symbols and representations can be socially shared and transmitted among the group. Further, by becoming imbued with language to provide explicit designations for meaning, actors have the conceptual tools to build more complex and intricate modes of conduct. Viewed in these terms, *meaning becomes a method of acting towards things*. Whereas activity is seen as having an experiential quality, it is in the articulation of *the linkages* between situations, activity, and consequences that people (linguistically) develop notions of reality (Biesta and Burbules 2003: 42–53).

Dewey insisted that scholars focus on the enacted outcomes that people associate with objects. Things are not inherently meaningful, but are given meanings by the ways that people locate these things within their ongoing realms of activity. Mead credited Dewey with the origination of meaning in the sense that he would later use it:

> The title that Dewey gives to these objects of thought is 'meanings'; and by this title and his account of the origin and function of meanings he brings them within the field of conduct, and in so doing this adds another category to reality – the category of the social. For meanings arise only through symbols – language is of course a system of symbols par excellence. Only because one individual can point out certain characters to other individuals, and can point them out to himself, do these characters get isolated and attain the standing that makes them objects of thought. It is social conduct in its symbolic references to objects that endows them with meanings.
>
> (Mead 1936: 77–8)

Thus, Dewey was a major influence on Mead's conception of social psychology and the understanding of how knowledge is arrived at within the functional parameters of the human group. However, Mead would develop pragmatist ideas even more so in the direction of sociology, and develop extensive theories of the self in the community, as well as argue for the generation of knowledge as a product of collective social action.

George Herbert Mead

George Herbert Mead (1863–1931) was the most influential of the pragmatists to sociology, probably because of the success of the publication of his lectures in *Mind, Self and Society* (1934) and his influence on famous sociologists at Chicago, most notably, Herbert Blumer. Having studied under the neo-Hegelian Josiah Royce at Harvard, Mead pursued graduate studies in Germany with Wilhelm Wundt and Wilhelm Dilthey (1833–1911). Robert C. Prus (1996) has drawn attention to some of the more striking affinities of the works of Mead (especially *Mind, Self and Society*) with Dilthey's (1978) analysis of human knowing and acting. While there are few references to Dilthey in Mead's works, Mead was no doubt influenced by him (see Puddephatt, forthcoming), and it seems that many of Mead's students at Chicago, including Blumer, were exposed to some of Dilthey's texts. Wundt also had a substantial influence on Mead. In his first volume of *Volkerpsychologie*, Wundt (1886/1897, 1900–20) emphasized the concept *volksseele* (that is, folk mind or social consciousness), which Mead largely endorsed. Wundt's influence was also apparent in Mead's (1934) reformulation of Wundt's 'concept of the gesture' and 'significant symbols'.

Mead (1934) began his analysis by arguing that there is a fundamental difference between the minds of lower animals and that of human beings. Lower animals act instinctively, and automatically respond to stimuli in the environment, such that their outward behaviour fully captures their conduct. As such, studying the conduct of lower animals using the principles of psychological behaviourism to measure stimulus–response patterns, as his student John B. Watson would do, makes a great deal of sense. However, using such an approach is wholly inadequate in considering human conduct, because of the unique qualities of the human mind.

Like Dewey, Mead argued that humans have the unique capacity to use symbols to represent and indicate phenomena to themselves and others in the environment in order to play out the probable consequences of action internally as lines of action are considered. This capacity for indicating symbolic representations to ourselves internally is enabled by the 'conversation of gestures' present in social interaction. By learning how to make mutual indications towards things through patterns of gestures with others, individuals also learn to make symbolic indications to themselves. It is this ability to make use of these shared symbolic representations in forming conduct that forms the unique basis of the human mind. Only once we have developed the social capacity for making mutual indications and engaging in linguistically mediated social interaction can we gain the ability to use these tools for individual reflective thought. Thus, human reflective intelligence is an inner dialogue that is enabled by the social community, in that individuals make indications to themselves on the basis of the symbolic representations furnished by the group.

Like the other pragmatists, Mead located 'meaning' in the resultant consequences brought about by executing a particular line of action. Thus, the meaning of an act takes shape in the course of social interchange, while the subsequent understanding of that act is represented symbolically by human groups in the form of an idea. This concept is often confused by many contemporary sociological accounts of Mead's theory, but Mead was quite clear in maintaining that the meanings of social acts can be unconscious and implicit as well as conscious and explicitly defined. He wrote:

> Much subtlety has been wasted on the problem of the meaning of meaning. It is not necessary, in attempting to solve this problem, to have recourse to psychical states, for the nature of meaning, as we have seen, is found to be implicit in the structure of the social act, implicit in the relations among its three principle individual components: namely, in the triadic relation of a gesture of one individual, a response to that gesture by the second individual, and completion of the given social act initiated by the gesture of the first individual. And the fact that the nature of meaning is thus found to be implicit in the structure of the social act provides additional emphasis upon the necessity, in social psychology, in starting off with the initial assumption of an ongoing social process of experience and behaviour ... upon which the existence and development of their minds, selves, and self-consciousness depend.
>
> (Mead 1934: 81–2)

This essential component of Mead's assumptions – that practical human interaction in the form of action and adjustment comes before and sets the stage for the consciously held and shared meanings that may arise – was echoed in his earlier work *Essays in Social Psychology*, which was more recently published (Mead 2001: 3–17). This book is very useful in that, unlike *Mind, Self and Society*, the passages were written by Mead himself and indicate his early thoughts on the relationship between the meanings implicit in social action and the implications of this for the development of mind and self.

Posed against atomistic theories of society that would see society as an amalgamation of independent and autonomous individuals, Mead argued that society always predates the individual, and hence, selves must emerge as products of social communities. Much as it is only possible to develop reflective intelligence as a result of social experience and the acquisition of language, selves can only come into definition in accordance with relationships to others through social interaction. As such, selves emerge and then flexibly develop as they are socialized, with meanings gained through linguistic discourse and practical social experience in the community. Mead wrote:

> The language process is essential for the development of the self. The self has a character which is different from that of the physiological organism proper. The self is something which has a development; it is not initially there at birth, but arises in the process of social experience and activity.
>
> (Mead 1934: 135)

Since people are capable of 'taking the role of others', to view themselves as an object, they look to the social community for a definition of their own identity. By gleaning information from the social responses of group members, the self comes into definition. As a result, the individual can plan future conduct in ways that are perceived to coalesce more with the expectations of others in an effort to gain positive social rewards. Actions are taken into account from the perceived standpoint of significant particularized others (for example, friends and family members) or from an imagined 'generalized other' representing a typical or role-specific viewpoint. Thus, making decisions in a baseball game requires the individual to take on the attitude of generalized others in terms of their positions, and hence their roles in a specific play.

This self-regulation happens not only in the presence of others, but also in solitary conduct, since the actions of the self as an object are always assessed using the language and viewpoints obtained from the social group. Mead wrote, 'Self-criticism is essentially social criticism, and behaviour controlled by self-criticism is essentially behaviour controlled socially' (1934: 255). As individual selves encounter new definitions and meanings about themselves and others, their conception of how they fit in relation to others changes as well. As such, the individual's role (and sense of self) will change with the acquisition of new experiences and social situations in the course of its development.

Pragmatism as an empirical venture: Cooley, Blumer and Chicago School ethnography

The works of Peirce, James, Schiller, Dewey and Mead are of great value not only for exposing the major flaws that characterize empiricist and idealist approaches to the study of the human condition, but also for articulating the foundations of human lived experience and the associated matters of reality, speech, process, agency, activity and community. However, it can be acknowledged that none of these pragmatist philosophers implemented the pragmatist maxim of testing things out in more sustained ways with the aid of an empirical methodology (see Durkheim 1913–14/1983). Thus, it is with Charles Horton Cooley, Herbert Blumer, and the broader Chicago-style emphasis on ethnographic inquiry that American pragmatist theory most explicitly began to achieve its potential as a comprehensive realm of scholarship.

Although highly attentive to the enabling features of language and the importance of social process for comprehending the human condition, Charles Horton Cooley (1864–1953) also made a major methodological contribution to pragmatist social thought through his emphasis on the use of 'sympathetic introspection' (that is, ethnographic research) as the primary basis for learning about human group life (Cooley 1909, 1922, 1926, 1928). If scholars were to comprehend humans more genuinely, to know people more adequately, Cooley stipulated that it would be necessary for researchers to attend centrally to the day-to-day lives and experiences of the other. This meant spending time with and dialoguing extensively with people in an open, receptive fashion in order to more effectively learn about their activities and viewpoints. Further, Cooley importantly showed how this mode of inquiry could be applied to all realms of human association, including more complex instances of organizational life.

Cooley seems most well known to sociologists for his conception of the 'looking glass self', which refers to the notion that people are able to gain a definition of their own self by seeing their reflection in the reactions and viewpoints of others. Cooley wrote that for individuals, 'each to each a looking glass, reflects the other that doth pass' (1922: 184). Like Mead, he developed a fundamentally sociological conception of the self that is formed by the individual from the perspectives of the imagined viewpoints of the surrounding community. Thus, Cooley refused to construct any theoretical separation between the self and community, since both are seen to be outcomes of the same fundamental social process.

This process of social adjustment and self-development is most consequential for Cooley amidst people's socialization within their 'primary groups', where as a 'result of intimate association, psychologically, is a certain fusion of individualities into a common whole, so that one's very self, for many purposes, at least, is the common life and expression of the group' (Cooley 1909: 23). It is here where the individual develops the most foundational and consistent understandings and feelings of self, and thus where a more stable identity is generated. As individuals mature and enter into other social domains they will change, but the most formative definitions of self (including fundamental conceptions of morality and character) emerge through these early interchanges with significant others. It is this sympathetic understanding and adjustment of the individual to societal others that forms a cornerstone assumption in Cooley's thought (Hammersley 1981).

Still, Cooley's most significant contribution to pragmatist conceptions of social psychology may be his emphasis on empirically studying the very social processes he addressed. The following passage anticipated the base of Chicago-school ethnography in the spirit of Robert E. Park, along with Herbert Blumer's later emphases on exploration and inspection:

> Sympathetic introspection, putting himself in intimate contact with various sorts of persons and allowing them to awake in himself a life similar to their own, which he afterwards to the best of his ability, recalls and describes. In this way, he is more or less able to understand – always by introspection – children, idiots, criminals, rich and poor, conservative and radical – any phase of nature not wholly alien to his own. This I conceive to be the principal method of social psychology.
>
> (Cooley 1909: 7)

Thus, Cooley rejected the long-held tradition of the 'self-absorbed' philosopher in favour of analysing the nature of community in life in detailed and direct terms. Since the imaginations that people carry in their heads about others are the most important 'facts of society', they must be investigated in rigorous ways if we are to understand human conduct and the collective activities of social groups. It is the method of sympathetic introspection, whereby through sustained inquiry and observation we gain greater understanding of and insight into the life-worlds of the other in the participants' own terms, that represents the fundamental research priority for the social sciences.

Building on Mead's social behaviourism, Cooley's notions of sympathetic introspection, and the broader tradition of ethnographic research that was emerging at the University of Chicago, it was Herbert Blumer (1900–1987) who most directly and effectively synthesized pragmatist emphases about the nature of human group life with a methodological agenda designed to study this accordingly (Blumer 1969, 2004). It was also Blumer (1969) who formulated an exceptionally succinct, clear, and coherent set of pragmatist assumptions undergirding the production of activity within the interactionist tradition:

> Symbolic interaction rests in the last analysis on three simple premises. The first premise is that human beings act toward things on the basis of the meanings they have for them … The second premise is that the meaning of

> such things is derived from, or arises out of, the social interaction that one has with one's fellows. The third premise is that these meanings are handled in, and modified through, an interpretative process used by the person in dealing with the things he encounters.
>
> (Blumer 1969: 2)

Not only was Blumer highly mindful of the emergent, actively configured aspects of community life, he was also explicitly attentive to the obdurate features of human lived experience – the variety of continuities and associated resistances that people encounter as they deal with the life-worlds in which they find themselves (Blumer 1969; Prus and Dawson 1996).

Attentive to community life 'in the making', Blumer was intensely concerned with examining instances of particular phenomena in attempts to better understand and articulate the more abstract conceptual forms or generic essences. For Blumer, the task of the social sciences very much revolved around the development of concepts whose integrity (validity) is to be more or less continuously assessed against actual instances. Concepts are to be articulated (and continually adjusted) to better approximate the materials that researchers encounter in the course of achieving intimate (intersubjective) familiarity with the people who engage the great many life-worlds that constitute communities in the making. In addition, attending more fully to the enacted features of pragmatism, Blumer pursued the task of defining the foundations of a social science that is fully and explicitly attentive to the interlinkages of theory and action within the context of human lived experience:

> Let me begin by identifying the empirical world of human beings. This world is the actual group life of human beings. It consists of what they experience and do, individually and collectively, as they engage in their respective forms of living; it covers the large complexes of interlaced activities that grow up as the actions of some spread out to affect the actions of others; and it embodies the large variety of relations between the participants.
>
> (Blumer 1969: 35)

> One should not blind oneself to the recognition of the fact that human beings in carrying on their collective life form very different kinds of worlds. To study them intelligently, one has to know these worlds, and to know the worlds one has to examine them closely.
>
> (Blumer 1969: 39)

> The research scholar who engages in direct examination should aim at

> casting his problem in theoretical form, at unearthing generic relations, at sharpening the connotative reference of his concepts and at formulating theoretical propositions. Such analysis is the proper aim of empirical science, as distinguished from the preparation of mere descriptive accounts.
>
> (Blumer 1969: 43)

As with the American pragmatists, Blumer (1928, 1969) recognized that the perspectives and practices of quantitative science may be of great practical value in certain realms of the human-object sphere (especially as this pertains to matters of human physiology, the physical sciences and material technologies). However, he insisted that any science has the fundamental obligation of respecting its subject matter. It was on this basis that he so strenuously objected to the baseline inadequacies of any 'social science' that disregards the foundational features of human group life (that is, language, intersubjectivity, interpretation, action and interaction).

In contrast to many other approaches in the social sciences, a pragmatism informed by the methodological emphases of Cooley and Blumer:

- attends to the full range of human association – as in cooperation, loyalty, conflict, competition, and influence and resistance
- acknowledges the human interchanges that take place in all realms of human group life (as in religion, deviance, work and recreation)
- is mindful of the many levels of interchange in which community life takes shape (from large scale instances of collective behaviour to large organizations, small group interchanges and solitary activity)
- maintains a secular or pluralist (versus moralist, advocacy) perspective on human group life
- focuses on the matters of activity, language and intersubjectivity, deliberation and agency, work and resistance, relationships and all other enacted instances of collective ventures.[8]

Conclusion

Focusing on pragmatism as the study of human knowing and acting as this pertains to the ongoing accomplishment of community life and everyday life, we have approached pragmatist social theory in historically informed terms, addressed the intersubjectivist, actively engaged features of human group life, and established the empirical foundations of a pragmatist social science. In the process, we have situated pragmatist social thought in the broader, more enduring sets of debates about the nature of knowledge (epistemology) that have characterized Western social thought over the millennia. Whereas an awareness of the divisions implied in empiricist, idealist and pragmatist approaches to the human condition is fundamental to a more adequate understanding of the evolution and central emphases of the humanities and social sciences more generally, it should also be recognized that without an explicit emphasis on studying phenomena in instances and attending to the comparisons and conceptual inferences thereof, pragmatism would remain an idealist approach.

Although the works of Peirce, James, Schiller, Dewey and Mead are remarkable for elucidating the principles of pragmatist thought amidst the heavy emphases on empiricist and idealist philosophies in the early 20th century, it was with the ethnographic emphasis that Cooley, Blumer and Chicago-style sociology brought to the pragmatist tradition that contemporary pragmatist thought more completely achieved its potential as an exceptionally authentic and enduring human science (Prus 2007b).

Relatedly, even though many features of pragmatist social thought can be found in other interpretivist approaches, perhaps most notably in the dramaturgical emphases of Kenneth Burke and Erving Goffman, and in the phenomenological positions adopted by Alfred Schutz, Peter L. Berger and Thomas Luckmann, and Harold Garfinkel, it was the pragmatist emphases on the developmental unity of activity, speech, objects and ongoing everyday life; on examining people's activities as these are developed in instances of human group life; and on developing concepts and connections thereof through comparative analysis, that pragmatist social thought as represented in Chicago-style symbolic interactionism is so entirely relevant for the human sciences.

Far from representing the unique product of a historically situated democratic society, an individualistic or subjectivist approach, or a philosophy without empirical substance, pragmatist scholarship, with its emphasis on examining everyday life as a phenomenon 'in the making', has the potential to be of great value as a human science for all generations to come.

Notes

1. As is the case for many co-authored statements, we each contributed to different sections of this chapter. The overarching framework of the chapter, the discussion of the classical Greek roots of pragmatism and the contributions of Ferdinand Schiller and Herbert Blumer were developed primarily by Robert C. Prus. The discussions of Charles Sanders Peirce, William James, John Dewey, George Herbert Mead and Charles Horton Cooley were generated primarily by Antony Puddephatt.
2. Although an emergent process in itself, American pragmatism appears to have been derived more vaguely from an assortment of European, predominantly British and

German, sources. For some other accounts of American pragmatism, see Moore (1910), Durkheim (1913–14/1983), Scheffler (1974), Murphy (1990), Biesta and Burbules (2003) and Reynolds (2003). For some other commentaries on pragmatism, see Wiley (1994, 2006), Joas (1996), Archer (2003), Alexander (2004), and Shalin (2007).

3. See Puddephatt (forthcoming) for an outline of Mead's neglected sociological analysis of scientific knowledge.
4. To a very large extent, Peirce's subsequent writings revolve around his attempts to clarify what he termed the pragmatist (and, later, the 'pragmaticist') position.
5. See James's references to Immanuel Kant in James (1975b: 268–9; Appendix I (here quoted from James, 'Philosophical Conceptions and Practical Results' (1898/1967)).
6. It appears that James worked with a prepublication copy of Schiller's (1907) *Studies in Humanism*. James (1907) not only had correspondence with Schiller, he also explicitly cited particular chapters in Schiller's work and incorporated many of these ideas into major sections of his own pragmatism. Schiller, who very cogently rejected idealist and rationalist standpoints, based much of his analytic work on the Greek philosopher Protagoras, who adopted the position that 'man is the measure of all things'.
7. Dewey's (1934) *Art as Experience* is comparatively unknown to social scientists, including those working more directly in symbolic interactionism. Nevertheless, it constitutes one of Dewey's most articulate, focused and thorough considerations of human group life as a developmentally achieved and socially constructed realm of human endeavour.
8. Others who have contributed more notably to Chicago-style interactionism include Robert E. Park, Everett C. Hughes, Anselm L. Strauss, Tamotsu Shibutani, John Lofland, Howard S. Becker, Erving Goffman, Fred Davis and Jacqueline Wiseman. For a fuller indication of the broader set of scholars involved in developing Chicago-style interactionism, see Prus (1996, 1997) and Prus and Grills (2003)

Bibliography

Alexander, Jeffrey C. (2004) 'Cultural pragmatics: social performance between ritual and strategy.' *Sociological Theory*, 22 (4): 527–73.

Archer, Margaret (2003) *Structure, Agency and the Internal Conversation*. Cambridge: Cambridge University Press.

Aristotle (1984) *The Complete Works of Aristotle*. Princeton, NJ: Princeton University Press.

Biesta, Gert J. J. and Nicholas Burbules (2003) *Pragmatism and Educational Research*. New York: Rowman & Littlefield.

Blumer, Herbert (1928) *Method in Social Psychology*. Doctoral dissertation, University of Chicago.

Blumer, Herbert (1969) *Symbolic Interaction*. Englewood Cliffs, NJ: PrenticeHall.

Blumer, Herbert (2004) *George Herbert Mead and Human Conduct*. Walnut Creek, CA: AltaMira.

Cooley, Charles Horton (1909) *Social Organization: A Study of the Larger Mind*. New York: Shocken.

Cooley, Charles Horton (1922) *Human Nature and the Social Order*. New York: Shocken.

Cooley, Charles Horton (1926) 'The Roots of Social Knowledge.' *American Journal of Sociology*, 32: 59–79.

Cooley, Charles Horton (1928) 'Case study of small institutions as a method of research.' *American Sociological Review*, 22: 123–32.

Dewey, John (1896) 'The reflex-arc concept in psychology.' *Psychological Review*, 3: 357–70.
Dewey, John (1910/1975) *How We Think*. Amherst, NY: Prometheus.
Dewey, John (1922/2002) *Human Nature and Conduct*. Amherst, NY: Prometheus.
Dewey, John (1929/1958) *Experience and Nature*, 2nd edition. New York: Dover.
Dewey, John (1934) *Art as Experience*. New York: Penguin Putnam.
Dilthey, Wilhelm (1978) *The Critique of Historical Reason*, Chicago: University of Chicago Press.
Durkheim, Émile (1913–14/1983) *Pragmatism and Sociology*. New York: Cambridge University Press.
Hammersley, Martin (1981) *The Dilemma of Qualitative Method: Herbert Blumer and the Chicago Tradition*. London: Routledge.
James, William (1898/1967) 'Philosophic conceptions and practical results', in John J. McDermott (ed.), *The Writings of William James*. New York: Random House.
James, William (1907) *Pragmatism: A New Name for Some Old Ways of Thinking*. Cambridge, MA: Harvard University Press.
James, William (1909) *The Meaning of Truth: A Sequel to 'Pragmatism'*. Cambridge, MA: Harvard University Press.
Joas, Hans (1996) *The Creativity of Action*. Chicago: University of Chicago Press.
Mead, George Herbert (1930) 'The Philosophies of Royce, James and Dewey in their American setting.' *International Journal of Ethics*, 40: 211–31.
Mead, George Herbert (1934) *Mind, Self and Society*. Chicago: University of Chicago Press.
Mead, George Herbert (1936) *Movements of Thought in the Nineteenth Century*. Chicago: University of Chicago Press.
Mead, George Herbert (2001) *Essays in Social Psychology*. New Brunswick: Transaction.
Moore, Addison Webster (1910) *Pragmatism and its Critics*. Chicago: University of Chicago Press.
Murphy, John P. (1990) *Pragmatism: From Peirce to Davidson*. San Francisco: Westview Press.
Peirce, Charles Sanders (1878–1906/1934) *The Collected Papers of Charles Sanders Peirce*. Cambridge, MA: Harvard University Press.
Plato (1997) *Plato: The Collected Works*. Indianapolis, IN: Hackett.
Prus, Robert C. (1996) *Symbolic Interaction and Ethnographic Research: Intersubjectivity and the Study of Human Lived Experience*. Albany, NY: State University of New York Press.
Prus, Robert C. (1997) *Subcultural Mosaics and Intersubjective Realities: An Ethnographic Research Agenda for Pragmatizing the Social Sciences*. Albany, NY: State University of New York Press.
Prus, Robert C. (2003) 'Ancient forerunners', in Larry T. Reynolds and Nancy J. Herman-Kinney (eds), *Handbook of Symbolic Interactionism*. Walnut Creek, CA: Altamira Press.
Prus, Robert C. (2004) 'Symbolic interaction and Classical Greek scholarship: conceptual foundations, historical continuities and transcontextual relevancies.' *American Sociologist*, 35 (1): 5–33.
Prus, Robert C. (2007a) 'Aristotle's *Nicomachean Ethics*: laying the foundations for a pragmatist consideration of human knowing and acting.' *Qualitative Sociology Review*, 3 (2): 5–45.
Prus, Robert C. (2007b) 'The intellectual canons of a public sociology: pragmatist foundations, historical extensions, and humanly engaged realities', in Lawrence T. Nichols (ed.), *Public Sociology: The Contemporary Debate*. New Brunswick, NJ: Transaction.
Prus, Robert C. and Lorne Dawson (1996) 'Obdurate reality and the intersubjective other: the problematics of representation and the privilege of presence', in Robert C. Prus (ed.), *Symbolic Interaction and Ethnographic Research*. New York: State University of New York Press.

Prus, Robert C. and Scott Grills (2003) *The Deviant Mystique: Involvements, Realities, and Regulation.* Westport, CN: Praeger.
Puddephatt, Antony J. (forthcoming) 'George Herbert Mead: an early sociologist of scientific knowledge.' *Studies in Symbolic Interaction.*
Reynolds, Larry T. (2003) 'Intellectual precursors', in Larry T. Reynolds and Nancy J. Herman-Kinney (eds), *Handbook of Symbolic Interactionism.* Walnut Creek, CA: Altamira Press.
Scheffler, Israel (1974) *Four Pragmatists.* New York: Humanities Press.
Schiller, Ferdinand Canning Scott (1907) *Studies in Humanism.* London: Macmillan.
Shalin, Dimitri (2007) 'Signing in the flesh: notes on pragmatist hermeneutics.' *Sociological Theory*, 25 (3): 193–224.
Smith, John E. (1966) *The Spirit of American Philosophy.* New York: Oxford University Press.
Wiley, Norbert (1994) *The Semiotic Self.* Chicago: Chicago University Press.
Wiley, Norbert (2006) 'Peirce and the founding of American sociology.' *Journal of Classical Sociology*, 6 (1): 23–50.
Wundt, Wilhelm (1886/1897) *Ethics: An Investigation of the Facts and Laws of the Moral Life.* London: Swan Sonnenschein.
Wundt, Wilhelm (1900–20) *Volkerpsychologie: Eine Untersuchung der Entwicklungsgesetze von Sprache, Mythos und Sitte,* 10 vols. Leipzig: Engelmann & Kroner.

CHAPTER 3

Phenomenological Sociology
The Subjectivity of Everyday Life

SØREN OVERGAARD AND DAN ZAHAVI

Introduction

Does phenomenology have any insights or theoretical resources to offer the sociology of everyday life? In the present chapter, we suggest an affirmative reply to this question. This is not only because sociality is a central theme in phenomenology, but also because phenomenologists consistently emphasize the importance of examining the world, including social reality, just as we experience it in everyday life. Or, as many phenomenologists prefer to put it, phenomenology must examine the 'life-world'.

Phenomenologists generally stress that social reality should not be conceived as a fixed and objective external reality. Rather, social reality is essentially a product of human activity. *Inter alia* through processes of 'typification', we 'constitute' a meaningful social world around us. This is obviously not the achievement of isolated individuals acting alone; most of our typical assumptions, expectations and prescriptions, indeed, are socially derived. However, phenomenological sociologists insist that we must not downplay the role of individual subjectivities. Social reality cannot be reduced to relations between individual subjects; yet without the latter – that is, without *intersubjectivity* – there is ultimately no social reality. As we shall see in the present chapter, phenomenology continues to be of relevance to the sociology of everyday life and has the resources to respond to the criticisms typically directed against it.

The phenomenological movement

The movement of phenomenology is more than a century old. In fact, the inauguration of the movement can be dated precisely to 1900–01, the years in which the two parts of Edmund Husserl's (1859–1938) *Logical Investigations* were published. Husserl was originally a mathematician, whose interests in the foundational problems of mathematics led him to logic and philosophy. Despite the title, *Logical Investigations* does not merely address logical problems narrowly conceived. Rather, Husserl advanced what he believed was the right approach to philosophical problems in general: instead of resorting to armchair theorizing and speculation, we must consult 'the things themselves', or that which 'manifests itself' or 'gives itself' (Greek: *phainomenon*). On this basis, Husserl claimed that the traditional notion of the mind as an inner, self-contained realm is misguided. Rather, the mind is in various ways directed upon objects external to it. Influenced by the Austrian psychologist and philosopher Franz Brentano (1838–1917), Husserl labelled this object-directedness 'intentionality'. To watch a soccer game, to want a new bicycle, and to recall last year's summer holidays, are examples of different experiences that have the character of 'intentionality', of being directed at an 'object' (the soccer game, a new bicycle and last year's holidays, respectively).

Logical Investigations made Husserl widely known, and contributed to the formation of phenomenological schools in Göttingen, where Husserl himself taught from 1901, and Munich, where among others Max Scheler (1874–1928) advocated a phenomenological approach. However, in his second magnum opus, entitled *Ideas Pertaining to a Pure Phenomenology and to a Phenomenological Philosophy I* (1931/1982), Husserl pushed his phenomenology in a direction that many other phenomenologists considered problematic.

Logical Investigations had emphasized a purely descriptive approach, and Husserl had remained neutral on the question concerning the ontological status of the mind (or consciousness) and its objects. Many phenomenologists in Göttingen and Munich had consequently regarded *Logical Investigations* as fully compatible with their own realist views. In this context, 'realism' is the view that the nature and existence of reality is completely independent of the mind. In *Ideas*, however, Husserl argued that the world is 'constituted' by consciousness or 'transcendental subjectivity'. Although Husserl denied that transcendental subjectivity 'creates' the world in any conventional sense, his new position did imply that the world cannot be conceived of as completely independent of a world-cognizing subject. This 'idealism' was unacceptable to many of the original adherents of the phenomenological movement. Yet even though Husserl, in later works such as *Cartesian Meditations* (1964/1995) and *The Crisis of European Sciences and Transcendental Phenomenology* (1935/1970), increasingly emphasized that transcendental subjectivity must be embodied and embedded in a community of subjects, he never abandoned the 'transcendental phenomenology' introduced in *Ideas*.

After Husserl became professor of philosophy in Freiburg in 1916, the phenomenological movement became increasingly influential outside the old phenomenological strongholds. In Freiburg, Husserl became acquainted with the young philosopher Martin Heidegger (1889–1976), who soon convinced Husserl of his great potential. When Husserl retired in 1928, he appointed Heidegger as his successor. By then, Heidegger was already something of a celebrity in philosophical environments across Germany, in particular on account of his unorthodox but enormously popular lectures. Heidegger's early masterpiece *Being and Time* (1927/1962) is undoubtedly an important phenomenological work; but it is questionable to which extent Heidegger remains faithful to Husserl's programme (see Overgaard 2004).

Being and Time revolves around an extremely complex problem which Heidegger labelled 'the question of the meaning of Being'. Central to this question is an analysis of the peculiar mode or manner of being that characterizes the human being (or *Dasein*, as Heidegger preferred to say). In continuation of Husserl's analyses of intentionality, Heidegger claimed that the human being cannot be understood independently of the world in which they are experientially and practically engaged. As he put it, the being of *Dasein* is 'Being-in-the-world'. Heidegger was particularly concerned with emphasizing the practical involvement of humans in their environment. A human being is not primarily a spectator in their environing world, but an agent in it; and the world is not a collection of neutral objects or things, but more like a web of functional relations between practical 'tools' or 'equipment'.

It is in the space between Husserl and Heidegger that we must locate the main inspiration for the later French phenomenologists. Emmanuel Lévinas (1906–1995) studied philosophy in Freiburg when Heidegger succeeded Husserl. Even though the ostensible topic of Lévinas's dissertation *The Theory of Intuition in Husserl's Phenomenology*, published in 1930 (1930/1995), was Husserl's thought, Heidegger's influence was pronounced. Moreover, Husserl and Heidegger remained essential interlocutors in Lévinas's later works, such as *Totality and Infinity* (1969) and *Otherwise than Being or Beyond Essence* (1974), in which he attempted to develop an independent phenomenological ethic centring on the notion of respect for other human beings.

Jean-Paul Sartre's (1906–1980) phenomenological magnum opus *Being and Nothingness*, published in 1943, drew upon Husserl, Heidegger and Hegel, in an attempt to articulate a radical distinction between consciousness, which Sartre labelled 'Being-for-itself', and all types of objective being, which he collected under the heading 'Being-in-itself' (Sartre 1943/1956). Maurice Merleau-Ponty's (1908–1961) phenomenology of body and perception, elaborated in the 1945 masterpiece *Phenomenology of Perception*, was to some extent a continuation of Husserl's later works. But Heidegger's influence was also tangible, not least in Merleau-Ponty's contention that the phenomenon of human embodiment is an aspect of the structure that Heidegger calls 'Being-in-the-world' (Merleau-Ponty 1945/1962).

The influence of phenomenology, however, extends beyond philosophy. Philosophical phenomenology offers general ideas of relevance to the social sciences (anthropology, economy, law, political science, and so on).[1] But in addition to this, there are phenomenological traditions in psychology and psychiatry, and more relevant in the present context, there is a distinct phenomenological approach to sociology, which was developed by Alfred Schutz (1899–1959) and his students. Schutz's main inspiration was drawn from Husserl's later thoughts on intersubjectivity and the life-world. In the next sections, we shall briefly sketch these ideas.

Phenomenology and intersubjectivity

It is sometimes claimed that phenomenology has nothing valuable to offer sociology. Jürgen Habermas, for example, accused Husserl's philosophy – and by extension phenomenology as such (Habermas 1992: 42) – of being solipsistic, that is, of being able to conceive of the existence of only one single subject (*solus ipse* is Latin for 'only I'). Thereby, Habermas obviously questioned the relevance of phenomenology for social thought in general.

However, there is reason to regard Habermas' claim with a good deal of scepticism, for the criticism seems based on a misunderstanding of the phenomenological perspective on sociality. Instead of viewing the individual and society – or subjectivity and sociality – as mutually exclusive options, phenomenology explicitly attempts to combine them. Husserl's claim that a subject can only be a world-experiencing subjectivity insofar as it is member of a community of subjects (Husserl 1964/1995: 139) suggests a key phenomenological claim: the individual subject qua world-experiencing is dependent on other world-experiencing subjects. But on the other hand, we should not downplay the role of the individual subject. Phenomenology insists on understanding sociality in its most fundamental form as *intersubjectivity* (see Zahavi 2001a). It only makes sense to speak of intersubjectivity if there is a (possible) plurality of subjects, and intersubjectivity can therefore neither precede nor be the foundation of the individuality and distinctness of the various subjects. Thus, we cannot invoke the notion of intersubjectivity without committing ourselves to some form of philosophy of subjectivity. Yet, on the other hand, Husserl maintains that a sufficiently radical and thorough phenomenological reflection leads us not only to subjectivity, but also to intersubjectivity (Husserl 1925/1962: 344). Accordingly, he sometimes refers to his project as that of sociological transcendental philosophy (Husserl 1925/1962: 539), and states that a full elaboration of transcendental philosophy necessarily involves the move from an egological to a transcendental-sociological phenomenology (see Zahavi 1996, 2001b).

The life-world

As part of their ongoing concern with the relation between science and experience, phenomenologists have often emphasized the importance of the 'life-world'. The life-world is the world we ordinarily take for granted, the pre-scientific, experientially given world that we are familiar with and never call into question. The life-world needs rehabilitating because, although it is the historical and systematic sense-foundation for science, the latter has forgotten or ignored the life-world. Even the most exact and abstract scientific theories rely on the type of pre-scientific evidence that the life-world offers. And life-worldly evidence does not merely function as an indispensable but otherwise irrelevant station that we must pass through on the way toward exact knowledge; rather, it is a permanent source of meaning and evidence (Husserl 1935/1970: 126).

In pursuit of exact knowledge, science has made a virtue of its radical transcendence of bodily, sensory, and practical experience, but in the process it has overlooked the extent to which it is made possible by those kinds of experience. When experiments are designed and conducted, when measurements are noted down, when results are interpreted, compared and discussed, scientists rely on the common life-world and its common kinds of evidence. Even though scientific theories transcend the concrete, perceptible life-world in terms of precision and degree of abstraction, the life-world remains the meaningful foundation and ultimate source of evidence (Husserl 1935/1970: 126). However, the relation between science and the life-world is not static but dynamic. Science is founded on the life-world, and bit-by-bit it may, as it were, sink into the ground on which it stands. With the passing of time, theoretical assumptions and results may be absorbed by everyday practice and become part of the life-world.

When phenomenologists emphasize the significance of the life-world it is not at the expense of science. Phenomenologists have no desire to deny the immense value of science, and they agree that science has the potential to profoundly expand and alter our conception of reality. They do reject, however, the tendency within the natural sciences to advocate scientism and objectivism. A critical attitude towards the scientist self-image of science is one thing, and hostility toward science as such is a very different thing. Phenomenology has none of the latter. It is no coincidence that a famous manifesto of Husserl's was entitled *Philosophy as a Strict Science*.

According to scientism, it is natural science alone that decides what is real; reality is thus identical with what can be conceived and explained by natural science. Historically, reflections of this kind led to the claim that only the form, size, weight and movement of an object – that is, those characteristics that, in principle, could be described quantitatively with mathematical exactness – were objective properties. On this view, colour, taste, smell, and so on, were considered merely subjective phenomena that lacked real, objective existence.

In the course of centuries, this classical distinction between primary (or objective) qualities and secondary (or subjective) qualities has consistently been radicalized. Ultimately, it was not merely the objectivity of certain characteristics of the appearing object that was questioned, but rather the objectivity of anything that appeared. The appearance or manifestation as such was regarded as subjective, and it was this appearance, this phenomenal manifestation as such, which science, according to its understanding of itself, had to reach beyond in order to achieve knowledge of the real nature of things. A consequence of this view is that the world in which we live is very different from the world that the exact sciences describe, the latter having an exclusive claim to reality. The life-world, by contrast, is a mere construction, a result of our response to the stimuli we receive from physical reality.

Phenomenology, however, rejects the idea that natural science is the sole judge of what is real and what is not, and that all concepts that we wish to take seriously must be reducible to concepts of the exact sciences. According to phenomenology, the exact sciences do not describe a world that is different from the ordinary world. Rather, they simply employ new methods to describe and explain the world we already know, and thereby enable us to obtain more precise knowledge about it. The scientific ambition of describing reality objectively – that is, from a third-person point of view – is a thoroughly legitimate one. Yet we should not forget that any objectivity, any explanation, understanding and theoretical construct, presupposes a first-person perspective as its permanent ground and precondition. To that extent the belief that science can provide an absolute description of reality – a description purged of any conceptual or experiential perspective – is an illusion. Science is rooted in the life-world: it draws upon insights from the pre-scientific sphere and it is conducted by embodied subjects. For the phenomenologists, science is not simply a collection of systematically related, well-established propositions. Rather, science is something that people do; it is a particular – markedly theoretical – way of relating to the world.

Phenomenology does not attempt to explain human nature through science. Rather, it aims to make sense of scientific rationality and practice through detailed analyses of the cognizing subject's various forms of intentional experience. A central task is thus to give an account of how the theoretical attitude that we adopt when we are doing science – including sociology – arises out of, as well as influences and changes, our everyday 'being-in-the-world'. The phenomenological examination of the life-world obviously constitutes an important part of this project. Husserl himself articulated the basic ideas for such an analysis, and other phenomenologists such as Heidegger and Merleau-

Ponty, made important contributions. All of these thinkers, however, considered the analysis of the life-world a mere part of a larger philosophical project. A more independent interest in the phenomenology of the life-world – in particular its social structure – is found, above all, in Alfred Schutz and his successors within *phenomenological sociology*.

The phenomenological sociology of everyday life

Among the key figures in phenomenological sociology are Alfred Schutz (1899–1959), author of the works *The Phenomenology of the Social World* (1932/1972), *Collected Papers I–III* (1962–1966), and *The Structures of the Life-World*, co-authored by Thomas Luckmann and published in 1973; Peter L. Berger (b. 1929) and Thomas Luckmann (b. 1927), authors of the book *The Social Construction of Reality: A Treatise in the Sociology of Knowledge* (1966/1991); and finally Harold Garfinkel (b. 1917), whose most important publication in this context is *Studies in Ethnomethodology* (1967). These will be dealt with below.

Alfred Schutz

Alfred Schutz is often referred to as the founder of phenomenological sociology.[2] Schutz originally studied law and obtained his PhD from Vienna in 1921. Subsequently, he worked in a bank, however, and it was not until 1943, after his emigration to the United States, that Schutz obtained a part-time position at a university, the New School for Social Research in New York. In 1952 he became professor at the same institution.

Schutz was initially inspired by Max Weber's interpretive sociology. However, although Weber regarded meaningful action as the central topic of the social sciences, and although he emphasized the importance of an explicit thematization of the meaning that the individual actor attributes to his or her own action, he did not examine the constitution of social meaning as such, and was generally uninterested in fundamental questions in epistemology and the theory of meaning. It is precisely this gap that Schutz attempts to fill by combining Weber's sociology with Husserl's phenomenological methodology (Schutz 1932/1972: 13).

Schutz claimed that we experience the world as containing various relatively distinct and independent provinces of meaning (Schutz 1962: 230). Dreams, for example, have their own unique temporal and spatial 'logic'. The same goes for children's play, stage performances, religious experiences and so on. According to Schutz, science and research too take place within a distinct province of meaning. One region has a special status, however, and that is the life-world. This is not only because it is the region in which we spend most of our lives. Equally important is the fact that each of the other regions, or limited 'realities', is a modification of the life-world. The 'realities' of science and of dreams, for example, are regions that we enter by 'bracketing' or 'switching off' in some way the quotidian life-world; and to that extent they both fundamentally presuppose the reality of the life-world (Schutz 1962: 231–3; see Berger and Luckmann 1966/1991: 39–40). Following Husserl, Schutz employed the term *epoché* for such 'switching off'. When we dream, for example, we perform an *epoché* on the rules that in everyday reality govern the identities of persons and places. Most of us are thus familiar with dreams in which an event that takes place in one country switches to another location, without this being perceived as particularly odd within the universe of the dream.

Since it is the life-world rather than the mathematicized world of science that constitutes the frame and stage of social relations and actions, the sociologist, Schutz argued, should take his or her point of departure in the former. What is needed is a systematic examination of everyday life, and this requires a new type of sociological theory. Schutz's concrete contribution here was twofold. First, he aimed to describe and analyse the essential structures of the life-world. Second, he offered an account of the way in which subjectivity is involved in the construction of social meaning, social actions and situations – indeed social 'worlds'. Relying on Husserl's analyses of intentionality and the life-world, Schutz accordingly claimed that the social world reveals and manifests itself in various intentional experiences. Its meaningfulness is constituted by subjects, and in order to understand and scientifically address the social world it is therefore necessary to examine the social agents for whom it exists as such.

It is partly for this reason that Schutz claimed that the subject matter of the social sciences is more complex than that of the natural sciences. As he put it, the social sciences must employ 'constructs of the second degree' (Schutz 1962: 6), because the 'objects' of these sciences – social agents – themselves employ 'first-order constructs' of the reality around them. Of course, the social sciences must satisfy the same sorts of requirements as other empirical sciences: scientific results must be controllable and reproducible by other scientists working in the field, and scientific theories must be precise, consistent and so on (Schutz 1962: 49–52).

Schutz also stressed that social scientists and natural scientists alike are motivated by other, more theoretical interests than the everyday person is guided by. The everyday person is an agent rather than a theoretical observer; they have practical interests and are normally guided by common-sense knowledge and understanding. The social scientist, by contrast, is not an agent in the social relations they study. A scientific researcher, regardless of whether they study social hierarchies in Scottish factories or electrons and amino acids, is an observer, not a participant. Schutz thus insists that the social scientist must maintain a distance from the phenomena studied. However, the social sciences examine human beings in manifold social relations, and human agents have interests, motives, self-interpretation and an understanding of the world they live in – all of which must be taken into account if we want to understand social reality in its full concretion (Schutz 1962: 6; Gurwitsch 1974: 129).

This radically distinguishes social science from natural science: the latter obviously has no need to take into account the self-understanding and self-interpretation of the objects studied (electrons and amino acids have no self-understanding). Schutz thus emphatically rejected reductionist programmes, such as behaviourism and positivism, which attempt to reduce human action to observable behaviour and stimulus–response mechanisms. The social scientist must construct credible models of everyday agents – models that include such things as consciousness, motives and understanding. The task is to make explicit the meaning and significance these structures and relations have for the observed agents *themselves* (see Schutz 1964: 7).

For Schutz, the investigation of intersubjectivity – in particular, of how one subject has experiential access to another subject, and how a community of 'we' is constituted – had a central place in sociological theory (see Schutz 1932/1972: 97–9). A further task is to give an account of how a multitude of experiences can constitute the structures of meaning that make up social reality. As Schutz wrote, every science of social meaning refers back to our meaning-constituting life in the social world: to our everyday experience of other persons, to our understanding of pre-given meanings, and to our initiation of new meaningful behaviour (Schutz 1932/1972: 9).

Schutz's phenomenological perspective thus emphasized that the primary object of sociology is not institutions, market conjunctures, social classes or structures of power, but *human beings*, that is, acting and experiencing individuals, considered in their myriad relations to others, but also with an eye to their own, meaning-constituting subjective lives. Schutz's point, of course, was not that sociology should have no interest whatsoever in institutions, power structures, and the like. Rather, he merely insisted that a concept such as 'power structure' must be regarded as a sort of 'intellectual shorthand', which can be useful for certain purposes, but must never lead us to forget that, in the end, power structures presuppose experiencing, interpreting and acting individuals (Schutz 1962: 34–5; 1964: 6–7).

Along with Husserl and other phenomenologists, Schutz thus understood sociality as intersubjectivity – that is, as something that is ultimately anchored in individual subjects.

According to Schutz, each of us experiences our social environment as structured in 'strata' or 'layers' around ourself. Temporally as well as spatially, these layers are, for each individual, structured with that individual as the centre. With regard to the temporal structure, Schutz distinguished between three layers or spheres:

> In the dimension of time there are, with reference to me in my actual biographical moment, 'contemporaries', with whom a mutual interplay of action and reaction can be established; 'predecessors', upon whom I cannot act, but whose past actions and their outcome are open to my interpretation and may influence my own actions; and 'successors', of whom no experience is possible but toward whom I may orient my actions in a more or less empty anticipation. All these relations show the most manifold forms of intimacy and anonymity, of familiarity and strangeness, of intensity and extensity.
> (Schutz 1962: 15–16; see Berger and Luckmann 1966/1991: 46–9)

With regard to my contemporaries, there are various layers of 'spatial' proximity and distance, familiarity and strangeness. Some people are part of my immediate environment. Schutz said that I have a 'face-to-face' relationship with those people, but this expression is intended to refer to 'a purely formal aspect of social relationship equally applicable to an intimate talk between friends and the co-presence of strangers in a railroad car' (Schutz 1962: 16; see Berger and Luckmann 1966/1991: 43–6).[3] Obviously, even in the course of a whole lifetime, I have this sort of spatial proximity with only a very small percentage of the population of the world. This does not mean, however, that the rest of humanity is not part of my environing world at all. There is some mutual contact and influence, however vague, indirect and insignificant, between most of my contemporaries and me.

According to Schutz, the experience of the life-world is a process of typification. We employ a repertoire of maxims and recipes – a type of practical 'know-how' – for understanding and dealing with the world and other people. Objects in the life-world are not simply unique, individual entities, but 'mountains', 'trees', 'houses', 'animals' and 'people'. No matter what we encounter, it is something whose more or less general 'type' we are familiar with. A person who has only very limited knowledge of trees can perhaps not tell whether the tree passed in the woods is an elm or a beech, but sees it immediately as 'a tree'. In other words, we have a kind of immediate knowledge about how to understand our environment. The primary source of this knowledge is previous experience – both experiences we have had ourselves, and experience transmitted to us by others.

Obviously, typifications also play an important role in our social life. We immediately experience others in a typified manner: not only people with whom we are personally acquainted or bump into on the train, or with whom we communicate via the Internet, but also people with whom we never have any direct contact; indeed, we even typify in various ways our predecessors and possible successors. In fact, we do not only experience objects and living creatures as typified, but also actions, situations, motives, personalities, and so forth. Schutz wrote:

> Putting a letter in the mailbox, I expect that unknown people, called postmen, will act in a typical way, not quite intelligible to me, with the result that my letter will reach the addressee within typically reasonable time. Without ever having met a Frenchman or a German, I understand 'Why France fears the rearmament of Germany'. Complying with a rule of English grammar, I follow a socially approved behaviour pattern of contemporary English-speaking fellow-men to which I have to adjust my own behaviour in order to make myself understandable. And, finally, any artefact or utensil refers to the anonymous fellow-man who produced it to be used by other anonymous fellow-men for attaining typical goals by typical means.
>
> (Schutz 1962: 17; see Schutz 1932/1972: 185)

An action such as putting a letter in the mailbox involves a typification of other people and their motives in time and space. I implicitly assume that certain typical other people have certain typical motives (for example, that they want to do their job well) and therefore will perform certain typical actions in such a way that my letter will arrive at its destination. According to Schutz, another element in this pattern of typification is an assumption that others have 'systems of relevancies' that are similar to our own (Schutz 1962: 12); in other words, that others will by and large consider those things important that we ourselves regard as important.

Of course, Schutz does not claim that we implicitly assume that others' interests, projects and tastes are exactly like our own. Rather, he is trying to direct attention to something much more fundamental. If I send a letter to China, for example, I assume that Chinese postal workers will consider the address written on the envelope more important than, say, the size or colour of the envelope, when determining to which part of China the letter should be sent. According to Schutz, this idea about the 'congruence of the systems of relevancies' is part of a larger complex of implicit assumptions, which he called the thesis of 'the reciprocity of perspectives' (Schutz 1962: 11, 147). We do not merely assume that our systems of relevancies are in tune, but also that we would view things in the same way if we could view them from other people's perspectives. This point applies not only to spatial perspectives, but also to culturally, historically and biographically conditioned 'perspectives'.

As an agent in the life-world, however, I not only typify others. For example, my very imperfect understanding of the motives and actions of postal workers will lead me to typify some of my own actions when posting a letter. I try to write in such a way that a typical postal worker will be able to decipher my handwriting; I write the address in a typical place on the envelope, and so on. Briefly put, I try to make myself the typical 'sender of a letter' (see Schutz 1962: 25–6).

In connection with his analyses of the typifying assumptions that are implicit in any life-worldly action, Schutz also offered a close analysis of the *motives* for actions. He argued that we need to distinguish between two types of motives: 'in-order-to' motives and 'because' motives. An agent's in-order-to motive is what they want to achieve with the action – their aim or purpose. From the perspective of the agent, the in-order-to motive is thus directed at the future, that is, at the state of affairs that the action is supposed to realize. The because motive, in contrast, has to do with the agent's past and the circumstances that made them seriously consider the course of action adopted.

Schutz's favourite example involved a person who commits murder in order to obtain the victim's money. The in-order-to motive is straightforward: the purpose is to obtain money. The because motive is rather more complex, in that it includes all the factors that contributed to putting the agent in a situation where he or she could project and carry out this action. A problematic childhood and drug addiction may, for example, be part of the because motive. In ordinary language, both types of motive can be expressed by 'because' utterances, while only in-order-to motives can be expressed by 'in-order-to' utterances. It makes sense to say both 'I hit him because I wanted his money' and 'I hit him because I was abused as a child', but only the former sentence can be turned into an 'in-order-to' sentence. 'I hit him in order to get his money' makes perfect sense; 'I hit him in order to have been abused as a child' does not (Schutz 1962: 69–72).

My aims and interests decide how I experience things and people around me. As already suggested, these interests are mainly practical rather than theoretical (Schutz 1962: 208). Thus, although I have many levels of typification at my disposal, my interest usually picks out one such level as salient. With regard to some people and objects, I am only interested in certain typical features or aspects, whereas other things may not interest me in their typicality, but only in their uniqueness. My interest in the postal worker usually does not go beyond his or her typical motives and actions qua postal worker: blood type and hobbies, for example, are of no interest to me. In fact, it would not matter much if pigeons or robots rather than human beings delivered my letters, as long as something 'performed' certain typical actions in such a way that my letters would reach their addressees.

If I encounter a large, growling animal in the woods on a dark night, this creature does not strike me as an example of a spatially extended thing, but as a dangerous animal. The book a good friend gave me as a birthday present ten years ago, on the other hand, is not for me a typical 'book', nor is it, more specifically, 'a copy of *The Brothers Karamazov*' which could simply be replaced by another, identical copy. Rather, for me this object is unique. The same obviously goes for my friends and family. I do not regard them as 'mammals', specimens of *homo sapiens* or 'postal workers', who could in principle be replaced by other specimens of the type (Schutz 1962: 8–10).

These ways of understanding my environment are generally so natural and familiar to me that I never pause to reflect on them. As Schutz often put it, I take them *for granted*, without questioning their validity, and without subjecting them to scrutiny (Schutz 1962: 74). Like Husserl, Schutz called this unquestioning and uncritical attitude to our environment the 'natural attitude' (see Husserl 1931/1982: §27). When I am naturally attuned, the entire system of practical knowledge or 'know-how', to which my typifications belong, remains in the background, as it were. This is obviously connected with the practical focus of the everyday subject: we have letters to send, groceries to buy, children to take to school and so on. These activities and the various projects of which they form part guide our interests and priorities. Our practical knowledge, including the various typifications, is a tool that we employ immediately and take for granted in order to navigate in the life-world and accomplish our aims.

Our background knowledge, however, is not immune to revision. As long as my typifications help me achieve my aims and objectives, they will remain in force; but if they are repeatedly defeated, I will typically revise them. As Schutz put it, our background knowledge is taken for granted, but only 'until further notice' (Schutz 1962: 74; Berger and Luckmann 1966/1991: 58). If, for example, I repeatedly experience that the addressees do not receive my letters, I will revise some of my assumptions concerning typical postal workers and their typical motives. On the other hand, I can only deal with such a situation by relying on other assumptions and typifications. I may file a complaint with Royal Mail, for example, thereby tacitly assuming that certain officials will react in certain typical ways (read my complaint, rather than simply ignore it). Alternatively, I may decide that from now on I will use electronic mail only, thereby assuming typical courses of action on the part of my Internet service provider, and so on. Thus, even if individual typifications are only taken for granted 'until further notice', it would be practically impossible to abandon them unless other typifications and assumptions at the same time remained in operation. Schutz accordingly concluded that within the context of a world it is taken for granted that I can question and doubt individual cases. The life-world itself is the undoubted 'foundation of any possible doubt' (Schutz 1962: 74).

We perceive, experience and understand in accordance with normal and typical structures, models and patterns, which previous experiences have inscribed in our subjective lives (Schutz 1962: 7–10). These structures and models prescribe what we should do in a particular situation, and they give us a sense that we can count on social reality, that it is reliable and can be comprehended, and that others experience it as we do. Obviously, intersubjectivity plays an important role in this. The stock of typical assumptions, expectations and prescriptions, which I make use of with complete naturalness, is for the most part socially derived and socially accepted.

Normality is also *conventionality*, which essentially transcends the individual person. My relations with others go as far back as I can remember, and my understanding is structured in accordance with the intersubjectively handed-down ways of understanding, which I have acquired through my upbringing and through learning a language (Schutz 1962: 13–14; see Berger and Luckmann 1966/1991: 150–3). The same goes for a wide range of my opinions and actions. As Husserl had previously pointed out, beside the influences of concrete individual others, there are the more indeterminate, general commands that custom and tradition issue: 'one' thinks this about that; 'one' holds a fork like this, and so on (Husserl 1989: 281–2; Heidegger 1927/1962: 149–68). In sum, it is from others that I learn what is normal – in particular those others that are closest to me, those who raise me and those I grow up together with and live with. I am thereby part of a common tradition that, through a chain of generations, stretches back into a distant past.

My background knowledge, implicit assumptions, expectations and so on, are hence not primarily *mine*, understood as my own personal and unique constructions. On the contrary, they are *social* constructions. In connection with this general point, Schutz subjected *knowledge* to a close analysis. He focused on three aspects of the socialization of human knowledge: its *structural* socialization, its *genetic* socialization and its social *distribution* (Schutz 1962: 11).

As for the structural aspect, Schutz emphasized that the knowledge we have is knowledge that others could have as well, if they had access to the same facts as we have access to. Conversely, I could know what others know, if only I could view things from their perspective, with their background knowledge, and so on. This is, of course, connected with the point already mentioned about the 'reciprocity of perspectives'. Knowledge, however, also has a social genesis, in that, as mentioned, most of our knowledge has been transmitted to us through others (parents, friends and teachers, who were themselves taught by teachers, and so on).

Finally, Schutz emphasized that knowledge is socially distributed. This claim includes the obvious point that most of us know something about certain things, but very little about other things. A person can be an expert in Slavic languages and have no idea what to do if he cannot start his car. Fortunately, others (mechanics) do know how to deal with this sort of thing. And most of us have sufficient knowledge, even outside our fields of expertise, to get by in everyday life. We know how to fill up the tank and check the oil; and besides, we have some rough knowledge of how to find someone who can fill the gaps in our own stock of knowledge (Schutz 1962: 14–15).

The successors of Schutz

With Schutz's immigration to the United States shortly before the Second World War, American social scientists were introduced to phenomenological sociology. Nevertheless, it took considerable time for Schutz's perspective to achieve any real impact on American sociology. There are several reasons for this. First, Schutz only became a full-time professor after more than ten years in the United States. Second, he was attached to the New School for Social Research in New York, which at that time was not regarded as a prestigious institution. Third, Schutz's publications were not very successful. The English translation of his early book *The Phenomenology of the Social World* was only published posthumously; while he had begun a similarly comprehensive and systematic account of his ideas after migrating to the United States, he was unable to complete it; and his papers were primarily published in philosophical rather than sociological journals. Finally, as a result primarily of misunderstandings, Schutz fell out with the influential Harvard sociologist Talcott Parsons.[4] Despite all of this, Schutz managed, albeit with some delay, to influence the American sociological scene, and it was thus in the United States that two new phenomenological sociologies were first introduced: the *sociology of knowledge* and *ethnomethodology*.

Schutz repeatedly pointed out that the social distribution of knowledge is a topic that has been insufficiently studied – a topic that would deserve the title 'sociology of knowledge' (Schutz 1962: 15, 149; 1964: 121). Originally, the sociology of knowledge was a discipline that primarily addressed epistemological issues, such as how true knowledge is acquired, by which methods, and so on. Its focus was on theoretical ideas and the knowledge of the 'elite' – that is, the established sciences, the cultural elite, and so on. Schutz, however, emphasized that the mechanic and the supermarket checkout assistant also have their 'knowledge' and that such knowledge is just as legitimate an object for a genuine sociology of knowledge as is the knowledge of the scientific and cultural elite. Besides, it is not the task of sociology as an empirical science to address general epistemological questions. Rather, in Schutz's view, sociology should focus on the life-world as it is experienced by everyday subjects (Schutz 1962: 144–5).

These ideas were taken up by Peter L. Berger and Thomas Luckmann in *The Social Construction of Reality: A Treatise in the Sociology of Knowledge*. This influential book attempted to combine Schutz's phenomenological outlook with the symbolic interactionism of George Herbert Mead.[5] But Berger and Luckmann also drew upon German anthropology and figures such as Max Scheler, Helmuth Plessner and Arnold Gehlen, as well as Karl Marx, Max Weber and Émile Durkheim. Berger and Luckmann were born in Austria and Slovenia, respectively, but both migrated to the United States, and studied with Schutz at the New School for Social Research.

Berger and Luckmann sought to apply the theoretical perspective of phenomenology to crucial notions such as identity, socialization, social roles, language and normality/abnormality. They claimed that it is the task of the sociology of knowledge to analyse the societal conditions for the formation and maintenance of various types of knowledge, scientific as well as quotidian. Berger and Luckmann thus widened the focus of the sociology of knowledge beyond the question of the social distribution of knowledge that Schutz had singled out as the central problem (Berger and Luckmann 1966/1991: 28). But they shared Schutz's basic intuitions. The sociology of knowledge is, briefly put, interested in how knowledge is produced, distributed and internalized; it examines how the validity of any form of knowledge (that of the Tibetan monk no less than that of the US businesswoman or the criminologist) becomes socially established (Berger and Luckmann 1966/1991: 15). But as they also stressed:

> the sociology of knowledge must first of all concern itself with what people 'know' as 'reality' in their everyday, non- or pre-theoretical lives. In other words, common-sense 'knowledge' rather than 'ideas' must be the central focus for the sociology of knowledge. It is precisely this 'knowledge' that constitutes the fabric of meanings without which no society could exist.
>
> (Berger and Luckmann 1966/1991: 27)

This project involves a challenge to any objectivist and positivist social theory. Berger and Luckmann rejected any attempt to view social reality as an objective entity, as a non-human or supra-human thing (1966/1991: 106). As they wrote, the social order is a product of human activity; it is neither biologically determined, nor in any other way determined by facts of nature: 'Social order is not part of the "nature of things", and it cannot be derived from the "laws of nature". Social order exists only as a product of human activity' (Berger and Luckmann 1966/1991: 70). The task of social theory is to provide an account of how human beings, through manifold forms of interaction, create and shape social structures and institutions, which may first have the character of a common, intersubjective reality, but eventually become 'externalized' and achieve objective reality. As Schutz would also have said, this happens largely through institutionalized typifications (Berger and Luckmann 1966/1991: 85–96). Through institutionalization, human activity is subjected to social control. The constructed social structures define what is normal, and sanctions are introduced to maintain the social order and avoid digression. With time, institutions come to appear inevitable and objective. Yet:

> It is important to keep in mind that the objectivity of the institutional world, however massive it may appear to the individual, is a humanly produced, constructed objectivity .... The institutional world is objectivated human activity, and so is every single institution .... The paradox that man is capable of producing a world that he then experiences as something other than a human product will concern us later on. At the moment, it is important to emphasize that the relationship between man, the producer, and the social world, his product, is and remains a dialectical one. That is, man (not, of course, in isolation but in his collectivities) and his social world interact with each other. The product acts back upon the producer.
>
> (Berger and Luckmann 1966/1991: 78)

Social reality is thus not only an externalized and objectified human product; it acts back upon human beings. It does so not only in the sense that we may feel it as an oppressive external force that we cannot resist, but also in the sense that social reality is something individual human beings 'internalize'. We are not raised outside society, but grow up in it. And as we grow up and mature, we take over from others (and make our own) a language, roles, attitudes and norms (see Berger and Luckmann 1966/1991: 149–57). Human society, Berger and Luckmann emphasized, must therefore be 'understood in terms of an ongoing dialectic of the three moments of externalization, objectivation and internalization' (Berger and Luckmann 1966/1991: 149).

The Social Construction of Reality became very popular in the late 1960s and in the 1970s, and was the book that made Schutz's ideas accessible to a wider audience. Another brand of US sociology that received crucial impulses from Schutz was the ethnomethodology introduced by Harold Garfinkel in the early 1960s.[6] Garfinkel was influenced by Husserl, Merleau-Ponty and Heidegger, but his main inspiration came from Schutz, Aron Gurwitsch and Talcott Parsons. Unlike Berger and Luckmann, Garfinkel was never a student of Schutz; but Garfinkel's approach to sociology nevertheless betrayed an important Schutzean inspiration. While Schutz remained a social *theorist*, however, Garfinkel applied phenomenological ideas in carrying out actual empirical research.

Briefly put, the task of ethnomethodology is to examine how social agents structure their social environment in a meaningful way. Like Schutz, the ethnomethodologist seeks to view things from participants' perspectives, and attempts to understand how their life form can be viewed as a result of their interaction with each other. The point is not to establish whether a given life form is 'true' or 'false', but rather to determine how agents have formed the interpretations and opinions that they hold. Ethnomethodology regards social structures (roles, institutions and systems of cultural meaning and value) as products of social interaction, rather than as pre-existing and determining factors. Social reality is thus conceived of as a fragile and vulnerable construction. It is a construction that is actively maintained by the participants.

According to Garfinkel, we are all busy constructing a world in which we feel at home. As also emphasized by Schutz, this happens in part via a process of typification. We make use of various routines and maxims in coping with social reality. These routines and maxims are gradually internalized and thereby recede from our view. In this way, the preconditions for our production of social meaning and order become inaccessible to us. Our understanding can never be made completely explicit and will always involve a horizon of background assumptions. But ethnomethodology has developed special techniques to reveal the practices that people engage in when establishing a social order. One such technique involves creating situations in which our normal background assumptions are undermined and thereby made explicit.

In one experiment, Garfinkel asked his students to act like guests in their own homes and record the reactions of their family members. These reactions varied from confusion to anger, and thus, according to Garfinkel, illustrated the fragility of the social order: an order that we ourselves help to produce, but which we nevertheless tend to take for granted (Garfinkel 1967: 42–3).

A famous empirical study informed by phenomenological ideas is Aaron V. Cicourel's study of the treatment of juvenile delinquents in two Californian cities. According to Cicourel, the process of classifying a young person as a delinquent crucially involves certain background assumptions on the part of police officers, probation officers, court officials and others. The police may, for example, have a tendency to pick out likely candidates on the basis of an implicit picture of the 'typical delinquent'. The picture includes such factors as family background, school performance and ethnicity. By applying such 'typifications', police officers and others involved make sense of the cases they are faced with (Cicourel 1976). A similar approach is adopted in J. Maxwell Atkinson's work on suicide statistics (1978). Atkinson found that coroners often rely on 'common-sense theories' about suicide and its causes when determining whether a particular death should be classified as a suicide or an accidental death – theories that to a remarkable extent converge with the typical picture of suicide propagated by news media. For coroners as well as for other agents, Atkinson suggests, such theorizing 'provid[es] for the social organization of sudden deaths by rendering otherwise disordered and potentially senseless events ordered and sensible' (1978: 173).

Phenomenology and ethnomethodology have often criticized sociologies that attempt to analyse social reality in terms of various pre-defined categories, such as gender, class struggles, and the like. The claim is that such a procedure theorizes about the world instead of describing it. This critique suggests the phenomenological point that sociology must return to 'the things themselves', to the 'phenomena'. Rather than moulding the social world to fit various pre-defined theoretical categories, we ought to examine how people themselves experience their social reality. For ethnomethodology, the main sociological task is thus to understand how social agents themselves cope with the task of describing and explaining the order of the reality in which they live.

Criticism of phenomenological sociology

Let us briefly consider some of the criticisms that phenomenological sociology has met with. Nick Crossley (1996: 95–8) lists a number of allegedly problematic features of Schutz's work, one of which merits consideration here.[7] According to Crossley, 'Schutz tends to stick to the sorts of relationship which an individual takes to other individuals or groups at the expense of a consideration of relationships, practices and processes viewed from the trans-individual position of the systems which they form' (1996: 98). In other words, Schutz seems to adopt an 'individualist' perspective and thereby loses sight of the way 'the community itself functions as a system, perpetuating itself through space and time' (Crossley 1996: 98).

A phenomenological reply to this criticism consists of two parts. First, we should not think that Schutz's shortcomings are necessarily the shortcomings of the phenomenological perspective as such. Thus, even if it is correct that Schutz failed to consider the community as a system that perpetuates itself through space and time, this need not be because of his commitment to phenomenology. In fact, Berger and Luckmann, in Part Two of *The Social Construction of Reality*, give detailed consideration to how society perpetuates itself as an impersonal, 'trans-individual' system.

That said, however, Crossley does have a point. As readers of the present chapter may have noticed, some sort of emphasis on the individual person or subject is found in all the phenomenological thinkers we have considered – from Husserl, through Schutz, to Berger and Luckmann and Garfinkel. The phenomenologists, however, would insist that this is ultimately no ground for criticism. A society cannot be reduced to the sum of its individual members;

but on the other hand, the phenomenologists maintain that there is no society without individual subjects. To speak of a 'social system' in the absence of a robust notion of individual subjects makes little sense; for in what sense would the system in question be *social*? What could make it social except the fact that it involves (which is not the same as: 'can be reduced to') individual subjects standing in various relations to each other? A community of *no one* is hardly a *community*. An impersonal 'system' will never yield a society. For that, we need the *interpersonal* – and without the *personal*, there is no interpersonal (see Overgaard 2007, esp. chapter 5).

As another general criticism of phenomenology, we might maintain that its strengths could easily become its weaknesses. The phenomenological rehabilitation of the life-world, and the insistence on the importance of the everyday human being and their 'common-sense' knowledge, may seem to verge on celebrating the ordinary or mediocre. For example, the idea that commonsense knowledge is as legitimate a sociological theme as is scientific knowledge may seem to imply that these two kinds of knowledge are equally valuable. But, if so, the phenomenological perspective would implicitly legitimize intellectual laziness. Other critics have claimed that phenomenological sociology is conservative, that it implies a defence of the status quo – even when status quo is an unjust social order. Finally, the phenomenological emphasis on subjectivity as active and creative must not lead to blindness regarding the manifold ways in which individuals can be subjected to, and controlled by, institutions or other individuals.

However, phenomenology has largely pre-empted these criticisms. The notion that the phenomenological sociologist must primarily examine the everyday person, and that they must take seriously this person's 'knowledge' and perspective, is fully compatible with maintaining a critical distance. Schutz himself stressed that the sociologist must be an observer of, rather than a participant in, the social phenomena examined. And he emphasized the fact that our common-sense knowledge is limited and incomplete. A phenomenologist such as Heidegger couples an examination of the everyday human being and its 'average' understanding with a rather critical perspective on this everyday understanding (allegedly superficial and with a tendency to rely on hearsay) (Heidegger 1927/1962: 210–19). Indeed, Heidegger emphasized that the everyday subject may be blinded by habit and convention (1927/1962: 149–68). Thus, a phenomenological examination of the everyday subject need not glorify or idealize it. Similarly, a descriptive analysis of social reality as it is need not legitimize it. On the contrary, a sober description is an important element in any rational deliberation on what, precisely, ought to be changed about the status quo.[8]

Ultimately, however, the phenomenologists would insist that it is not an option to devalue entirely – let alone reject – our ordinary everyday knowledge. For even scientists and political revolutionaries *must* rely on this knowledge in the greater part of their lives. Moreover, in spite of its many imperfections and limitations, this knowledge is usually adequate enough for practical purposes. Nor, as already mentioned, is it an option to ignore completely the individual subject or to insist that they are nothing but a plaything in the hands of society. As individual subjects we are not merely subjected to the social reality in which we live; we also take part in its creation and maintenance. And for that very reason it is possible for us to change it. As Berger and Luckmann wrote, 'However objectivated, the social world was made by men – and, therefore, can be remade by them' (1966/1991: 106).

Conclusion

Let us briefly recapitulate some of the crucial features of phenomenological everyday life sociology. First, all phenomenologists share an insistence on description and a resistance toward theoretical speculation. A second important feature of phenomenological sociology is its emphasis on the need to take everyday life seriously. The 'naturally attuned', practically oriented commonsense person and their experienced life-world is the primary object of sociology. Thirdly, phenomenology maintains that an examination of sociality and social reality has to take subjectivity into account. Human subjectivity is not merely moulded and determined by social forces. In interaction with others, subjectivity also shapes social reality.

Phenomenological sociologists have consistently issued warnings against the tendency to substantialize and reify social matters and they have offered a corrective to traditional positivistic research methodologies. Societal reality, including institutions, organizations, ethnic groupings, classes, and so on, must be regarded as a product of human activity. The sociological task is to understand the workings of this productive or constitutive process. No account of everyday social life can be complete if it does not take into account the contribution of individual subjectivities. This is the fundamental message of phenomenological sociology.

Notes

1. Natanson (1973) contains papers addressing concretely the significance of phenomenology to various social sciences.
2. See Barber (2002) for an excellent introduction to Schutz. Schutz's paper 'Commonsense and scientific interpretation of human action' contains a concise account of the main tenets of his phenomenological sociology.

3. It is thus essential to make a sharp distinction between Schutz's notion of the 'face-to-face' relation and Lévinas' notion of 'face to face'. The latter is a communicative social relation with a special ethical status (see Lévinas 1969).
4. An account of Schutz's influence on American sociology, including the factors that impeded and delayed it, is found in Psathas (2004).
5. The title of Berger and Luckmann's 1966 book was later appropriated by the movement of *social constructivism*. Yet, most social constructivists do not regard themselves as phenomenologists, and phenomenologists do not necessarily share the relativism and nihilism advocated by some social constructivists.
6. Ethnomethodology is discussed in detail elsewhere in this book. We shall therefore restrict ourselves to mentioning a few points that illustrate Garfinkel's debt to Schutz.
7. Crossley's other points concern omissions or limitations in Schutz's work that have little to do with his phenomenological perspective as such; most of the defects, indeed, are remedied in Berger and Luckmann (1966/1991).
8. Cicourel's study illustrates the critical potential of phenomenological descriptions of the status quo.

Bibliography

Atkinson, J. Maxwell (1978) *Discovering Suicide: Studies in the Social Organization of Sudden Death.* London: Macmillan.

Barber, Michael (2002) 'Alfred Schutz', in Edward N. Zalta (ed.), *The Stanford Encyclopaedia of Philosophy* [online] http://plato.stanford.edu/archives/win2002/entries/schutz/

Berger, Peter L. and Thomas Luckmann (1966/1991) *The Social Construction of Reality: A Treatise in the Sociology of Knowledge*. Harmondsworth: Penguin.

Cicourel, Aaron V. (1976) *The Social Organization of Juvenile Justice*. London: Heinemann.

Crossley, Nick (1996) *Intersubjectivity: The Fabric of Social Becoming.* London: Sage.

Garfinkel, Harold (1967) *Studies in Ethnomethodology*. Englewood Cliffs, NJ: Prentice-Hall.

Gurwitsch, Aaron (1974) *Phenomenology and the Theory of Science.* Evanston, IL: Northwestern University Press.

Habermas, Jürgen (1992) *Postmetaphysical Thinking: Philosophical Essays.* Cambridge: Polity Press.

Heidegger, Martin (1927/1962) *Being and Time.* Oxford: Blackwell.

Husserl, Edmund (1925/1962) *Phänomenologische Psychologie (Husserliana IX).* The Hague: Martinus Nijhoff.

Husserl, Edmund (1931/1982) *Ideas Pertaining to a Pure Phenomenology and to a Phenomenological Philosophy: First Book.* Dordrecht: Kluwer Academic.

Husserl, Edmund (1935/1970) *The Crisis of European Sciences and Transcendental Phenomenology.* Evanston, IL: Northwestern University Press.

Husserl, Edmund (1964/1995) *Cartesian Meditations: An Introduction to Phenomenology.* Dordrecht: Kluwer Academic.

Husserl, Edmund (1989) *Ideas Pertaining to a Pure Phenomenology and to a Phenomenological Philosophy: Second Book.* Dordrecht: Kluwer Academic Publishers.

Lévinas, Emmanuel (1930/1995) *The Theory of Intuition in Husserl's Phenomenology*. Evanston, IL: Northwestern University Press.

Lévinas, Emmanuel (1969) *Totality and Infinity: An Essay on Exteriority.* Pittsburgh: Duquesne University Press.

Lévinas, Emmanuel (1974) *Otherwise than Being or Beyond Essence*. Pittsburgh: Duquesne University Press.

Merleau-Ponty, Maurice (1945/1962) *Phenomenology of Perception*. London: Routledge & Kegan Paul.

Natanson, Maurice (1973) *Phenomenology and the Social Sciences, Vols I–II*. Evanston, IL: Northwestern University Press.

Overgaard, Søren (2004) *Husserl and Heidegger on Being in the World*. Dordrecht: Kluwer Academic.

Overgaard, Søren (2007) *Wittgenstein and Other Minds: Rethinking Subjectivity and Intersubjectivity with Wittgenstein, Lévinas, and Husserl. New York:* Routledge.

Psathas, George (2004) 'Alfred Schutz's influence on American sociologists and sociology.' *Human Studies* 27: 1–35.

Sartre, Jean-Paul (1943/1956) *Being and Nothingness: An Essay on Phenomenological Ontology*. New York: Philosophical Library.

Schutz, Alfred (1962) *The Problem of Social Reality: Collected Papers I*. The Hague: Martinus Nijhoff.

Schutz, Alfred (1964) *Studies in Social Theory: Collected Papers II*. The Hague: Martinus Nijhoff.

Schutz, Alfred (1966) *Studies in Phenomenological Philosophy: Collected Papers III*. The Hague: Martinus Nijhoff.

Schutz, Alfred (1932/1972) *The Phenomenology of the Social World*. London: Heinemann Educational.

Schutz, Alfred and Thomas Luckmann (1973) *The Structure of the Life World*. Evanston, IL: Northwestern University Press.

Zahavi, Dan (1996) 'Husserl's intersubjective transformation of transcendental philosophy.' *Journal of the British Society for Phenomenology*, 27 (3): 228–45.

Zahavi, Dan (2001a) 'Beyond empathy: phenomenological approaches to intersubjectivity.' *Journal of Consciousness Studies*, 8 (5–7): 151–67.

Zahavi, Dan (2001b) *Husserl and Transcendental Intersubjectivity*. Athens, OH: Ohio University Press.

CHAPTER 4

Symbolic Interactionism

The Play and Fate of Meanings in Everyday Life

DENNIS D. WASKUL

Introduction

Reflect, for a moment, on the meaning of a kiss. Think about it. For my part, every morning when my young children leave for school they get a kiss goodbye – it is an important part of my good wishes for a fantastic day. Those kisses are not unlike the 'good night kiss' I give them before bed, only then I am wishing for the sweetest of dreams (and a full night's sleep!). All of these kisses are similar to a kiss I give my wife – namely, the kiss we share just before departing for work. My wife and I share other kinds of kisses too. Indeed, in Part II (Chapter 3) of *Kama Sutra*, Vatsyayana lists a total of seven kinds of intimate kisses; like most long-term lovers (I presume), my wife and I have discovered all of those and then some others as well (and we did not need a book to do it, nor did we write about them). But we do not need to get too personal (nor so sloppy), do we? Among people who are perhaps more bio-hygienic and less publicly intimate, it is not uncommon to observe the 'blowing' of kisses. A blown kiss is a playful expression that could mean many things. And, surely, kisses that are blown have advantages; amongst them is neither juicy saliva nor possible unwanted tongue!

But wait. All flesh and fluids aside, there is more to a kiss than these acts of kissing themselves. A kiss is no mere noun or verb – is it also a metaphor, and one complete with a variety of slang idioms. Once again, think about it. To be told to 'kiss off' means something antithetical to what the physical act of kissing would seemingly imply. Moreover, and inexplicably, a 'kiss ass' means something different than being told to 'kiss my ass!' In fact, is being a 'kiss ass' not a whole lot like 'kissing up'? If so then, generally speaking, by 'kissing up' are we not headed in the wrong direction if we truly wish to 'kiss ass'? No? Vexing, is it not?

Reflecting on these various meanings of a kiss I think we can see, rather clearly, the fundamental relevance of symbolic interaction in everyday life. As a verb or noun, the meaning of a kiss is defined in *action*. What a kiss means depends on *how* it is performed, with *whom* and in what *context* – varied combinations result in varied meanings unto what is, basically, the same act (but they are not the same at all). Furthermore, what a kiss 'is' cannot be disentangled from what that kiss *means*, and this is something we simply cannot understand by regarding a kiss as a mere physical action; a simple puckering of our lips, often against a person or object, and frequently concluded with a smacking sound. In addition, and more than an action, a kiss is a significant symbol – namely, it is a word. The word 'kiss' is deployed to convey a variety of creative meanings that are artfully fashioned in everyday life. Those phrases, too, are defined in symbolic interaction. For example, what does it mean when someone says 'kiss my ass!'? It might be an insult, or perhaps a playful expression between friends who, because of their close relationship, can light-heartedly tease one another. Here too, the meaning of a phrase as simple as 'kiss my ass' depends on *how* it is stated, by *whom* and in what *context*. In other words, a kiss – be it an action or a word – is defined in symbolic interaction.

Symbolic interaction is something people *do* in everyday life. It is the active, reflexive, creative and communicative doings of people in which meaning is *fashioned* – a uniquely human quality that bestows the capacity for both self and society at the most fundamental level. Symbolic interaction is also a perspective and analytical method for doing social science and understanding our social, cultural and communicative worlds. In this chapter I focus on symbolic interactionism as a perspective and method and, as will be obvious, it is fundamentally a *sociology* of everyday life. Indeed, '[s]ymbolic interactionism is widely regarded as the most sociological of all social psychological theories' (Reynolds and Herman-Kinney 2003: 7). Although many symbolic interactionists do not consider themselves social psychologists, symbolic interactionism is, at its core, *pragmatic* and thus everyday life is necessarily its chief subject. But I am already getting ahead of myself ...

Definitions, central tenets and key principles

'Symbolic interaction' was first coined by Herbert Blumer (1900–1987) in 1937 – but he would later regard it as a 'somewhat barbaric neologism that I coined in an offhanded way' (Blumer 1969: 1). Indeed, Blumer's *Symbolic Interactionism* (1969) more than compensates; anything but 'barbaric' and 'offhanded' the book is not only a classic, but perhaps the most seminal text for students of symbolic interaction. No other text more clearly defines the perspective and method of symbolic interaction, and few others are more widely cited among students of symbolic interaction. For these reasons, let us begin with a brief overview of some of Blumer's most central ideas.

However, we should first start with a definition, or at least an attempt at one. This is somewhat tricky; symbolic interaction is a diverse perspective that can be defined in various ways. Although interactionists agree that symbolic interaction is a distinct conceptual and methodological framework for doing sociology, there is no universally agreed definition. Therefore, perhaps a definition of symbolic interaction is best produced in a manner that is pragmatic and plural: symbolic interaction is an approach that, among other things, emphasizes the active processes by which people craft social worlds, create meaning, accomplish self, define situations and engage in cooperative, situated and structured joint action.

Not satisfying? I suspect not, and that is understandable. A more complete understanding of symbolic interaction requires, not a definition, but a close examination of the central and guiding premises of this perspective and method – which is precisely what Blumer (1969: 2) suggests: '[S]ymbolic interactionism rests in the last analysis on three simple premises.' Collectively, these premises succinctly define the perspective and method:

- 'Humans act toward things on the basis of the meanings that the things have for them.'
- 'The meaning of such things is derived from, or arises out of, the social interaction that one has with one's fellows.'
- 'These meanings are handled in, and modified through, an interpretive process used by the person in dealing with the things he encounters' (Blumer 1969: 2).

Because these widely cited premises collectively define symbolic interaction better than any other statement, let us explicate what Blumer means and how these premises uniquely position symbolic interaction as a distinct perspective from other sociological and psychological approaches to understanding.

The first premise is, arguably, the most important to symbolic interaction. The fact that humans act toward things on the basis of the meanings things have for them states, first and foremost, the *centrality of meaning* to the perspective and method of symbolic interaction – it is also, as I will soon illustrate, a simple enough premise to both understand and observe in everyday life. 'Yet, oddly enough, this simple view is ignored or played down in practically all of the thought and work in contemporary social science and psychological science' (Blumer 1969: 2). As Blumer explains:

> [M]eaning is either taken for granted and thus pushed aside as unimportant

> or it is regarded as a mere neutral link between the factors responsible for human behaviour and this behaviour as the product of such forces. We can see this clearly in the predominant posture of psychological and social sciences today. Common to both of these fields is the tendency to treat human behaviour as the product of various factors that pay upon human beings; concern is with the behaviour and with the factors regarded as producing them. Thus, psychologists turn to such factors as stimuli, attitudes, conscious or unconscious motives, various kinds of psychological inputs, perception and cognition, and various features of personal organization to account for given forms or instances of human conduct. In similar fashion, sociologists rely on such factors as social position, status demands, social roles, cultural prescriptions, norms and values, social pressures and group affiliation to provide such explanations. In both such typical psychological and sociological explanations the meaning of things for the human beings who are acting are either bypassed or swallowed up in the factors used to account for their behaviour.
>
> (Blumer 1969: 2–3)

Clearly, Blumer positions symbolic interaction as an alternative to both mainstream psychological and sociological approaches to understanding human activity – and it does so by taking the position that 'the meanings that things have for human beings are *central* in their own right' (Blumer 1969: 3, emphasis added). Simply put, what things are is less important than what things mean. Take, for example, 'the finger'. Our middle finger is just a finger – remarkably like the finger next to it. But, to many people, 'the finger' means something that has little to do with fingers at all; to 'give' someone 'the finger' is a gesture that conveys meaning. Thus, to regard 'the finger' – the 'middle finger' – as *just* a finger is to miss the point altogether.

Blumer further differentiates symbolic interaction from mainstream psychological and sociological approaches in his second premise. By stating that the meaning of things is derived from, or arises out of, social interaction Blumer identifies the *origin of meaning*. Here, too, Blumer (1969: 3) contrasts the perspective and method of symbolic interaction to 'two well-known traditional ways of accounting for the origin of meaning' and explains:

> One of them is to regard meaning as being intrinsic to the thing that has it, as being a natural part of the objective makeup of the thing. Thus, a chair is clearly a chair in itself, a cow a cow, a cloud a cloud, a rebellion a rebellion, and so forth .... The meaning emanates, so to speak, from the thing and as such there is no process involved in its formation .... This view reflects the traditional position of 'realism' in philosophy – a position that is widely and deeply

> entrenched in the social and psychological sciences. The other major traditional view regards 'meaning' as a psychical accretion brought to the thing by the person for whom the thing has meaning .... An expression of constituent elements of the person's psyche, mind or psychological organization.
>
> (Blumer 1969: 3–4)

Blumer contrasts symbolic interaction from these two dominant views by locating the origin of 'meaning as arising *in* the process of interaction between people .... Thus, symbolic interactionism sees meanings as social products, as creations that are formed *in and through the defining activities of people as they interact*' (Blumer 1969:4–5, emphasis added) – a premise that owes deeply to the pragmatist tradition of symbolic interaction, which will briefly be explained later.

Once more, we can use the middle finger as an example. For many people, the meaning of the middle finger is offensive. Crudely stated, to 'give' someone 'the finger' is tantamount to saying 'f*ck you'. That meaning, however, is not of the finger itself: no amount of dissection of the flesh, blood and bones of one's finger will ever uncover the 'f*ck you' part of this anatomy, for it is not anatomical at all; when born into this world the doctors did not say 'Oh no, not another one with one of *those* fingers!' When someone gives us 'the finger' we are not potentially insulted because they showed us that piece of flesh. Instead, we are potentially offended because of what 'the finger' means.

This is what Blumer suggests in his first premise. Here Blumer is suggesting something else: the meaning of 'the finger' is not culturally predetermined or programmatic either – it is *situated* and *emergent*; its meaning is actively defined *in* the processes of interaction and *between* people. For example, I am likely to be offended if I am given 'the finger' by a stranger with a scornful look on his face; I am likely to laugh and regard it as a sign of camaraderie if a friend gives me the same finger in a bout of playful banter. This is what Blumer (1969: 5) implies by meaning being 'formed in and through the defining activities of people as they interact'. The meaning of 'the finger' is neither automatic nor culturally preset; it depends on who is giving me the finger, under what circumstances, in what context, and so on.

Finally, Blumer's third premise differentiates symbolic interaction even further: '[T]he use of meanings by a person in his [or her] action involves an interpretative process' (Blumer 1969: 5). This interpretive process is nothing less than communication – and especially people communicating with *themselves* – in which meanings are 'more than an arousing or application of already established meaning' (Blumer 1969: 5). Instead, it is a creative, active and 'formative process in which meanings are used and revised as instruments for the guidance and formation of action' (Blumer 1969: 5). While the first premise establishes the centrality of meaning to symbolic interaction, and the second premise identifies the source, this third premise contends that 'meanings are handled *flexibly* by the actor in the course of forming his [or her] action' (Blumer 1969: 6, emphasis added).

Here, too, 'the finger' is a good example. All that I have already suggested indicates that 'the finger' is subject to 'the play and fate of meaning' (Blumer 1969:18) – the finger, like a kiss, might mean many things, depending on how it is interpreted by people who flexibly and creatively communicate. 'The finger' might be a gesture that is offensive, playful, defiant, a sign of solidarity, a warning, an expression of frustration or any number of other possible meanings that necessarily hinge on an *interpretive* process.

Consistent with these basic premises, symbolic interactionism is loosely organized around central tenets. Robert C. Prus (1996: 15–17) identifies six: human group life is intersubjective, multi-perspectival, reflexive, activity-based, relational and processual. These six tenets are, for the most part, also reflected in (or related to) Jerome G. Manis and Bernard N. Meltzer's (1978: 6–8) seven central principals of symbolic interactionism:

- Distinctively human behaviour and interaction are carried on through the medium of symbols and their meanings.
- The individual becomes humanized through interaction with other persons.
- Human society is most usefully conceived as consisting of people in interaction.
- Human beings are active in shaping their own behaviour.
- Consciousness, or thinking, involves interaction with ourselves.
- Human beings construct their behaviour in the course of its execution.
- An understanding of human conduct requires study of the actors' covert behaviour.

By use of these general assumptions, tenets and principals – which, as I hope is clear, represent both a perspective and a method – symbolic interactionists examine a wide range of topics by use of a variety of research methodologies. In terms of research methodology, '*the symbolic interactionist perspective does not have a method that at the same time does not belong to non-interactionist perspectives*' (Maines 2003: 11, original emphasis). However, it is also true that the majority of interactionist research is, in fact, qualitative – but this does not preclude quantitative and even experimental research designs (see, for example, Miller 2000; Ulmer and Wilson 2003).

Furthermore, David R. Maines is also correct when he states that '*symbolic interactionism does not have a content that is any different from the content of general sociology*' (Maines 2003: 7, original emphasis). For this reason, the substantive focus of symbolic interaction is as deep and wide as the discipline of sociology itself. Indeed, Larry T. Reynolds and Nancy Herman-Kinney's (2003) *Handbook of Symbolic Interactionism* is meaty – over 1000 pages in girth. Part Six is an overview of major substantive areas and 'is the largest and most diverse section of this handbook' – 12 chapters written by 16 authors – and yet is it is merely a '*sample* of *some* of the areas of inquiry that have seized the intellectual attention of symbolic interactionists' (Reynolds and Herman-Kinney 2003: 687, emphasis added). Reynolds and Herman-Kinney (2003: 687) readily admit that 'there are many more substantive areas of interactionist interest worthy of consideration', but the list of chapter topics is lengthy already: deviance, collective behaviour, race and ethnic relations, gender, emotions, social movements, the life course, childhood, sport and leisure, occupations and professions, applied sociology, community and urban life. The list could have also easily included communications, mass media, popular culture, sexualities, sociology of the body, health and medicine, and death and dying. Clearly, the methodological and substantive focus of symbolic interaction is synonymous with sociology itself – symbolic interactionists merely seek to describe, explain and understand by use of a unique perspective that is fundamentally grounded in the dynamics of everyday life.

Influences and forerunners

Like many (if not all) conceptual frameworks, 'symbolic interactionism can be seen to have an affinity with a number of intellectual traditions' (Plummer 1996: 226). Reynolds (2003a) provides an excellent overview of some of the more important precursors: evolutionism, German idealism, Scottish moralism, pragmatism, and functional psychology. All of these, among others (especially the works of Georg Simmel, existentialism and phenomenology) are worthy of discussion, but for our purposes we shall briefly address the school of thought that has had the greatest influence on what would become symbolic interaction: pragmatism. I shall also provide a brief overview of the two most central pragmatists who would greatly influence symbolic interaction: Charles Horton Cooley (1864–1929) and George Herbert Mead (1863–1931).

Because pragmatism is covered at length elsewhere in this book, I shall keep my discussion concise – and that's a good thing; pragmatism is not 'a single unified body of philosophic ideas' (Martindale 1960: 297). This loosely bound philosophical school of thought is really more a variety of related ideas than a coherent and organized paradigm. Moreover, it is an approach that 'had always sought to demonstrate its worth in practice' (Reynolds 2003a: 45) rather than in philosophical tomes per se. In fact, it is ironic that Mead (1936: 97) – widely regarded as the most influential pragmatist on what would become symbolic interaction – himself defined pragmatism 'as a pseudo-philosophic formulation of that most obnoxious American trait, the worship of success'. Nonetheless, Reynolds (2003a: 45) succinctly identifies key assumptions of pragmatism – four of which are most central to symbolic interaction:

- Human beings are active and creative agents.
- The world people inhabit is one they had a hand in making. And it, in turn, shapes their behaviour. They then remake it.
- Subjective behaviour does not exist prior to experience but flows from it. Meaning and consciousness emerge from behaviour. An object's meaning resides not in the object itself but in the behaviour directed toward it (Manis and Meltzer 1978: 3).
- The examination of social issues and the solution of practical problems must be the real focus of philosophical endeavour (Lauer and Handel 1977: 10).

These core pragmatic principles are a nucleus of ideas that remains central to symbolic interaction – and that should be no surprise. The two early pragmatic philosophers whose work would influence symbolic interaction the most – Cooley and Mead – were themselves heavily influenced by their cohort of pragmatists, namely Charles Sanders Pierce, William James and John Dewey.

Charles Horton Cooley is regarded as one of 'the first to pioneer the (then unnamed) theory of symbolic interaction' (Plummer 1996: 226). Cooley's most significant contributions to sociology include a view of society that is mentalistic in character and construction, as well as a framework that conceives of individuality as a part of social order – two sides of the same coin. These are most clearly seen in Cooley's famous 'looking-glass self', which has 'three principal elements: the imagination of our *appearance* to the other person; the imagination of his [or her] *judgement* of that appearance; and some sort of self *feeling*, such as pride or mortification' (Cooley 1902: 87, emphasis added). In this way, Cooley's approach proposes that 'the imaginations which people have of one another are the solid facts of society'; that 'persons and society must be studied primarily in imagination' (Cooley 1902: 86). As Thomas J. Scheff (2005: 147) suggests, among Cooley's key contributions is a view of self-consciousness as a 'continually monitoring self from the point of view of others' and that 'living in the minds of others, imaginatively, give rise to real and intensely powerful emotions'. Indeed, this is also the major shortcoming of Cooley's perspective, which has been legitimately criticized as excessively solipsistic:

> If imaginations are the solid facts of society, it seems to follow that there are

> as many societies are there are individual imaginations. If our imaginations differ, how can we get beyond these differences and to what do we refer these differences in order to build general knowledge of society.
>
> (Stryker 1980: 27)

Mead's contributions to what would become symbolic interaction do not suffer from this shortcoming; Mead transformed this 'inner structure of the theory of symbolic interaction, moving it to a higher level of theoretical sophistication' (Martindale 1960: 329). And, certainly, no other philosopher is more closely associated with symbolic interaction. 'So powerful was Mead's influence that many interactionists, and other sociologists as well, regard him as the one "true founder of the symbolic interactionist tradition"' (Reynolds 2003b: 67).

Mead's significance to symbolic interaction is interesting, if not somewhat satirical, considering that at the time of his death he had not authored a book. Mead had written many articles on a wide variety of subjects, but they were often obscure and difficult to follow – he never produced a systematic and comprehensive theoretical framework (Fine and Kleinman 1986), not during his lifetime at least. Published after his death, and based on transcripts of his lectures, class notes taken by his students, unpublished papers and incomplete manuscripts, Mead's most important contributions are a series of books: *The Philosophy of the Present* (1932), *Mind, Self and Society* (1934), *Movements of Thought in the Nineteenth Century* (1936) and *The Philosophy of the Act* (1938). Of these four books sociologists are most familiar with *Mind, Self and Society* (1934), which is also the most noteworthy for symbolic interaction. Indeed, Mead's conception of mind, self and society are so central to symbolic interaction that I shall detail this 'holy trinity' later in the chapter. For now it is sufficient to identify Mead's more general ideas.

Mead asserts that society is possible because people interact cooperatively, which in turn is made possible because humans have the unique capacity to take the role of the other. In short, Mead argues that 'the real basis of social life is found in the capacity to take the role of the other' (Reynolds 2003b: 69). Likewise, this same capacity is the essence of self: 'If you can act toward yourself as you have toward others, you possess a self' (Reynolds 2003b: 73). In these external and internal communicative acts:

> we are more or less seeing ourselves as others see us .... We are calling out in the other person something we are calling out in ourselves, so that unconsciously we take over these attitudes. We are unconsciously putting ourselves in the place of others and acting as others act.
>
> (Mead 1934: 68–9)

This reflexivity is also what Mead means by 'mind' – which is a *process* and not a thing. Indeed, reflexivity is so central to Mead's conceptions of mind, self and society that it is unfortunate that the word 'unconscious' is chosen for the quote above. Upon close examination little of Mead's thought hinges on unconsciousness – it is, in fact, overwhelmingly based on *active agency*.

Regardless, Mead details a framework that magnifies the importance of significant symbols (especially language), communication (especially internalized communication and as both the ability to take the role of the other as well as the ability of socialized people to be objects unto themselves), how social processes bestow the capacity for selfhood, and the significance of reflexive thought to both self and society (as well as the very capacity for either).

It would ultimately, however, be Mead's star student who would champion his ideas, and indeed coin the term 'symbolic interaction'. That person, of course, was Herbert Blumer whom we have already discussed. Indeed, Blumer's efforts in *Symbolic Interactionism* might be regarded as a grand and ultimately successful scheme to make Mead's insights less philosophical and more sociological:

> My purpose is to depict the nature of human society when seen from the point of view of George Herbert Mead. While Mead gave human society a position of paramount importance in his scheme of thought he did little to outline its character. His central concern was with cardinal problems of philosophy .... In making his brilliant contributions along this line he did not map out a theoretical scheme of human society. However, such a scheme is implicit in his work.
>
> (Blumer 1969: 61)

Mind, self and society: the interactionist holy trinity

Central to symbolic interaction are the ways the perspective has formulated conceptions of mind, self and society. Although to deem these a 'holy trinity' is a bit melodramatic, it is hard to deny that these related concepts are among the most central to the perspective – understanding them, and the relationships between them, is key to the framework of symbolic interaction. In this section, I shall give a brief overview of these essential concepts. My intent here is not to focus narrowly on Mead's conceptions of mind, self and society (in spite of his significant book of the same name). Instead, I utilize these three concepts to illustrate how symbolic interaction frames and approaches key dynamics of everyday life; I also give a brief and selected review of some relevant scholarship related to each of these conceptualizations.

Mind

'Mind', writes Bernard N. Meltzer (2003: 253), is 'an integral concept within the interactionist frame of reference [that] implicates most other central concepts of the perspective'. However, unlike other key concepts 'mind receives relatively little direct, explicit attention in interactionist research' (Meltzer 2003: 253). Meltzer accounts for this irony by indicting the abstract and complex character of mind in symbolic interactionism, the multiplicity of forms that mind can take and the many manifestations of mind. All of these are likely culprits. I suggest another possibility. Mind receives little direct attention in symbolic interactionist research because mind is *the* process that implicates self and society, and is therefore so fundamental that it is difficult to isolate meaningfully.

Regardless, in symbolic interactionist thought, mind is a verb – not a noun (Meltzer 2003; Strauss 1978). Simply put, mind is something people *do*. Consistent with John Dewey's (1887/1967) perspective on perception, mind is an *activity*. We do not 'have' a mind, instead we engage in minded acts or, more accurately, acts of 'minding'. Minding is, fundamentally, a reflexive act which, as Meltzer (2003) rightly suggests, is an antithesis of René Descartes's dictum. Descartes would have us believe 'I think therefore I am.' In symbolic interaction it is the other way around: 'I am therefore I think.' The seemingly simple capacity to state 'I am' is a quintessential reflexive act, the very substance of thought itself. More specifically, mind is a *communicative* process which to Mead in particular, is both emergent and constituted by language and significant symbols: 'Only in terms of … significant symbols is the existence of mind … possible; for only in terms of … significant symbols can thinking – which is simply an internalized or implicit conversation – take place' (Mead 1934: 47).

In this way, significant symbols (especially language) are 'both the means for expression of our thoughts and the means for the very existence, or creation, of our thoughts' (Meltzer 2003: 261). It is also for these reasons that 'minding' is an acquired capacity – a faculty that emerges in socialization and is deeply connected to language acquisition. Thus, minding is of social and cultural origin, owing first and foremost to society and culture (that is, the unsocialized have no mind) – but once acquired, minding is what allows people to transcend society. But, more than just an internalized conversation, mind is also 'that which enables the individual to take the attitude of the other toward himself' (Mead 1934: 38), without which neither self nor society are possible.

Eviatar Zerubavel (1991) neatly illustrates the central role of significant symbols – especially language – in taken-for-granted but central acts of minding. Zerubavel effectively argues that language guides our classification of experience because things only become meaningful when placed into categories (and primarily in processes he coins as 'lumping' and 'splitting'). These are inevitably arbitrary acts; largely a matter of lingual convention. Yet, think about some of the examples Zerubavel gives: it is only through language and specifically the word 'alcohol' that we regard wine as a beverage more like vodka than grape juice. It is only through language that we think adding cheese to a hamburger makes it a 'cheeseburger' – a rather arbitrary convention since adding lettuce to a hamburger does not make it a 'lettuceburger'. Itisonlythroughlanguagethatyoucanreadthissentence; only those who possess the language can see the spaces that are missing – and that is an active act of minding. Thus, in acquiring a language people not only acquire the means for communication, but also a profound (but subtle) capacity to perceive reality in socially accepted ways; being able to 'see' the world through active yet socialized mental lenses (Zerubavel 1991).

Self

To Mead (1934), the self is that which is object unto itself – simultaneously both knower and known. Furthermore, this 'self, as that which can be an object to itself, is essentially a social structure, and it arises in social experience' (Mead 1934: 140). Like Cooley, Mead concludes that 'it is impossible to conceive of a self arising outside of social experience' (Mead 1934: 140). In other words, we cannot do self all by ourselves; instead self is both personal and communal all at once. And, like mind, self is also acquired through socialization and equally a verb: self is not something people 'have' so much as it is something that people do, and primarily in communicative acts (with our self and others). Furthermore, self is fluid, emergent and multiple:

> We carry on a whole series of different relationships to different people. We are one thing to one man [or woman] and another thing to another .... We divide ourselves up in all sorts of different selves with reference to our acquaintances .... There are all sorts of different selves answering to all sorts of different social reactions .... A multiple personality is in a certain sense normal.
>
> (Mead 1934: 142)

In short, selfhood is understood in the plural; we all harbour a vast multiplicity of selves as we are one thing to some people and someone else to others.

Unlike mind, self is a concept that is extensively explored. In fact, self has a fair claim to being among the most widely explored concept in interactionist research. Therefore, and perhaps for this reason, self is a concept with a variety of formulations. Andrew J. Weigert and Viktor Gecas (2003) provide an extremely useful framework for understanding the variations of interactionist conceptions of self. Weigert and Gecas identify three variations of symbolic interactionist understandings of self; I shall briefly summarize each.

The symbolic interactionist approach to self that is most closely tied to the works of Blumer regards *self as process*. From this point of view, self is always becoming, always a 'self creating process' (Weigert and Gecas 2003: 270) – something that people perpetually do in ongoing, situated and emergent joint acts. The central feature of 'self as process' is that self emerges and is experienced primarily in taking the role of the other. Symbolic interactionists who emphasize 'self as process' seek to show how selves develop, are maintained and affect their environments (Weigert and Gecas 2003).

A classic example of 'self as process' in the empirical literatures of symbolic interaction might be Howard S. Becker, Blanche Geer, Everett C. Hughes and Anselm L. Strauss's (1961) study of medical students, their subculture and the socialization that transforms them from a student to a professional doctor. Another excellent empirical example of 'self as process' can be seen in Norman K. Denzin's (1987) 'recovering alcoholic self'. Denzin explores a process of self-transformation among participants in Alcoholics Anonymous (AA) which parallels Mead's stages in the acquisition of self. Participants in AA first learn a language of significant symbols by which they imitate and mimic the words, actions and feelings of other members of AA. They then learn how to take the attitudes of specific members of AA as a kind of anticipatory socialization to their emerging recovering alcoholic self. Finally, the alcoholic self fully emerges once the individual is able to take the attitudes of AA – the community in the collective – as a generalized other. Consistent with Mead, but pushing ideas in important directions that would anticipate other interactionist approaches to selfhood (more fully developed a decade later), Denzin's (1987) brilliant analysis hinges on processes of storytelling (a narrative 'self in process') in which the old self of the alcoholic is continually juxtaposed with the new self of the recovering alcoholic.

A second variation of symbolic interactionist conceptions of self owes to works inspired by Erving Goffman and the dramaturgical genre. This approach emphasizes self as producer – self as a character that results from enacted scenes, dramatic action, appearances, impressions and presentations (Weigert and Gecas 2003). The difference here is subtle, but consistent with Kenneth Burke's (1969) dramaturgical emphasis on agency (which Goffman would share) – an emphasis on how things are done. In short, this is self as dramatic affect. Whereas 'self as process' emphasizes role taking, 'self as producer' magnifies selfhood as something that results from what people do. Goffman states it best when he writes that self is:

> a *product* of a scene that comes off, and is not a *cause* of it. The self, then, as a

> performed character, is not an organic thing that has a specific location, whose fundamental fate is to be born, to mature, and to die; it is a dramatic effect arising diffusely from a scene that is presented, and the characteristic issue, the crucial concern, is whether it will be credited or discredited.
>
> (Goffman 1959: 252)

One example of 'self as producer' might be seen in Patricia A. Adler and Peter Adler's (1989) conceptions of the 'glorified self' – although here, in their study of college athletes, this glorified self is largely fashioned of media constructions that are intoxicating caricatures of the athletes themselves. Furthermore, this form of a 'glorified self' is a dramaturgical affect that is not entirely of the athlete's own making – and it acts back to constrain athletes in troubling ways. Perhaps a more direct example of 'self as producer' might be seen in how people fashion a self in Internet environments (see Waskul 2003; Waskul and Douglass 1997; Waskul, Douglass and Edgley 2000). Who are we when online? The Internet, after all, is not a physical location – 'cyberspace' is not so much a physical thing as it is a concept that contains shared meanings, understandings and information (Waskul 2003), and it is crafted purely of communication in words and images. Likewise, when people communicate on the Internet, they interact with others and create personally meaningful selves – but these selves are not embodied in the flesh – *they are presented and preformed in words and images alone*. Like face-to-face interactions, Internet selves emerge through interaction with others – but on the Internet people literally write themselves into existence in a medium where they would not exist otherwise. Perhaps nowhere else are the dynamics of 'self as producer' more evident than on the Internet.

A third symbolic interactionist variation on self owes primarily to the 'Iowa School' (briefly discussed later) which, in contrast to the Chicago School (championed by, for instance, Blumer), represents a more structural and often quantitative approach to symbolic interaction. This point of view emphasizes *self as product* (Weigert and Gecas 2003). Closely associated with the works of Manford Kuhn and Sheldon Stryker, this structural form of symbolic interaction emphasizes roles and especially how roles both link people to social systems *and* bestow identity. From this point of view, role–person mergers (Turner 1978) represent an essential core to (and of) selfhood.

One rather complete empirical example of 'self as product' is in Dennis D. Waskul's (1998) ethnography of camp staffing. In this study, Waskul examines processes of self-transformation as participants at a resident camp produce a camp staff identity. Isolated among themselves and living in the wilderness for months, these staff members craft a role for themselves in an emergent 'wilderness community' which differs qualitatively from outside worlds and selves. In adopting these roles, and largely in a process of 'role-making' (Turner 1978), the camp staff role and identity gradually merges with the person and thus results in often profound transformations of self. However, at the end of the camping season, individuals leave the wilderness and return to their everyday life and the old selves of that world. In short, roles and identities are put on and taken off in processes that implicate the self (sometimes profoundly).

Society

Blumer suggests that definitions and understandings of society must consider how 'human beings, individually and collectively, *act* in society' (Blumer 1969: 89, emphasis added). This point of view is the hallmark of how symbolic interactionists conceive of society: it is both social and processual (Katovich and Maines 2003) and deeply grounded in the pragmatist tradition. Blumer bluntly states it best: 'It is the social processes in group life that creates and upholds the rules, not the rules that create and uphold group life' (Blumer 1969: 19).

From this point of view, Michael Katovich and David Maines (2003: 292) nicely summarize the symbolic interactionist perspective on society as an approach that emphasizes 'society-in-the-making rather than society-by-previous design'. At the core of this 'society-in-the-making' is an emphasis on choice namely that 'choice making allow[s] interactionists to "see" a society in the making in the context of negotiated agreements between representatives of institutions' (Katovich and Maines 2003: 293). Blumer's posthumously published *Industrialization as an Agent of Change* (1990) is perhaps one of the best examples; an ambitious exploration of how people bring about change in ongoing and emergent processes that are defined in the adjustments that people make.

In short, like all other aspects of symbolic interactionism, society is seen as an emergent and situated process. This framework does not preclude stability, for that too is an emergent and situated process. Indeed, society is symbolic interaction (Blumer 1969) and '[w]hatever is "there" exists in a process made up of people who behave together to create situational objectives' (Katovich and Maines 2003: 304).

Variations: symbolic interactionisms

The major schools and varieties of symbolic interaction are not easy to identify; '[t]here is simply not a great deal of consensus among interactionists concerning whether one can meaningfully speak of real varieties or schools of symbolic interactionism' (Reynolds and Herman-Kinney 2003: 85). Still, although they may not be distinct varieties or 'schools' in any rigid or mutually exclusive sort of way, we can nonetheless reasonably characterize 'variations' of symbolic interaction in at least two methodological and conceptual ways. On one hand, we can reasonably identify what are called the 'Chicago School' of symbolic interaction and the 'Iowa School' of symbolic interaction. On the other hand, and in a more conceptual way, we can also follow Thomas J. Scheff's (2005) suggestion and characterize variations of symbolic interaction into two other forms – one associated with Mead and Blumer, and the other with Cooley and Goffman. In this section I briefly review all four variations.

It is sensible to conclude that symbolic interaction was born in Chicago. The University of Chicago was home to John Dewey, William I. Thomas, and most significantly, George Herbert Mead and Herbert Blumer. But this is perhaps not so exceptional; some suggest that almost every major sociological subfield was developed at Chicago (Kurtz 1984). Nonetheless, the guiding philosophy of the Chicago School of symbolic interaction is pragmatism and their preferred methodologies were field studies. Although not strictly or entirely ethnographic, these field studies were largely naturalistic, and many classics were produced (for example, Nels Anderson's *The Hobo* (1923), Paul Cressey's *The Taxi-Dance Hall* (1932), Frederic Thrasher's *The Gang* (1927)).

But these influences were prior to the Second World War; to many Herbert Blumer is 'the postwar Chicago interactionist' (Musolf 2003). Blumer's approach to symbolic interaction would become most closely associated with the Chicago School – one that emphasizes process, emergence, situated joint acts, and the fluid play and fate of meanings in everyday life. This approach would also favour qualitative if not ethnographic methods because:

> the crucial limit to the successful application of variable analysis to human group life is set by the processes of interpretation or definition that goes on in human groups. The process, which I believe to be the core of human action, gives a character to human group life that seems to be at variance with the logical premises of variable analysis.
>
> (Blumer 1969: 132)

For this reason, the Chicago School of symbolic interaction is an approach that regards 'behaviourism, positivism and quantitative methods – indeed any method that apes the natural sciences, which treat human behaviour as just another datum to code the frequency of while ignoring human agency, consciousness, reflection, covert behaviour and minded activity – as inadequate' (Musolf 2003: 111–12).

The Iowa School of symbolic interaction is sadly mischaracterized (Buban 1986), owing primarily to Bernard N. Melzer and John W. Petras's (1970) reading of the alleged division between Chicago and Iowa schools. Originally led by Manford Kuhn, the Iowa School is, in fact, consistent with Mead's framework – Kuhn merely sought to transform the eloquent but largely abstract framings of Mead (and as articulated by Blumer) into a grounded and scientific approach that is precise, measurable, observable and can withstand the rigours of empirical demonstration and testing. Kuhn and his students sought to:

> establish the Iowa School of symbolic interaction as a bona fide scientific enterprise in social psychology. Kuhn believed that the hard work of an interactionist and pragmatic science (Mead 1938) would prove invaluable and would replace the more esoteric expressions of interactionist ideas.
> (Katovich, Miller and Stewart 2003: 120)

Kuhn would initially ground these efforts in systematic studies of the self, but in a far more codified manner than proposed by Blumer. Kuhn's approach would locate self as a set of statuses and identities, plans of action, values and definitions (Spitzer, Couch and Stratton 1971). The 'twenty statements test' (Kuhn and McPartland 1954) is easily the most well known of these efforts. In the 1970s, shortly after Kuhn's death, the Iowa School would be led by Carl Couch and shift to systematic and even laboratory studies of the processes and structures of coordinated interaction – namely, 'how interactors constructed social acts' (Katovich et al. 2003: 123).

While Blumer focused on how shared meanings led to joint action, from the perspective of the post-1970 'new Iowa School', Blumer failed to problematize interaction itself. Borrowing loosely from Simmel's framework of social forms, 'the central theme running throughout the Iowa School of thought is the notion of *structure*' (Katovich et al. 2003: 124, original emphasis):

> [T]he emphasis on symbolism, so pronounced in Chicago School ethnographies, became attenuated in favour of an emphasis on interactional elements of sociation .... The Chicago School emphasized the symbolic meanings of the act, whereas the New Iowa School accented its interactional elements.
> (Katovich et al. 2003: 126)

In this way, although the methods and emphasis are different, Iowa School interactionists share the same goals and conceptual frameworks as any other symbolic interactionist. Indeed, Iowa School symbolic interaction builds from *both* Mead and Blumer. But, with its emphasis on structure and a more cosy relationship with quantitative and laboratory methods, the Iowa School of symbolic interaction articulates a Simmelesque approach that does not deny, but rather explores, universal applications and generic conditions (Katovich et al. 2003).

In contrast to these widely cited variations, Thomas J. Scheff (2005) presents a compelling and perhaps less polemical way of seeing variations of and within symbolic interactionism. Scheff suggests that:

> [t]he prevailing line in symbolic interactionism follows Mead's theory of role-taking, as articulated by Blumer. Blumer was Mead's bulldog, relentlessly explaining Mead's basic thesis. This line elaborates on a single idea – that thought, self and society are a product of role taking – and feeling and emotion played very little part. But Cooley's framework was larger, since it referred to both thought and feelings.
>
> (Scheff 2005: 148)

Scheff proposes a persuasive argument – that there are two 'lines' of symbolic interactionism. One line is consistent with Mead and Blumer, and it is overwhelmingly based on role taking. We acquire a self by taking the role of the other with increasing degrees of sophistication; thinking is talking to our self, which is also a form of role taking; in society we are able to communicate and act cooperatively because of our ability to take the role of the other. From this Median–Blumerian line of symbolic interaction role taking is, clearly, the central premise – the very building block of human activity – and neither Mead nor Blumer had much to say about emotions.

On the other hand, for Cooley emotions are central. Moreover, 'Cooley focused on specific emotions, pride and shame' (Scheff 2005: 148). Indeed, 'Cooley was quite blunt in naming pride and shame, with no hesitation or qualification. For him, both of these emotions arose from self-monitoring, the process that was at the centre of his social psychology' (Scheff 2005: 149). Scheff suggests that, for Cooley, pride and shame are basic social emotions, which can also be seen to form the basic structure of Goffman's writing (particularly his earlier works). Even a casual reading clearly reveals how Goffman explored emotions, as well as thoughts and actions, but was especially interested in embarrassment, shame and humiliation. This second line of symbolic interactionism is owed to Cooley and Goffman, and hinges on a different central premise, namely one that is 'built around the dynamics of the looking-glass self, and Goffman's extension of it into … the management of the resulting emotions' (Scheff 2005: 163).

The past, present and future of symbolic interactionism

I shall conclude this chapter with brief reflections on the past, present and future of symbolic interactionism. While the past and present are relatively easy to characterize, future casting always entails some precarious guesswork. However, it is worthwhile to entertain those possibilities because, frankly, there are significant changes between symbolic interactionism's past and present – ones that signal a future that is less certain and considerably more diffuse.

A quarter of a decade ago, symbolic interactionism was labelled 'the loyal opposition' (Mullins 1973): a kind of separatist movement that was a part of a general reorientation of sociology in the 1960s into a discipline that is more inclusive of critical, qualitative and non-positivist perspectives. In this milieu, '[s]ymbolic interaction served as a convenient and welcoming home for many sociological "malcontents", frustrated by functionalist orthodoxy' (Fine 1993: 63) – and interactionists crafted a new vision for contemporary sociology. The Society for the Study of Symbolic Interaction (SSSI) was established in 1974. Three years later SSSI launched its own journal, *Symbolic Interaction*. SSSI and *Symbolic Interaction* were the hub of interactionism's place in sociology – collectively they were the cornerstones of a 'tight social network with a clear theoretical and research focus' (Fine 1993: 62). Much has changed since then.

Gary Alan Fine (1993) has suggested four processes that have altered the contemporary character of symbolic interactionism: fragmentation, expansion, incorporation and adoption. By 'fragmentation' Fine refers to a shift from '[w]hat used to be a fairly narrow, tightly focused perspective [that] now might be faulted for deemphasizing the traditional problems of situational definition, negotiation, impression management and meaning creation that once animated symbolic interaction' (1993: 64) – a kind of splintering as well as diversifying of interactionist interests. Related to this fragmentation is a simultaneous 'expansion' into new terrain for legitimate interactionist research – topics 'distinctly outside of what symbolic interactionists had once typically claimed for their domain' and to such an extent that symbolic interaction has indeed succeeded in connecting 'to the broad span of academic knowledge' (Fine 1993: 65). In this process, interactionists have 'incorporated' ideas and concepts from Marxist and critical theories, functionalism, Lev Vygotsky, Jean Piaget and many, many others. Likewise, those who do not self-identify as interactionists have 'adopted' key concepts and ideas, often with 'little knowledge of classic symbolic interaction' (Fine 1993: 66). The result is a decidedly 'new look' in which symbolic interaction has simultaneously (and ironically) triumphed, disappeared and deceased:

> If the goal of symbolic interaction is to maintain itself as a distinctive oppositional movement, then it has failed, with more and more outsiders addressing central issues and more and more insiders stepping outside the boundaries, not caring about their badges of courage. Yet, if the ultimate goal

> is to develop the pragmatic approach to social life – a view of the power of symbolic creation and interaction – then symbolic interaction has triumphed gloriously.
>
> (Fine 1993: 81)

In the final analysis, it's a little of both but neither.

For these reasons symbolic interaction may have, in fact, become a *silently* dominant perspective in sociology – and largely among sociologists who are 'unaware interactionists' (Maines 2003: 8). Ideas, concepts and propositions that were once unique to symbolic interaction now permeate the literature of general sociology (Maines 2003). A good example is the journal *Symbolic Interaction*. *Symbolic Interaction* was launched as a separatist if not sectarian outlet for works of symbolic interactionists; it was regarded as 'our' journal (Maines 2003). But, since then, it has morphed into a mainstream journal. By 2006 *Symbolic Interaction* was publishing high-quality empirical and theoretical works (and had an acceptance rate of a rigorous 8.6 per cent) and ranked in the top quarter of sociological journals (see Maines 2001, 2003). Likewise, contemporary interactionists find a warm welcome for their scholarship in a wide number of journals – many of which have a recent history of editors who are themselves interactionists (*Journal of Contemporary Ethnography*, *Qualitative Sociology Review*, *Qualitative Sociology*, *Social Psychology Quarterly*, to name a few). It is becoming harder and harder to precisely identify just who, or what, qualifies as symbolic interaction(ists) – a clear sign that symbolic interaction has become conventionalized and its practitioners are producing works with a wide range of uses and applications.

What, then, may we suggest about the future of symbolic interaction? Those who have speculated are unsure (see Fine 1993; Maines 2001, 2003) and rightly so! Forecasting is risky. Besides, the future of symbolic interaction will be written by a hitherto unnamed 'third wave' of interactionists. If we regard the 'first wave' as the masters (Herbert Blumer, Erving Goffman, Manford Kuhn, Carl Couch, Greg Stone, Anselm L. Strauss and so on), then the 'second wave' are primarily their students (Gary Alan Fine, David R. Maines, Norman K. Denzin, Peter Hall, Howard S. Becker and so on). Framed in this way, and with no intentions of being divisive, the 'third wave' has distinct characteristics: they have no personal memories of the masters whose works are only known to them in the trace records of publications; they have no personal memories or allegiances to the splits and turns that have allegedly 'fragmented' the perspective; they have no personal memories nor vested interests in symbolic interaction as an oppositional movement – indeed, third-wave interactionists have never known a sociology that was not a generally warm and inclusive discipline for symbolic interaction.

Where, then, will that 'third wave' take symbolic interaction? It is hard to tell, but there is some evidence of a 'renewed pragmatism' – a serious, yet critical, re-examination of the classic literatures, central tenants and key ideas. Some of them are challenging the anthrocentric bias of symbolic interaction by extending key principles to non-human animals (see Irvine 2004; Sanders 2003). Such work is controversial among interactionist insiders – but we cannot deny that these scholars are crafting and articulating a form of symbolic interaction that is loaded with immense possibilities. Some of them are critical of symbolic interaction, and often drawing from the classic works of Charles Sanders Pierce, are pointing out the significance of other forms of meaning-making, such as the iconic and indexical (see Vannini and Waskul 2006a, 2006b; Waskul and Vannini 2008; Waskul, Vannini and Wiesen 2007). In these and many, many other ways the future of symbolic interactionism seems hopeful.

Bibliography

Adler, Patricia A. and Peter Adler (1989) 'The glorified self: the aggrandizement and the constriction of self.' *Social Psychology Quarterly*, 52(4): 299–310.

Becker, Howard S., Blanche Geer, Everett C. Hughes and Anselm L. Strauss (1961) *Boys in White*. Chicago, IL: University of Chicago Press.

Blumer, Herbert (1969) *Symbolic Interactionism – Perspective and Method*. Berkeley, CA: University of California Press.

Blumer, Herbert (1990) *Industrialization as an Agent of Change* (ed. Thomas Morrione and David R. Maines). New York: Aldine de Gruyter.

Buban, Steven (1986) 'Studying social processes: the Chicago and Iowa schools revisited', in Carl Couch, Stanley Saxton and Michael Katovich (eds), *Studies in Symbolic Interaction: The Iowa School*. Greenwich, CT: JAI Press.

Burke, Kenneth (1969) *A Grammar of Motive*. Berkeley, CA: University of California Press.

Cooley, Charles H. (1902) *Human Nature and Social Order*. New York: Scribner.

Denzin, Norman K. (1987) *The Recovering Alcoholic*. Thousand Oaks, CA: Sage.

Dewey, John (1887/1967) 'Psychology', in *John Dewey: The Early Works 1882–1898*, Vol. 2. Carbondale, IL: Southern Illinois University Press.

Fine, Gary Alan (1993) 'The sad demise, mysterious disappearance and glorious triumph of symbolic interaction.' *Annual Review of Sociology*, 19: 61–87.

Fine, Gary Alan and Sherryl Kleinman (1986) 'Interpreting the sociological classics: can there be a true meaning of Mead?.' *Symbolic Interaction*, 9(1): 129–46.

Goffman, Erving (1959) *The Presentation of Self in Everyday Life*. Harmondsworth: Penguin.

Irvine, Leslie (2004) 'A model of animal selfhood: expanding interactionist possibilities.' *Symbolic Interaction*, 27 (1): 3–21.

Katovich, Michael and David R. Maines (2003) 'Society', in Larry T. Reynolds and Nancy Herman-Kinney (eds), *Handbook of Symbolic Interactionism*. New York: Rowman & Littlefield.

Katovich, Michael, Dan Miller and Robert Stewart (2003) 'The Iowa School', in Larry T. Reynolds and Nancy Herman-Kinney (eds), *Handbook of Symbolic Interactionism*. New York: Rowman & Littlefield.

Kuhn, Manford and Thomas McPartland (1954) 'An empirical investigation of self-attitudes.' *American Sociological Review*, 19: 68–76.

Kurtz, Lester (1984) *Evaluating Chicago Sociology*. Chicago, IL: University of Chicago Press.

Lauer, Robert and Warren Handel (1977) *Social Psychology: The Theory and Application of Symbolic Interactionism*. Boston, MA: Houghton Mifflin.

Maines, David R. (2001) *The Faultline of Consciousness: A View of Interactionism in Sociology*. New York: Harper & Row.

Maines, David R. (2003) 'Interactionism's place.' *Symbolic Interaction*, 26 (1): 5–18.

Manis, Jerome G. and Bernard N. Meltzer (eds) (1978) *Symbolic Interactionism: A Reader in Social Psychology*. Boston, MA: Allyn & Bacon.

Martindale, Don (1960) *The Nature and Types of Sociological Theory*. Boston, MA: Houghton Mifflin.

Mead, George H. (1932) *The Philosophy of the Present*. Chicago, IL: University of Chicago Press.

Mead, George H. (1934) *Mind, Self, and Society: From the Standpoint of a Social Behaviourist*. Chicago, IL: University of Chicago Press.

Mead, George H. (1936) *Movements of Thought in the Nineteenth Century*. Chicago, IL: University of Chicago Press.

Mead, George H. (1938) *The Philosophy of the Act*. Chicago. IL: University of Chicago Press.

Meltzer, Bernard N. (2003) 'Mind', in Larry T. Reynolds and Nancy Herman-Kinney (eds) *Handbook of Symbolic Interactionism*. New York: Rowman & Littlefield.

Meltzer, Bernard N. and John W. Petras (1970) 'The Chicago and Iowa schools of symbolic interactionism', in Tamatsu Shibutani (ed.), *Human Nature and Collective Behavior*. Englewood Cliffs, NJ: Prentice-Hall.

Miller, Dan (2000) 'Mathematical dimensions of qualitative research.' *Symbolic Interaction*, 23 (4): 399–402.

Mullins, Nicholas (1973) *Theories and Theory Groups in Contemporary American Sociology*. New York: Harper & Row.

Musolf, Gil (2003) 'The Chicago School', in Larry T. Reynolds and Nancy Herman-Kinney (eds), *Handbook of Symbolic Interactionism*. New York: Rowman & Littlefield.

Plummer, Ken (1996) 'Symbolic interactionism in the twentieth century: the rise of empirical social theory', in Bryan S. Turner (ed.), *Blackwell Companion to Social Theory*. Oxford: Blackwell.

Prus, Robert C. (1996) *Symbolic Interaction and Ethnographic Research*. Albany: University of New York Press.

Reynolds, Larry T. (2003a) 'Intellectual precursors', in Larry T. Reynolds and Nancy Herman-Kinney (eds), *Handbook of Symbolic Interactionism*. New York: Rowman & Littlefield.

Reynolds, Larry T. (2003b) 'Early Representatives', in Larry T. Reynolds and Nancy Herman-Kinney (eds), *Handbook of Symbolic Interactionism*. New York: Rowman & Littlefield.

Reynolds, Larry T. and Nancy Herman-Kinney (eds) (2003) *Handbook of Symbolic Interactionism*. New York: Rowman & Littlefield.

Sanders, Clinton (2003) 'Actions speak louder than words: close relationships between humans and nonhuman animals.' *Symbolic Interaction*, 26 (3): 405–26.

Scheff, Thomas J. (2005) 'Looking-glass self: Goffman as symbolic interactionist.' *Symbolic Interaction*, 28(2): 147–66.

Spitzer, Stephan, Carl Couch and John Stratton (1971) *The Assessment of Self*. Iowa City, IA: Sernoll Press.

Strauss, Anselm L. (1978) *Negotiations: Varieties, Contexts, Processes and Social Order*. San Francisco, CA: Jossey Bass.

Stryker, Sheldon (1980) *Symbolic Interactionism: A Social Structural Version*. Menlo Park, CA: Benjamin Cummings.

Turner, Ralph H. (1978) 'The role and the person.' *American Journal of Sociology*, 84 (1):1–23.

Ulmer, Jeffery and Mindy Wilson (2003) 'The potential contributions of quantitative research to symbolic interactionism.' *Symbolic Interaction*, 26 (4): 531–52.

Vannini, Phillip and Dennis D. Waskul (2006a) 'Symbolic interaction as music: esthetic constitution of meaning, self and society.' *Symbolic Interaction*, 29 (1): 5–18.

Vannini, Phillip and Dennis D. Waskul (2006b) 'Body-ekstasis: socio-somatic reflections on surpassing the dualism of body-image', in Dennis D. Waskul and Phillip Vannini (eds), *Body/Embodiment: Symbolic Interaction and the Sociology of the Body*. Aldershot: Ashgate.

Waskul, Dennis D. (1998) 'Camp staffing: the construction, maintenance and dissolution of roles and identities at a summer camp.' *Sociological Spectrum*, 18(1): 25–53.

Waskul, Dennis D. (2003) *Self-Games and Body-Play: Personhood in Online Chat and Cybersex*. New York: Peter Lang.

Waskul, Dennis D. and Mark Douglass (1997) 'Cyberself: the dynamics of self in online chat.' *The Information Society* 13 (4): 375–97.

Waskul, Dennis D., Mark Douglass and Charles Edgley (2000) 'Cybersex: outercourse and the enselfment of the body.' *Symbolic Interaction*, 23 (4): 375–97.

Waskul, Dennis D. and Phillip Vannini (2008) 'Smell, odor and somatic work: sense-making and sensory management.' *Social Psychology Quarterly*, 71 (1): 53–71.

Waskul, Dennis D., Phillip Vannini and Desiree Wiesen (2007) 'Women and their clitoris: personal discovery, signification and use.' *Symbolic Interaction*, 30 (2): 151–74.

Weigert, Andrew J. and Viktor Gecas (2003) 'Self', in Larry T. Reynolds and Nancy Herman-Kinney (eds), *Handbook of Symbolic Interactionism*. New York: Rowman & Littlefield.

Zerubavel, Eviatar (1991) *The Fine Line: Making Distinctions in Everyday Life*. New York: Simon & Schuster.

CHAPTER 5

Existential Sociology

The Self Confronts Society

JOSEPH A. KOTARBA

Introduction

The word 'existentialism' conjures up all kinds of romantic, mysterious and even adventurous images. We see stylish, French intellectuals casually enjoying their Beaujolais on a warm afternoon in a quaint café on a busy Parisian boulevard in the Left Bank, engaged in animated political and philosophical discussion. We see university students, gathered together in a salon at the Sorbonne, alternating sips of *café au lait* with hardy, unfiltered Gauloises, contemplating the notion of meaning and commitment. We see the stately yet worried professor, adorned with appropriate leather patches on his tweed sports coat, concluding a lecture with an exclaimed '*C'est absurd!*'

Those of us who borrow from existential thinking when forging our version of everyday life sociology admit to the allure of existentialism as a cultural and intellectual style. I succumbed to this infatuation, if you will, on a trip to Paris several years ago. There was something special, even exciting, about navigating around St Germain des Prés on a Friday evening, with my trusted Frommer's guide firmly in hand, when my wife and I fell upon the Café de Flore. The café is a bit touristy now, but it remains the spot where Jean-Paul Sartre wrote his famous trilogy, *Les Chemins de la Liberté* (*The Roads to Freedom*) at his table – *sacré bleu!*

Existential thought, especially in its philosophical versions, has served more as a source of inspiration for existential sociology than as an intellectual doctrine to be followed religiously. Consequently, existential sociology has remained an intellectually elusive perspective. Existentialists reject the formulation of all-encompassing global theories. Instead, they adhere to the individualistic ethos of existentialism by developing their own particular ways of writing about phenomena of personal choice. This can be seen in the way the modal format for publishing existential sociology is the edited book, not the unified and heavily integrated textbook (see, for example, Douglas and Johnson

1977; Douglas, Adler, Adler, Fontana, Freeman and Kotarba 1980; Kotarba and Fontana 1984; Kotarba and Johnson 2002). Existential sociology functions best as an orientation to the everyday life world, a particular set of questions we pose to the people in whom we are fascinated. In the parlance of the sports journalism, existential sociology consists of a particular 'take' on everyday life. The purpose of this chapter is to outline the major features of that 'take'.

'Existential sociology is defined descriptively as the study of human experience-in-the-world (or existence) in all its forms' (Douglas and Johnson 1977: vii; see also Fontana 1980). A key feature of experience-in-the-(contemporary)-world is change. Existential sociologists expect if not assume change to be a constant feature of people's lives, their sense of self, their experience of the social world, the other people that populate the social world, and the culture that provides meaning for life. Everyday life is more than merely situational and problematic; a point on which all the varieties of everyday life sociology generally agree. Everyday life is *dramatic* and experienced as such. In contrast to Erving Goffman's (1959) dramaturgical model of social life, the drama that existential sociologists see in everyday life does not follow anyone else's script. The actor is simultaneously writer, producer and actor on a stage not necessarily of their own choosing, but a stage that cannot simply be exited without confrontation with the owner (for example, agents of social control). To paraphrase an existential philosophical truism, the person in contemporary everyday life is forced to perform.

At a more historical level, existential sociology can be seen as part of the broad evolutionary change occurring in Western thought over the past few centuries (Kotarba 1979: 348). Ever since the Copernican revolution supplanted the Aristotelian belief in an inalterable and immutable universe, modern thought has progressed from the search for absolute and eternal ideas to a reconceptualization of reality as change, flux, complexity and uncertainty. Franklin L. Baumer has referred to this historical trend as the movement from 'being to becoming', that is, to 'a mode of thinking that contemplates everything – nature, humanity, society, history, God himself – *sub specie temp oris*, as not merely changing but as forever evolving into something new and different' (Baumer 1977: 20). As we will see, the notion of becoming is very much central to existential sociology.

In the remainder of this chapter, I shall describe the major features of existential sociology. First, I describe the evolution of existential thought into a sociological perspective addressing contemporary social phenomena. Second, I explain the way emotions fill everyday life and impact social relations and human activity. Third, I examine the main concept in existential sociology – the existential self – and how it provides a useful basis for conducting research on human experience in-the-world. Fourth, I describe the impact postmodern thinking has had on the existential sociology project, as well as points of convergence between the two. Finally, I describe the current movement in existential sociology towards more policy-related research and writing.

Existential (social) thought

Existentialism gained its greatest popularity and acceptance in the years after the Second World War, at first in Europe, and then several years later in the United States (Johnson and Kotarba 2002). The writings of French philosopher and writer Jean-Paul Sartre (1905–1980), as well as the novels and essays of Albert Camus (1913–1960), are among the most important reasons for existentialism's initial popularity and acceptance. Existentialism is both a philosophy and something other than a philosophy, and it is very important to see and understand each of these aspects. It is a philosophical perspective in that it has a series of well-developed arguments and positions on the questions and issues that have been central to philosophy as a discipline since the times of the Greek sophists and philosophers 3000 years ago (Johnson and Kotarba 2002: 3).

Existentialism is additionally something other than a philosophical position or perspective. It is a sensibility, a way of life, a passion for living, an orientation to the flux and emergence of actual lived experience. The formal literature of the existentialist tradition is known by its emphasis on these central themes: the nature of the individual; the central role of the passions and emotions in human life; the nature and responsibilities of human freedom; and the irrational aspects of life (Johnson and Kotarba 2002: 4). On all of these issues there are many books, novels, essays, articles, treatises, plays, films, paintings, sculptures and dances. The important influences of existentialism on all of these aspects of intellectual and artistic life testify to the power of this orientation. But the power of the existentialist sensibility continues to reside in the questions it poses for us. Who am I? What is the nature of human life and experience? What is my place and purpose in this larger scheme of things? How should I understand the world?

The questions posed by existentialists extend beyond philosophical or academic ones. These are questions about how to live, how to feel and what to think about one's situation. Diverse existentialisms have arisen to address these questions and they all express a certain attitude of rebellion. It is a rebellion against the received and inherited 'wisdom' of one's culture, against what most people think, against what most intellectuals consider true, against the 'herd mentality' and its 'popular culture', against conformity. From this, it is not surprising that existentialists have aligned themselves with the full range of human values and opinions, including fundamentalist Christianity, anti-Christianity, atheism, humanism, communism, anti-communism, socialism, anti-socialism, left-wing politics, right-wing politics, anti-politics, pro-democracy and anti-democracy. Even on some of the fundamental intellectual or philosophical issues, existential thought runs the full gamut: Sartre says that individuals have 'absolute freedom', whereas for German philosopher Friedrich Nietzsche (1844–1900), freedom is a 'philosophical myth' (Johnson and Kotarba 2002: 5).

The nature of human freedom and agency

Existentialist ideas began influencing the social sciences more than four decades ago. In 1962 Edward A. Tiryakian published *Sociologism and Existentialism*, an influential work of sociological theory, which sought to resolve two very different ways of thinking about human social life and existence. The first is 'sociologism', a term commonly associated with the seminal sociological scholarship of Émile Durkheim (1858–1917). The idea behind sociologism is very simple to grasp: individuals do not matter very much. Social reality is a reality *sui generis*, or in and of itself, to use Durkheim's phrase. The larger social structures of society are seen as superseding and transcending the lives and meanings of individuals, and are not dependent on individuals in any meaningful way. Societies and cultures are seen to achieve stability, change, transform and disintegrate largely independent of the wills, intentions, choices and decisions of individuals. This is the key idea for those who are 'structuralists' in the social sciences, and such thinkers have traditionally dominated academic thought. The second perspective is that of 'existentialism', and this view tends to place a much greater emphasis on individuals, their choices, their responsibilities, their passions, their decisions, their cowardice, their virtues and so on. In his book, Tiryakian proposed to bring these two seemingly incompatible perspectives together in a manner that would retain the integrity of each (Johnson and Kotarba 2002: 5).

In the earliest collection of essays, Jack D. Douglas and John M. Johnson's (1977) *Existential Sociology*, the authors engaged structuralists and other cultural determinists, stressing the relative freedom of individuals, and the partial independence of individuals from their social and cultural contexts. They emphasized that social and cultural realities are not determined, but rather they are socially constructed, meaning that the agency, choice, will, intention and interpretation of actual individuals are decisive for the determination of meaning. That early work additionally stressed the relative independence and dominance of feelings and emotions over thoughts and cognition, and in addition their relative independence and dominance over values.

The second major collection, Joseph A. Kotarba and Andrea Fontana's (1984) *The Existential Self in Society*, focused on the primary concept in existential sociology, the self. The authors described various strategies individuals use to construct their self, within a variety of social and cultural contexts, and the ways in which feelings and emotions impact this construction. The empirical studies reported in these essays illustrate the great value of locating actual studies in the specific situations of everyday life, and the difficulties of creating facile generalizations from them. Topics ranged from commercial blood donors, abused and battered women, and being a former nun, to wheelchair athletes and the homosexual self-identity. These studies and others surely do not yet provide a definitive theoretical synthesis of the nature of the self in all possible social circumstances. Nevertheless, they clearly illustrate the great analytical benefits that can be obtained from actual, empirical studies in concrete situations.

Affect in everyday life

Sociologists have only recently paid serious attention to the study of feelings and emotions, as well as their central role in the formulation of everyday social life. Modern philosophical analysis of affect can be traced at least as far back as Jean-Paul Sartre's (1949) attempt to write a comprehensive analysis of a wide range of emotions and to justify their place in human life. Jack D. Douglas (b. 1937) has championed the study of feelings and emotions in the social sciences (see, for example, Douglas 1977: 3–73). His efforts, and those of his students, have led to widespread acceptance of the legitimacy among sociologists of the empirical study of emotions.

Douglas was thus instrumental in setting the stage for serious sociological analysis of the centrality of feelings and emotions in everyday social life. Enlightenment thinkers set the stage for modern behavioural and medical science by arguing for the supremacy of reason over feelings. In the midst of this over-rationalized view of life, Douglas (1977: 3) strongly reminded other sociologists to take seriously the notion of *brute bring*, the core of feeling and perception that is our innermost selves, our beings. He argued that we must recognize the crucial role that passions, feelings and emotions play in social life:

> Love and hate, ecstasy and agony, pleasure and pain, lust and satiety, hope and despair, sympathy and spite, full and hungry, tasty and foul, comfort and discomfort. These and a vast number of other feelings, named and unnameable, are the core of our being, the stuff of our everyday lives. They are the foundations of all society.
>
> (Douglas 1977: 51)

Douglas, along with other intellectuals such as Michael Foucault (1976), usually equated feelings with dark passions and lusts, and viewed them as unfairly stifled and squelched by social conventions, rules and reason. Douglas described emotions as 'the "darker" side of human experience' (1977: 10), powerful forces overwhelming reason and impelling action, but at the same time more authentic and more important than reason. He pointed out that reason and feeling usually occur together, yet reason should serve as a guide to the expression and gratification of human desires. He essentially turned the cultural anti-emotion, pro-reason bias on its head.

More recent writings on feelings and social life have reminded us of both the existence and value of positive feelings and emotions in everyday life. For example, Candace Clark (2002: 155) notes that, because of emotions such as greed, envy, pride, powerlust, shame, anger, enmity and hate, social life is fraught with the potential for deception, interpersonal abuse and violence. However, if we look for emotions of connection we can still find evidence of them – self-sacrifice, caring for others, and myriad acts of micro-heroism that protect and promote others at our own expense. Emotions such as gratitude, liking, love, obligation, respect, concern and sympathy all foster social cohesion and social bonds. Emotions, then, are not only inevitable and not only forces destructive to the social order. Emotions are also essential for forming and perpetuating human societies.

The existential self

Apart from a growing interest in emotions and feelings, there is within sociology today also a movement toward renewed interest in the concept of the self (Kotarba 1984: 222). Many influential works on the self have been published in recent years, reflecting a healthy diversity in analytical goals and perspectives. Some writers have rejuvenated the discussion of George Herbert Mead's classic philosophical analysis of the self-concept, especially his interpretation of the socially learned as opposed to the creative aspects of self-definition (for example, Carveth 1977). Others have attempted to apply more recent insights from phenomenological thought to understanding the cognitive structures of the self (for example, Kovit 1980). We have also witnessed the emergence of new models of the self, such as Ralph H. Turner's (1976) *impulsive self* and Louis A. Zurcher's (1977) *mutable self*, which attempt to account for the strategies used by people today to anchor their personal sense of being in a rapidly changing social world.

An interesting question is why this renewal of interest in the self-concept is occurring today. There are two explanations. First, this renewed interest parallels and to some degree results from the dramatic surge of interest in self-actualization and development that is occurring within popular culture – a development that is not only monitored but nurtured by the mass media. Second, researchers and analysts in several academic disciplines have been finding that traditional models of conceptualizing the self are inefficient, and have been seeking new methods for understanding the self. Social psychologists who study the self-concept by means of objectified measures and scales, for example, have found that these highly quantitative methods cannot account for the immense complexity of the self. Even Morris Rosenberg (1979), one of the major scholars in positivistic research on self-esteem, has warned his colleagues that self-esteem cannot explain much of the variance in people's actual behaviour.

Thus, popular and professional interest in the self has undoubtedly contributed to the emergence of the existential model of the self. But those of us who conduct social research under the rubric *existential sociology* have also felt the need for a new model of individual experience, primarily as a result of what we have been discovering about contemporary social life. The constant, and occasionally dramatic, changes occurring in our social rules, values, institutions and life-styles encourage exploration of the contrasts and innovations in social life, and make the search for conceptual universals seem, for the moment, premature.

Since existential sociology is designed to monitor closely the tone of, and trends in, contemporary life, our attention has been drawn especially to the many people in all walks of life who are dissatisfied with both their own sense of who they are and society's demands of who they should be. Furthermore, we have been finding that new social forms, whether they are entirely innovative or simply reconstructions of existing social forms, are reflections of new and innovative ways in which members of our society are coming to think and feel about themselves. The conceptual relationship between innovative social forms and changes in our selves is complex. But it is clear that many members of our society are actively seeking new ways of fulfilling and expressing themselves.

The following definition of the existential self is intended to display the relative fluidity of the modern self and to account for the internal as well as external manifestations of the process of making sense of one's being. *The existential self refers to an individual's unique experience of being within the context of contemporary social conditions, an experience most notably marked by an incessant sense of becoming and an active participation in social change.* The following is a brief discussion of some of the major features of this existential self.

The existential self is embodied

Being-within-the-world means that feelings and primordial perception precede rationality and symbol use and, in fact, activate them. My research on chronic pain (Kotarba 1977, 1983, 2004) clearly illustrates the limitations of the rational/scientific/medical strategies for making sense of and mastering bodily afflictions. Chronic pain refers to severe experiences of physical discomfort that fail either to heal naturally or to respond to normal medical intervention. Common types of chronic pain include lower back pain, migraine headaches and postoperative pain. Most people in Western societies, regardless of social class, will consult modern medicine when they hurt and the pain does not easily go away by itself. Again, most people are raised to trust modern medicine, as Talcott Parsons (1951) stated in his classic formulation of the concept of the *sick role*. As pain continues and the suffering person's physicians are unable to relieve it by means of medicine, physical therapy or surgery, the person is likely to abandon unquestioned faith in modern medicine in favour of whatever alternative healing modalities promise help (for example, chiropractic, faith healing and holistic health care). Middle-class people will consult indigenous folk healers. Medical doctors themselves will even consult their traditional, professional enemies – chiropractors – on the sly when their pain will not go away. Most telling, people in pain will reject their physicians' rationalistic explanations for intractable pain. As I indicate:

> The person with chronic pain adopts the definitions of others when they are meaningful to the management of the pain. But this is frontwork, not reality. The primary definition of being sick comes from the person's body. Even the social definition, 'it's all in your head' (or more professionally, 'psychosomatic disease') that refers *directly* to the self is disregarded.
>
> (Kotarba 1977: 272)

We cannot reasonably deny bodily feelings because the body is the fundamental experience of human life. Brute being is the foundation and overriding reality of life. As a result, the person with chronic pain seeks various modes of cure and adjusts their everyday life in response to the dictates of the body, whether or not the dictates of others correspond.

In developing an understanding of the chronic pain experience, we must remember that bodily distress is an existential feeling of the self. If the pain is not reflected in their outward identity, the person decides whether or not to make the pain an element of social interaction. If they decide to make the pain known to others, in order to enlist their help in managing the pain, the reactions of others are evaluated according to their usefulness to them. Throughout the experience with pain, the person is primarily motivated to interact with healers by feelings of pain, trust, hope and fear. It is up to the individual to make sense of their pain. Thus, the embodied self negotiates the appropriateness of social reactions according to its own feelings and sensations.

The existential self is becoming

The notion of *becoming* is one of the most important ideas in existentialist thought. Jean-Paul Sartre, in his philosophical and literary writings (see, for example, Sartre 1949), argued dramatically that we are condemned to be free, condemned to choose continually who we are because existence in itself is empty and meaningless. The French philosopher Maurice Merleau-Ponty (1908–1961) takes a more moderate view, and one more conducive to the sociological perspective, by insisting that our becoming must be grounded in the real (read social) world if we have any intention of being effective in coping with the given world (1962). The individual is encouraged by the brute reality of life to acquire some distinctive style of self-actualization:

> The very notion of freedom demands that our decision [on how to approach the world] should plunge into the future, that something should have been *done* by it, that the subsequent instant should benefit from its predecessor and, though not necessitated, should be at least required by it .... A decision once taken and action once begun, I must have something acquired at my disposal, I must benefit from my impetus.
>
> (Merleau-Ponty 1962: 437)

Freedom, therefore, is viable only to the degree that it allows us to control the goals of our endeavours and to utilize them for our own personal growth. Put differently, existentialism presents an image of the self-to-society relationship that is quite apropos to today's world: the image of the self *confronting* society. We constantly attempt to shape and manipulate society – that is, society as we experience it – in order to have it as a resource for fulfilling our most basic needs and desires.

The self is not only in a state of constant becoming throughout life, but is actualized only through social roles that must be shaped and even created to meet the needs that emerge as the self confronts itself (see Yalom 1980). The most obvious reason that the self is grounded in a constant state of becoming is the aforementioned *embodiment* which forms the core of our existence. The body is not only the source for unending and ever-changing feelings and emotions and the criterion by which we evaluate the objects in our world; it also provides life events that may either threaten the self or open the way to self-fulfilment. The act of selling our blood plasma does both, as Wendy Espeland (1984) indicates. The primary motive for engaging in this practice is quite often to get money, but the 'respectable' donor must develop intricate strategies for counteracting the stigma associated with 'prostituting the lifestream of the body'.

The dramatic experience of the meaninglessness of human life has been a recurring topic of interest among writers as they attempt to come to grips with it by means of concepts like *reflexivity* (Mehan and Wood 1975) and *absurdity* (Lyman and Scott 1970). The affective result of meaninglessness can be either pleasurable or painful, depending on the social context within which it occurs. Robert J. Lifton (1976: 3–34) elegantly describes the pleasurable encounter with meaninglessness as 'experiential transcendence', which is a state so intense that in it time and death disappear. When we achieve ecstasy or rapture, the restrictions of the senses – including the sense of mortality – no longer exist. Poetically and religiously, this has been described as 'losing oneself'. It can occur not only in religious or secular mysticism but also in song, dance, battle, sexual love, childbirth, athletic effort, mechanical flight, computer gaming or in contemplating works of artistic or intellectual creation. This state is characterized by extraordinary psychic unity and perceptual intensity. But there also occurs, as we hear described in drug experiences, a process of symbolic reordering. We feels ourselves to be different after returning from this state.

The experience of meaninglessness can be quite painful when an individual becomes the victim of external, harmful forces, which destroy the security of self. In this situation, the person will seek out social forms that can assist in reconstructing the self and in eliminating the threat. The notion of being a victim and the interpretive basis for it is the theme of John M. Johnson and Kathleen Ferraro's (1984) research on battered women. An individual who is suffering intense physical abuse may not automatically adopt the self-definition 'victim'. A married woman, for example, may be battered by her husband for years but not come to define herself as a 'victim' until certain events elicit introspective redefinition and a confrontation with self; for example, a sudden change in the severity of the beatings may denote a threat to her very life. At this point, the content of the woman's previously secure sense of self as a 'happily married woman', 'good Christian' or 'deserving of punishment' is destroyed, and she may become willing to let third-party interveners (for example, shelters) help to restore her sense of self-integrity and protect her from further abuse.

The existential self becomes or evolves continuously throughout life. Joseph A. Kotarba (2002a, 2002b) has described the way rock 'n' roll music informs the becoming of self among middle-aged people in our society. Lay and professional observers alike have long noted the significance of rock 'n' roll music to teenagers. Similarly, sociologists have demonstrated increasing interest over the years in rock 'n' roll music as an indicator of dramatic changes occurring in the social and cultural worlds of teenagers (see Coleman 1961; Epstein 1994). Yet, the same observers have generally ignored an important element of social and cultural change: rock 'n' roll is no longer limited to, nor is it solely the possession of, teenagers. The original generation of rock 'n' rollers, the 'baby boomers', are now parents and in some cases grandparents themselves. The music and musical culture they grew up with has stayed with them and has become the soundtrack of US culture. Rock 'n' roll can affect adults' sense of self in many ways: as continuing rock 'n' roll fans; as parents of rock 'n' roll fans, as adults who construct lifestyles and work styles incorporating rock 'n' roll, as citizens contending with the political and ethical issues surrounding rock 'n' roll, and simply as people who, over the course of their lives, have come to use rock 'n' roll as a source of meaning for their joys and their sorrows.

Finally, a somewhat benign force that impels us to redefine the self is one that most of us experience at one time or another: *the fear of boredom*. A smoothly functioning social system, one that provides for people's material needs and offers excessive levels of security for the self, can lead to what William Simon and John Gagnon (1976: 361) referred to as the 'anomie of affluence', which occurs 'precisely when the objects or experiences that have symbolized achievement become part of the easily accessible and therefore unspectacular, everyday quality of life'. The anomie of affluence can lead to a stagnant sense of self, which the person can attempt to alleviate by rejuvenating the search for self-fulfilment through over-consumption, withdrawal from competition for culturally approved goals, pursuit of the unconventional and so on. The wellness movement is a contemporary example of the ways in which people in late capitalistic Western society attempt to perfect the self by perfecting the body both in terms of health but also in terms of appearance (Kotarba and Bentley 1988).

The inner self

The self is the focal point of all aspects of being: values, creativity and emotions. The self is also the arena for the ongoing conflict between the individual and society. The self now operates in a complex, ever-changing, postmodern, high tech and media-dominated world. One of the strengths of existential sociology, however, is its argument that the actual experience of self – the *inner self* – remains a deeply personal and to some degree primitive phenomenon regardless of the sophisticated social and contexts within which it is found.

Jack D. Douglas has sculpted the idea of the inner self in many of his works. He pays allegiance to the symbolic interactionist policy of defining the self in terms of *process* or *becoming*, yet he also argues for the importance of *being* in terms of the reality of *human nature* – a heretical term in normal interactionist and sociological circles. Instead of focusing on the most visible, social, empirically retrievable and codable aspects of self, Douglas dwells on the deepest, almost hidden and perhaps darkest aspects of the self.

In his work, Douglas has explored the inner self through such dramatic phenomena as suicide (Douglas 1967) and the social dynamics of southern California nude beaches (Douglas and Rasmussen 1977). More recently, he has been investigating mundane and pervasive social phenomena such as love, sex and intimacy (Douglas and Atwell 1988) in order to arrive at generic principles of self. Furthermore, he argues that scientists, psychologists, psychiatrists, mass media observers and others have distorted our understanding of love and Eros by simply equating these complex phenomena with sex.

According to Douglas, the inner self serves as a set of general guidelines that orient the individual toward the world and others. At the centre of the inner self is the experience of *brute being*, a complex of feelings and primitive emotions that form the essence of life (Douglas 1977: 15). This is not to say that feelings or emotions somehow cause human behaviour. On the contrary, modern existence requires a finely orchestrated and cooperative performance by feelings, thoughts and values in order to master modern life. Nevertheless, 'feelings are the *vital* aspects of our sense of self' (Douglas 1984: 85). Ideas and values guide us in choosing the social forms or styles that hopefully fulfil basic emotions, 'but it is our basic emotions that orient or guide our will in choosing what kinds of actions to perform' (Douglas 1984: 84). Love, intimacy, sex and subsequent feelings – affects that are intrinsic to embodiment – are the most powerful of our vital emotions. The viable and healthy inner self belongs to the individual who is able to control threats of self-degradation and loss of self-integrity. The secure self is then able 'to grow, to create, to expand' (Douglas 1984: 97).

The existential self and agency

A person's ability to perceive situations and to respond to them rationally, affectively and orally is at the core of the existential self. The term *agency* summarizes this complex of human potential. Within existential sociology, agency is not the equivalent of the popular expression *free will*, for the latter term implies human activity devoid of the social, historical, political and cultural constraints in operation on everyday life. The concept of the existential self's emphasis on agency can temper overly behaviourist or deterministic models of self, especially as they appear in medical settings.

An example is the experience of women living with HIV/AIDS and their efforts to manage their affliction. I recently conducted a study of these women with a team of nurses. Nurses use the concept of *inner strength* to describe 'the psychological and emotional resources available to women to help fight if not overcome serious illness' (Kotarba et al. 2003: 90). The concept of the existential self offers a strategy for conceptualizing and a method for studying inner strength as a process of *becoming*, as opposed to a thing-feature of a person's character.

Existential sociology posits the person as a social actor who faces and attempts to master everyday life dilemmas. The person seeks meanings (for example, values, rules, definition and attitudes) from others to complement deep feelings in order to deal with these dilemmas. The actor manages meanings by embedding them in stories that form the substance of social life. Therefore, a revised and more theoretical conceptualization of inner strength is 'the different ways women with serious illnesses experience and, subsequently, talk about the deepest, existential resources available to and used by them to manage severe threats to body and self' (Kotarba et al. 2003: 94). By integrating the two concepts, we were able to analytically locate women at the centre of their coping and sense-making activities. By encouraging the women in the study to tell their own stories of living with and trying to make sense of serious illness, it was possible to empower them methodologically.

In our interviews with the women, they related three types of story about their experiences of inner strength: *faith stories*, which recount the ways reliance upon a higher power (spiritual or religious) provide a sense of *inner strength*; *character stories*, which recount the ways women experience *inner strength* as a resource available to them before as well as during their illness; and *uncertainty stories*, which recount the ways women perceive their *inner strength* as problematic. In all three types of story, the women describe *inner strength* as an accomplishment or process requiring collaboration with others.

The existential self and social change

The two concepts most commonly used for discussing the relationship between social change and the individual are *culture* and *role*. We can define social change as the significant alteration of the content of a culture (see Moore 1963). Numerous theories have been proposed to explain social change. Some are based on the natural evolution of society, others on the advancement of science and technology or on the diffusion of economic resources and other processes in the social structure. All of these theories view the effects of social change on the individual or the self as essentially a reordering or elimination of traditional expectations of individual behaviour or social roles, and the institution of new role expectations.

From the existential perspective, however, the self is seen as an active agent in the process of social change. Our understanding of social change – and therefore of its perceived consequences – is grounded in our interpretation of events in the world as changing. Furthermore, the interpretation or definition of 'social change' is elicited largely by the person's concern for the becoming of self within the context of what are perceived to be uncertain social conditions.

By focusing on the self, we can arrive at the following model of social change. The individual perceives an uncertainty or change occurring in the segments of the social world that impinge on their existence. This uncertainty, whether it is 'real' or imagined, can occur at the level of technology, attitudes, values, rules or any other realm of social life. What is crucial is that the individual views these changes as critically relevant to maintaining a coherent and satisfying sense of self. This relevance can take two forms. The individual may decide that uncertainty in social conditions leaves existing modes of self-actualization obsolete. Or the individual may perceive new possibilities for self-actualization emanating from changing social conditions. In either case, the individual will actively seek new means for self-actualization, usually in the form of new social roles. This search is likely to be a collective endeavour, for the individual will either actively cooperate with others, who are experiencing similar concerns for self and are therefore instituting new social forms, or they will passively share in new social forms created by others. The process is then perpetuated when these new social forms provide still other individuals with a new basis for perceiving uncertain social conditions.

To provide an example, Terra McDaniel (2002) examined ethnographically the process by which young adults, with unfulfilled spiritual hunger, organize indigenous churches. Creating a house church is an effort to collectively resolve the tension between spiritual hunger and increasingly unrewarding membership in the large traditional denominations. The personal objective is to sculpt a moral and spiritual self that is resilient to the pressures of the contemporary secular world. The house church movement associated with Evangelical Christianity is a relatively new religious phenomenon, but one whose roots can be traced back to the earliest days of the Church (circa 50 AD).

In the United States, such house churches are one type of what Robert Wuthnow (1994) refers to as spiritual 'small groups'. These groups have become popular in the days of mega churches, urban sprawl and the subsequent longing for community which, for many, is not satisfied by attending a traditional church. The growing house church movement is characterized as having a commitment to orthodoxy in beliefs combined with a more relaxed and innovative approach to worship. Fuelled by a desire for a spirituality that is relevant to everyday life, members of Haven in the Montrose are making fundamental alterations to traditional church structure to create what Leonard Sweet (1999) calls an 'ancientfuture' church. This church neither embraces old means wholly nor completely rejects them. Members are committed to the Bible as God's words to humanity and Jesus's style of evangelism and discipleship. However, they abandon many of the practices of the 20th-century church, including the strict hierarchy between clergy and laity and the displacement of worship from daily life to something that only happens on a given day (Sunday), time (11 am) and place (church sanctuary).

They remain engaged in postmodern culture by creating a web page, communicating frequently via email and using popular movies, music, and art to emphasize spiritual themes. They incorporate psychological understandings in both their leadership training and their interactions with visitors and members. They exemplify what Anthony Giddens (2000: 427) calls 'the duality of structure'. They draw upon all the stocks of knowledge available to them in theology, psychology, education and the religious writings associated with several different denominations. Combining these in new and innovative ways, they are creating a new kind of church that is a bricolage of these and diverse other sources. They break bread together, but the bread is often taken out of the microwave oven or brought home from a fast food restaurant. This church is founded upon mentoring and community rather than preaching and pews. As they do this, their senior pastor says they continually sense that they are 'building the bridge as they cross it' (McDaniel 2002: 140).

The postmodern turn in existential sociology

How was it possible for existentialists in the post-Second World War years to produce scholarly, literary and artistic works that spanned the entire range of human values? How could existentialists be Christians, atheists, humanists and Buddhists? How could they be socialists, communists, capitalists and communitarians? How could they be found on the left wing of politics as well as on the right wing? How could they belong to fundamentalist house churches and to the drug-pervasive techno/rave movement? One answer to these questions emphasizes what these various existentialisms share in common – the primordial feeling that, in Sartre's words, 'existence precedes essence'. This means that men and women are thrown into the world, into real, specific situations, and only by living in and dealing with these situations do they thereby define their nature. It really matters little whether God does or does not exist; either way, men and women are confronted with the same fundamental questions. What does all this mean? What am I to make of this? What do I do next? (Johnson and Kotarba 2002: 8–9).

Unsurprisingly, the conceptual and topical inclusiveness of existential sociology sounds a lot like the postmodern appreciation for *pastiche* and *bricolage* (Denzin 1997). There are other distinctive similarities between the two perspectives, such as distaste for the master narratives of the Enlightenment (for example, socialism and democracy) and an appreciation for rich and metaphoric writing. In fact, the advent of postmodern thinking in sociology over the past 15 years provides many useful ideas for the continuing evolution of existential sociology.

Perhaps the most obvious if not most important similarity between postmodernism and existential sociology is the heavy emphasis both place on understanding the mass media. According to Jean Baudrillard (1983), postmodernism sees the mass media as virtually synonymous with culture in late capitalistic society. In existential sociology, the mass media are becoming one of the most compelling audiences to the self. Further, existential sociologists are very interested in examining the growing place electronic communications – ranging from cellphones to the Internet – play in contemporary everyday life.

One of the most fruitful points of compatibility between existential sociology and postmodernism, however, is in the area of research methods. Both perspectives agree that there is no inherent hierarchy of methods in terms of power or truthfulness. Research is inherently political and practical, and it is designed and conducted for practical reasons (for example, journal editorial policies and contract obligations to funding agencies) (see Douglas 1976). Both perspectives also agree that the composition and style of research reports and the dissemination of research findings are personal to the writer (see Kotarba et al. 2003). Finally, both perspectives argue that the researcher has an extremely wide range of presentation styles to choose from, many of which can be borrowed from the humanities as well as the social sciences.

Performance ethnography, for example, is a postmodernist technique which allows the researcher to present findings and analysis through a theatrical format (Denzin 1997). I have developed this idea into the concept of *synthetic performance ethnography*, in which the sociologist wears two hats: as a producer of art and as an analytical and critical observer of that art. The case in point is my 'Black Men, Black Voices' project, in which I produce programmes consisting of varieties of African-American music for audiences primarily in the community, not the academy. As a sociologist, I was then able to observe self-identity work among African-American male artists across generations and musical styles (for example, blues, zydeco and rap) as they interact naturally as performers (see Kotarba 1998).

Similarly, Andrea Fontana (2002: 201–18) has argued for the value of the short story in portraying ethnographic research in existential sociology. Ethnographies tend to weave together a continuous sense of reality. When we present an ethnographic account, the readers are shown this chronological flow of events, a smooth story that moves from beginning to end. Erving Goffman (1974) tells us that the ethnographer fills in the gaps in reality, making it appear seamless. Fontana's study of Bonneville Speed Week reminded him that reality is much more fragmented. To borrow a metaphor from Bonneville Speed Week, reality is like a carburettor – it starts, it stops, it goes again, it races, it sputters.

The search is for a better way to portray the fragmented reality of everyday life. Fontana looks to the short story format for an answer.

Short stories are fairly new in sociology, and not yet widely accepted in the discipline (Fontana 2001). The postmodern turn in everyday life sociology occasioned the writing of stories and poems to report ethnographies, thus bridging the existential notion of being-in-world with the postmodern one of reporting-one's-being-in-the-world. Postmodern ethnographers turn a mirror upon themselves and thereby question their authority to be the voice through which the accounts of the members of everyday life are to be reported. They become much more sensitized to the fact that their interaction with the subjects is not one in which the ethnographer tries hard not to influence the world they are studying, but a collaborative created effort between researcher and subjects (Gubrium and Holstein 1997).

Politics, power and policy in the postmodern world

Recent work among some of the major thinkers in existential sociology has attempted to apply the insights and methodologies of the perspective to the solution of current social problems. Although existential sociology began largely as a way to study micro-social life, recent work has taken the following programmatic definition originally fashioned by Douglas (1977) to heart: *Existential sociology is defined descriptively as the study of human experience-in-the-world (or existence) in all its forms. Politics, power and policy reside in the same everyday life world as personal feelings and perceptions*. Existential sociology views macro phenomena like politics and power as practical processes and tasks that are conducted and accomplished by real people in concrete situations. Following the existential notion of agency, politics becomes an organized method for people to manage personal feelings, perceptions and objectives. The clarity of existential sociology's almost journalistic style provides a useful platform for critiquing complex political issues while at the same time formulating accessible policy recommendations. Here are three topics to illustrate this action.

The politics of popular music

The techno/rave scene in popular music is a good example of the type of contemporary political phenomenon that can be analysed effectively through the existential sociology perspective. Musically, techno/rave is electronic dance music. Socially and politically, it remains a paradox. Although it may appear to be a very individualistic if not narcissistic leisure activity, its supporters in the United States and in Europe see a radically new style of politics in it. Critics claim that youthful techno/rave enthusiasts have given up on the politics of their (baby boomer) parents by disregarding traditional youth values such as a revolt against tradition or rebellion and commitment to changing the world. These critics argue that, instead, technoids surrender to consumption, hedonism, conformity and a weariness of politics. According to Ronald Hitzler and Michaela Pfadenhauer (2002: 87), however, technoids reject their parents' politics by 'dancing on the ruins of industrial civilization' instead of fighting the ruins. Conventional political strategies evolve into *existential strategies*, by which youths struggle dramatically for individuality through obstinate aesthetic tendencies, private preferences or simply conspicuous patterns of consumption. Although young people may distance themselves from traditional political institutions, they nevertheless struggle in a political sense for (their right to) their own life.

My own ethnographic study of the evolution of the rave scene over time is an illustration of the way the nature of the audience-to-the-self has changed considerably from immediate other in face-to-face interaction to a mass/electronically mediated source of self-meaning as a current theme in existential sociology (Kotarba 1993). The youthful rave partier in 1993 learned the values of the drug subculture from baby boomer parents, often inadvertently. Current rave partiers are also heavily influenced by Internet sites that help them sort out their place in the scene. Similar to the techno/rave scene in Western Europe, the rave culture in the United States has been constantly infiltrated by political ideologies ranging from national politics to environmental concerns.

The 'e-audience'

David L. Altheide (2002) has written extensively on an emerging phenomenon he calls the 'e-audience' as a new type of community. He argues that this evolving phenomenon challenges the existential self by adding another forum for identity play. He defines the e-audience as 'those individuals who dwell partially in cyberspace and engage in substantial amounts of electronic interaction and communication (e.g., email, net surfing and specific internet use, pagers, cell phones, etc)' (Altheide 2002: 41). A distinctive feature of this audience is a sense of control and entitlement to communicate, whereby the communicative act is demonstrated and displayed to self and others through electronic technology. This audience is constantly interactive, but does not exist in relation to a fixed medium, for example television. Rather, this audience is very active and reflexive, meaning that it takes into account other communication experiences and renderings of them in other mass media and popular culture. Moreover, the communication process transcends work and play. The e-audience has an elusive membership that is controlled by a meaningful interaction process involving audience expectations, anticipated audience responses and identity formation in everyday life contexts that extend increasingly to familiarity, ownership and use of information technology. Despite its elusiveness, the e-audience may contain seeds for contemporary political action.

Myth, greed and fear in everyday politics

Feelings and emotions also function as the building blocks for higher-order social institutions. Three very recent works illustrate dramatically how hubris among leaders can lead to the establishment of non-sustainable welfare state systems; how fear is the stuff by which the mass media create images of risk in everyday life; and how primitive myths can supports the intricate social institution of capital punishment. Jack D. Douglas's magnum opus, *The Myth of the Welfare State* (1989), is a detailed description of the historical consequences of societal leaders ignoring the true features of human nature. Over-rationalized state bureaucracies, whether in the United States or the old Soviet Union, are managed by leaders who have little practical knowledge of the economy, culture and history of the people they control. Douglas proposes that we can save society by reshaping policy to focus on fundamental self-interest and social concern.

David L. Altheide's *Terrorism and the Politics of Fear* (2006) chronicles the many different ways politicians and other decision makers extend and intensify their control over their constituents by manipulating and overstating fear, most recently the fear of terrorism. One of the most powerful analyses in the book focuses on the ways Pat Tillman, a former NFL football player who enlisted in the army and died in Afghanistan, was socially constructed as a hero to be exploited by the mass media and even by Tillman's alma mater, Arizona State University. Moreover, John M. Johnson and Rudolph J. Gerber's *The Top Ten Death Penalty Myths* (2007) systematically dismantles ten myths used by law enforcement officials and politicians to create fear among the public and to misrepresent the death penalty as a public policy issue. Contrary to official views and propaganda, the death penalty does not foster community bonding, does not deter crime and does not provide emotional closure for suffering families. As is evident from these studies, existential sociology flourishes, reaches and incorporates ever-new topics of interest, and in the process, sets new agendas for sociology and society alike.

Conclusion

I hope this presentation of existential sociology portrays it as an exciting approach to understanding everyday life. Sociologists who work under this rubric walk the fine line between a frank observation of social life as complex, emergent and somewhat unpredictable, and the goal of capturing it through analysis and description.

In the preface to the most recent collection of essays, *Postmodern Existential Sociology*, my co-editor John M. Johnson and I argue that one very distinctive feature of existential sociology that unifies its adherents is its inclination to provide us with a *romantic* way to appreciate everyday life (Johnson and Kotarba 2002). By romantic, we are referring to the way existential sociology celebrates the dramatic, aesthetic, adventurous and creative aspects of society. Existential sociology does this not only by studying the exotic and newsworthy, but also by looking for these features and finding them in the most common and unnoticed aspects of regular people's lives.

The authors of the chapters in our book felt that revisiting existential sociology is intellectually timely. Other disciplines and arts continue to acknowledge the value of existentialism's focus on the individual's search for meaning in an otherwise problematic world. There is a bit of a renaissance occurring in existential thinking. There is, for example, renewed interest in the work of Friedrich Nietzsche, whose work served as a precursor to existentialism through its illumination of the dark and non-rational side of man. Richard Foreman's New York off-Broadway play, *Bad Boy Nietzsche*, resurrects the spirit of Nietzsche for a new audience seeking understanding for the classic as it is experienced in the 21st century.

There has been consistent interest in existential philosophy, especially as it relates to other philosophical developments. Maurice Merleau-Ponty is a philosophical mainstay in existential philosophy. For example, Thomas Busch and Shaun Gallagher's (1992) edited volume on Merleau-Ponty links his writing on hermeneutics with postmodernism, and reaffirms the centrality of temporality and corporeality to philosophical discourse.

Historical events also draw us to a reconsideration of existentialist thought. The revitalization of intellectual life in the recently democratized central and eastern European societies has freed writers there to explore pro-individualistic and anti-collectivist paradigms such as existentialism. For example, Leszek Dziegel's *Paradise in a Concrete Cage* (1998) is a first-person account, written by this well-known Polish ethnographer, of the strategies developed by intellectuals in the post-Second World War Poland to maintain a semblance of individuality and intellectual legitimacy within that grey and depressing Stalinist era.

Ultimately, existential sociology will, however, only prosper to the degree that its proponents and adherents continue to refresh the perspective through constant surveillance of our rapidly changing social life.

Bibliography

Altheide, David L. (2002) 'Toward a mapping of the mass media and the 'e' audience', in Joseph A. Kotarba and John M. Johnson (eds), *Postmodern Existential Sociology*. Walnut Creek, CA: Alta Mira.

Altheide, David L. (2006) *Terrorism and the Politics of Fear*. Lanham, MD: Alta Mira.

Baudrillard, Jean (1983) *Simulations*. New York: Semiotext(e).

Baumer, Franklin L. (1977) *Modern European Thought*. New York: Macmillan.

Busch, Thomas and Shaun Gallagher (eds) (1992) *Merleau-Ponty: Hermeneutics and Postmodernism*. Albany, NY: State University of New York Press.

Carveth, Donald (1977) 'The Hobbesian Microcosm: On the Dialectics of Self in Social Theory.' *Sociological Inquiry*, 47: 3–12.

Clark, Candace (2002) '"Taming the 'brute being": sociology reckons with emotionality', in Joseph A. Kotarba and John M. Johnson (eds), *Postmodern Existential Sociology*. Walnut Creek, CA: Alta Mira.

Coleman, James S. (1961) *The Adolescent Society*. Glencoe, IL: Free Press.

Denzin, Norman K. (1997) *Interpretive Ethnography: Ethnographic Practices for the 21st Century*. Thousand Oaks, CA: Sage.

Douglas, Jack D. (1967) *The Social Meanings of Suicide*. Princeton, NJ: Princeton University Press.

Douglas, Jack D. (1976) *Investigative Social Research*. Beverly Hills, CA: Sage.

Douglas, Jack D. (1977) 'Existential sociology', in Jack D. Douglas and John M. Johnson (eds), *Existential Sociology*. New York: Cambridge University Press.

Douglas, Jack D. (1984) 'The emergence, security, and growth of the sense of self', in Joseph A. Kotarba and Andrea Fontana (eds), *The Existential Self in Society*. Chicago, IL: University of Chicago Press.

Douglas, Jack D. (1989) *The Myth of the Welfare State*. New York: Transaction.

Douglas, Jack D., Patricia A. Adler, Peter Adler, Andrea Fontana, C. Robert Freeman and Joseph A. Kotarba (1980) *Introduction to the Sociologies of Everyday Life*. Boston: Allyn & Bacon.

Douglas, Jack D. and Freda C. Atwell (1988) *Love, Intimacy and Sex*. Beverly Hills, CA: Sage.

Douglas, Jack D. and John M. Johnson (eds) (1977) *Existential Sociology*. New York: Cambridge University Press.

Douglas, Jack D. and Paul K. Rasmussen (1977) *The Nude Beach*. Beverly Hills, CA: Sage.

Dziegel, Leszek (1998) *Paradise in a Concrete Cage*. Krakow: Arcana Press.

Epstein, Jonathan (ed.) (1994) *Adolescents and Their Music*. New York: Garland.

Espeland, Wendy (1984) 'Blood and money: exploiting the embodied self', in Joseph A. Kotarba and Andrea Fontana (eds), *The Existential Self in Society*. Chicago, IL: University of Chicago Press.

Fontana, Andrea (1980) 'Toward a Complex Universe: Existential Sociology', in Jack D. Douglas, Patricia A. Adler, Peter Adler, Andrea Fontana, C. Robert Freeman and Joseph A. Kotarba: *Introduction to the Sociologies of Everyday Life*. Boston: Allyn & Bacon.

Fontana, Andrea (2001) 'Salt fever: an ethnographic narrative in four sections.' *Studies in Symbolic Interaction*, 24: 147–63.

Fontana, Andrea (2002) 'Short stories from the salt', in Joseph A. Kotarba and John M. Johnson (eds), *Postmodern Existential Sociology*. Walnut Creek, CA: Alta Mira.

Foucault, Michel (1976) *The History of Sexuality, Vol. 1: An Introduction*. Harmondsworth: Penguin.

Giddens, Anthony (2000) 'The time–space constitution of social systems', in Peter Kivisto (ed.), *Social Theory*. Los Angeles: Roxbury.

Goffman, Erving (1959) *The Presentation of Self in Everyday Life*. New York: Anchor.

Goffman, Erving (1974) *Frame Analysis*. New York: Harper & Row.

Gubrium, Jaber F. and James Holstein (1997) *The New Language of Qualitative Methods*. New York: Oxford University Press.

Hitzler, Ronald and Michaela Pfadenhauer (2002) 'Existential strategies: the making of community and politics in the techno/rave scene', in Joseph A. Kotarba and John M. Johnson (eds), *Postmodern Existential Sociology*. Walnut Creek, CA: Alta Mira.

Johnson, John M. and Kathleen Ferraro (1984) 'The victimized self: the case of battered women', in Joseph A. Kotarba and Andrea Fontana (eds), *The Existential Self in Society*. Chicago, IL: University of Chicago Press.

Johnson, John M. and Rudolph J. Gerber (2007) *The Top Ten Death Penalty Myths: The Politics of Crime Control*. New York: Praeger.

Johnson, John M. and Joseph A. Kotarba (2002) 'Postmodern existentialism', in Joseph A. Kotarba and John M. Johnson (eds), *Postmodern Existential Sociology*. Walnut Creek, CA: Alta Mira.

Kotarba, Joseph A. (1977) 'The chronic pain experience', in Joseph A. Kotarba and John M. Johnson (eds), *Postmodern Existential Sociology*. Walnut Creek, CA: Alta Mira.

Kotarba, Joseph A. (1979) 'Existential sociology', in Scott G. McNall (ed.), *Theoretical Perspectives in Sociology*. New York: St. Martin's Press.

Kotarba, Joseph A. (1983) *The Chronic Pain Experience*. Beverly Hills, CA: Sage.

Kotarba, Joseph A. (1984) 'A synthesis: the existential self in society', in Joseph A. Kotarba and Andrea Fontana (eds), *The Existential Self in Society*. Chicago, IL: University of Chicago Press.

Kotarba, Joseph A. (1993) *The Rave Movement on Houston, Texas*. A Report to the Texas Commission on Alcohol and Drug Abuse, Austin, Texas.

Kotarba, Joseph A. (1998) 'Black men, black voices: the role of the producer in synthetic performance ethnography.' *Qualitative Inquiry*, 4(3): 389–404.

Kotarba, Joseph A. (2002a) 'Baby boomer rock 'n' roll fans and the becoming of self', in Joseph A. Kotarba and John M. Johnson (eds), *Postmodern Existential Sociology*. Walnut Creek, CA: Alta Mira.

Kotarba, Joseph A. (2002b) 'Rock 'n' roll music as a timepiece.' *Symbolic Interaction*, 25(3): 397–404.

Kotarba, Joseph A. (2004) 'Professional athletes' injuries: from existential to organizational analysis', in Kevin Young (ed.), *Sporting Bodies, Damaged Selves: Sociological Studies of Sports-Related Injury*. Oxford: Elsevier.

Kotarba, Joseph A. and Pamela Bentley (1988) 'Workplace wellness and the becoming of self.' *Social Science and Medicine*, 26(5): 551–8.

Kotarba, Joseph A. and Andrea Fontana (eds) (1984) *The Existential Self in Society*. Chicago: University of Chicago Press.

Kotarba, Joseph A., Brenda Haile, Peggy Landrum and Debra Trimble (2003) 'Inner strength and the existential self: improving managed care among HIV + women through the integration of nursing and sociological concepts.' *Research in the Sociology of Health Care*, 21: 87–106.

Kotarba, Joseph A. and John M. Johnson (eds) (2002) *Postmodern Existential Sociology*. Walnut Creek, CA: Alta Mira.

Kovit, Leonard (1980) 'The phenomenology of self.' *Reflections*, 1: 23–37.

Lifton, Robert J. (1976) *The Life of the Self*. New York: Simon & Schuster.
Lyman, Stanford M. and Marvin B. Scott (1970) *A Sociology of the Absurd*. New York: Appleton-Century-Crofts.
McDaniel, Terra (2002) 'Community and transcendence: the emergence of a house church', in Joseph A. Kotarba and John M. Johnson (eds), *Postmodern Existential Sociology*. Walnut Creek, CA: Alta Mira.
Mehan, Hugh and Houston Wood (1975) *The Reality of Ethnomethodology*. New York: Wiley.
Merleau-Ponty, Maurice (1962) *The Phenomenology of Perception*. London: Routledge & Kegan Paul.
Moore, Wilbert (1963) *Social Change*. Englewood Cliffs, NJ: Prentice-Hall.
Parsons, Talcott (1951) *The Social System*. New York: Free Press.
Rosenberg, Morris (1979) *Conceiving the Self*. New York: Basic Books.
Sartre, Jean-Paul (1949) *Nausea*. New York: New Directions.
Simon, William and John Gagnon (1976) 'The anomie of affluence.' *American Journal of Sociology*, 82(2): 154–76.
Sweet, Leonard (1999) *Soul Tsunami*. Grand Rapids, MI: Zondervan.
Tiryakian, Edward A. (1962) *Sociologism and Existentialism*. Englewood Cliffs, NJ: Prentice-Hall.
Turner, Ralph H. (1976) 'The real self.' *American Journal of Sociology*, 81: 989–1016.
Wuthnow, Robert (1994) *'I Came Away Stronger': How Small Groups are Shaping American Religion*. Grand Rapids, MI: Eerdmans.
Yalom, Irving D. (1980) *Existential Psychotherapy*. New York: Basic Books.
Zurcher, Louis A. (1977) *The Mutable Self*. Beverly Hills, CA: Sage.

CHAPTER 6

Critical Everyday Life Sociologies

Problematizing the Everyday

MICHAEL E. GARDINER

Introduction

The purpose of this chapter is to introduce the reader to the rudiments of a critical theoretical tradition with respect to the study of everyday life. Insofar as this approach is of mainly Marxian (or at least Marxist-influenced) and German providence, it originates, not surprisingly, in the work of Karl Marx (1818–1883) and Friedrich Engels (1820–1895), then stretches to Georg Simmel (1858-1918) and Georg Lukács (1885–1971), culminating in the so-called 'Gnostic Marxism' of Walter Benjamin (1892–1940).

Such a theory is characterized by certain distinctive preoccupations. First, any discussion of 'everyday life' in this context is inseparable from a political project that seeks to unveil and critique what it takes to be the debased, routinized and ideological qualities of daily existence in modern capitalist society, but also to locate certain emancipatory tendencies within this selfsame terrain. This orientation can be summed up in the phrase 'everyday utopianism' (see Gardiner 1995, 2004). The second thing to note is that as a result of this expressly political stance, each of the major figures of this tradition cultivates an *ambivalent*, and hence *dialectical,* attitude towards the everyday. Yet, as we shall see, precisely how this ambivalence is registered in the work of any given thinker varies considerably.

Finally, each of the theorists to be discussed here grappled, although some more explicitly and self-consciously than others, with how everyday life has been changed in the transition from a premodern to modern society. This involves analysing the nature of capitalism as an economic system, especially how the commodity-form dominates day-to-day social life. But it is also concerned with the ways in which the culture of modernity and the process of modernization more generally have insinuated themselves into the everyday. This pertains to such phenomena as the secularization and rationalization of the social world; the condensation of time/space through emerging technologies of transportation and communications; the demise of relatively stable, premodern identities and the concomitant growth of individualism; a pervasive urbanization process; and the concentration and centralization of political power, institutional structures and capital, to name only the most salient.

Hence, for the theoretical tradition discussed here, everyday life cannot simply be taken-for-granted: it must be 'problematized', rendered strange or unfamiliar, in order to grasp how it is influenced by a wide range of sociocultural, political and economic factors. Even within this relatively coherent body of ideas, that is to say, the everyday must be regarded as a 'contested and opaque terrain, where meanings are not to be found ready-made', as Ben Highmore (2002a: 1) puts it. Despite this contestation, what I hope to demonstrate in the following discussion is that this critical intellectual tradition continues to have much of value to tell us about the nature of everyday life, its still relatively unknown qualities and untapped possibilities.

Karl Marx: the 'religion of everyday life'

The fundamental ambivalence regarding everyday life mentioned above can be seen clearly in the writings of Karl Marx himself, as well as those of his close collaborator, Friedrich Engels. Marx, as is well known, wanted to combat the spectral abstractions of his German idealist predecessors, predominantly G. W. F. Hegel, as well as the no less reductive materialism of Ludwig Feuerbach and other such pretenders to Hegel's throne. To this end, Marx admonishes us to turn our thoughts away from arcane theological and philosophical debates in order to grasp actual social practices and relationships as these are located in the sphere of daily existence. To focus exclusively on rarefied ideas, or on 'man [*sic*, and *passim*]-in-general', was not only to misunderstand profoundly the true nature of human beings and their social relations. It was, in Marx's opinion, to contribute actively to the enslavement of the working class in alienated conditions of existence that were almost entirely beyond their understanding or control.

So convinced was Marx that critical theory had to be anchored in tangible problems and relationships that he typically construed the phenomenon of 'ideology' as a body of representations that functioned to deflect attention away from the realities of concrete social life toward ghostly abstractions and idealizations. In the realm of ideology, he reasoned, real socio-economic contradictions and conflicts were 'solved' at the level of the imaginary or fantastical. This notion is rendered most explicitly in an early text that remained unpublished in Marx and Engels's lifetime, *The German Ideology*, where it is argued that capitalist social relations encourage a systematic misunderstanding of the world and our place in it, through a process of inversion or reversal.

In evoking the famous metaphor of the 'camera obscura', a device that projects an inverted image through a pin-hole opening, Marx and Engels sought to convey the notion that such ideological transpositions prompt social actors to attribute the determination of history and society wholly to ideas, and the philosophical or religious systems that correspond to them, rather than the social organization of economic production. So, ideology in classical Marxism is a form of representational distortion that results from this (structurally induced) tendency in capitalist society to reverse the true state of affairs, thereby buttressing the prevailing system of class division and exploitation.

For Marx, the critique of ideology could not remain on the level of obscure philosophical debate; it had to be rooted in an investigation of the specific material conditions that fostered 'consciousness and its products', together with the practical transformation of the material conditions of class society. The ultimate goal was to allow people to realize themselves in free, conscious activity, unencumbered by the dull compulsion of alienated economic activity: 'Human emancipation will only be complete when the real, individual man has absorbed into himself the abstract citizen', write Marx and Engels (1978: 46), when in their 'everyday life [they] become a *species-being*'.

Marx's critique of ideology is premised also on the Hegelian distinction between 'real relations' and 'phenomenal forms', an idea developed most fully in the famous short chapter in Volume I of *Capital* entitled 'The fetishism of commodities and the secret thereof'. According to Marx, capitalism had transformed personal worth into exchange value. The result is that the so-called 'cash nexus' mediates virtually all human activities and interactions, and trumps other, more qualitative, sociocultural values and interests. But this has a positive side: by stripping away all semblances of past tradition and religious beliefs, of sentimentality and bourgeois talk of 'morality', modernity has forced human beings to come to grips with their actual conditions of life.

Unfortunately, the potential for this kind of sober and realistic assessment of the world, and what might be done to change it, is at least partially blocked by the cognitive dislocation encouraged by the fetishism of the commodity. Marx theorizes that the commodity form induces a kind of 'collective amnesia' with regard to the origins of the commodity, whether it is a table, toothbrush or shoe. Although he is vague as to the actual psychological mechanisms involved, Marx suggests that the spontaneous 'commonsense' generated by capitalism prevents us from looking beyond the surface appearance of the commodity so as to grasp the underlying socio-economic relations that, in reality, produced it. The result is that value appears to emanate magically from the commodity itself, or else the result of the quantity of money spent in purchasing it within ritualized exchanges of the capitalist marketplace, instead of corresponding directly to the amount of socially organized labour that created it. Accordingly, a relation that involves fundamentally the interaction of *people* within determinate socio-historical contexts takes on the appearance of a relation entirely between *objects*. As Michael Billig notes, Marx locates the concealment of socio-economic realities in:

> the intercourse of everyday life. Custom, or habit, fixes a price to commodities; and, in consequence, the hidden secret disappears from awareness. Marx's brief remarks contain an implicit psychology: custom sets routines, for which we use 'obvious' commonplace notions, but these notions drive from awareness the full nature of these routines. In this way, there is a link between custom and lack of awareness, so that an unconsciousness is built into the accomplishment of social customs.
>
> (Billig 1999: 316)

Billig goes on to argue that Marx's remarkable insight here is not followed up with a coherent explanation of how mundane routines of economic intercourse bolster this kind of 'amnesia' on a day-to-day basis, apart from implying that commodity fetishism operates in a quasi-Freudian way to 'repress' (or at least sublimate) a conscious awareness of the realities of capitalism. However, Marx does make it clear that it is not only in the everyday consciousness of people that this bedazzlement by surface appearances and the resultant social 'forgetting' is registered. It is found equally in all manner of scholarly doctrines, such as bourgeois economics (which also fails manifestly to understand how value is produced), and such philosophies as British empiricism or Comtean positivism. This helps to explain why Marx routinely excoriated these theories: by shifting attention away from the true nature of social life under capitalism towards various fanciful abstractions, fetishes and hobby-horses, such doctrines play a crucial role in the legitimating of class domination.

The 'cure' for such pathology is similar to Marx's treatment of Hegel's philosophy of spirit: since it is now standing on its head, it must be returned to its feet. The supposed autonomy of ideological systems must be rejected decisively, and replaced by empirical socio-historical research into the production and reproduction of human life within particular historical circumstances – what Marx referred to as the 'study of actuality'. In opposition to the pseudo-science of positivism, he argued that genuine science had to penetrate the realm of surface appearance to grasp the constitutive relations and structures that generate such appearances, and which are not always available to direct sensory experience. Marx followed Hegel here in believing that 'what is concretely true is so only as a totality', wherein the specificities of everyday lived experience had to be related to a wider whole, in order to acquire coherence and meaning. Genuine knowledge, in Marx's opinion, therefore represented a fusion of the empirically sensuous and the philosophically abstract, a dialectical movement that takes up key elements of the everyday and its contradictions, moves them to a higher level of conceptualization and understanding, and then spirals back to the concrete to reproduce in thought a 'rich totality of many determinations' (Marx 1989: 44).

It is at this point where Marx's ambivalence towards the everyday comes to a head. We cannot ignore or trivialize the everyday, because daily life is where humanity's essential powers and 'species-activity' is located and expressed fundamentally. Yet, we also need to understand capitalist modernity as a complex, historically situated totality, with the practical goal of ending the systematic oppressions and alienations of class society and realizing the full range and wealth of human potentialities. We require a dialectical science that neither 'primly abstracts' from the 'extended wealth of human activity', nor remains entangled in mere phenomenal appearance. This represents a 'real science with a genuine content', as Marx says in the '1844 manuscripts', which must also supersede 'false appearance and deception, this autonomization and fossilization of the various social elements of wealth in relation to each other, the personification of things and the reification of production relations, this religion of everyday life', as he put it later in Volume III of *Capital* (Marx 1967: 830). Everyday life is both the cause of and prophylactic for mystified and fetishized social relations, something to be celebrated, but also criticized and ultimately transfigured.

Throughout his writings, Marx sought to maintain the integrity of each of the two distinct threads with regard to this mode of dialectical inquiry, the particular and the everyday versus the general and theoretical. In practice, however, the more he turned his attention toward the study of the broad sweep of history and the inner workings of the capitalist mode of production, the more the earlier preoccupation with the qualities and problems of everyday experience became supplanted by the grand abstractions of political economy. This economistic bent in the work of the later Marx helps to explain why 'Western' Marxism became concerned increasingly with the nature of lived experience and human subjectivity in the context of urban modernity. Despite this produced shift in focus, the tension or ambivalence regarding everyday life that marked the original writings of Marx and Engels continued throughout the work of the various Western Marxists of the 20th century. Arguably the key figure in the shift from classical to Western Marxism is Georg Lukács. Before we discuss his contribution to a theory of everyday life, however, a detour through the ideas of Simmel is required.

Georg Simmel: the 'technology of metropolitan life'

Georg Simmel was an oddball genius and a prolific, wide-ranging thinker who blurred the lines between various academic genres and styles of exposition. Despite periodic flashes of interest in his work, he remained a marginal figure within the German intellectual establishment during his lifetime. Nevertheless, Simmel had an enormous impact on an entire generation of Central European scholars, including such luminaries as Benjamin, Ernst Bloch, Martin Heidegger, Siegfried Kracauer, Georg Lukács and Karl Mannheim, not least because many of them attended his seminars at Berlin University before the First World War. Lukács (1991: 145) himself referred to Simmel as 'the most important and interesting transitional phenomenon in all of modern philosophy'. His use of the word 'transitional' is significant, because Simmel is arguably the crucial link between the writings of Marx and Engels and the Western Marxists with respect to everyday life.

Although Marx did formulate initially the theories of alienation and commodity fetishism, he focused primarily on how these related to capitalist economic processes. Simmel, by contrast, sought to grasp modernity as a distinct socio-cultural formation that transformed daily life and engendered a wide range of new affective, behavioural and sensory effects. And, although Simmel never declared himself a Marxist explicitly, it is clear nonetheless that in suggesting that his sociology builds 'another storey beneath historical materialism', he saw no essential contradiction between the tenets of Marx and his more 'culturalist' and social-psychological orientation. Finally, he shared the ambivalence that the Marxist thinkers discussed here evinced regarding the nature and fate of everyday life in the modern world.

Simmel is important because he developed an innovative phenomenology of culture that sought to grasp how the diverse practices, spaces and objects in an urbanized everyday life manifested latent significances. As he argued in his 1900 masterwork *The Philosophy of Money*, the diagnostician of modernity can find in each particle of daily life 'the totality of its meaning'. Such a novel sociological method focuses on the formal properties of given modes of 'sociation', by which he meant 'styles' or 'forms' of life, and relate them to their intellectual and historical contexts. For Simmel, accordingly, the study of the everyday is analogous to the microscopic analysis of cells in biology. Just as with their biological counterparts, social 'cells' interact with each other continuously, in the innumerable fleeting and more enduring interactions that make up day-to-day city life.

But although Simmel detects a connection between the micro- and macroscopic in such myriad details, he does not counsel us merely to glimpse the societal whole in each of its component parts, because the everyday must also be understood contextually: '[To] the adequately trained eye the totality of beauty, the complete meaning of the world as a whole, radiates from every single point' (Simmel 1968: 69). Simmel sought to understand the very 'everydayness' of mundane social existence, not only to see in the objects and passing moments of daily life a sign of something 'deeper' or more 'fundamental'. His methodology is therefore rigorously anti-reductionist. Like each spot of light and colour in a kaleidoscope that reveals a hidden pattern when brought into correct alignment, Simmel's 'sociological impressionism' privileges neither the isolated detail nor the abstract system (see Frisby 1992). Rather, each is part of a mutually revealing dialectic of interpretation that produces 'snapshots' of everyday life in the modern world, but taken from the 'standpoint of eternity'. It was not the value of any particular interpretation of an empirical phenomenon that interested Simmel, whose voluminous writings range over such diverse topics as fashion, the domestic interior, gossip, holidays and the figure of the stranger. Rather, what tickled his fancy was the attempt to develop a new and more modern approach to sociological inquiry, in tandem with an innovative style of exposition better suited to the subjective experience of modernity.

Simmel's desire to develop a new style of sociological writing was animated by his proto-existentialist concern for the fate of human freedom and ethics in the context of modernity. This brings us to the notion of the 'tragedy of culture', which has proven to be enormously influential within Western Marxism. In *The Philosophy of Money*, Simmel (1990) suggests that, under capitalism, the products of culture are separated from practical human activity, and confront human beings as objective, anonymous forces. Accordingly, human relationships become subject to a process of instrumentalization and intellectualization; as Simmel puts it, 'one may characterize the intellectual functions that are used at present in coping with the world and in regulating both individual and social relations as *calculative* functions' (in Frisby 1984: 108). The result is that objective culture becomes separated from human subjectivity, and the scope for individual autonomy and creativity becomes severely attenuated. This is the tragedy and conundrum of modern life: that although ultimately the product of active human praxis, the world we create is presented to us as something bereft of intrinsic meaning and coherence, and hence often as alien and threatening. Again, the main difference between Simmel's account of reification and Marx's theory is that the latter tended to restrict alienation to the commodity-form and economic production, whereas for Simmel – presciently, to say the least – it permeates all domains of modern society.

The reifications induced by the money economy clearly weighed on Simmel's ethical sensibilities. Capitalist rationalization not only results in the alienation of the individual producer from the object, as Marx noted; it also encourages the transformation of human subjectivity into what Simmel describes as 'cool reserve and anonymous objectivity'. The latter is summed up in his phrase the 'blasé attitude', a 'distracted' and calculating psychological orientation towards the world. That is, we can only deal with rapid social change and the fragmentation of subjectivity if we cultivate this mode of blasé detachment, which allows us to maintain a buffer between ourselves and the world of others. We can flourish in dense and chaotic urban settings because we are largely indifferent to the fate of those around us, and we do this by shaping our psyche in line with the sort of calculating mentality demanded by a money- and commodity-based economy. This is so not least because, under modernity, human purpose and action is mediated increasingly by objects, rather than other people, and technical considerations of efficiency and narrowly goal-oriented behaviour tend to supplant relationships of an ethical and qualitative nature.

In particular, Simmel is fascinated by the extent that *money*, although the ultimate symptom and symbol of human reification, becomes the common substratum of value for virtually all social actors. Because it can be converted into any commodity imaginable, money has a dehumanizing effect; to paraphrase Marx, money transcends things like inherited status or even natural ability, and can make the ugly person beautiful, the dullard fascinating. Yet money also has strangely egalitarian effects. Because it is the generality that mediates all particularity, the crucial nexus that binds modern society together, money can be the means through which a near infinity of human needs and desires are satisfied (or at least pursued), which has the paradoxical outcome of 'levelling out' conventional social distinctions. Furthermore, money is an infinitely transmutable phenomenon which can impart value to the most diverse contents imaginable, a veritable Nietzschean 'transvaluation of all values', making possible ever-changing material realities, experiences and worldviews.

Simmel also has a dialectical view of the nature of life in the modern metropolis. The sheer compactness of the urban environment, the tremendous multiplicity of groups and individuals we interact with on a daily basis, and the compression of time and space by various modernizing and technological processes mean that everyday life in the contemporary city is marked by a constant bombardment of the senses. But the results are contradictory: along with overstimulation and the blasé attitude that is an adaptive response to it, comes an inestimable richness and variety of objects and experiences. Modern urban 'nomadism' does bring with it negative consequences, such as the breakdown of traditional social support networks, or the demise of the sort of existential and cosmological certitudes of the past. And certainly, we all have to adjust to the abstract and quantitative aspects of mass urban existence – Simmel mentions, for example, the growing importance of clock time as a way of synchronizing everyday life and the wider social world. However, exactly how any given individual adapts to these conditions, there is much leeway: the very universality and objectivity of modern existence allows for the cultivation of a wide range of subjective orientations, thereby encouraging 'qualitative differences' between diverse groups and persons that had not existed previously. Modernity frees up hitherto repressed human potentials, encourages a broader and more cosmopolitan outlook, and breaks down the stultifying prejudices and blind spots inherited from more hide-bound, traditional societies. Everyday life becomes a kind of individual project, a 'work of art' constituting an end to itself, accomplished through the refinement of individual tastes and dispositions symptomatic of the general 'aestheticization' of daily existence under modernity.

Simmel's work might have been compatible broadly with Marxism on the level of general theories and concepts, but he was not attracted to the doctrine of revolutionary social change, and his political sympathies were always more reformist than radical. He maintained a complex and dialectical view of modern urban life, juxtaposing positive and negative factors without ever arriving at some overarching synthesis in which all such tensions and contradictions are resolved. Yet, on balance, Simmel was relatively upbeat about the prospects for humanity under modernity, especially with regard to the expanding horizons of individual freedom and the possibilities for self-expression through the aestheticization of daily life. He did not regard modern society as a utopia *per se*, but he did feel it was guided by a utopian ideal, in that the supersession of tradition raised the possibility of the secular realization of what were once exclusively theological ideals of plenitude and fulfilment.

> Modern salvation was achieved when a person's being formed a unified whole, radiating a consistent personal style from an unseen central point. Simmel was making a call for peaceful cultural anarchy in which freely interacting individuals would not hinder one another's self-realization.
>
> (Liebersohn 1988: 154)

In promoting this sort of 'everyday utopianism', Simmel showed himself to be resolutely anti-metaphysical: for him, the possibilities of human freedom had to be sought through ethical and aesthetical reflection and action in the here and now, in tandem with certain tendencies that modernity manifested and that could not be blithely ignored.

Georg Lukács: the 'riddle of the commodity-structure'

It is clear from the above discussion that Simmel maintained an even-handed and dialectical view of modernity. As such, it may seem strange that when the

First World War began in earnest, after some initial hesitation, he embraced the war effort of the Central Powers. Simmel saw in the conflagration the promise of 'authenticity', by overcoming the 'tragedy of culture' he identified with the modern experience and the forging of a new German identity rooted in a collective struggle guided by transcendental, anti-materialistic values. Yet, this was a common enough position at the time: even the left-wing German Social Democratic Party, which sent delegates to a large European peace conference shortly before the conflict broke out, voted enthusiastically for war credits, mass conscription and the extensive militarization of German society.

In judging his work as a whole, however, we can conclude that Simmel was not attracted particularly to the pessimism and irrationalism of his romanticist contemporaries, and nor was he implacably anti-capitalist. On the other hand, what Georg Lukács himself once described as 'romantic anti-capitalism', the belief that modern capitalism had created a soulless, mechanical civilization in the place of an organic and integrated premodern community, was very widespread at the time. For complex reasons that cannot be chronicled here (see Sayre and Löwy 1984), a romantic anti-capitalism replete with strikingly Messianic elements, the latter referring to a belief in 'end-time' (the culmination, fulfilment or negation of history in a manner that transforms present-day conditions and ushers in a radically different form of human existence), played an influential role in European social thought during the late 19th and early 20th centuries. It left its mark on the writings of such thinkers as Ferdinand Tönnies, Ernst Troeltsch and Gustav Landauer, as well as Lukács – and, albeit in a quite different way, Walter Benjamin.

Michael Löwy (1980: 106) has identified two central features of the Messianic impulse during this period: first, *restoration*, a heartfelt yearning for a lost Edenic paradise or 'Golden Age'; and second, *utopia*, the desire to re-establish this paradisiacal condition at some future time. This somewhat contradictory synthesis of conservative and revolutionary impulses is the defining characteristic of modern Messianism, which often borrowed directly from elements of Judaism. Unlike its Christian counterpart, which was more concerned with spirituality and the ultimate fate of individual souls, Jewish Messianism was avowedly collectivist, 'this-worldly', and apocalyptical. It argued that only a catastrophic transformation of a degraded secular world could reverse humanity's fall from a prelapsarian state of grace and reunite a fractured and tragically flawed cosmos. Messianism was therefore irrevocably opposed to any form of reformism or ameliorism. In this aggressively revolutionary form, it represented a profound challenge to many of the central assumptions of modernity, especially the Enlightenment faith in the unbroken continuity of progress and the irreversible improvement of humanity's lot in every conceivable field of endeavour.

For his part, Lukács agreed with many disillusioned intellectuals of his generation that they were living in an age of intense cultural and spiritual crisis. Especially in his early, pre-Marxist writings, he argued that capitalist civilization represented a brazenly materialistic and God-forsaken social order that had destroyed the last vestiges of genuine community. At this time, Lukács subscribed to an essentially dualistic worldview, which projected a stark contrast between a debased world of mundane bourgeois existence on the one hand, and a Platonic realm of absolute values and quasi-existentialist 'authenticity' on the other. These two domains were, in his mind, totally opposed; there was no possibility of traversing the gap between them. This dualism was the major source of Lukács's tragic vision, which for him entailed a retreat into a highly personalistic mysticism tempered by bouts of pessimistic despair, in which he felt it necessary to bear 'all suffering on the path through clarity toward redemption' (Lukács in Löwy 1979: 95).

However, he did envisage a partial deliverance from the inauthenticity of everyday life through aesthetic experience. For Lukács, the aesthetic sphere contained genuine values, and was separate from the philistine, 'dishonest' realities of daily existence. Art was a repository of authenticity not only because it could evoke vividly such past 'Golden Ages' as pre-classical Greece, but also in that it held out the possibility of realizing such a paradisiacal state in the future. In his 1916 *The Theory of the Novel*, for example, Lukács (1971a) asserted that we are presented with a vision of genuine community in such premodern literary works as the Homerian epic. In the epic landscape, there is no dichotomy between self and world; meaning is immanent in the community and in the wider environment, and, as such, each aspect of life relates organically to a wider, cohesive totality from which it derives its significance. Although this immanent unity has since been shattered by the emergence of capitalist society and egoistical individualism, it continues to linger on as a distant, collective memory of paradise lost – in the novel, for example, which is the literary form of the bourgeois period *par excellence*.

Ultimately, however, Lukács came to regard such purely aesthetic solutions to the degraded character of everyday life as unsatisfactory. Rather than being galvanized patriotically by the carnage of the First World War, as was Simmel, Lukács was disturbed deeply by the conflict. Finding succour in the apparent triumph of the 1917 Russian Revolution, he came to the conclusion that art, in and of itself, could not redeem debased social conditions. Whereas his youthful 'ethical pessimism' saw no possible way of broaching the duality between the 'Is' of mundane existence and the 'Ought' of idealist philosophies, once Lukács committed himself to the communist cause, he discovered a tangible agent of redemption: namely, the revolutionary proletariat. Accordingly, the everyday was viewed increasingly by Lukács, not so much as a sphere of metaphysically 'inauthentic' existence, but as the primary social terrain wherein class contradictions were manifested and a militantly anti-capitalist consciousness might be generated.

Influenced by the anarchism and revolutionary syndicalism of Mikhail Bakunin, Rosa Luxemburg and Georges Sorel, Lukács' idiosyncratic Marxism took on an apocalyptical character. There was no room for compromise when it came to the complete transcendence of capitalism, mainly, *contra* Simmel, because there was nothing faintly worthwhile or redeemable about such a socio-economic system. Since capitalism could only be understood as a totalizing structure in which the logic of commodity production seeped into every nook and cranny of daily existence, it could never be reformed, but only destroyed root and branch, and replaced entirely by socialism. 'The real contribution of the capitalist epoch to the construction of the future consists in its creating the possibilities of its own collapse and in its ruins, even creates the possibilities of the construction of the future', as Lukács (1973: 19) writes in his 1920 essay 'The old culture and the new culture'. In essence, the Russian Revolution became a source of redemptive hope for Lukács, and Vladimir Lenin himself represented a Messiah-like figure.

These diverse influences crystallized in his 1923 work *History and Class Consciousness*. Here, Lukács develops an account of reification and alienation derived mainly from his reading of the passage in Marx's *Capital* on commodity fetishism, together with Simmel's musings on the 'tragedy of culture'. To reiterate, commodity fetishism occurs when social actors are alienated from the things they produce, and thus fail to recognize the intrinsically social character of commodities in the conduct of ritualized economic exchange. People come to view their social interactions as relations between *things*, and hence as natural, eternal and unchangeable, which encourages their submission to these exploited and degraded conditions. Reification, as Lukács (1971b: 197) puts it, is therefore the 'necessary, immediate reality of every person living in capitalist society'. In order to liberate humankind from such mystified beliefs about the nature of these social processes, Lukács argued it was the central task of the proletariat to challenge this 'metaphysical passivity' by developing a revolutionary class consciousness and confronting the ossified structures of bourgeois power. In so doing, the proletariat would overcome the painful separation between subject and object caused by capitalism, and thereby fulfil its 'pre-ordained' historical mission. Following successful revolutionary transformation, social contradictions would be reconciled or superseded in the Hegelian sense, and a unified, organic social totality would replace the fragmentation and dissonance engendered by modern capitalism.

In Lukács's writings from this period, his views on the everyday and its relationship to utopia acquire a definite socio-political content. Yet, at the same time, they retain the Messianic and eschatological flavour of his earlier, pre-Marxist work. The major difference is that the goal of transcending everyday life and resurrecting genuine community is legitimated by reference to a Marxist, as opposed to an explicitly theological, vocabulary. Simmel, it will be recalled, saw in the *Gesellschaft* of urban, capitalist existence the possibility of enhanced personal freedom and self-expression, in which a successful balance could be achieved between social interests and individual desires and impulses. For Lukács, by contrast, the daily life of modernity was so debased that redemption would only be possible by superseding the everyday completely, through a 'leap' into a completely different kind of community – or, to be more precise, a *return* to what is essentially a romanticized, pastoral and pre-capitalist society.

In defining capitalism as a form of spiritual and social decay, rather than as a contradictory social formation containing within itself both destructive and liberatory forces, and in maintaining the belief that history would culminate in a revivified *Gemeinschaft* that would reconcile subject and object, Lukács subscribed to a position that was undialectical and ahistorical in the extreme. In the words of Harry Harootunian, Lukács failed manifestly to grasp the everyday as:

> a coherently worthy subject of investigation and instead looked to the larger structures of the social totality whose behaviour would reveal the impending collapse of the capitalist mode of production and its social formation. Structures offered entry to concrete and material reality while experience was often relegated to ideological reflection. In this sense, the everyday was subsumed under capitalism and modernity, consciousness and experience frozen in a reified state that, according to Lukács, only the proletariat – despite being transformed into the figure of a 'dehumanized commodity atrophying the 'soul' – was still able 'to rebel against reification', unlike the bureaucrat whose 'thoughts' and 'feelings' have been objectified through and through.
>
> (Harootunian 2000: 71–2)

Walter Benjamin: the 'dream-houses of the collective'

However flawed, Lukács' theory of reification paved the way for Western Marxists to understand daily life within modern urban settings in terms of commodification. To comprehend the everyday, it was realized that we need to confront the status of the objects in our profane experience as commodities, and with how their effects are registered in human consciousness, social behaviour and cultural forms.

The central members of the Frankfurt School picked up on this notion, and made it an essential part of their studies. As an example, in his book *Minima Moralia* Theodor W. Adorno voices his distaste for the 'withering away of experience', which he believes to be a consequence of 'identity-thinking', the tendency under modernity to conflate the 'real' with a totalizing system of static concepts and ideas. Identity-thinking was, in his opinion, made possible by the abstract equivalence between all things promoted by exchange value, especially in the form of money, wherein the particular and the concrete are homogenized and effectively destroyed (see Adorno 1974). At the same time, however, the Frankfurt School agreed with Lukács that reification was an all-encompassing process, and that 'false consciousness' had become so pervasive and deep-rooted that the oppressed could no longer comprehend their experience of alienation, much less do something about it. Transitory moments of non-alienation could only be glimpsed furtively in the most *avant-garde* of artworks and theoretical reflections – aesthetic and intellectual practices which, by virtue of their very complexity and symbolic opacity, resisted absorption into the 'culture industry'.

In abandoning the search for tendencies of progressive social change within the everyday itself, and refusing the Lukácsian 'solution' of seeing in the revolutionary proletarian (and later the Communist Party) an escape from a routinized and commodified daily existence, the central thinkers of the Frankfurt School viewed the everyday as essentially irredeemable. This left them no option but to fall back onto a kind of Weberian pessimism and baroque cultural criticism which displayed many elitist and anti-populist tendencies.

Although a peripheral member of the Frankfurt School who was influenced strongly by *History and Class Consciousness*, Walter Benjamin took a very different path with regard to the question of everyday life. For him, it *was the everyday world itself* that was open to redemption, to positive transformation, although he would hardly dispute the notion that the highest achievements of art or critical intellectual inquiry were integral to a fully lived human existence. It may well be the case that what is repressed in modernity is precisely 'the force of the prosaic, the counter-authenticity [of] the texture and rhythm of our daily lives and decisions, the myriad of minute and careful adjustments that we are ready to offer in the interests of a habitable world', as Michael André Bernstein (1992: 182) writes. Benjamin also knew, however, that everyday life in the modern world was not lacking completely in emancipatory possibilities. Although he was not as upbeat as Simmel about modernity, he did believe that there were always hidden 'constellations' of qualitative meaning and subterranean rumblings of dissent in the margins and interstices of the modern capitalist city. In the minutiae of daily life, the very 'banality' of which is worth savouring, we can find numerous gestures, practices and symbols that are not entirely overshadowed by the logic of the commodity form. As an example, boredom was for Benjamin a peculiarly modern refusal to conform to the omnipresent compulsion to consume passively an ever-expanding range of goods and services, and hence was an expression of non-alienated experience (see Moran 2003).

How, specifically, does Benjamin approach the everyday? In his eclectic and wide-ranging writings, he rarely evokes the term 'everyday life' or theorizes about it explicitly, as others have noted (see Roberts 1999: 21). Yet, it is equally apparent that a preoccupation with daily existence constitutes something of a *leitmotiv* for Benjamin, especially in his later writings. This orientation was precipitated at least in part by his encounter with Marxist playwright Bertolt Brecht (not to mention Benjamin's *paramour* at the time, the Latvian communist Asja Lacis), and the growing militancy of his politics, especially after the collapse of Germany's Weimar Republic and the rise of Nazism in the early 1930s. Benjamin's project can therefore be read as a 'heterogeneous project for rescuing the everyday life of modernity from silence', as Ben Highmore (2002b: 61) neatly puts it.

Part and parcel of this 'heterogeneous project' involves assessing the nature of human experience and the ways it has been transformed in the wake of capitalist modernization, but also how the everyday has been ignored or disabused by most Western philosophical traditions. As to the latter, although it undoubtedly contributed to the advancement of individual freedom and critical reason, Benjamin argues that the Enlightenment encouraged a regrettable narrowing and impoverishment of what it means to be 'human'. Kant, for example, acknowledges everyday life as an intrinsic part of human experience, but relegates it to a 'lower order' of being than reflective, abstract cognition.

Echoing Ernst Bloch's assertion that a critical Marxism must incorporate both the 'cold stream' of logical investigation and analytical rigour and a 'warm stream' of passionate utopian speculation, Benjamin (1983–84a: 51), argues instead that the 'source of experience lies in the totality of experience'. Insofar as myriad passions, epiphanies and irrationalities are as much a part of the 'systematic continuum' of life as our capacity for rational cognition, we need to realize that all such elements contribute to the vast array of meanings and narratives we create out of the 'raw material' of our daily lives. The alternative to the Enlightenment tendency to project abstract standards of truth on to the world is to try to close the gap between representation and the sensuously experiential, to understand the world in theoretical terms, but to not lose sight of the concreteness of things, their 'everydayness'.

This is evidenced in Benjamin's affinity for the oral medium, insofar as he privileges the mimetic power of spoken language over its purely communicative or semiotic function. Moreover, Benjamin not only sought to come to grips with the concrete in conceptual terms: he conveys the bodily and the experiential through his very *style* of written expression. Benjamin's prose 'attempts to restore the various dimensions of the sensual through its direct and transparent expression, which constantly evokes a world in which both the sensuous and non-sensuous correspondences are manifest', as Anson Rabinbach asserts. It is 'perhaps the most visual and corporeal philosophical prose we possess. He calls forth something we all desire, but can no longer retrieve: the ability to "speak in pictures"' (Rabinbach 1979: 11).

Benjamin was therefore concerned deeply with the problem of actually representing the everyday, not only in writing but in such newer mass media techniques as film, photography or radio. He was transfixed by Brecht's dictum that 'truth is concrete', and that it is best expressed through the vehicle of 'coarse thoughts', which 'have a special place in dialectical thinking because their sole function is to direct theory toward practice' (Benjamin 1978: 199).

Although he was undoubtedly a master of the prose tradition of classical German philosophy – many, for example, have blunted their intellect on his first book on the *Trauerspiel*, or German tragic drama – in such later works, Benjamin tried to develop a quite different method. In his massive, unfinished study of the 19th-century Paris arcades, for example, he engaged in the montage-like juxtaposition of relatively unembroidered descriptions and reportages with a minimum of interpretive overlay. The idea was that readers could forge their own 'constellations' of meaning out of these 'dialectical fairy tales', which might serve to heighten their awareness of history and the need for collective political praxis (see Benjamin 1999).

We shall return to this point shortly, but, for the moment, it is worth mentioning that Benjamin's approach here has many similarities with Simmel's focus on the everyday minutiae of capitalist modernity. Like Simmel, Benjamin tried to create a new kind of philosophically informed cultural criticism that took as its object not the supposedly noble ideals and platonically eternal values of conventional Western thought, but rather the commonplace things and practices of present-day life. Benjamin agrees with Simmel that the exploration of the modern everyday must occur on two different levels: first, in terms of material culture and the built environment (specifically, the capitalist city); and second, with respect to how this urban setting impacts on human psychology, bodies and social interactions.

Simmel argues that, as mentioned above, the continuous rush and tumult of life in the capitalist metropolis bombards the human sensory apparatus, to which individuals adapt psychologically by developing a 'blasé' attitude of emotional distance and self-interested, rational calculation. In a manner consistent with his 'Marxist turn' of the 1930s, Benjamin largely agrees with this, but places considerably more emphasis on how capitalist industrialization and routinization effectively re-engineers the human psyche and corporeal habitus. Mechanization and repetitive motion becomes a generalized metaphor for life under modernity, not simply about the labour process *per se*. 'The shock experience which the passer-by has in the crowd', writes Benjamin (1968: 176), 'corresponds to what the worker "experiences" at his machine'. And, *contra* Simmel, these forces had to be contested and transformed, not merely adapted to. For Benjamin, people's actions in both their working and everyday lives become increasingly automatized: they are more and more 'massified', constituting an 'amorphous crowd of passers-by', rather than a true community. Such a 'mass' consists of people uniformly similar in dress, use of facial expressions and spoken idioms: they are more interchangeable, yet at the same time increasingly isolated from each other.

Nonetheless, the basic idea is the same in the respective writings of Simmel and Benjamin: that alienation and reification ultimately have a socio-economic foundation, although its effects pervade the modern social world, and one significant result is a stereotypical everyday consciousness and manner of bodily deportment that is characterized by habituated 'distraction'. Such a distracted mode of being does present the individual with certain coping mechanisms: it allows us to better cushion ourselves from the continual shocks and traumas of modernity, to 'roll with the punches' of rapid social changes that can be disorienting and anomic in the extreme. But such adaptations are acquired at tremendous cost: as the fabric of traditional social relations unravels and nothing is left but the cash-nexus, the collective rituals and traditions that bound premodern societies together, and that had transmitted coherent, shared life narratives from generation to generation, are effectively lost. (Benjamin suggests that such modern-day rituals as popular festivals and celebrations are datum of 'remembrance', and exhibit a faint connection to an earlier way of life.) These forms of collective solidarity and affirmation are replaced in the modern world by social atomization, the fragmentation of experience, and an egotistical, almost solipsistic individualism. As such, we are 'increasingly unable to assimilate the data of the world around [us] by way of experience' (Benjamin 1968: 158).

In many respects, Benjamin's assessment here is not terribly different from that of Lukács. But they part company in at least one crucial respect: whereas Lukács' romantic anti-capitalism leads him to yearn for a reconstructed social totality modelled on the supposedly *Gemeinschaft* communities of premodern times, for Benjamin the task is one of locating in the shards and fragments of modern everyday life the resources for future social transformation. Such a project necessarily involves a radical *break* with past traditions. In other words, to redeem tradition, especially the suffering of innumerable past generations, it must be destroyed. So Benjamin does not prompt us to look backwards at a

'Golden Age' of presumptively genuine community, but rather to detect the pulse of utopian energies in the here and now (and in the most unlikely of places), to tap into these forces, revivify them, and link them to transformative political praxis.

The essential premise here is that there have existed in the collective consciousness of humanity since time immemorial countless dreams and 'wish-images' of a free human society founded on equality and universal material abundance. But, although rooted in a timeless past, what is important to Benjamin about such wish-images is that they are anticipations (*pace* Bloch) of a transformed *future* society, and hence a kind of 'dreaming forward', or 'future nostalgia'. Paradoxically, the actual *content* of these wish-images of a future society is culled from the symbols and narratives of an archaic 'Ur-history' of humankind – the 'lost paradise' of a primitive egalitarian society. However, they also envision the radically new, and do not merely recapitulate endlessly an idealized past history. 'In the dream in which every epoch sees in images the epoch that follows, the latter appears wedded to elements of Ur-history, that is, of a classless society', as Benjamin (1973: 159) says.

Such wish-images are best understood as sparks or flashes of insight and awakening that are spurs to practice, not 'blueprints' of some sort of fully imagined, perfect society of the future. As such, Benjamin's position here escapes the charge of 'social engineering' that is often levelled at utopianism. Furthermore, these visions can only be realized successfully if wedded to the immense technological potential of modernity. What Benjamin called the 'phantasmagorical' qualities of the commodity world – especially the visual consumption of signs and images, ranging from the physical organization of the 19th-century Parisian arcades to fashion and advertising – have drained the utopian dream of its creative, anticipatory core and inculcated a debilitating 'false consciousness'. The wish-image continues to channel utopian desire, but in the form of a commodity fetish that can only be satisfied through a 'distracted' and atomized consumption of the superabundant commodities, mass spectacles and entertainments proffered by capitalist modernity.

The result is that the social world once again became mythified, congealed into a barren landscape of naturalized, eternal forms, and separated from concrete praxis by an 'epic distance' in which blind fate is felt to control human destiny. Hence, it is increasingly difficult to escape the sense that capitalist social relations are part of the inherent order of things, a fossilized 'second nature', and seemingly impervious to revolutionary transformation.

Although Benjamin continued to believe that modern technology harboured certain emancipatory possibilities, he also felt that the material realization of utopia through advanced technology is encumbered or 'fettered' by archaic productive and class relations under capitalism. Benjamin speculated that what was required was a realignment of technical organization with a new sociocultural habitus that was appropriate to the accelerated tempo and shocks of modern everyday life. But to achieve this goal we must challenge decisively the re-entrenchment of a mythological consciousness that lies at the very heart of modern industrial society, to clear away the 'underbrush of delusion and myth' (Benjamin 1983–1984b: 2). He felt that the ethos of modernity took the form of a seductive narrative of infinite progress and ceaseless growth – an 'empty, homogeneous time' – in which human agency and collective will are abandoned to an inescapable fate. Individuals are condemned to engage in the ceaseless, repetitive production and consumption of ostensibly new goods and services, in a manner akin to Nietzsche's doctrine of 'eternal recurrence', and to squander their creative energies in reified and alienated sociocultural forms. (Here, we see the influence of Simmel's notion of the 'tragedy of culture', but in much more rhetorically dramatic and unequivocal terms.)

But how did Benjamin propose to counter this process of 'mythification' and the social 'forgetting' that it induces? Unlike Lukács, or other members of the Frankfurt School, Benjamin found succour in the dreams, wish-images and artefacts of the everyday mass culture of the modern city. The task at hand for him was one of rescuing the 'truth-content' of such images from the phantasmagoria of the commodity and the mythification of the social world. This meant tearing these profane objects and images out of the monolithic continuity of 'official' history with a 'firm, apparently brutal grasp' (Benjamin 1983–84b: 22), and to juxtapose them with both older and more contemporaneous narratives and images.

The most apt metaphor of this approach was one of the collector or 'ragpicker', a figure who sifts through the scraps and debris of modern everyday life in order to glean what is worthwhile out of what has been discarded or forgotten. These 'rescued' objects and images can be read as ciphers of different times and experiences that are currently 'out of fashion' – in other words, here we can find multiple temporalities and historical possibilities coexisting in the same range of material artefacts. As such, the ragpicker's task becomes, in the words of Ben Highmore (2002b: 65), one of 'cataloguing the broken promises that have been abandoned in the everyday trash of history'. If successful, such a 'profane illumination' might unleash the collective energies of the proletariat and the technological possibilities of modernity in a manner akin to the 'splitting of the atom'. Although influenced by the montage techniques of the surrealists, Benjamin parted company with their tendency to wallow in fantasy and chance encounters, arguing that only a *critical, rational knowledge* of society and history can break through the reified and mythified structures of capitalist modernity, draw together the threads of scattered memories and images into a coherent narrative, and unlock the hidden potential of the dream state, thereby quite literally 'awakening' the working masses from their slumber.

Benjamin's descent into the 'Ur-history' of modern everyday life was intended to strip official history of its ideological legitimations and facilitate the transmission of a 'counter-tradition' of suffering and revolt, in which the 'secret agreement' between the generations of past and present would be consummated. This helps to explain the urgency of his injunction that humankind not squander the precious legacy of the 'weak messianic power' with which it has been endowed. And, although Benjamin drank from the same well-spring of 'romantic anti-capitalism' as did Lukács, their understanding and usage of such ostensibly theological motifs as 'redemption' or the 'Messianic' diverged significantly. Whereas Lukács sought to reconcile subject and object in a restored organic community, Benjamin harboured considerable doubts regarding the Hegelian desire for a reconciliation of all contradictions and the goal of reconstituting a lost totality. Instead, Benjamin subscribed to what Adorno once termed a 'negative theology', which looked for signs of utopian possibility within marginalized or suppressed human experiences and in the fleeting images of popular culture.

There are no certitudes for Benjamin here: any attempt to redeem the fragmented and reified world of capitalist modernity was fraught with innumerable missteps and blindspots, and there is certainly no quasi-theological insight into the direction of history to rely on. It was an unequal struggle in which the enemy had not 'ceased to be victorious', a sober assessment that explains his self-described 'radical pessimism'. Yet, Benjamin was also acutely aware that the price to be paid for the failure to redeem the semantic potentials of the past, and to achieve the classless utopia through the 'definitive interruption' of the present historical continuum, was a regression to a new and even more virulent form of barbarism: namely, National Socialism.

Despite his frequent use of religious and theological tropes, Benjamin is therefore a profoundly anti-theological thinker, as reflected in his suggestion that the 'order of the profane cannot be built upon the idea of the divine Kingdom, and therefore theocracy has no political, but only a religious meaning' (Benjamin 1979: 155). Utopia does not represent the end-point of the self-propelled 'juggernaut' of capitalist modernity, or the inexorable unfolding of some divine plan. It is understood by Benjamin to be a uniquely human achievement, one that can only be constructed collectively out of the fabric of modern everyday life.

Conclusion

This chapter has focused on three central thinkers – Marx himself, Lukács, and Benjamin, along with a key 'transitional' figure, Simmel – as their ideas bear on a critical understanding of 'everyday life'. It was noted that they share certain overlapping positions, such as their determination not to regard the everyday as a 'backdrop' for ostensibly more important social institutions or activities. Rather, they tend to see the everyday as a crucial site of ideological contestation and the formation of mass consciousness, wherein essential human powers and characteristics are formulated and expressed. As such, the everyday does not consist only in habitualized or taken-for-granted behaviours and attitudes, but can also be the locus of counter-ideological insights and emancipatory tendencies that can be identified and potentially activated by rigorous sociocultural research. This stance is reflected in a constitutive ambivalence all of them have regarding the everyday, albeit in different ways and degrees.

At the same time, there are some important differences. For example, Lukács saw the only hope for a transformed social world, through which an irredeemably debased everyday life could be transcended, in the Messianic figure of Lenin and the dynamo of world communism. Benjamin, by contrast, cleaves to a position that owes more to Simmel than to Lukács: he regards the objects, images and practices of modern everyday life as a crucial repository of the collective dreams and wishes of humankind for a free and egalitarian society, which, if properly understood and translated effectively into political action, could help to jumpstart social transformation. The upshot is that Benjamin develops an approach to the study of everyday life that is considerably more nuanced and dialectical than that of Lukács, or even, for that matter, Marx and later Frankfurt School figures. Consequently, of the theorists discussed here, Benjamin's ideas are arguably best suited to the articulation of a radical cultural politics that takes the 'everyday' as both its primary focus and essential point of departure.

Regardless of such differences and similarities, the core notion developed here – that the everyday is permeated with political and ideological meanings, and constitutes the fundamental ground on which both domination and resistance are exercised – is one that continues to resonate in critical social thought to this day. For, as Michael Billig (1999: 313) notes convincingly, insofar as commodities have acquired even more 'transcendental' qualities in an allegedly postmodern consumer society than the laissez-faire capitalism of the 19th century, once 'freed from the necessity of appearing "Marxist", these ideas may be particularly valuable for understanding the [everyday life] conditions of today'.

Bibliography

Adorno, Theodor W. (1974) *Minima Moralia: Reflections From a Damaged Life*. London: Verso.

Benjamin, Walter (1968) *Illuminations: Essays and Reflections*. New York: Schocken.

Benjamin, Walter (1973) *Charles Baudelaire: A Lyric Poet in the Era of High Capitalism.* London: Verso.
Benjamin, Walter (1978) *Reflections: Essays, Aphorisms – Autobiographical Writings.* New York: Schocken.
Benjamin, Walter (1979) *One Way Street and Other Writings.* London: Verso.
Benjamin, Walter (1983–84a) 'Program of the coming philosophy.' *The Philosophical Forum*, 40 (1–2): 41–54.
Benjamin, Walter (1983–84b) 'Theoretics of knowledge; theory of progress.' *The Philosophical Forum*, 40 (1–2): 1–40.
Benjamin, Walter (1999) *The Arcades Project.* Cambridge, MA: Harvard University Press.
Bernstein, Michael André (1992) *Bitter Carnival: Ressentiment and the Abject Hero.* Princeton: Princeton University Press.
Billig, Michael (1999) 'Commodity fetishism and repression reflections on Marx, Freud and the psychology of consumer capitalism.' *Theory and Psychology*, 9 (3): 313–29.
Frisby, David (1984) *Georg Simmel.* London: Tavistock.
Frisby, David (1992) *Sociological Impressionism: A Reassessment of Georg Simmel's Social Theory*, 2nd edition. London: Routledge.
Gardiner, Michael E. (1995) 'Utopia and everyday life in French social thought.' *Utopian Studies*, 6 (2): 90–123.
Gardiner, Michael E. (2004) 'Everyday utopianism: Lefebvre and his critics.' *Cultural Studies*, 18 (2–3): 228–54.
Harootunian, Harry (2000) *History's Disquiet: Modernity, Cultural Practice, and the Question of Everyday Life.* New York: Columbia University Press.
Highmore, Ben (2002a) 'Introduction: questioning the everyday', in Ben Highmore (ed.), *The Everyday Life Reader.* London: Routledge.
Highmore, Ben (2002b) *Everyday Life and Cultural Theory: An Introduction.* London: Routledge.
Liebersohn, Harry (1988) *Fate and Utopia in German Sociology, 1870–1923.* Cambridge, MA: MIT Press.
Löwy, Michael (1979) *Georg Lukács: From Romanticism to Bolshevism.* London: New Left Books.
Löwy, Michael (1980) 'Jewish messianism and libertarian utopia in Central Europe (1900–1933).' *New German Critique*, 20: 105–15.
Lukács, Georg (1971a) *The Theory of the Novel.* London: Merlin Press.
Lukács, Georg (1971b) *History and Class Consciousness: Studies in Marxist Dialectics.* Cambridge, MA: MIT Press.
Lukács, Georg (1973) *Marxism and Human Liberation: Essays on History, Culture and Revolution.* New York: Delta.
Lukács, Georg (1991) 'Georg Simmel.' *Theory, Culture and Society*, 8: 141–50.
Marx, Karl (1967) *Capital Vol. III.* New York: International Publishers.
Marx, Karl (1989) *Readings from Karl Marx* (ed. Derek Sayer). London: Routledge.
Marx, Karl and Friedrich Engels (1978) *The Marx-Engels Reader, 2nd Edition* (ed. Robert Tucker). New York: W. W. Norton.
Moran, Joe (2003) 'Benjamin and boredom.' *Critical Inquiry*, 45 (1–2): 168–81.
Rabinbach, Anson (1979) 'Critique and commentary/alchemy and chemistry: some remarks on Walter Benjamin and this special issue.' *New German Critique*, 17: 3–14.
Roberts, John (1999) 'Philosophizing the everyday: the philosophy of praxis and the fate of cultural studies.' *Radical Philosophy*, 98: 16–29.

Sayre, Robert and Michael Löwy (1984) 'Figures of romantic anti-capitalism.' *New German Critique*, 32: 42–92.

Simmel, Georg (1968) *The Conflict in Modern Culture and Other Essays.* New York: Teachers College Press.

Simmel, Georg (1990) *The Philosophy of Money*, 2nd edition. London: Routledge.

PART II
FERMENTATION

CONTENTS

CHAPTER 7

French Sociologies of the Quotidian

From Dialectical Marxism to the Anthropology of Everyday Practice

DEREK SCHILLING

Introduction

Sociological theories of the quotidian in France are inextricably bound up with the pioneering work of Marxist philosopher Henri Lefebvre (1901–1991), whose *Critique de la vie quotidienne* (*Critique of Everyday Life*) effectively introduced to social analysis two terms – 'the everyday' and 'everydayness' – that had held scant currency in a tradition concerned more with 'elementary rules' (Émile Durkheim) and 'total social facts' (Marcel Mauss) than with mundane existence.

Drafted at the close of the Second World War and published in 1947, the first volume of what would become a four-decade project in historical dialectics[1] reprises and updates Karl Marx and Friedrich Engels's theses on alienation and class struggle with a mind to transforming the false consciousness that plagues men and women under conditions of modernity. For Lefebvre, everyday life was not synonymous with banality or boredom, though it did comprise such attitudes; nor was it restricted to material conditions of the kind that can be apprehended by statistics or surveys on standards of living. Rather, everyday life was a complex 'level' that had to be grasped dialectically, in its evolving historical relationship to superstructures and ideologies as well as in its immediate, lived aspect.

What the author foregrounds across *Critique of Everyday Life* is the progressive impingement of technical rationality, bureaucracy and organized consumption on the 'styles of life' that had lent premodern rural and urban communities their vitality. Lefebvre argues that in spite of standardization, an unalienable human 'residue' persists, and it is this neglected remainder that harbours the prospect of transformed, demystified existence. This insight philosopher Maurice Blanchot (1907–2003) would hail as a major achievement, for it pointed towards a radically other place from which to critique philosophy, starting from immediate socio-historical facts that had gone all but unnoticed (Blanchot 1969/1993).

By the close of the 1960s, Lefebvre's theses on the 'society of directed consumption', the urban festival and sexual liberation enjoyed a broad public in France and Western Europe.[2] They were met with moderate enthusiasm from research sociologists, in part because of the author's longstanding ties to the French Communist Party[3] but also because the 'revolutionary romanticism' of this former French Resistance fighter was at odds with the newly dominant structuralist paradigm in which Lefebvre saw a belief in technical rationality gone awry. *Critique of Everyday Life* would become nonetheless an indispensable reference for the several approaches to the quotidian that emerged in France after the historical watershed of May 1968.

Among the most salient of these – the 'reverse anthropology' of the interdisciplinary collective Cause Commune, Michel de Certeau's theory of 'everyday practices' and Michel Maffesoli's 'polyphonic' analysis of sociality – none merely parrots or reprises Lefebvre, and none preserves his Marxist dialectical framework. Instead, these thinkers set forth independent paradigms which variously account for the quotidian as a source of undisclosed signification in an anaesthetized realm of spectacle (Cause Commune); as a repository of 'inventiveness' and popular resistance (de Certeau); or as a theatrical space within which the masses cynically assert a healthy distance from ideology (Maffesoli). If Lefebvre cannot be said to play the epochal role that Michel Foucault (1984) attributes to Karl Marx, Sigmund Freud or Ferdinand de Saussure as creators of a 'discourse', he would remain for subsequent generations an authority – now a tutelary source of inspiration, now a rival to be reckoned with.

By setting its sights on a historical totality even as it valorized ground-level occurrences, *Critique of Everyday Life* demonstrated the fallacy of any unmediated approach that would construe the everyday as a 'purely' empirical object. Instead of breaking up reality into a series of specialized inquiries, materialist dialectics, which conjoins the particular and the general, observable fact and concept,[4] stood to disengage everyday life from positivism and to unveil the critical, transformative potential Marx and Engels long ascribed to it. This insistence on dialectics – what Michael E. Gardiner (2000) calls the 'ambivalence' of thinking the everyday – explains why empirical study appears not to have been the strong suit of French quotidian sociologies, Lefebvre's work on rural France for the Centre National de la Recherche Scientifique (CNRS) in the 1940s and 1950s or the many projects housed by the Centre d'Etudes sur l'Actuel et le Quotidien[5] notwithstanding. Hierarchies in the university have meant that fieldwork is subordinate to speculative research; institutionally, this division of labour replicates the divide between *culture savante* and *culture populaire*, between theory and folk anthropology. Thus, in contrast to an Anglo-American ground-up tradition of participant observation, where theoretical insights may result from the collation of multiple neighbourhood studies or demographic surveys, French approaches to quotidian sociology have by and large produced *schemes of thought* for conceptualizing everyday life. How does the everyday both reflect and escape modern structures of technical rationality and their attendant ideologies? What relationships obtain between existence as it is planned and as it is lived? To what extent do individuals remain passive as they go about their daily tasks?

In the survey of French everyday life sociologies that follows, I shall place particular emphasis on Lefebvre's Marxist paradigm, followed by discussions of three less explicitly political reckonings from the 1970s, a decade which marks a high point in contemporary reflection on the quotidian. I have chosen to retain only those figures whose appeals to the everyday or to everydayness as a guiding category are explicit. To be sure, proponents of 'reverse' or 'reflexive' anthropology since 1980 such as Gérard Althabe, Daniel Fabre and Marc Augé in particular have lavished attention on 'ordinary' objects, but as these figures have not seen fit to advance a theory of the quotidian as such, their efforts are peripheral to the conceptual dialogue sustained here.

Henri Lefebvre: Marxist humanism and dialectics

Critique of Everyday Life appears first as a defence of concrete human reality against attempts to 'mystify' individual consciousness and to mask those ingrained mechanisms of capitalist organization that in Marx's reading produce alienation in its many forms. In the mid-20th century, reflects Henri Lefebvre, the French working class is unable to see the full measure of its subjugation; palliated by popular wisdom and folk sayings, it interprets its suffering as the expression of a natural, if not divine order. To the extent that it confuses capitalism with the whole of human reality, it neglects the manifold historical possibilities that technical progress affords. Working from this negative diagnostic towards the goal of realizing Marx's ideal of 'total man', Lefebvre adopts in his 1947 'Introduction' to the *Critique* a threefold aim:

- to establish, over against both bourgeois speculative reason and orthodox Marxism, the primacy of dialectical reason for understanding 'impure' everyday life as part of the totality

- to combat the subjugation of the proletariat by 'demystifying' it and rekindling the class solidarity needed to effect change
- to observe and analyse those facets of human reality that are ignored by the disciplines the better to prepare the transformation of everyday life through praxis.

Lefebvre's 'sociology' thus breaks with the French university tradition of the Third Republic (Émile Durkheim receives only a passing mention in Lefebvre (1947/2008: 148)) to continue the work of Marx and Engels, for whom 'sociology' was inseparable from philosophy and political struggle. Notably, Lefebvre makes no distinction, as would Louis Althusser, between Marx's early 'humanistic' or political writings and the 'scientific' ones inaugurated by the *Grundrisse* and pursued in *Capital*. Alienation, false consciousness, the labour theory of value, commodity fetishism, the money-form, the dialectic of nature – all these elements co-shape Lefebvre's thought, which integrates to varied effect the nascent modern research sociology of the questionnaire and the interview. Yet, it is the dialectical method that remains front and centre throughout the *Critique* to the detriment of a clear research proposal.

Mystification and total man

Lefebvre opens his 'Introduction' of 1947 by adducing the decadence of French bourgeois society, which he sees as mired in the psychological schemata of 19th-century literature. Exemplified by the seer-like poet Arthur Rimbaud, whose cult of sensorial disorientation stops just short of self-induced neurosis, or by André Breton's neo-romantic surrealism, literature stands guilty of encouraging mental confusion, of convincing individuals that the 'beyond' alone should command their attention (Lefebvre 1947/2008: 133). What is forgotten is the immediately visible: the newly tilled field, the bustling street or the factory floor. Lefebvre argues that with the triumph of rationalism, the pursuit of transcendence can no longer furnish meaning: only the collective realization of humankind's potential to transform nature can accomplish this. All the same, film makers, dramatists and novelists, rather than speak to basic human needs, suggest that the paroxystic moments of existence are alone desirable. The mass of individuals hence buy into a dualistic idea of selfhood, wherein 'poetic' or 'metaphysical' states of being promise liberation from concrete reality. 'The theory of superhuman moments is inhuman', objects Lefebvre (1947/2008: 140), claiming that only in the apparently 'inauthentic' realm of everyday life can dis-alienated existence be achieved.

As a communist writing in the mid-1940s, Lefebvre had to contend with the holistic notion of society defended by bourgeois idealists. To be true, the totality must be grasped not through rhetoric or statistics, but dialectically, in contact with the conflicted 'impurity' of the everyday. No less an adversary than idealism is a dogmatic materialism that purports to explain the world through formulas, for example, superstructure as a 'reflection' of economic base, the withering of the state, the dialectical 'leap' from quantity to quality. Marxism can in Lefebvre's view serve as the foundation of modern sociology only on condition that it be understood not as doctrine, but as a self-critical means to comprehend and transform everyday life.

Despite the historic post-war gains of the French Communist Party, Lefebvre entertains few illusions as to the proletariat's role as a vanguard class in France; revolution is not the issue and, in light of Josef Stalin's experiment, certainly not the answer. The proletariat nonetheless bears immense historical possibility, for even as it is crushed by the capitalist system, it retains its 'fundamental health' through daily creative activity on the assembly line, in the workshop or in the fields (Lefebvre 1947/2008: 143). Manual labour enables men and women to avoid the traps of 'private consciousness', while workers' unions and political organizations allow for discussion and improvement of labour and living conditions. If workers find therein the means to combat alienation, the bourgeois intellectual who joins them is by contrast condemned to unhappy consciousness: rather than superseding class, they merely 'break' with it.

Its potential for self-renewal aside, the proletariat remains by and large 'mystified', opposing little resistance to a system that, under modernity, admittedly affords it increased comforts. 'Mystified consciousness', which Lefebvre had explored in the 1930s with philosopher Norbert Guterman, describes the contradiction in bourgeois society between belief and fact, perception and reality. We think we know ourselves, but this knowledge is the product of interpretations whereby we misjudge our objective condition. Workers may well have the same abstract rights as any other citizen, explains Lefebvre, but until they demand political and legal justice their 'equality' is but a fiction. Likewise, so long as they see substandard labour conditions as the working person's fate, rather than as violations of human dignity, they will not understand why collective struggle is necessary (Lefebvre 1947/2008: 146). Yet, the task of re-establishing true class-consciousness is stymied by the equation drawn in advanced capitalist societies between 'being' and 'having'. We pain to conceive of social life outside the money form, which, according to Marx's idea of reification, masks the social relations congealed in the products of human labour. Reduction of biological, social and psychological needs to the sole need for money makes it difficult to think about equity in human terms, outside the top-down models of taxation and state redistribution or of nationalization of private property.

The inventory of culture

Critique of Everyday Life thus attempts to establish Marxism anew as the critical knowledge of everyday life (Lefebvre 1947/2008: 148). Subscribing to Marx's dictum that the purpose of philosophy is not to interpret the world but to change it, it advocates a 'new man' who thinks 'level with the real' (Lefebvre 1947/2008: 226); to this tenet Lefebvre adds that the only true transformations are those that cut across the substance of the everyday (Lefebvre 1947/2008: 228).

To organize and orient collective struggle, then, the sociologist must first answer the basic question: *how is it precisely that we live?* Here, Lefebvre calls for a four-part 'inventory' of French culture, which must have struck the empiricists of the day as unmanageable in the extreme. First, through interviews and observations of individuals, the critique aims to reconstitute daily existence (living conditions, life trajectories, decisions) as it is lived and perceived, in particular by women who are victim to the discourse of 'personal sacrifice' and who, as child-rearers, housekeepers and employees, bear the brunt of everydayness (Lefebvre 1947/2008: 271n.6). Second, the critique should describe the components of an ordinary day, which understood socially rather than as a component of 'individual experience' is anything but banal. (Lefebvre mentions the way in which economic trusts – today's multinationals – shape our lives without our knowledge.) Third, the sociologist asks what traits leisure and sociability take on in different national contexts. Fourth and finally, the critique attempts to reintroduce those very contents that consumer society tends to repress, namely a distinctive style or 'art of living' rooted in popular solidarity and the village or urban festival.

It is little surprise that the results of this vast inventory scarcely materialized. Defining attainable research objectives was perhaps not a priority for Lefebvre; establishing the critique of everyday life as a means of surpassing philosophy arguably was. In the second volume of the *Critique* published in 1961, Lefebvre addresses the opposition to his object of study among the various disciplines. For historians, everyday life connotes the anecdotal dust of history, which has little bearing on the event;[6] for philosophers from Plato to Martin Heidegger it is 'inauthentic' existence, deprived of truth and prior to being; for the social scientist, it is a non-quantifiable, non-observable generality; for the structuralist, it fails in its informality to compose an organized system; for the Marxist ideologue, it is an 'idealistic deformation' that masks the rift between the working class and the bourgeoisie, who in fact share nothing; for the militant communist, finally, it must disappear with the advent of revolutionary consciousness (Lefebvre 1961/2002: 17ff).

To these arguments Lefebvre objects that not only is everyday life immanent to all human activity – 'it surrounds us [and] besieges us, from all sides'

(Lefebvre 1961/2002: 41) – it also performs an *indirect* critique of those specialized forms of knowledge that depreciate it. Whence the ambivalence of the critique of everyday life, which is at once the repudiation of all that is burdensome and intolerable in ordinary existence *and* the spontaneous critique that everyday life itself exacts on that which purports to rise above it. Ethics and epistemology go hand in hand in Lefebvre's promotion of a forgotten remainder or 'common denominator' of all knowledge. Ben Highmore cogently refers to this move as a 'perceptual reversal' constitutive of theories of everyday life generally, where foreground and background are suddenly inverted (Highmore 2002: 27).

Levels, tactics and spontaneity

The second volume of the *Critique* trilogy, entitled *Foundations for a Sociology of the Everyday* (1961/2002), sets forth a complex programme for modern research sociology based on a 'grid of levels in everyday life' (Lefebvre 1961/2002: 124–5) while taking stock of France's swift post-war modernization. Since the war, Lefebvre notes, some of the 'unevenness' of French class society has disappeared; the ordinary housekeeper, for instance, has seen her daily burden lightened by the advent of new consumer durables. Yet such 'improvements' do not abolish the everyday, rather, they 'colonise' everydayness in the name of consumer society (Lefebvre 1961/2002: 11). New questions and new sources of alienation arise: Which product to buy? How to conform to the images that appear in advertisements? What to do with 'free' time on a tight income? Instead of encouraging spontaneous social praxis, leisure society creates widespread feelings of emptiness by imposing constraints of its own.

Similarly, if mechanization relieves the factory worker of the most gruelling physical tasks, at the same time, by converting them into a technical appendage, it erodes the sense of craftsmanship and of the 'job well done'. In light of such transformations, which are always two-sided, sociologists must be wary of constructing 'facts' that leave consciousness and unintended consequences aside. They should take a middle road between philosophical meditation on the one hand and specialized field research on the other. The study of needs, for example, should focus not on the availability of cars, washing machines and televisions to average wage earners, but on the dialectic between *need* as a spontaneous expression of human existence, and *desire*, the fleeting 'wants' that are exacerbated through the fantasy of enjoyment (Lefebvre 1961/2002: 11). Lefebvre remarks that in present consumer society, desires are progressively decoupled from real needs; inversely, real needs no longer naturally produce desires. Everyday life is made homogenous, cleansed of any style.

Central to Lefebvre's analyses in the second volume is the idea of 'level'.

Were the sociologist to define the everyday as a fixed set of daily activities or gestures, he would encourage a restrictive functionalism at odds with a dialectical understanding of everyday life (Lefebvre 1961/2002: 43). The everyday is better seized as a level of existence, which individuals variously sink below or rise above in their life course. Those who are 'immersed' in everydayness live in close contact with the concrete; pushed to act by basic needs, they experience social existence as cyclical and deeply repetitive. For those who dwell outside everydayness, such as intellectuals, statespeople or members of high society, basic material constraints are lifted and a linear, project-oriented time dominates (Lefebvre 1961/2002: 51–2).

A second description of the everyday as level emerges in relation to 'tactics' and 'strategies', two keywords borrowed from military theorist Carl von Clausewitz. Social groups, Lefebvre writes, coalesce around shared projects: a goal to be attained, a common adversary to be defeated. When, in situations of 'extreme tension, turmoil and intense social activity' (Lefebvre 1961/2002: 135), a group puts into motion a concerted *strategy*, its existence becomes historical, such that everyday life is suspended and transformed. By contrast, when existence stagnates, the everyday becomes one-sided and 'lapses into triviality'. The quotidian sociologist, then, should seek out reality in-between the trivial and the strategic, 'on the level of *tactics*, of forces and their relations, and of stratagems and suspicions' that have not yet coalesced (Lefebvre 1961/2002: 135).

One implication of the idea of 'immersion' in everydayness is that much of what transpires in daily life is not visible to social actors themselves, much less to their adversaries. This insight informs the perspective of de Certeau, who, taking von Clausewitz in a different direction, describes how the weak use their innate 'tactical' sense to outsmart the power-based 'strategies' of institutions. But it is Lefebvre's belief in the inherent spontaneity of the everyday that would prove most influential to later thinkers. Reflecting on the tendency of bureaucracy to establish itself as a self-perpetuating 'system' even as it meets real objectives, Lefebvre writes:

> [Bureaucracy] never succeeds in 'organizing' the everyday completely; something always escapes it, as bureaucrats themselves ruefully admit. The everyday protests; it rebels in the name of innumerable particular cases and unforeseen situations. Beyond the zone bureaucracy can reach, or, rather, in its margins, the unformed and the spontaneous live on. There is something tenaciously resistant within this organized or possibly overorganized sphere, which makes form adapt and modify.
>
> (Lefebvre 1961/2002: 64–5)

Beneath the multiple encroachments of capitalist and socialist systems alike, a non-dominated sector persists. To develop knowledge of this neglected sector in order to prepare the lasting transformation of social relations and of private consciousness is the explicit aim of the *Critique*.

Dialectical anthropology and fieldwork

Lefebvre aligns his approach *in fine* with neither philosophy nor sociology, but with a humanistic 'dialectical anthropology' at odds with orthodox Marxism, which he sees as over-emphasizing productive labour's role in human endeavours (Lefebvre 1961/2002: 95). This orientation again speaks to the fraught relationship of the *Critique* to empirical study: fieldwork is conceived as praxis, or active intervention in the everyday with the 'tools of knowledge' that dialectics affords. Like the anthropologist, Lefebvre sees mutual understanding as the goal of any cultural encounter. In interview situations, the investigator should defer to the language of their subject and 'involve and compromise himself within the dialogue' (Lefebvre 1961/2002: 103); in place of closed questionnaires, an open exchange where 'participants talk about this and that' is desirable, for it better exposes each party's real investments in and attitudes towards everyday life. Empirical critique must broach 'intermediate' realities neither too broad (for example, 'society' and 'the working class') nor too restricted (sub-groups) and should incorporate techniques of what Pierre Bourdieu calls 'objectivation', that is, it must factor into analysis the tactics and strategies of the interviewer and their interlocutors (Lefebvre 1961/2002: 107).

Whether Lefebvre ultimately succeeds in 'pushing philosophy from its pedestal and realizing it as a vision of transparency in everyday human relations' (Lefebvre 1961/2002:136) is, for practising sociologists, perhaps beside the point. His defence of dialectical anthropology as the only 'objective' science puts a more difficult challenge to the corporation, however. Is thinking the totality a condition *sine qua non* for attaining insight into the quotidian? Must sociology supersede itself to achieve the status of a truly human science, and if so, at what cost, given that the critique of 'mystifications' can become an ideology of its own? Concepts and processes remain primary throughout the *Critique*, and it is telling that several empirical projects, like the one on women's magazines Lefebvre announced in 1958, were described only to be abandoned. The meta-critical tone of the *Critique*'s culminating volume, which was published in 1981 on the heels of key works by de Certeau and Maffesoli, suggests that positive knowledge of the everyday must constantly be deferred: just as the dialectician's 'object' begins to coalesce, new conditions appear that require its re-evaluation. Lefebvre's fear was that technical rationality would colonize the everyday not only as lived reality but also as concept: indeed, by the turn of the 1980s the 'positive knowledge' sought by the specialists of micro-history, micro-sociology or micro-psychology had, in his view, obscured the critical and political potential of the everyday 'to the vanishing point' (Lefebvre 1981/2005: 4).

Legacies of the Critique

The notoriety enjoyed by *Critique of Everyday Life* in the English-speaking world is little reflective of its long-time status in France. Published from 1958 by the independent Parisian publishing house L'Arche, the work enjoyed a small but committed readership, one which did not see Lefebvre's communism and unswerving faith in dialectics as a hindrance. Later connections with the Situationists and a post as head of sociology at Nanterre, where he mentored Jean Baudrillard and May 1968 firebrand Daniel Cohn-Bendit, meant that Lefebvre was able to reach a broad student public. As Michael E. Gardiner has written, through his 'optimistic and essentially populist stance', the philosopher:

> escapes the charges of elitism and intellectualism that are often (with some justification) levelled at the Frankfurt School. At the same time, however, Lefebvre rejects the widespread proclivity within contemporary cultural studies to interpret the process of meaning-creation that accompanies cultural consumption as essentially liberatory in nature.
>
> (Gardiner 2000: 85)

The everyday thus remains an ambivalent 'mixture of repressive and emancipatory qualities' (Gardiner 2000: 86).

While Lefebvre's legacy in France is primarily linked to the urban studies journal *Espaces et sociétés* (founded in 1970), in the Anglophone world a sympathetic reappraisal of Western Marxism and a groundswell of interest in popular culture and in the urban/rural divide has, since the early 1990s, transformed the *Critique* into a touchstone for cultural studies. Ben Highmore's *Everyday Life and Cultural Theory*, which paints Lefebvre as a thinker of social heterogeneity (Highmore 2002: 119), and Kristin Ross's (1994) history of French modernization and uneven development, *Fast Cars, Clean Bodies*, are noteworthy examples. If we can agree, as Highmore (2002: 25) writes, that 'everyday life might be the name for the desire of totality in modern times', then Lefebvre is unarguably the French thinker who realized that desire most fully.

Cause Commune: uncovering the infra-ordinary

Ephemeral as it was, the interdisciplinary journal *Cause Commune*, founded in 1972 by sociologist Jean Duvignaud (1921–2007) and architect Paul Virilio

(1932–), displayed a deep commitment to Lefebvre's goal of drawing attention to the forgotten 'remainder' of everyday life. The aim of the journal, to which Lefebvre himself contributed on occasion, was to question received ideas about European culture to open the way for an 'anthropology of modern man' [*sic*] and an 'investigation of everyday life at all levels' (*Cause Commune* 1972–74: 1).

This appeal to anthropology, which would be borne out after 1980 by the shift in the social sciences towards reflexive anthropology and proximate ethnography, can be explained by two factors. First, researchers steeped in a humanist tradition that drew on the 'soft' techniques of participant observation felt disaffected from modern research sociology in which quantitative analysis and complex models buttress a scientific agenda. A more sympathetic attitude that connects with the thick detail of everyday life in its 'lived-ness' was a desirable alternative to such discourses. Second, a decade after France's African colonies won political independence, European anthropologists were increasingly aware of their complicity with colonial power relations, and well-disposed to returning from faraway locales to perform fieldwork 'at home'. In a 1972 roundtable discussion with *Cause Commune*'s editors, Georges Balandier insists that anthropologists were uniquely equipped to assess Western modernity because, unlike sociologists for whom alterity often translates into deviance, they are trained to interpret minute cultural elements whose meaning is not readily apparent. By turning their gaze towards their society of origin and making the familiar appear unfamiliar, anthropologists can aid Western society in overcoming its 'primary narcissism' or the misperception that the schemes of thought it devises to understand itself are sufficient (*Cause Commune* 1972–74: 10).

Cause Commune's point of entry for a reverse cultural analysis was the 'infra-quotidian' or 'infra-ordinary', a realm of existence which, like background noise, goes all but unnoticed precisely because it is unremarkable. The journal's contributors variously aligned this notion with a creative imaginary that lay below theatricalized interactions and habits (Duvignaud) or with a critique of Western scientific imperialism (Virilio). But the notion is best expounded in the 1973 essay 'Approaches to what?' by Georges Perec (1936–1982), a writer who had participated in Lefebvre's *Groupe d'études sur la vie quotidienne* in 1960 and who, with *Things: A Story of the Sixties* (1965/1999), had garnered a reputation as a Barthesian literary sociologist of sorts. That brief novel of 1965 retraces the struggles of a French couple who are smitten with consumer desires but who pain to make ends meet (perversely enough, they are employed in the burgeoning field of market research!).

If *Things* performed an exhaustive description of consumer society's discursive commonplaces (Schilling 2006), 'Approaches to what?' insists instead on the collective need to 'question' the objects, rhythms, gestures and lived spaces that compose everyday life. Arguing that the media invariably equate the spectacular and the noteworthy, the exceptional and the meaningful, Perec adduces a collective anaesthesia that leaves subjects unable to register the existence of a vast cultural 'residue' (Perec 1965/1999: 205). Lefebvre's stamp is evident here, and it is to this reservoir of meaning that all individuals must attend should they wish to escape the stultifying effects of spectacle. Free of the pessimism of Guy Debord's 'critique of separation' expounded in *The Society of the Spectacle* (1967/1977), Perec's text stresses the need to undo habit to better access a new language of social being:

> How are we to speak of these 'common things', how to track the down rather, flush them out, wrest them from the dross in which they remain mired, how to give them a meaning, a tongue, to let them, finally, speak of what is, of what we are?
>
> (Perec 1965/1999: 206)

A three-fold programme emerges, namely to take stock of, question and describe that which 'goes without saying'. The author's contention is that the unnoticed will regain meaning only if we prove ourselves able to be 'astounded' by it and see within these shared elements a framework for collective memory. Echoes can be discerned here of Bertolt Brecht, Marcel Mauss and Maurice Merleau-Ponty. Perec borrows from the dramatist the dialectical technique of estrangement by which the banal reverts into the unexpected; from the ethnologist, the need for the minute description and classification of ordinary objects and gestures; and from the phenomenologist, the conviction that the act of describing the world undoes its familiarity to produce wonderment.

What Perec's essay promotes is, in sum, consciousness-raising divorced from revolutionary politics (after 1968, subversion appears a safer bet), a commitment to open-ended questioning and a playful approach to the lived environment through which the subject reinvents patterns of use and even the functions of objects. This democratic programme culminates in *Species of Spaces and Other Pieces* (1974/2007). Subtitled 'A journal of a space user', the work unfolds in telescopic fashion the frames of reference – from the written page, the bed and the bedroom, to the city, country, nation and beyond – in which the discovery of self and world transpires. Again, it is the 'unnoticed' that is subjected to reflection, on uses proper and improper, the dulling nature of habit and alternative modes of dwelling, as in Virilio's own investigations on the theme 'living the inhabitual' (*Cause Commune* 1972–74: 13–16).

Its humour and pluralist humanism aside, Perec's literary anthropology gives rise to a weak descriptivism that does not attend to social processes, rules or representations. It presupposes a de-ritualized, classless social sphere in which actors, for all their inventiveness, remain users and consumers at base, wedded as they are to instruction manuals and to the implacable order of things. When Perec did venture into the field, as in the case of one three-day descriptive experiment conducted at the Saint-Sulpice square on the Left Bank, the resulting text – 'Attempt to exhaust a Parisian place' (*Cause Commune* 1975: 59–108) – reflects a now frenzied, now poised attempt to capture the movement of pedestrian and vehicular traffic; the social disappears as such behind the verbally transcribed background noise of the city square. No doubt the value of such a writerly approach for social science generally lies in its very accessibility: without making any claims to objectivity or truth, Perec unveils the basic human need to attend to those immediate, shared elements of a culture that are all but repressed in the contemporary era of mediated spectacle and that, viewed in an inquisitive light, by no means 'go without saying'.

Cause Commune was short-lived; just nine issues of the eponymous journal appeared, followed in the mid-1970s by a handful of paperbacks on the themes of decay, nomadism and cunning among others. The last of these, *La ruse*, extends Hellenists Marcel Détienne and Jean-Pierre Vernant's discussion of trickery in Ancient Greece to modern societies. 'Doesn't an unspoken casuistry allow most humans to circumvent rules, and this, without entering into the game of obedience and transgression?', we read in the volume's preface. 'Don't such re-appropriations characterise collective life at least as much as ritual does?' (*Cause Commune* 1977: 8). The choice of theme is revealing to the extent that both Maffesoli and de Certeau would see as 'cunning' the modus operandi of ordinary individuals. Witness Balandier's appreciation of the manner in which contemporary youth subvert social norms through 'indirect action', so many 'ruses [that] consist in corroding from the inside that which can't be attacked head-on' (*Cause Commune* 1977: 29). For Duvignaud, it means 'getting around the structure of conventional ideas, rules and values' and 'bringing to the surface ... forms, symbols and gestures that lend the trivial world a richer image of its own life', so as to make real 'the fascinating utopia of unthought ideas and ways of being'(*Cause Commune* 1977: 120).

If the utopianism of *Cause Commune* is Lefebvrian in origin, this insistence on the imaginary and on neglected, low-level forms of resistance (in lieu of frontal political action) is consonant with Maffesoli's and de Certeau's iterations of the everyday at the close of the decade. With the demise of class struggle and revolution as a means of transforming the everyday, sociologists are well served to measure in what ways humans, who are creative, polytheistic beings at base, withstand attempts to limit their existence from above. The break with the class-based paradigm is clear in this anthropological turn, which again views social science as suspect and humanistic critique as necessary.

De Certeau's theory of everyday practices

If, for many observers, Lefebvre included, the historic weeks of May 1968 had failed to bring about durable change in social relations, for Michel de Certeau (1925–1986) they represented an epochal 'capture of speech'. The countless graffiti of 1968 championing self-management, anti-authoritarianism and untrammelled desire confirmed the innate productivity of 'dominated' individuals who, in the right circumstances, could turn the tables on their oppressors. The resourcefulness of French demonstrators reflected a utopian desire for living otherwise and to conceive of culture 'in the plural', outside its restrictive definition by the ruling elites.

Preceding the crisis of 1968, de Certeau, a Jesuit brother, had spent much of the 1960s researching mysticism, possession and religion. On the basis of his perceptive analysis of May 1968, *La prise de la parole* (*The Capture of Speech*), he was retained as an advisor to the French Ministry of Culture, which invited him to break with the quantitative models often used to study reading or viewing habits and with the official ministerial practice of cultural 'democratization', that is, bringing theatre, classical music and museums to the people (Dosse 2002: 444). In this context, de Certeau began to lay the groundwork for a pluralistic theory of everyday practices that the eclectic *L'invention du quotidien: arts de faire* (1980) would expose in full one decade later. The work's English title, *The Practice of Everyday Life*, is incomplete: taking as his object a host of 'ways of doing' that range from walking and reading to storytelling and cooking, the author aims to uncover the inherent yet unseen 'inventiveness' of everyday life.

Practice as interstitial creativity

De Certeau aptly conceives the creativity of ordinary practices in response to Michel Foucault's analysis of knowledge and power relations in *Discipline and Punish* (1975) and to Pierre Bourdieu's structuralist explanations of social practice. Rejecting a vision of a social world in which disciplinary mechanisms perfected in schools, prisons, asylums and hospitals leave individuals all but powerless, he maintains that subjects invariably find room for manoeuvre in the non-dominated everyday. The seemingly limitless extension of what Foucault terms 'micro-technologies of power' may well limit opportunities for action, but it cannot account for the ways in which subjects who operate in the 'interstices' of 'established technological networks' (de Certeau 1980/1984: 49) routinely skirt the imposed order. In contrast to the burdensome strategies that emanate from institutions, the ordinary practices of the 'weak' – de Certeau's stand-in for the popular class – are 'tactical'. Lacking a proper place from which to assert their legitimacy, tactics amount to seizing the opportune moment the better to subvert power relations, as in the case of assembly-line workers who in their overseer's absence craft an object for personal use from scraps picked up off the cutting floor.

The introduction of time as *kairos* rather than *chronos* to guide creative action allows de Certeau to offer a corrective to Pierre Bourdieu's structuralist paradigm. He criticizes the author of *Outline for a Theory of Practice* (1973/1977) for insisting on the 'reproduction' of unconscious structures and for assuming the passivity of individuals, whose undertakings would express a pre-existing 'habitus'. Circular explanations such as Bourdieu's leave the observer blind to those behaviours and activities that do not conform to preordained patterns. Moreover, where Bourdieu implicitly claims theoretical mastery over the subjects whose practices he describes, de Certeau refuses to place himself above the everyday, for this can only produce a 'fiction' of objective knowledge, 'a strategy of intellectual bluff and counter-bluff', as Jeremy Ahearne (1995: 153) puts it.

From a ground-level perspective it becomes possible to perceive in everyday practices not *docta ignorantia*, but the knowing creativity of individuals who endlessly reinvent stratagems to circumvent existing limits (de Certeau 1980/1984: 56). Everyday life by nature is, then, lived against the grain: each act of consumption is a selective re-appropriation, a proof of the vitality of bricolage, which Claude Lévi-Strauss had aligned with the production of myths in 'primitive thought'. The notion that individuals reinterpret rather than execute blindly their daily tasks may seem self-evident, but in the late 1970s in France such a thesis ran sharply against the structuralist doxa. Valorising the act *qua* act in place of the impersonal codes and signifying systems that for structuralist thinkers determine what it is possible or impossible to do and to say (a 'grammar of practice'), de Certeau seems to reintroduce variation, indeterminacy and human agency. Like Richard Hoggart, he brings optimism to the study of popular sociability, long dominated by the pessimism of the Frankfurt School which saw in the 'culture industry' a means to pacify the masses.

Observing the everyday: empiricism and inventiveness

De Certeau's ground-level approach is arguably more amenable to fieldwork than Lefebvre's dialectical sociology, for if practices are observable, concepts and mediations are less so. The difficulty lies in translating theoretical insight into usable terms, a challenge that the authors of *Habiter, cuisiner* (*Living and Cooking*), the empirical companion volume to de Certeau's text, take up with mixed results (de Certeau, Mayol and Giard 1980/2002). As Michael Sheringham notes (2006: 240, 246), Pierre Mayol's description of the workings of 'accommodation' and 'recognition' in Lyon's working-class district of La Croix-

Rousse is closer in spirit to the Bourdieu of *Distinction* (1979/1984) than to de Certeau. Take, for example, Mayol's explanation of the social control exerted by the street on its users, who find within an expression of the social contract:

> The dweller, as an immediately social being caught in a relational public network he or she has not completely mastered, is taken care of by the signs that secretly order him or her to behave according to the requirements of propriety. The latter occupies the place of law, a law stated directly by the social collective that is the neighbourhood, of which no one dweller is the absolute keeper, but to which all are urged to submit, in order, quite simply, to make everyday life possible.
>
> (de Certeau et al. 1980/2002: 36)

Mayol's discussion of the structuring effects of the neighbourhood chimes with much of the sociological literature from the 1950s to the 1970s. The use of sexual innuendo, whether in public or among the members of a groups, the work of codes of honour and 'recognition', the ambivalence of alcohol as a 'socializing dynamic', and the implicit 'social contract' that governs all interactions are themes familiar to any reader of Paul-Henri Chombart de Lauwe, Howard S. Becker, Richard Hoggart or Pierre Bourdieu. If Mayol's findings are valuable with respect to local history – note the painstaking descriptions of a typical *canut* apartment and its furnishings (de Certeau et al. 1980/2002: 62–70) – and to the evolution of working-class solidarity in a newly modernized France, the reader may fail to discern their connection to de Certeau's problematics of inventive appropriation. To argue, for example, that window-shopping on Saturdays goes 'beyond' the consumerist paradigm by making possible 'the appropriation of urban space through the desire of an itinerant subject' (de Certeau et al. 1980/2002: 102) is jargonizing in the extreme, and the conclusion according to which 'the urban neighbourhood is the place for a decisive social apprenticeship' leading to 'the apprenticeship of everyday life' may strike readers as a truism (de Certeau et al. 1980/2002: 113). What Mayol most consistently asserts are the conditions of possibility for normal social functioning.

Inventiveness and creativity are more centrally at issue in the parallel empirical study of culinary practices by Luce Giard, who argues that for the 'socially invisible' woman housekeeper, ordinary practices, however fleeting, 'are often the only place of inventiveness available to the subject' (de Certeau et al.1980/2002: 155). In sharp contrast to the artistic freedom and masculine prestige of restaurant cuisine, ordinary cooking is scorned as monotonous and considered to be bound strictly to necessity (de Certeau et al. 1980/2002: 156–7). But it is here that creativity takes root through shared knowledge. While there is little point in disputing Giard's claim that home cooks are good improvisers whose time-honoured gestures enrich the social fabric (de Certeau et al. 1980/2002: 213), it is worth asking whether the pleasure experienced by some women in perfecting a dish or sharing recipes offsets the alienation that daily confinement to the kitchen brings. Writing in a reverential and celebratory tone, Giard tends to elevate the mundane through a surfeit of poetry: 'Each meal demands the invention of an alternative mini-strategy, when one ingredient or the proper utensil is lacking' (de Certeau et al. 1980/2002: 157).

Populism and resistance

The gap in the two volumes of *The Practice of Everyday Life* between a 'theory' and 'practice' of everyday practices was perhaps inevitable; as Michael Sheringham (2006: 239) points out, the theoretical volume had yet to be published when Mayol and Giard began their studies under de Certeau's guidance. Given the limited methodological insights afforded by the monographs on neighbourhood solidarity and cooking, however, it is tempting to conclude that the empirical studies that best resonate with *The Practice of Everyday Life* are, on the one hand, those that directly inspired de Certeau, like Jean-François Augoyard's work of 1979 on the 'rhetoric' of foot traffic in a modern housing project (Augoyard 1979/2007), and, on the other, works of Anglo-American cultural studies from the 1980s and 1990s that developed de Certeau's boundless insights.

The extraordinary enthusiasm with which Volume I of *The Practice of Everyday Life* met upon publication in 1984 in English translation (more than 30,000 copies sold) (Dosse 2002: 426) was linked to the impression that de Certeau had restored agency to common users. An exponent of an anti-institutional populism who saw in anti-colonialist struggles from the 16th century to the present deep challenges to Western rationality (Dosse 2002: 427), de Certeau was cast in the United Kingdom and the United States, where he spent the last part of his career, as a leader in a struggle which extended to feminist movements and subaltern studies, while his model of creative appropriation would closely inform sociological approaches to youth subculture and to the media in particular. The explanation of televisual 'consumption' in terms of a 'hidden productivity' took on great resonance in the work of John Fiske and Henry Jenkins among others.

Readers of *The Practice of Everyday Life* may wonder whether translating de Certeau's ethnography of actions into the language of active resistance does not overly magnify the book's claims. To equate unnoticed 'interstitial' activities with resistance is to run the risk of heroicizing what is effectively a non-encounter between dominant and dominated; if the dominated are allowed from time to time to outsmart their dominators, it is perhaps because the latter know that the gains of the former are short-lived. But as Jeremy Ahearne persuasively argues, even if we admit that the 'redistribution of cultural practices' signalled by de Certeau is 'largely "symbolic"', it is these very symbolic divisions between legitimate and illegitimate practices that 'constitute the operative fabric of modern democratic societies' (Ahearne 1995: 188). De Certeau's intervention, then, though divorced from party politics, is in some respects no less political than Lefebvre's.

It remains that *The Practice of Everyday Life* conceives of everyday practice negatively, as that which escapes the grid of technical rationality. Cultural critic Kristin Ross offers an abrasive but apposite assessment of the work's legacy: 'By concentrating on the periphery and only on the peripheries, cultural analysis derived from de Certeau ends up with a lot of pinprick operations separated from each other in time and space' (Ross 1996: 71). The interstices, we may infer, are narrower and less significant than de Certeau wished to believe; qualifying everyday creativity as creative 'bricolage' or 'poaching' on the master's terrain scarcely assuages the fear that rationality has a near-total grasp of the social, and that power relations will hold fast. Even as de Certeau explores non-determined social facts, then, his position remains wedded to the instrumentality of the user and, *nolens volens*, to a de-historicized productivist/consumerist paradigm.

Michel Maffesoli's rituals of passive resistance: the persistence of the social

If the release of Michel Maffesoli's *La conquête du présent: pour une sociologie de la vie quotidienne* (*The Conquest of the Present*) in 1979 was less eventful than that of de Certeau's treatise the following year, retrospectively it is a no less a milestone in the development of quotidian sociology in France. Where de Certeau, after drafting a local theory of ordinary creativity, turned towards other objects in the closing years of his life, Maffesoli (b. 1944) would develop across ten volumes a singularly comprehensive explanation of how the social endures in and through everyday life. The fact that his works, unlike those of Lefebvre and de Certeau, have not been taken up by Anglo-American practitioners of cultural studies reflects the expectation that thinkers of the everyday take a 'radical' political stance. Though Maffesoli took an early interest in Marx and the Situationists during his student days in Strasbourg, his essays enter in dialogue with the grand European tradition of Ferdinand Tönnies, Max Weber, Georg Simmel, Émile Durkheim, Marcel Mauss and Vilfredo Pareto among others. Wary of semiotics, Lacanian psychoanalysis and various iterations of Marxism that were his generation's touchstones, he insists above all on the ethical dimension of the everyday:

how do play and ritual allow groups and individuals to co-exist in the dynamic construct that Maffesoli terms 'sociality' or 'communalized empathy'? (Maffesoli 1988/1996: 136).

The non-logical present

The frame of reference of *The Conquest of the Present* is anti-historical, or better, deeply anthropological. It valorizes shared collective impulses which surge up cyclically to disturb the all too seamless narratives of progress to which the West is held in thrall. Maffesoli argues that the credence given to linear patterns, for example the Christian eschatology that leads from dereliction to salvation or the Marxist narrative of alienation, revolution and liberation, creates an ideological blind spot. As soon as lived time is conceived as purposive and heterogeneous, it becomes difficult to perceive the structuring role of the present, namely of those recurrent elements that assure, in their chaotic interplay, the continuity of the social. Sociality, whether expressed in ritualized repetition, exuberance or violence, is for Maffesoli 'sovereign' by nature, for it resists the attempts of transitory powers to subordinate it.

Like Weber before him, Maffesoli recognizes, *pace* Hegel, that the real cannot be equated with the rational. Even in periods in which rationality dominates, an incongruous residue composed of collective and individual passions and vital forces persists (whence the many social engineering disasters of the 20th century). What Pareto calls 'non-logical' actions are ubiquitous in daily life – the 'rational social actor' is a convenient myth – and it is through these contents, which resist easy representation that the social whole coheres. Hedonism is a case in point. In Maffesoli's neo-pagan framework, the will to enjoyment of the masses, which the author links to Tönnies's *Wesenwille* or collective essential will (Maffesoli 1979/1998: 44), is a sign not of depravity or ignorance but of robust social health. To experience pleasure in the here and now is a means of coping with human finitude but also of debunking ideologies that emphasize sacrifice and deferred gratification. Because the masses live at one with the 'tragic sentiment' of the present (Maffesoli 1979/1998: 36), they know best how to seize the moment in its concrete sensuality.

We might object that such a celebration of the present, which Maffesoli (1979/1998: 39) terms an 'enlightened sensualism', translates to disaffection from the political and hence from a meaningful, shared future. The author argues that the masses, quite to the contrary, prove their wisdom whenever they turn a deaf ear to politicians: aware from experience of how empty most campaign promises are, they will not invest themselves in a cause that will likely produce few tangible rewards before it is replaced by another, no less transient cause. Theirs is a 'creative relativism' rooted in an 'active passivity', rather than in acquiescence or Nietzschean *ressentiment* (Maffesoli 1979/1998: 169). For even as they appear to subscribe to official values, the masses keep their distance, viewing as suspect all top-down attempts to unify the social whole around an ideal. This corner-café cynicism reflects deep connections to the local environment, which, imperfect as it may be, is what matters in the end. 'The dry goods store, shops, squares, markets and public places create so many unadorned occasions to experience the crucial problem of time's passage', writes Maffesoli (1979/1998: 87) of the city or town, which becomes the 'nodal point' for sociality.

Cunning and ethics

Since play and resourcefulness are central to Maffesolian sociality, comparison with de Certeau's notion of popular tactics is instructive. Both thinkers view cunning (*la ruse*) as what defines the operative mode of ordinary actors and *kairos* as the seat of opportunity in daily life. But where de Certeau conceives everyday practices as a structural response to the rational programming of the everyday, Maffesoli evokes an ethical need for outsmarting natural and social constraints, in keeping with the Weberian polytheism of human values. The proof that individuals wilfully skirt 'normative external obligations' (Maffesoli 1979/1998: 61) lies in the fact that even as they are quick to cheat the (impersonal) system, they are remarkably faithful to their peer groups and kin. Where de Certeau lends everyday gestures a 'poetic' aspect largely as a function of their statistical unpredictability, Maffesoli sees in them the strivings of impassioned individuals who live out the 'poetry of existence' (Maffesoli 1979/1998: 63). Gestures are not micro-sociological data to be subjected to quantitative or functional analysis, but phenomenological reflections of the imaginary, affect and fiction, which introduce in everyday life a 'doubled' or 'duplicitous' space of freedom. In sum, if the organic vitality of the masses cannot be reduced to 'ways of doing', it is because the masses act primarily by *not* participating. For Maffesoli, whose debt to Gilbert Durand's *Anthropological Structures of the Imaginary* (1969) runs deep, investment in the present bespeaks an 'empirical surrealism' through which individuals draw on a collective bank of images and myths to save themselves from boredom (Maffesoli 1979/1998: 95–6).

Interaction rituals

Maffesoli further distances himself from Lefebvre and de Certeau in his emphasis on appearances and theatricality in face-to-face interactions. Objective science, he argues, fails to acknowledge that in the lived realm there is no 'truth' behind appearances. The surface play of masks and simulacra, the endlessly reprised game of 'as if', the presentation of self and other as a function of stereotypes and archetypes – these phenomena cannot be discounted, for it is through them that 'being' is realized and made visible (Maffesoli 1979/1998: 149). Whence the need for a 'sociology of circumstances' (Erving Goffman's term) that takes stock of the anecdotes and banal situations that compose human existence (Maffesoli 1979/1998: 26).

There is to Maffesoli's mind little point in seeking to discern the intentions or consciousness of social actors when what determines the outcome of interpersonal exchanges is, following Goffman, an interplay of ritualized roles, a 'spectacle' that exhausts itself in the present of its unfolding. To Goffman's analyses Maffesoli brings a postmodern twist, one consonant with Jean Baudrillard's own musing on signs: social life is a game of masks and simulacra which know no referents (Maffesoli 1979/1998: 142–3). The paradoxical foundation of social life in the play of appearances has as its corollary the omnipresence of spectacle in society. 'Rational' behaviours are the exception, not the norm; voting for one candidate over another in an important election may be less a measured decision than a passionate one. Despite the abuses to which spectacle is put by ideologues intent on rousing the masses from their passivity, Maffesoli does not denounce it as a tool for manipulation. Spectacle is simply the outward form that sociality adopts in the everyday to protect the collective from the fear of imminent death (Maffesoli 1979/1998: 163).

By denying any group a role in making history and by identifying the everyday with dynamic stasis, Maffesoli sets himself apart from Lefebvre's leftist tradition, which thought the quotidian in tandem with socio-political transformation. His concept of 'conflicted equilibrium' or 'differentiated harmony' is telling in this regard. Social dynamism, like the play of affects, depends for Maffesoli on what the 19th-century utopian Charles Fourier called an 'enhanced play of differences' that enables the 'acceleration of relations between different groups' (Maffesoli 1979/1998: 49, 136). Whereas traditional societies thrive upon internal differences in titles or caste, modern democratic societies have eradicated distinctions to an extent that all social beings are reduced to a lowest common denominator, hence producing a one-dimensional whole at odds with Max Weber's 'polytheism' of human values. To conclude from this that Maffesoli joins a chorus of anti-democratic thinkers is to forget that the sociologist's object is not how things should be, but how things are or appear to be. Rather than prescribe, Maffesoli limits himself to describing a chaotic, imperfect sociality, which is shaped as much by cruelty and violence as by democratic longings.

It is, in the end, the temporal aspect of Maffesoli's project that gives it its singularity. In contrast to the future-oriented 'possibilism' of Lefebvre,

Maffesoli cautiously decouples the present from past and future and affirms the homogeneity of lived time, which is swiftly expended through play, ritual and duplicity (1979/1998: 193). If these processes and attitudes do not afford political or economic liberation, they do assure individuals and the 'tribes' they increasingly form (Maffesoli 1988/1996) a distance from which to preserve their sense of self, an 'aloofness' that guarantees the continuation of sociality as a dynamic but stable whole. By recognizing the sovereignty of the everyday in the face of 'deadly impositions' from above, the sociologist recalls the existential import of those 'micro-attitudes, small-scale creations, periodic and ephemeral situations' (Maffesoli 1979/1998: 190) that form a discrete counter-power. The masses, in this iconoclastic view, are most effective in maintaining sociality not because of what they do or would like to be doing, but because they prefer not to participate, believe or protest. Perhaps those who dwell in the quotidian are not so very alienated in the end? Such is the post-historical perspective that came to the fore some three decades years after Lefebvre's opening salvo.

Conclusion

The present survey has explored the rich dialogue that French thinkers have entertained with the quotidian since the Second World War. Given the widely different valences ascribed to everyday life by a Lefebvre or a Maffesoli, it is worthwhile to underscore in conclusion those traits that seem to characterize French quotidian sociologies generally.

First, the high degree of state centralization in France, coupled with the central place of revolution and collective struggle in politics, have meant that the everyday cannot be conflated with 'private life' or 'individual experience', as is the case in the United Kingdom or North America. In the French context, what Louis Althusser calls 'state ideological apparatuses' are so present in the public domain that whatever organic impulses everyday life may contain are reorganized from above. Even those practices that appear 'spontaneous' are affected by the pervasive logic of rationality, and it is the resulting reduction of the social to mundane repetition – to an everydayness without respite – that the authors reviewed above attempt to combat.

Second, inspired by the anthropologist's example, French sociologists have devised a battery of techniques and approaches through which to locate the everyday firmly in observable, lived reality even as they recognize its conceptual import. There results a productive tension between empiricism and theory, one which is largely unresolved.

Finally, from the historical standpoint it should be clear that the events of May 1968 mark a watershed not just in national culture but in the orientation of everyday life sociologies themselves. In the wake of 1968, the future-oriented praxis of Lefebvre yields to an anthropological description of 'background noise' (*Cause Commune*); celebration of the popular class as productive non-producers (de Certeau) or as individuals cynically bound to enjoyment (Maffesoli) replaces Marx's injunction to change the world, instituting in the space of a once-politicized everyday a new ambivalence.

Notes

1. Lefebvre, who considered *Critique of Everyday Life* an 'unending' project, published an expanded edition of Volume I in 1958, followed by Volume II in 1961 and Volume III in 1981.
2. By 1972, *La vie quotidienne dans le monde moderne* (*Everyday Life in the Modern World*, 1967), a favourite among students on the eve of May 1968, had been translated into Portuguese, English, German and Spanish (Shields 1998: 199).
3. In 1958 Lefebvre was excluded from the Parti Communiste Français (PCF) for his heterdox (that is, anti-Stalinist) views.
4. On Lefebvre's approach to the dialectic, see Shields (1998: 109–26).
5. The Research Centre on the Contemporary and the Everyday, founded in 1982 by Michel Maffesoli and Georges Balandier.
6. The Annales School of Ferdinand Braudel and Lucien Febvre, which looked into the 'structures of everyday life', was the exception; see Schilling (2003: 26–30).

Bibliography

Ahearne, Jeremy (1995) *Michel de Certeau: Interpretation and its Other*. Cambridge: Polity Press.

Augoyard, Jean-François (1979/2007) *Step by Step: Everyday Walks in a French Housing Project*. Minneapolis: Minnesota University Press.

Blanchot, Maurice (1969/1993) 'Everyday speech', in *The Infinite Conversation*. Minneapolis: Minnesota University Press.

Bourdieu, Pierre (1973/1977) *Outline for a Theory of Practice*. Cambridge: Cambridge University Press.

Bourdieu, Pierre (1979/1984) *Distinction: A Social Critique of the Judgment of Taste*. London: Routledge.

Cause Commune (1972–1974) Nine issues. Paris: Denoël/Gonthier.

Cause Commune (1975) *Le pourrissement des sociétés*. Paris: UGE.

Cause Commune (1977) *La ruse*. Paris: UGE.

De Certeau, Michel (1980/1984) *The Practice of Everyday Life*. Berkeley, CA: University of California Press.

De Certeau, Michel, Pierre Mayol and Luce Giard (1980/2002) *The Practice of Everyday Life*, Vol. II: *Living and Cooking*. Minneapolis: University of Minnesota Press.

Debord, Guy (1967/1977) *The Society of the Spectacle*. Detroit: Red & Black.

Dosse, François (2002) *Michel de Certeau: le marcheur blessé*. Paris: La Découverte.

Foucault, Michel (1984) 'What is an author', in Paul Rabinow (ed.), *The Foucault Reader*. New York: Pantheon.

Gardiner, Michael E. (2000) *Critiques of Everyday Life*. London: Routledge.
Highmore, Ben (2002) *Everyday Life and Cultural Theory: An Introduction*. London: Routledge.
Lefebvre, Henri (1947/2008) *Critique of Everyday Life*, Vol. I: *Introduction*. London: Verso.
Lefebvre, Henri (1961/2002) *Critique of Everyday Life*, Vol. II: *Foundations for a Sociology of the Everyday*. London: Verso.
Lefebvre, Henri (1981/2005) *Critique of Everyday Life*, Vol. III: *From Modernity to Modernism (Towards a Metaphilosophy of Daily Life)* [1981]. London: Verso.
Maffesoli, Michel (1979/1998) *La conquête du présent: pour une sociologie de la vie quotidienne*. Paris: Desclée de Brouwer.
Maffesoli, Michel (1988/1996) *The Time of the Tribes: The Decline of Individualism in Mass Society*. Thousand Oaks, CA: Sage.
Perec, Georges (1974/2007) *Species of Spaces and Other Pieces*. Harmondsworth: Penguin.
Perec, Georges (1967/1999) *Things: A Story of the Sixties*. London: Vintage.
Ross, Kristin (1994) *Fast Cars, Clean Bodies: Decolonization and the Reordering of French Culture*. Cambridge, MA: MIT Press.
Ross, Kristin (1996) 'Streetwise: the French invention of everyday life.' *Parallax*, 2: 67–75.
Schilling, Derek (2003) 'Everyday life and the challenge to history in modern France.' *Diacritics*, 33(1): 23–40.
Schilling, Derek (2006) *Mémoires du quotidien: les lieux de Perec*. Villeneuve d'Ascq: Presses Universitaires du Septentrion.
Sheringham, Michael (2006) *Everyday Life: Theories and Practices from Surrealism to the Present*. Oxford: Oxford University Press.
Shields, Rob (1998) *Lefebvre, Love and Struggle: Spatial Dialectics*. London: Routledge.

CHAPTER 8

Erving Goffman

Self-Presentations in Everyday Life[1]

SØREN KRISTIANSEN

Erving Goffman: the lone wolf of sociology

The Canadian-American sociologist and social psychologist Erving Goffman (1922–1982) is today considered one of the most significant sociological analysts in the field of modern everyday life. Goffman, who studied sociology in the 1940s, earned his PhD from the University of Chicago and later became professor at the University of California, Berkeley, and at the University of Pennsylvania. Several of his books have gained recognition far beyond the field of sociology. *The Presentation of Self in Everyday Life* (1959) and *Asylums* (1961a), probably the most well-known among his books, have been translated into several languages and have exerted considerable influence on sociologists and other scholars worldwide.

Other works by Goffman have left indelible marks upon the field of (micro)sociology. This, for instance, is true of *Interaction Ritual* (1967), *Behaviour in Public Places* (1963a), *Relations in Public* (1971) and *Frame Analysis* (1974). With his incisive powers of observation and linguistic versatility, Goffman was able to discern the significance of microscopic and seemingly trivial aspects of people's face-to-face interactions, and several of Goffman's concepts, such as 'impression management', 'stigma', 'total institutions' and 'frames', have gradually been incorporated into the professional vocabularies of sociologists and other scholars and professionals.

Goffman's sociology is concerned with one of the most elementary forms of social life – the human encounter; that is, situations in which people cooperate towards maintaining a mutual focus of attention. In Goffman's (1983a) view, this cooperation involves maintaining a unique 'interaction order', and at the crux of this order, another of Goffman's important figures evolves, that is, his unique concept of the self. For him, the self is not a question of the individual's inner experience, but very much a socially situated and changeable product. In order to describe and analyse the processes and products of the interaction order, Goffman utilized different conceptual metaphors, among which the most well-known are the metaphors of the theatre, the game and the ritual. With these metaphors, Goffman employs a distancing analytic method, so to speak: viewing the commonsense world from an outside system of relevance (Kristiansen and Mortensen 2005).

Although Goffman was known as 'an independent spirit, impossible to classify' (Hacking 2004: 292), there have been numerous attempts to label him within the constraints of established traditions and paradigms. Some have discussed the phenomenological aspects of his work (for example, Lanigan 1988); others have categorized him as a microfunctionalist (Chriss 2003); while others again have dubbed him a symbolic interactionist (Zeitlin 1973). Goffman himself refused to contribute to these efforts at classifying him; yet, in one interview, he characterized his own work as an 'urban ethnography' following in the wake of the tradition of field study developed by Everett C. Hughes (1897–1983) at the University of Chicago (Verhoeven 1993).

The fact that Goffman's thinking has been influenced by the intellectual milieu at the University of Chicago is probably beyond doubt. Along with figures such as Howard S. Becker (b. 1928), Harold Garfinkel (b. 1917) and Herbert Blumer (1900–1987), Goffman came to represent an interactionist surge in sociology, which with its predilection for ethnographic methodology, social microdynamics and qualitative data represented a substantial counter-movement to the Parsonian structural functionalism which, on the American continent, reached its pinnacle in the 1950s.

Besides being inspired by the academic environment later to be known as the 'Chicago School', Goffman was also influenced by several classical thinkers in sociology. Thus, from Georg Simmel (1858–1918) he obtained his interest in social forms as well as the microscopic and molecular processes of social life. From Émile Durkheim (1958–1917), Goffman adopted the concept of ritual, which he used to shed light on the affirmation of the self and the moral dimension in interactions of daily life. Along with his interest in the 'social order', the inspiration from Durkheim led Goffman away from a 'pure' interactionism towards a variant of microstructuralism which is not first of all interested in how people create social situations, but more in the structure, syntax and organization predominant in human encounters. As Goffman himself writes in the preface to *Interaction Ritual*: 'Not, then, men and their moments. Rather moments and their men' (Goffman 1967: 3). Apart from being inspired by these two prominent thinkers, Goffman obviously found stimulation in existentialism's conception of the absurd nature of modern life as well as in the way ethology analyses patterns of interaction, especially the idea of the development of personal territories.

Shortly before his death in May 1982, Goffman presented a lecture in Lyon to a group of French sociologists under the heading 'Microsociology and History'.[2] Here we encounter one of Goffman's trademark understatements when he says that:

> the major part of the works I have authored make no contribution to the study of everyday life .... Most of what I have done has to do with forms of interaction; and the ones I have concerned myself with are, in my opinion, the fundamental ones.
>
> (Goffman 1983b)

The latter is no doubt correct, but to say that Goffman has not contributed to the study of everyday life truly seems a massive meiosis. Goffman was indeed concerned with the study of everyday life, more specifically with the parts of it 'which pertains to face-to-face interactions' (Schwartz and Jacobs 1979: 192). This chapter seeks to illustrate Goffman's understatement through an introduction of the most important themes and prominent concepts in Goffman's analyses of modern everyday life.

The chapter is laid out in four parts. The first part presents the dramaturgical perspective which unfolds in *The Presentation of Self in Everyday Life*; the second part introduces Goffman's analyses of social interaction based on games theory; the third part outlines Goffman's use of Durkheim's concept of ritual; while the fourth part concerns a cornerstone theme in Goffman, that is, the production and maintenance of the social self. The chapter will thus present an introduction to Goffman's analysis of the social organization behind the face-to-face interactions of everyday life.

Everyday life as drama

The Presentation of Self in Everyday Life is probably Goffman's most famous book and also the book that introduces his unique, distancing analytical method. This is where Goffman expounds his so-called 'dramaturgical perspective' on people's face-to-face interactions. The book was first published in 1956 in a series of research publications from the University of Edinburgh. A revised edition was published in 1959. The differences between the two editions consist in part of minor cosmetic changes, but there are also more important differences in the views of the self and the dramaturgical metaphor itself. Whereas the first edition presents an optimistic view of the theatrical metaphor and an exposition of the self as a hidden manipulator, this interpretation is modified and nuanced in the 1959 edition, introducing the idea that we all, as interacting beings, present a multitude of selves, each self expressing certain aspects of us as persons (Manning 1991: 77). The book is notably based on experiences garnered from a field study in the Shetland Islands, which formed the empirical basis for Goffman's PhD dissertation, and as such it can be seen as a theoretical expansion of many of the concepts (impression management, performance, discrepant roles and so on) that were initially expounded in that thesis.

In his preface, Goffman characterizes the book as a sort of 'handbook' presenting a sociological perspective that may be used to study the social lives of human beings. The social life is defined as the type of mutual influencing that takes place between people who are in immediate physical vicinity of one another. The sociological perspective to which Goffman refers is the dramaturgical perspective; employing this, he wishes to seek out certain fundamental, dramaturgical principles. Using the dramaturgical principle, he sets out to analyse how a human being in 'ordinary work situations presents himself and his activity to others, the ways in which he guides and controls the impression they form of him, and the kinds of things he may and may not do while sustaining his performance before them' (Goffman 1959: 8).

In the introductory chapter, Goffman hypothesizes that when an individual is in the immediate physical presence of other people, they will unavoidably (and utilizing various techniques) seek to control the impression of themself gathered by the others present. Obversely, those present will seek to form an impression of who and what this particular individual is, and for that purpose, they may employ a number of different types of sign vehicles, each saying something about the person concerned. In this connection, Goffman introduces a distinction between the information we 'give' and the information we 'give off'. The first information concerns traditional communication, since it regards the verbal or non-verbal symbols we consciously use in order to convey a specific meaning. The other form of information consists of the signs and expressions emitted unwittingly and unconsciously by individuals, signs which the surroundings perceive as characteristic for that person (Goffman 1959: 14). In face-to-face interactions we are thus involved in two forms of communication and we reciprocally seek to learn about each other by noting the many bits of information imparted directly as well as through inference from appearances and non-intended information.

Thus, *The Presentation of Self in Everyday Life* is about performances and about how we all, through certain dramaturgical practices and by utilizing the props at hand, exert our influence on how the others present perceive or define the situation at hand. According to Goffman, an important part of this performance is a person's *front*, consisting of the attitudes, presence and 'expressions' which we – consciously or unconsciously – use in order to construct a certain image of who we are (Fine and Manning 2003: 46). Thus, as Goffman's analysis points out, a person's chances of being taken seriously – say, as a university teacher – depend not only on the clarity and logic of their presentation, but also eminently relies on that person's presence and comportment. With regard to the distinction between the signs and expression that are 'given' versus those 'given off' respectively, the university teacher's work consists in an effort to control the audience's access to and perception of information so that the signs consciously emitted will be interpreted by the audience as signs that are (unconsciously) revealed and therefore are an expression of that person's 'true' identity (Fine and Manning 2003: 46). For the university teacher, this may in actual fact be about convincing the audience that the voluminous tomes that they have laboriously stuffed with innumerable post-its and flagged annotations and meticulously arranged in a bewildering chaos on the desk and lectern are an expression of a completely natural and immediate part of their personality.

The core analytic unit in Goffman's *The Presentation of Self in Everyday Life* is the 'social encounter'; that is to say, the situation that arises when people interact with each other face-to-face. The crucial task for participants in interaction, in Goffman's view, is to express and maintain a 'definition of the situation'. With our actions and gestures, we unavoidably make suggestions as to how the situation at hand is to be defined and thus as to how others are to perceive and treat us. We engage in what Goffman calls 'impression management' whenever we seek to influence the perceptions of the situation gathered by the others. Usually, Goffman asserts, the various definitions of the situation proffered by the others present will to a certain degree be in accord. This is not to say that a total and complete consensus prevails, but that those present will subdue many of their most sincere emotions and present a view of the situation which the others are presumed to be able to accept. A certain form of 'modus vivendi' rules in which those present each make their own contribution to a common definition of the situation, which also comprises an agreement concerning this definition to avoid open conflict (Goffman 1959: 21). Hence the goal is to sustain a common definition of the situation, ensuring that the participants know what norms are in effect and thus how to behave accordingly.

A similar line of thought is found in *Frame Analysis* (1974), in which Goffman uses the 'frame' concept to describe the fact that we almost automatically interpret social situations within significance-providing frames, which assist us in understanding and defining what is going on as well as the identities of those taking part. For Goffman, frames constitute 'the principles of organization which govern events – at least social ones – and our subjective involvement in them' (Goffman 1974: 11). This means, among other things, that the way in which a given activity is framed determines how the individuals engaged in that event relate to the activity and to each other. Needless to say, a social event or situation which is framed as a 'serious and demanding, professional endeavor' will entail that participants relate to each other and to the situation in a specific way; a way which would be markedly different if the activity were to be framed as 'entertainment' or 'play'. In other words, frames contribute to defining situations and thus help the participants determine which rules apply in this particular context.

As we may surmise, the definitions of situation contain a moral component in the sense that individuals have a morally founded right to expect to be treated according to the social markers they present, implicitly or explicitly. At the same time, as interacting actors we are also under an obligation to really be who we pretend to be:

> When an individual projects a definition of the situation and thereby makes an implicit or explicit claim to be a person of a particular kind, he automatically exerts a moral demand upon the others, obliging them to value and treat him in the manner that persons of his kind have a right to expect.
> (Goffman 1959: 24)

With the dramaturgical framework outlined in *The Presentation of Self in Everyday Life*, Goffman wishes to analyse how individuals cooperate in an effort to sustain definitions of situations that preserve the 'faces' of those participating, thus ensuring that they each get what they deserve. In this context it should be mentioned that Goffman's concept of 'face' differs from the conventional use of the term. An individual's face, in Goffman's terminology, is not only a question of physiognomy, but is also emphatically a social and emotional construct; the concept thus comprises the image we conjure up of ourselves and which others (usually) help us to maintain. Among other things, the book describes the preventive measures taken in order to avoid embarrassing breakdowns; the *defensive practices* employed to protect one's own definitions of the situation and face and the *protective practices* used to save other people's definitions and faces; as well as the dramaturgical problems encountered by people when the actors of daily life engage in their craft in the presence of others (Goffman 1959: 24–6).

The dramaturgical model of the face-to-face interactions of everyday life is unfolded in *The Presentation of Self in Everyday Life* through six chapters dealing with, in turn, performances, teams, regions and region behaviour, discrepant roles, communication out of character and the art of impression management. A performance is about making an impression on those present and notably about asserting – to ourselves and to the others – that we are who we profess to be. An individual's facade will help them to stage the specific performance; which is to say that a person's expressive equipment (clothes, gender, position, and so on) act as that person's auxiliary tools in expressing their message.

Another component of a performance is the 'idealization' or the fact that, as a performer, we are prone to give the audience an impression superior to what reality will verify. Goffman illustrates this concept with tales of domestic performances in Scotland, where 'the average laird and his family lived far more frugally in the ordinary way than they did when they were entertaining visitors'. This includes situations where dinner served by five or six servants and all the adherent pomp and circumstance consisted of nothing but oatmeal and pickled herring in different guises (Goffman 1959: 47).

'Teams', or perhaps rather 'teamwork', is another dramaturgical principle; with this, Goffman is referring to the fact that performances are not always rendered by individuals, but sometimes by several people together. According to Goffman (1959: 85), a team is 'any set of individuals who cooperate in staging a single routine'. The staff at a psychiatric hospital ward, like the one studied by Goffman in *Asylums* (1961a), may be thought of as a team cooperating to sustain what Goffman calls the 'medical-service definition of the situation', which involves the idea of so-called 'rational, empirical treatment'.

Under the concept of 'regions', Goffman presents his renowned distinction between the 'scene' or the *front region* and the *back region*. These concepts are often also referred to as *frontstage* and *backstage*, respectively. The front region is the area where the specific performance takes place and which is placed before an audience. Here, the performers play out their roles and adjust their performances according to the prevailing norms. The back region is the area to which the performer can withdraw; providing the opportunity to relax, rehearse and recharge.

Particularly interesting situations are the transitions from the front region to the back region. By studying these transitions you will be able to detect 'a wonderful putting on and taking off of character' (Goffman 1959: 123). A good example is provided by George Orwell who describes how waiters change character by moving from the hotel kitchen to the dinning room: 'As he passes the door, a sudden change comes over him. The set of his shoulders alters; all the dirt and hurry irritation have dropped off in an instant. He glides over the carpet, with a solemn priest-like air' (Goffman 1959: 23).

'Discrepant roles' are about how certain persons may 'learn about the secrets of the team' and therefore may constitute 'threats to their privileged position' (Goffman 1959: 143). Gumshoes, snitches or field researchers 'under cover' are all immersed in discrepant roles and constitute a potential risk for the entire team because it is no longer in full control of its secrets.

'Communication out of character' refers to those parts of the participants' expressions that will often contradict and compromise the performance of the moment because they are alien to it. Goffman uses this term to describe the fact that the performance of the moment does not constitute the only reality of the team members. They may, for instance, step aside from this reality and malign the audience (*treatment of the absent*) or make use of secret and implied communication (*team collusion*) even as the official performance unfolds.

With the final concept, 'impression management', Goffman wishes to describe the control over impressions made, which is necessary during the interaction sequence in order to avoid a breakdown of a situation or embarrassing episodes. This, among other things, refers to dramaturgical loyalty, dramaturgical discipline and dramaturgical thoughtfulness. 'Impression management' signifies how players – through their utterances, body language, attire, and so on – seek to gain control of the impression gathered by the audience; but also intimates the collaboration expected on the part of the audience, say, by ignoring or forgetting about a performer's slips, contradictions and so on.

Thus, the picture of the social interactions of everyday life established in *The Presentation of Self in Everyday Life* is a picture of staged negotiations or exchanges. As performers, we must offer something that everybody else will appreciate or reward. In other words, our presentations of self (and thus our identity efforts) have to be adapted to the expectations of the audience being present at any given time. Different situations have different adherent audiences and thus different expectations, which is why the images presented by us are constantly adapted to the social situations we take part in. Thus, in his analysis in *The Presentation of Self in Everyday Life*, Goffman demonstrates how the social interactions of everyday life should not only be construed as a game of masks where we deliberately seek to hoodwink each other, but also as a functional process where individuality and social order are united in an endless process of dramatization (Münch 1986: 53).

Everyday life as a strategic game

As is evident, Goffman's *The Presentation of Self in Everyday Life* is devoted to how, in the interactions of everyday life, we process information about ourselves and others and how we play roles and present ourselves in front of each other. Influenced by Thomas Schelling (b. 1921), a game theoretician, Goffman in his later writings introduced what is best described as a game-theoretical perspective on the face-to-face interactions of everyday life. This perspective is especially evident in the publications *Encounters* (1961b), *Strategic Interaction* (1970) and finally in the extended essay 'Where the action is' from *Interaction Ritual* (1967).

The first essay in *Strategic Interaction* deals with what Goffman calls 'expression games'. With this concept, Goffman refers to the situations in which we reciprocally seek to decode and manipulate the information about ourselves available in that situation. As participants in such 'expression games', we are, says Goffman, a kind of agents of everyday life:

> In every social situation we can find a sense in which one participant will be an observer with something to gain from assessing expressions, and another will be a subject with something to gain from manipulating this process. A single structure of contingencies can be found in this regard which renders agents a little like us all and all of us a little like agents.
>
> (Goffman 1970: 81)

In the second essay, entitled 'Strategic interaction', Goffman is seemingly not as interested in how we reveal, expose or manipulate information, but more concerned with how we strategically plan and execute our actions in the most rational manner (Jacobsen and Kristiansen 2002: 107). Here he seeks to identify the different aspects that the strategic player must take into consideration when he or she wants to plan actions in the most rational way, involving the situational counterpart and the situation itself. In this context, that means in the way leading to the highest degree of personal gain (recognition). Below is a description of the most important of these strategic aspects:

- *The other's moves*: here, the objective is to analyse the counterpart's potential motives and possible alternate moves.
- *The operational code*: that is, the counterpart's way of playing the game; his or her style of playing and goals.
- *The opponent's resolve*: meaning an assessment of the counterpart's willpower and ability to continue the game despite personal costs.
- *The other's information state*: the knowledge that the counterpart possesses. Any potential move must be built up around the counterpart's thoughts/knowledge.
- *The opponent's resources*: it is important to know about the possible aids which the counterpart (and the actor him/herself) have at their disposal when making your next move.

Phrased differently, the individual player must take several things into consideration when planning and executing the most rational actions. The player must make the necessary calculations concerning the other players in the game and, based on these calculations, must make the requisite moves. However, the characteristic feature of this game is that while player A tries to see through player B's motives, intentions, resources and stockpile of information, player B is all the while simultaneously attempting to discern A's motives, intentions, and so on (Jacobsen and Kristiansen 2002: 108). Based on this, Goffman claims that strategic interaction occurs when persons:

> find themselves in a well-structured situation of mutual impingement where each party must make a move and where every possible move carries fateful implications for all of the parties. In this situation, each player must influence his own decision by his knowing that the other players are likely to try to dope out his decision in advance .... An exchange of moves made on the basis of this kind of orientation to self and others can be called strategic interaction.
>
> (Goffman 1970: 100–1)

In other words, as participants in the game we are all at the mercy of the same game based on our *mutual assessment*. This ongoing surveillance is reciprocal, and thus the power being exerted in people's interaction is in a certain sense democratic, since the surveillance is a two-way street, so to speak. Goffman stresses that we enter into a type of shared destiny during everyday interactions in which our moves entail consequences not only for ourselves, but for the other players as well. Our ability to act rationally, and thus strategically maximize our own gains, pointedly depends on our ability to assess and predict the thoughts and actions of the other persons involved (Jacobsen and Kristiansen 2002: 109). But, as George Herbert Mead (1863–1931) has said, strategic interaction also comprises gaining influence on the situation by putting 'ourselves in the others' place' and making use of this knowledge in planning our own moves.

In his rather lengthy essay, 'Where the action is', Goffman analyses the social interactions of human beings in light of the game metaphor. His point of departure is the concept of *action*, which in this context refers to the often problematic chance- or risk-involving activities initiated for the sake of entertainment or excitement. Goffman's concept of action refers to those moments where people, just like the gambler in the casino, throw themselves into the game, place their bets and reap their rewards or suffer their losses. Although modern everyday life does not present the same obvious physical elements of danger or risk as in earlier, pre-civilized ages, this life is not, in Goffman's view, totally devoid of risk. Human encounters and social situations may be momentous and dangerous games in the sense that we may both win (praise, recognition or dignity) and lose (become embarrassed, lose face or composure).

Hence Goffman is not interested in the situations, activities and contexts which directly and quite patently appeal to the human thirst for excitement and taking risks, such as the aforementioned casino, race tracks, parachuting, mountaineering, and so on. Rather, his interest lies in the action revolving around human nature or the human ability to display self-control and dignity, often in the face of stress and momentous 'fatal' situations. As Goffman sees it, our studies of situations of everyday interaction can lead us to pinpoint the so-called *character contests*; that is, the little social games, battles or disputes which we now and then 'fight out' with each other and which are about demonstrating self-control and a strong character at the other's expense. Everyday life provides many opportunities for fighting such battles:

> Whenever individuals ask for or give excuses, proffer or receive compliments, slight another or are slighted, a contest of self-control can result. Similarly, the tacit little flirtations occurring between friends and between strangers produce a contest of unavailability.
>
> (Goffman 1967: 240)

Thus, the character contest is Goffman's term for situations where we, as a result of modern life's lack of palpable danger and excitement, embark on risk-laden behaviour in relation to other people for the purpose of adding value to our own character. Some people engage in this type of behaviour more than others; some will indefatigably burst into heated remonstrations in the face of all their potential character-related losses and winnings. Yet, if you manage to maintain a clear head and carry yourself with a certain dignity, chances are you may win something; needless to say, if you lose composure or display signs of weakness, the risk of losing is imminent.

It should also be mentioned that when Goffman speaks of strategic interaction and uses the game metaphor in relation to social life (Goffman 1970: 113–14), he is well aware that empirical reality rarely presents us with such 'pure games'. Everyday games play out within the framework of a panoply of limiting as well as opportunity-laden social norms; in 'Where the action is', Goffman also mentions how character contests will only surface periodically, because people in everyday life fundamentally desire to sustain peace and ritual order.

A crucial point made by Goffman is that it is the definition of situation that orchestrates how you are expected to comport yourself; and that this definition thus has a moral component in the sense that those participating have a right to be appreciated according to the social indicators they presume to possess. In this way, there is an implicit coercion, often with a moral slant, involved in the situation. It is the definition of situation that decides how we are to act, which roles we should play and what demeanour we should assume. So while we constantly make strategic deliberations in focused interactions, and while we sometimes act in a calculating manner in order to gain 'character winnings', and while there may well be an ongoing mutual surveillance or spying, all these efforts are made within a framework involving certain moral norms. This naturally leads us to another central theme in Goffman's writings, the question of the normative and moral regulation of the interactions of everyday life.

Interaction rituals of everyday life

The American sociology professor and Goffman interpreter Randall Collins (1986, 1988, 1996) singles out Goffman's authorship as a consistent Durkheimian sociology; justifying his claim by citing Goffman's recurrent interest in norms and in what you might call the moral order of social interaction. Goffman's inspiration from Durkheim is seen as early as in his PhD dissertation where he partly blames Max Weber and George Herbert Mead for the neglectful treatment sociology has afforded to the ritual aspects of interaction:

> The ritual model for interaction has been poorly treated in the literature, perhaps because of the stress given be G. H. Mead and by Weber to the fact that a social relationship, and hence social interaction, was a product of *two* persons taking *each other*'s actions into consideration in pursuing their own action. This stress seems to have given an instrumental flavour to our thinking about the kinds of consideration we show in regard to others: the implication is that we *take into consideration* the actions of others (the better to achieve our personal ends, whatever these may be) and not so much that we *give consideration to others*. By 'consideration' we have come to mean calculation, not considerateness.
>
> (Goffman 1953: 103)

Durkheim's sociology of religion gives Goffman the theoretical bricks with which to construct a perspective on social interaction that stresses the ritual solicitude and respect we display daily towards one another as 'sacred objects'. This line of thinking can also be found in *The Presentation of Self in Everyday Life,* and is expressed in its clearest and most explicit form in Goffman's analyses of the so-called interaction rituals of everyday life (Goffman 1967). In his essay 'On face work', Goffman states the following reasons for his use of the concept of ritual:

> I use the term *ritual* because I am dealing with acts through whose symbolic component the actor shows how worthy he is of respect or how worthy he feels others are of it .... One's face, then, is a sacred thing, and the expressive order required to sustain it is therefore a ritual one.
>
> (Goffman 1967: 19)

Goffman's interaction rituals are to be construed as a form of rules or codes applying to everyday life, manifesting themselves in stereotypical behavioural sequences and patterns of speech. Among the ways in which they express themselves are through the small and seemingly insignificant courtesies that we daily extend to each other. Goffman (1967: 47) expands further on Durkheim's conception of the sanctity of the soul, and claims that the faces of modern individuals have a kind of sacred character. This sanctity must be protected, affirmed and maintained; we do this, Goffman says, by observing certain, apparently insignificant, interaction rituals.

Thus, by using the concept of ritual, Goffman indicates that many of the interactions of everyday life are indeed symbolic actions, the purpose of which are to endorse our faces and social reality. By treating each other with respect and dignity, by turning away our attention whenever others are about to lose face, in short, by engaging in face work we are actually protecting each other and the social reality involving us (Jacobsen and Kristiansen 2002: 37). It is the observance of this ritual (co)operation, these many and varied interaction rituals, that makes Goffman assert that the individual, in modern society, has taken the place of the gods. As Goffman sees it, many gods have disappeared, 'but the individual himself stubbornly remains as a deity of considerable importance' (Goffman 1967: 95). However, as Norwegian sociologist Dag Album (1996: 133) has pointed out, it is not people's uniqueness or individuality that is celebrated in the interaction rituals of everyday life. Rather, what is venerated is their commonality, that which they have in common with everybody else; and it is through his analysis of the microscopic celebrations of commonality in everyday life that Goffman demonstrates how society's social order and structures are continually being reproduced.

Hence among Goffman's notable achievements is to have focused our attention on the significant, yet often unnoticed, *rituals* of everyday interaction. He demonstrated how, on the micro-level, these rituals are part and parcel of what ensures that we have decent intercourse with each other; and how, on a more global level, they form part of the 'glue' maintaining cohesion in society at large. The interaction rituals that interest Goffman do not express themselves as explicit and verbalized injunctions or prohibitions, but come in the form of more or less unpremeditated ways of treating one another. When we meet an acquaintance in the street, we greet that person with a gesture or our voice and we may enquire as to how things are going. On the other hand, when meeting strangers, we glance downwards or elsewhere before getting too close so as not to invade that individual's personal space.

Goffman has a poignant description of this kind of courteous civility or 'civil inattention' in *Behaviour in Public Places*:

> What seems to be involved is that one gives to another enough visual notice to demonstrate that one appreciates that the other is present (and that one

> admits openly to having seen him), while at the next moment withdrawing one's attention from him so as to express that he does not constitute a target of special curiosity or design. In performing this courtesy the eyes of the looker may pass over the eyes of the other, but no 'recognition' is typically allowed. When the courtesy is performed between two persons passing on the street, civil inattention may take the special form of eyeing the other up to approximately eight feet, during which time sides of the street are apportioned by gesture, and then casting the eyes down as the other passes – a kind of dimming of lights.
>
> (Goffman 1963a: 84)

According to Goffman, this interaction ritual may be the most overlooked, yet it is nonetheless a ritual constantly regulating the social interaction of human beings (1963a: 84). As the example indicates, interaction rituals are to a large extent directed at showing the other person respect. The goal is to avoid intrusion and thus an invasion of the others' right to a private life. Differently put, the rituals ensure protection for the individual, but they are also part of what regulates the way we enter into relations with one another. In this context, Goffman speaks about *opening moves* and *clearance signs*; thereby referring to the different ways (typically by glances) we ask for contact and signal that we are available to each other.

There are also rituals hinging upon the respect with which we should introduce ourselves. Because it is not enough to display respect for others, in order to receive the necessary recognition and acceptance from others, you must also be able to comport yourself in a respectful manner. In Goffman's analysis, we are interconnected through the interaction rituals whereby we respect, sustain and acknowledge the images or faces that we mutually present to one another. As has been mentioned, the rituals primarily involve protecting and caring for each other's faces; on a more general level, the ritual obligations serve to maintain a moral order.

Another among Goffman's main achievements springs from his endeavour to integrate the question of feelings into microsociological theory. For Goffman does not confine himself to enumerating specific behavioural codes, strategies and processes; he is also interested in people's feelings as a crucial interaction component. Some, including Swedish social psychologist Thomas Johansson (1999: 89), maintain that Goffman's analysis of the ritualization of everyday life exposes the emotional handling or 'emotionology' that helps individuals cope with the unpredictable nature of modernity. Much of this endeavour revolves around protection – protecting yourself, each other and thus in a wider sense the social order – against threats and collapse.

In his essay 'Embarrassment and social organization', Goffman (1967) analyses how social interaction eminently strives to avoid the embarrassment that arises whenever an individual's self is threatened or discredited. In interaction situations, the individual is expected to project a self suitable for the occasion into the interaction though the 'expressive implications of his stream of conduct'. More or less consciously, the individual will thus project a self into social situations, and the other players' contribution to that social situation is, according to Goffman, attuned to and composed of the demands thus projected.

Needless to say, each individual wants to avoid to experience or express embarrassment; consequently, most people seek to avoid situations that threaten their own projected self as well as the self projected by the other players. This may be achieved by projecting a relatively 'humble' self into the interaction and not overplaying your hand, so to speak. It may also be done by deliberately charting a course skirting potentially dangerous situations; and, finally, by showing consideration or tactful tolerance towards others. However, situations may arise where certain events raise serious doubts as to the claims an individual has put forwards concerning his or her self. The situation is disrupted because the presuppositions on which it rested are seemingly no longer valid. These individuals therefore feel shame or embarrassment. As Goffman sees it, such feelings not only perturb the person whose self has been threatened. Often the confidence in a person who pretends to be tactful but actually causes the other person to lose face is weakened far more than trust in the person who is at first discredited.

People may also become embarrassed and flustered when persons who do not usually interact informally suddenly find themselves in situations where the option of informal discussion cannot be ignored. When the cleaning lady and the CEO meet in the elevator, they may experience an awkward moment because, in adapting to this moment's demands, they have to, in a manner of speaking, abandon their usual roles. They may attempt to meet each other in an informal chat, but both may also feel uneasy at the situation because they have to sacrifice their roles, so to speak. In this, Goffman sees the social function of embarrassment; according to him it is not an irrational impulse, but forms part of a group of actions that may be spontaneous, but are no less mandatory than the other, conscious acts which contribute to maintaining the social structure.

Had the CEO in the elevator encounter insisted on his superior right to recognition – adhering to the principle that the nature of the work done determines a person's status – and had the cleaning lady on her part demanded an equal status according to the principle that belonging to the firm entitles you to such equal treatment, then the conflict between two opposite social principles of organization would have been expressed openly in the situation. But because both parties become embarrassed and thus temporarily sacrifice themselves, Goffman notes that 'only' they and the ongoing social encounter are compromised. Thus, the individuals' embarrassment serves a function: In the example mentioned, it contributes towards maintaining or protecting the social structure, since it prevents that otherwise inevitable clashes between the organizational principles of different systems are expressed too manifestly in the social encounter. As Goffman comments at the end of his essay: 'Social structure gains elasticity; the individual merely loses composure' (1967: 112).

Besides describing and analysing the microscopic interaction rituals and emotionology of everyday life, Goffman also, as a kind of 'microsociological Linné' (Collins 1988: 43), develops an array of conceptual classifications and taxonomies. From Durkheim, Goffman (1967: 73) adapts the fundamental differentiation between positive and negative rituals. According to Durkheim, positive rituals are a kind of mandatory rules prescribing preferred modes of behaviour, while the negative rituals are overt prohibitions or taboos. Goffman rephrases these concepts into *presentational rituals* which 'encompass acts through which the individual makes specific attestations to recipients concerning how he regards them and how he will treat them in the on-coming interaction' (1967: 71). According to Goffman (1971), one variety of the positive rituals are the so-called *supportive interchanges*, that is, the little actions and behavioural patterns with which we display respect and courtesy towards others and which primarily revolve around preventing interactional crises or 'ritual imbalance'. Goffman calls the negative rituals *avoidance rituals* and they primarily concern keeping others at a distance and avoiding violation of what Simmel has called people's 'ideal sphere' (Goffman 1967: 62). The people in the above-mentioned example are thus participants in an avoidance ritual aimed at mutually respecting each other's ideal sphere.

Of course, interactions in everyday life do not unfold without breakdowns, awkwardness, embarrassment, violations and crises. Everyday life presents us with situations where individual faces are violated to a degree making it awkward bordering on unbearable for the individual violated as well as for the other participants. These situations call for what Goffman has labelled 'remedial interchanges'. Remedial interchanges are sequences of behaviour or procedures that help people to repossess lost faces and thus re-establish the situation as a whole. The person responsible for the violation or crisis may be confronted with negative sanctions explicitly and directly. Situations may also arise where the gravity of the violation is not greater than that the situation can be repaired through almost imperceptibly directing the common attention focus of all participants in other directions. If the violation cannot be ignored, the general rule is that the violator is given the chance to make good on the damage. Through remedial rituals, he or she will offer compensation to the violated party as well as to the overall situation. This may be through an explicit and public apology. In doing so, not only is the violated party's face and the overall situation provided with compensation and repaired; the violator, through his or her violation, has often also violated him- or herself, and if the apology is recognized and accepted, this also restores his or her own self.

As mentioned, Goffman was particularly concerned with the positive, motivational and supportive rituals. To him, the social interactions of everyday life are not an ongoing, comforting and unproblematic process that participants may enter into risk-free. A number of potential threats and dangers lurk in these social interactions of everyday life and they demand constant attention (see Burns 1992: 26). The main part of the interaction rituals, that Goffman devotes his attention to, concerns how this fragile order unremittingly and often by insensible degrees has to be repaired and maintained.

The interaction rituals contribute towards facilitating the interaction in different ways. As has been mentioned, there are rituals that contribute to soliciting togetherness and semaphore availability (Goffman 1963a, 1971); similarly, there are rituals for 'closure'; there are rituals for repairing broken-down situations (Goffman 1971) and there are conversation-regulating rituals (Goffman 1981). You may say, as does Dag Album (1996: 133ff), that Goffman with his ritual metaphor, and thus his focus on the everyday ceremonials, demonstrates how in everyday social encounters, we make a certain sacrifice or pay a particular price for ensuring the problem-free proceedings of that encounter and interaction. This sacrifice or price is our humble and decent behaviour, our display of a respectable and comprehensible personality. In return for making this sacrifice, we may expect a certain amount of security and social recognition.

Goffman's analysis of the ritualized unfolding of our face-to-face interactions should be viewed in a context that also involves his efforts to sketch the outline of a so-called 'interaction order'. As has been mentioned, in his inaugural lecture as President of the American Sociological Association, which he – since he was at an advanced stage of cancer – never had the opportunity to deliver, he tried to define the interaction order as an order with its own processes and rules. Here, rituals play a decisive role because in Goffman's view (1983a), they are the ones ensuring, maintaining and repairing the necessary flow of the interactions. The rituals help the interacting actors to remain constantly anchored in a normative structure and thus safeguard that we as individuals are not adrift as isolated islands, but that we interact with each other in a decent and civilized manner.

The performed self

Goffman's analysis of role-playing and the interaction rituals of everyday life are closely intertwined with another key theme in his authorship, namely the question of the self. As mentioned, Goffman in *The Presentation of Self in Everyday Life* analyses how we, through our quotidian performances for each other, seek to create a certain impression of ourselves in our surroundings. Our daily role-playing is an imperceptible and not always conscious process, focused on creating and maintaining identities and images of ourselves and each other, whereby together we simultaneously sustain a type of social order. Goffman's self is a social and permutable factor, the object of constant negotiations between the owner of the self and the social audience. Goffman is interested in the sociological self and pointedly in the social self; not the self perceived as the individual's inner experience of this self. Perhaps one may even say that Goffman, with the analyses offered in *The Presentation of Self in Everyday Life* and, not least, in the essay on 'role distance' (Goffman 1961b), undermines perceptions of the self as being identical with an underlying 'personality'.

This decidedly sociological and situational perspective finds its expression, among other places, in his analyses of the stage arrangements, the expressive equipment and the relationship between the performer and the social audience. The self is the result, so to speak, of the negotiating process unfolding between a performer presenting a face and an audience receiving and reacting to this presentation of self. The audience may reject or accept this presentation of self proposed by the performer; the crucial point here is that the Goffmanian self is the *product* of these seemingly insignificant exchanges. This being said, it should at the same time be emphasized that Goffman distances himself from a thoroughly symbolic interactionist view of the self in his understanding of the presentations of self proffered by individuals, attaching more importance to the demands of the situation at hand than to the symbolic processes of communication and interpretation (Miller 1982: 124). Towards the end of *The Presentation of Self in Everyday Life*, Goffman expresses his view of the social self quite clearly:

> While this image is entertained *concerning* the individual, so that a self is imputed to him, this self itself does not derive from its possessor, but from the whole scene of his action, being generated by that attribute of local events which renders them interpretable by witnesses. A correctly staged and performed scene leads the audience to impute a self to a performed character, but this imputation – this self – is a *product* of a scene that comes off, and not a *cause* of it. The self, then, as performed character, is not an organic thing that has a specific location, whose fundamental fate is to be born, to mature and to die; it is a dramatic effect arising diffusely from a scene that is presented, and the characteristic issue, the crucial concern, is whether it will be credited or discredited.
>
> (Goffman 1959: 244–5)

Goffman thus stresses that analyses of the self should not focus on its proprietor. He specifically states that the self's proprietor is 'the peg on which something of collaborative manufacture will be hung for a time' (1959: 245). By this, Goffman is alluding to the fact that the self is produced or emerges as part of a scene performed by a team; a team making use of the available props and whose performance is interpreted and accepted by an audience. Thus, according to Goffman's analysis, the self of a person should not be understood as a driving force behind an individual's activities and behaviour. We do not behave as we do because we *have* a certain self. The self, as stated by Goffman above, should be seen as a 'dramatic effect'; that is, as something which is created by a person's performance and collaboration with others.

As is evident, the self is social because it is inextricably connected to social arrangements expressing themselves with the aid of socially constructed 'tools', and it is dependent upon an interpreting audience. Moreover, it can be surmised that Goffman differentiates between the individual as a *performer* and the individual as a *character* (Goffman 1959: 244ff). This differentiation reflects the implicit and earlier mentioned duality in Goffman's conception of the self, meaning that the self on the one hand should be understood as a product of a specific scene, while on the other hand the self should be seen as an impression fabricating performer bent on staging, alone or together with a team, a particular performance. In Goffman's view, the incessant role-playing of everyday life receives its particular character due to the twin nature the self has as performer and as character.

Thus, in *The Presentation of Self in Everyday Life*, Goffman demonstrates how people as active performers and partially as manipulative actors go about staging their role-playing and trying to embody the socially produced and socially situated roles in ways forming the basis of a unique identity of self. In the essay entitled 'Role distance' (1961b), Goffman pursues a similar line of thought. Here he analyses how we, as interacting actors, may deal differently with the socially situated roles we accept or are placed in; and how through the way we choose to deal with these roles, we may convey a certain self to the social surroundings. We may engage in the role, be completely devoured by or immersed in the role or we may distance ourselves from it. By relating to the roles, we actively try to relate to the self which they imply.

In certain contexts, the person will accept the role and be completely immersed in it, like the perfect waiter or three-to-four-year-old children on a merry-go-round. In other situations, we may try to distance ourselves from the role and from the socially situated self as well, in an effort to signal to the surroundings that we are in fact something else and more than what the social role would seem to imply. With his concept of 'role distance', Goffman thus refers to the actors' ability to drive a wedge in between themselves and the socially situated role; or rather, between themselves and the actual self that the role implies and which should be valid for everybody accepting it and acting it out. Thus, role distance is the prerequisite for both filling out and entering into social roles while at the same time expressing a unique personality (Goffman 1961b).

Goffman's social or interactional self is seen by several authors (including Schwalbe 1993; Tseëlon 1992) as a precursor for the postmodern idea of the self. This is, of course, because Goffman concerns himself with the images of self produced in social situations and interactions and not with a permanent, continuous and underlying factor. The Goffmanian self is, like in the postmodern turn, decentred and thus only exists as a panoply of socially situated roles, albeit with an added personal touch. However, this is not to say that Goffman rejects any idea of an inner self having a more stable nature. In *Stigma* (Goffman 1963b: 129ff), he actually uses the concept 'ego identity'. But as a sociologist, his overall interest lies in understanding the connection between the self and the social surroundings; thus, when he introduces the concept of 'ego identity', it is primarily in order to discuss how the identities of stigmatized individuals are influenced by relations to and influences from the social surroundings.

Conclusion

As is evident from the above, you will find in Erving Goffman a roster of concepts and perspectives for understanding many of everyday life's social interactions and occurrences, which at first sight seem insignificant and trivial. He points our attention to the existence of a particular order of interaction characterized by rules and dynamics entirely its own, loosely linked to society's macrostructures. Thus, Goffman places himself at the centre of everyday life sociology, which can generally be said to place an interest in people's brass-tacks social life alongside of, intertwined with or opposed to society's political, economic or cultural macrostructures (Kristiansen and Mortensen 2005).

Utilizing his metaphorical re-descriptions of the social interactions of everyday life, he reveals how much social interaction is about ensuring the maintenance and proceedings of social situations as such; and how everyday life is permeated by a social order sustained by microscopic rituals and dramatic techniques. Furthermore, Goffman points out how emotions, or rather the handling of emotions, play a crucial role for maintaining this order. One of the ways social situations differ from each other is according to the feelings that may be shown and how this display of emotions should take place; and with his analysis of the 'social organization of embarrassment' he demonstrates how the experience of embarrassment or awkwardness plays a part in asserting and protecting the social structure.

Goffman's analyses of everyday life are eminently about the situated self, about how the self is interconnected with the social dimension; or rather how the self is performed, threatened and affirmed in social situations. With his analyses, he demonstrates how the role-playing of everyday life is poignantly concerned with the construction and maintenance of a meaningful identity and how we all, through collaborative processes, sustain, adjust and repair each other's faces as well as the social encounters themselves. By applying a variety of metaphors (the theatre, the strategic game and the ritual) as a point of departure for his analyses, Goffman manages to demonstrate how staging, manipulation, trust and morals are interconnected components in the social interactions of modern everyday life.

If you can speak of a bona fide 'Goffman-effect' in sociology, you would have to distinguish between three different kinds of 'effects'. First, as has been pointed out by Anne Rawls (2003: 216), it is difficult to be a sociologist at all today without using some sort of Goffmanian thinking. Rawls here refers not least to Goffman's sociological understanding of the self. Second, it can be noted that Goffman's perspective and concepts are found in many empirical studies, not least in studies of everyday routines and places (see, for example, Birenbaum and Sagarin 1973). Goffman's acute sense of the significance inherent in the seemingly trite occurrences of everyday life has inspired researchers to study different types of human social situations and encounters, say, between clients and case workers (Berg Sørensen 1995), modes of interaction and interaction rituals between cancer patients in hospitals (Album 1996) or funeral ceremonies (Turner and Edgley 1976). In Denmark during the 1970s, Goffman was an important theoretical inspiration for different critical institutional studies (see Gregersen 1975), and in parts of the Danish 'Power report', Goffman's perspective and concepts also play an important part (Järvinen, Larsen and Mortensen 2002). Third, it should be highlighted that Goffman's sociology is crucial to several modern sociological syntheses of theory; for example, Anthony Giddens's (1984) theory of structuration and Jonathan H. Turner's (2002) integrated theory of social interaction.

Notes

1. English translation by Mark Hebsgaard.
2. The lecture was originally translated simultaneously from English into French by Belgian sociologist Yves Winkin.

Bibliography

Album, Dag (1996) *Nære fremmede: Patientkulturen i sykehus*. Otta: Tano.

Berg Sørensen, Torben (1995) *Den sociale samtale: Mellem klienter og sagsbehandlere*. Århus: Forlaget Gestus.

Birenbaum, Arnold and Edward Sagarin (1973) *People in Places: The Sociology of the Familiar.* London: Nelson.

Burns, Tom (1992) *Erving Goffman*. London: Routledge.

Chriss, James J. (2003) 'Goffman as a microfunctionalist', in A. Javier Treviño (ed.), *Goffman's Legacy*. Lanham, MA: Rowman & Littlefield.

Collins, Randall (1986) 'The passing of intellectual generations: reflections on the death of Goffman.' *Sociological Theory*, 4: 106–113.

Collins, Randall (1988) *Theoretical Sociology.* San Diego: Harcourt Brace.

Collins, Randall (1996) 'Theoretical continuities in Goffman's work', in Paul Drew and Anthony Wootton (eds), *Erving Goffman: Exploring the Interaction Order.* Cambridge: Polity Press.

Fine, Gary Alan and Philip Manning (2003) 'Erving Goffman', in George Ritzer (ed.), *The Blackwell Companion to Major Contemporary Social Theorists*. Oxford: Blackwell.

Giddens, Anthony (1984) *The Constitution of Society.* Cambridge: Polity Press.

Goffman, Erving (1953) *Communication Conduct in an Island Community.* PhD dissertation, Department of Sociology, University of Chicago.

Goffman, Erving (1959) *The Presentation of Self in Everyday Life*. Harmondsworth: Penguin.

Goffman, Erving (1961a) *Asylums: Essays on the Social Situation of Mental Patients and Other Inmates*. Harmondsworth: Penguin.

Goffman, Erving (1961b) *Encounters: Two Studies in the Sociology of Interaction*. Indianapolis: Bobbs-Merrill.

Goffman, Erving (1963a) *Behavior in Public Places: Notes on the Social Organization of Gatherings*. New York: Free Press.

Goffman, Erving (1963b) *Stigma: Notes on the Management of Spoiled Identity.* Harmondsworth: Penguin

Goffman, Erving (1967) *Interaction Ritual: Essays on Face-to-Face Behavior*. New York: Pantheon.

Goffman, Erving (1970) *Strategic Interaction*. Philadelphia: University of Pennsylvania Press.

Goffman, Erving (1971) *Relations in Public: Microstudies of the Public Order.* New York: Harper & Row.

Goffman, Eving (1974) *Frame Analysis: An Essay on the Organizaion of Experience*. Boston: Northeastern University Press.

Goffman, Erving (1981) *Forms of Talk*. Philadelphia: University of Pennsylvania Press.

Goffman, Erving (1983a) 'The interaction order.' *American Sociological Review*, 48: 1–17.

Goffman, Erving (1983b) 'Microsociologie et historie', in Philippe Fritsch (ed.), *Le Sens de L'ordinaire*. Paris: Editions du Centre National de la Recherche Scientifique.

Gregersen, Bo (ed.) (1975) *Om Goffman – 11 artikler*. Copenhagen: Hans Reitzels Forlag.

Hacking, Ian (2004) 'Between Michel Foucault and Erving Goffman: between discourse in the abstract and face-to-face interaction.' *Economy and Society*, 33: 277–302.

Jacobsen, Michael Hviid and Søren Kristiansen (2002) *Erving Goffman: Sociologien om det elementære livs sociale former*. Copenhagen: Hans Reitzels Forlag.

Järvinen, Margareta, Jørgen Elm Larsen and Nils Mortensen (eds) (2002) *Det magtfulde møde mellem system og klient*. Århus: Aarhus Universitetsforlag.

Johansson, Thomas (1999) *Socialpsykologi: Moderna teorier och perspektiv*. Lund: Studentlitteratur.

Kristiansen, Søren and Nils Mortensen (2005) 'Hverdagslivssociologi', in Anders Esmark, Carsten Bagge Laustsen and Niels Åkerstrøm Andersen (eds), *Socialkonstruktivistiske analysestrategier.* Roskilde: Roskilde Universitetsforlag.

Lanigan, Richard L. (1988) 'Is Erving Goffman a phenomenologist?' *Critical Studies in Mass Communication*, 5: 335–45.

Manning, Phil (1991) 'Drama as life: the significance of Goffman's changing use of the theatrical metaphor.' *Sociological Theory*, 9: 70–86.

Miller, Diane L. (1982) 'Ritual in the work of Durkheim and Goffman: the link between the micro and the macro.' *Humanity and Society*, 6: 122–34.

Münch, Richard (1986) 'The American creed in sociological theory: exchange, negotiated order, accommodated individualism and contingency.' *Sociological Theory*, 4: 1–60.

Rawls, Anne Warfield (2003) 'Orders of interaction and intelligibility: intersections between Goffman and Garfinkel by way of Durkheim', in A. Javier Trevino (ed.), *Goffman's Legacy.* Lanham, MA: Rowman & Littlefield.

Schwalbe, Michael L. (1993) 'Goffman against postmodernism: emotion and the reality of the self.' *Symbolic Interaction*, 16: 333–50.

Schwartz, Howard and Jerry Jacobs (1979) *Qualitative Sociology: A Method to the Madness.* New York: Free Press.

Tseëlon, Efrat (1992) 'Is the presented self sincere?.' *Theory, Culture and Society*, 9: 115–28.

Turner, Jonathan H. (2002) *Face to Face: Toward a Sociological Theory of Interpersonal Behavior.* Stanford, CA: Stanford University Press.

Turner, Ronny E. and Charles Edgley (1976) 'Death as theater: a dramaturgical analysis of the American funeral.' *Sociology and Social Research*, 60: 377–92.

Verhoeven, Jef C. (1993) 'An interview with Erving Goffman.' *Research on Language and Social Interaction*, 26: 317–48.

Zeitlin, Irving (1973) *Rethinking Sociology: A Critique of Contemporary Theory.* New York: Appleton-Century-Crofts/Meredith.

CHAPTER 9

Ethnomethodology

Respecifying the Problem of Social Order

STEPHEN HESTER

Introduction

'Ethnomethodology' is a discipline that is both within and alternate to the discipline of sociology. Its central focus is on a domain of phenomena that sociology failed to notice even as that domain was and remains the irremediable foundation of its very own inquiries. The actual term 'ethnomethodology' was coined by Harold Garfinkel (b. 1917) in the early 1950s to make reference to recognizably methodological concerns and aspects of jury deliberations that had been tape recorded (Garfinkel 1967, 1974; Hill and Crittenden 1968). Thus, jurors are concerned with such methodological matters as the adequacy of descriptions and accounts, the fairness of conclusions and decisions, the legality of decisions, the truth and falsity of accounts, what could be demonstrated and treated as evidence, what could be taken as fact or discounted as opinion, and so forth. By extrapolation, if not yet by empirical investigation, these methodological aspects of jury deliberations could apply to any social activity.

The wider origins of ethnomethodology lie in Garfinkel's engagement with the social theory of Talcott Parsons (1902–1979) and with the phenomenology of Edmund Husserl (1859–1938), Alfred Schutz (1899–1959) and Aron Gurwitsch (1901–1973). The conjunction of these specific and wider origins constituted the 'discovery' of a domain of social action and social order hitherto unnoticed by sociologists – the world of daily life as it is experienced and accomplished by members of society – and led to the opening up of this domain as a site for empirical research.

Since its beginnings in the 1950s and 1960s and its elaboration in the decades that followed, ethnomethodology has both retained the key thematics and commitments established in the initial pioneering studies of Garfinkel (1967), and at the same time, has diversified into a family of convergent yet distinctive strands. In this chapter I identify ethnomethodology's phenomena, describe the diversity of its programme, outline its analytic procedures and consider two exemplary classic studies in order to illustrate how ethnomethodology can assist us in understanding everyday life.

Ethnomethodology: respecifying the unnoticed

In making sense of ethnomethodology, it may be helpful to begin with the parts of the word itself. As the 'methodology' part suggests, 'ethnomethodology' involves the study of methods. As far as the 'ethno' part is concerned, the meaning here is drawn from the so-called 'ethno' disciplines, such as ethno-botany, ethno-musicology, ethno-economy and so on, wherein investigations into a variety of people's knowledge systems and cultural practices (botanical, musical, economic, and so on) were undertaken, much as anthropologists and ethnographers had studied foreign cultures and societies.

So 'ethno' refers to the people who are members of some culture or society, where membership is conceived in terms of sharing a common culture, a mastery of a shared language, a common collection of practices and a 'common-sense knowledge' used in doing things and in making sense of things. However, where many of these ethno-inquiries had then made comparisons between such indigenous knowledge and practice and that of 'Western' rationality, sometimes not without aspersions of inferiority or primitivism, ethnomethodology is entirely indifferent to any such possible rankings of knowledge and practice. Whatever the 'ethno' methods are that people use, for whatever activities, they are interesting in their own right, they require understanding 'from within' the cultural practices that exhibit their use and are not to be evaluated in terms of their shortcomings compared with other methods that might be deployed.

There remains, of course, the question of just what 'methods' are being talked about here. The methods are those used to do 'concrete', that is to say specific ordinary, activities such as having a conversation, reading the newspaper, having a family dinner, teaching a school or university class, singing in a choir, playing in a band, finding a parking space, discovering a new object in outer space; the list is as endless as the activities that human beings engage in. Most humans can do at least some of these and, of course, the constituent activities of which these are composed, but fewer know how to play music in a band or be a competent astronomer. Whether they are simple or complex, the point is, however, that they have to be accomplished and such accomplishment involves the use of methods of one sort or another. Without them, there would be no social activities, no 'society' for sociologists or anyone else to study.

Even so, it may be asked, are there not already available books on how to do (at least some of) these things in the library or bookstore? Is it not the case that if a person wants to find out more about learning to play music, establish a productive vegetable garden or acquire a reputation as a charming and polite host or hostess of dinner parties, then all they have to do is consult an appropriate instruction manual? Is it not the case that many, perhaps all, of the so-called 'professions' have such manuals to instruct the novice in the ways and means of their passage to professional qualification? Furthermore, is it not also the case that when it comes to the more complex tasks involved in medicine, scientific research, writing English literature, learning a foreign language and so on, where matters are not reducible to a manual, there are courses of guided instruction to assist the neophyte in acquiring the requisite skills? Clearly, whether the task is simple or complex, the answer is in the affirmative, and if the descriptions of methods contained in these various 'literatures' were sufficient for the task of understanding just how these activities are done, then ethnomethodology would arguably be redundant before it had even begun its inquiries. The plain fact, of course, is that much more can be said about how these things are done than is contained in training manuals, assembly instructions, procedural guidelines, recipes, musical scores, health and safety rules, building regulations and other types of lay and professional instruction, and it is in this 'much more' that ethnomethodology is interested. What, then, does this 'much more' consist of?

The 'much more' of interest to ethnomethodology is what remains unnoticed, taken for granted and yet relied upon not only in the kinds of instructional literatures just mentioned but also in the literature of ethnomethodology's 'home discipline' of sociology itself. For the former literatures, a vast amount of knowledge and a huge range of methodical competences are presupposed in relation to such activities as 'following an instruction', 'singing in tune', 'improvising', 'reading', 'understanding the meaning of regulations', 'measuring a distance', 'aligning objects', 'interpreting machine read-outs', and 'talking about the results'.

Anyone who has used, for example, furniture assembly diagrams can acknowledge, with little reflection, the 'effort' (especially first time through) that is required to make sense of the arrows, representations of objects and bits of equipment and the meanings of the words used in the instruction leaflet. Likewise, they will know that much of what is needed to do the task of assembly is not actually mentioned; the reader is expected to provide this competence and knowledge – ethno-methods – in and through which the instructions can be understood and applied to the materials at hand. These actual ways of 'translating' the instructions into real-time practical action are left unexplicated by the manual, even as they are relied upon as common-sense everyday practical expertise in reading, understanding and applying the text's instructions. What is 'much more' than manuals of instruction, then, is what is required and used to make the instructions actually happen as furniture assembly, as music (see Hester and Francis 2007), as a classroom lesson, as doing a chemistry experiment and so forth; it is the knowledge that people use to make sense of instructions in the first place and then in applying them to the task and in the circumstances at hand.

As ethnomethodological investigations into this domain of unnoticed methodological expertise show, there is a vast amount of taken-for-granted knowledge and practical know-how that the members of society make use of in conducting their everyday practical affairs. The task, for ethnomethodology, is to describe in detail just what is involved, just what is used, in any particular case, to make 'following instructions' happen. However, this is not to say that ethnomethodology pursues detail for its own sake and merely offers a supplementary literature to instruction manuals. There are deeper, more foundational reasons for its focus on the taken for granted, the unnoticed and the presupposed than that it so happens that these methodical matters are left out of instructional literatures. This, then, brings us to the sociological literature, and it is to ethnomethodology's relationship to sociology that the discussion will now turn.

Ethnomethodology and sociology

There are at least two 'deeper' reasons for ethnomethodology's interest in taken-for-granted knowledge and methodical practice. The first of these is that such knowledge and practice is foundational; it is presupposed not only in ordinary instructional literatures but also by sociology itself. From its very beginnings, sociology attempted to set itself apart from common-sense and ordinary practical reasoning, insisting that as a discipline it would come up with reliable knowledge of the social world through the application of special 'systematic' methods of inquiry and theoretical frameworks. If sociology was to become a social science, so the argument went, it would have to transcend mere common-sense understandings of the world. This was the position adopted by Émile Durkheim (1858–1917), who proposed to establish a scientific sociology whose subject matter was a distinctive realm of social facts explainable via statistical techniques by other social facts (see Durkheim 1952, 1966). Whilst quantitative methods may no longer be subscribed to as preferred practice in sociology, the commitment to theoretical explanation remains.

Sociology, as any textbook on the subject will reveal, is overwhelmingly a theoretical discipline. This means that the sociologist makes use of a theoretical perspective in making sense of what is going on in society and in explaining relationships between social facts. Following Durkheim, sociology assumes that the solution to the problem of social order lies in something exterior to the concrete activities and situated actions of the members of society. Even social constructionists, who emphasize the role of 'human agency' in social life, nevertheless then situate such agency in theoretically stipulated wider webs of social order to which human agents unwittingly contribute.

However, despite its scientific pretensions and despite its commitment to a theoretical solution to the problem of social order, sociology has always been dependent on the world of everyday life. This is evident in how it takes for granted the availability of its objects of inquiry, in its own 'mastery of natural language', in its use of common-sense practical reasoning and practical action, and in its methods of inquiry. Appreciation of this rootedness or embeddedness of sociology goes at least as far back as the work of Alfred Schutz (1962, 1964, 1966, 1967), who brought Edmund Husserl's (1970) phenomenological perspective to bear upon the foundations of the social sciences, showing that like the natural sciences, the social sciences too were grounded in and dependent upon the world of everyday life or *Lebenswelt.* Sociology uses common-sense reasoning and everyday language as foundational resources for its inquiries, and yet it had failed to consider this, not only in terms of its role within social life but also in connection with its own activities.

The second reason for ethnomethodology's interest in taken-for-granted knowledge and methodical practice is that because sociology insisted on a solution to the problem of social order that was based on scientific methodology and theoretical explanation (what Garfinkel (2000: 94) refers to as 'formal analytic representational theorizing'), it missed the orderliness of the concrete, ordinary activities comprising social life. In its presumption that there was a stable foundation of objects, activities, categories of person, social settings and facts in the world, like families, classrooms, courtrooms, hospitals, doctors, police officers, lessons, trials, arguments, conversations and so on, and that they are available for study and theoretical explanation, sociology failed to appreciate that the phenomena of this stable foundation were already orderly in that they were intelligible, recognizable and accountable as just those phenomena.

In other words, theoretical conceptions of social order take for granted and ignore the already available orderlinesses of social life; they necessarily ignore how the ordinary activities of everyday life are produced so as to be available as those things in the first place. Furthermore, that they were available means that they must have been produced *somehow*. Where, then, sociology begins with the social facts of everyday life and seeks to account for them in terms of other social facts, ethnomethodology recommends a return to the social facts themselves and asks instead: how are these recognizable social facts produced, or more precisely, how is a particular social fact, such as a specific classroom lesson or an event within a lesson, produced? It directs its analytic attention to how particular instances of intelligible – that is, for the members or participants – factual activity are accomplished. Thus, where sociology seeks explanations of social facts in other facts that are external to them, ethnomethodology directs attention to the internal organization of facts.

While it is perhaps a 'condition' of practical sociological inquiry to ignore these 'foundational' common-sense matters (Garfinkel 1986), for ethnomethodology these resources are to be turned into topics of inquiry (Zimmerman and Pollner 1971). Where conventional sociology relies upon and yet ignores the domain of everyday life, ethnomethodology turns the organization of the ordinary activities making up that life into phenomena for investigation. A contrast, then, between theoretical orderliness and everyday or 'concrete' orderliness lies at the heart of the difference between sociology and ethnomethodology. Thus, as Garfinkel (1991, 1996) has pointed out, it is widely assumed within sociology that there is 'no order in the plenum'. To the contrary, for ethnomethodology, the very availability and intelligibility of social activities *for the members of society* constitutes a demonstration that there is indeed order in the plenum, in the concreteness of everyday social life. Furthermore, the 'ordinary' members of society seem to have little trouble carrying on their affairs without the use of professional sociological theories (Francis and Hester 2004). It is also quite clear that professional sociologists themselves make use of everyday language and common-sense knowledge in finding their way about in the social world and in conducting their investigations.

This shift or transformation of the orderliness of ordinary, concrete activities of social life from being taken-for-granted to being the focus of detailed attention has been described with the concept of 'respecification' (Garfinkel 1991; Button 1991; Zimmerman and Pollner 1971). It involves turning what sociology treats as a taken-for-granted resource into a topic of ethnomethodological enquiries. As Graham Button indicates, it is to respecify the problem of social order. The respecification is one from order-as-a-theoretical-phenomenon to order 'in-and-as-of-the-workings-of-ordinary-society' (Button 1991: 6). Furthermore, this respecification does not mark merely a difference in how social order is conceptualized since that would be simply to replace one theoretical framework with another. Instead, ethnomethodology's respecification of the problem of order is radically methodological; it locates social order in the specifics of whatever is actually done in and as of *particular instances* of social activities. Social order, in other words, is to be discovered in the detail of just how intelligible, accountable social activities are accomplished. The ethnomethodological researcher is therefore enjoined to investigate the production of social order as it happens *in situ*.

Finding phenomena of order

The 'central recommendation' of ethnomethodology's programme is stated on the first page of Garfinkel's first book *Studies in Ethnomethodology* (1967). There he writes:

> The following studies seek to treat practical activities, practical circumstances and practical sociological reasoning as topics of sociological study, and by paying to the most commonplace activities of daily life the attention usually afforded extra ordinary events, seek to learn about them as phenomena in their own right. Their central recommendation is that the activities whereby members produce and manage settings of organised everyday affairs are identical with members' procedures for making those settings 'account-able'.

This emphasis upon 'accountability' lies at the heart of ethnomethodology and its respecification of the problem of social order. There are two aspects to the notion of accountability. The first refers to the ways in which the members of society, sociologists included, make use of their common-sense knowledge and practical reasoning in making sense of things. The second refers to how persons produce their actions in the world such that they make sense to others as just those actions. More recently (Garfinkel and Wieder, 1992; Garfinkel, 2000), this emphasis on accountability has been re-described as a concern with the accomplished character of 'phenomena of order'.

If this is 'ethnomethodology's programme', then how is it to be carried out? As Douglas W. Maynard and Steven E. Clayman (1991) have indicated, ethnomethodology has a history of diversity both in terms of what has been studied and the nature of methods used to accomplish the investigations. In terms of the former, ethnomethodology has indeed developed and diversified.

Garfinkel's (1967) early studies established the two-fold concern with accountability. Thus, he reported investigations of how persons in various settings made sense of others' talk and action, as in their use of the reciprocity of perspectives, interpretive procedures such as the documentary method of interpretation, the use of common-sense models of social conduct in jurors' decision making and the use of common-sense conceptions of social structure in coding practices. His study of the transsexual Agnes in 'passing' as a normal, natural female established the ethnomethodological study of accountability in terms of how people produce actions that make sense to others. In these various studies the 'what happened', the 'what someone meant', the 'what something is', the 'what they are talking about', the 'who or what someone is', the 'how should it be done' are explored in terms of their situated accomplishment of members' practical action and practical reasoning.

The two sides of accountability were then taken up by the 'first generation' of Garfinkel's students and colleagues. Don Zimmerman (1971), for example, respecified 'rules' as a members' phenomenon, describing their actual use in making sense of and in organizing interaction within a public assistance agency. Similarly, D. Lawrence Wieder (1974) explored how the inmates of a 'halfway house' made use of an 'inmate code' in making accountable various forms of conduct found there and in accomplishing (that is, making accountable) a variety of interactional activities. In another example, Melvin Pollner (1974a, 1974b, 1978, 1987) investigated 'mundane' reasons (members' orientations to the reality or facticity of phenomena) in the resolution of 'reality disjunctures' (discrepant vrsions of the 'same' event) in traffic court. Members' assumptions about what was true, real and factual were thus shown to be pivotal in making sense of 'what happened' and, by the same token, making accountable the courses of practical action and practical reasoning constitutive of courtroom argument and judicial decision making.

It was also during the 1960s that another of Garfinkel's colleagues, Harvey Sacks, invented conversation analysis, and with colleagues Gail Jefferson and Emanuel Schegloff developed the discipline into what many have said is ethnomethodology's finest achievement. In Sacks' hands, the work of conversation analysis is indeed distinctively ethnomethodological, and this can be seen in his concern to locate 'conversational objects' and their uses in accomplishing a variety of conversational activities (Sacks 1992a, 1992b). These conversational objects were explored in two interrelated strands of Sacks' work: the sequential organization of conversational interaction and the categorical organization of description and other actions within conversation.

The first of these is discussed in the chapter by Paul ten Have in this book and so I shall not comment upon it here. The second, however, has now developed into a distinctive genre of ethnomethodological inquiry in its own right, known as 'membership categorization analysis' (MCA). Sacks' work in this area initially inspired a series of studies in 'MCD analysis' during the 1970s and 1980s, particularly in the United Kingdom by, for example, Wes Sharrock (1974) on the association of knowledge with and its 'ownership' by incumbents of membership categories, Rod Watson (1978, 1983, 1986) on such activities as calling for help, blame allocation and motive imputation, Mick Atkinson (1980) on the conversational use of the 'natural lifetime' or stage of life device, Edward C. Cuff (1994) on the use of categories in talk about family problems in a radio programme, George Payne (1976) on the beginning of a classroom lesson, and Lena Jayyusi (1984) on 'categorization and moral order'.

Research on membership categorization then developed during the 1990s under the rubric of MCA (Eglin and Hester 1992; Hester and Eglin 1997; see also Watson 1997), in studies by Carolyn Baker (1997), Susan Danby and Carolyn Baker (1998, 2000), Stephen Hester (1992, 1994, 1996, 1998, 2000, 2002) and Hester and David Francis (1994, 1996, 2000, 2001, 2002, 2003) on categorical activities in educational settings, Peter Eglin (2002) and Eglin and Hester (1999a, 1999b, 2003) on 'gendering work' and the use of membership categories in media accounts of events, and Derek Edwards (1998), Edwards and Elizabeth Stokoe (2007) and Stokoe (2003) on the use of identity categories in relationship counselling and gender categories in neighbourhood disputes. In recent years, conversation analysts, whose work had hitherto focused more or less exclusively on sequential topics, have begun to take an interest in matters of categorization and person reference (see Schegloff 2007a, 2007b). The field is one of lively debate, with Rod Watson (1997) and others, for example, arguing that the separation of MCA from sequential analysis has had a detrimental effect, especially on the latter.

Conversation analysis and MCA do not, of course, exhaust the kinds of activities that may be investigated by ethnomethodologists, and neither do they exhibit the limits of the kinds of orderlinesses that may be produced in and as human activity. Accordingly, another way of doing ethnomethodology is that known as the 'studies of work programme'. In part, this programme owes its origins to Garfinkel's original problematics in exploring the accountable work of jurors, coders, suicide prevention workers and social scientists. The programme was then developed by Garfinkel and his students during the 1970s (for example, Garfinkel 1986) and later in the United Kingdom and elsewhere. In contrast to mainstream studies of work, those working in this programme made serious attempts to study the 'missing whatness' of workplace activities, such as astronomy (Garfinkel, Lynch and Livingston 1981), mathematics, physics and chemistry (Livingston 1986, 1999, 2007), neurochemistry (Lynch 1985), lawyers' and judges' work (Lynch 1997; Burns 1996, 1997, 2001), computer programming (Button and Sharrock 1995), human–computer interaction (Luff and Heath 1993), entrepreneurial work (Anderson, Hughes and Sharrock 1989), mammography (Slack, Hartswood, Proctor and Rouncefield 2007), air traffic control (Anderson, Sharrock and Watson 1989), teaching and classroom management (Macbeth 1990, 1991, 1992, 1994), amongst many others (see Button 1993).

Furthermore, this strand of ethnomethodology is not limited to 'occupational' activities. Its central focus is less on *occupational* work than it is on the *work* that is involved in producing the orderliness of any accountable activity. Accordingly, in addition to specifically occupational tasks, studies have been done of many other activities, including playing basketball (Macbeth undated), learning kung fu (Girton 1986), playing jazz piano (Sudnow 1978), playing with a pet dog (Goode 2007), reading (Livingston 1995), reading introductory algebra (Sharrock and Ikeya 2000), walking in public places (Hester and Francis 2003) and various other forms of embodied everyday action.

Finally, mention should be made of that aspect of ethnomethdology's programme that has sought, drawing on the ordinary language philosophy of Ludwig Wittgenstein (1889–1951) as well as on ethnomethodology, to respecify cognitive and psychological conceptions of the mind, mental activities, memory, thought and emotion. A particularly notable exponent here is Jeff Coulter (for example, 1982, 1989, 1999), the key thematic being to respecify hitherto mental, cognitive and psychological events and processes as members' phenomena at the level of language use and social interaction.

Research methods in ethnomethodology

When the research methods used in these investigations are considered, more diversity is encountered. Garfinkel's original (1967) studies, for example, were done using so-called 'breaching experiments', interviews and observation. Some of the early studies (Wieder 1974; Zimmerman 1971; Zimmerman and Wieder 1977; Stoddart 1974) involved methods conventionally regarded as ethnographic. However, this description of ethnomethodologists' methods needs to be approached with caution; the reader should not be misled into thinking that, like mainstream sociology, ethnomethodology subscribes to the view that a set of special research techniques are required to obtain data relevant to its investigations.

John Hughes and Wes Sharrock (2007: 264) capture concisely the character of ethnomethodology's position on 'methods of data collection'. Their central point is that 'data collection methods' in ethnomethodology are not distinct from everyday 'methodical' practices. Everybody observes, talks to others and establishes relationships with others, so there is nothing special about ethnomethodological observation, ethnomethodologists' conversations with research subjects or the ways in which ethnomethodologists build interpersonal relationships with other people. However, this is not to say that 'anything goes' when it comes to the data that ethnomethodologists work with.

What ethnomethodology does insist upon are certain *sorts* of data on the one hand and a particular kind of *relationship* to them on the other. If the ethnomethodologist wishes to understand how social activities are *actually* produced, the data should preferably be naturally occurring. As for the ethnomethodologist's relationship to this data, it is both policy and practice to insist that the ethnomethodologist know the data *from within*, that is, as a member with respect to the activity in question; the researcher should have a certain familiarity with or acquire an immersion in the activity being investigated. It is only via such immersion that the knowledge acquired of the activity is *insider's knowledge*.

Garfinkel and Wieder (1992: 182) refer to this insistence on immersion as the 'unique adequacy requirement of methods'. This refers to the requirement that the analyst must have or acquire an 'insiders" or members' competence if they are able 'to recognize, identify, follow the development of or describe phenomena of order" (Garfinkel and Wieder 1992: 82); the analyst must have at least a competence in the activity as it is ordinarily understood. The point of 'vulgar' competence is that it enables the researcher to understand what is happening in the data that has been obtained. For many activities, of course, analysts already possess such competence, but for many others they may not, and it is for this reason that an immersion must then be acquired. So for conversation, say, one must be competent in being conversational, knowing how to have a conversation ordinarily understood. However, whereas conversation analysis trades upon and topicalizes ordinary competencies possessed by any competent conversationalist, the analysis of, for example, reasoning in chemistry or mathematics, kung fu, playing jazz piano or making a pass in basketball demand a grasp of skills beyond those of everyday conversational expertise. It is for this reason that 'immersion' is a prerequisite for analysing and reflecting upon the production of such specialized activities. It is only through immersion that the researcher can become as familiar with the methods involved in the production of these activities as they are with the methods of ordinary conversation.

Furthermore, data can be about the person themselves or others. In the case of themselves, the analyst turns their own participation/understanding into data. This is known as self-reflective analysis; it refers to a mode of inquiry in which the researcher's own understandings and activities provide the phenomena for analysis. In other words, the researcher's own understandings, reasoning and/or action are treated as data. Whether the data examined pertains to themselves or to others, it is incumbent on the analyst to provide the data that is being analysed. This methodological requirement was developed by Harvey Sacks and his colleagues in the interest of conducting rigorous analyses of conversational data; that is, analyses could be checked against the original data, rather than the reader having to rely upon the analysts 'word for it', that the data, for example, what was said and what was done, was as the analyst claimed. For this reason, transcripts and photographs are standard accompaniments of ethnomethodological analyses.

Analysing phenomena of order

Acquisition of a 'vulgar' competence is a prerequisite for analysis. It allows the process of analysis to begin. Once data has been obtained, the question becomes one of how to analyse them. A first thing to say here is that the analysis that is possible will depend on the nature of the data. The order that may be found there is, so to speak, already in the materials that have been recorded and transcribed and so one cannot sensibly go looking for orderliness that may not be there. For many, there is a preference for 'perspicuous sites', namely those where 'academic', 'philosophical', 'theoretical' and 'methodological' can be readily respecified as members' phenomena and as 'the work of the streets'. Clearly, some settings may be more perspicuous than others when it comes to such phenomena of order. Different situations and settings, and different acts and activities, will then differ in terms of their perspicuity for the analysis of different phenomena of order. Where the perspicuity of a setting or situation is already known, then this will obviously be helpful in the researcher's selection of research site if they already have in mind a particular kind of orderliness. On the other hand, through a strategy of 'unmotivated looking' (Sacks 1984: 27), the perspicuity and hence achieved orderliness of some phenomena is a discoverable matter.

Whatever specific orderlinesses may be located in the materials available, a core analytic mentality anchors the ethnomethodologist's approach to them. The key notion is of 'production'; social activities have the intelligibility that they have by virtue of the ways in which they are done by whoever is doing them. In this regard, attention is focused on how social activities are produced from within. This raises the question of just what this production consists of. In other words, how do people make sense of and produce sensible social activities, and what, specifically, do they use to do this? This stance is the basic investigative attitude of ethnomethodology. There are, furthermore, analytical procedures that may be followed in order to 'make visible' the phenomena of interest and then to analyse it. The procedures involve starting out with what anyone can observe about some situation or activity and then turning 'what is observably the case' into a topic for analysis, where the observable features of social life are treated as 'productions' of the parties to them.

Accordingly, ethnomethodology involves three methodological steps:

1. Notice something that is observably the case about some talk, activity or setting.
2. Pose the question: how is it that this observable feature has been produced such that it is recognizable for what it is?
3. Consider, analyse and describe the methods used in the production and recognition of the observable feature.

In other words, then, ethnomethodology starts out with what might be called the 'common-sense appearances of the social world' and then seeks to describe how they will have been produced 'from within' such that they do indeed have the appearances they have. Observations, then, are not the product of specialized sociological techniques; they are the 'available observations' that anyone can, and expectably does, make. Observations are not an end of inquiry; they are the starting point for what might be called 'constitutive analysis'.

Whether the three-step method is applied self-reflectively or to the conduct of others, the 'vulgar competence' assured by the unique adequacy requirement of methods will provide for a members' sense of what is being accomplished in and as of the activity under consideration. Familiarity with the activities provides the necessary mundane sense of 'what is going on' and 'what is observably the case' which can then topicalized. The question then becomes: how is what is observably the case accomplished, methodically speaking? This requires being able to describe the operation of methods in producing particular instances of phenomena.

As the discussion so far will have implied, if not explicitly articulated, ethnomethodological analysis pertains to particular instances of orderliness rather than to general characterizations of order production. This orientation to the accountability and accomplished orderliness of specific instances of talk and embodied action marks a key contrast between ethnomethodology and, for example, phenomenological sociology and symbolic interactionism. Particular instances of an activity will already possess orderly features that it is the task of the analyst to discover and then to describe in such a way that they 'preserve and display those orderly features'. As Doug Benson and John Hughes (1991: 131) put it: 'The ethnomethodological objective is to generate formal descriptions of social actions which preserve and display the features of the machinery that produced them.' Alternatively put, what is required is that the analyst's description of the machinery used to produce an action is uniquely adequate to account for the instance in question; it should be adequate to the task of providing for *just this* actual case.

Two exemplary studies

At this point, the discussion will now turn to an examination of exemplary studies. The first consists of the classic so-called 'breaching experiments' by Garfinkel (1967). The second is a classic piece by Sacks (1974), 'The analysability of stories by children', a study conducted within what is now known as 'membership categorization analysis'.

The breaching experiments

Although the breaching experiments are no longer much used in ethnomethodological research, they nevertheless were a milestone in the development of ethnomethodology, and any introductory discussion of ethnomethodology would be incomplete without mentioning them in some detail. Their significance is that they demonstrated conclusively that there was indeed a domain of common-sense knowledge that the members of society relied upon in recognizing and producing the activities making up the everyday world. They are reported in several chapters of Garfinkel's *Studies in Ethnomethodology*. As he points out:

> In accounting for the stable features of everyday activities, sociologists commonly select familiar settings such as familial households or work places and ask for the variables that contribute to their stable features. Just as commonly, one set of considerations are unexamined: the socially standardised and standardising, 'seen but unnoticed,' expected, background expectancies as a scheme of interpretation. With their use actual appearances are for him recognizable and intelligible as the appearances-of-familiar-events. Demonstrably, he is responsive to this background, while at the same time he is at a loss to tell us specifically of what the expectancies consist. When we ask him about them he has little or nothing to say.
>
> (Garfinkel 1967: 36)

Faced with this reticence, Garfinkel (1967: 37) opted 'to start with familiar scenes and ask what can be done to make trouble'. His hope was that:

> the operations that one would have to perform in order to multiply the senseless features of perceived environments; to produce and sustain bewilderment, consternation, and confusion; to produce the socially structured affects of anxiety, shame, guilt and indignation; and to produce disorganised interaction should tell us something about how the structures of everyday activities are ordinarily and routinely produced and maintained.
>
> (Garfinkel 1967: 37–8)

Accordingly, in one 'demonstration' Garfinkel had his students engage an acquaintance or friend in an ordinary conversation and then without indicating that what they were doing was at all unusual, ask the friend or acquaintance to clarify the sense of their remarks. For example:

> 'Case 1':
> The subject was telling the experimenter, a member of the subject's car pool, about having had a flat tire while going to work the previous day.
> S: I had a flat tire.
> E: What do you mean, you had a flat tire?
> She appeared momentarily stunned. Then she answered in a hostile way: What do you mean, 'What do you mean?' A flat tire is a flat tire. That is what I meant. Nothing special. What a crazy question!

'Case 3':
On Friday night my husband and I were watching television. My husband remarked that he was tired. I asked, 'How are you tired? Physically, mentally, or just bored?'
S: I don't know, I guess physically, mainly.
E: You mean that your muscles ache or your bones?
S: I guess so. Don't be so technical.
(*After more watching*)
S: All these old movies have the same kind of old iron bedstead in them.
E: What do you mean? Do you mean all old movies, or some of them, or just the ones you have seen?
S: What's the matter with you? You know what I mean.
E: I wish you would be more specific.
S: You know what I mean! Drop dead!

The point of these demonstrations is that they show quite clearly that the 'subjects' expected the students to understand what they meant even though they did not say what they meant in so many words. They expected the students to 'fill in' the meaning of the utterances without further ado. They expected them, in other words, to bring the same 'natural attitude' to bear upon their talk as they intended themselves.

Similarly, in another set of 'demonstrations', students were asked to look at what went on in their own homes as if they were strangers or 'boarders'. Like the first of demonstrations examined above, the results were that the students became acutely aware of the ordinary, commonplace ways in which household activities were normally done. That is to say, because they were looking at what was happening as 'strangers', they could no longer take for granted the knowledge and the practices that made possible 'everyday family life' as these students knew it. By 'stepping outside' they were able to notice the taken-for-granted assumptions, knowledge, methods and practices that had hitherto been used in the 'unnoticed' constitution of the everyday activities comprising family life. In short, the point that needs to be taken is that through his experiments Garfinkel succeeded in opening up as a domain of empirical inquiry the methodical accomplishment of everyday activities through 'seen but unnoticed' practices. The following study is an example of one way in which research in this domain was then carried out.

The baby cried …

The procedure for analysis used by Sacks is the three-step procedure mentioned earlier. Thus, Sacks starts with an observable 'outcome' and then seeks to describe the methods whose use will have produced that outcome. Sacks had previously used the procedure in his analysis of the 'Search for help' and various other observable events. In connection with the children's story, 'the baby cried, the mommy picked it up', Sacks focuses on the activity of 'making sense'. The sense in question is Sacks's own and hence the study is an example of 'self-reflective analysis' even though, as Sacks points out, the sense that he makes, as a member of his culture, is a sense that 'anyone' could and most likely would make of the events recounted in the story. As Sacks (1974: 216) says, the sense that he makes of this story is that the 'baby' in question is the baby of the 'mommy' who is mentioned in the story and that she picked it up because it was crying, as is a common occurrence in caring for little babies. This sense, he argues, is one which any member of our culture would make because of what everybody knows about the categories, the relationships and the activities mentioned in the story. Furthermore, as he indicates, this 'common sense' is not articulated in so many words in the story, but is 'filled in' by its hearers and readers. The question then is: what is the nature of this work of 'filling in' or 'sense making' that enables this common-sense understanding to be produced?

In answering this question, Sacks spells out the constituents of a 'machinery' or collection of methods through which the activity of sense making may be done and whose use in this instance will produce the particular sense in question. The first component of this machinery is 'membership categories'. These are basically social types of person (see Schutz 1967), such as 'farmer', 'singer', 'janitor', 'uncle' and 'birdwatcher'. The second component consists of 'membership categorization devices'. These refer to 'category collections' or collections of membership categories that 'go naturally together' in terms of our natural everyday language for describing and referring to people. Thus, in the category collection 'family' it is natural or common-sensical to assume that this includes such categories as 'baby', 'mother', 'father', 'aunt', 'uncle' and so forth, but not, say 'teacher'. The latter does not 'sound' like a member of the collection 'family'. Conversely, it is hearable as a category from the collection 'educationists', along with 'teaching assistant', 'lecturer' and 'professor', but not 'mother'.

In addition to membership categories and membership categorization devices, Sacks mentions two 'rules of application' for the use of membership categories. The 'economy rule' states that in describing persons, a single category will suffice. For example, if someone is doing the activity of introducing their new girlfriend or boyfriend to their other friends, then they do not have to mention all of the categories with which they might possibly be described. To do so would seem oddly redundant, though there may also be occasions when a preference for more than a single category will be evident, for example in discussions between teachers, psychologists and other welfare workers which focus on 'problem' children and their families. Second, there is the 'consistency rule' which holds that:

> If some population of persons is being categorized, and if a category from some device's collection has been used to categorize a first member of the population, then that category or other categories from the *same* collection may be used to categorize further members of the population.
>
> (Sacks 1974: 219)

This means, for example, that if a first person has been categorized as a 'goalkeeper', then further persons in the population being described may be referred to by that category or other categories of a collection of which they and 'goalkeeper' are co-members. In the context of the collection 'footballers' or 'football team', for example, the other categories that are relevant, given the use of 'goalkeeper', are 'centre forward', 'midfield player', 'full back' and so on. There is also a consistency rule corollary or 'hearer's maxim' related to the consistency rule. This holds that: 'If two or more categories are used to categorize two or more members of some population, and those categories can be heard as categories from the same collection, then: hear them that way' (Sacks 1974: 219–20).

Sacks also speaks of 'category-bound activities'. These are activities that are common-sensically associated with particular membership categories. For example, police officers 'arrest' people, judges 'sentence' convicted criminals and doctors 'treat' the sick. Such activities, furthermore, as Watson (1978, 1983), Hester and Eglin (1997) and Payne (1976) have all indicated, comprise just one class of 'category predicates' which are those features (activities, attributes, entitlements and so on) that are expectably and properly associated with persons who are the incumbents of particular categories.

Given these 'procedural devices' of categories, collections, rules of application and category predicates, it can now be shown how they are used to produce an understanding of the story 'the baby cried, the mommy picked it up'. Thus, the consistency rule corollary, or the hearer's maxim, is used to hear the baby and the mommy as co-members of 'family'. That is, if these two categories *can* be heard as categories belonging to the same collection, then: *hear them that way*. This, it seems, is what 'we' naturally do and the use of this method can be understood to adequately account for how the categories 'baby' and 'mommy' are heard as going together.

However, as Sacks indicates, there is more to it than this apparently straightforward consistency. Both 'baby' and 'mommy' could under some circumstances be heard as categories belonging to collections other than that of family. For example 'baby' could be a term of endearment between lovers or a derogatory description of an adult who is crying. The particular sense of 'baby' as referring to that category from the stage of life device known as 'very young child' is producible by virtue of the relationship between categories and activities. Thus, the reference to 'crying' provides us with a clue as to the identity of the person engaged in this particular activity. This is because crying can be heard as just the sort of thing that babies do, for example when they are tired, hungry or uncomfortable; crying is a category-bound activity of 'baby'.

Sacks suggests here that hearers will make use of a viewer's maxim which states that if this is an activity that can be seen to be done by the incumbent of a category to which it is bound, then see it that way. The same procedure may be used to understand the activity of 'picking up' as being bound to the category 'mommy', as meaning caring for babies who cry (as opposed, hypothetically, to refer to picking up litter or picking up people in bars). Accordingly, then, we can understand the baby not as a lover or a 40-year-old 'whinger' but as a very young child, and we can understand the 'mommy' as a woman who has a baby and who is taking care of that baby because it is crying. These senses 'reinforce' our common-sense understanding of the category identities and their relationship in the story. So the 'baby' is a very young child and the 'mommy' is the 'mommy' of the 'baby' who cries.

Conclusion

This chapter has discussed the approach known as ethnomethodology. It began by indicating the domain of phenomena that ethnomethodology seeks to investigate – the taken-for-granted methods used by members of society in accomplishing the intelligible 'social facts' of everyday life. It was pointed out that even as sociology relies upon the readily available social facts of everyday life, it failed to investigate them or even to acknowledge their orderliness. For sociology, the 'real' orderliness of the world was something to be reached via the use of 'systematic' methods of research and the application of sociological theories to interpret and explain the 'data' acquired by such research. Ethnomethodology contests this particular vision of social order, and has sought instead to respecify the 'problem of social order' as a members' problem, thereby initiating a programme of inquiry into the achieved order of social activities, whatever they may be.

The specific and wider origins of this programme were discussed, and the diversity of approaches now comprising the discipline of ethnomethodology was outlined. Its notable continuity with conversation analysis, especially in the work of Sacks, was emphasized. Methodological continuities across the diverse forms of ethnomethodological inquiry, with respect to both finding phenomena of order and analysing those phenomena, were then considered. It was indicated that the fundamental 'analytic mentality' of ethnomethodology starts from the position that observable and available 'social orders' are the products of the 'work' that the members of society who are engaged in them do. The task, then, is to make visible this work.

Several strategies for achieving this were then discussed. It was emphasized that because the orderliness of social life in ethnomethodological analysis is always a situated orderliness, ethnomethodologists consistently set themselves the task of adequately describing and accounting for particular instances of phenomena, in contrast to the tendency amongst varieties of 'interpretive sociology' for generalized and decontextualized analysis. The two exemplary studies by Garfinkel and by Sacks discussed in the final part of the chapter, exhibit this commitment to studying the – often unnoticed – 'local production of social order'.

Bibliography

Anderson, Bob, John Hughes and Wes Sharrock (1989) *Working for Profit: The Social Organisation of Calculation in an Entrepreneurial Firm.* Aldershot: Avebury.

Anderson, Bob, Wes Sharrock and Rod Watson (1989) 'Utterances and operations in air traffic control.' *Language and Travail*, 221–34.

Atkinson, Mick (1980) 'Some practical uses of a "natural lifetime".' *Human Studies*, 1: 33–46.

Baker, Carolyn (1997) 'Ticketing rules: categorization and moral ordering in a school staff meeting', in Stephen Hester and Peter Eglin (eds), *Culture in Action: Studies in Membership Categorization Analysis.* Lanham, MD: University Press of America.

Benson, Douglas and John Hughes (1991) 'Method: evidence and inference – evidence and inference for ethnomethodology', in Graham Button (ed.), *Ethnomethodology and the Human Sciences*. Cambridge: Cambridge University Press.

Burns, Stacy (1996) 'Lawyers' work in the Menendez brothers' murder trial.' *Issues in Applied Linguistics*, 7: 19–32.

Burns, Stacy (1997) 'Practicing law: a study of pedagogic interchange in a law school classroom', in Max Travers and John F. Manzo (eds), *Law in Action: Ethnomethodological and Conversation Analytic Approaches to Law.* Aldershot: Dartmouth.

Burns, Stacy (2001) '"Think your darkest thoughts and blacken them": judicial mediation of large money damage disputes.' *Human Studies*, 24: 227–49.

Button, Graham (1991) 'Introduction: ethnomethodology and the foundational respecification of the human sciences', in Graham Button (ed.), *Ethnomethodology and the Human Sciences.* Cambridge: Cambridge University Press.

Button, Graham (ed.) (1993) *Technology in Working Order: Studies of Work, Interaction and Technology.* London: Routledge.

Button, Graham and Wes Sharrock (1995) 'The mundane work of writing and reading computer programs', in Paul ten Have and George Psathas (eds), *Situated Order: Studies in the Social Organisation of Talk and Embodied Activities*. Lanham, MD: University Press of America.

Coulter, Jeff (1982) *Rethinking Cognitive Theory*. London: Macmillan.

Coulter, Jeff (1989) *Mind in Action.* Cambridge: Polity Press.

Coulter, Jeff (1999) 'Discourse and mind.' *Human Studies*, 23: 163–81.

Cuff, Edward C. (1994) *Problems of Versions in Everyday Situations.* Lanham, MD: University Press of America.

Danby, Susan and Carolyn Baker (1998) 'How to be masculine in block area.' *Childhood,* 5: 151–75.

Danby, Susan and Carolyn Baker (2000) 'Unravelling the fabric of social order in block area', in Stephen Hester and David Francis (eds), *Local Educational Order: Ethnomethodological Studies of Knowledge in Action.* Amsterdam: John Benjamins.

Durkheim, Émile (1952) *Suicide: A Study in Sociology.* London: Routledge & Kegan Paul.

Durkheim, Émile (1966) *The Rules of Sociological Method.* New York: Free Press.

Edwards, Derek (1998) 'The relevant thing about her: social identity categories in use', in Charles Antaki and Sue Widdicombe (eds), *Identities in Talk.* London: Sage.

Edwards, Derek and Elizabeth Stokoe (2007) 'Self-help in calls for help with problem neighbours.' *Research on Language and Social Interaction,* 39(4): 9–32.

Eglin, Peter (2002) 'Members' gendering work: "women", "feminists" and membership categorization analysis.' *Discourse and Society,* 13: 819–25.

Eglin, Peter and Stephen Hester (1992) 'Category, predicate and task: the pragmatics of practical action.' *Semiotica,* 88: 243–68.

Eglin, Peter and Stephen Hester (1999a) 'Moral order and the Montreal massacre: a story of membership categorization analysis', in Paul L. Jalbert (ed.), *Media Studies: Ethnomethodological Approaches.* Lanham, MD: University Press of America.

Eglin, Peter and Stephen Hester (1999b) 'You're all a bunch of feminists: categorization and the politics of terror in the Montreal massacre.' *Human Studies,* 22: 253–72.

Eglin, Peter and Stephen Hester (2003) *The Montreal Massacre: A Story of Membership Categorization Analysis.* Waterloo, ON: Wilfrid Laurier University Press.

Francis, David and Stephen Hester (2004) *An Invitation to Ethnomethodology: Language, Society and Social Interaction.* London: Sage.

Garfinkel, Harold (1967) *Studies in Ethnomethodology.* Englewood Cliffs, NJ: Prentice-Hall.

Garfinkel, Harold (1974) 'On the origins of the term "ethnomethodology"', in Roy Turner (ed.), *Ethnomethodology: Selected Readings.* Harmondsworth: Penguin.

Garfinkel, Harold (ed.) (1986) *Ethnomethodological Studies of Work.* London: Routledge & Kegan Paul.

Garfinkel, Harold (1991) 'Respecification: evidence for locally produced, naturally accountable phenomena of order, logic, reason, meaning, method, etc. in and as of the essential haecceity of immortal ordinary society: (1) An announcement of studies', in Graham Button (ed.), *Ethnomethodology and the Human Sciences.* Cambridge: Cambridge University Press.

Garfinkel, Harold (1996) 'An overview of ethnomethodology's program.' *Social Psychology Quarterly,* 59: 5–21.

Garfinkel, Harold (2000) *Ethnomethodology's Program: Working Out Durkheim's Aphorism.* Lanham, MD: Rowman & Littlefield.

Garfinkel, Harold, Michael Lynch and Eric Livingston (1981) 'The work of a discovering science construed with materials from the optically discovered pulsar.' *Philosophy of the Social Sciences,* 11: 131–58.

Garfinkel, Harold and D. Lawrence Wieder (1992) 'Two incommensurable, asymmetrically alternate technologies of social analysis', in Graham Watson and Robert M. Seiler (eds), *Text in Context: Contributions to Ethnomethodology.* Newbury Park, CA: Sage.

Girton, George (1986) 'Kung Fu: toward a praxiological hermeneutic of the martial arts', in Harold Garfinkel (ed.), *Ethnomethodological Studies of Work.* London: Routledge & Kegan Paul.

Goode, David (2007) *Playing with My Dog, Katie: An Ethnomethodological Study of Canine–Human Interaction*. Ashland, OH: Purdue University Press.

Hester, Stephen (1992) 'Recognizing references to deviance in referral talk', in Graham Watson and Robert M. Seiler (eds), *Text in Context: Contributions to Ethnomethodology*. Newbury Park, CA: Sage.

Hester, Stephen (1994) 'Les categories en contexte', in Bernard Fradin, Louis Quere and Jean Widmer (eds), *L'enquête sur les catégories*. Paris: Ecole de Hautes Etudes en Sciences Sociales.

Hester, Stephen (1996) 'Laughter in its place', in George Paton, Chris Powell and Stephen Wagg (eds), *The Social Faces of Humour*. Aldershot: Arena Press.

Hester, Stephen (1998) 'Describing deviance in school: recognisably educational psychological problems', in Charles Antaki and Sue Widdicombe (eds), *Identities in Talk*. London: Sage.

Hester, Stephen (2000) 'Motives, morality and membership categorisation in referral talk', in Stephen Hester and David Francis (eds), *Local Educational Order: Ethnomethodological Studies of Knowledge in Action*. Amsterdam: John Benjamins.

Hester, Stephen (2002) 'Bringing it all back home: selecting topic, category and location in TV news programmes', in Stephen Hester and William Housley (eds), *Language, Interaction and National Identity: Studies in the Social Organisation of National Identity in Talk-in-Interaction*. Aldershot: Ashgate.

Hester, Stephen and Peter Eglin (eds) (1997) *Culture in Action: Studies in Membership Categorisation Analysis*. Lanham, MD: University Press of America.

Hester, Stephen and David Francis (1994) 'Doing data: the local organisation of a sociological interview.' *British Journal of Sociology*, 45 (4): 675–95.

Hester, Stephen and David Francis (1996) 'Reality analysis in a classroom storytelling.' *British Journal of Sociology*, 48 (1): 95–112.

Hester, Stephen and David Francis (2000) 'Ethnomethodology, conversation analysis and "institutional talk".' *Text*, 20: 391–413.

Hester, Stephen and David Francis (2001) 'Is institutional talk a phenomenon? Reflections on ethnomethodology and applied conversation analysis', in Alec W. McHoul and Mark Rapley (eds), *Talk in Institutional Settings*. London: Continuum International.

Hester, Stephen and David Francis (2002) 'Category play in a school staff-room.' *Ethnographic Studies*, 5: 42–55.

Hester, Stephen and David Francis (2003) 'Analysing visually available mundane order: a walk to the supermarket.' *Visual Studies*, 18(1): 36–46.

Hester, Stephen and David Francis (2007) 'Analysing orders of ordinary action', in Stephen Hester and David Francis (eds), *Orders of Ordinary Action: Respecifying Sociological Knowledge*. Aldershot: Ashgate.

Hill, Richard J. and Kathleen S. Crittenden (eds) (1968) *Proceedings of the Purdue Symposium on Ethnomethodology*. Purdue: Institute for the Study of Social Change, Department of Sociology, Purdue University, Ashland, OH.

Hughes, John and Wes Sharrock (2007) *Theory and Methods in Sociology*. Basingstoke: Palgrave/Macmillan.

Husserl, Edmund (1970) *The Crisis of European Sciences and Transcendental Phenomenology*. Evanston, IL: Northwestern University Press.

Jayyusi, Lena (1984) *Categorization and Moral Order*. London: Routledge & Kegan Paul.

Livingston, Eric (1986) *The Ethnomethodological Foundations of Mathematics*. London: Routledge & Kegan Paul.

Livingston, Eric (1995) *An Anthropology of Reading.* Bloomington, IN: Indiana University Press.
Livingston, Eric (1999) 'Cultures of proving.' *Social Studies of Science*, 29: 867–88.
Livingston, Eric (2007) 'Circumstances of reasoning in the natural sciences', in Stephen Hester and David Francis (eds), *Orders of Ordinary Action: Respecifying Sociological Knowledge.* Aldershot: Ashgate.
Luff, Paul and Christian Heath (1993) 'System use and social organisation: observations on human–computer interaction in an architectural practice', in Graham Button (ed.), *Technology in Working Order: Studies of Work, Interaction and Technology*. London: Routledge.
Lynch, Michael (1985) *Art and Artifact in Laboratory Science: A Study of Shop Work and Shop Talk*. London: Routledge & Kegan Paul.
Lynch, Michael (1997) 'Preliminary notes on judges' work: the judge as a constituent of courtroom hearings', in Max Travers and John F. Manzo (eds), *Law in Action: Ethnomethodological and Conversation Analytic Approaches to Law.* Aldershot: Dartmouth.
Macbeth, Douglas (1990) 'Classroom order as practical action.' *British Journal of Sociology of Education*, 11: 189–214.
Macbeth, Douglas (1991) 'Teacher authority as practical action.' *Linguistics and Education*, 3: 281–313.
Macbeth, Douglas (1992) 'Classroom "floors": material organizations as a course of affairs.' *Qualitative Sociology*, 15 (2): 123–50.
Macbeth, Douglas (1994) 'Classroom encounters with the unspeakable: "Do you see, Danelle?".' *Discourse Processes*, 17: 311–35.
Macbeth, Douglas (undated) 'Basketball notes.' Unpublished manuscript.
Maynard, Douglas W. and Steven E. Clayman (1991) 'The diversity of ethnomethodology.' *Annual Review of Sociology*, 17: 385–418.
Payne, George (1976) 'Making a lesson happen', in Martyn Hammersley and Peter Woods (eds), *The Process of Schooling.* London: Routledge & Kegan Paul.
Pollner, Melvin (1974a) 'Mundane reasoning.' *Philosophy of the Social Sciences*, 4: 35–54.
Pollner, Melvin (1974b) 'Sociological and common-sense models of the labelling process', in Roy Turner (ed.), *Ethnomethodology: Selected Readings*. Harmondsworth: Penguin.
Pollner, Melvin (1978) 'Constitutive and mundane versions of labelling theory.' *Human Studies*, 3: 285–304.
Pollner, Melvin (1987) *Mundane Reason: Reality in Everyday and Sociological Discourse.* Cambridge: Cambridge University Press.
Sacks, Harvey (1974) 'On the analysability of stories by children', in Roy Turner (ed.), *Ethnomethodology: Selected Readings*. Harmondsworth: Penguin.
Sacks, Harvey (1984) 'Notes on methodology', in J. Maxwell Atkinson and John Heritage (eds), *Structures of Social Action: Studies in Conversation Analysis.* Cambridge: Cambridge University Press.
Sacks, Harvey (1992a) *Lectures on Conversation, Volume One.* Oxford: Blackwell.
Sacks, Harvey (1992b) *Lectures on Conversation, Volume Two.* Oxford: Blackwell.
Schegloff, Emanuel (2007a) 'A tutorial on membership categorisation.' *Journal of Pragmatics*, 39: 462–82.
Schegloff, Emanuel (2007b) 'Categories in action: person-reference and membership categorisation.' *Discourse Studies*, 9: 433–61.
Schutz, Alfred (1962) *Collected Papers, Volume One.* The Hague: Martinus Nijhoff.
Schutz, Alfred 1964) *Collected Papers, Volume Two.* The Hague: Martinus Nijhoff.
Schutz, Alfred (1966) *Collected Papers, Volume Three.* The Hague: Martinus Nijhoff.

Schutz, Alfred (1967) *The Phenomenology of the Social World.* Evanston, IL: Northwestern University Press.

Sharrock, Wes (1974) 'On owning knowledge', in Roy Turner (ed.), *Ethnomethodology: Selected Readings.* Harmondsworth: Penguin.

Sharrock, Wes and Nozomi Ikeya (2000) 'Instructional matter: readable properties of an introductory text in matrix algebra', in Stephen Hester and David Francis (eds), *Local Educational Order: Ethnomethodological Studies of Knowledge in Action.* Amsterdam: John Benjamins.

Slack, Roger, Mark Hartswood, Rob Proctor and Mark Rouncefield (2007) 'Cultures of Reading: On Professional Vision and the Lived Work of Mammography', in Stephen Hester and David Francis (eds), *Orders of Ordinary Action: Respecifying Sociological Knowledge*. Aldershot: Ashgate.

Stoddart, Kenneth (1974) 'The facts of life about dope: observations of a local pharmacology.' *Urban Life and Culture*, 3: 179–204.

Stokoe, Elizabeth (2003) 'Mothers, single women and sluts: gender, morality and membership categorisation in neighbour disputes.' *Feminism and Psychology*, 13: 317–44.

Sudnow, David (1978) *Ways of the Hand: The Organization of Improvised Conduct*. London: Routledge & Kegan Paul.

Watson, Rod (1978) 'Categorisation, authorisation and blame-negotiation in conversation.' *Sociology*, 12: 105–13.

Watson, Rod (1983) 'The presentation of victim and motive in discourse: the case of police interrogations and interviews.' *Victimology*, 8: 31–52.

Watson, Rod (1986) 'Doing the organization's work: an examination of a crisis intervention centre', in Sue Fisher and Alexandra D. Todd (eds), *Discourse and Institutional Authority*. Norwood, NJ: Ablex.

Watson, Rod (1997) 'Some general reflections on "categorisation" and "sequence" in the analysis of conversation', in Stephen Hester and Peter Eglin (eds), *Culture in Action: Studies in Membership Categorisation Analysis.* Lanham, MD: University Press of America.

Wieder, D. Lawrence (1974) *Language and Social Reality: The Telling of the Convict Code.* The Hague: Mouton.

Zimmerman, Don (1971) 'The practicalities of rule use', in Jack D. Douglas (ed.), *Understanding Everyday Life*. London: Routledge & Kegan Paul.

Zimmerman, Don and Melvin Pollner (1971) 'The everyday world as a phenomenon', in Jack D. Douglas (ed.), *Understanding Everyday Life*. London: Routledge & Kegan Paul.

Zimmerman, Don and D. Lawrence Wieder (1977) '"You can't help but get stoned": notes on the social organization of marihuana smoking.' *Social Problems*, 25: 198–207.

CHAPTER 10

Conversation Analysis

Analysing Everyday Conversational Activities

PAUL TEN HAVE

Introduction

'Conversation', people talking together, seems to be the prime type of event in everyday life. As soon as people who know each other meet, they start talking, and even strangers often use face-to-face situations – occasions in which they can see and hear each other – to strike up a conversation. So 'having a conversation' is among the most quotidian of events. For a long time, however, it seemed to be so 'ordinary' that social scientists did not consider it a topic for serious attention. Even linguists focused on written language rather than spoken. And when what people were saying was taken into consideration, it was the content, what they were saying, that was mostly attended to, rather than how they spoke together. In other words, the ways in which people talk together is a prime example of 'the unnoticed', and therefore the study of the organization of talk-in-interaction, of conversation, is one of the major 'sociologies of the unnoticed'.

The main initiative in this field was taken by a few young sociologists in the early 1960s, Harvey Sacks (1935–1975) and Emanuel A. Schegloff (b. 1937). Against a background of a range of intellectual inspirations, they used recent technological innovations that allowed easy-to-use audio recording to develop new insights into the intricacies of spontaneous interactional talking, leading to a research tradition that is now known as *conversation analysis* (CA). To a certain extent, this label is misleading, as CA research is not only focused on 'conversation', informal talk among peers, but also on many other types of incidence of people talking together, such as interviews, formal meetings and talk while working. In this chapter I describe the emergence and development of CA, its specific methodological approach, some of its core concepts and a few major applications.

What is conversation analysis?

As noted above, conversation analysis has become the established label for a quite specific approach to the analysis of interaction, which emerged in the 1960s in the work of Harvey Sacks and his co-workers Emanuel A. Schegloff and Gail Jefferson (1938–2008) (see Sacks 1992). Its basic interest was sociological: understanding social order. As such it was inspired by the sociological perspective of Erving Goffman (1922–1962) and the ethnomethodology as developed at the time by Harold Garfinkel (b. 1917). Sacks and Schegloff both studied with Goffman in Berkeley. What they took away from him was, at least, that direct interaction between people could be a sensible topic for sociological investigation. They did, however, take a path different from his, both theoretically and methodologically. In these respects, they were more strongly influenced by Garfinkel's 'ethnomethodology', which (to formulate it in a simplifying way) focuses on the 'methods' members of society use to constitute social situations as somehow 'orderly'. For many, CA is still a part of ethnomethodology, but it has also been developed as a relatively independent pursuit.

'Conversation', or as it later came to be called, *talk-in-interaction*, was chosen as a field of exploration because the creation and maintenance of social order could be studied in detail by inspecting recordings of actual interactions. As it developed, the method of CA was refined and has attracted a still growing number of practitioners, not only from sociology, but also from linguistics, anthropology, communication studies and psychology. Its original impetus and way of working has, however, remained essentially the same. CA's interest is primarily *procedural* and *organizational.* That is, its goal is to specify the ways in which participants moment by moment organize their talking together, for instance who is to take a turn at speaking after the present speaker, and when, about what, how problems of understanding are to be managed, and so on. As in ethnomethodology generally, there are two sides to this, generic and occasional; which resources are available in the culture at large, and how are they used at this particular moment.

Later developments

While CA's general approach has remained essentially the same since about 1975, there have been important later developments in the way in which these essential insights could be applied. In its earliest phases, CA's originators and students used a wide range or interactional data, especially telephone calls, but also for instance group therapy sessions, in order to explore generic aspects of talk-in-interaction. This kind of work is still being done today and I call it pure CA. It means that the researcher abstracts, to a certain extent, from the specific setting of the talk, at least analytically. Aspects of the situation may be considered in order to understand what is going on, but are not, as in other approaches, used to explain the conduct of the interactants. In other words, its focus is on the local, moment-by-moment production of social order.

In the late 1970s, some researchers, such as John Heritage (b. 1946) and Paul Drew (b. 1948), started to use CA's general approach to elucidate interactional aspects of the workings of specific institutions such as court sessions or medical consultations. In such studies, which I call applied CA, the analytic focus shifts to explore institution-specific interactional formats, involving, for instance, asymmetrical distributions of action-types, such as questions (see Drew and Heritage 1992; Heritage and Maynard 2006).

A second trend that started in the late 1970s was the use of video rather than just audio data, which stimulated researchers such as Charles Goodwin (b. 1943) and Christian Heath (b. 1952) to systematically consider the *visual* aspects of face-to-face talk in interaction. What these studies show is that the findings of the earlier phase of CA studies, based on audio recordings, were still valid for face-to-face encounters, but that participants in such situations use additional visual cues to organize their interactions, such as gestures and gaze direction. They also showed that, and how, talk and bodily activities of various sorts tend to be quite subtly coordinated (see Goodwin 2000; Heath 2004).

A third development emerged during the 1980s and 1990s which, in a way, combined the earlier two, as some researchers started to use video to study work activities in technologically complex environments. They showed that, and how, workers in such situations not only coordinated talk and bodily activities, but also various complex manipulations and consultations of technical artefacts, such as computers and telephones. In order to understand and analyse such complex activities researchers needed to go beyond the recordings, by doing fieldwork, observations and informal interviews, in such settings. They had to acquire setting-specific membership knowledge before they could make sense of their audiovisual data. This kind of work now carries the label of *workplace studies* (see, for instance, Heath and Luff 2000).

As CA became more prominent in the later 1990s, researchers with a background in other disciplines than sociology started to explore the possibilities of using it to tackle problems in or relevant to the home disciplines. Linguists, for instance investigated relationships between grammar and talk-in-interaction, as grammar can be seen to offer a set of specific resources to the organization of interactional talk, while some grammatical structures can be analysed as emerging from interactional constraints and possibilities (see Ford, Fox and Thompson 2002).

A very important consequence of CA's focus on the *organization* of talk is that it tends to be critical of a major feature of Western cultures to understand actions primarily in terms of *individual* mental dispositions, such as attitudes, cognitions and internalized norms and values. This tendency is observable both in everyday life and in a discipline like psychology. The empirical approach of CA has therefore been quite attractive to psychologists who were equally critical of their discipline's individualistic and mentalistic bias, and who propose what they call a 'discursive psychology' (see te Molder and Potter 2005).

In a similar way, speech conventionally tends to be seen as an individual production. Therefore, the study of communication problems involving people with impaired capabilities, for instance, has been dominated by research submitting such individuals to individual tests in laboratory settings. CA studies, however, have shown that such people and unimpaired care givers were often able to communicate much better than such tests would predict (see Goodwin 2003). In short, the specific approach of CA has proven to be able to elucidate a wide range of 'local' and 'situational' phenomena which escape established views: really a sociology of the unnoticed.

Methodological approach

The 'unconventional' character of CA, noted above, emerged from the ability of its originators, Sacks and Schegloff, to use the inspirations that they had encountered to study the most ordinary events in detail. In most current approaches in the social sciences, what are studied are indications of, or reports on, 'theorized' objects, that is as presupposed and pre-conceptualized phenomena. Inspired by ethnomethodology, which in turn was inspired by phenomenology, the originators of CA turned their attention to interactional phenomena themselves. The technology that made this possible was audio recording. It facilitated the detailed study of talk, by repeated listening, both individually and collectively, and by transcription. It was only in this way that they could go beyond the what of talk to look at the how.

Since then, CA research has remained essentially a *data-driven* endeavour. It starts with the inspection of data. Researchers in CA work on audio or video recordings of interactions that are naturally occurring, which means that they are not arranged or provoked by the researcher, as in experiments or interviews. For CA as such, 'pure CA', there are in principle, and often in practice, no further requirements or limitations, although for specialized forms of 'applied CA' it makes sense to collect recordings of specific types of situation.

Such recordings are then carefully transcribed, using a set of conventions developed by Gail Jefferson, sometimes referred to as the Jefferson System.

Apart from the words as spoken, these conventions allow the researcher to highlight a range of production details concerning timing, intonation and so on. While such details are not ordinarily taken into consideration in most kinds of social science research, they have been proven to be quite often important for the organization of the interaction (see Jefferson 1985, 2004; see also the explication of transcription in the next section).

Exhuming 'the unnoticed' can be done in various ways. Sacks and Schegloff, while quite erudite, 'bracketed' their vast knowledge of a range of literatures in order to be able to take a fresh look at the practices of interactive talking. A similar strategy is still often recommended for CA, in what is called 'unmotivated looking', that is without a pre-specified problem or question in mind. This does not deny the fact there is a broadly focused interest in CA in the how of interactional organization. Furthermore, now that there is a well-defined and elaborate 'tradition', the CA look is structured by an extensive conceptual apparatus, which it would be silly to ignore (see the section on concepts below). So while much is already known about the organization of interactive talk, the interest in much current work in CA is still to discover previously unnoticed phenomena, but at the same time researchers also want to extend and refine what is known, or to apply CA to new areas. The 'news' that CA can offer to existing non-CA knowledge is often that such knowledge is too 'simple' in the sense that it ignores or glosses over the actual details of interactive talk, or/and that it starts from and is limited by current cultural, mostly individualistic and mentalistic preconceptions.

The analytic strategies practised in CA can take a variety of shapes as far as they relate to pre-existing knowledge. To simplify matters, I shall concentrate my discussion on a relatively pure form of 'unmotivated looking'. Here the researcher starts with inspecting some recordings and/or transcript looking for episodes that seem somehow interesting, maybe puzzling or especially apt. That episode should be analysed in depth using CA's conceptual repertoire. As I have argued elsewhere (ten Have 2007), such an analysis essentially takes two steps, which I call 'understanding' and the 'analysis' proper.

Listening to the recording and reading the transcript, the analyst first tries to *understand* what the interactants are doing 'organizationally' when they speak as they do. They may, for instance, be requesting information, offering to tell a story or changing the topic. Such understandings will be based, at first, on the researcher's own membership knowledge, as, we might say, a 'cultural colleague' of the speakers. Second, however, the analyst will check the sequential context and especially the uptake of the utterances in question in subsequent talk, immediately following or later in the conversation, for instance by granting a request. Understanding the actions, while not the purpose of the research, is a necessary requirement for the next step, the analysis proper, which is to formulate the *procedures* used to accomplish the actions-as-understood. As noted, CA's interest is organizational and procedural. The ultimate object of CA research is what Schegloff has called the *procedural infrastructure of interaction*, and in particular, the practices of talking in conversation. This means that conversational practices are not analysed in terms of individual properties or institutional expectations, but as situated accomplishments.

Such an analysis results in an analytic formulation of a device, a typical sequence, whatever, which may be reported as such in a single case study. Most of the time, however, the researcher will go on to inspect other cases, which may be relevantly compared to the first one. This may lead to a confirmation, reformulation, a specification or a differentiation into types. The researcher may formulate conditions for, and effects of, the device or sequence – in general, its functions. This more extended type of research is often called a *collection study*. The idea is that the analysis of a first case can be used as a starting point for a more systematic exploration of an emerging analytic theme. The researcher searches an available data set of newly collected data for instances that seem to be similar to the 'candidate phenomenon', the first formulation of the theme, as well as data that seem to point in a different direction, so-called deviant case analysis. In short, the researcher builds a collection of relevant cases in search of patterns that help to elucidate some procedural issues.

This suggests a kind of principled independence of a single research project from existing knowledge, but this is not the case for all CA reports. An investigation may take off from an issue internal to the CA tradition, or even from some problematic or idea external to it.

Transcription

In order to understand what CA is all about, it is essential to consider the activity of transcription, which is to produce a textual rendering of the recorded interaction. In this process of 'entextualization' it is inevitable that some kinds of information are lost, while others are highlighted. In other words, transcriptions are essentially selective; they reflect the underlying theoretical orientation and particular interests of the researcher. In the CA tradition this selectivity has, as mentioned, been institutionalized in a set of transcript conventions developed by Jefferson. This Jeffersonian transcription system suggests which aspects of the interaction as recorded should be noted and made available for consideration though particular symbols and formattings. To get an idea of what transcription in the CA context is all about, it seems best to quote an example. Box 10.1 gives an example of a transcript by Jefferson, which shows some of the most frequently noted details of talk-in-interaction:

Box 10.1

Extract 1, quoted from Jefferson (2002: 1346)
((Co-workers Maggie and Sorrell went to a wedding reception where Maggie had some sort of momentary blackout and felt ill. Next morning she phones Sorrell at work to say that she will not be coming to work, is going to the doctor))
(1) Maggie: .hh because I (.) you know I told Mother what'd ha:ppened yesterday
(2) there at the party,
(3) Sorrell: [°Yeah.°]
(4) Maggie: [a : :] n d uh, .hhhhh (0.2) uh you know she asked me if it was
(5) because I'd had too much to dri:nk and I said no=
(6) Sorrell: =[No ::::::.]
(7) Maggie: =[because at the t]i:me I'd only ha:d,h you know that drink 'n
(8) a ha:lf when we were going through the receiving line.
(9) Sorrell: Ri:ght.

The extract is introduced, within double brackets, with a description of the interactional context, to assist the reader in understanding the episode. In the actual transcript a number of special symbols are used to render the specific, hearable details of the speech production. Space considerations prohibit a full explanation of these, but I shall just note some of the more important ones.

Underlining indicates stress, and we can see in the example that the speakers use stress to 'shape' their contributions' emotional meaning. Square brackets are used to indicate those parts that were spoken in overlap, so Sorrell's 'supportive' contributions in lines 3 and 6 are spoken while Maggie continues her story. In interaction the *timing* of one utterance in relation to others is essential. When one utterance follows another very quickly, this is indicated by equal signs (=), so Sorrel's 'No' comes in 'early', thereby emphasizing her agreement. It is also prolonged, as indicated by the colons: 'No ::::::.' Punctuation markers are used to indicate intonation; a ? a rising one, a comma a non-final flat one, and a dot a downward falling tone. The dot-preceded .hhh, finally, render an 'inbreath', which is often done as a speaker starts speaking, thereby 'claiming' the next turn.

I shall now discuss some of these interactional phenomena in a more systematic fashion by explicating and illustrating some of CA's core concepts.

Core concepts

During CA's first decade, its originators explored a range of conversational materials from an 'organizational' perspective. These explorations resulted in the conceptualization of a few essential 'organizations' that conversationalists could be seen to use in designing their talking together. This conceptualization has since been extended and refined, but it is still basic to the analytic apparatus of current CA. In this section, it will be explicated by using some data extracts for illustrative purposes.

Turn-taking organization

Quite early on, Sacks formulated two essential properties of 'conversation': overwhelmingly, there is one and only one person speaking at a time, while speaker change generally recurs with minimal gap and minimal overlap (Sacks 1992, 2004; Sacks, Schegloff and Jefferson 1974). These properties are seen as a continuous *achievement* of the parties to the conversation, which they accomplish *together* on a turn-by-turn basis, or, more precisely, at any 'transition relevance place' (TRP), at the end of any 'turn constructional unit' (TCU). A 'turn' consists of one or more of these 'units', which may consist of just one word or a clause or a sentence. These are constructed in such a way that their possible end, their 'completion point', can be roughly expected by the other(s). On its completion, another speaker may have been selected by the current speaker, may 'self-select' or the current speaker may continue talking (see Sacks, Schegloff and Jefferson 1974).

Let's take another look at extract 1. In lines 1 and 2 we have a first turn by Maggie: '.hh because I(c) (.) you know I told Mother what'd ha:ppened yesterday there at the party,'. After a hearable inbreath (.hh), which is quite common a start of a turn, she utters 'because I', which is obviously incomplete, although it is followed by a short pause. Then she says 'you know', which involves her recipient, and which is also quite common as a within-turn interjection. Then follows 'I told Mother what'd ha:ppened yesterday', which on the face of it might be a complete turn, but does not have a final intonation. There follows, in any case, an addition: 'there at the party,'. The comma in the transcript indicates that it produced with a kind of intermediate or 'semi-final' intonation. So its character as a TRP is a bit dubious.

In line 3 Sorrel, the recipient of Maggie's turn, then produces a softly spoken (indicated by the degree signs) '°Yeah.°'. This may be called an 'acknowledgement token' or in Schegloff's (1982) terms a 'continuer'. It acknowledges receipt, understanding and/or acceptance of the other's turn so far, but does not claim a turn at speaking for itself. In so doing, it allows the other to continue speaking. In fact, in line 4, Maggie starts to continue her turn in overlap with Sorrel, and she does this in a rather marked way, an 'and' with a prolonged vowel in overlap with Sorrel's '°yeah.°', a rather long inbreath, a short pause, and two filler-like items: '[a : :] n d uh, .hhhhh (0.2) uh you know'. We may speculate that these details are symptoms of a slight difficulty in the organization of turn-taking at this point.

Maggie continues her turn, in lines 4 and 5, with: 'she asked me if it was because I'd had too much to dri:nk and I said no'. The moment she has said this (indicated by the equal signs), Sorrel comes in with an emphatically intoned 'No ::::::.' (line 6). This, as Jefferson stresses in her paper, is not an acknowledgement, but a rather strong alignment with Maggie's point of view, as she has been a witness to the scene reported. Sorrel's 'No ::::::.' is produced in overlap with the start of a further continuation by Maggie in lines 7 and 8: 'because at the t]i:me I'd only ha:d,h you know that drink 'n a ha:lf when we were going through the receiving line.' Note that this time she produces a final intonation (marked by the point). Now Sorrel produces a confirming 'Ri:ght.'

I assume that this short discussion of just one fragment has been enough to demonstrate that in any particular case, issues of turn-taking, who is to speak when and for how long, are intimately bound up with what is being talked about and the relationship between the speakers that builds up while they are talking. That was, of course, a rather special episode in which Maggie continued telling her little story, while Sorrel's contribution was limited to short supportive and affiliative items. In many cases, the distribution of turns is more equal, as we shall see when we look at extract 2 in the next sub-section.

Sequence organization and repair

Right from the start of CA, another aspect of the organization of talk-in-interaction emerged as a crucial one: the interconnection between subsequent utterances. At first, this was discussed in term of 'paired-actions'. Later a technical concept was developed: 'adjacency pair', which can be defined as a two-part sequence in which the first part makes relevant the production of a second pair part of the type suggested by the first part to follow immediately after the first one, as in question–answer, greeting–greeting, invitation–acceptance/declination (see Schegloff and Sacks 1973: 295–6; Schegloff 2007:13–27). When a speaker produces an utterance that is recognizable as a first pair part of a certain type, the addressed recipient is expected to respond in a fitting manner, like in 'what time is it?' / 'Three o'clock'. If an answer is not forthcoming, the recipient is 'accountable' for its absence, which can be honoured by giving an excuse, for instance, like 'I don't have my watch with me, sorry.' A two-part sequence consisting of just one adjacency pair can be expanded in various ways, for instance by a 'pre-sequence', like 'may I ask you a question?' / 'yes', an 'insertion sequence' like 'wait a moment' / 'sure' between the first and second pair parts of the base sequence, or with a 'post-expansion', as in 'thank you' / 'that's OK'/'bye' (see Schegloff 2007).

Let's take a look how sequence organization is 'done' in an actual stretch of talk, the start of a telephone conversation between two ex-partners about the return of their son from the mother to the father (Box 10.2).

Box 10.2

Extract 2, quoted from Schegloff (2007:42–3)
(0) ((ring))
(1) Marsha: Hello:?
(2) Tony: Hi: Marsha?
(3) Marsha: Ye:ah.
(4) Tony: How are you.
(5) Marsha: Fi::ne.
(6) (0.2)
(7) Marsha: Did Joey get home yet?
(8) Tony: Well I wz wondering when 'e left.
(9) (0.2)
(10) Marsha:.hhh Uh:(d) did Oh: .h Yer not in on what ha:ppen'.(hh)(d)
(11) Tony: No(h)o=
(12) Marsha: =He's flying.
(13) (0.2)
(14) Marsha: En Ilene is going to meet im:.Becuz the to:p wz ripped
(15) off'v iz car which is tih say someb'ddy helped th'mselfs.
(16) Tony: Stolen.
(17) (0.4)
(18) Marsha: Stolen.=Right out in front of my house.

The sequence starts with the telephone ring, which represents an 'action', which Schegloff (1968) has characterized as a 'summons', which makes relevant an answer, here given with a 'Hello:?' on line 1. Together, the ring and the hello constitute a summons–answer sequence, a typical way to start an interaction. Next we get a question-intoned 'Hi: Marsha?', followed by a 'Ye:ah.'; an identification followed by a confirmation. Then a third 'adjacency pair' is produced: 'How are you.', followed by 'Fi::ne', a how-are-you sequence. With these absolutely routine sequences the scene is set for the actual business of the call (see Schegloff 1986).

These small explications should suffice, for the moment, to demonstrate what CA is after: the actual doing of interaction is organized by way of a concerted application of more or less conventional 'formats', or 'devices', adapted to the local circumstances. So for any utterance one can ask what is the *action* that it performs in the sequential context in which it is produced, which predominantly involves the immediately previous actions.

A possible effect of the condition that we are dealing with an *inter*action, involving more than one party, is that what a speaker projects may be taken up in a non-projected manner. Consider the space after Marsha's 'Fi::ne.' in line 5 (the 0.2 in line 6 indicates a pause of two-tenths of a second). Several things *could* have happened there. Marsha could have asked 'and how are you?', as quite often such inquiries are reciprocated. Or, Tony, being the initiator of the call, could have produced an account for the call, a reason-for-the-call, thereby initiating a first topic. What happens instead is that Marsha, after a small moment, as Tony does not take a turn, continues by asking a substantial question: 'Did Joey get home yet?' (line 7). And then Tony, instead of answering that yes/no-question directly, produces what Schegloff calls a 'counter', 'Well I wz wondering when 'e left.' (line 8). Apparently, this was his reason-for-the-call, which also implies that Joey has not arrived yet, so in a way it is an answer after all. Next, after another small pause in line 9, Marsha produces a quite complicated turn, '.hhh Uh:(d) did Oh: .h Yer not in on what ha:ppen'.(hh)(d)' (line 10). So she infers from Tony's counter that he has not been informed about recent changes in Joey's travel plan, which is promptly confirmed in Tony's emphatic 'No(h)o' (line 11). Marsha's inference about Tony not being informed, reported in line 10, is an implicit offer to tell him 'what happened', and his confirmation, in line 11, works as an acceptance of that offer, a 'go-ahead'. Together, these two utterances work as an offer–acceptance adjacency pair, a 'pre-sequence' that prepares the actual telling, which does indeed follow, starting with a conclusion (in line 12), to be followed with a more extended explication (not fully quoted in the extract). So what we can see in this extract is how the two interactants, in their unique circumstances, use very general sequence formats, conceptualized here as various types of adjacency pairs, to constitute a shared understanding of the situation as it has developed, an achieved intersubjectivity.

Very special kinds of sequence, 'repair sequences', are designed to solve various problems of hearing or understanding a preceding utterance, the so-called 'trouble source'. In the simplest case, the speaker who produced this utterance corrects this problematic utterance him- or herself, a case of self-initiated self-repair. But another may also initiate repair, for instance by saying 'what?'. When the original speaker then gives the same or a corrected version, we have other-initiated self-repair; otherwise we can get other-initiated other-repair. In general self-repair is 'preferred' and others tend to provide space for it, before they initiate or even do the repair themselves (Schegloff, Jefferson and Sacks 1977). Box 10.3 provides a rather simple example.

Box 10.3

Extract 3, quoted from Schegloff (2007:105)

(1)	*Bet*	*Was last night the first time you met Missiz Kelly?*
(2)		*(1.0)*
(3)	*Mar*	*Met whom?*
(4)	*Bet*	*Missiz Kelly.*
(5)	*Mar*	*Yes.*

The utterance on line 1, a first-pair-part, turns out to be the trouble source, as there is not an immediate answer (line 2). On line 3 we see a repair initiator, with the repair following on line 4, after which the addressee is able to complete the adjacency pair with an answer on line 5. The repair sequence (lines 3 and 4) is inserted into the base adjacency pair (lines 1 and 5). Repair sequences can be initiated at any time and they inevitably 'interrupt' the flow of the interaction.

Turn design and preference organization

After a discussion of turn-taking, and one of the activities of constructing sequences of turns, I now turn to the ways in which turns themselves are designed. What we have seen in considering the extracts discussed so far is that speakers seem to design their turns quite carefully in order to accomplish locally relevant tasks effectively. Look again, for instance, at the three short contributions of Sorrel in extract 1: "°Yeah.°" (line 3), 'No ::::::.' (line 6) and 'Ri:ght.' (line 9). Not only their explicit 'content', but also their 'placement' in relation to the talk by the primary speaker, and their intonation, display her sensitivity to Maggie's expressed concerns, and in so doing accomplish her alignment with her friend. We can say that the intimate friendship of the two is produced in and by such displays of caring for each other. For extract 2, it may be suggested that the parties take care to manage the tensions inherent in their being ex-partners and co-parents in a bearable manner.

What these cases, and the remarks I just made, demonstrate is the significance of the CA concept of 'recipient design', defined as 'a multitude of respects in which talk by a party in a conversation is constructed or designed in ways which display an orientation and sensitivity to the particular other(s) who are the co-participants' (Sacks et al. 1974: 727). The sensitivity displayed in the design of turns concerns not only the other(s) as a person in a relationship, but also, as noted above, their specific 'placement'. This is especially prominent in second-pair-parts of adjacency pairs, in the ways in which they relate to the first-pair-part to which they reply. For many types of first-pair-parts there are alternative types of responses, and these tend to be differently 'valued', one being in some way positive, or 'preferred', while the other is valued negatively; it is 'dispreferred'. When a request is made, for instance, granting is preferred and declining is dispreferred. This is not a matter of personal preference, but what might be called a structural or cultural one.

In extract 1 we saw the working of another preference, the preference for agreement. Maggie's story clearly projected an agreement as its 'preferred' response, and Sorrel provided that response promptly, with one-word turns: '°Yeah.°' (line 3), 'No ::::::.' (line 6), and 'Ri:ght.' (line 9). This is a general property of preferred responses: they come like that, fast and short. Dispreferred responses, on the other hand, are designed very differently. They tend to be delayed in various ways, by pauses, inbreaths, hesitations and positive prefaces, while they are also mostly followed by an account.

In extract 2, line 8, Tony's 'counter' is formulated as: 'Well I wz wondering when 'e left.' A first observation is that he starts with 'Well'. This is one of a restricted set of words that are often used to preface a 'dispreferred' response. It delays that response a bit, but it also suggests that the speaker 'steps back' a bit, we could say, indicating that what follows is a reconsidered message, rather than a spontaneous reply. Furthermore, note that he uses a past tense, 'wz' (was), marking that what he says reports on a (mental) event that existed before this particular moment. Marsha's response to this: '.hhh Uh:(d) did Oh: .h Yer not in on what ha:ppen'.(hh)(d)' (in line 10) is also marked as special in a number of ways. It starts with a hearable inbreath and an 'Uh:', both of which delay the core part of the turn, typical of dispreferred turns. Then we get 'did' projecting a sentence which is not forthcoming, but instead she utters an 'Oh:'. John Heritage (1984) has abundantly demonstrated that 'oh' is used to indicate a 'change-of-state' of the speaker, like receiving new, unexpected information. Here it may be used to note that Tony's lack of information on the changed travel plan surprises her as she had expected Joey to call his father to tell him about it. Finally, note that at the end of her turn, there is a small bit of laughter, indicated in the transcript as '(hh)', and note also that in his immediate response (in line 11), Tony also laughs a bit: 'No(h)o'. In this way, the two share a bit of amusement or 'lightness' while dealing with these complicated misunderstandings. Details of turn design, then, add layers of meaning to the verbal exchanges, far beyond just the words spoken. It is part of CA's core business to exhume such subtleties by very careful listening, transcribing and analysing.

With these short sketches, I hope to have achieved a basic understanding of some of the core concepts used in CA as they can be used to explicate generally unnoticed but real-world subtleties of verbal interaction. For reasons of space, I have left many more detailed concepts unmentioned and unexplicated. I refer the reader to the list of references for pointers to other sources in which these can be found.

Visual aspects of face-to-face encounters

In the first decade of its existence, CA was almost exclusively based on audio recordings. While this is not a problem with the telephone conversations that were mostly used, for face-to-face interactions researchers could not investigate the visual cues that evidently play an important role in such encounters. When video technology became available during the 1970s some people, most prominently Charles Goodwin and later Christian Heath, began to apply CA methods and concepts to video-recorded interactions. Goodwin's studies showed clearly that and how visuals do play an important role in the organization of face-to-face encounters. His findings do not seem to invalidate the results of earlier, audio-based studies, however, but they do provide an extremely valuable addition to what was already known.

To take a simple type of case, non-verbal actions can fit into action sequences that also include verbal utterances. The handing over of the salt at a dinner table can be a fitting second-pair-part in a request sequence. More importantly, the bodily activities that accompany verbal expressions often have an impact on the production and reception of those expressions. Speakers can select a recipient by their gaze, and often make an effort to 'get' the gaze of their intended recipient, for instance by restarting their utterance. Looking at someone functions as an 'attention display' for what that person is doing and saying. Pointing at something, whether explicitly by a pointing gesture, or more implicitly by looking at an object, often works to have the others present shifting their attention in the direction of the pointing. Other aspects of bodily behaviour, like facial expressions, body attitude and walking, are also important, but gestures and gazing seem to be the easiest to investigate (see Goodwin 2000; Heath 2004).

Nowadays, most CA researchers work with video recordings when they study face-to-face encounters. Not all of them focus explicitly on visual aspects; they may use the visual features just as an aid or addition to their understanding of the scenes analysed for their vocal interaction. Quite often, however, most prominently in workplace studies (discussed later in this chapter), attending to bodily actions is an essential part of the analysis. On the other hand, those who concentrate on vocal interaction as such may prefer to use telephone data, and you may have remarked that the transcripts I have used above were from telephone calls.

Applied CA: institutional interactions

In my rendering of CA so far, I have concentrated on the type of conversation analysis that is focused on the analysis of the organization of talk-in-interaction as such, what I call 'pure CA'. Since the late 1970s, however, quite a lot of CA work has acquired what might be called a 'double focus': while still analysing the organization of interactive talking, it has also attended to the functions of such talk in the wider setting in which it occurred. Some of the settings investigated in this way are courtrooms, news interviews, standardized survey interviews and medical consultations.

These 'institutional interactions' could often be characterized in terms of a special turn-taking system, which involves a specialization of turn-types for the different categories of participants in those encounters. In news interviews, for instance (see Clayman and Heritage 2002), the interviewer is asking questions, while the interviewee is limited to giving answers. It can often be observed that interviewers produce quite long introductory statements, during which the interviewees do not react, until finally a recognizable question is voiced, after which the interviewee produces an answer in which they may also take issue with some aspects of the introductory statement.

In medical consultations, to take another example (see ten Have 2006; Heritage and Maynard 2006), patients are generally expected to present their complaints and answer questions about their symptoms. When they depart from those restrictions, for instance by suggesting a diagnosis, they often do this hesitantly, showing that they recognize the 'dispreferred' status of such actions *for them*. It is also clear, however, that the specific character of such restrictions depends on the phase of the encounter. So in the diagnostic phase, patients tend to accept the diagnosis as a matter of course, while in the treatment phase they are often much more active, as physicians seek their acceptance of the treatment proposal.

It should be noted that patterns like the ones just mentioned are not just a matter of determinative cultural conventions, but rather indicative of oriented-to interpretative frameworks. So, for instance, an interviewee may interrupt on occasion an interviewer's introductory statement in order to show his or her utter disagreement with its presuppositions. Furthermore, local circumstances, including prominently the course of the interaction so far, may have an observable impact on how contributions to the interaction are produced. Anssi Peräkylä (2006), for instance, found that patients tended to react in an extended fashion to diagnostic statements by the physician when the latter explicated the evidence for it, rather than when the physician just asserted the diagnosis.

With these few remarks, we have to leave this important branch of applied CA. As can be seen from the examples above, these studies mostly investigated interactions between institutional agents and another persons who, in one way or another, were a 'client' of that institution. This is different in the type of research to be discussed next.

Applied CA: workplace studies

While applied CA studies of agent–client interactions limit themselves mostly to audio or video recordings, a different kind of study of work settings emerged in the late 1980s. In addition to video recordings, these studies also used ethnographic fieldwork. The studies focused mostly on rather specialized activities, involving complex technological support devices like computers and various communication technologies, such as control rooms for public transport facilities (see Heath and Luff 2000). Video is used because these activities often take place in a group setting involving team members and extensive use of various technological artefacts. Analysing such activities requires, on the one hand, visual access to the local environment in order to study bodily actions and non-vocal exchanges *in situ*, and on the other, a deeper, locally specialized understanding of the activities under study than is generally used for agent–client interactions.

Some kinds of participant observation, as well as studying relevant documents and interviewing experts, are the means used to acquire the required background for really understanding what is going on. To mention one example, Maurice Nevile (2004) collected his core data for his studies of 'talk-in-interaction in the airline-cockpit' by videoing the activities of flight crews on scheduled flights by commercial airlines. But before he even approached the airlines to ask for their cooperation, he prepared his research by extensively reading whatever he could find about the operation of commercial airlines, training and operations manuals, official accident reports and so on He also watched available information videos showing pilots at work, visited conferences and talked to research psychologists working with flight crews and accident investigators.

In such workplace studies, the concepts, findings and methods of CA are 'applied' as part of a wider undertaking which is broadly inspired by ethnomethodology. I shall just mention a few general insights that can be gained from these studies. First, it is clear that such specialized (team)work requires an experience-based practical knowledge that goes far beyond what can be acquired through formal instruction in a non-work setting. Second, effective teamwork requires not only the individual worker's understanding of the task-at-hand, but also an understanding *at a glance* of what others are doing. A lot of actual coordination of activities occurs in an implicit fashion, often by seeing in peripheral vision or by overhearing talk and adapting one's own activities accordingly. So, for instance, the worker in a London Underground control room, who has the task to make announcements to the travelling public, knows from observing and overhearing his colleagues at work on some crisis situation what to announce, to whom, and when, without getting a request to do so (see Heath and Luff 2000). Third, formal accounts of work activities cannot make this 'hidden work' and the competencies involved in it visible to outsiders, including the 'overseeing' management (see Whalen and Vinkhuyzen 2000).

In order to illustrate how CA figures in this more encompassing endeavour, let me refer shortly to some of Nevile's (2004) findings when studying airline cockpits. In the first part of his book, he analyses the use of personal pronouns 'I', 'you', and 'we'. Some of these uses are officially prescribed in the relevant manuals, while others are voluntary, impromptu and chosen on the spot. They function, in any case, as designators of local and momentary cockpit identities, with associated tasks and responsibilities. So when 'I' is used, for instance, the speakers claims an individual action, responsibility or experience, while 'we' suggests a collective, team reality, while 'you' assigns a task to the other pilot.

In the second part, Nevile discusses a range of concrete examples to examine how pilots coordinate their talk and non-talk activities as they perform the routine tasks necessary to fly their plane. Such coordination is essential in maintaining a shared understanding of 'where they are' in the flight and 'what has to be done' then and there, as pilots have to perform their tasks with split-second precision and strictly in sequence, one after the other. In doing this work, talk is just one of the resources that participants use and orient to. Others include gaze direction, gesture and placement and movement of parts of the body, such as head, arm, hand, leg and eyebrows.

In the third and final part of his book, Nevile widens his perspective on talk in the cockpit to investigate how it is coordinated with talk to participants outside the cockpit, such as air traffic controllers and cabin crew members. Again, the issue is that the two pilots have to attain and demonstrate a shared understanding of the local consequences of the outside talk, which they can do by internal talk and/or non-vocal, but visible activities. Investigation of such fine-tuned activities requires very finely detailed transcriptions of talk with descriptions of the associated activities.

To give an impression of how this is done, I quote one of Nevile's examples in Box 10.4, which in the text is accompanied by a picture of the pointing finger:

Box 10.4

Extract 4, quoted from Nevile (2004: 131)

C = Captain
PNF = Pilot not flying
FO = First officer
PF = Pilot flying

```
(1)            (50.3)
(2) C/PNF:     one thousand to altitude.
               ⥣-----------------⥣
(2a) C/PNF:    ((moves right hand up from lap, then left to right, at
               chest height, with index finger extended))
                           ⥣--------------⥣
(2b) C/PNF:                ((holds right hand still, just to the right
                           of own chest, index finger points to
                           FO/PF's side of main instrument panel))
                                   ⥣
(2c) C/PNF:                        ((moves right hand down and left,
                                   back to right leg))
(3)            (3.2) = (0 > 1.4 > 2.4 > 3.2))
                           ⥣----------⥣
(4)                        ((sound of altitude alert buzzer))
(5) FO/PF       >alert (.) for level (.) two fi::ve zero
(6)            (27.5)
```

The arrows indicate the moment in the talk at which the non-vocal activities start or stop.

It should be clear by now that workplace studies are a rather demanding kind of CA study, but it is to my mind also extremely rewarding and necessary because it reflects the subtle but too often ignored or unnoticed complexity of specialized work.

Applied CA: impaired communication

In early CA the analytic attention was not directed to the conditions so much as to the 'internal workings', so to say, of conversational interactions. One field of applied CA in which such conditions are in focus is that in which the interactions involve at least one person whose communicative capabilities are in one or another way impaired. Charles Goodwin, for instance, has studied interactions involving one person who, after a severe stroke, could only speak three words, 'yes', 'no' and 'and', voice nonsense syllables with meaningful intonation, and gesture with one hand. Goodwin (2003: 91) notes that the fact that he could speak just these three words specifically seems crucial as 'yes' and 'no' are typically used as second-pair-parts in adjacency pairs, while 'and' ties other units of talk. He adds:

> This vocabulary set presupposes that its user is embedded within a community of other speakers. His talk does not stand alone as a self-contained entity, but emerges from, and is situated within, the talk of others, to which it is inextricably linked.

In his video-based case study, Goodwin shows how this is possible, as the members of the impaired person's family are able to solve the puzzles created by his gestures and voicings against the background of their known-in-common knowledge of their experiences of the previous few days. Furthermore, as they are intimately aware of the limited possibilities of the aphasic, they can design their own utterances, especially their first-pair-parts, in such a way that the aphasic can respond sensibly with one of his three available words or a gesture.

The results of case studies by other CA researchers of situations involving other kinds of impairment point in the same direction. The achievement of collaborative understanding requires not only a lot of patience by the participants, but also intimate knowledge of concrete situations and recent experiences as well as the limitations and possibilities of the impaired other. Studying impaired communication as it happens in everyday real-life situations between intimates differs enormously from the usual ways in which the abilities of impaired communicators are assessed 'officially', and leads to different results. The standard way in which such assessments are produced is to place the subject in an experimental situation and give them a set of separate standardized communicative tasks to perform. Without the continuity of a sensible sequence and the familiarity of the participants as real-life partners, it is no surprise that the impaired function is often assessed as much poorer than it actually is in the person's ordinary life.

This is not to deny that interactions in which at least one participant is aphasic or otherwise communicatively impaired differ in many ways from those in which all participants are normally competent. There will, for instance, be many more repair sequences, which can be quite long. Therefore, it may be more difficult to stay on one particular topic. These repair sequences may be concerned with a production difficulty, like searching for a word, or with 'guesses' offered by the recipients of an unclear utterance. Aphasics tend to use rather general expressions, 'general meaning lexical items' like pronouns or words like 'thing' and 'do', where others would select a more precise and specific one. This can create difficulties for co-participants who will have to guess what is meant, which again may take time before mutual understanding is achieved. It should be stressed, however, that the basic mechanisms used in these conversations are the same as those in ordinary circumstances. In other words, the basic issues and solutions of turn-taking, sequence organization, repair and so on that are operative in ordinary conversations, are also at work in 'impaired' circumstances. It is sad and frustrating for impaired speakers, when all too often this basic competence is not recognized as such. One of the specialists in this area, Ray Wilkinson, recently remarked:

> A notable feature of the application of CA to aphasia is the fact that this approach has been used within intervention studies and has been incorporated, to some extent at least, into the everyday clinical practice of some professionals (primarily speech and language therapists) working with people with aphasia.
>
> (Wilkinson 2006:108)

We may hope that this usage will spread over the coming years, to the benefit of the people concerned, as well as CA itself.

Conclusion

Since the time that the first steps toward CA were taken in the 1960s, it has developed in numerous directions, although its basic ideas have stayed essentially the same. And while it originated within a sociological framework, it has spread to quite a lot of different disciplines. It has therefore not been possible in the limited space of this chapter to present a complete picture of these developments and disciplinary connections. There are, for instance, many linguists interested in the actual use of language in interactional situations who work within CA or who have incorporated ideas from CA into their own work (see Ford et al. 2002). Similarly, there are psychologists who have developed a branch called 'discursive psychology', which has taken on board a lot of CA conceptually and methodologically (see ten Have 2007: 54–7; Wooffitt 2005).

For applied CA, I had to limit my treatment to just three of the most prominent fields of application, but there are many others in which CA is used, for instance in education (classroom interaction, second language learning) and communications (meetings, negotiations and so on). CA has also been used in gender studies. Schegloff (1997) has stressed that when CA is used in the service of such wider concerns, it is important to *first* analyse the interactions 'in their own terms', so to speak: that is, focusing on participants' own local orientations as visible in their situated interactions and the local uptake of these. It has to be demonstrated, in other words, that an issue like 'gender' is relevant in some way to that interaction as such, and not just a projection of an analyst's private interests. Recent contributions to what is called 'feminist CA' prove that this can be done, with interesting and sensible results for both feminism and CA (see Speer 2005 for an overview and Kitzinger 2005 as a recent example). The same point can, of course, be made for other general issues such as power relations, social inequality and social problems.

In sum, CA offers a conceptual framework and an established methodology to explicate a level of social organization which is conventionally 'unnoticed', while it is, at the same time, unavoidably used by everybody who performs as a member of society by talking and doing other things in interaction.

Bibliography

Clayman, Steven and John Heritage (2002) *The News Interview: Journalists and Public Figures on the Air*. Cambridge: Cambridge University Press.

Drew, Paul and John Heritage (eds) (1992) *Talk at Work: Interaction in Institutional Settings*. Cambridge: Cambridge University Press.

Ford, Cecilia E., Barbara A. Fox and Sandra A. Thompson (eds) (2002) *The Language of Turn and Sequence*. New York: Oxford University Press.

Goodwin, Charles (2000) 'Practices of seeing: visual analysis – an ethnomethodological approach', in Theo van Leeuwen and Carey Jewitt (eds), *Handbook of Visual Analysis*. London: Sage.

Goodwin, Charles (ed.) (2003) *Conversation and Brain Damage*. New York: Oxford University Press.

Heath, Christian (2004) 'Analysing face-to-face interaction: video, the visual and material', in David Silverman (ed.), *Qualitative Research: Theory, Method and Practice*, 2nd edition. London: Sage.

Heath, Christian and Paul Luff (2000) *Technology in Action*. Cambridge: Cambridge University Press.

Heritage, John (1984) 'A change-of-state token and aspects of its sequential placement', in J. Maxwell Atkinson and John Heritage (eds), *Structures of Social Action: Studies in Conversation Analysis*. Cambridge: Cambridge University Press.

Heritage, John and Douglas W. Maynard (eds) (2006) *Communication in Medical Care: Interaction Between Primary Care Physicians and Patients*. Cambridge: Cambridge University Press.

Jefferson, Gail (1985) 'An exercise in the transcription and analysis of laughter', in Teun A. van Dijk (ed.), *Handbook of Discourse Analysis*, Vol. III. London: Academic Press.

Jefferson, Gail (2002) 'Is "No" an acknowledgment token? Comparing American and British uses of (+)/(-) tokens.' *Journal of Pragmatics*, 34: 1345–83.

Jefferson, Gail (2004) 'Glossary of transcript symbols with an introduction', in Gene H. Lerner (ed.), *Conversation Analysis: Studies from the First Generation*. Amsterdam/Philadelphia: John Benjamins.

Kitzinger, Celia (2005) 'Heteronormativity in action: reproducing normative heterosexuality in "after hours" calls to the doctor.' *Social Problems*, 52: 477–98.

Nevile, Maurice (2004) *Beyond the Black Box: Talk-in-Interaction in the Airline Cockpit*. Aldershot: Ashgate.

Peräkylä, Anssi (2006) 'Communicating and responding to diagnosis', in John Heritage and Douglas W. Maynard (eds), *Communication in Medical Care: Interaction Between Primary Care Physicians and Patients*. Cambridge: Cambridge University Press.

Sacks, Harvey (1992) *Lectures on Conversation*, 2 vols. Oxford: Blackwell.

Sacks, Harvey (2004) 'An initial characterization of the organization of speaker turn-taking in conversation', in Gene H. Lerner (ed.), *Conversation Analysis: Studies from the First Generation*. Amsterdam/Philadelphia: John Benjamins.

Sacks, Harvey, Emanuel A. Schegloff and Gail Jefferson (1974) 'A simplest systematics for the organization of turn-taking for conversation.' *Language*, 50: 696–735.

Schegloff, Emanuel A. (1968) 'Sequencing in conversational openings.' *American Anthropologist*, 70: 1075–95.

Schegloff, Emanuel A. (1982) 'Discourse as an interactional achievement: some uses of 'uh huh' and other things that come between sentences', in Deborah Tannen (ed.), *Analyzing Discourse: Text and Talk*. Washington, DC: Georgetown University Press.

Schegloff, Emanuel A. (1986) 'The routine as achievement.' *Human Studies*, 9: 111–51.

Schegloff, Emanuel A. (1997) 'Whose text? Whose context?.' *Discourse and Society*, 8: 165–87.

Schegloff, Emanuel A. (2007) *Sequence Organization in Interaction: A Primer in Conversation Analysis*, Vol. 1. Cambridge: Cambridge University Press.

Schegloff, Emanuel A., Gail Jefferson and Harvey Sacks (1977) 'The preference for self-correction in the organization of repair in conversation.' *Language*, 53: 361–82.

Schegloff, Emanuel A. and Harvey Sacks (1973) 'Opening up closings.' *Semiotica*, 8: 289–327.

Speer, Susan A. (2005) *Gender Talk: Feminism, Discourse and Conversation Analysis*. London: Routledge.

Te Molder, Hedwig and Jonathan Potter (eds) (2005) *Conversation and Cognition*. Cambridge: Cambridge University Press.

Ten Have, Paul (2006) 'On the interactive constitution of medical encounters.' *Revue Française de Linguistique Appliquée*, 11 (2): 85–98.

Ten Have, Paul (2007) *Doing Conversation Analysis: A Practical Guide*, 2nd edn. London: Sage.

Whalen, Jack and Eric Vinkhuyzen (2000) 'Expert systems in (inter)action: diagnosing document machine problems over the telephone', in Paul Luff, Jon Hindmarsh and Christian Heath (eds), *Workplace Studies: Recovering Work Practice and Informing Systems Design*. Cambridge: Cambridge University Press.

Wilkinson, Ray (2006) 'Applying conversation analysis to aphasic talk: from investigation to intervention.' *Revue Française de Linguistique Appliquée*, 11 (2): 99–110.

Wooffitt, Robin (2005): *Conversation Analysis and Discourse Analysis: A Comparative and Critical Introduction*. London: Sage.

CHAPTER 11

The Sociology of the Absurd

'An Absurd Man in an Absurd World'

MICHAEL HVIID JACOBSEN

Introduction

Absurdist writer Albert Camus (1913–1960) described his nihilistic novel *The Stranger* as 'a study of an absurd man in an absurd world'. In this book and many others, Camus depicted how the inhabitants of the modern world were experiencing a new malaise materializing in their futile search for meaning, feelings of loss and in their search for identity being increasingly alienated. He insisted that the 20th century marked a turning point in the values and ethics of human society, a radical departure from enchanted and community-based traditional society now setting humanity loose – to absurdity. This diagnosis sets the somewhat sombre tone for this chapter, dealing with one of the most overlooked and least recognized perspectives within everyday life sociology, namely the 'sociology of the absurd'.

Perhaps the sociology of the absurd qualifies as the most infinitesimal perspective or approach in sociology because only a book or two has been written within the direct scope of the perspective provided by the original proponents and only a handful of articles or books dealing with, applauding or critiquing the perspective have subsequently been published. As a consequence, it is a forgotten perspective seldom discussed in social theory and hardly ever directly utilized in actual social research. Moreover, references to readings from the sociology of the absurd will only rarely appear in university teaching curricula with the consequence that new generations of sociologists remain largely ignorant of this position.

Does this mean that the sociology of the absurd is utterly unimportant and useless for sociologists? A resounding 'no' must be the answer – an answer I shall seek to justify below. It ought to be a truism that the importance or usefulness of theories or perspectives is not always matched or measured by their popularity or the piles of works published in their honour. This chapter seeks to rectify sociology's negligence of this overlooked perspective by introducing the sociology of the absurd as one among many everyday life perspectives. It draws on a range of conventional sociological sources, but also represents a perspective that in originality and creativity has covered terrain left uncharted and untouched by more orthodox everyday life theories.

First, the intellectual ancestry and the proponents of the sociology of the absurd is presented. This is followed by an excursion into the substantial areas of theorizing to which the sociology of the absurd has contributed, and by a section dealing with how the sociology of the absurd can be put into action in actual research. Subsequently, I deal with some central points of criticism raised against the sociology of the absurd. Finally, an assessment of the continued relevance for sociology of the sociology of the absurd is presented.

The intellectual ancestry of the absurd

The sociology of the absurd is a product or phenomenon of the experimental and progressive *Zeitgeist* of the late 1960s. It can be ranked among the avant-gardist 'new sociologies' emerging during this period, and among those critical of the status quo of mainstream sociology especially on the American continent. These new sociologies reacted to the dominance of the so-called 'orthodox consensus', consisting of functionalism, neopositivism and modernization theory (Giddens 1979), especially in American sociology throughout the 1950s and 1960s. Many of the new sociologies were also so-called 'creative sociologies' because they emphasized a creative and active image of the human actor and their meaning-creating capacity as the cornerstone of social order. Among these new sociologies ranked ethnomethodology, symbolic interactionism, phenomenology and other more micro-oriented perspectives (Morris 1977). Although these positions and traditions were not entirely new, the reception and backing they received especially in these early years was unprecedented in sociology.

Among them also ranked the sociology of the absurd as the invention of Stanford M. Lyman (1933–2003) and Marvin B. Scott at that time employed at University of California and Sonoma State College respectively. Their research agendas primarily evolved around empirical studies of racial issues, student revolts and gambling behaviour (see Lyman 1972, 1974; Scott and Lyman 1970; Scott 1968) and therefore it was unsurprising that they would eventually venture into a more theoretical/conceptual enterprise culminating in the book *A Sociology of the Absurd*. The backbone of the sociology of the absurd is exactly this collection of essays, published by Lyman and Scott in 1970, and reissued in an expanded edition in 1989, dealing with a variety of topics, some of which will be dealt with more substantively below.

The sociology of the absurd is sometimes referred to as 'neo-interactionism' because it takes the conventional interactionist perspective of studying social interaction in natural settings further, and provides a more hybrid perspective on everyday life, incorporating insights from a variety of sources. As the interactionists, the absurdists define themselves as belonging to the strand of anti-positivist movements in sociology, together with for example ethnomethodology and phenomenology (Lally and Preston 1973). This anti-positivism can be seen in the sources of inspiration drawn upon by the absurdists. Apart from borrowing heavily from interactionism, phenomenology, existentialism and ethnomethodology, they were also inspired by game theory, conflict theory, dramaturgy, absurdist literature and artistic and creative input from for example surrealism. Therefore, the sociology of the absurd is a synthetic approach, a collage or a colloid, as Edward A. Tiryakian (1973) observed.

The 'theatre of the absurd', according to Martin Esslin (1991), such a prominent and provocative presence among the performing arts during the 1950s and 1960s, constituted another of the major sources of inspiration for Lyman and Scott, and was responsible for the original naming of their perspective. Their overall point of departure was an understanding – stemming from absurdist philosophy, poetry and performative arts – that the world is without meaning. Absurdity – what Tiryakian regards rather as ambiguity – is thus a cardinal fact of life for the absurdists, referring to the non-existence of any objective meaning independent from the social actors establishing meaning in and by their actions and interactions in everyday life. Albert Camus especially was instrumental in providing lucid descriptions of this inherent meaninglessness and absurdity of life (Sagi 1999), but the unmistakable presence of insights from a long list of scholars, writers and performers can be excavated implicitly or explicitly from the intellectual lineage of sociology of the absurd. They include Jean-Paul Sartre, Søren Kierkegaard, Karl Jaspers, Samuel Beckett, Erving Goffman, Harold Garfinkel, Alfred Schutz, Maurice Merleau-Ponty, William Shakespeare, Nicolas Evreinoff, Georg Simmel, Max Weber, Max Frisch, Ludwig Wittgenstein, Edmund Husserl, Luigi Pirandello, Harold Pinter, Eugène Ionesco, Franz Kafka, the Marquis de Sade and Friedrich Nietzsche.

Lyman and Scott, however, name Florentine political philosopher Niccolò Machiavelli (1469–1527) as 'the father' of the sociology of the absurd and as providing the most comprehensive worldview for the absurdists (Lyman and Scott 1970: 12–27). The reason for Machiavelli's centrality to the sociology of the absurd is, according to them, first and foremost because his ideas were conceived in a time and place (15th-century Italy) apparently resembling the time and place of their own writings – a social milieu permeated by fundamental pluralism, fragmentation and accompanying social conflict (Lyman and

Scott 1970: 213–14). Moreover, central to Machiavelli's understanding of social life is the omnipresence of power – defined as the capacity to impose one's will on the behaviour of others – and power, as Machiavelli shows in *The Prince*, can in a world of *fortuna* and arbitrariness be exercised most effectively and prudently by resort to *virtù* (princely virtue). According to him, *virtù* (which should perhaps be translated as virility rather than virtue) consists of the human actor's facing up to the world, of his ability to obtain his goals and ambitions by way of cunning, reason, strategy and also by resort to a certain amount of cynicism and brutality. *Virtù* is contrasted with fortune, fate or being a victim of circumstances; it is a matter of being able to act otherwise, of being able to reach one's objectives by whatever means necessary.

Everyday life through such a Machiavellian lens consists of deception, lies and broken promises, and the demands on Machiavelli's Prince are transformed by the sociology of the absurd into the demands on everyman. *Virtù* is an art that in everyday encounters may be brought into use through such tactics as have been termed 'impression management', 'face work', 'masking' or 'role manipulation', and here the absurdists are especially indebted to the Machiavellian aspects of Erving Goffman's work on self-presentation (Lyman and Scott 1970: 20), to which I return below.

From more conventional everyday life sociology, the absurdists name Georg Simmel's (1908/1955) understanding that one of the fundamental forms of sociation is conflict as a precursor for their own line of thinking. Conflict in interaction or the struggle to define the situation according to the absurdists create victors but also victims: 'In the arena of face interaction, there are no crimes without victims' (Lyman and Scott 1970: 40). Simmel also substantiates the micro interactional insight of the absurdists that 'society … is only the synthesis or the general term for the totality of these specific interactions … "Society" is identical with the sum total of these relations' (Simmel 1907/1978: 175).

Society does not exist 'out there' but is constituted by constantly interacting human actors. Also from Simmel, the notion of the 'adventure', the episodic and periodic character of everyday life, is incorporated into Lyman and Scott's situational approach. From Erving Goffman, as mentioned, they borrow the idea of managing appearances and identity manipulation in everyday life (Goffman 1959). In their reading of Goffman, however, they tend to ignore the more Durkheimian aspects of ritual care and moral obligation which are also part and parcel of Goffman's universe, when writing that 'Machiavelli's prince and Goffman's social actor have no interior specifications. Rather situations define them' (Lyman and Scott 1970: 20).

From Harold Garfinkel and the ethnomethodologists, the absurdists derive their focus on the routine grounds of everyday action and the insistence on the inherent meaninglessness of the world, leading to a preoccupation with how –

through which methods – people create meaning and construct social order as they go along. Despite such somewhat eclectic, and sometimes selective, reading, Lyman and Scott succeed in creatively drawing together different theoretical positions and constructing an important and innovative perspective on contemporary everyday life.

Conceptualizing the absurd

The late 1960s was a time of social upheaval, a time of confronting ingrained values and norms, of new social and political movements, of the appearance of new forms of life and of new ways of thinking. In the vortex of this development, the sociology of the absurd attempted to describe and conceptualize this new social environment and man's role within it, in what could, at first glance, be regarded as negative terms. And true, absurdists, poetic as well as philosophical, have often described the world as full of suffering, loss, death, despair, nausea and misery. Martin Esslin captured this world of absurdity confronting man in the 20th century by stating, 'When it is no longer possible to accept complete closed systems of values and revelations of divine purpose, life must be faced in its ultimate, stark reality' (1991: 401). When God is dead, as Nietzsche noticed, when there is no providential or metaphysical meaning, and when all traditional systems of thought are undermined, repudiated or found ineffective, humans must establish meaning by and through themselves. The sociology of the absurd follows this lead but turns it from a defeatist attitude into a constructive sociological agenda. Already on the first page of their manifesto *A Sociology of the Absurd*, the absurdists attest how this new wave of thinking, to which they subscribe, tries to understand and appreciate the inherent absurdity of life:

> The term 'absurd' captures the fundamental assumption of this new wave: *The world is essentially without meaning*. In contrast to that sociology which seeks to discover the *real* meaning of action – a sociological reality, such as the *functional* meaning of social behaviour – this new sociology asserts that all systems of belief, including that of the conventional sociologists, are arbitrary. The problems previously supposed to be those of the sociologists are in fact everyday problems of the ordinary man. It is he who must carve out meaning in a world that is meaningless. Alienation and insecurity are fundamental conditions of life – though, they are experienced differently by individuals and groups – and the regular rehumanization of man is everyman's task.
>
> (Lyman and Scott 1970: 1; original emphasis)

Six central tenets may be extracted from this programmatic statement of the absurdists:

- Human existence is in essence absurd and meaningless (dominated by *fortuna*).
- It is so, although to varying degrees, for everybody.
- The problems of creating meaning are not exclusively sociological but relate to everyman.
- The human responses to meaninglessness is alienation, uncertainty, conflict and confusion.
- It is therefore up to human beings themselves individually or collectively to counter this fateful absurdity and create meaning (through *virtù*).
- This can be achieved, for example, by active intervention and/or strategic and reflexive efforts aimed at the rehumanization of life – that is, giving meaning to the meaningless.

Since all systems of belief are deemed arbitrary, and since there is no inherent 'real' or essential meaning to the world, the human actor is empowered to construct the meaning of the world himself: 'It is the meaningless-world-made-meaningful which is the strategic research site for the sociology of the absurd' (Lyman and Scott 1970: 27). The ontological foundation for the absurdists is therefore the human meaning-creating capacity – the ability to carve out meaning where meaninglessness prevails.

Regarding the aforementioned rehumanization of the world as the task of everyman, the absurdists are not concerned with instigating rebellion or inspiring revolt in order to attain such rehumanization. Because being anti-realists, anti-functionalists and anti-positivists forsaking everything that might hamper, constrain or limit humanity's potential or freedom to transcend the absurdity of the world, the aim of the absurdists is to provide descriptive knowledge of the social world enabling human actors to navigate in the world and act accordingly. Throughout their work, the absurdists therefore construct typologies and conceptual schemes of the everyday world showing ways to act (for instance, counter, minimize or avoid the inherent absurdity of life). In order accurately to describe man's struggle with this absurdity of life, the absurdists focus extensively on topics such as power, conflict, drama, strategy and manipulation, culminating in consecutive situations, episodes and encounters:[1]

> If life consists of encounters, episodes, and engagements, among persons pursuing goals of which they are consciously aware, or about which they can be made aware, then it appears that the fundamental structure of human action is *conflict*. This is true even if individuals are pursuing the same ends, since each is out to

> maximize his own interests. Thus, even two lovers in an erotic embrace, as Simmel once noted, may be regarded in conflict since each may be seeking to outdo the other in demonstrating affection or providing the other with feeling.
>
> (Lyman and Scott 1970: 5)

As mentioned above, this Simmel-inspired focus on conflict – human beings as in conflict with society, with nature and ultimately with themselves – constitutes a fundamental template for comprehending social life which, coupled with Goffman's metaphor of the drama, provides the absurdists with a dramatic image of the world and a dramatic image of humanity. However, Lyman and Scott ask:, 'Has not Goffman, in swinging the pendulum away from Parsons' over-socialized view of man, moved too far in the direction of an over-dramatized image of man?' (1970: 24). Their answer is:

> It is not that all men are clever calculators constantly matching wits with other men, or that they all boldly stride out with stratagems to challenge fate. Rather, they succeed or fail according to whatever they can do and its effects on situation and chance.
>
> (Lyman and Scott 1970: 25)

When describing and conceptualizing the world in such conflictual and dramatic terms, the absurdists seek to provide a sober and deep-drilling description of social life which refrains from privileging or prioritizing the perspectives of specific groups, ideologies or power formations in society. They therefore espouse relativism, egalitarianism and perspectivism in depicting, analysing and understanding the world of everyday life:

The world has no objective meaning. We can study the social world from the point of view of the superior or the subordinate; of the lover or his mistress; of the bourgeoisie or the proletariat; of management or labour; of the deviant or of the person who labels them deviant, and so on. What is important is that we should have a perspective, but the particular perspective employed is irrelevant to the rectitude of theorizing. We can make true statements from any perspective, including those not consonant with any available ideology (Lyman and Scott 1970: 16).

Therefore, the absurdists privilege no particularistic perspective – no vantage point on the social world may, from a moral or valuative perspective, be deemed better or more correct than another. All perspectives are equal, none being superior or inferior to any other. As is evident, because the absurdists take people's meaning-making attempts as their starting point, they represent a radical constructivist perspective on ontology as well as on epistemology – a constructivism that permeates their substantial contributions to a wide range of specific topics and themes related to everyday life.

Encountering the absurd

How do the absurdists encounter this everyday world of absurdity, and how do they create meaning out of a world deemed devoid of meaning? As such the problems of meaning confronting the sociological absurdist are no different from the problems of meaning confronting every human actor. Making sense and constructing meaning is everyman's task. Thus, Lyman and Scott assert that the absurdists reject 'the a priori existence of a determined world discovered by the sociologists. It regards man as an actor who builds up his actions on the basis of his goals and his continuing attempts to define and redefine the situation' (Lyman and Scott 1970: 8). The sociologist's perspective on the world is no more privileged than any other, but it may provide important insights into aspects of human sociality that would otherwise remain undiscovered. Taking drama and conflict as the outset of description and analysis, the absurdists proceed to provide a multitude of conceptual and descriptive tools for making sense of the social world. Below I shall therefore illustrate with five concrete cases from the writings of the sociology of the absurd – territorial claims, time tracks, accounts, troubled identities and games – how an absurd approach may enhance our conceptualization and understanding of these central aspects of everyday life. These conceptualizations and understandings may later be used to inspire or guide actual empirical research.

Territorial claims

Human freedom of action and meaning-creation in the face of absurdity are closely connected to territorial occupation. Due to the transformation of modern society, the turn to absurdity, the absurdists claim that 'in contemporary society it appears that men acknowledge increasingly fewer free territories for themselves. Free territory is carved out of space and affords opportunities for idiosyncrasy and identity' (Lyman and Scott 1970: 89). Apart from this diagnostical statement on the decreasing amount of free space available to people in modern society, Lyman and Scott also make a more substantial contribution to the formal theorization and conceptualization of space and territoriality, something they regard as a neglected dimension in sociology.

Obviously inspired by Goffman's notion of 'the territories of the self', Lyman and Scott therefore offer a typology of territories. Different types of territories from everyday life may be used for presenting, claiming and defending self or confronting others:

- *Public territories* are those areas of social life to which individuals may claim access based on citizenship and to which certain freedoms but also certain restrictions on behaviour apply. Such areas include public parks, the streets, the pavement and other publicly accessible spaces. In public areas certain codes of conduct may be invoked but public territories may also be subject to transformation into so-called 'home territories' if homeless people, for example, occupy the pavement or if demonstrators decide to squat empty public buildings. As Lyman and Scott observe, such public territories often function as testing grounds for challenges to authority.

- *Home territories* are areas where the regular participants have a relative degree of freedom of behaviour and a sense of intimacy and control over the use of the area. Examples of such territories are makeshift club houses of children, hobo jungles, beggars occupying the pavement, the local bars of football supporters and discos of sexual minorities. Home territories may function as 'identity pegs' for their regular users through either 'colonization' or 'sponsorship'.
- *Interactional territories* are those mobile and often fragile gatherings that may coagulate and disperse swiftly, and such territories are often surrounded by a social membrane – for instance, a group of people standing in a chit-chatting circle at a party who are momentarily somewhat isolated from the rest of the guests. Unwanted company intruding or invading such groups exemplifies offences against such interactional territories.
- Finally, *body territories* refer to the space occupied by the human body and the anatomical space of the human organism. It also refers to the space immediately surrounding the body as a moving vehicle in everyday life which Edward T. Hall (1969) termed the 'intimate sphere'. Such space may be infected or contaminated by unwanted contact if for example rape or violence takes place, or less dramatically, by unwanted touches or inappropriate intimacies. Body territory can also be transformed into home territory by a lover through the sexual act or intimate caresses.

To claim a territory is also to claim and defend an identity for oneself. Therefore, battles concerning territorial rights often concern claims to certain identities: for example, homosexuals who establish a gay bar in order to live out their sexual preferences perhaps in a hostile heteronormative society. All territories are subject to *violations, contamination* or *unwarranted use*, which can be countered by strategies such as *turf defence, insulation* or *linguistic collusion*, or by claiming free territory through *manipulation, adornment* or *penetration* strategies. Lyman and Scott's intention with proposing all these many concepts is to illustrate how territorial claims present ways to confront absurdity and to claim control of the absurd circumstances of life. They finally suggest that such 'micro-sociological studies of territoriality .... may be extrapolated to an analysis of macro-sociological inquiries especially in the realm of international affairs' (Lyman and Scott 1970: 109) – something Lyman himself later attempted in his study of NATO and Germany (see Lyman 1995).

Time tracks

Not only territory but also time, another of the Kantian *a priori* forms of perception, is important to the absurdists, as shown in their analysis of so-called 'time tracks'. Their interest in temporal aspects of social life also connects to life's inherent absurdity – life is absurd because man is confronted with death, and time is therefore a scarce resource to human beings and of utmost importance. Lyman and Scott define time tracks as:

> [T]emporal periods employed by individuals, groups, and whole cultures to designate the beginnings or the determination of things .... The time track concept presupposes that social actors conceive of periods as characterized by a dominant event or type of event, activity or type of activity, thought or type of thought .... Since social behaviour takes place on time tracks, any social system may be conceived as an arrangement or time-specific activities .... Time tracks are products of cultural definitions; they conceive of life as divided into temporally specific, qualitatively different event activities.
>
> (Lyman and Scott 1970: 189–90, 211)

Examples of such time tracks, encircling social behaviour and a characteristic of any social system, are what in the history books has been called the Great Depression, starting with the stock market crash in 1929 and ending in 1933 with F. D. Roosevelt's 'New Deal'; the era of disco music being associated with the opening of Studio 54 in New York in 1977 and ending with its closing down in 1986; or something as mundane and everyday as the duration of a love affair or that a semester starts in September and ends in December. In short, time tracks organize our perception and memory of the events taking place in the world by designating beginnings and terminations of things. They point to 'the historicity of social phenomena, the rhythms of activities, and the tempos of life' (Lyman and Scott 1970: 190).

In order to conceptualize the varieties of activity within such time tracks, such 'social time', Lyman and Scott suggests two dimensions or continua of paired concepts to highlight differences within time tracks: *humanistic–fatalistic* and *continuous–episodic*. The former continuum concerns the degree of human autonomy and free will in decisions and events, whereas the latter continuum concerns the duration – or perceived duration – of the behaviour taking place. Humanistic time tracks are those in which individuals feel in control of events and in which personal choice or decision making dominate, whereas fatalistic time tracks are those in which individuals experience obligations, pressures or compulsion to act a certain way. On the other continuum, continuous time tracks are, for example, an occupational career gradually taking an individual up the corporate ladder, whereas episodic time tracks are those events that seem unconnected to past and future, such as a one-night stand or other 'one-off' happenings.

Time-tracks serve as means to conceptualize how people comprehend and experience the events of an absurd life, thereby seeking meaning amidst meaninglessness. As Lyman and Scott observe, while some people may be more inclined to conceive the world from a fatalistic perspective in which they are the victims of the inconveniences of time (for instance, 'life is a rat race'), other segments are more prone to conceive life positively as adventurous, exhilarating and euphoric, in which the individual is in charge of their own fate. The same goes for the continuous–episodic continuum diversifying people's conception of time. Lyman and Scott conjure up a reservoir of central concepts intended to capture how people comprehend and react to time, and how they enter and terminate time-tracks. Finally, they remark how 'time tracks divide life into feeling-activity states, and provide for man the crucial element of action or inaction' (Lyman and Scott 1970: 212).

Accounts

What the ethnomethodologists term 'accounts' is also part and parcel of the absurdists' quest to provide an answer to the question of *how* social order or society is possible. An account, as 'the slightest of interpersonal rituals', as 'talk', is defined by the absurdists as a 'linguistic device employed whenever an action is subjected to valuative inquiry', a 'statement made by a social actor to explain unanticipated or untoward behaviour', whereby the actor verbally seeks to bridge the gap between action and expectation (Lyman and Scott 1970: 111–12). Accounts testify to human meaning-bestowing capacity and to their need to comprehend the actions of self and others.

Accounts belong to the so-called 'vocabularies of motive' described by C. Wright Mills (1940), the delineation of which makes it possible to form an analysis of the integrating, controlling and specifying function that certain types of speech fulfil in socially situated actions, such as those analysed by the absurdists. Lyman and Scott differentiate between different types of accounts – *excuses* and *justifications* – which are both invoked whenever a person has done something wrong, bad, unacceptable or unexpected and needs to provide some explanation for their actions. The former, excuses, may be subdivided into four specific forms: *appeal to accidents, appeal to defeasibility, appeal to biological drives* and *scapegoating*. All these different kinds of excuses with their different motivations tell us something about how people seek to explain their behaviour to others. Appeals to defeasibility, for example, will be invoked whenever some 'mental defect' can be said to interfere with people's actions and their responsibility for the consequences of these actions. Appeals to defeasibility have, in most societies, been institutionalized in codes of law as 'temporary insanity' which might exempt culprits from punishment and excuse their actions.

Justifications, like excuses, consist of socially approved vocabularies that are intended to neutralize an act, its perpetrator or its consequences, when it is called into question. In this case both excuses and justifications are past-oriented, but contrary to excuses, justifications are aimed at asserting the positive value of an act in the face of a claim to the contrary. Where excuses are defensive, justifications are more offensive. Justifications rest on so-called 'techniques of neutralization' such as *denial of injury, denial of victim, condemnation of condemners* and *appeal to loyalties*, which all, while recognizing the impermissibility of an act, still seek to invoke special circumstances accounting for why something impermissible did happen.

Let us dwell on one of these – *denial of the victim*. Some of the top Nazis captured by the Allies towards the end of the Second World War and who were subsequently prosecuted at the Nuremberg Trials did not attempt to excuse their actions but sought to justify them by reference to the fact that the victims, the Jews, deserved the injury inflicted upon them – 'they had it coming'.

Besides such 'techniques of neutralization', Lyman and Scott also list *sad tales* and claims to *self-fulfilment* as types of justification. Sad tales, through a selected arrangements of facts from a dismal personal past (such as a miserable childhood) seek to explain an individual's present status, and claims to self-fulfilment describes a situation in which individuals point to their unfulfilled desires or to a wish to relinquish the reins as reasons for their actions (for example, living out homosexuality or becoming a drug user).

Accounts may be delivered in a variety of ways, and Lyman and Scott list these as *intimate, casual, consultative, formal* and *frozen* styles. Accounts – as excuses or justifications – may also be either honoured or not depending on the specific 'background expectancies' of the participants in conversation. When honoured, accounts may be said to be efficacious in restoring situations and in maintaining equilibrium. When not honoured, accounts may lead to conflict, strife or collapse of conversation or relationships because they are regarded as either 'illegitimate' or 'unreasonable'. Strategies for avoiding giving accounts – and thus for being accountable for actions – include *mystification, referral* or *identity-switching*. Accounts, in short, are rituals that may uphold and preserve or threaten to undermine and jeopardize sociality in everyday encounters.

Troubled identities

Accounts are especially important when dealing with deviant identities because people who are labelled 'deviant' will often seek to avoid the stigma attached to their person or appearance by giving specific types of accounts or by displaying only positively evaluated parts of their selves. Deviants will often experience paranoia because of the innate human fear of being exposed, ridiculed or embarrassed, and Lyman and Scott observe how homosexuals, paranoids and other stigmatized identities 'continually regard their social world as problematic and thus exhibit heightened awareness of it' (Lyman and Scott 1970: 77). They aspire to describe what the labelled or deviant person *thinks* about how to hide potential discrediting attributes, and they focus especially on paranoids and homosexuals as two such types of deviants. In this they rely on a game model of social life in which life is regarded as an 'information game', to which I return specifically below.

Whereas deviant people may seek successfully to hide discrediting information about themselves, other participants in the situation may want to reveal or disclose discrediting information or confirm their suspicions about the deviant. 'Passing' – the ability successfully to present a desired (non-deviant) identity – is therefore a delicate balancing act for deviants who may develop paranoia, hyperconsciousness, suspicion awareness and insecurity arising from such situations. As a consequence, deviants will tend to be more strategic, more vigilant, more suspicious and more careful in their social contacts and responses, and they therefore develop a game-strategic understanding of most social relationships. Moreover, deviants require an ambivalent 'double identity' – one reserved for contacts with other deviants and one reserved for contact with non-deviant groups.

According to Lyman and Scott, 'normal' or 'non-deviant' identities may also occasionally give rise to feelings of suspicion and paranoia, and thus it is not just those with troubled identities who experience uneasiness in everyday life or need to 'pass' (see also Renfrow 2004). Paranoia, anxiety and 'stage fright' – once again a dramaturgical framework is invoked by the absurdists – are part and parcel of the performances everybody puts on every day in their claims to identity.

Stage fright especially attests to a fundamental aspect of ordinary social interaction: the problem of sustaining the claim to a desired identity. Stage fright is generated and experienced in one of two ways: either the knowledge in advance that a situation will open up the self to total inspection, or anticipating that a slip, mistake or flaw will suddenly thrust a person into a position that invites challenges to a claimed identity, or both. Stage fright is primarily part of 'critical performances', in which claims to and the recognition of identity are of the utmost importance to the actors. Here the actor may seek to manipulate body, props or territories in order to present a desired self that is ultimately accepted and verified.

Different specific strategies may be deployed by the human actor when struck by stage fright in everyday life. The first strategy is to prevent stage fright from emerging in the first place by way of *rehearsals, preparations* and *practice.* A second strategy concerns attempts to conceal stage fright when it occurs and to prevent it from erupting in ways that endanger performance or discredit identity. A third kind of coping strategy can be employed by way of conceiving *rescue* or *restorative devices,* allowing victims of stage fright to be 'saved' from anxiety and embarrassment either by themselves or by the other participants. The absurdists – in their focus on identity and the ability to manage identities – attest to the importance of the human ability to 'keep cool' as a fundamental aspect of modern everyday life (Lyman and Scott 1970: 145–57; Stearns 1994) in which keeping cool concerns the ability to manipulate and control one's self in the situational and episodic identity games that constitute everyday life encounters.

Games

Erving Goffman once famously stated, 'Not, then, men and their moments. Rather moments and their men' (1967: 3). Since the absurdists subscribe to a Machiavellian conflict-oriented and strategic understanding of the world, they also attest to such a Goffmanian episodic character of social reality and a corresponding situational or moment-oriented approach to understanding society. As Lyman and Scott establish, 'Since the world is created anew in each encounter, it is precisely these engagements that form the comprehensible units for sociological investigation' (1970: 23). These moments, situations and engagements 'created anew in each encounter' that constitute the absurdists' conception of everyday life – not as historical *longue durée* but as short-lived episodes – are conceptualized as contests or games involving two or more parties or groups in mutual communication. Therefore, a game framework or typology is suggested in which everyday encounters are regarded as strategic games through which participants figuratively 'bracket' or think of the situation as a game:

> A game may be said to be under way ... when at least one actor in an encounter perceives a situation as problematic, estimates his own and others' construction of self and situation, and undertakes a line of action designed to achieve a goal or goals with respect to the situation.
>
> (Lyman and Scott 1970: 75)

The absurdists differentiate between several different types of such games:

- *Face games*, which consist of participants manoeuvring in order to maximize their own realization of a valued identity while simultaneously seeking an equilibrium that permits other participants to achieve the same. Face games come in two kinds: defensive, in which the participants seek to protect their own identities against external damage or spoilage, and protective, in which participants seek to prevent damage done to the identities of others. Face games involve different types of challenges, avoidances, moves, offerings, responses and restorative actions that will ultimately decide the outcome of the game.
- *Relationship games* which consist of participants aiming to create, maintain, attenuate or terminate personal relationships such as love affairs, employments or friendships. Lyman and Scott distinguish between positive and negative relationship games, where the former (consisting of 'introduction', 'invitation' and 'acceptance' moves) are concerned with creating or buttressing certain relationships, while the latter (consisting of an 'opening-terminating gambit', a 'supportive response' and an 'acceptance of termination') are concerned with terminating or attenuating relationships. Relationship games are balancing acts because the lines separating trust and distrust, formality and informality, the intimate and the distanced in social relationships are always delicate.
- *Exploitation games* which consist of participants seeking compliance from others in order to maximize their own positions of power, status and influence in relation to one another. As such, exploitation games are power contests whose outcome, on the outset, is unpredictable and which consist of conflicting framing attempts on behalf of the would-be-exploiter and the would-be-exploited. Typical exploitation games involve a dichotomy of reward and punishment.
- *Information games* which consist of participants attempting either to conceal or to uncover certain kinds of knowledge about each other. In this sense, the information game is a kind of 'metagame' because it encompasses all other types of game and because everybody in everyday life consciously reveals and conceals only selected parts of their personality or life story to or from others. Information games begin when an actor perceives how information they wish to keep secret is being sought, and commence with a sequence of 'control moves', 'covering moves', 'uncovering moves' and 're-covering moves'. Information about others can be obtained through a variety of sources ranging from 'interviewing' and 'spying' to 'seduction' and 'coercion'.

All of five themes delineated above – territorial claims, time tracks, accounts, troubled identities and games – are distinctive features of the way in which the absurdists in an analytically dramatic manner conceptualize and map everyday life. How would they then insist on investigating this dramatic everyday world in actual sociological research?

Investigating the absurd

In *The Myth of Sisyphus* Camus set the tone for the way absurdists approach the social world as human beings and investigate it as sociologists: 'For the absurd man it is not a matter of explaining and solving, but of experiencing and describing. Everything begins with lucid indifference' (Camus 1955/2000: 87). Therefore, the absurdists are not engaged in instigating rebellion or preaching revolt; they are neither policy-oriented nor action researchers, as many radical sociologists were at that time. Moreover, they hold no aspirations to alter the social world they encounter through social scientific interference.

The sociology of the absurd is a thoroughly analytical and descriptive enterprise which favours qualitative research designs. As Lyman and Scott contend:

> The most appropriate way to gather data for use in studies of the Absurd is by unobtrusive observation of natural settings or by examining reproductions of natural settings – movies, taped conversations, and so on ..... Today's democratized prince cannot really be comprehended by survey research.
>
> (Lyman and Scott 1970: 27)

The sociology of the absurd also rests on the classic interactionist dictum that sociologists should engage with and immerse themselves in the natural social environment but refrain from over-identifying with the subjects studied. An 'involved distance' is their preferred research strategy – involvement rather than identification. Consequently, the absurdists also pay homage to the notion of 'ethnomethodological indifference' according to which the sociologist should refrain from normative evaluation of the appropriateness, importance, necessity or value of the actions and behaviour observed (Garfinkel and Sacks 1970: 345). Moreover, there is an everyday egalitarianism in the sociology of the absurd, taking Alfred Schutz's idea that we are all sociologists to its radical extremes. Thus, the absurdists turn their backs on any notions of the sociologist being superior to or more advanced in escaping absurdity than the ordinary person. Sociologists should strive to be careful observers but not be misled into conceiving of themselves as social reformers, muckrakers, social engineers or meliorists (Lyman and Scott 1970: 10). From this anti-meliorism, however, it does not follow that the absurdists are out of touch with or ignorant of what happens to people in everyday life. Rather Lyman and Scott state that the sociologist of the absurd:

> must be a careful observer in any situation, and his awareness and exact description of the political, legal, social, and moral restraints on the individual is part of his task .... [He must] locate the person precisely in the continuum between humanism and fatalism. He must uncover ideology and utopia in each man, wish and transfiguration in each situation. The Sociologist of the Absurd, by his very description of society, by his everlasting unfolding and illumination of the modes and styles of social order, can summon men to build the world of their dreams, but he cannot build it for them.
>
> (Lyman and Scott 1970: 10)

One way to 'summon men to build the world of their dreams' is paved with 'defamiliarization', which is a main strategy deployed by the absurdists when seeking to comprehend and describe their subject matter – the everyday lives of human actors. By this strategy they aspire to make the familiar world appear strange (Lyman and Scott 1970: 27). When the world is made to appear strange to us we may suddenly stop to think – and perhaps act. The absurdists therefore state that 'the everyday world provides situations from which truth might be extracted by those who would take the trouble to look with the attitude appropriate to witnessing human and divine performances: wonder, astonishment and naïve puzzlement' (Lyman and Scott 1975: 2). In short, it is a matter of *not* taking the world for granted in order to understand it, transcend it and act in it. Like the human actors living in everyday life, the sociologist investigating everyday life must therefore try to create or carve out a sense of coherence and meaning from the fragmented, confused subjective encounter with an absurd world, thereby allowing for some sort of transcendence.

Transcending the absurd

The sociologists of the absurd, like most absurdist novelists and poets, take as their starting point of analysis the existential absurdity of human life. Moreover, what could be termed the 'institutional absurdity' of modern life (Goodwin 1971) – that there is a deep-seated and deepening dissonance, contradiction, conflict and chasm between man and society – is also part and parcel of their whole perspective. The absurdists therefore represent a dialectical line of thinking in highlighting the dilemmas and discrepancies between the conditions people create, the contradictions of these conditions and their attempts to transcend or annul the absurdity of life through action. Therefore, Glenn A Goodwin observes how for absurdists:

> the final and definitive synthesis – 'the good life' – is an impossibility. Choosing to act in the face of this realization, it is argued, becomes the determinant of man's freedom. In other words, man's choosing to act, *with the definitive understanding that his action will resolve nothing*, is what determines his freedom .... Predicated on this realization, social man consciously creates dissonance to which he can then react, and thus he achieves a semblance of meaning.
>
> (Goodwin 1971: 832; original emphasis)

The creation of dissonance and the continuous struggle to solve conflict, confront anomalies or bridge contradictions are fundamental to the absurdists' view of humanity's task in the world. People are more dissonance seekers than consonance seekers. A person actually never is – they are always becoming through their endless, Sisyphean struggle to tackle absurdity. Because the world is absurd, it is each person's own personal responsibility to make sense of the world and to carve out islands of meaning in a sea of meaninglessness. Because reality holds no inherent, absolute or objective meaning in store for human actors, and because this lack of meaning may frustrate, infuriate or create a sense of loss, apathy and confusion, they will have to conjure up meaning for themselves. Therefore, the absurdists present an everyday life consisting of people struggling, competing and fighting. As a consequence, none of the quotidian cosiness of many other everyday life perspectives is anywhere to be found.

But how may people then possibly tackle the inherent existential and institutional absurdity of modern living? Although he rejected suicide as an answer to life's inherent absurdity, Albert Camus seemed to point to defeatism as the most appropriate response to absurdity, when stating that 'there is thus a metaphysical honour in enduring the world's absurdity. Conquest or role-playing, multiple loves, absurd revolt are tributes that man pays to his dignity in a campaign in which he is defeated in advance' (1955/2000: 86). And as such Camus was right – the absurdity of everyday life cannot be entirely defeated or eliminated, merely momentarily postponed or transcended, thereby opening up to new conditions of absurd living. An answer to the question 'Can absurdity ever be transcended?' would therefore be: to some extent, but not definitively. As Lionel Rubinoff explained:

> Instead of facing up to the absurd, we either counterfeit or ignore it. Many of our current myths and images of man [such as underlie the practice of the

> social sciences] have been surreptitiously manufactured for the purpose of counterfeiting the experience of the absurd. I propose to confront the absurd directly by imaginatively living through it .... A mind which has achieved a ... critical awareness of the absurd ... may be said, therefore, to have transcended it.
>
> (Rubinoff in Goodwin 1971: 836)

The idea of sociology as a saviour in the face of absurdity or suffering does not appeal to the absurdists because sociologists – like ordinary men – are incapable of releasing people (including themselves) from their sense of absurdity or ambiguity. Sociology is itself caught up in the selfsame absurdity and only vicariously, through analyses of absurdity, manages to escape the absurd. For ordinary people, rebellion, fight or the ability to say 'no' may therefore prove to be the ultimate means to transcend the absurd. The human being as a rebel, as Camus would have it, or as a 'primitive rebel' in the words of Eric Hobsbawm, fits the absurdists' strategic worldview well. Those unable to rebel, to say 'no', or at least to present a convincing self – manipulated or genuine – and who are therefore incapable of taking advantage of or mastering the art of virtù in their contact with others remain the perpetual losers in the game of social interaction:

> Such people are the oppressed, the down-trodden, the people who walk in despair .... Such people live in an anomic world, not knowing whether life is a function of chance, opportunity or fate. They have their entrances and exits, but these are determined and involuntary – all else is waiting and wondering.
>
> (Lyman and Scott 1970: 23)

As mentioned, despite their preoccupation with conceptual and typological development and refinement, the absurdists have surprisingly not been particularly successful in proving a paradigm or general framework for carrying out empirical work within sociology, and only a minority of scholars have utilized this perspective for empirical analysis. One of the few studies in which an absurd perspective has been used is one by Dragan Milovanovic and Jim Thomas (1989) empirically highlighting the absurdity of conditions of life and the efficacious action of so-called 'jailhouse lawyers'. Drawing upon a body of absurdist assumptions, they illustrate – based on interviews with inmates in maximum security prisons in the United States in the 1980s – how prisoners use the law to counter, and successfully suspend, the absurdity of dehumanized life in prison. Through strategic action, reason and cunning the prisoners are able to avoid oppression and keep absurdity at bay. Instead of silently acquiescing and surrendering, they confront the very base of absurdity – the authorities, the system's 'looping policies' and existing definitions of power – by way of litigation and constant appeals to the law. Milovanovic and Thomas's analysis might fruitfully be extrapolated to struggles against absurdity in many other institutional settings apart from the 'total institution' of the prison, by showing how people continuously and laboriously seek to rehumanize a dehumanized existence.

Critiquing the absurd

As mentioned above, the amount of work carried out by way of, or research conducted within the framework provided by, the sociology of the absurd remains surprisingly limited (for a few exceptions, see for example Brown and Lyman 1977; McDavitt 1999; Shoham 1974/2006).[2] This also means that criticisms voiced against the perspective of the absurdists remain rather limited in sociology. However, I shall briefly summarize some of the main points of critique raised against the sociology of the absurd throughout the years.

First, the *critique of conservatism*: because it is not aimed at social meliorism, social improvement or social engineering, the sociology of the absurd – together with symbolic interactionism, phenomenology and ethnomethodology – is accused of being part of a conservative mentality detrimental to critical sociological theorizing and of being unable to advance social critique, for example of social inequality and political stratification (McNall and Johnson 1975).

Second, the *critique of subjectivism/situationalism*: because they primarily focus on the microscopic aspects of society, the human experience of life through the episodes and situations of everyday life, thereby presumably neglecting social and political structure at the macroscopic level, the absurdists are criticized for subscribing to a micro-reductionism or a 'dictatorship of the subjective' (Goodwin 1971: 835). Following this, by neglecting macro structure, socialization, social integration, systemic reproduction and other more macro-oriented topics, the absurdists are accused of moving social analysis towards situationalism and of privileging an 'under-socialized' image of humanity. Robert S. Broadbent (1974) as well as Barry Schwartz (1971) in their respective reviews of *A Sociology of the Absurd* both characterized the image on humanity as expounded by the absurdists as such an 'under-socialized conception of man', supplementing Dennis H. Wrong's (1961) classic critique of the 'over-socialized conception of man' in structural functionalism – each being guilty of excessive simplification.

Third, the *critique of exoticism*: because they often deal with difficult passing scenarios, deviance and conflicts, the absurdists' perspective might be blamed for overlooking the overwhelming normality and triviality of everyday life. For example, Broadbent commented how 'the absurdists only deal with problematic, unordinary, volatile situations such as homosexual "passing", paranoia and other exotic behaviours' (1974: 39). Zygmunt Bauman was also critical of ethnomethodology's tendency to focus on the exotic and extraordinary instead of the ordinary and mundane. This is something that could easily be extended to the sociology of the absurd, which might also be castigated for reproducing such a:

> particular knack for descending to the level of 'everyday life' from the abstract heights of the official sociology inhabited by imaginary homunculi. But it is a strange everyday life they descend to: hardly anybody eats there his everyday bread, even less bakes it, let alone earns it – though, as a naïve observer would say, eating and baking and earning bread seem to constitute eighty per cent of the everyday life of eighty per cent of everyday people.
>
> (Bauman 1972: 196)

By focusing excessively on the exotic, the extraordinary and the problematic aspects of everyday life, the absurdists may rightfully be blamed for committing the same error as the ethnomethodologists – the mundane, ordinary and trivial character of everyday life is displaced from the realm of normality, which most of us experience most of the time, to the realm of abnormality, which constitutes merely a fragment of most encounters of most people in most parts of the world of the everyday.

Assessing the absurd

The aforementioned points of criticism naturally attest to important shortcomings, limitations, problems and pitfalls in the perspective on everyday life, and society more generally, provided by the sociology of the absurd. However, as I have attempted to show above, the absurdists offer an original, provocative and refreshing approach to a variety of topics, themes and agendas within everyday life sociology. Although this approach, in a limited sense, may be counted among or labelled 'everyday life sociology', the sociology of the absurd also contains certain aspects of a political sociology. For example, Edward A. Tiryakian in his review of Lyman and Scott's book appraisingly remarked on the originality of their perspective for practising political sociology:

> The only thing they are not doing, I might suggest, is a sociology of the absurd; rather, it might be better to think of their essays as providing a new and possibly radical conception of political sociology, one based on situational analysis rather than on more staid institutional analysis.
>
> (Tiryakian 1973: 221)

Indeed, the sociology of the absurd does provide a conceptual and analytical peephole into the situational micropolitics (the dramas, conflicts and strategies) of everyday life rather than a bird's-eye view on the macro politics of national or international institutions often found in conventional political science or political sociology. In many ways, the essays of the absurdists supplement these 'grand' political sociologies with a much-needed emphasis on situational everyday politics.

In a more general sense, at the time of its culmination, the sociology of the absurd anticipated much of what later became conceptualized under the acclaimed headings of 'postmodernism', 'social constructivism' and 'deconstructivism' (see Carney 1998; Rose 2003). Therefore, the sociology of the absurd can be seen as a much-neglected forerunner to postmodernism as well as a critical corrective to some of the ideas advanced by postmodernists. For example, according to Lyman in his collection of essays in *Postmodernism and a Sociology of the Absurd*, the absurdists converge with – and stands as a precursor to – postmodernists in claiming that, first, although the world has no ultimate ontological or objective meaning, it still almost everywhere seems to make sense to human actors; and second, the self and society are social constructions (Lyman 1997: 13). The sociology of the absurd, just like many varieties of postmodernism and social constructivism, is as I have shown preoccupied with how human actors create, construct and interpret the meaning of the reality they take part in. Lyman's social constructivism is unambiguous when he states, 'To put it bluntly, it is not the social construction of reality – suggesting another ontological reality is out there and independent of the social – rather, it is that the social construction is reality' (1997:14). At the same time, however, Lyman rejects the radical constructivist or postmodernist notion of the 'death of the subject' – to the sociology of the absurd, the subject, the human actor, is still very much alive and kicking in everyday life (Lyman 2001).

Overall, the absurdists have been instrumental in highlighting the everyday as an arena of drama and conflict as a supplement to conventionally less conflict-oriented and more consensus-focused perspectives such as symbolic interactionism and phenomenology. They provide a multitude of pioneering analytical frameworks and many imaginative 'sensitizing concepts' (Blumer 1954) capable of inspiring the sociological imagination of students and scholars alike to carry out studies within the situational-interactional realm with a keen eye to drama, conflict, strategy and continuous human meaning-creation. These anchor points or metaconcepts – many of which have been presented above – should inspire concrete research agendas. Possibilities abound of using the conceptual arsenal of the absurdists in connection with actual empirical research, regardless of whether it deals with 'normal' or 'deviant' identities and situations.

Although it mostly speaks in the past tense of the sociology of the absurd, and although protagonists of the perspective are increasingly difficult to spot in contemporary sociological landscape, absurdist thinking still inspires theorists and thinkers around the world. In 2001, the online community The New Absurdists was founded, through which writers and scholars exchange ideas and interpretations and engage in analyses on the Internet based on an absurdist perspective. It is my firm belief that analyses of everyday life may benefit – and indeed gain strength and vigour – from incorporating insights from the sociology of the absurd.

Notes

1. It is important to emphasize that although the situational analysis of the absurdists focuses extensively on episodes and encounters, they do recognize how:

   > the episode does not arise full-blown without connections to past or future. Rather man brings to it his memories, perceptual apparatus, and wishes, hopes and dreams. And if he has no particular wishes or goals in an episode, he may just muddle through it, piecing it together as he goes, and, perhaps, not reflecting too much about it.
   >
   > (Lyman and Scott 1970: 25)

   Thus, we are not dealing with situational constraint, as it were, but rather an analytical privileging of situational aspects of social life.
2. Another exception to the otherwise sparse attention devoted to the sociological absurdists is Daniel J. Boorstin's (1969/1970) somewhat obscure exposition in *The Sociology of the Absurd, or the Application of Professor X*, which, to my knowledge, was not originally inspired by or associated with Lyman and Scott's development of the sociology of the absurd.

Bibliography

Bauman, Zygmunt (1972) 'Culture, values and science of society.' *University of Leeds Review*, 15 (2): 185–203.

Blumer, Herbert (1954) 'What is wrong with social theory?' *American Sociological Review*, 19: 3–10.

Boorstin, Daniel J. (1969/70) *The Sociology of the Absurd, or the Application of Professor X*. London: Thames & Hudson.

Boudon, Raymond (1977) *Effets pervers et ordre social*. Paris: Presses Universitaires de France.

Broadbent, Robert S. (1974) 'Notes on the sociology of the absurd: "an undersocialized conception of man".' *Pacific Sociological Review*, 17 (1): 35–45.

Brown, Richard H. and Stanford M. Lyman (eds) (1977) *Structure, Consciousness and History: New Writings in the Sociology of the Absurd*. Cambridge: Cambridge University Press.

Camus, Albert (1955/2000) *The Myth of Sisyphus*. Harmondsworth: Penguin.

Carney, Larry S. (1998) 'On being anchored in an absurd world.' *International Journal of Politics, Culture and Society*, 11 (3): 517–23.

Esslin, Martin (1991) *The Theatre of the Absurd*. Harmondsworth: Penguin.
Garfinkel, Harold and Harvey Sacks (1970) 'The formal properties of practical actions', in John C. McKinney and Edward A. Tiryakian (eds), *Theoretical Sociology*. New York: Appleton-Century-Crofts.
Giddens, Anthony (1979) *Central Problems in Social Theory*. Berkeley, CA: University of California Press.
Goffman, Erving (1959) *The Presentation of Self in Everyday Life*. Harmondsworth: Penguin.
Goffman, Erving (1967) *Interaction Ritual: Essays on Face-to-Face Behavior*. New York: Pantheon.
Goodwin, Glenn A. (1971) 'On transcending the absurd: an inquiry in the sociology of meaning.' *American Journal of Sociology*, 76 (5): 831–46.
Hall, Edward T. (1969) *The Hidden Dimension*. London: Bodley Head.
Lally, Jim and David L. Preston (1973) 'Anti-positivist movements in contemporary sociology.' *Journal of Sociology*, 9 (2): 3–9.
Lyman, Stanford M. (1972) *The Black American in Social Thought – New Perspectives on Black America*. New York: Putnam.
Lyman, Stanford M. (1974) *Chinese Americans*. New York: Random House.
Lyman, Stanford M. (1995) *NATO and Germany: A Study in the Sociology of Supranational Relations*. Fayetteville: University of Arkansas Press.
Lyman, Stanford M. (1997) *Postmodernism and a Sociology of the Absurd and Other Essays on the 'Nouvelle Vague' in American Social Science*. Fayetteville: University of Arkansas Press.
Lyman, Stanford M. (2001) *Roads to Dystopia: Sociological Essays on the Postmodern Condition*. Fayetteville: University of Arkansas Press.
Lyman, Stanford M. and Marvin B. Scott (1970) *A Sociology of the Absurd*, 1st edition. New York: Appleton-Century-Crofts.
Lyman, Stanford M. and Marvin B. Scott (1975) *The Drama of Social Reality*. New York: Oxford University Press.
Lyman, Stanford M. and Marvin B. Scott (1989) *A Sociology of the Absurd*, 2nd edition. New York: General Hall.
McDavitt, Joanne M. (1999) *Fragments: The Social Construction of the Absurd and the American War in Vietnam*. Unpublished PhD dissertation, Boston College.
McNall, Scott G. and James C. M. Johnson (1975) 'The new conservatives: ethnomethodologists, phenomenologists and symbolic interactionists.' *Insurgent Sociologist*, 4: 49–65.
Mills, Charles Wright (1940) 'Situated actions and the vocabularies of motive.' *American Sociological Review*, 9: 904–13.
Milovanovic, Dragan and Jim Thomas (1989) 'Overcoming the absurd: prisoner litigation as primitive rebellion.' *Social Problems*, 36 (1): 48–60.
Morris, Monica B. (1977) *An Excursion into Creative Sociology*. Oxford: Blackwell.
Parsons, Talcott (1949) *The Structure of Social Action*. Glencoe, IL: Free Press.
Renfrow, Daniel G. (2004) 'A cartography of passing in everyday life.' *Symbolic Interaction*, 27(4): 485–506.
Rose, William (2003) 'Postmodern subjects: on Lyman's sociology of the absurd.' *International Journal of Politics, Culture and Society*, 16 (4): 569–86.
Sagi, Avi (1999) *Albert Camus and the Philosophy of the Absurd*. Amsterdam: Rodopi.
Schwartz, Barry (1971) 'Critique of the sociology of the absurd.' *American Journal of Sociology*, 77: 153–6.
Scott, Marvin B. (1968) *The Racing Game*. Chicago, IL: Aldine.
Scott, Marvin B. and Stanford M. Lyman (1970) *The Revolt of the Students*. Columbus, OH: Charles E. Merrill.

Shoham, Shlomo G. (1974/2006) *Society and the Absurd: A Sociology of Conflictual Encounters*. London: Sussex Academic Press.

Simmel, Georg (1907/1978) *The Philosophy of Money*. London: Routledge & Kegan Paul.

Simmel, Georg (1908/1955) *Conflict and the Web of Group Affiliations*. New York: Free Press.

Stearns, Peter N. (1994) *American Cool: Constructing a Twentieth-Century Emotional Style*. New York: New York University Press.

Tiryakian, Edward A. (1973) 'Review of Stanford M. Lyman and Marvin B. Scott: *A Sociology of the Absurd*.' *Contemporary Sociology*, 1 (3): 220–1.

Wrong, Dennis H. (1961) 'The oversocialized conception of man in modern sociology.' *American Sociological Review*, 26: 183–93.

Part III
Dissemination

CONTENTS

CHAPTER 12

Scandinavian Everyday Life Sociologies

Routines, Ruptures and Strategies

ANN-DORTE CHRISTENSEN

Introduction

Scandinavian everyday life research is not a new research area. Long before the notion of everyday life was known and the methods to investigate it were formally developed, a few pioneers had conducted and disseminated research in everyday life and folk culture in Scandinavia – first and foremost Norwegian social and cultural scientist Eilert Sundt (1817–1875), who is considered the founder of sociology in Norway. Sundt was mainly interested in folk history, and he literally walked from village to village and studied customs and practices. He focused on contemporary ethnic minority groups (gypsies), on life expectancy, marital relations, morals and hygiene. Sundt used quantitative methods (in the form of extensive recording of facts) as well as qualitative methods in relation to conversations and other forms of expression (such as songs). Danish cultural historian Frederik Troels-Lund (1840–1921) is another example of early research in folk culture. His main work *Dagligt Liv i Norden* (*Daily Life in the Nordic Countries*, 1914–15) contains cultural historical descriptions based on detailed information about housing conditions, clothing and nutrition as well as significant events from birth to death.

However, it was not until the late 1960s and early 1970s that everyday life research as we understand it today had its real breakthrough in Scandinavia. Norwegian social anthropologist Marianne Gullestad (1946–2008), who was one of the prominent researchers in the field, emphasized that the focus in Scandinavian everyday life research was empirical research and an institutional rooting in studies of the home. In the 1980s home, family and the intimate sphere were formulated in contrast to the 'big' society and bureaucratic organizations, but Gullestad was also aware that idyllizing the home sphere is an inherent risk in the perspective of everyday life (Gullestad 1989: 175). I shall return to this later.

Another characteristic trait of Scandinavian everyday life research is its specific focus on gender. Of course, this follows naturally from having the family as the point of departure, but also from the social and academic context in which the theories are developed: that is, where the active women's movement as well as the emerging gender studies from the 1970s put the spotlight on the political and social significance of the family and the intimate sphere, for instance power relations between the genders (Holter 1975). This means that in a Scandinavian context there has been a strong interconnection between the development of feminist research and the development of everyday life research.

My point of departure in this chapter is two different Scandinavian traditions that concentrate on everyday life.[1] In the first part of the chapter I introduce and discuss the most widespread tradition in Scandinavian everyday life research: research in everyday life drawing on inspiration from phenomenology, for instance the heritage of Alfred Schutz, Agnes Heller, Peter L. Berger and Thomas Luckmann. The research by Marianne Gullestad and Danish cultural sociologist Birte Bech-Jørgensen (b. 1939) is presented as examples from this tradition, which is characteristic in that it combines the development of concepts with empirical research in 'the hidden society' or 'taken-for-granted' experiences. Moreover, the Nordic Research Group for the New Everyday Life will be presented as an example of a common Scandinavian contribution to everyday life research, and of everyday life research based on a critical perspective and a vision to create a new and better everyday life.

The second part of the chapter discusses the structural life-mode analysis developed by Danish ethnographer Thomas Højrup (b. 1953). In contrast to most everyday life research, Højrup's approach is based on a Marxist understanding of the mode of production as a fundamental basis for different types of 'life-modes' (such as wage earner or self-employed). Højrup synthesizes the traditions of historical materialism with a specifically Danish model of life-modes into ideal types in order to grasp the differences in people's cultural orientation, attitudes, expectations and values, emerging primarily from the relation between work, family and leisure time.

The final section of the chapter assesses strengths and weaknesses in Scandinavian everyday life research, and discusses how this research tradition has contributed to the understanding of modern, complex and multicultural societies.

The legacy from and challenges to phenomenology

The renewed interest in everyday life research in Scandinavia gained a foothold in studies and publications especially in the 1980s. It manifested itself as a reaction to the relatively strong influence from Marxist and structuralist theories since the late 1960s and the 1970s, but also in the focus that the emerging women's and gender research put on the understanding of social relations from the late 1970s to the early 1980s with respect to civil society, family and informal work.

Among the more sociologically oriented contributions to this interest in the everyday, let me mention *Dagliglivets organisering* (*The Organization of Everyday Life*) (Wadel 1983), *Vardagsverklighet och struktur* (*Everyday Reality and Structure*) (Ahrne 1981) and *Kultur och arbete* (*Culture and Work*) (Liljeström 1981). But the growing focus on everyday life also entered more narrowly defined fields, for example studies of local communities and close surroundings, which were continuations of some of the key studies of the fringe regions of Northern Norway conducted by Norwegian social scientist Ottar Brox as early as the 1960s (Brox 1966).

The everyday life perspective also took a central position in the 1980s in relation to the growing focus on technology. The Danish Research Council launched a large project on technology and everyday life under the Technology-Society initiative. The project examined questions of theoretical understandings and empirical analyses of the impact of technological innovation on everyday life (see Cronberg and Sangregorio 1981; Cronberg 1986).

Finally, the establishment of the Nordic Research Group for New Everyday Life had a major impact on everyday life research. The main ambition of the group, which was funded by the Nordic Council of Ministers, was to develop a model for integrating the most important functions of everyday life: care, work and housing. It was also a characteristic of the group's work that it had a normative objective, namely to strengthen integration and cohesion in the 'new' everyday life. This constitutes part of the background for the positions and perspectives that developed throughout the 1980s and 1990s in different Scandinavian countries.

Marianne Gullestad's and Birte Bech-Jørgensen's approaches to everyday life studies have a number of common elements related to the theoretical link to phenomenology and the combination of empirically in-depth analyses and conceptual development. Both are inspired by Schutz's concepts of 'common sense', 'world within reach' and 'the natural attitudes' in which bodily movement, actions and intersubjectivity are localized in time and space. Both focus on 'ordinary people' and emphasize broad definitions of everyday life as the life lived every day with other people (Bech-Jørgensen 1994a, 1997a, 1997b; Gullestad 1984/2002, 1989). Finally, both are examples of the empirical tradition that characterizes Scandinavian everyday life research and thus of the growing attention the notion of everyday life attracted in theory and research practice in the 1980s. However, Gullestad and Bech-Jørgensen also differ on significant points concerning the relationship between empirical depth and theoretical development, as we shall see below.[2]

Around Norwegian kitchen tables in Bergen

Gullestad's first comprehensive study of everyday life was based on a two-year anthropological field study of family life and friendships of young working-class mothers in the suburbs of Bergen, the second largest city in Norway. The main results were published in the book *Kitchen-Table Society* (Gullestad 1984/2002). In contrast to many other studies of gender relations at this time, Gullestad did not base her perspective on oppression of women and power relations between the genders. Instead she focused on the perspective of the actors themselves, and contributed to the debate by providing a detailed account of how a small group of young mothers occupied themselves in everyday life. The empirical method was participant observation combined with a few structured interviews. The practical and symbolic focus was the kitchen table, where Gullestad either listened carefully to the women's conversations about everyday life or participated in the conversations and used them as informal interviews.

For instance, Gullestad wrote about her encounter with Elizabeth, who had two children and worked two hours every afternoon as a charwomen:

> When I rang her doorbell, a tall, slim girl, 25 years of age, with long fair hair opened the door. That morning she was dressed in very tight navy blue corduroy jeans, blue sweater and a blue white shirt. Around her neck she had a thin gold chain with a piece of jewellery made of gold and a pearl. She gives the impression of being neat and at the same time modern and youthful. She has a charming and bright smile, but this smile also reveals some bad teeth. Her first words, after having asked me to come in, were: 'Would you like some coffee?' I accepted. In the months to come I was offered coffee many times in the kitchens and living rooms of different homes in this and similar cooperative apartment houses in Bergen. The time between 11 a.m. and 2.30 p.m. is the time for informal visits and coffee klatches. Elisabeth had finished the morning house-work. Her five-year-old boy was playing in the neighbourhood with his friends. She had just put her one-year-old daughter to bed with her bottle to have her usual morning nap of a couple of hours.
>
> (Gullestad 1984/2002: 38)

Through her analysis Gullestad made young working-class women's subcultural way of life visible. It was emphasized that they saw themselves as decent, respectable and ordinary people. One central point was that the young women had well-developed relations and social networks in the local community. Together with the family these networks constituted their most important framework for orientation and identity, and in contrast to middle-class women these working-class women had low expectations and values linked to careers in the labour market. Instead, their primary expectations and values were linked to home and family.

It is interesting that Gullestad, as opposed to other local studies, concluded that these young women did not feel isolated, but were rather closely linked to various networks in the local community. Finally, she highlighted how the young women were circumscribed by their class in all significant attitudes of their lives: child practices, the importance of cleanliness, what they considered good taste and so on (Gullestad 1984/2002: 136).

In her other books *Kultur og hverdagsliv* (*Culture and Everyday Life*) (1989) and *The Art of Social Relations: Essays on Culture, Thought and Social Action in Modern Norway* (1992), Gullestad further developed her everyday life concept based on, among other things, the studies in Bergen. In the former book, the empirical focus was still family and care, with particular emphasis on home, care work and children as active participants in society. This was examined via for example an analysis of the significance of the babysitter role – a phenomenon Gullestad encountered in the previously mentioned kitchen table field study. In the latter book, Gullestad more explicitly examined how 'ordinary' people's 'ordinary' lives can affect the study of society's overall modernization processes. She was very critical of the wide gap between the 'system' and close personal relations in everyday life, which is reproduced over and over in Scandinavian as well as in international research (Gullestad 1992: 59).

In her book from 1989, Gullestad discussed more explicitly the notion of everyday life – both theoretically and in terms of applicability and operationalization in connection to empirical analyses. She criticized the traditional approaches to everyday life, because she found that it was reduced to an 'organizational residual category' that is looked at from above. This is not least true in the widely used analytical model that divides society into three spheres: state, market and family/civil society. Although the model opens up to include family and civil society, Gullestad found it incomplete: first of all because it cannot contain the 'grey zone' surrounding the family – social networks, kinship, informal organizations, immediate environment, local community and so on; and second, because it encourages a focus on one of the three societal spheres and not on the interplay, movements and interaction among the three spheres.

Gullestad's alternative was to see society 'from below'; not as a sphere in itself but as cutting across all three spheres. With reference to Agnes Heller, she emphasized that everyday analyses will often have *a substantial focus on the home*,[3] because this is where we move around every day and where we always return to. According to Gullestad, a focus on 'the intimate' and the family does not imply that we lose sight of 'the big perspectives'. On the contrary, she argued that precisely because it is in the home and everyday life that people connect and unite the different roles and fora in which they participate, these areas of life are also suitable for studying large historical questions of civilization (Gullestad 1989: 26).

Gullestad called this emphasis on defining everyday life as both something transversal and something substantial the *dual determination of everyday life*. In relation to empirical analyses she suggested a distinction between two analytical dimensions. The first dimension concerns the daily organization of activities, such as social networks or kinships based on ordinary people's own notions (for instance about cooking and child care). As an alternative to the common social science categorizations, Gullestad suggested, for example, the intersection between biology and culture (birth, death, cleanliness, cooking, and so on) or activity systems (such as those associated with child or elder care.). The second dimension has to do with analysing people's endeavours to establish cohesion in life. It is a characteristic of these endeavours that they cut across different social factors (workplace, school, home, family and so on), but as mentioned the home remains the fundamental substantial field.

Finally, it should be mentioned that in her book *Everyday Life Philosophers: Modernity, Morality and Autobiography in Norway* (1996) Gullestad combined the everyday life approach with biography research. The point of departure was four of 630 contributions submitted by 'ordinary people' to an autobiography competition. She especially highlighted the notion of values and how 'taken-for-grantedness' changes, where for instance 'being of use' is replaced by 'being myself'. Already in this book she encouraged people to see Norway as a multicultural society. She followed up on this angle in some of her later books, which I discuss in the last section of the chapter.

What are young Danish unemployed women doing?

Birte Bech-Jørgensen has conducted several empirical analyses of everyday life, but here I shall mainly discuss her largest and most comprehensive study of 57 young unemployed women between the age of 16 and 24, which she carried out from 1982 to 1984 (Bech-Jørgensen 1990a, 1990b, 1994a). The main question in the analysis was, what are they doing when they seem to be doing nothing? For example, the author wondered why the young unemployed women did not do all the things they had wanted to do, but never had time for, when they went to school or worked every day. Why didn't they meet with other unemployed people; why didn't they go out; why didn't they do sports, and so on? Bech-Jørgensen was critical of simply concluding that it is a general question of bodily and mental withdrawal, and instead decided to find out what these women do when they seem to be doing nothing.

It is a methodological point that Bech-Jørgensen focuses on *ruptures* in everyday life in the form of unemployment. She thus wants to grasp the changeability in everyday life by examining what she calls shifts in the symbolic order of taken-for-grantedness, which are the fundamental conditions in everyday life in the form of repetitions, recognitions and routines. The point is that it is easier to grasp this taken-for-grantedness when it is changing, and that it provides an opportunity to analyse how the conditions of everyday life are recreated and redefined. Like Gullestad's analysis from Bergen, the analysis of the unemployed women was also rooted in the home. Bech-Jørgensen also emphasized that the home is not a separate societal arena, but has precisely the cohesive and condensing function where the symbolic order of home becomes the central condition of unemployed life. The young women's daily activities are not only situated in time, but also in space – primarily the home, but also that of the residential area of the city. Bech-Jørgensen wrote about the home:

> The symbolic order of the home is continually changing. The changes are externally determined by the ways in which these conditions are handled. This is exemplified by the ways in which most of the young mothers tried to recreate their positions inside the symbolic order of the home. They did so by means of the magic of consumption: When they happened to buy too much, namely when they bought clothing and small toys for the children, underwear for their husbands or cheap small wares for the home, or when they anticipated wishful situations by buying things to set a scene for these situations, they intended to reproduce the position of the caring mother in the symbolic order of the home. Some of them also tried to reproduce another position, namely that of a respectable woman in the neighbourhood. The means was a re-ordering of the home space, for example through buying new furniture. As their income was very low, some of these young mothers threw themselves into irrecoverable hire-purchase systems.
>
> (Bech-Jørgensen 1994a: 293)

One of the most important empirical findings of the study was the analysis of different strategies utilized by the unemployed women, manifesting themselves in different symbolic expressions in relation to the home. One form of strategic expression was 'the presentable home', that did not reveal its occupants were unemployed; another form of strategic expression was 'the messy home', where unemployment manifested itself as laziness and sluggishness; a third form of strategic expression had to do with what people have always done, for example leave the home and connect with the world and normal daily activities and routines – in other words maintain the symbolic order of taken-for-grantedness.

Besides the in-depth analysis of the young women's everyday strategies,

Bech-Jørgensen was interested in developing concepts of everyday life, partly in the form of a clarification of definitions, partly in the form of a reformulation of some classic concepts from Alfred Schutz's and Agnes Heller's works on everyday life. As far as the definition of everyday life is concerned, her point was that:

> everyday life cannot be defined in sociological terms. Everyday life can be described as a life we recreate and reproduce every day. What can be defined, I propose, are the conditions of everyday life, and the ways in which these conditions are handled. The symbolic order of taken-for-grantedness is the fundamental condition of everyday life.
>
> (Bech-Jørgensen 1994a: 291)

She was emphasizing that it is the so-called unperceived or unnoticed activities that make daily activities possible.

Although Bech-Jørgensen was basically inspired by Schutz (1975), she also criticized his notion of 'the natural attitudes', which he saw as the very foundation of everyday life. According to him, what is not experienced as natural is not included as a part of everyday life. Schutz's understanding of everyday life therefore cannot accommodate the analyses of the social conditions that Bech-Jørgensen pointed to as significant. Instead she turned to Heller's (1970/1984) theory and her so-called paradigm of human conditions, which is an ideal typical model for everyday life.[4]

Based on her empirical findings among the young unemployed women, Bech-Jørgensen transformed Heller's abstract philosophical categorizations into sociological concepts about the conditions for everyday life. She distinguished between three analytical levels:

- *the symbolic order of taken-for-grantedness*: a general level based on repetition and recreation of the taken-for-grantedness of everyday life in the form of unperceived activities – routines, traditions and rituals
- *the universes of meaning*: like Heller's second sphere of objectivations for-itself, this level is associated with conscious acts that can give everyday life meaning and explain the meaninglessness of life
- *social institutions*: social, economic, political and legal-administrative structurings of human activities (Bech-Jørgensen 1994a: 170ff).

Since this extensive analysis, Bech-Jørgensen has worked empirically with everyday life research based on the concepts developed. From 1996–2002 she headed the research project The Qualified Everyday Life, concerned with marginalized and excluded groups, such as the homeless, as a point of departure. However,

Bech-Jørgensen finds the description of the homeless stigmatizing and chooses to call them 'unusual people' to signal that they live according to different norms and customs than the usual ones (Bech-Jørgensen 2003:15). The purpose of this project was to develop new ways of organizing these unusual people's everyday lives based on cases in Copenhagen and Aalborg. As part of a broad analysis of the groups' everyday lives, the project also included neighbours and people who live close to the homes, drop-in-centres, workshops and shops used by the excluded.[5]

Strengths and weaknesses in phenomenological everyday life research

If we take a look at the works of Gullestad and Bech-Jørgensen discussed here, they illustrate the strengths and weaknesses of much phenomenological everyday life research. At the empirical level, they are very thorough and detailed analyses which manage to grasp routines and repetitions in everyday life and also place focus on the integrative mechanisms and strategies of action that are developed as part and parcel of everyday life's strength and empowerment. In both analyses the point of departure is groups of women (young working-class women; young unemployed women) whose everyday lives are often invisible or treated as a residual category.

Both Gullestad and Bech-Jørgensen also maintain Heller's focus on the family. This can be seen as a strength because it is made visible how the home as a central arena may create cohesion in everyday life. However, it is also in their views of the family that we have registered the most important differences between the two researchers: Gullestad emphasized family and networks in the local community as a collective strength for the young women, whereas Bech-Jørgensen emphasized the family as a potential frame for the young women's isolation in the 'enclosedness' of the home. This might be a result of temporal and geographical differences between the two studies, but it could also be a result of different methodological approaches to the analysis of everyday life. In my opinion, Gullestad was more successful than Bech-Jørgensen in combining the everyday life approach 'from below' with a more collective and structural level. Even Gullestad's term 'kitchen table society' signals more community than isolation. It is also noteworthy that Gullestad's analysis put heavy emphasis on, for instance, the class aspect.

The primary strength in Bech-Jørgensen's analysis is the extensive development of concepts; the weakness is the insufficient linking of family life and other spheres (such as the labour market and state). When Bech-Jørgensen analysed the 'home' (the enclosedness), it was considered as being outside of institutions, and she did point out that 'in modern societies the socially generated institutions split up everyday life – they produce a fragmentation' (Bech-Jørgensen 1994a: 176). The argument is that institutions are disembedded from local contexts. But I would argue that the institutions could have an integrating function in local communities as well, since many of them (such as schools and day-care institutions) constitute a framework for everyday repetitions by establishing a link to the family. More specifically, it seems strange that Bech-Jørgensen by and large ignored the young women's relations to the day-care institutions attended daily by their children, or the women's own relationships with, for instance, unemployment institutions. It is somewhat paradoxical that she did not integrate the institutional perspective into her analysis, because in her more theoretical considerations and in the analytical model she developed, she emphasized the significance of social institutions as a structuring framework of everyday life activities.

Fundamentally, the strength in both Gullestad's and Bech-Jørgensen's analyses is grounded in their ability to grasp the symbolic order of taken-for-grantedness and thus unperceived activities in the form of everyday routines, traditions and rituals. As far as the theoretical development of the concepts is concerned, the two researchers supplement each other. As concerns Gullestad, I would emphasize her ability to maintain the transversal perspective on different social factors through a view from below with the family as the pivot. As concerns Bech-Jørgensen, I would mention her ability to analyse and conceptualize the unperceived activities and the symbolic order of taken-for-grantedness. This corresponds to the first level in Bech-Jørgensen's own analytical model, as described above, whereas the two other levels are somewhat weaker in her analysis.

To conclude this part of the chapter about phenomenological everyday life research, I now turn to the Nordic Research Group for the New Everyday Life and their visions.

A new everyday life – realities and visions

The work carried out under the auspices of the Nordic Research Group for the New Everyday Life is interesting for several reasons. First, the research group over many years worked systematically with the everyday life perspective on an interdisciplinary basis across the Nordic countries.[6] Second, the group did not simply want to analyse everyday life as it unfolded. Instead the work was based on a clearly defined normative foundation, with criticism of the current fragmented everyday life and formulated visions for a new (and better) everyday life. This vision was initially linked to contemporary feminist visions of a society based on children's needs and daily reproduction, but the group's ideas about the new everyday life had a much broader scope, related particularly to feminist research. The group wrote that they:

> shared a common feeling of dissatisfaction with the current urban and social planning and its consequences. They also shared the conception that the present reality is not the only possible one. The goal of the conference was not to document the present situation ... but to discuss visions and strategies. How would we like it to be – and how shall we act in order to get there?
>
> (Research Group for the New Everyday Life 1991: 9)

The group's critical point of departure was that everyday life is split into time, space and individuals. Life in the workplace and in production may develop without consideration of the values that exist in intimate face-to-face relations in everyday life. Likewise, society is characterized by a number of divisions, for example in terms of geography, age and not least gender. The group emphasized that women's lives especially are associated with primary responsibility for care and life in the home, but are separated from work life and without independent control.

The purpose of a new everyday life is to break with these divisions and develop cohesive everyday cultures. As a central element the group emphasized that closeness is an important pivot in a number of key areas: between dwelling, work and recreation; between reproduction and production; between different age groups, and between genders. To achieve this cohesion, the group proposed to build up a so-called intermediary level for change, situated between the structural frames and the individual everyday life. This concerns the social and material conditions organized around local homework, local care, local production and local management. The research group found that the core in these activities is care (home care and child care), and they argued that more of society's activities should be rooted in this intermediary level if we want to create a new everyday life based on integration and cohesion instead of division and fragmentation (Research Group for the New Everyday Life 1987: 36ff). They asserted that:

> the intermediary level is the missing link between the household and society. The intermediary level has the advantage of more people and consequently a broader competence and larger resources than a single household. In relation to the 'big society' and solutions from above, the intermediary level has the advantages of closeness and first hand experience. The solutions can be better adapted to the real needs, and the available resources are used better.
>
> (Research Group for the New Everyday Life 1991: 27)

From where we stand today, parts of these visions for the new everyday life may seem banal and outdated: for instance the unequivocal linking of women to care, which is no longer a Scandinavian reality since a growing number of men now participate in care work. I include the group's contribution here because its work has had great significance for the development of Scandinavian everyday life research. I also want to emphasize it as an asset that the group cultivates an everyday life perspective that accommodates the conditions related to macro, meso and micro levels of analysis. For although visions about the new everyday life are rooted at the dynamic intermediary level with an emphasis on the meso level, macro conditions in the form of structural frames and micro conditions in the form of individual everyday life are also discussed. It is thus an analytical model that focuses on different levels and at the same time connects a 'from below' and a 'from above' perspective on everyday life. The approach is close to that of Gullestad's analytical model, and she did in fact explicitly mention that she was inspired by the group's work.

Structural life-mode analysis

It can be argued whether structural life-mode analysis is a theory about everyday life. In any case, both its point of departure and its analytical methods are fundamentally different from the dominant micro-oriented or phenomenologically inspired everyday life analyses described above. I choose to present structural life-mode analysis here because it offers an alternative perspective and useful analytical tools in terms of thematizing life styles and daily life: for instance, differences between various social groups, and the relation between work and family life.

Structural life-mode analysis was developed by Danish ethnographer Thomas Højrup, starting in the book *Det glemte folk: Livsformer og centraldirigering* (*The Forgotten People: Life-Modes and Central Direction*, 1983). Højrup later developed the theory with, among others, Lotte Rahbek Christensen (see Højrup 1995; Christensen and Højrup 1989). The Forgotten People was a large research project aimed at developing methods to create greater cohesion between the life-modes and living conditions of different social groups. The project was intended to be used in, among other things, regional planning. The empirical point of departure was Salling, an area in Northern Jutland in Denmark with a large provincial town – Skive – as well as small towns and rural districts (including coastal areas with fishing). Højrup's work with establishing an analytical framework for the project is the primary ingredient in life-mode analysis, an empirical analysis that has been used not to develop but only to test and exemplify theory. Højrup's subproject unfolded into a comprehensive analysis of the very different life-modes and struggles to preserve these life-modes in the community. The theoretical inspiration or backbone was its structural Marxism, dialectics and logics with a strong rooting in theory of science (Højrup 1983:13).

According to Højrup, being able to talk about everyday life in a systematic way without losing yourself in minor details or random facts is decisive. The primary objective of life-mode analysis is therefore to grasp theoretical contrasts in the population's everyday lives. The basic premise of the theory is that each life-mode has its own conceptual world – its own way of understanding itself and its surroundings. Thus, our concepts and values are products of cultural life-modes. Consequently, to understand the differences between life-modes, it is necessary to first grasp the different conceptual worlds that 'determine' the different cultural orientations. The conceptual worlds and the cultural practices are fundamentally rooted in social formation and the different modes of production. This highlights the structural point of departure and the basic connection between mode of production, cultural practice and subjective orientations.

At the overall level of analysis Højrup distinguishes between two modes of production that characterize Western capitalist societies: first, the dominant capitalist mode of production, and second, the subordinate simple commodity production. The two modes of production (and the differences between them) make up the foundation of the different life-modes, in which a specific mode of production requires specific life-modes to reproduce itself. Likewise, a specific life-mode determines specific political, economic and legal organizations in order to exist.

In the *capitalist mode of production*, the producers do not own the business organizations and they do not possess the skills to enter into all elements of production. Producers own only their labour power, which they make available in return for a wage income with which they can buy goods. This mode of production is linked to life-mode 2 and life-mode 3. In *simple commodity production*, the individual producer owns their business or property and possesses the skills required to perform the entire work process. This often refers to small production units, such as family farms or cooperatives. Business economy and private economy cannot be separated, and the producer typically specializes in one type of product. This mode of production is linked to life-mode 1 (Højrup 1983: 39ff, 2003a: 18ff).

In the more detailed description of the three life-modes, Højrup emphasizes the relation between the three basic elements: work, family and spare time, which are analysed within the relationship of means and ends (Højrup 1983, 2003a). Let us turn to the three life-modes in order to see what according to Højrup specifically characterizes them.

Life-mode 1: the self-employed

The life-mode of the self-employed is literally full-time work, with no distinction between work and spare time. In this type of business (of for instance fishers, farmers or small tradespeople) the whole family is usually involved, and those involved possess the necessary skills. The same principles apply to, for instance, production collectives, although their base is not the family. Business and private economy cannot be separated. There is no distinction between work and spare time/family life. Farmers and fishers do not 'go home from work'; instead 'freedom' means making your own decisions, 'being your own boss'. In this life-mode, the concept of work and its cultural content is completely different from that of wage earners. Means and ends are closely related: the goal is to stay independent, and the business is the means.

Life-mode 2: the wage earners

In contrast with life-mode 1, wage-earning workers in life-mode 2 are connected with the buying and selling of their labour skills in the capitalist mode of production. Work and spare time are sharply separated. You work in order to obtain something else. You sell your work hours to obtain the means to reach the end, which is spare time. In your spare time you can spend the wage you earn at work. Employers and employees are divided into 'them' and 'us'. What you do during work hours is basically not important. The important thing is to get as high a wage as possible and enough spare time in which to 'live'. Højrup here distinguishes between different types of spare time in terms of degree of consumption and desire to 'expand' one's spare time (for example, buying a larger home or expensive travel).

Life-mode 3: the career professionals

This life-mode is also linked to the capitalist mode of production. Compared with life-mode 2, the great difference is that the means–ends relation is fundamentally different. as work is seen as the goal and spare time as the means. In contrast to the wage-earner mode, there is no clear separation between work and spare time – rather spare time is used to recharge for work. The goal is engagement and success, and spare time is also geared to this. Career professionals are highly qualified people who are involved in running a business. There is no 'us' and 'them' in relation to management – the carriers of this life-mode identify with management. The key words here are competition and individuality – not solidarity.

As mentioned, it is important to keep in mind that these life-modes are not empirical units but ideal-typical categories. It is the theoretical, not the actual, empirical differences that are interesting. For example, differences in the means–ends relations may offer a fruitful basis for thematizing theoretical contrasts between the life-modes. It is also important to point out that the life-modes rarely exist in any pure form; they will often be mixtures.

An important element in a life-mode analysis is thematizing the ethnocentrism of the life-modes, where the different means–ends relations in terms of work and spare time mean that bearers of the three life-modes have difficulties in understanding each other's priorities. For example, bearers of the wage-earner mode will have a hard time understanding the self-employed because they work all day and never relax. Likewise, bearers of the self-employed life-mode will have a hard time understanding the priorities of the two other modes. They will see wage work as a defeat because wage earners cannot take care of themselves; they will see them as wage slaves, and look down on intellectual work (life-mode 3) because it does not involve physical effort.

Since 1983, the three basic life-modes have made up the core of Højrup's theoretical work. However, he has since developed the theory further by incorporating among other things state theory, and emphasizing the correlation between family forms, life-modes and state forms, including the determination of what characterizes a welfare state and the challenges to this state form (Højrup 2003b, 2006). I shall not go into more detail here, but instead move on to how life-mode analysis has contributed to the study of family and gender.

Life-modes, gender and family

In continuation of Højrup's three basic life-modes, Lone Rahbek Christensen has developed two so-called female life-modes. The point of departure is a complementary gender understanding and the different meanings of family in the three life-modes. In the self-employed life-mode, the family is often part of the same unit as the business. In the wage-earner mode, the family is linked to spare time, and family and work are sharply separated. In the career professional life-mode, the family is a support base – the means that support the career focus. Here too, family and work are linked (Christensen 1987: 27ff).

Based on this, Christensen developed two specifically female life-modes: the housewife praxis and the home-front praxis, which of course are also theoretical categories and not empirical forms of female/male work. The *housewife praxis* is linked to the wage-earner family: the home is related to the means and family time to the ends. Christensen emphasizes the housewife mode as a theoretical category, which is contingent on somebody providing for the family (via wage work) and somebody building and maintaining the family materially (through practical chores) and immaterially (being together). There are different types within the housewife praxis, based on the balance between home and family time (Christensen 1987: 61ff). The *home-front praxis* is also linked to family and provision, but is based on the premise that career professionals – unlike wage earners – only sell their labour power on specific qualifications and limited time. For the career professional there is more involved – first and foremost respect, which is not only linked to wage work, but also to the family in the form of style: clothes, house, car and so on. The home-front praxis 'woman' is there to assist the career 'man', and she is thus co-producer of his image. Their relation is teamwork – her effort in the family is part of his success, and his success is her means (to preserving the family and its status) (Christensen 1987: 87ff).

In her argument for constructing the two female life-modes, Christensen enters into a critical dialogue with gender research, which she argues has tended to homogenize women and thus overlook women who are primarily linked to housework, assisting wives, part-time work and so on (Christensen 1987: 11). She also emphasizes the theoretical status of the two female life-modes. Still, it is obvious that the theoretical construction as well as the empirical examples remain based on stereotypical views of women's and men's roles which correspond poorly with the actual development in the Scandinavian welfare states. This is true for the three main life-modes (primarily associated with men) and the two supplementary life-modes (primarily associated with women).

I would argue that all five life-modes contain important analytical aspects, but in their construction they should be disassociated from such stereotypical gender conceptions. It is evident that life-mode analysis has not been based on frameworks developed within gender studies, which we have seen was the case for the phenomenologically inspired everyday life research.

The Danish sociologist Anne-Dorthe Hestbæk has made an important contribution. In a qualitative analysis of parenthood in different types of families with young children, she combines life-mode analysis with the perspective of modernity. The basic assumption is that parenthood is influenced by modern society, but that the traits of modernity have various manifestations in the specific life-modes. Hestbæk's analysis is based on, first, the life-modes' understanding of variations, and especially how they are expressed in values and practice in relation to parenthood. Second, it is based on the discussion in modernization theory of the relationship between tradition and change in terms of, for example, gender equality, negotiation and reflexivity. The analysis shows that the life-mode approach applied in this nuanced way can serve as a good analytical tool for understanding variations between modern families.

Hestbæk's study indicates that there are important differences between families where degrees of modernization are concerned. The least modernized families are those that are bearers of the wage-earner life-mode. Even in dual wage-earner couples, the negotiation space between the genders is very limited, just as the division of labour in the home is often based on traditional gender relations. The most modernized families are dual-career families and families and couples with self-employed women (see Hestbæk 1995, 1998).

To conclude on life-mode analysis, I want to emphasize that its strength is the structural point of departure and its insistence on the relation between modes of production and the cultural expressions and values in work, family and spare time. As ideal types the life-modes' theoretical differences therefore constitute an excellent analytical tool for highlighting contrasts and differences in everyday life – from the self-employed life-mode as it manifests itself in the marginal areas among fishers and farmers with a low degree of modernization, via life-modes that are bearers of traditional wage-earner values, to modern career professional life-modes as they are expressed in the cities. Likewise, the principles in life-mode analyses may be suitable for analysing tensions and contrasts within specific parts of the population.

The weakness in this type of analysis is the static and apparently unchangeable approach, which leaves very little room for the subjects in the structural determination of the life-modes. The room for changes within the life-modes is extremely limited, just as historical changes (for instance, in wage work) are difficult to conceive. This static perspective is particularly evident in the perception of gender, where especially the praxis in female life-modes are founded on an antiquated and stereotypical view of gender that leaves little or no room for the fundamental changes in women's and men's lives. Hestbæk's alternative contribution, which combines life-mode analysis with the understanding of modernity, is a good example of how a more dynamic application of the theory can be fruitful.

Concluding perspectives and current challenges

What are the specifically Scandinavian contributions to everyday life research, and what are the current challenges? First and foremost, I see it as a strength that Scandinavian studies of everyday life to a large extent are based on synthesizing research where general theories and concepts of everyday life are further developed through empirical analyses. The result is, first and foremost, enriching insights into 'ordinary people's' everyday lives, whether it is around the kitchen tables in Bergen, in marginal areas in Northern Norway or along the Danish west coast, in unemployed women's everyday strategies or as insights into unusual people's daily rhythms and routines. Second, the research has led to extensive development of concepts either through thematization of what Gullestad calls concepts of everyday life or through developments and reformulations of some of the classic concepts, as Bech-Jørgensen has done.

Another characteristic of the phenomenologically inspired Scandinavian everyday life theory is that its point of departure is the home. It is remarkable that although the home is at the centre of attention, it is treated in different ways and assigned different meanings in relation to social interaction and patterns of action. As we have seen, Gullestad sees home and family life as a collective strength and as a gathering point that condenses all other social spheres, whereas Bech-Jørgensen is aware of the 'enclosedness' of the home and the danger of isolation from the surroundings. This dual perspective emphasizes that the home in modern societies can be an arena both for isolation, and for intimate relations in daily life which constitute the framework for collective organizations in the local community.

I also want to draw attention to the fact that most Scandinavian everyday life research has advocated a holistic perspective on everyday life. A good example is the Research Group for the New Everyday Life, whose visions emphasize the creation of an intermediate level that connects micro, meso and macro perspectives. The same goes for Gullestad's analytical models, which maintain family, home and intimate networks in a close interplay with labour market and social institutions.

In the same way – but from a fundamentally different theoretical point of departure – Højrup's structural life-mode analysis is based on a holistic perspective on everyday life. He starts out from the significance of general modes of production for differences in cultural orientations, as links between means and ends in the relation between work, family and spare time. As ideal-types the life-modes constitute a useful analytical tool for thematizing contrasts between specific social groups, and also for examining the tension between tradition and modernity within and across the life-modes. This is not least true in the later versions, which combine life-mode analysis with a gender and modernity perspective.

Overall, Scandinavian everyday life theories thus still have a lot to offer contemporary sociological research that is interested in ordinary people's unusual everyday lives, their rhythms, repetitions, routines and ruptures. A pertinent question is, however, whether everyday life theories as we know them today have the capacity to relate to modern complex and multicultural societies. Are the everyday life theories in their particular focus on 'ordinary' people's 'ordinary' lives capable of questioning prevalent everyday knowledge through critical reflection on people's values and prejudices?

This is a topic Gullestad discussed in depth in her last two books, among other things by criticizing her own 'bottom up' perspective (Gullestad 2002, 2006). Here she argued that culture and everyday life researchers may have contributed to preserving exoticizing perceptions of ethnic minority groups as 'the others'. The reason is that the constructions of national borders, race and ethnicity are not only associated with politics and economy; they are also to a large extent rooted in all those practices that are plausible structures for imagining the categories of race, gender, culture and nation – for example, in terms of belonging, inclusion and exclusion (Gullestad 2006: 34). The point is that the cultural world-views that are drawn out of culture and everyday life studies, for instance of ethnic minority groups, often serve to maintain rather than change interpretive frames that reinforce the gap between 'us' and 'the others'. It happens among other things because a lot of the research on ethnic minority groups in Scandinavian countries is written for 'us' about 'them'. Research 'from below' does not only require thorough knowledge of the people and their actions; it is also based on scientific theories and interpretations that are influenced by common perceptions on, for instance, homogeneity in the Nordic countries or implicit arguments that we have to think of 'our own' first.

Gullestad therefore warns against linking the tendencies towards diversity in everyday life unequivocally with ethnic minority groups, and recommends the following in order to renew everyday life research so that it does not confirm, but rather challenges existing prejudices. Place more analytical emphasis on questioning prevalent everyday knowledge; focus less on differences between 'us' and 'them', focus more on differences within each ethnic minority group as well as within the majority groups; and get a better analytical grasp of the power relations associated with gender, race, ethnicity and social class as they are expressed in the interplay between local, national and transnational processes. This convincing argument about the need for an intersectional approach to everyday life research illustrates that contemporary Scandinavian everyday life research is also closely related to developments within feminist research where intersectional approaches to gender and other categories (like class, race, and ethnicity) have replaced the original focus on women and women's everyday lives.

Notes

1. I want to thank Sara Marie Jensen, who has worked as a student assistant searching for literature and working out a bibliography on Nordic everyday life research which has been very useful to my work on this chapter (see Jensen 2008).
2. For the debate between Gullestad and Bech-Jørgensen, see e.g. two articles in the journal *Dansk Sociologi* from 1994 (Gullestad 1994; Bech-Jørgensen 1994b).
3. As we shall see later, Bech-Jørgensen also maintains the substantial focus on the home. She emphasizes that the division between residence, home and residents is an expression of socially generated conditions in modern everyday life. She also refers to Ivan

Illich's (1986) metaphor on the residence as a garage where family members are parked at nights and weekends, because in daily activities there is a division between family residence, workplaces, child-care institutions and so on (Bech-Jørgensen 1994a).

4. Heller's paradigms of human conditions include three spheres: (1) the sphere of objectivations in-itself; (2) the sphere of objectivations for-itself; (3) the sphere of objectivations for-and-in-itself. (These spheres are inspired by the Marxist notions of *an sich/für sich*.) The first sphere refers to unreflected given skills like language, customs and use of tools – according to Heller the backbone of everyday life. The second sphere is related to conscious acts and meaningful worldviews in relation to art, science, religion and philosophy. This is where the cultural surplus in everyday life gathers. The third sphere contains socially created institutions, which can cause objectivations both *an sich* and *für sich*, depending on the degree of oppression in the system (Heller 1970/1984:118ff).
5. Some of the most significant main results from the project 'The Qualified Everyday Life' are published in Bech-Jørgensen (1998, 2001a, 2001b, 2003); Jørgensen (1998, 2006); Svendsen-Tune (2002) and Dengsøe (2000).
6. The following researchers participated in the Research Group for the New Everyday Life: from Denmark: Birte Bech-Jørgensen, Tarja Cronberg and Hedvig Vestergaard. From Finland: Liisa Horelli and Kirsti Vepsä. From Norway: Sigrun Kaul and Anne Saeterdal. From Sweden: Ingela Blomberg, Birgit Krantz and Inga-Lisa Sangregorio. The group was cross-disciplinary and represented sociology, psychology, political science, physical planning, architecture and macro-economy (Research Group for the New Everyday Life 1984, 1987, 1991).

Bibliography

Ahrne, Göran (1981) *Vardagsverklighet och struktur*. Göteborg: Korpen.

Bech-Jørgensen, Birte (1990a) 'The impossibility of everyday life', in Flemming Røgilds (ed.), *Every Cloud has a Silver Lining*. Copenhagen: Akademisk Forlag.

Bech-Jørgensen, Birte (1990b) 'What are they doing, when they seem to do nothing?', in Jari Ehrnrooth and Lasse Siurala (eds), *Construction of Youth*. Helsinki: VAPK-Publishing.

Bech-Jørgensen, Birte (1994a) *Når hver dag bliver hverdag*. Copenhagen: Akademisk Forlag.

Bech-Jørgensen, Birte (1994b) 'Hverdagslivets kvaliteter: Et svar til Marianne Gullestad.' *Dansk Sociologi*, 2: 61–8.

Bech-Jørgensen, Birte (1997a) 'Individualization and post-traditional communities', in Catharina J. Christensen (ed.), *The Meeting of the Waters: Individuality, Community and Solidarity*. Copenhagen: Scandinavian University Press.

Bech-Jørgensen, Birte (1997b) 'Symbolsk orden og hverdagskultur', in Ann-Dorte Christensen, Anna-Birte Ravn and Iris Rittenhofer (eds), *Det kønnede samfund: Forståelse af køn og social forandring*. Aalborg: Aalborg Universitetsforlag.

Bech-Jørgensen, Birte (1998) 'Hjemløses boliger', in Birte Bech-Jørgensen and Søren Kristiansen (eds), *Sociale perspektiver*. Aalborg: Forlaget ALFUFF.

Bech-Jørgensen, Birte (2001a) *Nye tider og usædvanlige fællesskaber*. Copenhagen: Gyldendal.

Bech-Jørgensen, Birte (2001b) 'Forskning og hverdagsliv' and 'Brobyggerselskabet – de udstødte: En introduktion.' *Social Kritik*, 73.

Bech-Jørgensen, Birte (2003) *Ruter og rytmer – om brobyggerne, frontfolket og de hjemløse*. Copenhagen: Hans Reitzels Forlag.

Brox, Ottar (1966) *Hva skjer i Nord-Norge?* Oslo: Pax.

Christensen, Lone Rahbek (1987) *Hver vore veje: Livsformer, familietyper og kvindeliv*. Odense: Etnologisk Forum.

Christensen, Lone Rahbek and Thomas Højrup (1989) 'Strukturel livsformsanalyse.' *Nord Nytt: Nordisk Tidsskrift for Folkelivsforskning*, 37: 53–91.

Cronberg, Tarja (1986) *Teorier om teknologi og hverdagsliv*. Copenhagen: Nyt fra Samfundsvidenskaberne.

Cronberg, Tarja and Inga-Lisa Sangregorio (1981) *Du sköna nya vardag*. Stockholm: Prisma.

Dengsøe Poul (2000) *Hverdagsliv på Vesterbro – fra folkeligt kvarter til moderne bydel*. Aalborg: Aalborg Universitetsforlag.

Gullestad, Marianne (1984/2002) *Kitchen-Table Society: A Case Study of Family Life and Friendships of Young Working-Class Mothers in Urban Norway*. Oslo: Universitetsforlaget.

Gullestad, Marianne (1989) *Kultur og hverdagsliv: På sporet av det moderne Norge*. Oslo: Universitetsbiblioteket.

Gullestad, Marianne (1992) *The Art of Social Relations: Essays on Culture, Thought and Social Action in Modern Norway*. Oslo: Universitetsforlaget.

Gullestad, Marianne (1994) 'Misjonerende sosiologi: Innlegg som førsteopponent ved Birte Bech-Jørgensens disputats på Københavns Universitet 21. januar, 1994.' *Dansk Sociologi*, 2: 42–56.

Gullestad, Marianne (1996) *Everyday Life Philosophers: Modernity, Morality and Autobiography in Norway*. Oslo: Universitetsforlaget.

Gullestad, Marianne (2002) *Det norske sett med nye øyne: Kritisk analyse av norsk innvandringsdebatt*. Oslo: Universitetsforlaget.

Gullestad, Marianne (2006) *Plausible Prejudice: Everyday Practices and Social Images of Nation, Culture and Race*. Oslo: Universitetsforlaget.

Heller, Agnes (1970/1984) *Everyday Life*. London: Routledge & Kegan Poul.

Hestbæk, Anne-Dorte (1995) *Forældreskab i 90'erne*. Copenhagen: Socialforskningsinstituttet, Rapport 95: 5.

Hestbæk, Anne-Dorte (1998) 'Parenthood in the 1990's: tradition and modernity in the parenthood of dual-earner couples with different life-modes.' *Childhood*, 4: 463–91.

Holter, Harriet (1975) *Familien klassesamfunnet*. Oslo: Pax.

Højrup, Thomas (1983) *Det glemte folk: Livsformer og centraldirigering*. Copenhagen: Statens Byggeforsknings Instituts Forlag.

Højrup (1995) *Omkring livsformsanalysens udvikling*. Copenhagen: Museum Tusculanum Press.

Højrup, Thomas (2003a) *State, Culture and Life-Modes: The Foundations of Life-Mode Analysis*. Aldershot: Ashgate.

Højrup, Thomas (2003b) *Livsformer og velfærdsstat ved en korsvej? Introduktion til et kulturteoretisk og kulturhistorisk bidrag: Stats- og Livsformer 5*. Copenhagen: Museum Tusculanum Press.

Højrup, Thomas (2006) 'Forskningsoversigt – etnologiske studier i stats- og livsformsteorien', in Astrid Jespersen et al. (eds), *Verden over: En introduktion til stats- og livsformsteorien i dens aktuelle anvendelse i etnologien*. Copenhagen: Museum Tusculanum Press.

Illich, Ivan (1986) *Køn*. Copenhagen: Tiderne Skifter.

Jensen, Sara Marie (2008) *Bibliografi over nordisk hverdagslivsforskning* (unpublished).

Jørgensen, Anja (1998) *De fattige og udstødte i Aalborg by – et socialhistorisk tilbageblik*. Aalborg: Forlaget ALFUFF.

Jørgensen, Anja (2006) *Når kvarteret opdager sig selv*. Aalborg: Aalborg Universitetsforlag.

Liljeström, Rita (1981) *Kultur och arbete*. Malmø: Liber Förlag/Sekretariatet för framtidsstudier.

Research Group for the New Everyday Life (1984) *Det nya vardagslivet: Forskargruppen för det nya vardagslivet*. Kommittén för Jämställdhetsfrågor, Nordisk Ministerråd, Nord.

Research Group for the New Everyday Life (1987) *Veier til det nye hverdagslivet*. Kommittén for Jämställdhtsfrågor, Nordisk Ministerråd, Nord.

Research Group for the New Everyday Life (1991) *The New Everyday Life – Ways and Means*. Copenhagen: Nordic Council of Ministers.

Schutz, Alfred (1975) *Hverdagslivets sociologi*. Copenhagen: Hans Reitzels Forlag.

Svendsen-Tune, Stine (2002) *Skæve hverdagsliv*. Aalborg: Aalborg Universitetsforlag.

Troels-Lund, Frederik (1914–15) *Dagligt liv i Norden i det sekstende aarhundrede*, 7 vols. Copenhagen: Gyldendal.

Wadel, Cato (1983) *Dagliglivets organisering*. Oslo: University Press.

CHAPTER 13

The Sociology of Emotions

Managing, Exchanging and Generating Emotions in Everyday Life

POUL PODER

Introduction

This chapter introduces three major theoretical perspectives within the sociology of emotions in order to illuminate how everyday life is profoundly emotional. The main point is to demonstrate how these perspectives from the sociology of emotions significantly supplement more cognitively oriented approaches to everyday life such as phenomenology, symbolic interactionism and existentialism.

In order to do so, I first introduce Arlie R. Hochschild's theory of emotional experience as a product of the interaction between cultural 'feeling rules' and 'display rules', and individuals' 'emotion management' aimed at feeling and showing what is considered appropriate in the given situation. As an illustration of this cultural and dramaturgical perspective, I discuss Hochschild's analysis of how emotions of love and care are influenced by emotion management aimed at adapting to changing cultural understandings of love and care.

Second, I introduce Candace Clark's theory of how emotions are part of a socio-emotional economy according to which individuals exchange emotions or 'emotional gifts' in accordance with their 'place' in micro-hierarchies of everyday life. This theory is useful in explaining how emotions are exchanged between individuals in their micro-political standing in relation to each other. Acts and expressions of niceness and gratitude are better understood as part of a certain economy than as something expressed indiscriminately and gratuitously.

Third, I draw on Randall Collins's ritual theory of how emotions arise in interaction rituals characterized by common, focused attention and group emotion and 'emotional energy' resulting from particularly strong and successful interaction rituals. Collins's theory is used to explain how everyday life rituals further an ongoing generation of emotional energy, which is crucial in understanding the formation of the agency of individuals. My argument is here that agency must also be understood as emotional rather than merely a mind phenomenon.

Finally, in the conclusion I discuss how the presented perspectives supplement other approaches to everyday life, and I give a few suggestions as to how the sociology of emotions can contribute to the sociological understanding of everyday life. However, the chapter begins with a short section that explains the phrase 'the sociology of emotion', outlines a basic definition of the concept of emotion and presents the main theoretical perspectives of 'the sociology of emotions'.

The sociology of emotions

In order to understand the 'sociology of emotions', it is necessary to consider the role of emotions in sociology in an overall sense, since the sociology of emotions is best understood as a reaction to how sociology has developed in an emotion-neglecting direction. In sociology's constitutive phase, classical sociologists such as Émile Durkheim, Georg Simmel and Max Weber were all, one way or the other, concerned with understanding emotional dimensions of social and moral life (Shilling 2002). Durkheim's concern with the ritual generation of social sentiments and symbols is but one example of how modern sociology in its beginning was attentive to emotional qualities of social life.

However, as sociology developed after the writings of these classics, it largely came to ignore the emotional dimensions of social life (Shilling 2002; Stauth and Turner 1988). This neglect formed the background on which the sociology of emotion emerged as a sub-discipline starting in the 1970s (Barbalet 1998; Flam 2000, 2002; Kemper 2000; Thoits 1989; Turner and Stets 2005). The rise of such a sub-discipline was led by a group of sociologists, who wanted to correct this neglect of sociological theory and research. Yet the sociologists identifying themselves as 'sociologists of emotions' were and are still not united in a single, coherent theoretical perspective. The sociology of emotion encompasses a variety of sociological perspectives and is therefore not comparable to a particular theoretical tradition such as, for example, the phenomenological tradition.

Researches within the sociology of emotion camp deal with issues such as the emotional basis of solidarity in groups; how outcomes of social interaction determine emotions; the normative regulation of emotions and emotional regulation; the socialization of emotions via the transfer of meaning to physiological experience; how emotional experience varies according to, for example, social class, occupation, gender, race/ethnicity, and emotions in wider social and political processes of stability and change (Kemper 2000: 45).

Emotion defined

Emotion as a category contains various meanings and dimensions as it is applied within biology, anthropology, psychology, affective neuro-science and the social sciences. Consequently, there is no firm definition, but many emotion researchers and theorists tend to agree that three types of data are significant in defining emotions. First, there is a behavioural level evidenced in, for example, facial expressions or aggressive posture. Second, there are physiological data such as high pulse rate or sweaty palms that are associated with a 'rush' of emotion. Third, there is also the subjective or inter-subjective level of experiential knowledge or interpretation of emotion, as when we are aware of feeling, for example, angry or disappointed (Gibson 1997: 214).

Moreover, different emotions arise in response to different meanings. They tend to be elicited by particular types of events: 'Grief is usually elicited by personal loss, anger by insults or frustrations, joy by success, etc.' (Frijda 2007: 5). Emotion is generally understood as states of a limited duration – ranging from a few minutes to a few hours – which have one or more causes that can be identified. Emotions are thought to be states that link events with what is of concern for the feeling person, and they work as evaluative signals indicating something of relevance to the self. Furthermore, emotions dispose plans or establish an orientation towards other persons. These are two fundamental ways in which emotions are significant in social life (Oatley, Keltner and Jenkins 2006).

Constitutive of the sociology of emotion is the insight that emotion is defined by social context. Emotion is not purely a psychological or biological phenomenon located within the individual personality or the biological body. Emotions reside both in experiencing individuals and in their social relations (Barbalet 1998: 79). But both experiential and contextual elements of emotion are necessary to conceptualize emotion as a social phenomenon. Emotion cannot be reduced to its person-bound indicators if we understand social context as a constitutive part of emotions. Understanding emotion sociologically means seeing emotions as referring not merely to the individual's bodily and psychological changes but also to changes in the social context.

Main theoretical perspectives

The issue of social context and how it influences emotional experience and its expression is what all sociological approaches to emotions conceptualize one way or another. Broadly speaking, social context refers either to social and historical (macro) conditions such as economy, ideology and culture which shape how emotions unfold in interaction, or to micro-conditions on the level of interaction itself such as for, example, how the concrete setting affects what is experienced and how it is displayed.

A recent and thorough review of existing sociological theories of emotions suggests seven theoretical approaches, which I mention briefly to indicate the richness of the sociology of emotions:

- *Dramaturgical and cultural theories* which underscore how people's behaviour is often a strategic performance in front of an audience composed of others. Cultural beliefs and norms about which emotions and expressions are appropriate in the particular situation and script for the performance of the individuals.
- *Ritual theories* that emphasize how individuals rhythmically synchronize their responses to each other and how emotions and emotional energy are engendered through a moment-by-moment responsiveness.
- *Symbolic interactionist theories* focus on identity and self-conceptions as the regulators of behaviour. When people can reaffirm identity in a situation, they feel positive emotions, and conversely, they feel negative emotions when their self-conception is threatened in the situation.
- *Symbolic interactionist theories* incorporating psychoanalytical ideas which add to the interactionist approach in that individuals often invoke defence mechanisms which distort their experience and expression of emotion when the self is not confirmed.
- *Exchange theories* focusing on how individuals respond emotionally as they receive or do not receive expected and desired resources, or on how emotions themselves are resources to be exchanged.
- *Structural theories* which concentrate on how individuals' places or positions in social structures influence what they feel. When others' responses confirm someone's position, positive emotion is expected, while negative emotions are aroused if such confirmation is lacking.
- *Evolutionary theories* seek to understand how human emotionality has evolved as a result of natural selection. However, within sociology, evolutionary theories are concerned with how underlying biological mechanisms interact with socio-cultural formations to generate emotional responses, rather than being a new manifestation of biological determinism (Turner and Stets 2005: 23–5).

In the remainder of this chapter I introduce theoretical perspectives belonging to the dramaturgical and cultural, the ritual and the exchange clusters, as these three perspectives explain significant emotional processes of everyday life.

Managing feelings according to culture

In this section I draw on Arlie R. Hochschild's (b. 1940) classic theory of emotion management, which can help us understand how emotions, which are often taken for granted as more or less automatic and biologically hardwired reactions, are also the result of various forms of emotion work/management activities by the feeling individual. Hochschild's theory casts light on how emotions of love and care are not natural reactions, but heavily mediated by culture and individuals' active emotion management. Consequently, feelings of everyday life are changing as culture changes – something which I discuss by introducing Hochschild's analysis of the cooling of modern culture with respect to feelings of love and care.

Hochschild's theory has been described as a dramaturgical and cultural type of theory (Turner and Stets 2005), but I also want to emphasize how it further develops the interactionist perspective as it highlights how everyday life is also about management of emotions and not merely about self-indication and interpretation (Blumer 1986) or 'impression management' (Goffman 1959).

According to Hochschild, how emotions of love and care are lived and experienced is a matter of culture. Culture defines certain assumptions about how and when to feel these emotions and how to express them, as culture defines basic assumptions concerning human attachment. One example of such a premise is the idea that between partners, and between parents and children, love is or should be unconditional. Love is something the child can expect to be given by parents. It is not something the child should do something in particular to earn. This cultural assumption of unconditional love influences how we feel in certain situations. The child who is not met with unconditional love will most likely feel wounded. And the parents will most likely try to make themselves feel more loving. In other words, different cultures define different basic notions concerning humans and what they need. A culture defines a particular notion of the self which influences how we think and feel about, for example, love. If humans are basically thought of as self-enclosed and independent in a particular culture, this may weaken the idea of others as being very significant as love partners to the individual (Hochschild 2003: 14).

As people live in particular societies, communities or groups, part of their cultural and social context is a *culture of emotion*. Such culture consists of ideas of what feelings are *feelable* in particular social situations. For example, to have the expectation that your wedding will be the happiest day of your life implies that you rely on a prior notion of what feelings are culturally available to be felt

(Hochschild 2003: 121). A culture of emotion is like an emotional dictionary which expresses the idea that there are given, emotional experiences within the group of people belonging to this culture. In a very basic sense, the particular culture of emotion of, for example, teenagers in Western culture delineates what kind of emotional experiences teenagers can expect to have. A culture of emotion also consists of ideas about how to recognize and label a particular feeling. One kind of culture devises one set of emotions as possible and imaginable concerning love between two people, whereas another kind of culture may dispose a quite different set of imaginable and expectable emotions. Moreover, a culture of emotion also contains ideas on how people *should* feel and how they *should* express emotions. It contains ideals or norms concerning, for example, how love should be practised. An example could be the common, Western and romantic idea that people should not pay money to receive love from another human being. Love should be practised not as a money transaction, but as a relationship between two free and mutually devoted individuals.

Consequently, Hochschild writes about 'feeling rules' understood as ideal expectations entertained by groups of people, which reflect forms of social memberships. Feeling rules are social guidelines telling how we wish to feel in particular situations. Indication of the existence of such rules is our talk about rights and duties linked to certain emotions, when we, for example, insist that 'we have a right to be angry at someone' in certain situations. She also writes about 'display rules', which refer to cultural expectations that we will express certain feelings on certain occasions – for instance, sorrow at a funeral. People recognize such rules when we inspect how we assess our feelings, how other people evaluate our emotional display and expressions, and by sanctions issued from them or ourselves. Take as an example when parents tell the disappointed birthday child that she ought to feel more grateful for her presents, or at least reduce her display of disappointment. People monitor others' and their own emotions in view of the specific situations they act in, and the cultural feeling rules and display rules that define what it is appropriate to feel in given situations, and how it is appropriate to express these emotions.

Summing up, the culture of emotion influences emotional life by expressing what emotional experience is expectable and realistic, and by expressing normative ideals of what to feel and how to express emotions in particular situations. In brief, emotions are not automatic reactions, but neither are they solely a product of the cultural socialization which individuals acquire.

Emotion management

Hochschild stresses that emotion is a complex response, partly determined by our 'emotion management', which is defined as 'the management of feeling to create publicly observable facial or bodily display' (Hochschild 1983: 7) and to create feelings other than those we have momentarily (Hochschild 1983: 219). Hochschild's theory does not merely focus on management aiming at impression management in relation to others, it also focuses on the inner work individuals do in order to make themselves feel other emotions than they do momentarily. Emotion work or management is 'activity' on the self of which the individual need not be aware:

> We can try to induce feelings that we don't, at first, feel, or to suppress feelings that we do. We can – and continually do – try to shape and reshape our feelings to fit our inner, cultural guidelines. These acts of emotion management are sometimes successful; often they are hopeless. But however hopeless, such acts provide a clue to who we are trying, inside, to be; an emotional 'strategy' as a larger plan, guiding acts of emotion management.
>
> (Hochschild 1998: 9)

'Emotion management' refers to the fact that emotion is co-constructed through our attempts to feel and express emotions that are considered appropriate in particular situations. Having and feeling emotions is an experience constituted in relation to socially defined and distributed 'feeling rules'. Such rules suggest what to feel and how to display emotions in particular situations. Emotion management or work is directed towards bringing emotion in line with the feeling norms of the situation. This work highlights the efforts rather than the result of the efforts. Even when there is no successful result of the management activity, the pure effort at it demonstrates that we are guided by ideal expectations about our emotions. According to Hochschild, feelings are not stored 'inside' us independently of our acts of management:

> Both the act of 'getting in touch with' feeling and the act of 'trying to' feel may become part of the process that makes the thing we get in touch with, or the thing we manage, into a feeling or emotion. In managing feeling, we contribute to the creation of it.
>
> (Hochschild 1983: 17–18)

In order to analyse different instances of emotion work, Hochschild distinguishes analytically between commonly applied *techniques of self-management* for changing, altering, modifying, repressing, dissolving and/or creating emotions in order to cope with demands, expectations and tensions of particular situations:

- a cognitive technique where people try to change images, ideas and thoughts

in order to alter the emotions related to these 'cognitive' constructs – for example, when a person thinks about a threatening situation as 'challenging' in order to try to feel better about it
- a bodily technique where people try to alter bodily symptoms of emotion by, for instance, attempting to breathe more slowly or control nervously shaking hands
- an expressive technique where people alter expressive gestures in order to change their inner emotion, when they smile or cry in order to feel better in a particular situation (Hochschild 1979: 562).

According to Hochschild, emotions come about through intricate and often unnoticed emotion work, but with her perspective and analytical concepts it is possible to untangle how this takes place. We can thereby show how often taken for granted emotions are not unmediated, automatic reactions, but how they are influenced by a particular culture surrounding the feeling individuals. However, Hochschild does not assume that the human self can live up to every kind of feeling rule. Rather there is a tension between the individual's self and cultural demands for emotion management. Too much demand on having a service attitude towards customers makes employees feel stressed (Hochschild 1983).

As a way of conceptualizing this tension, Peter Freund has coined the concept of 'dramaturgical stress', which 'emanates from threats to self-other or group boundaries, or to the security of informational preserves – threats, in short, to ontological security' (Freund 1998: 267). Dramaturgical stress concerns the emotion work of protecting the boundaries of self and other, and is therefore implied in the dramaturgical quality of social life as such. Coping with dramaturgical stress implies emotion work which consumes energy, and the demands of control can become so great that individuals will suffer from heightened stress. This happens when the individual finds that their chosen performance conflicts with the idea of self that they are trying to maintain (Freund 1998: 281). Emotion work in order to maintain self-composure in situations of 'dramaturgical stress' is often unnoticed (Layder 1997: 58). Dramaturgical stress can arise in interaction with the rude customer who 'is always right' or as an effect of interpersonal competitiveness or hierarchical pressures (Freund 1998: 285).

In understanding how dramaturgical stress is distributed in socio-structural terms, it is useful to consider Hochschild's concept of 'status shields', which explains how there is a link between social status and individuals' emotions. She writes: 'The lower our status, the more our manner of seeing and feeling is subject to being discredited and the less believable it becomes' (Hochschild 1983: 173). Hochschild's study of flight attendants' emotional management or labour showed that female attendants were more subject to the displaced feelings of others. Customers let out their aggression and frustration more on female than male attendants.[1] Hochschild explains this difference by referring to the fact that women in general 'have far less independent access to money, power, authority or status in society' (Hochschild 1983: 163). The concept of status shield thus elucidates how macro-social status results in certain advantages at the level of interaction. A strong status shield means that someone's way of seeing and feeling in the world is not easily discredited, thus reassuring their sense of self. This idea of protection implied in the notion of status shield is understandable on the basis of an idea of the self as being preoccupied with maintaining its identity.

Cooling off

In the following section I draw on Hochschild's cultural and dramaturgical perspective by discussing her analysis of changes in contemporary culture, which focus on trends towards a cooling off concerning our ideas of love and care, so that we come to expect less warmth and devotion from others. The culture of emotion in this area is changing, she argues, based on an analysis of changes in the images of advice books on love life in contemporary Western capitalistic societies. This analysis can illustrate how everyday life and its central emotions are influenced by more comprehensive social, economic and cultural forces.

Advice books reflect a culture of emotion – certain expectations, a basic notion of the human self, and certain explicit or implied feeling and display rules. Advice books deal with how contemporary individuals (particularly females) should treat themselves and what they ought to expect from their intimate life. In Hochschild's view, traditional advice books advise women to suppress any assertion of individual will in order to bind themselves to their men and marriage, while more recent advice books advise women to suppress feelings that attach them too closely to men. Traditional books counsel women to accumulate domestic capital and invest at home, while contemporary modern books encourage women to invest in the self as a solo enterprise, and advocate an outlook on life characterized by emancipation and emphasis on open communication about wants and needs between partners. The most recent advice books call for more open and equal communication between men and women (Hochschild 2003: 14).

But this emancipated view on life legitimizes a cool look at humans as emotional beings, Hochschild argues. The ideal individual (woman) in recent advice books is invited to manage her needs more, to devote herself to ascetic practices of emotional control and to expect to exchange little love with other human beings (Hochschild 2003: 22). Modern advice books are cool in the sense of legitimizing and presuming that individuals get by with relatively little social and emotional support, and by presuming that they have fewer needs than was formerly the case, whereas the traditional advice books can be seen as warm because they legitimize a high degree of care and social support and offer a scope for human needs. To sum up, the advocating of equalized, modern love comes together with a legitimizing of detaching strategies to engage those equal bonds (Hochschild 2003: 15). Contemporary advice books legitimize strategic control over feelings rather than people expressing their emotional needs. According to Hochschild, the cool modern books are made up of images that prepare the way for a paradigm of distrust and caution. They portray human relationships in insecure market terms and contain images of 'me' and 'you' which are psychologically shallow (Hochschild 2003: 24).

In order to live up to the ideals of this new culture of emotion, people have to develop a capacity to endure emotional isolation, which requires forms of emotion management that make it possible to live up to the novel, cultural ideal of being an independent individual. An example of an emotion management technique that can be applied in order to implement this cultural ideal is the cognitive technique of thinking in certain ways in order to change your feelings. For example, you can downplay your expectations concerning a potential love partner and refuse ideas of engaging in long-term relationships.

The intention of this section has been to show how particular cultures of emotion are crucial in determining which emotional experiences are made possible. I introduced Hochschild's thesis of a shift in the cultural premises for human attachment. Her basic argument is that:

> helping and being helped are matters of such overwhelming importance that any cultural shift which 'thins out' the process, through which we give care to one another, or empties the content of help, should make us stop and think about where we are going.
>
> (Hochschild 2003: 14)

Summing up, this section has pinpointed how we can understand particular cultures of emotion as exerting influences on individuals' emotional everyday lives. Peoples' emotions arise as a consequence of their social interaction with others, which is shaped by the cultural ideas and rules that define the context of interaction. Emotion culture concerns certain deep, taken-for-granted assumptions about values of social life – such as assumptions concerning what kind of activities should not be monetarized in interaction between people.

Hochschild's theory can unravel what emotion culture implies in terms of feeling and display rules and certain forms of emotion management engaged by the individuals in the culture concerned. Her thesis of the cooling-off of our expectations concerning love and care causes people to engage in emotion management in order not to engage in more comprehensive and warm forms of giving care and experiencing love. Hochschild raises an important question as she points out the rise of a contemporary culture of avoiding, or at least down-playing, human attachment, and she points out how such a cultural development is associated with market-driven commercialization of care, exemplified by the expansion of a market of all sorts of therapy, which tends to replace therapeutic activities within relationships of family and friendship.

Exchanging emotions and feeling your place

The previous section argued in favour of seeing emotion as culturally mediated and regulated by feeling and display rules. In this section a further step is taken, as it is suggested that emotions are exchangeable resources in the 'socio-emotional economy' of everyday life. That most organizations are explicitly hierarchical should not make us believe that informal everyday life is necessarily beyond hierarchy. Everyday life may be more egalitarian in a formal sense, but it is still hierarchical in a socio-emotional sense. How this is the case I shall explain by drawing on Candace Clark's (b. 1945) theory of how the exchange of emotion between individuals is part of establishing micro-hierarchies in everyday life (Clark 1990). Her emphasis on the exchange of emotions gives a different perspective on everyday life, which is often seen as a sphere that is somehow outside or beyond economic exchange.

As argued by Hochschild, emotions are not to be understood as merely spontaneous and natural reactions. Clark argues that in order to understand emotions sociologically, we also need to see how emotions are implied in micro-political relationships of exchange. Focusing on the expression of sympathy, she argues that even such an expression is not a natural reaction or a clear-cut 'altruistic' action. Rather it is guided by cultural rules which regulate individuals' micro-political struggle for recognition. Even an emotion such as sympathy can be part of micro-political power that is exercised as a way of marking a particular position in micro-hierarchies.

The micro-political exchange of emotional gifts

In order to understand Clark's exchange theory of emotion, we need to emphasize her observation that a sense of obligation is crucial for social exchange, because no kind of economy could work without people feeling obligated towards others. Obligation motivates people to give and is therefore a central factor in creating a group and in conforming to group norms. When people do not act on their feeling of obligation, they feel guilty, which is another emotion-promoting conformity. A person would not be able to feel guilty about disappointing someone if they did not feel obligated towards this particular person. Consequently, the emotion of obligation incites people to share socio-emotional resources with each other (Clark 1997: 136).

Given such a sense of obligation, Clark can make another crucial point: 'Without display, the emotion is a social outcome, but not a social force. Showing sympathy literally forces people to interact. Because it is emblematic of a social bond, it often creates social integration and promotes solidarity' (Clark 1997: 56–7). Expressions of sympathy work as a social force as they obligate others to respond and thereby engage in micro-political interaction. In Clark's view, 'micro-politics' refers to the activity of changing and maintaining your place within the micro-hierarchy. It 'is behaviour aimed at getting, keeping, and sometimes giving up interpersonal power, through such activities as making place claims, negotiating and jockeying for position' (Clark 1997: 233). The position we give partners, business associates, parents, children and political leaders is, to a large extent, based on how we feel about them. Everybody is therefore attentive to how they can influence others' feelings. As actors, we express emotions towards others, which function as claims to certain positions. Emotions such as contempt, disgust, anger, gratitude, patience and sympathy can be used in subordinating others, asserting ourselves, or both.

This form of interaction is political as it concerns the exchange of resources such as love, attention, company, gratitude, sex, sympathy and esteem, which are central resources in everyday life relationships. Such emotions are emotional gifts which evoke positive emotion in others. To be such a gift-giver, you have to be an expert player in the socio-economy (not a chump who gives away indiscriminately and thereby makes the gift feel less valuable). As actors in the socio-emotional economy, individuals create margins or accounts of socio-emotional credits for each other; credits which can be held in reserve, cashed in, replenished or even used up entirely (Clark 2004: 418).

Through her empirical investigation of everyday life exchange of sympathy, Clark shows that showing sympathy is not necessarily an unambiguously good thing. Bestowing emotion gifts on others in the form of displaying sympathy, patience or gratitude has micro-political effects. She argues that showing sympathy can bring people closer to each other, while at the same time maintaining the distinctions in the group. This might seem paradoxical, but it should be recalled that micro-political effects of displays of sympathy reflect the fact that all human groups are both cohesive and stratified. Sympathy and other emotional gifts contribute to cohesion when the gifts are used with the aim of reducing a gap in micro-hierarchical relations; sympathy is one such way of directing positive emotions to others and thereby flattering them, 'buttering them up' and 'getting in their good graces'. Conversely, emotional gifts can lead to stratification when one actor bestows an emotional gift in a way that makes the recipient feel self-conscious or inadequate. Consequently, giving emotional gifts can have different effects in the relationship between receiver and giver. It can emphasize inequality, increase inequality, or minimize the degree of inequality.

Expressing sympathy can emphasize inequality when the sympathizing person expresses this in a manner that underlines that they certainly do not have the problem that the receiver of sympathy has. An example of increasing inequality could be when a powerful person gives another person a gift that they cannot in any measure reciprocate. Sympathy displayed in such a manner highlights that one party is sovereign or superior to the other. It emphasizes the inequality of the relationship in spite of possible benign intentions on behalf of the giver. Finally, sympathy can also be expressed in ways that minimize the degree of inequality. This can be achieved when sympathy and patience are expressed in such a way that the giver under-communicates their own advantages and the problems of the receiver. The gap in the micro-hierarchy can also be reduced by expressing attention and giving acknowledgement to people placed in subordinate positions.

Feeling your place in everyday life hierarchies

Inequality is a salient part of everyday life social relations, which is reflected in how we naturally talk about being 'down' or 'up', 'putting someone in his/her place', 'being put down', the 'pecking order' and many similar phrases. According to Clark, people *feel* their way through interaction with others, who let them sense their place through their display of emotion. Reading your place in the social configuration of places is a complicated activity, as the individual's effort to understand their proper place often differs from the other's idea of where they belong. Emotional signals such as unrest or guilt often tell the actor where to find their place in the situation or how the place has changed. In sum, emotions are crucial in finding out our position in the ongoing negotiation of place in everyday life.

We act on the basis of our sense of our appropriate *place*. 'Place' can be understood as a micro-level equivalent to social status in a society's stratification system. Where social status is a socially agreed-upon position, a place is a less defined position on the interactional level. Place relationships are in a state of flux, adjustment and alignment, and micro-hierarchies are less stable than stratification on a macro-level. While the macro-level social status of a person is without significance for their place, there is no simple one-to-one relationship between interactional 'place' and societal 'status'. Persons with the same social status can differ in the place they occupy in micro-hierarchies. Social place can be high while social status is low. An example of this can be the highly appreciated teacher among students and colleagues, who has little social status as they do not have a tenured position in the workplace (Clark 1997: 229–30).

Individuals' sense of place is *linked to identity*. When they feel 'out of place' – for example, put in place *under* the position they (believe they) deserve – they often strive to occupy a more prestigious place. The extent to which people can sustain an acceptable self-image (self-identity) depends on their ability to occupy acceptable positions/places in the situations, meetings and relations that form their overall life space. Individuals are not just sensitive about what rejections may tell us about them, rejections also indicate something about the social bond between them and others. Being very attentive to the distribution and order of places is therefore a sign of how people are attentive to the actual and changing character of the social bond. In short, they are cautious about even minor alterations in the differentiation of the social space, and they cannot orient themselves without this sensing, social and self-protecting activity (Clark 1997: 230–1).

Being attuned to the micro-hierarchical arrangements provides the individual with a chance of knowing or sensing what action to take towards others. The emotions that steadily arise and are experienced during interactions serve as a crucial function of making people adjust to each other. One example is that self-directed emotions of pride and other-directed emotions of admiration serve to mark and confirm the places of the feeling persons in their interaction. Feeling self-directed emotions like pride and satisfaction and other-directed emotions such as contempt often creates a subjective experience of superiority and potency, while feelings of embarrassment can form an experience of inferiority. Therefore, emotions can be said to mark social place by registering a person's relative placement in their psyche and body (Clark 1997: 233).

This behavioural orientation comes about in comparing ourselves with others and in the way we estimate our esteem/status in relation to them: 'In every encounter and relationship, each participant asks (among other things) who has a higher, social place and, for a given moment at least, each answers the question in his or her own way' (Clark 1997: 230). This kind of comparing and contrasting evokes emotions which provide information about where people stand. It is part of individuals' normal, intellectual equipment and not necessarily wilful acts. People may not be aware of their attempts to place themselves in relation to others and vice versa (Clark 1997: 230). Clark argues that this reading of place would not go on as smoothly as is actually the case in shifting micro-hierarchies of status and power if the reading process were merely a cognitive task of consciously monitoring signs of status and expectations, because this would not allow sufficient information to guide people's conduct (Clark 1997: 230).

The everyday life economy of places in micro-hierarchies

Clark's theory of the exchange of emotional gifts explains how emotions are essential in the production and reproduction of subtle connections and divisions in everyday life interaction. She explores how the display of, for example, sympathy has certain micro-political effects with respect to how everybody is settled in places more or less matching their identity. Her theory expands the sociological understanding of social connectivity and barriers, as it explains how displays of sympathy, patience or gratitude (emotional gifts) call forth responses to be understood in a micro-political perspective.

Clark's analysis of everyday emotions such as sympathy and gratitude shows how emotions are exchangeable as resources in a micro-political game of obtaining a valuable place. She shows how hierarchy is not a phenomenon that merely pertains to the macro-social world, as she illustrates how the everyday is also a micro-hierarchical sphere of social life. Clark's theory can therefore supplement other approaches to everyday life such as phenomenology and symbolic interactionism, which traditionally have not substantially theorized the issue of power (Craib 1992; Wallace and Wolf 1999). With the notion of the socio-emotional economy, Clark underlines how everyday life has its own socio-emotional economy guided by forms of give-and-take logics, which differs from the capitalist economy of money. By stressing the principle of obligation to exchange she explains how the display of emotion works as a social force, which incites others to respond.

The common-sense understanding of exchange suggests that exchange implies a balance of costs and benefits. However, when we recognize the various exchange principles, a more sophisticated model of social life emerges. Clark distinguishes between three different principles of exchange:

- *Complementary role expectations*: some people have to give other people particular benefits as their social role obliges them to do so (dominant in feudal and traditional society).
- *Reciprocity*: the person who gives is entitled to get something in return.
- *Beneficence*: a principle of giving what others need regardless of their position and ability to repay.

In understanding how people exchange sympathy, for example, Clark underlines that the principles become mixed: for instance, a principle of complementarity mixed with reciprocity, or reciprocity mixed with beneficence. The socio-emotional economy is guided by these exchange principles and by how the actual micro-hierarchy influences what the particular individual owes to others in terms of, for example, attention and gratitude. Moreover, Clark's theory explains how people use feelings to orient themselves in relation to others in the micro-hierarchies in which they find themselves.

Interaction rituals generate emotional energy

In their everyday life most people have been overwhelmed by, for example, anxiety, sorrow, despair, shame, shyness or modesty, which make them passive rather than energetic (Barbalet 1996). Colloquial expressions such as 'I don't have the energy', or 'it was very energizing to be together with these people' refer to energy as a resource that cannot be taken for granted. Energy is something we strive for, and in this section I explain how it can be understood as an outcome of everyday life interaction rituals, as explained by Randall Collins's (b. 1941) theory of 'emotional energy'. The main point of drawing on this theoretical perspective is to explain how individuals' agency can be understood as an outcome of particular emotional processes rather than as a stable feature of personality.

Collins warns against the error of identifying agency with the individual (2004: 6). Instead, he conceptualizes agency as 'the energy appearing in human bodies and emotions and as the intensity and focus of human consciousness, arises in local, face-to-face situations, or as precipitates of chains of situations' (Collins 2004: 6). Collins understands social interaction as a ritual which can generate different ritual outcomes as explained through the model shown in Figure 13.1 (2004: 48).

The right-hand column of the model predicts how ritual interaction generate various outcomes: feelings of membership or group solidarity; feelings of confidence, elation, strength, enthusiasm and initiative in taking action (emotional energy); symbols – visual icons, words, gestures – that members feel are associated with themselves collectively, and feelings of morality and a sense of rightness in adhering to the group. If the ritual interaction is part of a recurrent pattern, it may also contribute to the forming of common standards of morality among the participating individuals (Collins 2004: 49).

Building on Durkheim's theory of ritual, Collins argues that ritual interaction consists of four basic ingredients:

- Co-presence of at least two persons in the same place so that they affect each other by their bodily presence, whether they are aware of it or not.
- Participants have a sense of who is taking part, since there are boundaries to outsiders.

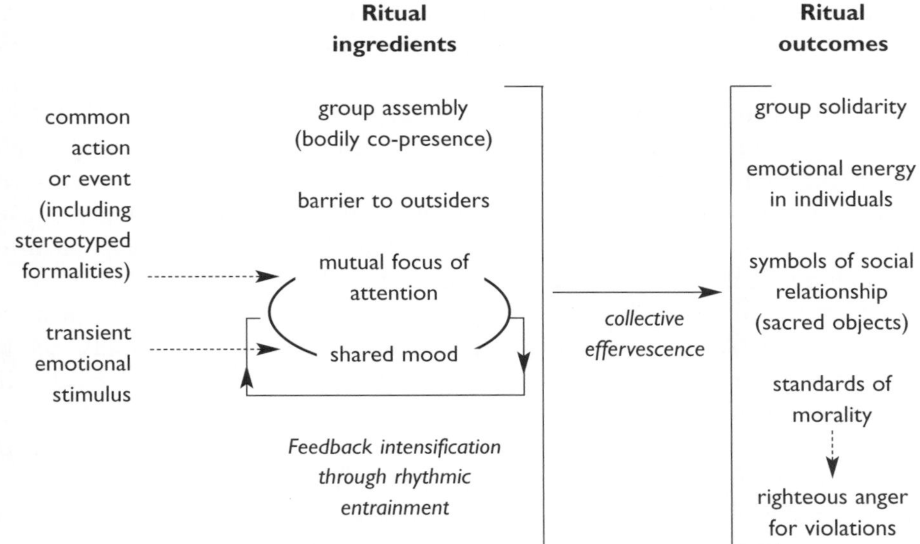

Figure 13.1 Interaction ritual
Source: Collilns (2004: 48).

- People have a focused attention upon the same activity or object, and in communicating this to each other, they are made aware of each other's focus of attention.
- People share a common mood or emotional experience (Collins 2004: 48). What particular emotion they feel is not significant, as it is the sharing or the contagion that is the crucial dynamic. When people are aware of each other's focus, they become caught up in each other's emotions: 'As a result, the emotional mood becomes stronger and more dominant; competing feelings are driven out by the main group feeling' (Collins 1990: 32).

Thus, bodily co-presence, barriers to outsiders, common action or event, mutual focus of attention and shared mood that might be triggered by a transient emotional stimulus needed to generate an interaction ritual. All these ingredients, in particular the last two, mutually reinforce each other. Individuals engage each other via embodied emotions, for instance by showing interest or lack of interest through bodily posture. Their embodied emotions work to engage and disengage others, and often operate more or less unnoticed (Freund 1998: 273; Goleman, Boyatzis and McKee 2002: 11).

In this context I want to emphasize emotional energy as an outcome of such ritual interaction. Emotional energy differs from episodic and dramatic emotions such as 'shouting or lashing out in anger, squealing and gesturing with joy, shrieking or running around in fear' (Collins 2004: 134). Emotional energy is a long-term consequence of interaction rituals that acquire a high degree of focused emotional entrainment. It is an emotional effect that stays after the individual has left the situation (Collins 2004: 134). When people think of the symbols stemming from successful ritual interaction, they will feel energized even after the interaction has faded away. Emotional energy can be indicated by, for example, bodily postures and movements such as erect posture, and moving firmly and smoothly (Collins 2004: 135–6).

According to Collins's theory, people are motivated to experience positive emotional energy or a sense of initiative and enthusiasm. Individuals seek to maximize their level of emotional energy if possible. Consequently, in Collins's theory agency is not a generic capacity of the individual. Rather it is particular situations that 'charge' individuals with agency in the form of emotional energy. While Collins assumes that people are generally after obtaining emotional energy, he is not suggesting that this energy is equally and freely distributed. It is more a part of power games, since emotional energy 'gives the ability to act with initiative and resolve, to set the direction of social situations *rather than to be dominated by others in the micro-details of interaction*' (Collins 2004: 134; emphasis added). In what Collins describes as 'carousing rituals' we have a situation in which individuals are dominated by the micro-details of interaction. In such rituals it is the people at the focus of everybody's attention who receive the recognition and thereby get most emotional energy out of the ritual:

> Those at the centre of sociable gatherings, with their situation-dominating talk, joking, gossiping, sexual flirtation, are those most prone to adopt fads; their central network-positions both enable them to do so quickly, and to reap the emotional energy and situational dominance of being local exemplars of widespread images of prestigeful behaviour.
>
> (Collins 2004: 338)

Collins contends that sociology has failed to be perceptive when it comes to understanding the structure of opposition set up by carousing as a pure form of situational stratification. Sociology should therefore investigate how pure sociability rituals involve a ranking between the popular and the unpopular, belles and beaus versus wallflowers and duds, the cool and the uncool, party animals and nerds, and so on. This dimension of stratification is very crucial as this overlooked kind of situational stratification is, for participants, often the most salient dimension of everyday life compared with the macro-structural stratification of class, ethnicity and gender (Collins 2004: 237–8).

The people who are subordinated in carousing rituals have little possibility of counteracting this differentiation in the distribution of energy. They cannot use their subordination, exclusion or dishonour as a basis for a collective identity. This is because achieving collective consciousness as being 'nerds', 'duds' or 'wallflowers' will only increase their dishonour (Collins 2004: 338). Everyday life consists of carousing rituals of various sociable situations where individuals gather in order to have a drink, take a smoke, have dinner or enjoy a party. Such rituals contribute to situational stratification of emotional energy among the participants, which is different from the commonly understood stratification of status groups on the macro-level of society. This everyday life stratification explains how emotional energy, such as confidence and enthusiasm, is a dynamic feature rather than located within more or less established personalities.

Emotional energy as a crucial ingredient in agency

Much sociological theory has understood agency as a generic capacity of individuals rather than as a dynamic capacity of social relationships in which individuals are enmeshed (Layder 2004). The consequence of these prior conceptions is that sociological understanding has not quite come to terms with the everyday life fact that it is a passive as much as an active subject we are dealing with.

Collins's theory of interaction rituals is one way of exploring how everyday life is an ongoing (re)generation of emotional energy (agency) through interaction rituals. His theory explains how everyday life dynamically charges and recharges people with a kind of emotional energy that is a precondition of their action(s). Understanding agency as a dynamic and emotional accomplishment, we can understand better why people differ in real life with respect to their agency.[2] Collins's perspective allows us to understand everyday life as consisting of interaction rituals that load people differently in terms of emotional energy. Resources are not merely macro-social phenomena or more tangible resources such as knowledge or money. Emotional energy is a resource generated and regenerated in and through various everyday life interaction rituals, and it should therefore not be understood as located or embedded in more or less energetic personality types.

Conclusion: the profoundly emotional character of everyday life

The overall point of this chapter has been to explore significant features of the profoundly emotional nature of everyday life. The theories and analyses presented question a view of everyday life as characterized primarily by taken-for-granted cognitive background assumptions and more or less emotion-free routines. Such a picture is too limited, as this chapter has explained how everyday life, in different ways, is profoundly emotional. Below I discuss how the contributions to the sociology of emotions presented here supplement other theoretical approaches such as phenomenology, symbolic interactionism and existentialism, but also the work of Erving Goffman. Moreover, I further outline how the sociology of emotions develops a sociological understanding of everyday life.

What seems to be routine everyday life interaction is often dramatic, as the interacting individuals are engaged in intensive emotion management which is required to make the interaction happen in appropriate and expected ways. In other words, individuals work on their feelings to feel and display the appropriate emotion in the situation. This emotion work is part and parcel of routine action, which often requires intensive emotion management which operates behind the visible front stages on which interaction appears.

Arlie R. Hochschild is inspired by Goffman's dramaturgical understanding of social interaction, which underlines how individuals are often engaged in managing the impression others might get of them (Goffman 1959). Goffman's analysis of everyday interaction accords a significant role to emotions in understanding the dynamic of interaction (Scheff 2006). In particular, he emphasizes the role of embarrassment and dishonour in understanding how much interaction is about confirming and protecting the face of the other. But Hochschild is critical of Goffman's methodological disregard of investigating subjectivity (Kleinman and Copp 1993: 15–16). Consequently, she expands Goffman's dramaturgical perspective by focusing the actor's inner work on their emotions. While her theory has been regarded as a further development of the tradition of symbolic interactionism (Wallace and Wolf 1999: 239), it is important to note that her approach to emotions and emotion management is more comprehensive than a traditional, symbolic interactionistic focus on meaning and interpretation as it unfolds at the interactional level (Blumer 1986: 78–89; Wallace and Wolf 1999: 227). This is because she, in what she describes as her 'interactional' theory, considers how structural conditions such as the job market and ideological issues of gender roles impinge on how cultural ideals of emotion management are established. In brief, Hochschild's theory explains actors' interaction with and on 'inner' emotional senses/signals and 'outer' structural, ideological and economical features of a given emotion culture.

By understanding emotions in the context of a socio-emotional economy, Candace Clark adds a new perspective to the sociology of emotions and other theoretical approaches to everyday life by explicating its socio-emotional economy. Emotions are seen as exchangeable resources which are crucial ingredients in the ongoing formation of micro-hierarchies. This micro-economic exchange approach to emotion counteracts a common-sense understanding of everyday life as characterized by more or less egalitarian relationships between interacting individuals.

Finally, Randall Collins's theory emphasizes how individuals become entrained in interaction rituals that can energize or de-energize them. On the basis of this theory, I have argued that agency has an unnoticed basis, since everyday life is about the ongoing generation of emotional energy such as enthusiasm and confidence. Everyday life has a dramatic character as individuals aim at becoming energized in sociable rituals of everyday life which cannot place each and every individual at the centre of attention. Moreover, Collins's theory stresses how people can be caught by emotional dynamics and how emotions can be contagious in a very impressive sense. According to ritual theory and contagion theory emotions work as forces that cannot be voluntarily chosen (see for example Hatfield, Cacioppo and Rapson 1994; Barsade 2000). This kind of theory therefore questions the overall importance of the existentialist idea of individuals as freely choosing beings. Collins's theory supplements theories such as phenomenology, symbolic interactionism and ethnomethodology which generally do not explore emotions and their role in basic processes of acting and interacting in everyday life (Craib 1992). In these traditions the stress is on the human mind – reflexivity, deliberation and intentionality – which is perceived as the faculty for agency (Charon 2001; Fuchs 2007). However, we can speculate a lot about our doing this or that, but such reflexivity does not in itself secure agency. It is one thing to have an intention, but another to carry it out. To do so we need emotional energy.

Each perspective has now been summarized through emphasizing what the emotion perspectives add to existing theories of everyday life. A few remarks on how the sociology of emotions can contribute to the understanding of everyday life remain to be made. The sociology of emotions has created a deeper understanding of everyday life by exploring specific emotions and their role in social processes. Jack Katz's (1999) study of a mundane phenomenon such as road rage or David Karp's (2001) study of how family members of the mentally ill persons construct limits to their sympathy to avoid being engulfed by the day-to-day suffering of a loved one are significant examples. So is Thomas J. Scheff's study of how shame, pride and rage are functional in the development and operation of interpersonal conflicts (Scheff 1990, 1997; Retzinger 1991).

Finally, I want to mention Stephanie Shields's study of the relationship between gender and emotion, which analyses how modern men and women are governed by different expectations concerning how to communicate their feelings. Gender and emotion are linked in a way that secures different styles of emotional expression for each gender position. Consequently, everyday life is not characterized by inexpressive males, but by males practising a certain 'manly emotion' style, which is about strongly felt emotion under control, 'and the stronger the felt emotion, the more clearly visible is the control of that intense experience. It is evident in a telegraphed style that conveys the felt emotion through economy of gesture, vocalization and facial expression' (Shields 2002: 173). This style is an underrated style as it lacks the 'size' and openness of expressiveness that is conventionally coded as 'emotional'. Consequently, masculinity is not about being unemotional, as it has conventionally been perceived. This style is a dominant cultural ideal with respect to work life and it differs from the 'extravagant emotion' style which is idealized with respect to family life. This style is more outspoken and expressive, and coded as 'emotional' in conventional terms. It is used to 'do' nurturance and linked to femininity. Yet, as none of those styles cover exclusively what men and women actually feel: they are challenged to try to find an appropriate mix of styles in securing a sense of genuine identity (Shields 2002: 174).

In sum, contemporary 'sociology of emotions' has investigated emotions in a more specific sense, and it thereby differs from classical sociologists' more vague treatment of emotional dimensions of social life. Fortunately, there is no reason to expect that the 'sociology of emotions' will stop this specifying endeavour. More likely, it will it continue to enrich the understanding of everyday life and other realms of social life.

Notes

1. Hochschild argues that:

> women tend to be more exposed than men to rude or surly speech, to tirades against the service, the airline, and airplanes in general .... Because her gender is accorded lower status, a woman's shield against abuse is weaker, and the importance of what she herself might be feeling – when faced with blame for an airline delay, for example – is correspondingly reduced. Thus, the job for a man differs in essential ways from the same job for a woman.
>
> (Hochschild 1983: 174–5)

2. Barbalet's theory of confidence, trust and loyalty as future-oriented, silent, social emotions is also useful for understanding the emotional character of agency (see Poder 2004, 2006), but given the limited space I have not introduced his theory here.

Bibliography

Barbalet, Jack (1996) 'Social emotions: confidence, trust and loyalty.' *International Journal of Sociology and Social Policy*, 16 (9–10): 75–96.

Barbalet, Jack (1998) *Emotion, Social Theory and Social Structure – A Macro-Sociological Approach*. Cambridge: Cambridge University Press.

Barsade, Sigal (2000) 'The ripple effect: emotional contagion in groups.' Yale SOM Working Paper No. OB–01.

Blumer, Herbert (1986) *Symbolic Interactionism – Perspective and Method*. Berkeley, CA: University of California Press.

Charon, Joel (2001) *Symbolic Interactionism – An Introduction, An Interpretation, An Integration*. Englewood Cliffs, NJ: Prentice-Hall.

Clark, Candace (1990) 'Emotions and micro-politics in everyday life: some patterns and paradoxes of "place"', in Theodore Kemper (ed.), *Research Agendas in the Sociology of Emotions*. Albany: State University of New York Press.

Clark, Candace (1997) *Misery and Company: Sympathy in Everyday Life*. Chicago, IL: Chicago University Press.

Clark, Candace (2004) 'Emotional gifts and 'you first' micropolitics – niceness in the socio-emotional economy', in Anthony Manstead, Nico Frijda and Agneta Fischer (eds), *Feelings and Emotions – The Amsterdam Symposium*. Cambridge: Cambridge University Press.

Collins, Randall (1990) 'Stratification, emotional energy and the transient emotions', in Theodore Kemper (ed.), *Research Agendas in the Sociology of Emotions*. Albany: State University of New York Press.

Collins, Randall (2004) *Interaction Ritual Chains*. Princeton, NJ: Princeton University Press.

Craib, Ian (1992) *Modern Social Theory – From Parsons to Habermas*. Englewood Cliffs, NJ: Prentice-Hall.

Flam, Helena (2000) *The Emotional 'Man' and the Problem of Collective Action*. New York: Peter Lang.

Flam, Helena (2002) *Soziologie der Emotionen*. Konstanz: UVK Verlagsgesellschaft.

Frijda, Nico (2007) *The Laws of Emotion*. London: Lawrence Erlbaum.

Freund, Peter (1998) 'Social performances and their discontents: the biopsychosocial aspects of dramaturgical stress', in Gillian Bendelow and Simon J. Williams (eds), *Emotions and Social Life – Critical Themes and Contemporary Issues*. London: Routledge.

Fuchs, Stephan (2007) 'Agency (and intention)', in George Ritzer (ed.), *Blackwell Encyclopaedia of Sociology*. Blackwell Reference Online.

Gibson, Donald (1997) 'The struggle for reason: the sociology of emotions in organizations', in Rebecca Erickson and Beverley Cuthbertson-Johnson (eds), *Social Perspectives on Emotion*, Vol. 4. Greenwich, CT: JAI Press.

Goffman, Erving (1959) *The Presentation of Self in Everyday Life*. Harmondsworth: Penguin.

Goleman, Daniel, Richard Boyatzis and Annie McKee (2002) *Primal Leadership – Realizing the Power of Emotional Intelligence*. Boston, MA: Harvard Business School Press.

Hatfield, Elaine, John Cacioppo and Richard Rapson (1994) *Emotional Contagion*. Cambridge: Cambridge University Press.

Hochschild, Arlie R. (1979) 'Emotion work, feeling rules and social structure.' *American Journal of Sociology*, 85(3): 551–75.

Hochschild, Arlie R. (1983) *The Managed Heart: The Commercialization of Human Feeling*. Berkeley, CA: University of California Press.

Hochschild, Arlie R. (1998) 'The sociology of emotion as a way of seeing', in Gillian Bendelow and Simon J. Williams (eds), *Emotions in Social Life – Critical Themes and Contemporary Issues*. London: Routledge.

Hochschild, Arlie R. (2003) *The Commercialization of Intimate Life – Notes from Home and Work*. Berkeley, CA: University of California Press.

Karp, David (2001) *The Burden of Sympathy: How Families Cope With Mental Illness*. Oxford: Oxford University Press.

Katz, Jack (1999) *How Emotions Work*. Chicago: University of Chicago Press.

Kemper, Theodore (2000) 'Social models in the explanation of emotions', in Michael Lewis and Jeanette M. Haviland-Jones (eds), *Handbook of Emotions*, 2nd edition. New York: Guildford Press.

Kleinman, Sherryl and Martha Copp (1993) *Emotions and Fieldwork*. London: Sage.

Layder, Derek (1997) *Modern Social Theory: Key Debates and New Directions*. London: UCL Press.

Layder, Derek (2004) *Emotion in Social Life – The Lost Heart of Society*. London: Sage.

Oatley, Keith, Dacher Keltner and Jennifer Jenkins (2006) *Understanding Emotions*. Oxford: Blackwell.

Poder, Poul (2004) *Feelings of Power and the Power of Feelings: Handling Emotion in Organizational Change*. PhD thesis, Department of Sociology, University of Copenhagen.

Poder, Poul (2006) 'Ingen frihed uden magt, ingen magt uden emotionel energi', in Michael Hviid Jacobsen and Poul Poder (eds), *Om Bauman – kritiske essays*. Copenhagen: Hans Reitzels Forlag.

Retzinger, Suzanne (1991) *Violent Emotions – Shame and Rage in Marital Quarrels*. London: Sage.

Scheff, Thomas J. (1990) *Microsociology – Discourse, Emotion and Social Structure*. Chicago, IL: University of Chicago Press.

Scheff, Thomas J. (1997) *Emotions, the Social Bond and Human Reality*. Cambridge: Cambridge University Press.

Scheff, Thomas J. (2006) *Goffman Unbound! A New Paradigm for Social Science*. Boulder, CO: Paradigm Press.

Shields, Stephanie (2002) *Speaking from the Heart: Gender and the Social Meaning of Emotion*. Cambridge: Cambridge University Press.

Shilling, Chris (2002) 'The two traditions in the sociology of emotions', in Jack Barbalet (ed.), *Emotions and Sociology*. Oxford: Blackwell.

Stauth, Georg and Bryan S. Turner (1988) *Nietzsche's Dance – Resentment, Reciprocity and Resistance in Social Life*. Oxford: Blackwell.

Thoits, Peggy (1989) 'The sociology of emotions.' *Annual Review of Sociology*, 15: 317–42.

Turner, Jonathan and Jan Stets (2005) *The Sociology of Emotions*. Cambridge: Cambridge University Press.

Wallace, Ruth and Alison Wolf (1999) *Contemporary Sociological Theory – Expanding the Classical Tradition*. Englewood Cliffs, NJ: Prentice-Hall.

CHAPTER 14

Social Semiotics

Constructing Stuff in Everyday Life

PHILLIP VANNINI

Introduction

Ageing $40 computer speakers, an open wallet displaying membership and credit cards, a tape recorder and scattered micro cassettes, bills, a book manuscript, and a faux hand-weaved basket litter my unusually clean and dust-free office desk today as I type away with the help of my laptop. My office chair adjusts to my back as I lean backwards to pause, immersed in thought over the next sentence. In the background the drier clunks and puffs with the morning load of clothes as the sprinkler awaits another go at the freshly planted backyard grass. Stuff. The world is full of it. Some we buy, some we freely collect, some we never become interested in collecting, some we carry with us at all times, and some we buy and sell. Hardly a moment of our day-to-day lives goes without it. We wear stuff to bead. We stuff our mouths. We stuff boxes. We watch stuff on television. We hang out, and do stuff like that. We fill our trunks and tanks with stuff. We carry stuff in bags. And come certain times of the year we collectively decide that it is time to get more stuff. How odd must we look to our animal companions as we fill our young ones' beds at night with stuffed pets, as we hang stuff on our house walls, or as we stuff our refrigerators and cupboards with stuff we will not immediately consume, and which will often go bad without ever being consumed.

Despite our lives being so full of stuff, as it turns out, we know very little about the significance of our day-to-day interaction with it. Indeed, we know so little that most people find it difficult if not downright impossible to describe the meanings of things. Give it a try. Ask a friend or a family member at the dinner table tonight, 'You know that tool you're using ... yeah, that fork you're holding ... what is the meaning of it? And that shirt you're wearing: what's the meaning of that?' Chances are they won't take you seriously. Why? Because you are supposed to know that the meaning of an object lies in its obvious functions. And they are too. And since we are all supposed to know what the meanings are of a lawnmower, toilet paper, a calendar, a train, or a padlock we simply never question them, never reflect on them, and never interpret them.

In this chapter I shall try and do so by reviewing the analytical perspective known as 'social semiotics': the interpretive and critical study of the resources we use in everyday life to construct meaning. After discussing the significance of social semiotics as an everyday life perspective I begin with an overview of social semiotics as a body of critical and interpretive theory, then examine it as a research strategy, and finally synthesize some research findings from recent semiotic studies of the unnoticed stuff of everyday life.

Social semiotics as an everyday life perspective

Why use social semiotics to understand stuff? Well, to begin with social semiotics is relatively unique amongst everyday life social theories and research strategies as it concerns itself with multimodal communication. Whereas most social theories focus on discursive interaction alone – communication that takes place by way of linguistic exchanges – social semiotics is best equipped for understanding different modes of expressing meaning through all the senses: the visual, the tactile, the aural, the gustatory and even the olfactory, either alone or in combination with one another. Because much of the stuff of everyday life is expressed and practised at a non-linguistic and complex multimodal level, social semiotics seems particularly adept at excavating much of the anthropological significance of the mundane. In other words, social semiotics is particularly useful in making mute mundane objects speak: in bringing their unnoticed significance and functionality to light.

Social semiotics seems particularly adept for the study of everyday life for other reasons as well. First, social semiotics is highly eclectic and it can be used easily in combinations with a broad variety of everyday life sociological perspectives such as symbolic interactionism, ethnomethodology, existential social theory, phenomenology, critical theory and cultural studies, and more. 'Social semiotics', Theo van Leeuwen (2005: 1) writes, 'can only come into its own when [it] fully engages with [other] social theory'. By itself it is nothing but a 'form of enquiry [which] does not offer ready-made answers'. Second, social semiotics stands in opposition to 'macro' semiotic perspectives which in their deterministic views posit social actors as passive users and objects of semiotic codes and forces. Third, social semiotics focuses on meanings in context and therefore on situated practices of communication, rather than merely on abstract, structural and formal grammar-like associations. Fourth, social semioticians – as opposed to other semioticians and similarly to students of discourse and conversation – posit that social actors reproduce larger linguistic and societal structures through everyday instances of speech and other multimodal interactions. Fifth, and lastly, we may say that – borrowing from Patricia A. Adler, Peter Adler and Andrea Fontana's (1987: 219) characterization of everyday life sociological perspectives – within social semiotics 'structure, organization, and order do not exist independent of the people that interact within them'. Everyday, communicative rituals make up society, and not vice versa.

As a semiotic theory, social semiotics is a perspective which concerns itself with the meanings of *signification.* In other words, in its most basic characterization it looks at associations of signs with their respective meanings, such as, for example, the link between a red light and the behaviour of halting at a traffic intersection. And as a social theory it focuses on signification as a social – rather than, say, purely structural linguistic – process based on conventions, dialogue, conflict, collaboration, interpersonal negotiations and so forth. Yet many theories in the social sciences do precisely this, and so what truly makes social semiotics unique – besides its emphasis on multimodal interaction – is its twofold profound attention to the functional materiality of semiotic resources in both their abstract potential and their concrete use.

To explain this further, let us introduce a basic concept in semiotics: the *sign.* Signs are associations between a referent (something that is meant) and a sign-vehicle (something that means, that stands for something else). To confuse things a bit, different semioticians use different terminology: referents are sometimes called 'signifieds' and sign-vehicles are sometimes called 'signifiers'. Regardless of the actual terms employed, signification is a pretty simple idea. For example, the English word 'tree' – made of the units T-R-E-E – is the sign-vehicle (or signifier) for those landscape-dotting green and brown wooden things (the referents, or signifieds).

Now, this is also where many semioticians disagree. For some, notably for the followers of *structuralist semiotics* or *semiology*, signifiers refer to mental concepts, not to actual material things. For them, therefore, the word 'tree' refers to whatever you cognitively associate that signifier with, and not to the actual leafy and wooden things. For others – mostly all social semioticians – instead, the opposite is true. Notwithstanding some subtle differences on this issue, social semioticians agree that abstract associations between signifiers and signifieds explain only part of the picture. Consequently, they feel that semiotic studies that focus on abstract rules regulating *denotation* – what a signifier refers to – or *connotation* – the meanings that a signifier may evoke amongst different interpretive communities – are by nature very limited. What they are limited to in fact is a study of a *theoretical semiotic potential* – a configuration of past uses and likely future uses of a semiotic resource.

While the study of theoretical semiotic potentials is interesting, social semioticians should keep in mind that semiotic resources 'may not be divorced from the concrete forms of social intercourse' (van Leeuwen 2005: 3). Rather than dwelling on the abstract nature of signs, social semioticians thus deal with the study of the ways in which 'people use semiotic *resources* both to produce communicative artefacts and events and to interpret them ... in the context of specific social situations and practices' (van Leeuwen 2005: xi; emphasis added). The situated study of semiotic resources allows social semioticians to zero in on the social regulation and negotiation of communication in all its situated diversity and idiosyncrasy rather than restrict semiotic investigation to the abstract and formal hermeneutics of semiotic codes or laws. Such an approach makes social semiotics an emblematic analytical perspective of the study of everyday social life.

Social semiotics: historical overview and basic theoretical components

A brief genealogy of social semiotic ideas

Social semiotics is a very young analytical perspective that is not to be confused with its older and more established cousin, the semiotics of the structuralist variety, which has deeply influenced decades of linguistic, sociological and anthropological research and theory. Structuralist semiotics, or semiology as it is sometimes called, is deeply influenced by the linguistic theory of Ferdinand de Saussure (1857–1913) (see Saussure 1959). In contrast, social semiotics is more influenced by the critical sociolinguistics of Mikhail Bakhtin (1895–1975) (e.g. Bakhtin 1965/1984, 1975/1981, 1979/1986) and Valentin Volosinov (1973),[1] the pragmatist philosophy of Charles Sanders Peirce (1839–1914) (see Peirce 1931), the functional linguistics of Michael A. K. Halliday (b. 1925) (Halliday 1978), the cultural theory of Roland Barthes (1915–1980) (see Barthes 1972), British cultural studies in general, and to some extent the post-structuralist thought of Michel Foucault (1926–1984) (see Foucault 1980).

Despite the long-standing tenures of Charles Sanders Peirce, Mikhail Bakhtin and Valentin Volosinov as some of the most recognized philosophers of the 20th century, and despite their formidable and distinctly unique contributions to the development of semiotic theory, social semiotics as we now know it cannot be said to have seen the light of day until 1988, with the publication of Bob Hodge and Gunther Kress's foundational book *Social Semiotics*. In that book Hodge and Kress took great pain to distance social semiotics from structuralist semiotics by outlining the analytical uniqueness of the former and its differences from the latter. From 1988 onwards, social semiotics has taken roots in a wide variety of interdisciplinary circles clustered around critical theory (Hodge and Kress 1988), media studies (Jensen 1995; Kress and van Leeuwen 1996), sociology (Gottdiener 1995), linguistics (Kress 2007a), literature and the fine arts (O'Toole 1994; Thibault 1991), and education (Lemke 1997). Today social semiotics has a flagship journal, *Social Semiotics*, a seminal textbook (van Leeuwen 2005) and a growing tradition of diverse empirical studies which primarily concentrate around cultural sociology, communication and cultural studies, as well as visual and material studies.

Historically, there have been at least three 'schools', or perhaps at least three 'circles', of social semiotic thought. The first two are identified by Theo van Leeuwen (2005: xi–xii) as the 'Sydney Semiotics Circle' in Australia and the European 'critical discourse analysis group'. A third, and more decentred and diverse, North American network is also alive. The three circles have operated in somewhat separate realms from one another, and it is only with the publication of the journal *Social Semiotics* that at least the first two have come into tighter contact.

The most influential school of social semiotic thought was undoubtedly that of the Sydney Semiotics Circle during the second half of the 1980s and throughout the 1990s. While influenced by the Prague School and by some of the work of Roland Barthes (1972), this circle had a uniquely Australian flavour due to the inspiration of Michael A. K. Halliday (1978) and his functional grammar tradition. Briefly (more on this and related points later), Halliday believed that the grammar of a language (and relatedly, social semioticians have argued, of an entire social and cultural organization) is not based in unchangeable codes or rules but rather in a system of resources for making meanings. Halliday's work was foundational in the research and theory of Theo van Leeuwen, Gunther Kress, Jim Martin, Paul Thibault, Anne Cranny-Francis, Jennifer Biddle, Terry Threadgold, Toby Miller and Radan Martinec. While Halliday's work was less central in the writings of Bob Hodge and Jay Lemke, they too can be said to have enjoyed an affiliation with the Sydney Semiotics Circle.

The European tradition of social semiotics is a bit more diffuse. Continental social semiotics borrows heavily from the Foucauldian version of critical discourse studies promulgated by Norman Fairclough. Fairclough (1995) following Foucault (1980) – and not unlike Volosinov (1973) – finds that power and meaning are inseparable. Discourse – that is, actual instances of communicative interaction – is deeply shaped by unequal arrangements of power. In light of that, all contexts of social interaction operate under what Hodge and Kress call a context-dependent 'logonomic system':

> A set of rules prescribing the conditions for production and reception of meanings; which specify who can claim to initiate (produce, communicate) or know

> (receive, understand) meanings about what topics under what circumstances and with what modalities (how, when, why). Logonomic systems prescribe social semiotic behaviours at points of production and reception, so that we can distinguish between *production regimes* (rules constraining production) and *reception regimes* (rules constraining reception).
>
> (Hodge and Kress 1988: 4)

Central socio-semiotic exponents of this interpretive and critical tradition are the likes of Malcolm Coulthard, Carmen Caldas-Coulthard, Lilie Chouliaraki, David Machin, Rick Iedema, Adam Jaworski, Ron Scollon, Tim Dant and Luisa Martin Rojo. Known widely for their contributions to critical visual semiotics are also Teal Triggs and Carey Jewitt (see van Leeuwen 2005). Even though the critical discourse studies tradition is rooted in continental origins it would be a mistake to conclude that the two groups differ from each other in any significant way. Sydney Circle scholars and European discourse scholars now work alongside each other in many universities (mostly English and Welsh) and on co-authored publications.

A looser but more distinct North American network has drawn upon the two traditions described above and pushed for a sociological agenda of its own. This network comprises amongst others urban and cultural sociologist Mark Gottdiener and interpretive sociologists like Eugene Rochberg-Halton, Norbert Wiley and myself, who have combined elements of social semiotics with the post-Marxist (in the case of Gottdiener) and the pragmatist and symbolic interactionist (in the case of the latter three) traditions. The presence of thinkers such as Charles Sanders Peirce and John Dewey and related pragmatist ideas is especially noticeable in the work of the latter three (see for example Halton 1986, 1995; Vannini 2004; Wiley 1994, 2006).

Even though social semiotics continues to grow in favour amongst young scholars and students, its fate ultimately resides in the ability of practitioners to maintain clean operational boundaries between it and the voracious behemoth that goes by the name of cultural theory. As opposed to much of contemporary cultural theory's fascination with speculation, social semiotics can and should continue to emphasize the situated study of semiotic resource use by developing a keener eye for methodological rigour, a deeper curiosity toward uncharted research topics, and a deeper appreciation of ethnographic knowledge.

Central theoretical premises

Structuralist semioticians have long believed that meaning arises out of a structure of oppositions. Such oppositions can be *paradigmatic* or *syntagmatic.* Let us take for example the word 'skirt'. Syntagmatically a skirt arises from the juxtaposition of the letters S-K-I-R-T. Such combination is different from and opposed to similar words, such as S-H-I-R-T, S-H-O-R-T-S and S-Q-U-I-R-T. You will find that when students of a foreign language first learn to tackle new words they are exposed to such syntagmatic associations in order to understand the important differences between words that are closely related in sound but not in meaning. It is not uncommon for a young language student to make mistakes that are simply ridiculous at the semantic level (like using the word 'squirt' instead of 'skirt' in a sentence) but are actually quite small from a sonorous perspective ('squirt' does sound a lot like 'skirt'). Paradigmatically instead – structural semioticians tell us – meaning emerges from differences along an axis of logical and semantic juxtaposition. Thus, again, we find that the meaning of the word 'skirt' may be taught by contrasting skirts with trousers, khaki shorts, Bermudas, jeans, dress pants and so on.

Oppositions are not only linguistic, but rather more broadly cultural as well. The structuralist tradition in anthropology is rich with systems of binary oppositions of values, social and moral norms, and even psycho-social entities that point to meaning as the outcome of a formal opposition of semantic and syntactic rules. Even though there are some onomatopoeic associations between signifiers and signifieds (for instance, 'the cat meowed as we left'), there are too few to be considered anything but exceptions, and therefore it can be said that in general meaning is arbitrary for structuralist semioticians. Indeed, we could very well agree that from now on women wear 'squirts' and that water guns 'skirt' water; all it takes is sufficient collective linguistic agreement.

Nothing could be further from the truth according to social semioticians. As Paul Thibault clearly tells us: 'Meanings are jointly made by the participants to some joint activity-structure. They are made by construing semiotic relations among patterned meaning relations, social practices and the physical-material processes which social practices organize and entrain in social semiosis' (1993). Meanings, in other words, are never arbitrary. Rather, they are the results of motivated choices guided by *interest* (Kress 1993). A social agent's interest, or a coalition of agents, could come into play at the *production level* (for instance, making a skirt reveals a certain attitude toward the appearance of a woman's body) or at the *consumption level* (for instance, a man could wear a skirt to make a challenging argument against heterosexism or perhaps to reveal a Scottish identity), or both in the same context (for instance, a skirt could be tailored in such a way as to objectify a woman's sexuality, and a woman could wear a skirt in such as way and in such a context to expose the male gaze in return).

Whereas structuralist semioticians tend to look for meaning in deep structures of semantic associations and differences, social semioticians look for meaning in social-meaning-making practices and in the contexts where these specific practices occur. Whereas a structuralist semiotician would look for meaning in abstract, universal and formal codes, a social semiotician looks for community-specific patterns and processes which distinguish that interpretive community from others. And whereas structural semioticians would agree that languages express or represent thoughts, social semioticians suggest that the social organization of thinking shapes both language itself and other, multimodal, forms of communication (Hodge and Kress 1988).

Arbitrariness is not the only aspect of structuralist semiotics that social semioticians have rejected. As Hodge and Kress (1988) have argued, social semiotics could be said to constitute a binary opposition of its own in relation to its structuralist counterpart. For example, whereas structuralists generally privilege the study of signifiers at the expense of signifieds, social semioticians constantly attempt to rediscover the relevance of signifieds, for example in their physicality and material design (Kress and van Leeuwen 1996). Whereas structuralists tend to focus on language and its deep structures of signification informing speech, social semioticians tend to focus on instances of speech and their effects on the larger linguistic order. Whereas structural semiotics concentrates on synchronic associations (that is, meanings at one point in time), social semiotics emphasizes the importance of diachrony (that is, semiotic transformations over time) (Lemke 2000; Vannini 2004, 2008). Whereas structural semioticians tend to look at signifiers as expressions of meaning in themselves, social semiotics tend to zero in on the exo-semiotic context, that is, the politico-economic, ideological, spatial, cultural context surrounding the process of semiosis (in other words, the process of meaning-making).

Rejecting the idea of arbitrariness translates into approaching the concept of *semiotic power* in radically different ways from those envisioned by structuralist semioticians. Not unlike Foucauldian scholars, social semioticians find that:

> power is centreless, heterogeneous, and it enables as much it negates, it facilitates as much it obstructs, it seduces as much it vexes, it constructs as much as it limits ... Power relations intersect in multiple ways delineating not constant conditions of dominations, but rather heteromorphous and localized dynamics constituted by and constituting global conditions.
>
> (Vannini 2004: 156)

This is a form of productive semiotic power, a form of power that 'doesn't only weigh on us as a force that says no, but that it traverses and produces things, it induces pleasure, forms knowledge, produces discourse' (Foucault 1980: 119).

Just like it is for Foucauldians, for social semioticians power is linked to knowledge because truths are but the effect of discursivity and multimodal communication. Such communication process unfolding in such practice field is the site where power struggles over competing definitions of meaning and the situation give rise to temporarily stable social organizations. These social organizations exercise their force by more or less successfully imposing their *ideological complexes*. An ideological complex is:

> a functionally related set of contradictory versions of the world, coercively imposed by one social group on another on behalf of its own distinctive interests or subversively offered by another social group in attempts at resistance in its own interests. An ideological complex exists to sustain relationships of both power and solidarity, and it represents the social order as simultaneously serving the interests of both dominant and subordinate ... Ideological complexes are constructed in order to constrain behaviour by structuring the versions of reality on which social action is based, in particular ways.
>
> (Hodge and Kress 1988: 3)

Ideological complexes are not fault-free mechanisms. They do not determine what people will do, feel or think at any given moment, and they are not forever lasting. Meanings of semiotic resources, therefore, are never controlled or entirely controllable. This is an important point which students often miss. Ideological complexes operate in subtle fashions and are always a form of meaning *potential* exercising a conditioning but not a determining force. It follows that a hegemony too is less powerful than sometimes students (and scholars alike) often think. In Norman Fairclough's words:

> Hegemony is leadership as well as domination, across the economic, political, cultural and ideological domains of a society. Hegemony is the power over society of a whole of one of the fundamental economically defined classes in alliance (as a bloc) with other social forces, but is never achieved more than partially and temporarily as an 'unstable equilibrium'. Hegemony is about constructing alliances, and integrating rather than simply dominating subordinate classes, through concessions or through ideological means, to win their consent.
>
> (Fairclough 1995: 76)

For social semiotics, in conclusion, everyday realities depend on the intersection of at least three forces. The first – in no particular order – force is that of the *grammar* of communication and the *materiality* of signifieds (Kress and van Leeuwen 1996; van Leeuwen 1999). By grammar of communication social semioticians intend the system of rules inscribed into texts and acts of communication. For example, by flipping a driver the bird in the middle of peak-hour traffic I am relying on the lexical rule which associates the middle finger with an insult, hoping that my gesture will be perceived as such by the addressee (rather than, say, be perceived as a friendly greeting). The fleshy materiality of the finger, in its erect, straight upward-pointing pose, also ensures that the energy behind the insult is conveyed in the most forceful manner (a slightly bent, glove covered pinkie finger would hardly have the semiotic power). Grammar rules and materiality do not determine actual meaning in advance, but certainly do condition the possibility that meaning will be interpreted as intended by its producer. Social semioticians have developed an extensive vocabulary of concepts for the study of such grammar of visual (Kress and van Leeuwen 1996), musical (van Leeuwen 1999) and aesthetic (O'Toole 1994) expression, amongst other modes.

The second force depends on the particularities of context. Within specific contexts logonomic systems prescribe and proscribe the conditions under which meanings are produced, distributed and consumed (Hodge and Kress 1988). Logonomic systems specify (more or less explicitly) who is legitimated to produce meaning, how, where, when and about what, as well as for whom meanings ought to be intended. Logonomic systems change over time, and so do meanings (Vannini 2008), yet as they change, their continued operation is ensured by changing socialization mechanisms through which rules are taught and learned. The deep contextuality of meaning, anchored by way of the functioning of the grammar of communication and the force of materiality and logonomic systems, shows how for social semioticians 'signs capture the articulation of universes of meaning and the material world' and how social semiotics 'accounts for the articulation of the mental and the exo-semiotic, material dimension of daily life along with signifying practices within the larger social context' (Gottdiener 1995: 171).

The third and final force is purely social and agentic. Despite the existence of context-bound rules and the conditioning imposed upon meaning by the grammar and physicality of signs, users may often be able to subvert inscribed meaning either accidentally (by way of confusion) or intentionally (hence, counter-hegemonically). This is an argument central in both Halliday's (1978) functional grammar – in which expression is always a potential awaiting employment and not finite meaning – and in Peircean semiotics – in which the meaning relies on the response. As you can see, social semiotics, at least from the theoretical angle used here, is not too different from other everyday life sociologies which emphasize contextuality, negotiation and agency. Yet, in addition, social semiotics offers a rich methodological vocabulary for the study of the expressive material of mundane life. To this vocabulary I now turn.

Socio-semiotic research strategies

As Theo van Leeuwen correctly notes, 'social semiotics is not "pure" theory' and nor is it a 'self-contained field'. Instead, social semiotics best 'comes into its own when it is applied to specific instances and specific problems' (van Leeuwen 2005: 1). Rather than a theory, or even rather than a distinct method of data collection, social semiotics can be said to be a *research strategy* which 'offers ideas for formulating questions and ways of searching for answers' (van Leeuwen 2005: 1). So, how is social-semiotic investigation done?

The activity of social semioticians first involves making an inventory of semiotic resources. By inventory I mean collecting, documenting and cataloguing (see van Leeuwen 2005) empirical data for the purpose of investigating their potential significance and actual use. Inventorying is guided by research needs and purposes. If an empirical research project requires understanding the meanings of a specific subcultural expression, for example, then inventorying will require collecting and cataloguing all expressions employed within such a subculture. In socio-semiotic research, rather than being random, therefore, sampling and data collection is driven by a study's design.

Data generally sought by social semioticians generally include semioticized and unsemioticized empirical material. Semioticized material is the type of data that consist of explicit and motivated traces of human communicative behaviour such as films, television series, songs, instruction manuals, diets, sculpture and bodily expressions. Unsemioticized data refers to material which has not been created by human practice. Social semioticians may be interested in unsemioticized material to understand the meanings inscribed into it not by its human producers (as there are none), but instead by its human consumers and by those who control the regime of consumption (think, for example, of the complex semiotic potential of land and landscape). Unsemioticized material is not to be confused with material designed for explicitly functional rather than symbolic purposes, like a common table fork for example. Even though much more symbolism can be inscribed in certain objects than others, all objects have semiotic potential, and for this reason all objects – material or metaphysical – may be objects of socio-semiotic analysis.

Because social semioticians over the years have developed a keen interest and refined their conceptual vocabulary to best understand multimodality rather than pure linguistic discursivity alone, most socio-semiotic analyses deal with multimodal material. Furthermore, because of the careful attention it has received over the last decade, visual data lend themselves particularly well to socio-semiotic investigation (see Jewitt and Oyama 2001; Kress and van Leeuwen 1996). In all of these cases, however, it is important to note that social-semiotic investigation is most effective when researchers need to deal with small amounts of data rather than with the large data banks typical of content analysis. In light of the above, it is not uncommon for socio-semiotic analysis to occur in combination with other methods such as content analysis or discourse analysis.

In a recent publication I introduced a systematic set of procedures for the combination between ethnography and social semiotics with the purpose of examining social agents' critical and interpretive activities as well as their context-specific use of semiotic resources (Vannini 2007). The potential of a socio-semiotic ethnography seems particularly useful for the further development of social semiotics as an everyday life sociological perspective. By shedding light on actual processes of engagement with the potential of semiotic resources, socio-semiotic ethnographies may – amongst other things – help combat hysterical moral panics over the passivity, over-conformity or vulnerability of audiences and consumers alike, so present in contemporary public and political debate. For example, by asking what it is that children precisely do with what they watch on television, Merris Griffiths and David Machin (2003) found that children are active agents who utilize television-based imagery and discourses to facilitate peer interaction and establish and maintain relationships, not unlike adults do. This type of research helps researchers to:

> move away from thinking about 'effects' and isolated demographic features of audiences [and] locate[s] television in culture as something that is part of people's usual everyday way of going about the business of fitting in, having a bit of fun, [and] understanding the way that the world and the people in it work.
>
> (Griffiths and Machin 2003:159)

While social semioticians are careful about not freezing the world into relationships based on simple linear cause and effect, it must be admitted that there is occasionally a dangerous tendency in social semiotics to privilege the study of not-always-so-clearly-defined multimodal communicative practices and discourses at the expense of how semiotic potential is actually realized through practice – thus emphasizing the importance and strength of the level of semiotic production. The ethnography of communication offers a way out of this dangerous zone by treating media as practice 'rather than a text or production process' (Couldry 2004: 129). The empirical utilization of a socio-semiotic ethnographic approach that is reflexive and attentive to the multiplicity of often contradictory meanings and discourses can help social semiotics advance deeper into the anthropology and sociology of lived experience and struggle (Vannini 2007). But let us now abandon this level of methodological generality, and examine instead some important socio-semiotic concepts for inquiry and some exemplary empirical studies.

Dimensions of social semiotic analysis

Following van Leeuwen (2005) I focus here on four dimensions of social semiotic analysis – discourse, genre, style and modality – as well as four social semiotic concepts: semiotic transformation, semiotic rules, multimodality and semiotic functions. The theoretical and empirical material I draw upon here pertains to the domain of material culture and popular culture, and focuses in particular on those studies and theoretical writings that touch upon substantive issues pertinent to the domain of day-to-day life. Even though most, if not all, of the writings presented below contribute to our understanding of two or more of the dimensions and concepts outlined above, for reasons of space for the most part I discuss individual studies only once and only in relation to the concept they pedagogically best illustrate.

Discourse

Discourse is talk, whether spoken or expressed through the written word. When social semioticians study discourse they study it as an expression of a socially constructed body of knowledge. To make their studies more manageable social semioticians study such discursive knowledge by zeroing on illustrative texts. For example, Hodge and O'Carroll (2006) interpret the meanings of multiculturalism in the Australian context by focusing on what they call expressions of 'borderwork': a multitude of texts which erect and dismantle boundaries between white Australians and 'the Other', while Cranny-Francis (1995) discusses representations and conceptualizations of the human body in academic discourse.

Central to the socio-semiotic examination of discourse is a focus on ideology (see for example Hodge and Kress 1988; Lemke 1995). Ideology enters everyday life through the operation of diverse bodies of discursive knowledge. Van Leeuwen (2005) lays out a clear framework for understanding the operation of discourse in everyday life. For him, following Foucault (1980), discursive knowledge is knowledge produced by social actors practising in specific social contexts with particular interests in mind. Understood this way, discourses work as plural resources for representing and constructing – and thus transforming – aspects of reality.

Discourses – van Leeuwen (2005) writes – have a history of their own, are distributed by a variety of agents through a multitude of media and are subject to realization in numerous ways. Other social semioticians follow this approach. Kress (2007a), for example, focuses on how ideologies enter social existence through everyday instances of speech, van Leeuwen and Machin (2007) examine multimodal representations of glocalized femininities in over 40 countries' editions of *Cosmopolitan* magazine, while Scollon (2003) and Jaworski and Pritchard (2005) analyse how space is shaped by discourses identifying the purposes that land and material landscape elements ought to serve. A related, but somewhat different, approach to discourse is adopted by Thibault (2006) in looking at the constitution of agency and consciousness through dialogue and children's play.

In all, this body of research and theory shows that discourses work by evaluating, representing and legitimizing social practices by regulating activities, the manners in which activities are carried out, what actors can participate, how they ought to present their roles and identities, what resources they can utilize, and when and where social practices should unfold (van Leeuwen 2005).

Genre

If discourses constitute the 'what' of communication, genres stand as examples of the 'how' of communication. Genres are categorical realizations of non-linguistic, linguistic and contextual features. In other words, genres are ideal 'types of texts' (van Leeuwen 2005: 122), and their typification resides in the fact that those who produce them follow rules common to other, similar texts in terms of content and form. Because social semioticians are interested in the functionality of semiotic resources, their interest lies primarily in what genres do, or better yet in what people do with the potential functions of genres. A classic example of the operation of semiotic genres in everyday life is that of 'speech acts' (Austin 1962). In arguing that language is not only and not always representational (and thus based on criteria of correspondence such as truth), John Austin identified certain speech acts that, rather than being true to what they refer to, construct realities of their own, such as apologies, declarations of intent, requests, offers and demands.

As opposed to conversation analysts, social semioticians have investigated a wide variety of genres, focusing for the most part on multimodal genres rather than speech alone. For example, Fiske and Hodge (1988) have looked at the narrative construction of Australian identity, together with the stereotypes associated with it, by examining popular culture texts. Scollon (1998) has looked at the intersection of mediated action and social practice by analysing news discourse, and van Leeuwen (1994) has examined in great detail the genre of media interviews, focusing on the context of the media interview as a unique form of conversation marked by specific semiotic rules, while Cranny-Francis (1992) has examined representation of gender in popular fiction. Amongst the most original of contemporary socio-semiotic studies is that of Jennifer Biddle (2007). Biddle conducted two years of fieldwork in Lajamanu, Australia, where she investigated the combination of body painting, singing and dancing in contemporary indigenous art from the great Australian desert. Her visual and performative ethnography reveal a sensuous engagement with Warlpiri women culture and the physicality of their unique genre of art. In sum, socio-semiotic analysis of genre reveals that genres format experiences and practices by laying out shared expectations on the form, and therefore on the potential for meaning, of semiotic resources.

Style

According to Hodge and Kress (1988: 79), style is a 'metasign'. In simpler terms, style is an ensemble of manners, an index of identity and expression. In socio-semiotic terms styles are broad signifying systems which link together smaller parts, turning them into concrete wholes. There are at least three kinds of style that interest social semioticians, according to van Leeuwen (2005: 140): individual style, social style and lifestyle.

Individual style is a matter of individual difference, of self-expression and impression management. A punk, for example, expresses their individuality by rejecting conformism to the masses and by denouncing all that is hegemonic, or mainstream, in terms of individual expression (see Gottdiener 1985). Punk, however, is also a collectively agreed-upon marker of social position, a sign of what people do as a result of group membership, and hence a social style. Expressing a social style is a common semiotic practice, a way of communicating a unique, but shared, ideology. As Hodge and Kress (1988: 79) write, 'Any group of any size needs markers of group membership to give it identity and cohesion, and to differentiate it from other groups.' Such common markers unite members of the same gender, class, and even regional group (for example by way of speaking with an accent) (see Hodge and Kress 1988). Finally, the concept of lifestyle is a combination of both social and individual style. In a consumer society lifestyle is expressed through forms of consumption stratified by taste, leisure patterns and attitudes (Gottdiener 2000a) and represented through such mundane choices as typographic font (van Leeuwen 2005), tanned skin (Vannini and McCright 2004), cars and bumper stickers (Noble and Baldwin 2001), sexual expressiveness (Machin and van Leeuwen 2005; Machin and Thornborrow 2006), and even urban architecture (Gottdiener 1995).

Modality

Another important concept in social semiotics is modality. Modality, as intended here, is not to be confused with multimodality. Modality is a measure of how true a representation is, in terms of both degree of truth and the mechanisms through which an impression of truth is achieved. Social semioticians, as you remember, believe that meaning is always interested, ideological, motivated. It follows that sign-vehicles, as Umberto Eco (1976) once put it, are always lies because they stand for something they are not. The task of social semioticians, therefore, becomes that of empirically investigating how communication leads to the achievement of putative realities – realities that are convincing enough for disbelief to be suspended. As van Leeuwen (2005: 160) explains, social semioticians 'are concerned not with the absolute truth but with the truth as speakers and writers and other sign producers see it, and with the semiotic resources they use to express it'.

Modality can be either linguistic or non-linguistic (that is, visual, abstract, sensory and naturalistic; see van Leeuwen 2005). Whereas discourse analysts generally focus on linguistic modality (for example how a text achieves authoritative force through written rhetorical means such as the use of the conditional, the subjunctive, and through subjective and objective modality), social semioticians focus on multimodal (that is, multimedia) texts. For example, in my research I have investigated modality in televised weather reports by examining how the use of illustrated maps, complex meteorological indicators, spectacular weather narratives and archival weather data lends an aura of scientific authority to what is essentially guesswork (Vannini and McCright 2007). In an earlier study instead I looked at how individuals minimize the stigma of 'fake-baking' (that is, artificial tanning) by downplaying the benefits of achieving an authentic tan through sunbathing (Vannini and McCright 2004).

In a different context, van Leeuwen (1999) has looked into the semiotic power of sound to achieve emotional effect and sensation – something which can be called 'sensory modality' or 'the effect of pleasure and displeasure' (van Leeuwen 2005: 170) achieved by the manipulation of semiotic resources like musical tones, rhythms, melodies and harmonies. Kress and van Leeuwen's (1996) research on the grammar of visual design is also critically important for understanding how still photography can communicate regimes of truth through such technics and techniques as articulation of photographic detail, use of background and foreground, colour saturation and differentiation, depth articulation, and articulation of light, shadow and tone. Also within the realm of both visual and multimodal communication figures the polemical critique of classist and racist ideology in South African film by cultural studies scholar Keyan Tomaselli (1988; also see Tomaselli and Shepperson 1991; Tomaselli 1996).

Semiotic transformation

Whereas attention in structural semiology is generally dedicated to how systems of meanings operate at any given point in time, social semioticians seriously concern themselves with how meanings and logonomic systems mutate over time. Diachronic (or longitudinal) analysis is not done at the expense of synchronic analysis, however, as a focus on both dimensions can coexist in most studies. As van Leeuwen (2005: 26) outlines, semiotic resources and logonomic systems can change for a variety of reasons, including the need for new resources and new ways of using existing resources. Change is not always possible, however. As I describe in a forthcoming article which looks at the example of fashion, certain contexts may be more or less open to change, and certain properties of those contexts may facilitate or prevent change (Vannini 2008). Regardless of the reasons and conditions of change, the process of meaning-making is itself grounded in time. As Hodge and Kress (1988: 163) have elegantly put it, following the Peircean vision of meaning as inevitably unfolding in time, 'time in semiosis is always history'.

Social semioticians have examined semiotic transformation in a wide variety of settings. Annemarie Jutel (2005) has analysed the changing meanings of fatness throughout history, and Kress (1999) has looked at the phonetic emergence of words and studied the significance of changes in spelling over time. In a different study he focused on changes in learning and pedagogy by focusing on changes in media literacy and the growth of multimodality in education (Kress 2003). In an insightful analysis bridging the domains of urban architecture, consumption and material culture, Gottdiener (2001) has examined the concept of 'theming' – typical for example in the design of theme parks, casinos and theme restaurants – and reflected on how it constructs collective memories of the past while simultaneously changing them in light of contemporary ideologies. Looking at technology and communication media instead, Scollon and Scollon (2004) have reflected at how the Internet has changed the sense of place in a small Alaskan town. As Lemke (2000) has remarked, because the flow of semiosis is always a transformation of its own grounding in history, an understanding of different scales of time is necessary to understand everyday interaction and to posit only one level of diachrony is as big a mistake as to focus exclusively on synchrony.

Semiotic rules

The concept of semiotic rules plays undoubtedly an important role in both structuralist and social semiotics. But whereas structural semioticians generally treat rules as universal, formal and abstract, social semioticians find them to be highly contingent on context and malleable by way of social interaction. In other words, in social semiotics rules do not rule people; rather people make rules. As van Leeuwen (2005: 47) explains, 'Rules, whether written or unwritten, are made by people, and can therefore be changed by people.'

Certainly, changing rules is a difficult process, and it is the more difficult as rules become institutionalized and protected. Yet rules can be negotiated and enforced differentially on the basis of idiosyncrasies and exceptions. For example, as Dennis Waskul and I have found (Waskul and Vannini, forthcoming), moral norms enforcing deodorizing and proscribing against body odours can be suspended and violated when all participants to social interaction agree that bad smell is to be expected and even to be interpreted as a positive sign (for instance, in contexts marked by competitive physical activity or after culinary feasts) or when local needs override global expectations (as in, for example, scent-free hospitals and workplaces).

Semiotic rules are of different types. Amongst the most common in social semiotics are lexicon and grammar rules. *Lexicon* rules stipulate what signifiers refer to. For example, in contemporary Western society artificially tanned skin connotes such things as physical appeal, a relatively affluent lifestyle and youth. *Grammar* rules instead stipulate how coherent messages can be built up with smaller semiotic resources. Again in the context of tanning for example, a tanned body is to be presented as a complex multimodal text composed in its whole of signs expressing its muscular fitness, sense of fashion, and other resources connoting a coherent lifestyle (Vannini and McCright 2004). While many rules of different types do exist, in general all rules work by way of at least five different types of resources, such as personal authority, impersonal authority, conformity, role modelling and expertise (van Leeuwen 2005). Rules and their use can be considered technologies of everyday life: an ensemble of technics and techniques by which people express lifestyles impressed by social norms and cultural values (see Dant 1999, 2005).

In a fascinating reflexive ethnography of the everyday social world of airports and airplanes, Gottdiener (2000b) examines the contextual, interpersonal and material rules regulating air flight and airport interaction. In these contexts, rules are social as much as they are semiotic, since they are constantly achieved by way of regulating the expressive features of material onboard airplanes and in airports. April Herndon (2005) has also shed light on the pervasiveness of semiotic rules and their ideological weight by uncovering the social inequalities behind the current US fight against obesity under the guise of health.

Semiotic functions

Finally, let us look at the idea of functionality. Let us take for example a common fork. A fork has an obvious functionality: it serves as a tool to pick up food with. That is its instrumental function: its most immediate, obvious, and taken for granted function. As a matter of fact you could even say that such function was inscribed into the fork by its designer, and that given its simplicity this is the only use, and the only meaning that it has. This would be a mistake, however. Short of suggesting that a fork could be used as a weapon (which it could, it's just that such a hypothesis completely decontextualizes the inscribed use of the fork and thus it is a bit beside the point), we could put our minds together and make an inventory of all the uses of a fork.

Thus, we may find that its strategic use in the house can be *regulative*, in that by placing a fork on the dining room table rather than on the kitchen table (or rather than on the floor), and on a specific corner of the table, a housekeeper tells a guest where food will be served. The fork may be used as a semiotic resource in an *informative* way as well, in that its size and shape may clue in the table guest as to the type of meal that will be served. The very shape of a common fork also has an *interpersonal* function. Forks are generally made for only one hand to hold them, hence limiting the commensality of a typical American or European meal. Compare for example the level of food sharedness that normally goes on in an Ethiopian meal, where the absence of forks enables people to feed with their hands off a common plate. Relatedly, a fork has a *personal* function as well. For a long time in college, my forks came from the university cafeteria. Definitely a sign of my class status, huh? A fork can also have a heuristic function, in that it can be used to find out about things. Think of how forks work as perfect tools for the poking of food open, like fish, which always seems cooked on the outside but offers no visible clues to its inside state of readiness. These are only six functions listed by van Leeuwen (2005: 76–7), and only six of many other functions to which semiotic resources can be put. The point here is that just as language is not only used in a referential function, material objects are not only used in an instrumental function.

As Mihaly Csikszentmihalyi and Eugene Rochberg-Halton (1981) have found, all kinds of domestic objects have all kinds of functions. They can be used to develop shared memories, to express identity, as extensions of the self, as symbols of class and status, as props for the performance of gender, and so forth. Something similar can be said about visual semiotic resources. Images can be used to educate but also to exclude and stereotype (Jewitt and Oyama 2001; van Leeuwen 2001). Similarly, multimodal semiotic resources like children's television programming can be used to entertain but can also be employed by children as tools to facilitate group cohesion (Griffiths and Machin 2003; also see Hodge 1986). Something similar can also be said about the human body, which arguably stands as the most malleable semiotic resources as all, open to use in innumerable functions (Thibault and Halliday 2004).

Social semiotics and the multimodality of everyday life

The empirical and theoretical attention that social semioticians have dedicated to multimodality over the years is an obvious indicator of the true strength and concentration of this perspective (see for example Baldry, Thibault and Lemke 2006; Cranny-Francis 2005; Gottdiener and Lagopoulos 1986; Jewitt 2008; Jewitt and Kress 2003; Kress 2004, 2007b; Kress and van Leeuwen 2001; Machin 2007). Whereas sociological investigation of social interaction has tended to restrict itself to the spoken and the written word, social semiotic analysis has blazed the territory of the visual, the rhythmical, the material, the olfactory, and much more, often in conjunction with one another too.

This is an important addition to our knowledge of everyday life. Symbols – linguistic symbols, that is – are but one type of signs (Peirce 1931). To truly understand human communication in all of its forms, social scientists must become able to relinquish methods that rely exclusively on the collection of words. The social semiotic attention to multimodal traces of human behaviour especially acquires a particular importance when we think of how everyday life is increasingly mediated by a plurality of media of communication, and how social interaction – as said in the beginning – is more and more surrounded by and enabled through deceivingly simple and yet so important 'stuff'.

In the end, what social semiotics can do to advance the sociological project of the study of everyday life is so important that mainstream sociologists cannot afford to miss it. It is no accident that one of the greatest founders of sociology, Charles Sanders Peirce (Wiley 2006), also figures as one of the most significant founders, if not *the* most significant founder, of social semiotics. Social semiotics has the tools to understand the materiality of semiotic resources, the significance of context-bound rules and conditions, and the importance of agency, as well as the openness to be mixed with a variety of research strategies and theoretical perspectives that sociologists are already familiar with.

Notes

1. While no conclusive evidence on this is available, many believe that Mikhail Bakhtin and Valentin Volosinov are actually the same person.

Bibliography

Adler, Patricia A., Peter Adler and Andrea Fontana (1987) 'Everyday life sociology.' *Annual Review of Sociology*, 13: 217–35.

Austin, John (1962) *How to Do Things with Words*. Boston, MA: Cambridge University Press.
Bakhtin, Mikhail (1965/1984) *Rabelais and His World*. Bloomington, IN: Indiana University Press.
Bakhtin, Mikhail (1975/1981) *The Dialogic Imagination: Four Essays*. Austin, TX: University of Texas Press.
Bakhtin, Mikhail (1979/1986) *Speech Genres and Other Late Essays*. Austin, TX: University of Texas Press.
Baldry, Anthony, Paul Thibault and Jay Lemke (2006) *Multimodal Transcription and Text Analysis*. London: David Brown.
Barthes, Roland (1972) *Mythologies*. New York: Hill & Wang.
Biddle, Jennifer (2007) *Breasts, Bodies, Canvas: Central Desert Art as Experience*. Seattle: University of Washington Press.
Couldry, Nick (2004) 'Theorising media as practice.' *Social Semiotics*, 14: 115–32.
Cranny-Francis, Anne (1992) *Engendered Fiction: Analyzing Gender in the Production and Reception of Texts*. Sydney: New South Wales University Press.
Cranny-Francis, Anne (1995) *Body in the Text*. Melbourne: Melbourne University Publishing.
Cranny-Francis, Anne (2005) *Multimedia: Texts and Contexts*. London: Sage.
Csikszentmihalyi, Mihaly and Eugene Rochberg-Halton (1981) *The Meaning of Things: Domestic Symbols and the Self*. Boston, MA: Cambridge University Press.
Dant, Tim (1999) *Material Culture in the Social World: Values, Activities, Lifestyles*. Buckingham: Open University Press.
Dant, Tim (2005) *Materiality and Society*. Buckingham: Open University Press.
Eco, Umberto (1976) *A Theory of Semiotics*. Bloomington, IN: Indiana University Press.
Fairclough, Norman (1995) *Critical Discourse Analysis: The Critical Study of Language*. New York: Longman.
Fiske, John and Bob Hodge (1988) *Myths of Oz: Reading Australian Popular Culture*. London: Allen & Unwin.
Foucault, Michel (1980) *Power/Knowledge*. Brighton: Harvester Press.
Gottdiener, Mark (1985) 'Hegemony and mass culture: a semiotic approach.' *American Journal of Sociology*, 90: 979–99.
Gottdiener, Mark (1995) *Postmodern Semiotics: Material Culture and the Forms of Postmodern Life*. Oxford: Blackwell.
Gottdiener, Mark (ed.) (2000a) *New Forms of Consumption*. New York: Rowman & Littlefield.
Gottdiener, Mark (2000b) *Life in the Air*. New York: Rowman & Littlefield.
Gottdiener, Mark (2001) *The Theming of America*. Boulder, CO: Westview Press.
Gottdiener, Mark and Alexandros Logolopoulos (eds), (1986) *The City and the Sign: An Introduction to Urban Semiotics*. New York: Columbia University Press.
Griffiths, Merris and David Machin (2003) 'Television and playground games as part of children's symbolic culture.' *Social Semiotics*, 13: 147–60.
Halliday, Michael. A. K. (1978) *Language as Social Semiotics*. London: Arnold.
Halton, Eugene (1986) *Meaning and Modernity*. Chicago, IL: University of Chicago Press.
Halton, Eugene (1995) *Bereft of Reason: On the Decline of Social Thought and Prospects for its Renewal*. Chicago, IL: University of Chicago Press.
Herndon, April M. (2005) 'Collateral damage from friendly fire? Race, nation, class, and the "war against obesity".' *Social Semiotics*, 15: 127–41.
Hodge, Bob (1986) *Children and Television: A Semiotic Approach*. London: Blackwell.
Hodge, Bob and Gunther Kress (1988) *Social Semiotics*. Ithaca, NY: Cornell University Press.
Hodge, Bob and John O'Carroll (2006) *Borderwork in Multicultural Australia*. New York: Allen & Unwin.

Jaworski, Adam and Annette Pritchard (eds) (2005) *Discourse, Communication, and Tourism*. New York: Multilingual Matters.

Jensen, Klaus B. (1995) *The Social Semiotics of Mass Communication*. London: Sage.

Jewitt, Carey (ed.) (2008) *A Handbook of Multimodal Analysis*. London: Routledge.

Jewitt, Carey and Rumiko Oyama (2001) 'Visual meaning: a social semiotic approach', in Theo van Leeuwen and Carey Jewitt (eds), *Handbook of Visual Analysis*. London: Sage.

Jewitt, Carey and Gunther Kress (2003) *Multimodal Literacy*. New York: Peter Lang.

Jutel, Annemarie (2005) 'Weighing health: the moral burden of obesity.' *Social Semiotics*, 15: 114–25.

Kress, Gunther (1993) 'Against arbitrariness: the social production of the sign as a foundational issue in critical discourse analysis.' *Discourse and Society*, 42: 169–93.

Kress, Gunther (1999) *Early Spelling: From Creation to Creativity*. London: Routledge.

Kress, Gunther (2003) *Literacy in the New Media Age*. London: Routledge.

Kress, Gunther (2004) *English in Urban Classrooms: A Multimodal Perspective on Teaching and Learning*. London: Routledge.

Kress, Gunther (2007a) *Language: A Semiotic View*. London: Blackwell.

Kress, Gunther (2007b) *Multimodality: Exploring Contemporary Methods of Communication*. London: Routledge.

Kress, Gunther and Theo van Leeuwen (1996) *Reading Images: The Grammar of Visual Design*. London: Routledge.

Kress, Gunther and Theo van Leeuwen (2001) *Multimodal Discourse: The Modes and Media of Contemporary Communication*. London: Arnold.

Lemke, Jay (1995) *Textual Politics: Discourse and Social Dynamics*. New York: Taylor & Francis.

Lemke, Jay (1997) 'Cognition, context, and learning: a social semiotic perspective', in David Kirshner and Aaron Whitson (eds), *Situated Cognition: Social, Semiotic, and Psychological Perspectives*. Hillsdale, NJ: Erlbaum.

Lemke, Jay (2000) 'Opening Up Closure: Semiotics Across Scales', in Jerry L. R. Chandler and Gertrudis van de Vijver (eds), *Closure: Emergent Organizations and their Dynamics* (Volume 901: Annals of the NYAS). New York: New York Academy of Science Press.

Machin, David (2007) *Introduction to Multimodal Analysis*. New York: Oxford University Press.

Machin, David and Theo van Leeuwen (2005) 'Language style and lifestyle: the case of a global magazine.' *Media, Culture and Society*, 27: 577–600.

Machin, David and Joanna Thornborrow (2006) 'Lifestyle and the depoliticisation of agency: sex as power in women's magazines.' *Social Semiotics*, 16: 173–88.

Noble, David and Rebecca Baldwin (2001) 'Sly chicks and troublemakers: car stickers, nonsense and the allure of strangeness.' *Social Semiotics*, 11: 75–89.

O'Toole, Michael (1994) *The Language of Displayed Art*. Leicester: Leicester University Press.

Peirce, Charles Sanders (1931) *Collected Papers*. Cambridge, MA: Harvard University Press.

Saussure, Ferdinand de (1959) *Course in General Linguistics*. New York: McGraw-Hill.

Scollon, Ron (1998) *Mediated Discourse as Social Interaction: A Study of News Discourse*. London: Addison-Wesley.

Scollon, Ron (2003) *Discourses in Place: Language in the Material World*. London: Routledge.

Scollon, Ron and Suzie Wong Scollon (2004) *Nexus Analysis: Discourse and the Emerging Internet*. London: Routledge.

Thibault, Paul (1991) *Social Semiotics and Praxis*. Minneapolis, MN: University of Minnesota Press.

Thibault, Paul (1993) 'Editorial: Social Semiotics.' *The Semiotic Review of Books*, 4. [Online] http://www.chass.utoronto.ca/epc/srb/srb/4-3edit.html

Thibault, Paul (2006) *Agency and Consciousness in Discourse: Self-Other Dynamics as a Complex System*. London: Continuum.

Thibault, Paul and Michael A. K. Halliday (2004) *Brain, Mind, and the Signifying Body: An Ecosocial Semiotic Theory*. London: Continuum.

Tomaselli, Keyan (1988) *The Cinema of Apartheid: Race and Class in South African Film*. Capetown: Smyrna Press.

Tomaselli, Keyan (1996) 'Politics of representation: semiotic struggles in South Africa.' *Caiet de Cinema*, 11: 1–20.

Tomaselli, Keyan and Arnold Shepperson (1991) 'Popularising semiotics: semiotics and social struggle.' *Communication Research Trends*, 11 (2). [Online] http://www.und.ac.za/und/ccms/socialsemiotics/popular.htm.

Van Leeuwen, Theo (1994) *The Media Interview: Confession, Contest, Conversation*. Sydney: New South Wales University Press.

Van Leeuwen, Theo (1999) *Speech, Music, Sound*. London: Palgrave Macmillan.

Van Leeuwen, Theo (2001) 'Semiotics and iconography', in Theo van Leeuwen and Carey Jewitt (eds), *Handbook of Visual Analysis*. London: Sage.

Van Leeuwen, Theo (2005) *Introducing Social Semiotics*. London: Routledge.

Van Leeuwen, Theo and David Machin (2007) *Global Media Discourse*. London: Routledge.

Vannini, Phillip (2004) 'Toward an interpretive analytics of the sign: interactionism, power, and semiosis.' *Studies in Symbolic Interaction*, 27: 151–76.

Vannini, Phillip (2007) 'Social semiotics and fieldwork: method and analytics.' *Qualitative Inquiry*, 13: 113–40.

Vannini, Phillip (2008) 'Blumer's thesis on fashion: toward a generic social process of semiotic transformation.' *Sociological Focus* (forthcoming).

Vannini, Phillip and Aaron McCright (2004) 'To die for: the semiotic seductive power of the tanned body.' *Symbolic Interaction*, 27: 309–32.

Vannini, Phillip and Aaron McCright (2007) 'Technologies of the sky: a socio-semiotic and critical analysis of weather discourse.' *Critical Discourse Studies*, 4: 49–73.

Volosinov, Valentin (1973) *Marxism and the Philosophy of Language*. New York: Seminar Press.

Waskul, Dennis and Phillip Vannini (forthcoming) 'Olfactory management as somatic work.'

Wiley, Norbert (1994) *The Semiotic Self*. Chicago, IL: University of Chicago Press.

Wiley, Norbert (2006) 'Peirce and the founding of American sociology.' *Journal of Classical Sociology*, 6: 25–50.

CHAPTER 15

Cultural Studies and Everyday Life

Tapping Hidden Energies

DAVID INGLIS

Introduction

Cultural studies ranks as one of the most vibrant and interesting new arrivals on the academic scene in the last few decades. Cultural studies scholars have often not been afraid to challenge what they see as some of the more hide-bound attitudes and practices of more conventional academia. From its very inception, back in the late 1950s, cultural studies has been pre-eminently a critical discipline, seeking to combat what it sees as outmoded approaches to the comprehension of human life and replacing them with new, more vital and more engaged forms of analysis and understanding.

Because cultural studies is self-consciously a highly engaged, often explicitly politicized, discipline, it has very often focused on processes of everyday life, seeking to demonstrate that these are often much more interesting, vibrant and sometimes socially subversive than both more conventional analytic approaches and hegemonic social discourses would have us believe. This chapter focuses on a number of important strains of cultural studies that have sought to identify and to tap into what they see as the hidden social and cultural energies of everyday activities, demonstrating the vivacity, creativity and thoughtfulness of these practices and rescuing them from the condescension of those, both inside the academy and outside, who see little value in such activities.

If I had to say which one element of cultural studies approaches to everyday life differentiated these from many or all more explicitly sociological approaches to quotidian matters, I would have to identify the distinctive cultural studies emphasis on everyday activities, and the people who carry them out, as being always potentially more socially critical, resistive and subversive than we might ever have guessed. While this emphasis on everyday resistance to forms of power has its problems, as we shall see below, nonetheless such a focus very usefully brings into the light certain features of everyday forms of existence that otherwise might have been underplayed or ignored, namely those which involve 'ordinary people' being more resilient and more critical of the world within which they live than we might otherwise have thought.

Not all forms of cultural studies deal explicitly with everyday-life contexts. This chapter examines those strands in cultural studies that have particularly homed in on such matters. In particular, the chapter examines the development of approaches to everyday life made by scholars in British cultural studies, Britain being the country where cultural studies first developed. The history of British cultural studies is in many ways the story of attempts to develop ever more sophisticated ways of understanding the cultural contours of everyday practices and attitudes (Tudor 1999). Some of these ways of thinking have been influenced by sociological concerns, some have been critical of what is taken to be sociology's lack of comprehension of the fine-grained details of human existence, and some have come to influence how some sociologists have come to view the world around them.

A particular concern of British cultural studies, as we shall see, has been the analysis of the ways in which forms of power can both structure the cultural features of everyday life and in turn be challenged and resisted by them. The theme of culturally mediated and expressed resistance to power is both one of the main distinctive features of British cultural studies and also arguably its most useful contribution to the study, sociological or otherwise, of everyday life.

In what follows, I first outline what cultural studies 'is' in the present day, before moving back in time in order to depict the initial roots of cultural studies' distinctive focus on everyday life contexts, namely the school of thought called 'culturalism'. I then turn to look at how British cultural studies evolved during the crucial period of the 1970s, coupling cultural themes to the richness of everyday contexts with sophisticated theoretical tools imported from continental Europe. Finally I look at how, since the 1980s, post-culturalist cultural studies have sought to demonstrate the often unexpectedly complex textures of everyday practices such as watching television. The chapter concludes with an assessment of the continuing importance of these sorts of cultural studies approaches for the sociological comprehension of everyday life.

What is cultural studies?

Cultural studies as an academic discipline and as an intellectual enterprise (or set of enterprises) can be regarded as having a number of key features (Inglis 2007). First, there is an emphasis on conceptual openness and fluidity. As it has developed, cultural studies has variously taken up, adapted and changed concepts, methods, problems and concerns from a diverse range of more 'orthodox' academic disciplines such as anthropology, history, literary studies, philosophy and sociology itself (Turner 1990: 1). Cultural studies can thus be described as being made up of a number of foci – problems, themes, theorizations and methods – drawn from different disciplines, such that 'there are no fixed boundaries and no fortress walls; theories and themes are drawn in from disciplines and may flow back in a transformed state to influence thinking there' (Baldwin et al. 2000: 41).

Second, cultural studies prides itself on embracing a wide range of theoretical and analytical perspectives, often said to be understandable from a great variety of different ways of thinking, such as Marxism, culturalism, linguistic structuralism and linguistic-philosophical post-structuralism and postmodernism, to name just some of the main possibilities available in the present day (Bennett 1998).

Third, it is often said that cultural studies can encompass the understanding of a very wide variety of things and their complicated relations with each other. For example, the statement of the aims of one of the field's flagship journals, called *Cultural Studies*, defines the task of the discipline as exploring 'the relation[s] between cultural practices, everyday life, material, economic, political, geographical and historical contexts'. On this view, cultural studies can examine just about everything in human life: nothing can, or should, be ignored.

Fourth, and finally, many cultural studies authors understand their own practices as being characterized by strong political engagements. Often cultural studies authors define their subject as one which, despite all its multiplicity, is centrally concerned with the relations that pertain between cultural forms and activities on the one hand, and forms and relations of power on the other. This in turn encompasses the analysis of power in its various and multiple forms, clustering around dynamics of class, gender and ethnicity, among other axes (Turner 1990: 5). Cultural studies authors also often say that their subject involves much more of a focus on political engagement in analysing and writing, as opposed to apolitical scholarship, than does any other discipline, including sociology. The contemporary British scholar Graeme Turner (1990: 227) speaks for many in the cultural studies field when he contends that cultural studies' 'commitment to understanding the construction of everyday life has the admirable objective of doing so in order to change our lives for the better. Not all academic pursuits have such a practical political objective.'

The political programmes expressed in cultural studies are all on the political left in one way or another, but they range from 'neomarxist socialist politics' to 'postmarxist identity-based politics' (Seidman 1997: 41). Regardless of the particular political position adopted, cultural studies authors also see themselves as engaging with what they see as vital and energetic cultural forms and activities – such as rap music lyrics, music videos and fan cultures – which can tell us a great deal about the contemporary world, and avoiding (and in fact, challenging) the often snobbish attitudes towards such things held by more established academic disciplines. Thus, cultural studies is not frightened of 'getting down and dirty' by analysing everyday practices and the sorts of popular cultural forms that other subjects (sociology perhaps included) might shy away from, because they think that such things are not worthy of study.

Culturalism and everyday existence

The idea that no cultural form or practice is below being studied, because even the most apparently debased and stupid cultural forms and practices can tell us something about how we live now, was first pioneered by those British scholars who advocated what subsequently became known as the 'culturalist' approach to social and cultural matters. In many ways, the beginnings of cultural studies as a set of distinctive approaches to cultural matters has its roots in Britain, and 'culturalism' generally figures in histories of cultural studies (such as Tudor 1999) as the very root from which later types of cultural studies sprouted. Culturalism as a way of thinking is associated with three major British thinkers of the post-war period, Richard Hoggart (b. 1918), Raymond Williams (1921–1988) and E. P. Thompson (1924–1993). Although their work varies somewhat in tone and substance, nonetheless the influential writings of these thinkers in the 1950s and early 1960s can be classed as 'culturalist' in that they all, in one way or another, asserted two key claims: first, that 'culture is ordinary', and second, that ordinary people are more creative and active in making their own lives than many intellectuals may think.

These characteristically culturalist claims were very much forged in reaction against the dominant views of what 'culture' is and what ordinary people ('the masses') were like in English society, and particularly in the universities, at that time. The dominant view, as expressed for example in the ideas of the very influential literary critic F. R. Leavis, was that while real 'culture', in the form of the more difficult 'high arts', was the preserve of a tiny minority of highly educated people, the rest of the population were content to watch the worst sorts of mass-produced culture – Hollywood films, paperback novels, sensationalist newspapers and so on – which had absolutely no intellectual or moral content whatsoever. Over time, 'mass culture', with its cheap thrills and tawdry shock-effects, not only came to dominate the lives of those lower down the social scale, it also slowly but inexorably began to infect the cultural lives of the elite too (Leavis 1932/1990: 67). The middle classes were becoming more and more corrupted by the ignorant and stupid modes of thought encouraged by mass culture, and thus were in danger of losing the morally responsible and sophisticated ways of thinking that were crucial if the overall society was not to become a wholly debased and philistine one.

This particular understanding of 'high art' being all that was good, and 'mass culture' being thoroughly bad, was a very common refrain from the intelligentsia in a range of countries throughout the first half of the 20th century (see Inglis and Hughson 2003). It ultimately derived from an idea of 'culture' that had first appeared in the earlier 19th century, as a reaction against what many intellectuals of the period perceived as the ugliness and money-obsessed nature of the new urban, industrial capitalist society that was emerging at that time. One of the most famous definitions of 'culture' in this vein was offered in the 1860s by the poet and educationalist Matthew Arnold (1822–1888). When he spoke of culture, Arnold referred to its qualities of 'sweetness and light', for in his view authentic culture was possessed of both great beauty and also profound intellectual insight. Arnold's (1869/1995: 199) famous definition of culture is that it is made up of 'the best which has been thought and said in the world', involving the finest and highest insights into human life that had ever been said and recorded: for example the art works of Michelangelo, the poetry of Shakespeare, the music of Beethoven. For Arnold, this sort of culture – high-minded, serious and insightful – was completely 'at variance with the mechanical and material civilisation' that he thought was dominant in England in his time (Arnold 1869/1995: 63).

This kind of thinking about culture proved to be very influential on later generations of English intellectuals, to the point that it had become a largely unquestioned orthodoxy by the 1950s. This was the background against which culturalism developed, as a rebellion against the elitism and often unthinking arrogance of the Arnoldian tradition, and its very negative understanding of anything that was not 'the best that has been thought and said'. For Arnoldian authors, everyday life was simply a debased and vulgar terrain within which every sort of stupidity was to be found. The culturalist writers of the 1950s took exception to the reactionary and elitist conception of everyday life, and endeavoured to show that it was a much more interesting locale than had previously been made out.

One of the central interventions in this regard was the early work of Raymond Williams, a scholar from a Welsh working-class background whose experiences at the elitist University of Cambridge had convinced him that the Arnoldian tradition was not just mistaken at the intellectual level, it was also an ideology that justified the ongoing privileges of elite groups in British society (O'Connor 1989). From his first book, *Culture and Society* (1958) onwards,

Williams was concerned to show that the word 'culture' had in essence been hijacked by elitist intellectuals wishing to push their own agendas. Williams, by contrast, wanted to show both how and why this had come about, and how the word could be redefined so as to capture more the vitality and creativity of the 'ordinary people' whom the Arnoldian tradition had dismissed as the unthinking masses. The main issue, as Williams saw it, was that the Arnoldian definition of culture completely severed it from any connections with human social relations. Culture, with a capital 'C', containing lofty ideas and aspirations, came to exist beyond and above 'Society', where the latter was defined as an everyday life characterized by ignorance, routinized thinking and the pursuit of money rather than goodness and beauty (Williams 1976). This conceptual division was subsequently falsely seen as being natural and inevitable, rather than as the product of particular historical conditions (Williams 1958: 43).

With these criticisms of the Arnoldian tradition, Williams was then able to assert that culture in fact is not a wholly isolated and specialized sphere, but rather is part and parcel of the 'whole way of life' of a given society. Williams insisted that far from seeing 'Culture' as a distinct entity (and with a capital 'C'), we should look at culture with a small 'c'. That way, we can recognize that social and cultural factors are always interrelated, and are not separate things, but are actually part of the same overall *socio-cultural process*. In the very appropriately-titled essay, 'Culture is ordinary' (1958/1989: 4), Williams argues that culture is not just 'the arts and learning' (which he defines as 'the special processes of discovery and creative effort'), it is also made up of the 'whole way of life', that is, the common ways of thinking and understanding in a particular society. Thus, on this view culture should be seen as both 'the most ordinary common meanings and the finest individual meanings'.

To see culture as 'ordinary' means seeing how both aspects of culture are fundamentally interrelated and inseparable. The culture of ordinary people and the specialist culture of the elite are part of the same everyday processes of cultural creation and recreation, not antithetical substances. Thus, what had previously been termed 'high culture' was actually part of the ordinary, everyday processes of social life. As a result, the culture of England is as much the product of the lives of working-class people living in the unfashionable provinces as it is of the fashionable, artistic producers drawn from the upper middle class. Much of Williams's later work was oriented towards showing how even the most apparently ethereal and distant activities, like the writing of literature, were in fact part of the everyday activities of human life.

On this basis, Williams was able to make an important point which was both theoretical and political at the same time. Williams denied there was such an entity as 'the masses'. Instead, cultural analysis must begin with the aim of studying real people living in real social and cultural circumstances (Williams 1961/1980: 48). Once this approach is adopted, we could say against elitist views of the ignorance of the 'common herd' that 'the telly-glued masses do not exist; they are the bad fiction of our second-rate social analysis' (Williams 1961/1980: 361).

Williams at this period in his writings did not entirely abandon all of the views of the Arnoldian tradition. He retained the Arnoldian belief that mass-produced commercial culture was in many ways objectively 'bad' – for example, the programming of commercial television, which was just beginning in Britain at this time, with its diet of undemanding entertainments such as soap operas and quiz shows. But the stupidities of this kind of culture are shifted away from the people who view it towards the capitalist culture industries that produce it, and in particular figures such as newspaper barons and other entertainment entrepreneurs (Williams 1961/1980: 366). This was one important feature of Williams's overall attempt to recuperate the 'whole way of life' of those people previously written off as the ignorant masses. A new focus on culture as the ordinary, day-to-day activities of human life was intended to show that far from being passive consumers of mass culture, 'ordinary' people could, indeed should, be examined in terms of the creativity and activity of their cultural and social lives.

The general philosophy of culturalism holds that human beings (almost) always have the capacity to rework the cultural habits they have hitherto been operating with such that they are not merely prisoners of the cultural system in which they live (Williams 1961/1980: 137). Another culturalist writer who made similar arguments to Williams was the historian E. P. Thompson, whose best-known work is *The Making of the English Working Class* (1963/1976). Thompson, a Marxist who had broken with the British Communist Party and its orthodox form of Marxist analysis, wished to set up a form of analysis of culture and society which emphasized Karl Marx's original stress on how history is *made* by ordinary people in their everyday struggles. The emphasis was to be shifted away from seeing (as in certain brands of sociology popular at the time, such as that of Talcott Parsons) abstract 'social structures' as determining how people lived their lives, towards examining how those people created and recreated social and cultural patterns. In terms of the sociological dualism of 'structure' and 'agency', Thompson definitely tended towards emphasizing the latter rather than the former.

Some of the same sorts of point were made by another foundational culturalist author, Richard Hoggart, whose book *The Uses of Literacy* (1957/1962) is one of the founding texts of the culturalist approach (see Jones 1994). One of the aims of the book was to identify the nature of an 'urban culture "of the people"' that had been created in the industrial towns and cities (Hoggart 1957/1962:

24). Similar to Williams's focus on a 'whole way of life', Hoggart described in great detail the everyday aspects of working-class culture, such as how meal-times were organized or how people conducted themselves in the front parlour of their houses. This accumulation of significant details was intended to create a picture of the richness of working-class life, and to show that far from being deadened and impoverished, it was full of subtleties and nuances that would never be observed by an unsympathetic, elitist mode of inquiry. Hoggart regarded this distinctive form of culture as having originally been created by working-class people as a means of accommodating themselves to, and making more comfortable, the often very harsh urban conditions of the 19th and early 20th centuries. A distinctive working-class culture had arisen as a result of the struggles of these people to make their lives liveable.

Hoggart has sometimes been accused of sentimentalizing this 'traditional' working-class culture, overemphasizing its positive aspects such as its strong sense of community and moral responsibility, and downplaying its more unpleasant aspects (drunkenness, wife-beating and so on). Yet his work also embodies what could be taken as one of the characteristic virtues of a culturalist approach: moving analytically away from *assuming* what the working classes are 'like', towards investigating empirically what activities and thoughts actually occur at the grass-roots level. Williams (1958/1989: 12) and other culturalists like Hoggart reject the untested Arnoldian assumption that 'the observable badness of so much widely distributed popular culture is a true guide to the state of mind and feeling, the essential quality of living of its consumers'. Or, as Hoggart (1970: 32) put it, the Arnoldian approach was based on a (false) claim that mass culture 'can be explained simply in commercial and economic terms; that it is wholly and deliberately a devised product, for an audience whose tastes are pretty exactly known'. Hoggart went on to argue that views 'like these … simplify the relationship between the producers and their audiences, the producers and their material, the audiences and the material, and the interactions between different forms and levels of taste'. Thus, in place of this misguided elitist form of thinking, cultural analysis has to involve detailed empirical research on how people actually live, for example, how they really make use of the cultural products they are offered by the culture industries.

Two further aspects of Hoggart's brand of culturalism are important in the present context. First, in his later work he went on to propose a culturalist methodology for comprehending the subtleties and details of life in particular everyday contexts. This method was in fact a development of one aspect of F. R. Leavis's version of literary criticism, the idea that in order really to understand the true significance of a book, you have to subject it to a 'close reading', investigating very carefully the nuances of every word and every sentence. Hoggart adapts this approach such that the analyst can 'read' the fine-grained particularities of life as it is felt, lived and experienced in particular micro-level contexts. In one of his later books he gives this example of the method he has in mind:

> You may find yourself intrigued by the charity shops which proliferate in British towns. Their different roles [in the life of the town] are quite hard to 'read'. Then one day, in a predominantly middle class town, yet another glance at the rack of discarded men's clothing holds your attention. You notice for the first time that much of that clothing, all freshly cleaned and ready to go on display, is casual wear, sports jackets … grey flannels, short leather coats, Barbour jackets – all of very good quality and all, you suddenly see, in styles adopted by elderly professional men. Then you have a vision of middle class widows clearing out their husband's wardrobes as soon as they can bring themselves to do it and carrying it all down to Oxfam [a well-known charity shop] or one of its cousins. A little, whole world.
>
> (Hoggart 1996:183)

Here we again see a distinctively culturalist emphasis, not just in Hoggart's focus on the minutiae of life in the charity shop, but also in the empathic attempt to understand 'from within' the emotional texture of human existence in that time and at that place. Such an approach has certain affinities both with the account of social action offered by the classical sociologist Max Weber and by the 'textualist' anthropologist Clifford Geertz.

The second facet of Hoggart's writings worth focusing on here is the culturalist emphasis on the creativity of ordinary people in how they deal with the social and cultural contexts in which they find themselves. Later scholars drew on the work of Hoggart, Williams and Thompson, and a particular area for later culturalist-inspired studies was the youth cultures that emerged in Britain from the 1950s onwards. Hoggart's work pointed towards a theme that would become central in cultural studies from the mid-1970s onwards, namely the idea that certain aspects of youth culture might display 'an unsuspected energy, an implicit criticism of … mass society … a thrust back from the grass roots, and a kind of imaginative inventiveness that nothing in our assumptions gave us reason to expect' (Hoggart 1982: 128). This point takes us on to the next phase of the history of cultural studies and its approaches to everyday life.

Power and resistance

It is frequently noted that cultural studies was first institutionalized in a university setting in the Centre for Contemporary Cultural Studies (CCCS), at the University of Birmingham, set up in the mid-1960s by Richard Hoggart. The Birmingham Centre became hugely influential from the mid-1970s onwards, by that time under the directorship of another distinguished scholar, the Jamaican-born Stuart Hall (b. 1932). The Centre became renowned for its empirical studies on youth cultures and other contemporary cultural phenomena, especially to do with ethnic groups, and also for its distinctive theoretical and conceptual innovations. The culturalist themes were now not just coupled to new analytical paradigms – the linguistic semiotics of Ferdinand de Saussure (1857–1913), the 'complex Marxism' of Louis Althusser (1918–1990), and the supple Marxism of Antonio Gramsci (1891–1937) – but were also criticized in light of these new ways of thinking.

The result was that from the later 1970s, 'subjectivity' and 'identity' became key areas of analytical inquiry over culturalism's concerns with 'ordinary culture' (Hall 1981), although culturalism's focus on the creative capacities of 'ordinary people' was still generally retained. Indeed, one of the distinctive features of the Birmingham approach to culture developed at this time was that it develops the culturalist focus on 'grass-roots creativity' through the means of pursuing such a theme through the sophisticated theoretical terminologies of both Gramsci's Marxism and Saussure's semiotics. (Althusser's Marxism, with its emphasis on how the structures of capitalist society very much construct individuals' capacities for thought and action, is much less useful in this regard.) One of the most important CCCS texts from this period is the collectively-authored *Resistance Through Rituals* (Hall and Jefferson 1976), which sets out and works through this new conceptual mixture.

Very briefly put, Saussure's semiotics concerns how particular systems of signs (*langue*), such as systems of language, very much shape how individuals use those systems to think and act (particular uses of *langue* by individuals being called acts of *parole*; for a full explanation, see Inglis and Hughson 2003). While Saussure's model emphasizes the power of *langue* over *parole*, we could reverse this emphasis and look at how active and creative individuals can change the various types of *langue* they use in and through their acts of *parole*. Thus, individuals can be creative users of the systems of signs they use – say to express themselves – rather than being the prisoners and puppets of those systems (Jameson 1972). This 'activist' reading of semiotics is one of the distinguishing features of Birmingham-style thinking about culture, as we shall see more concretely in a moment.

Also very briefly put, Gramsci's version of Marxism – written by the author when he was imprisoned by Mussolini's regime in the 1930s – was intended to develop a much more flexible version of Marxist thought than was on offer in more orthodox versions of Marx's ideas. Gramsci's (1971) analysis of 'hegemony' defines it as a condition whereby, first, the ideas of the ruling class in a society are to a large extent accepted by other classes in that society, such that those ideas just seem 'natural' and 'commonsense' rather than as the self-interested impositions of a ruling group; and second, the rule of the ruling class is regarded as legitimate by all the other classes. So far, this resembles closely Marx's ideas about the power of the ruling class being guaranteed by the power its ideologies have over the subordinate classes in society.

In Gramsci's terms, opposing forces and ideologies can be 'incorporated' into the ruling classes' system of power, effectively neutralizing dissent and opposition. However, Gramsci's innovation is to emphasize that in any actual society, matters are never clear-cut. There are always struggles and contradictions occurring, even if under an apparently placid surface of apparent social consensus. The ruling classes constantly have to win the consent of the other classes, because their power, their hegemony, is never simply guaranteed. The power of all powerful groups has to be constantly *achieved* and is certainly never guaranteed. Sometimes the ruling classes have to cut deals with the other classes in order to reach some kind of compromise with them. Sometimes, the ruling classes can lose their position of hegemony, and at that point a society moves into a condition of turmoil if not outright revolution (Harris 1992).

Gramsci himself wavered between a more pessimistic reading of capitalist society – where the ruling classes always seem eventually able to incorporate and tame subordinate class energies and opposition – and a more optimistic reading, whereby hegemony is thoroughly disrupted by cultural forces that are in opposition to it. These Gramscian themes were taken up by scholars associated with the Birmingham CCCS, and were often coupled with a version of Saussurean semiotics, such that creative acts of *parole* could challenge, and sometimes succeed in upsetting, the customary ways of thinking and acting that capitalist society presented as being simply 'natural' and inevitable. Sometimes grass-roots cultural activities could reveal the fabricated nature of what, under conditions of ruling-class hegemony, was passed off simply as common sense. In this way, cultural studies writers pointed to the ways in which everyday realities are both culturally constructed by particular forms of social power, and also open on occasion to contestation and disruption.

As I have noted, these sorts of theoretical themes were worked out in the collectively authored book *Resistance Through Rituals*, which endeavoured to apply them to the understanding of the nature of youth subcultures in Britain after the Second World War. Another study that takes up these sorts of themes is Dick Hebdige's (b. 1951) book *Subculture: The Meaning of Style* (1979), which presents an analysis of the cultural expressions of various British youth subcultures up until that time, such as Teddy Boys in the 1950s and punks in the later 1970s. For Hebdige, these subcultures pose a challenge to ruling class hegemony through indirect means, in particular through their styles of dressing:

> Style in subculture is ... pregnant with significance. Its transformations go 'against nature', interrupting the process of 'normalization'. As such, they are gestures, movements towards a speech which offends the 'silent majority', which challenges the principle of unity and cohesion, which contradicts the myth of consensus.
>
> (Hebdige 1979: 18)

In Hebdige's view, the aim of cultural studies is 'to discern the hidden messages inscribed in code on the glossy surfaces of style, to trace them out as "maps of meaning" which obscurely re-present the very contradictions they are designed to resolve or conceal' (Hebdige 1979: 18). In effect, Hebdige proposes a method of 'reading' the significance of subcultures, in that they are the points in cultural space where the fabricated, power-ridden nature of hegemonically structured 'common sense' and 'everyday reality' are momentarily revealed. For example, the punk's apparently 'outrageous' hairstyle and clothing are condemned by 'mainstream' norms of clothing and appearance; but what the punk's style reveals is that these apparently mainstream sartorial norms (such as men dressing 'respectably' in a suit and tie combination) are not just conventions rather than 'natural' ways of displaying oneself, they are also bound up with dominant modes of power (for instance, suits and ties being hegemonically defined as appropriate garb for the realm of business).

This kind of approach could be criticized for reading too much into the significance of youth subcultural dress codes: are the anti-hegemonic capacities of punk dress really what is motivating people to become punks? Is Hebdige just reading this into their behaviour? Is this not what the punks themselves intended to achieve? Is it valid to claim that their actions are unintentionally anti-hegemonic? Despite these and other related questions, Hebdige's analysis has clear affinities with the Situationists and other European critics of everyday life in its emphasis on revealing the fabricated nature of 'mainstream' practices and attitudes. After all, we could imagine a society where the mainstream dress sense was punk in nature, and where wearing a suit and tie was regarded as an outrageous provocation, thus indicating that what count as 'everyday' practices, in clothing or in any other terms, depend on what powerful groups have defined as 'normal'.

Another important figure in the development of cultural studies in Britain is Paul Willis (b.1945), a figure associated with the Birmingham CCCS, whose work indicates some of the developments there in the later 1970s and on into the 1980s and beyond. Willis's earlier work was focused on the Gramscian idea of 'incorporation', the idea that while cultural energies coming from people in subordinate classes might initially be capable of challenging the hegemonic status quo, they are often eventually channelled and controlled by the institutions that run in the interests of the ruling classes. In his classic study, *Learning to Labour* (1977), of working class 'lads' who were regarded by their teachers as the school troublemakers, Willis argued that the kinds of opposition and resistance to the school regime the boys participated in was ultimately of use to broader capitalist society. The boys engaged in all sorts of pranks and antics, centred around 'having a laff' as they put it, upsetting the authority of the teachers through all their misbehaviour and making life difficult for anyone who sought to impose regulations on them. The more conformist pupils in the school were also teased and bullied, and members of the 'bad boys' group themselves were subjected to mockery by each other. As Willis (1977: 33) noted, 'plans are continually made to play jokes on individuals who are not there: "Let's send him to Coventry when he comes", "let's laugh at everything he says", "let's pretend we can't understand and say 'How do you mean' all the time"'.

The lads' activities do embody a certain moral code – some people deserve ridicule more than others. 'Good' conduct in the eyes of the lads is bad conduct in the eyes of the teachers, the representatives of the wider 'official' world. The lads may have a great deal of fun, but in the end, in Willis's analysis of incorporation, they actually end up disadvantaging themselves, their behaviour leading to little or no qualifications, and thus eventually to a life of long-term unemployment or ill-paid unskilled labour. The capitalist economy 'needs' this class of people, because they will do the lowest level jobs that no one with qualifications would ever want to do. In the end, despite all the apparently 'oppositional' gestures of the lads against 'the system', the latter in the end always wins, because the resistance has been channelled to meet its ends.

This more pessimistic appraisal of grass-roots resistance to authority has been replaced in Willis's more recent work by a more optimistic evaluation of the everyday activities of working-class people. Developing a position that owes a great deal to the earlier culturalist authors described above, Willis (1990, 2005) now regards everyday life as being characterized by the 'common culture' of ordinary people, the ways in which people 'humanize, decorate and invest with meanings their common life spaces and social practices' (Willis 1990: 2). For Willis, this is the terrain of 'grounded aesthetics', ways of thinking, perceiving and evaluating that are just as 'creative' as the activities associated with 'high culture' and the art world. On this (culturalist, and in some ways Gramscian) view, ordinary people are just as inherently 'artistic' (creative, thoughtful, imaginative) as those persons conventionally defined as 'artists'. The ways they choose clothes, select music and discuss television programmes involve 'symbolic creativity' rather than passive acceptance of fads, fashions and opinions proffered by the culture industries. 'Grounded aesthetics' are the popular and everyday equivalents of 'high culture', but they go generally unnoticed and unreflected upon. Willis argues that there is tremendous creative energy in everyday activities such as decorating a home or choosing an ensemble of clothes from charity shops, forms of cultural innovation quite as vital – if not more so – than the officially sanctioned sphere of 'creativity', the art world.

In this regard, Willis's later work has much in common with the ideas of the French sociologist and philosopher Michel de Certeau (1925–1986), who has become one of the key thinkers associated with 'populist' versions of cultural studies (see below). For de Certeau (1997: viii) the everyday culture of the socially disadvantaged, far from being a site of total control by the social institutions of government and media, is in fact characterized by 'a proliferation of inventions in limited spaces'. In other words, people can respond to difficult and unpromising circumstances by developing certain means of coping with them, and certain ways of avoiding the worst aspects of what is imposed upon them by rules and authorities. As de Certeau (1984: xix) puts it, the 'weak ... continually turn to their own ends forces alien to them'. The socially disadvantaged can turn the workings of 'the System' to their own advantage, generally in ad hoc and fleeting ways. They are like poachers operating in woods run by and for the powerful, always finding ways of 'making do' and evading full regulation by the authorities.

An example of this sort of creativity in apparently adverse circumstances is a person who turns the impersonal space of a rented or local authority apartment into their own home by decorating and furnishing it in a manner of their own choosing. Working within the constraints set by the landlord or the authorities about what is permissible and what is not, the renter transforms with 'their acts and memories' a space that is not theirs into one that feels as if it is (de Certeau 1984: xxi). In the same vein, workers who have ways of evading the formal rules of the factory – making cigarette breaks last longer than they should, 'taking the piss' out of the foreman behind his back, using machinery and tools on the boss's time to make things for their own personal use – have found means of operating in the gaps between the regulations.

On this view, 'everyday culture' is made up of all the sly, cunning, unofficial and yet relatively invisible acts of those whom we might otherwise think were the most oppressed of all. Whatever we think of either de Certeau's claims (which are admittedly not greatly grounded in empirical evidence) or Willis's later work (which is more based on evidence), it nonetheless remains the case that they open up valuable vistas, which would otherwise be hidden from view, of contexts where all sorts of things might be going on that would be missed or misrepresented by more 'top-down' means of analysis.

Dealing with popular culture

In many ways, the mass media may be said to be perhaps *the* central social institution with which cultural studies has become concerned in the last 25 years or so. We can divide the study of the media into three basic elements – the analysis of media production, media texts and media audiences (or media consumption). While there has been a plethora of work in cultural studies in recent years on a very diverse range of media texts, much of the recent analysis of media production has been ceded to sociologists (see Golding and Murdock 2000). Beyond this, the most relevant work that has been done, as far as understanding cultural studies approaches to everyday life is concerned, has involved studies of media consumption and analyses of how audience members respond to media texts.

As we have already seen, the desire to ascertain how particular individuals and groups actually responded to and used the products of the mass media was a central concern of the culturalist authors. Both Hoggart and Williams argued that we cannot find out what people actually think and do just by inferring those things from analysing the kinds of films and television programmes they watch or the books and magazines they read. What goes on in everyday contexts of viewing and reading cannot simply be deduced from the messages in media texts themselves. Instead, we have to look at how people actually respond to, deal with, react to and possibly even alter the meanings they are being offered. As Hall (1981) phrased this approach in semiotic terms, media texts may well be 'encoded' with certain meanings, possibly hegemonic ones, by the people who make them (and they may well be unaware that they are doing this, so engrained are certain ideologies in their common-sensical views of the world). But while those processes may be going on at the production end of the media process, these messages are not necessarily 'decoded' (that is, listened to, interpreted, understood) by people in audiences in the ways that either the makers intended, or in manners that reflect and accept the ideologies 'built into' media texts.

One of the key studies in the development of this sort of cultural studies approach to media consumption was David Morley's (b. 1949) well-known study of different groups of viewers, all of whom watched the BBC current affairs programme *Nationwide* (Morley 1980). Morley's research team went into the houses of different types of people and observed how they reacted to and spoke about the programme. Morley found that how much or how little people agreed with the presentation of particular issues greatly depended on which social group they belonged to. Those with conservative political views, such as bank managers, generally had no problems with the presentation of stories about political and economic issues (such as the alleged influence of trade unions on government policies), while those with more left-wing views, such as trade union officials, were very concerned with what they regarded as 'right-wing bias' in such programmes. In the same vein, those occupying more 'comfortable' positions in society, such as white middle-class viewers, felt more accepting of the programme and the way it presented things than those in socially marginalized groups, such as black further education students from inner city areas, who generally rejected the programme and what it stood for as they saw it: middle-class and suburban values. As one of these students argued, the programme seemed not to reflect in any way their experiences and ways of life:

> It didn't show one-parent families, nor the average family in a council estate – all these people they showed seemed to have cars, their own home, property ... don't they ever think of the average family? .... And they show it ... like all the husbands and wives pitching in to cope with problems .... They don't show conflict, fighting, things we know happen. I mean it's just not, to me it's just not a true picture – it's too harmonious, artificial.
>
> (Morley 1981: 59)

The general point that Morley was making was that how people actually respond to what they view – or read, or listen to – depends greatly on what their social and cultural background is. How people make sense of what they are given by the mass media is made possible by the ideas and values they already possess, both from socialization as they have grown up and from the cultural situations they are part of in everyday life. The mass media may give people a plethora of messages, ideas and perspectives every day of their lives (Baudrillard 1987), but what they might take from that media exposure depends both on who they are and who they think they are.

As the discipline of cultural studies has developed over time in various different countries since the early 1980s, it has retained some of the themes and concerns of the Birmingham CCCS, but it has also developed other themes and has drawn upon other thinkers and ways of thinking. A striking case in point is of the English cultural and media studies author John Fiske (b. 1939), who has not only developed the sorts of ideas described above in provocative (some would say, foolhardy) ways, but also drawn on a notably diverse range of theoretical inspirations, a range that reflects the multiplicity of conceptual options cultural studies authors can choose from in the present day. Thinkers that Fiske has selected certain ideas from include the anthropologist Victor W. Turner, the sociologist Pierre Bourdieu, the social philosopher Zygmunt Bauman and the Russian literary philosopher Mikhail Bakhtin, as well as the culturalists described above, de Certeau and Gramsci.

Fiske's main (Gramscian) point is that it is wrong to regard forms of social power, created by certain institutions of the government and the media above all, as 'colonizing' everyday realms of action, thought and feeling. We must also account for forces of what Fiske (1993: 12) refers to as 'bottom-up' power, involving the struggles by 'ordinary' individuals and groups against 'imperialising power in one social context or another'. This sounds very much like

Gramscian analysis, and certainly Fiske's approach could be said to be a form of Gramscianism.

Likewise, Fiske (1987: 316) argues that television viewers engage in 'semiotic guerrilla warfare' (a term first used by the Italian semiotician Umberto Eco in the 1960s), by reinterpreting televized texts to their own liking and often in a way that is oppositional to the interests of programmers and, more broadly, the capitalist system. For Fiske, popular culture is a 'semiotic democracy' in which apparently subordinated persons and groups are empowered to make their own choices of products and interpretations of texts. Fiske's point here is to dispute the pessimism of cultural commentators on both the political left and right who have emphasized the putatively stupefying effects of popular culture. For Fiske, popular culture does not stupefy and enslave, it awakens and empowers; it does not becalm and pacify, it stirs and emboldens. As he puts the point in quite Gramscian terms, 'All popular culture is a process of struggle' (Fiske 1989: 28).

But Fiske pushes these ideas further than others have done, insofar as he implies that the power of social institutions never reaches into everyday viewing and reading practices, the realm of what he calls the 'popular economy'. This is a space which can 'be controlled by the subordinate [groups] who live within it', and is not successfully subjected to the strategies of the powerful (Fiske 1993: 12). It exists in opposition and antagonism to the other sort of space, the 'official' economy inhabited by media organizations, advertising agencies and other institutions of the powerful. The latter are fated forever to try to control the former, but are doomed to fail.

Here Fiske draws very much upon the ideas of Mikhail Bakhtin (1895–1975), an important Russian thinker of the 1930s whose work has many parallels with that of the contemporaneous Gramsci. Although in his famous work *Rabelais and His World* (1984), Bakhtin was referring to medieval society and the importance of carnival celebrations within it, his views are to an extent generalizable to all human societies, and certainly in Fiske's view to modern capitalist societies. Bakhtin (1984: 96) argued that culture is separated into two mutually antagonistic realms, 'the serious and the laughing aspect[s]'. The 'serious' world is made up of officialdom, government and bureaucracy; it is the realm of dominant groups and classes. These seek to control, but never fully succeed in reining in, the energetic cultural forces and modes of thought and expression associated with subordinate groups and classes. The broad masses of the people, far from passively accepting the ideas and values of dominant groups, are highly sceptical of those claims, often mocking and laughing at what they see as the pompous attitudes and activities of their supposed social superiors.

In this line of thought, there is such a thing as genuinely 'popular' culture; it is to be found in the habitual mocking of authority and sly anti-establishment humour of the lower classes and the socially disenfranchised. Fiske argues that there is indeed a truly 'popular' popular culture, one where the apparently socially subordinated are in fact always resisting the blandishments and threats of the powerful, a culture which is constantly mocking, disrespectful and above all not take in by the apparently dominant ways of thinking, acting and feeling.

Fiske (1989: 32) also draws upon some of de Certeau's ideas to depict what he takes to be the 'warfare' that constantly goes on between the 'official' and 'popular' economies. There is, in his view, a constant struggle between the controllers and distributors of cultural products on the one hand, who deploy 'strategies' to maintain their power and to manipulate those who purchase their products, and their audiences on the other, who can and do subvert the intended meanings and usages of these products by means of counter-hegemonic 'tactics'. For Fiske, young people hanging out in shopping malls are 'guerrillas par excellence' who consume the space and images but not the commodities of the mall (Fiske 1989: 37–8). Tactics employed by young people include shoplifting, occupying furniture in food courts and passageways intended for the use of paying customers, and wasting the time of shop workers, as there is no intention to purchase goods either at the time or on future occasions. Strategies deployed by management of stores and the mall to counter these tactics generally involve the increased use of security personnel to move youths on and to apprehend them when necessary. Again, following de Certeau, Fiske (1989: 38) sees youth as always being one step ahead, engaging in forms of 'trickery' which keep the powerful constantly guessing what they are up to and how their transgressive activities might be curtailed.

With Fiske's work, we come to a way of thinking that shares the emphasis of culturalist and Gramscian cultural studies on everyday life and activities as sites of means of resistance and contestation, but which has ditched the other emphasis that those approaches also retained, which concerns the possibility that lower-class struggles might end in failure and resistive energies might be curtailed, channelled and incorporated.

The work of Fiske (and indeed the later work of Willis too) has been dubbed by critics the 'populist' school of cultural studies, and has been charged by those critics of being guilty of a number of serious flaws. At a general level, it is alleged that the Fiskean approach has given up on, indeed has betrayed, the politically engaged critique characteristic of earlier cultural studies (Kellner 1995). More specifically, the severing of any connection between the two 'worlds' of the official economy and the popular economy could be seen as being based less on empirical evidence and more on unfounded theoretical assertion. Such a disconnection between these two levels of reality falsely postulates that the official economy can have no effects at all on the popular economy of 'ordinary' people and everyday life.

According to critics (such as McGuigan 1992) it would be very naive to think that viewers, readers and listeners always think just as they please and are never influenced by the media messages they receive. In addition to a focus on how people actively make sense of what is offered to them by the mass media, we would also have to examine the ways in which certain powerful interests can indeed influence everyday contexts of interpreting and understanding. Examining how on an everyday basis people make sense of, respond to, and give their opinions of stories they read or hear about, does not and should not rule out attempts to understand the various ways in which ideas, attitudes and experiences can be swayed, at least to some degree, by the media.

It is perhaps most reasonable to understand the operation of the media as *sometimes*, for particular reasons, having an identifiable effect on the thinking of *certain* people within *certain* social groups, and at other times having little or no discernible effect at all. Everyday reading, listening and viewing habits might plausibly be regarded as being neither wholly constructed nor at the same time totally unaffected by the messages of mass media texts. The overall point to make here is that viewing and reading habits are best understood as being complex in nature, and as Hoggart and Williams argued 50 years ago, what they involve cannot be prejudged one way or the other (Inglis 2005).

Conclusion

This chapter has examined some of the key contributions to the understanding of everyday affairs put forward by cultural studies scholars in Britain over the last five decades. Cultural studies during this time has developed a range of compelling ideas about everyday life, particularly stressing the richness and creativity of the cultural forces which are to be found in it, and how they may be drawn upon in order, explicitly or implicitly, intentionally or more unintentionally, to resist, challenge and disrupt the institutions, practices and thought-patterns of the socially powerful. This tradition of analysis, which begins with the work of the culturalists in the 1950s, continues to exert influence – sometimes acknowledged, sometimes not – on cultural studies in the present day.

The culturalist and post-culturalist strains in cultural studies offer an intriguing series of insights into the diverse and arguably unexpectedly fecund terrain of the ordinary spheres of human existence. More than that, they can be regarded as a corrective to more 'top down' approaches that see everyday affairs as being thoroughly structured by power relations. In this sense, the sorts of cultural studies approaches examined in this chapter can be seen as complementary to micro-sociological accounts of how macro-level modes of power are both enacted and challenged in micro-level contexts (Denzin 1992), while also emphasizing certain distinctive foci of their own. Far from being merely historical footnotes to the history of cultural studies, as some critics have asserted (see Inglis 2007), culturalist and post-culturalist cultural studies approaches remain very vital resources for understanding how, in even the most apparently banal and debased everyday contexts, there may be activities afoot that are much more rich, interesting and provocative than we might have initially guessed.

While such emphases have made their way into sociology in certain ways and in certain countries, in the future sociologists could profitably pay more attention to them, not least because they can both problematize and enrich conceptualizations of such phenomena as social structures and forms of social power. Likewise, cultural studies scholars themselves might pay some closer attention to the history of their own discipline, for if they wish to find inspiration for their studies of often partly hidden, sometimes wholly subterranean, cultural energies, they would do well to revisit the classic culturalist works which are their ancestral inheritance.

Bibliography

Arnold, Matthew (1869/1995) 'Culture and anarchy', in Stefan Collini (ed.), *Culture and Anarchy and Other Writings*. Cambridge: Cambridge University Press.

Bakhtin, Mikhail (1984) *Rabelais and His World*. Bloomington, IN: Indiana University Press.

Baldwin, Elaine et al. (2004) *Introducing Cultural Studies*, Revised 1st edition. Harlow: Pearson.

Baudrillard, Jean (1987) 'The ecstacy of communication', in Hal Foster (ed.), *Postmodern Culture*. London: Pluto Press.

Bennett, Tony (1998) *Culture: A Reformer's Science*. London: Sage.

De Certeau, Michel (1984) *The Practice of Everyday Life*, Vol. I. Berkeley, CA: University of California Press.

De Certeau, Michel (1997) *Culture in the Plural*. Minneapolis, MN: University of Minnesota Press.

Denzin, Norman K. (1992) *Symbolic Interactionism and Cultural Studies: The Politics of Interpretation*. Oxford: Blackwell.

Fiske, John (1987) *Television Culture*. London: Methuen.

Fiske, John (1989) *Understanding Popular Culture*. Boston: Unwin Hyman.

Fiske, John (1993) *Power Plays, Power Works*. London: Verso.

Golding, Peter and Graham Murdock (2000) 'Culture, communications and political economy', in James Curran and Michael Gurevitch (eds), *Mass Media and Society*. London: Edward Arnold.

Gramsci, Antonio (1971) *Selections from the Prison Notebooks*. London: Lawrence & Wishart.

Hall, Stuart (1981) 'Cultural studies: two paradigms', in Tony Bennett, Graham Martin, Colin Mercer and Janet Woollacott (eds), *Culture, Ideology and Social Process: A Reader*. London: Open University Press.

Hall, Stuart and Tony Jefferson (eds) (1976) *Resistance Through Rituals: Youth Subcultures in Post-War Britain*. London: Hutchinson.

Harris, David (1992) *From Class Struggle to the Politics of Pleasure: The Effects of Gramscianism on Cultural Studies*. London: Routledge.

Hebdige, Dick (1979) *Subculture: The Meaning of Style*. London: Routledge.

Hoggart, Richard (1957/1962) *The Uses of Literacy: Aspects of Working-Class Life with Special Reference to Publications and Entertainment*. Harmondsworth: Penguin.

Hoggart, Richard (1970) 'Literature and society', in *Speaking to Each Other, Volume II: About Literature*. Harmondsworth: Penguin.

Hoggart, Richard (1982) 'Humanistic studies and mass culture', in *An English Temper: Essays on Education, Culture and Communications*. London: Chatto & Windus.

Hoggart, Richard (1996) *The Way We Live Now*. London: Pimlico.

Inglis, David (2005) *Culture and Everyday Life*. London: Routledge.

Inglis, David (2007) 'The warring twins: sociology, cultural studies, alterity and sameness' *History of the Human Sciences*, 20 (2): 99–122.

Inglis, David and John Hughson (2003) *Confronting Culture: Sociological Vistas*. Cambridge: Polity Press.

Jameson, Frederic (1972) *The Prison-House of Language: A Critical Account of Structuralism and Russian Formalism*. Princeton, NJ: Princeton University Press.

Jones, Paul (1994) 'The myth of "Raymond Hoggart": on "founding fathers" and cultural policy.' *Cultural Studies*, 8 (3): 394–416.

Kellner, Douglas (1995) *Media Culture: Cultural Studies, Identity and Politics Between the Modern and the Postmodern*. London: Routledge.

Leavis, F. R. (1932/1990) *Fiction and the Reading Public*. London: Bellew.

McGuigan, Jim (1992) *Cultural Populism*. London: Routledge.

Morley, David (1980) *The 'Nationwide' Audience: Structure and Decoding*. London: British Film Institute.

Morley, David (1981) 'Interpreting television', in *Popular Culture and Everyday Life* (Block 3 of U203 *Popular Culture*). Milton Keynes: Open University Press.

O'Connor, Alan (1989) *Raymond Williams: Writing, Culture, Politics*. Oxford: Blackwell.

Seidman, Steven (1997) 'Relativizing sociology: the challenge of cultural studies', in Elizabeth Long (ed.), *From Sociology to Cultural Studies: New Perspectives*. Oxford: Blackwell.

Thompson, E. P. (1963/1976) *The Making of the English Working Class*. Harmondsworth: Penguin.

Tudor, Andrew (1999) *Decoding Culture*. London: Sage.

Turner, Graeme (1990) *British Cultural Studies: An Introduction*. London: Unwin Hyman.

Williams, Raymond (1958) *Culture and Society 1780–1950*. London: Chatto & Windus.

Williams, Raymond (1976) *Keywords: A Vocabulary of Culture and Society*. Glasgow: Fontana.

Williams, Raymond (1961/1980) *The Long Revolution*. Harmondsworth: Penguin.

Williams, Raymond (1958/1989) 'Culture is ordinary', in *Resources of Hope: Culture, Democracy, Socialism*. London: Verso.

Willis, Paul (1977) *Learning to Labour: How Working Class Kids Get Working Class Jobs*. Farnborough: Saxon House.

Willis, Paul (1990) *Common Culture: Symbolic Work at Play in the Cultural Activities of Young People*. Milton Keynes: Open University Press.

Willis, Paul (2005) 'Invisible aesthetics and the social work of commodity culture', in *The Sociology of Art: Ways of Seeing*. Basingstoke: Palgrave.

CHAPTER 16

Interpretive Interactionism

A Postmodern Approach to Everyday Life[1]

NORMAN K. DENZIN

Introduction

This chapter provides an introduction to understanding and appreciating contemporary everyday life through an interpretive interactionist, postmodern lens. With few exceptions, the rather considerable social science literature on qualitative research methodology and everyday life theory does not contain any extended treatment of the 'interpretive', existential point of view (see Johnson and Kotarba 2007; Kotarba 2007), nor is there any serious account that applies this perspective to the study of postmodern everyday life, to the personal troubles and turning point moments in the lives of interacting individuals. *Interpretive interactionism*, the topic of this chapter, attempts to fill this void.[2] It was, and remains, designed to provide students and scholars in the human disciplines with a relatively accessible description of the critical, existential and interpretive approaches to everyday life.[3] Interpretive interactionism attempts to make the world of lived experience directly accessible to the reader. It endeavours to capture the voices, emotions and actions of those studied. The focus of interpretive interactionist research is on those life experiences that radically alter and shape the meanings people give to themselves and their experiences in everyday life.

Therefore, interpretive interactionism is a special form of everyday life sociology. A dramaturgical sociologist or an ethnomethodologist, for example, focuses on the mundane, staged or taken-for-granted features of daily life. In contrast, the interpretive interactionist studies crises and problematic events in people's lives. These moments, which leave marks on people's lives, are called 'epiphanies', a topic to which I return later. Moreover, the everyday life world does not stand independent of human perception or experience. In these respects, interpretive interactionists find that their own worlds of experience are also a proper subject matter of inquiry. Unlike those sociologists who separate themselves from the worlds they study, the interpretive interactionists participate in the social world so as to better understand and express its emergent properties and features.

C. Wright Mills (1916–1962) states this position in the following words: 'The most admirable thinkers within the scholarly community .... do not split their work from their lives .... What this means is that you must learn to use your life experiences in your intellectual work' (1959: 195–6). Interpretive interactionism asserts that meaningful interpretations of human experience can only come from those persons who have thoroughly immersed themselves in the phenomenon they wish to interpret and understand. In short, we must write out of our own biographies!

In the last two decades there has been an explosion in the field of interpretive sociology and the interpretive, critical paradigms. Interpretive interactionism is part of that explosion. Indeed, like existential and postmodern everyday life sociology, it is part of a larger reformist movement which began at least two decades earlier. The interpretive and critical paradigms, in their several forms, are central to this movement. The appeal of critical interpretive studies across the social sciences and the humanities increases. Some term this the 'eighth moment of inquiry' (Denzin and Lincoln 2005: 20).[4] This is a period of ferment and explosion. It is defined by breaks from the past, a focus on previously silenced voices, a turn to performance texts, a concern with language, the media, the emotions, semiotics, cultural studies, moral discourse, pragmatism and phenomenological sociology. These concerns are folded into ongoing conversations about social justice, equity, democracy, race, gender, class, nation, freedom and community. In this 'eighth moment', at the beginning of the 21st century, there is a pressing demand to show how the practices of critical, interpretive, qualitative everyday life sociology can help change the world in positive ways. It is necessary to examine new ways of making the practices of critical qualitative inquiry central to the workings of a free democratic society. These are some of the issues that an interpretive interactionism attempts to address in a postmodern world.

In this chapter I present an overview of central aspects of this interpretive interactionism and attempt to illustrate its potential. My argument unfolds in several steps. I begin with C. Wright Mills. In *The Sociological Imagination* (1959) he challenged scholars in the human disciplines to develop a point of view and a methodological attitude that would allow them to examine how the private troubles of individuals, which occur within the immediate world of everyday life experience, are connected to wider public issues and to public responses to these troubles.

Mills's sociological imagination was biographical, interactional and historical. His was indeed a call for a postmodern, existential sociology (Kotarba 2007: vii; Johnson and Kotarba 2007: 8–9). Mills understood that human beings live in a secondhand world. Existence is not solely determined by interaction or by social acts. He put this forcefully: 'The consciousness of human beings does not determine their existence; nor does their existence determine their consciousness. Between the human consciousness and material existence stand communications, and designs, patterns, and values which influence decisively such consciousness as they have' (Mills 1963: 375).

Humans have no direct access to reality. Reality, as it is known, is mediated by symbolic representations, by narrative texts and by televisual and cinematic structures that stand between the person and the so-called 'real' world. This world can never be captured directly; we only study representations of it. We study the way people represent their experiences to themselves and to others. Experience can be represented in multiple ways, including rituals, myth, stories, performances, films, songs, memoirs and autobiographies. Experiences come in multiple forms: problematic, routine, ritual, liminal, epiphanic or turning point (see below). Mills wanted his sociology to make a difference in the lives that people lead. He challenged people to take history into their own hands. He wanted to bend the structures of capitalism to the ideologies of radical democracy. Despite the enormous influence of his work, there has never been a methodological discussion of how his theory and method might be put in place. This chapter on interpretive interactionism continues Mills's project by relating it to everyday life.

What is interpretive interactionism?

The perspective presented in this chapter is termed 'interpretive interactionism'. By this rather awkward phrase, as indicated above, I refer to the attempt to make the problematic lived experience of ordinary people visible to the reader. The interpretive interactionist interprets these worlds, their meanings and their representations. The research methods of this approach include performance texts, autoethnography, poetry, fiction, open-ended creative interviewing, document analysis, semiotics, life-history, life-story, personal experience and self-story construction, participant observation and thick description. As such, it is multi-methodological.

The term 'interpretive interactionism', as the above list of methods suggests, signifies an attempt to join traditional symbolic interactionist thought (Blumer 1969; Denzin 1992) with critical forms of interpretive inquiry, including reflexive participant observation and postmodern and literary ethnography, feminist, cultural studies, queer and critical race theory, naturalistic, constructivist and case studies, poetics, life stories and testimonies, creative and active interviewing, participatory action research, narrative, semiotic, interpretive and Foucauldian structural discourse analysis (see Denzin 2007 for a review), just to mention a few.

The interpretive interactionist heritage

Thus, the interpretive interactionist approach is associated with the works of a number of different scholars, including Karl Marx, George Herbert Mead, William James, Charles Sanders Peirce, John Dewey, Martin Heidegger, Hans-Georg Gadamer, Antonio Gramsci, Max Weber, Edmund Husserl, Jean-Paul Sartre, Max Scheler, Maurice Merleau-Ponty, Alfred Schutz, Roland Barthes, Jacques Derrida, C. Wright Mills, Jacques Lacan, Clifford Geertz, Donna Haraway, Patricia Hill-Collins, Gloria E. Anzaldua, bell hooks, Renato Rosaldo, Dorothy Smith, Jürgen Habermas, Stuart Hall, Herbert Blumer, Howard S. Becker, Erving Goffman, Harold Garfinkel and Anselm L. Strauss. It is present in a variety of disciplines such as communications, education, history, anthropology, psychology, sociology, political science, business studies, health and medicine, social work, English and comparative literature, and philosophy, to list a few.

It also goes by a variety of names, including interpretive anthropology or sociology, hermeneutics, cultural studies, phenomenology, symbolic interactionism, ethnomethodology, the case study method and Chicago School sociology. Yet it would be a mistake to categorize all of these approaches under the single label of 'interpretive interactionism'. There are as many differing interpretive perspectives in the social sciences as there are practitioners who utilize the critical, qualitative, naturalistic, literary methodology that defines the approach. Some aim for grounded theory. Others seek out generic processes and concepts. Some impose a grand theoretical structure upon the interpretive enterprise, seeking a totalizing theory of human societies, human actions and human history. Still others formulate ideal types and assess their theory-interpretive work in terms of such concepts as empirical adequacy and empirical validity. Some eschew such subjective concepts as self, intention, meaning and motive, and search only for invariant, publicly observable patterns of action. They seek to locate these patterns in the taken-for-granted structures of the everyday world of conversation and interaction. A book could be written on each of these several varieties of the interpretive approach in the human disciplines.

For obvious reasons, I offer *my* version of interpretation and give it the name 'interpretive interactionism'. This phrase signifies an attempt to join the traditional symbolic interactionist approach with the interpretive, phenomenological works of Martin Heidegger and the tradition associated with hermeneutics.

Interpretive interactionism also draws upon recent work in feminist social theory, postmodern theory and the critical-biographical method formulated by C. Wright Mills, Jean-Paul Sartre and Maurice Merleau-Ponty. It aims to create and construct studies, performances and texts which make sense of and criticize the postmodern period of human experience (Denzin 2003, 2008). A more formal definition of 'interpretive interactionism' is:

> Interpretive interactionism seeks to bring lived experience before the reader. A major goal of the interpretive writer is to create a text that permits a willing reader to share vicariously in the experiences that have been captured. When this occurs, the reader can naturalistically generalize his or her experiences to those that have been captured. This is what thick description does. It is a form of performative writing. It creates verisimilitude, a space for the reader to imagine his or her way into the life experiences of another. Thick descriptions capture and record the voices of lived experience or 'the prose of the world'.
>
> (Denzin 2001: 99)

As such, interpretive interactionist research has the following characteristics:

- It is existential, interactional and biographical.
- It is idiographic.
- It is based on sophisticated rigour and Jean-Paul Sartre's progressive-regressive method.
- It can be both pure and applied.
- It is anchored in the 'eighth moment' and builds on criticisms of positivism and postpositivism.
- It is concerned with the social construction of gender, history, power, emotion, effects and knowledge.

I shall here, in some detail, elaborate on each these characteristics of interpretive interactionism.

The existential, interactional and biographical text

The interactional text (Goffman 1983) is present whenever an individual is located in a social situation. It is ubiquitous. It is interaction itself. Interpretive interactionist studies collect and analyse existentially experienced, interactional and biographical texts. This is called 'doing existential ethnography' (Fontana 2007).

The works of Erving Goffman (1922–1982) and Harold Garfinkel (b. 1917) and their students are commonly associated with the study of face-to-face interaction and its interpretation (see Goffman 1959, 1961a, 1961b, 1967, 1971, 1974, 1981;

Garfinkel 1967; Garfinkel, Lynch and Livingston 1981). They have approached this topic from dramaturgical, linguistic, structural, cultural and phenomenological perspectives. They have shown how the world in front of us can be read and interpreted in terms of the rituals and taken-for-granted meanings that are embedded in the interaction process. They have disrupted this order so as to expose its underlying normative assumptions. They have stressed its socially constructed nature and they have examined its fragile features. They have connected the micro-world of interaction to the larger macro-structures of society, including gender, race and ethnicity, work, medicine, psychiatry, science, play and leisure.

There are three problems with this body of work, as it bears on the interpretive interactionist agenda. First, it is non-biographical and ahistorical. It does not locate interactional texts within the larger, historical social structure. Second, it seldom addresses existentially meaningful or relevant interactional experiences. Third, it inserts externally derived conceptual schemes into the reading of the interaction text. It typically reads interaction texts in terms of broader structural and ritual issues. It therefore seldom deals with the problem-at-hand as these problems are experienced and addressed by the interactants in question. In short, these authors study 'moments and their persons', not 'persons and their moments' of interaction.

Ideographic versus nomothetic research

Garfinkel's and Goffman's approaches to the interaction text are nomothetic and etic, and not ideographic and emic (Allport 1942; Pike 1954). Nomothetic studies seek abstract generalizations about phenomena and often offer non-historical explanations. Conversely, ideographic research assumes that each individual case is unique. This means that every interactional text is unique and shaped by the individuals who create it. This requires that the voices and actions of individuals must be heard and seen in the texts that are reported. Interpretive interactionist studies are ideographic and emic. While Goffman's and Garfinkel's work establishes the structural regularities present in interaction, their ahistorical, non-biographical stance does not permit the discovery of what a particular interactional moment means to its interactants. Their ability to speak to the epiphany or to the moment of existential crisis in a person's life is thereby severely restricted.

Naturalism, sophisticated rigour and the progressive-regressive method

Interpretive interactionists employ a strategy of research which is naturalistic and is located in the natural worlds of everyday social interaction. It tells stories. It relies upon 'sophisticated rigour' (Denzin 1989: 234–5), which is a commitment to make your interpretive materials and methods as public as possible. Sophisticated rigour describes work that employs multiple methods, seeks out diverse empirical situations and attempts to develop interpretations and personal stories grounded in the worlds of lived experience.

I have elsewhere advocated the use of Jean-Paul Sartre's (1963: 85–166) so-called 'progressive-regressive' method of analysis (Denzin 2001: 41). I have also termed this the 'critical-interpretive method'. The progressive-regressive/critical-interpretive method implements an emic framework. It seeks to situate and understand a particular class of subjects within a given historical moment. Progressively, the method looks forward to the conclusion of a set of acts or actions undertaken by a subject. The term 'progressive' refers here to the forward, temporal dimension of the interpretation process. Regressively, the method works back in time to the historical, cultural and biographical conditions that moved the subject to take or experience the actions being studied. By moving forward and backward in time the subject's projects and actions are situated in time and space. The unique features of the subject's life are illuminated in the interactional episodes that are studied.

Moreover, interpretive interactionism assumes that every human being is a so-called 'universal singular' (Sartre 1981: ix). No individual is ever just an individual. Each person must be studied as a single instance of more universal social experiences and social processes. The person, Sartre (1981: ix) states, is 'summed up and for this reason universalized by his epoch, he in turn resumes it by reproducing himself in it as a singularity'. Every person is like every other person, but like no other person. Interpretive interactionist studies, with the focus on the epiphany, attempts to uncover this complex interrelationship between the universal and the singular, between private troubles and public issues in a person's life. In this way, all interpretive interactionist studies are biographical and historical. They are always fitted to the historical moment that surrounds the subject's life experiences.

Pure and applied interpretive researchers

There are two basic types of interpretive researchers. One type engage in pure interpretation for the purposes of building meaningful interpretations of social and cultural problematics. These scholars aim to construct interpretations that are grounded in social interaction. For example, Anselm L. Strauss's work on chronic illness and medical technology has as its goal a grounded theory that 'accounts for a pattern of behaviour which is relevant and problematic for those involved' (Strauss 1987: 34). The second type of interpretive work is interpretive evaluation, or what Sherry B. Ortner terms 'addressing current social problems' (1997: 5). Such scholars conduct research on a fundamental social problem in order to provide policy makers with pragmatic, action-oriented recommendations for alleviating the problem. On the contrary, interpretive interactionist evaluation research, as a third option, is conducted from the point of view of the person experiencing the problem; it sides, not with policy makers, but with the underdogs who policy makers make policies for.

Criticisms of positivism and postpositivism

Traditional sociological research, in its various forms, has assumed that social processes can be captured within the strict cause and effect paradigm of positivism and postpositivism. This research paradigm assumes the following:

- 'Objective' reality can be captured.
- The observer can be separated from what is observed.
- Observations and generalizations are free from situational and temporal constraints: that is, they are universally generalizable.
- Causality is linear and there are no causes without effects, no effects without causes.
- Social inquiry is value-free.

The interpretive interactionist perspective opposes each of these assumptions. Interpretive interactionist studies replace the 'why' question with the 'how' question. That is, how is social experience or a sequence of social interaction organized, perceived and constructed by interacting individuals? How, then; not why.

Gender, history, power, emotion, effects and knowledge

The interpretive interactionist is sensitive to the social construction of gender, history, power, effects, emotion and knowledge. The feminist critique of postpositivism locates 'gender asymmetry' at the centre of the social world. It makes the doing of gender a basic focus of research (Olesen 2005). The gender stratification system means there is no gender-free knowledge.

Not only gender but also history is central to interpretive interactionism. History enters the research process in four ways. First, the events and processes that are studied unfold over time. In this sense they have their own inner sense of history or temporality. Second, these events occur within a larger historical social structure. This structure shapes, influences and constrains the processes under investigation. This structure includes language, in its various formations, micro- and macro-power relationships and taken-for-granted cultural meanings, which structure everyday social interactions and social experiences. History operates, third, at the level of individual history and personal biography. Each individual brings a personal history to the events that are under investigation. Fourth, the researcher has a personal, historical relationship to the interpretive process and this personal history also shapes research.

History interacts with power and emotionality. Power permeates every structure of society, including gender relations. For Michel Foucault (2000: 343) power exists as a process, in the dominance relations between men and women, between groups and institutions, and so on. Interpretive interactionist research also inevitably involves power. Discourses on truth and knowledge are implicated in relations of power. Micro-power relations influence every aspect of research. They exist at the level of the researcher gaining access to the field situation so that observations can be made. They exist, as a matter of course, in the world that is studied, for it is structured and organized in terms of authority relations. They exist in terms of the research formats, observational methods and experimental and quasi-experimental research designs the investigator employs. Science enters the research setting as power-in-practice. The researcher, that is, carries the power and prestige of science into the field.

Consequently, Foucault insists that we look at cultural forms and practices not in terms of their 'meanings' but in terms of their effects both on those to whom they are addressed and on the world in which they circulate. The effects of a discourse are seen in the experiences it produces. This focus on effects helps illuminate the importance of power within any system of discourse. Systems of meaning are always embedded in systems of domination and power.

Moreover, close inspection reveals that emotionality is everywhere present in interpretive interactionist research. It is present in the moods and feelings persons bring to the study. It is present in the lives of those who are studied. It is present in the interactions that go on between researchers and subjects. It is present in the observations that are gathered. It is part of power and of being powerful or powerless. An anatomy of power and feeling in the interpretive interactionist study reveals that detached, unemotional, purely cognitive interpretation is impossible.

Finally, knowledge is a belief, or set of beliefs, about a particular segment of reality. Knowledge is socially and politically constructed. Knowledge is intimately related to power. Those who have power create and then define the situations where knowledge is applied. Those with power determine how knowledge about situations is to be gained. Those who have power determine how knowledge will be defined. Those who have power also define what is and what is not knowledge.

How to open up the world to interpretation

As a distinctly qualitative approach to social research, interpretive interactionism attempts to make the world of lived experience visible to the reader. As indicated above, the focus of interpretive research is on those life experiences that radically alter and shape the meanings people give to themselves and their life projects. This existential thrust (Sartre 1956) sets this kind of research apart from other interpretive approaches which examine the more mundane, taken-for-granted properties and features of everyday life (see Garfinkel 1967; Goffman 1974; Johnson and Kotarba 2007). It leads to a specific focus on the 'epiphany'.

The subject's experiences and the epiphany

According to interpretive interactionism, those interactional moments that leave marks on people's lives have the potential of creating transformational experiences for the person. They are 'epiphanies'. In them personal character is manifested and made apparent. By recording and interpreting these experiences in detail the researcher is able to illuminate the moments of crisis that occur in a person's life. They are often interpreted, both by the person and by others, as turning-point experiences (Strauss 1959). Having had this experience, the person is never again quite the same.

Perhaps an example will make this concept of the epiphany more apparent. In the Christian religion the epiphany is a festival observed on 6 January, commemorating the manifestation of Christ to the Gentiles in the persons of the Magi. In this sense, the epiphany is a manifestation or sign of the Christian deity. Now consider the following moment in the life of the late Martin Luther King Jr. On the night of 27 January 1956 King, at the age of 26, had received several telephone threats on his life. Unable to sleep, doubting his place in the Montgomery bus boycott and his leadership position in the Southern Christian Leadership Conference, he sat alone at his kitchen table. He heard an inner voice that he identified as Jesus Christ. King stated: 'I heard the voice of Jesus .... He promised never to leave me, never to leave me alone.' The historian Howell Raines comments on the use of this episode in David J. Garrow's biography of King, *Bearing the Cross: Martin Luther King Jr. and The Southern Christian Leadership Conference*:

> Other biographers have noted this episode, but Mr. Garrow asks us to regard it as the transforming moment, the most important night in his life, the one he always would think back to in future years when the pressures seemed to be too great.
>
> (Raines 1986: 33)

Raines notes that King returned again and again in his later life to this epiphany, referring to it as 'the vision in the kitchen'.

James Joyce's *The Dubliners* (1906/1976) also employed this method of the epiphany. Indeed, he described his original notes for the book as epiphanies. Harry Levin discusses Joyce's use of this technique:

> Joyce underscored the ironic contrast between the manifestation that dazzled the Magi and the apparitions that manifest themselves on the streets of Dublin; he also suggested that these pathetic and sordid glimpses ... offer a kind of revelation. As the part, significantly chosen, reveals the whole, a word or detail may be enough to exhibit a character or convey a situation.
>
> (Levin 1976:18)

Consider another form of family or domestic violence, wife-battering. Here is an example of an epiphany as it is displayed in the life of a battered Korean wife. This woman is now separated from her husband:

> I have been beaten so many times severely in the early days of the marriage. But I would tell you the recent one. About 8 months ago, I was beaten badly. In the middle of the beating I ran out of the house .... But he followed and caught me. He grabbed my hair and dragged me to the house. He pushed me into the bathroom and kicked my body with his foot. My baby was crying .... Now I suffer from a severe headache. When I go out to the grocery store, I can't see items. I feel pain in my eyes. And I feel dizzy .... I can't forgive him! I hate, hate, hate him so much .... Is this because I was born a woman?
>
> (Cho 1987: 236)

Another battered wife described her experiences in the following words:

> He didn't let me sleep. We sat in the living room together from midnight till early in the morning. He forced me to sit down on the sofa while he drank beers. This went on for about a month. Every night he said the same story. It was like to turn on the recorder. He said that I am a ruthless bitch. He said he doubted if I was a virgin when I married him .... In the early days of the marriage, he used to force me to be naked and then he drank looking at me. Then he told me to dance.
>
> (Cho 1987: 231)

In these excerpts victims of family violence vividly report how they experienced battering. Their words bring the experience alive. These experiences became part of the turning-point moments in their relations with their husbands, and Joo-Hyun Cho (1987, 1988) has connected these experiences to the subsequent dissolution of these marriages.

Four experiential structures

It is possible to identify four major structures, types of existentially problematic moments or epiphanies in the lives of individuals. First, there are those moments that are major and touch every fabric of a person's life. Their effects are immediate and long-term. Second, there are those epiphanies that represent eruptions or reactions to events that have been going on for a long period of time. Third are those events that are minor, yet symbolically representative of major problematic moments in a relationship. Fourth, and finally, are those episodes whose effects are immediate, but their meanings are only given later, in retrospection, and in the reliving of the event. I propose to give the following names to these four structures of problematic experience: *the major epiphany, the cumulative epiphany, the illuminative, minor epiphany* and the *relived epiphany.* (Of course, any epiphany can be relived and given new retrospective meaning.) These four types may build upon one another. A given event may, at different phases in a person's or relationship's life, be first major, then minor, then later relived. A cumulative epiphany may, of course, erupt into a major event in a person's life. I here offer examples of each type.

In the major epiphany, an experience shatters a person's life and makes it never the same again. Martin Luther King Jr.'s hearing the voice of Jesus is an example. The cumulative epiphany occurs as the result of a series of events that have built up in the person's life. A woman, after years of battering, murders her husband or files for divorce. In the minor or illuminative epiphany, underlying tensions and problems in a situation or relationship are revealed. The account from Cho above, of the wife who was repeatedly battered by her husband, illustrates this form of the epiphany. As she stated, she had been beaten many times in the early days of her marriage. In the relived epiphany, a person relives, or goes through again, a major turning-point moment in their life. Cho's wife was reliving her last battering experience with her husband. Or consider the death of Michelle Rosaldo, a cultural anthropologist who fell to her death while on a field trip with her husband in 1981. The meaning of this death to her husband, Renato, was still being determined two years after it happened. The death was a major event in his life (Rosaldo 1984). It led him to reinterpret his entire relationship to the field of anthropology.

Let us take another example. Four persons are seated around a family kitchen table. A window looks out into the backyard onto a bird feeder. The individuals are Jack, a 55-year-old bachelor, his girlfriend, Shelly, Jack's mother Mae, and Paul, a 47-year-old recently divorced friend of Jack. Jack has brought his new girlfriend home to meet his mother. Paul has recently met Mae. Mae and Jack have been fighting for years over Jack's inability to settle down and become a respectable married man. The following conversation was reported:

Mae: *Looking out the window.* 'My word, that bird feeder's empty. Seems like it's always empty these days'.

Jack: 'I'll fill it, Ma. No problem. Birdseed still where it always was?'

Mae: 'Ya, now don't go and fill it more than half-way up. *Turning to Shelley and Paul, in front of Jack.* 'He never listens to me. He always spills seed on the ground. He's just like a little boy.'

Jack: *Goes out the backdoor, gets the birdseed from the wood shed, takes the sack of seed to the bird feeder, pulls the sack into the feeder, until it overflows, with seed streaming down to the ground.*

Mae: *Shouting, through the walls of the living room:* 'You idiot, I said half-full! Can't you remember anything! He never listens to me. It's always been like this. Why can't he do what I want him to?

This interaction between a mother and her son may be read as revealing underlying tensions and conflicts in their relationship. It is not a turning-point moment, yet it brings to the surface and illuminates what has been, in the past, a break or rupture in the relationship. The son has refused to live his life as his mother wants him to. His refusal to follow her instructions on how to put birdseed in the bird feeder symbolically speaks to this rupture. It is a minor epiphany.

Studying epiphanies

As the investigator grounds their study in lived experience, major, cumulative, minor and relived epiphanies will be observed and represented. Each of the above types of the epiphany must, as much as possible, be collected and studied within any interpretive interactionist investigation. This is the case if a thickly described and thickly interpreted picture of problematic experienced is to be produced. This is what is involved in doing 'existential ethnography'.

Locating the epiphany

The epiphany occurs in those problematic interactional situations where the subject confronts and experiences a crisis. Often a personal trouble erupts into a public issue, as when a battered woman flees her home and calls the police, or an alcoholic enters a treatment centre for alcoholism. Epiphanies occur within the larger historical, institutional and cultural arenas that surround a subject's life. The interpretive scholar seeks, as C. Wright Mills (1959: 5) observed, to understand 'the larger historical scene in terms of its meaning for the inner life and the external career of a variety of individuals'. This asks the scholar to connect personal problems and personal troubles to larger social, public issues. 'Troubles' are personal matters, like becoming an alcoholic or being a battered wife. 'Issues' have to do with public matters and institutional structures, like treatment centres for alcoholism or shelters for battered women. Troubles, Mills states:

> occur within the character of the individual and within the range of his [her] immediate relations with others; they have to do with his [her] self and those limited areas of social life of which he [she] is directly and personally aware .... A trouble is a private matter: values cherished by an individual are felt by him [her] to be threatened. Issues, on the other hand, have to do with matters that transcend these local environments of the individual and the range of his [her] inner life. They have to do with the organization of many such milieux into the institutions of an historical society as a whole .... An issue is a public matter: some value cherished by publics is felt to be threatened.
>
> (Mills 1959: 8)

Troubles are always biographical. Public issues are always historical and structural. Biography and history thus join in the interpretive process. This process always connects an individual life and its troubles to a public historical social structure. Personal troubles erupt in moments of individual and collective crisis. They are illuminated, often in frightening detail, in the epiphanies of a person's life. These existential crises and turning-point encounters thrust the person into the public arena. His or her problem becomes a public issue. Our task, Mills (1959: 226) argues, is to learn how to relate public issues to personal troubles and to the problems of the individual life.

Strategically, the researcher locates epiphanies in those interactional situations where personal troubles become public issues. They work back from the public to the private, seeking out persons whose troubles have come to the public's attention. Cho (1987), as I showed above, located battered women by going to a centre for battered women in Seoul. My own studies of alcoholism worked backward from treatment centres and Alcoholics Anonymous meetings to the personal lives of alcoholics (Denzin 1993).

Liminality, ritual and the structure of the epiphany

Epiphanies are experienced as social dramas; as dramatic events with beginnings, middles and endings. Epiphanies represent ruptures in the structure of daily life. Victor W. Turner (1986: 41) reminds us that the theatre of social life is often structured around a four-fold processual ritual model involving breach, crisis, redress, reintegration or schism. Each of these phases is organized as a ritual. Thus, there are rituals of breach, crisis, redress, reintegration and schism. Redressive rituals, for example, 'include divination into the hidden causes of misfortune, conflict, and illness' (Turner 1986: 41). Many rituals are associated with life-crisis ceremonies, particularly those of puberty, marriage and death. Turner contends that redressive and life-crisis rituals 'contain within themselves a liminal phase, which provides a stage ... for unique structures of experience' (1986: 41). Liminal phases of experience are detached from daily life and are characterized by the presence of ambiguous and monstrous images, sacred symbols, ordeals, humiliation, gender reversals, tears, struggle, joy and remorse. The liminal phase of experience is a kind of no-person's land 'betwixt and between the structural past and the structural future' (Turner 1986: 41). Epiphanies are such ritually structured liminal experiences that are connected to moments of breach, crisis, redress, reintegration and schism. It is as such that epiphanies must be studied by the interpretive interactionist researcher.

The mystory text and its performance[5]

A critical, performative social science grounded in interpretive interactionism attempts to create a writing form that captures the nuances of such epiphanies. The 'mystory' is one such form. The mystory is simultaneously a personal mythology, a public story, a personal narrative and a performance that critiques. It is an interactive, dramatic performance. The mystory is a montage text, cinematic and multi-media in shape, filled with sounds, music, poetry and images taken from the writer's personal history. This personal narrative is grafted into discourses from popular culture. It positions itself against the specialized knowledges that circulate in the larger society. The audience co-performs the text with the author, and the writer, as narrator, functions as a guide, a commentator or a co-performer.

Consider Hugo Campuzano's (2001) performance narrative 'In the name of tradition'. There are five speakers:

Speaker One: 'In the name of tradition, how much tradition should I follow? ... I have been in this country for 24 years I have grown up watching the Cosby Show, wearing Payless shoes.... I have lived with my Mexican family in a Mexican community. I have grown up eating tortillas, believing in the La Virgen de Guadalupe.'

Speaker Two: 'Don't get me wrong, I love being Mexican .... But I have to tell you, it is tough being Mexican. Take marriage, for example. My mom as told me ... that when I get married, I should go to Mexico and find myself a nice Mexican girl ..... She means I should go to Mexico ... and find a nice quiet girl who knows how to cook and clean .... How do I tell my mom I do not want someone like her?'

Speaker Three: *'Must tradition go on in the name of tradition?'*

Speaker Four: 'My mom's insistence that I marry a nice Mexican girl also makes me think about my sisters. Would she want my sisters to be nice Mexican girls? They have certainly been in training all their lives .... I remember a conversation I had a few years back with my siblings. We were talking about marriage and future families in this all-night conversation, everything that was coming out of our mouths was how we were not going to follow in our parent's footsteps. My brother and I were saying we were not going to be like our father, an authoritarian machista who uses the name of tradition to do things the way he wants to. My sisters were saying that they were not going be like our mother, a passive woman who in the name of keeping the family together ... participated in her own silencing. I guess there's just no room for tradition in my family.'

Speaker Five: *'Must tradition go on in the name of tradition?'*

Campuzano splits his voice into five speaking parts. This moves his narrative through a complex space. There are improvised elements in the performance. Each speaker brings a gendered presence and personal style of speaking to the text. At the same time, every person in the room, speaker or listener, brings to this text a set of personal memories involving family, tradition, marriage, mothers, fathers, daughters and sons. This means that Campuzano's mystory gets tangled up in other people's lives, unsettling and troubling these deep cultural narratives and myths surrounding duty and tradition and family.

In the mystory performance event a stage as such is not used; the wall between performers and audience disappears because all parties to the performance are also performers. The script puts into words the world of experience, actions and words that were, or could have been, and will be spoken here. The script, like Campuzano's, brings this world and its ethnodramas alive; reports on it, in some fashion; then criticizes the structures of power that operate therein. As Campuzano asks, 'Must tradition go on in the name of tradition?'

The text delineates specific characters, and these characters are caught up in dramatic conflict, which moves towards some degree of resolution at the end of the narrative. Simplistic characterizations based on traditional oppositions (male/female and so on) are avoided; difference, not conflict is privileged. There can be as many characters as there are readers available to do readings. The same reader can read the parts of the same and different characters. Every performance event is different; different readers, different lines, different meanings and different interpretations, yet in every instance a story is told and performed, a story with political consequences, a story that shows how the world can be changed, how it could be.

Of course, the mystory text is not easily constructed. It involves the hard interpretive work of editing personal, biographical reality. Editing biographical experience produces a dramatic reinterpretation of what has been felt and lived by the person, moments of crisis and pain. What will be edited is determined by what has been remembered, collected and written down, notes to the self, the *Rashomon* effect turned inside out. From the several layers and versions of the biographical field text, the writer aims to tell a story with some degree of dramatic power. Editing or crafting the text will involve many decisions. These include what words to put in the mouths of which characters, who the characters will be, and how many readers there will be. The focus is always on showing, not telling. Minimal interpretation is favoured; less is more.

The mystory text begins with those moments that define the crisis in question, a turning point or epiphany in the person's life. Gregory Ulmer (1989, 1994) suggests the following starting point:

> Write a mystory bringing into relation your experience with three levels of discourse – personal (autobiography), popular (community stories, oral history or popular culture), [and] expert (disciplines of knowledge). In each case, use the punctum or sting of memory to locate items significant to you.
> (Ulmer 1989: 209)

The sting of memory locates the moment, the beginning. Once located, this moment is dramatically described, fashioned into a text to be performed. This moment is then surrounded by those cultural representations and voices that define the experience in question. These representations are contested, challenged.

Mystories, liminality and utopia

Focusing on epiphanies and liminal moments of experience, the writer imposes a narrative framework on the text. This framework shapes how experience will be represented. It uses the devices of plot, setting, characters, characterization, temporality, dialogue, protagonists, antagonists and showing, not telling. As mentioned, the narration moves through a four-stage dramatic cycle, emphasizing breach, crisis, redress, reintegration or schism, and following Victor W. Turner (1986), this narrative model stresses conflict, tension, crisis and the resolution of crises.

Frederic Jameson (1990) reminds us that works of popular culture are always already ideological and utopian. Shaped by a dialectic of anxiety and hope, such works revive and manipulate fears and anxieties about the social order. Beginning with a fear, problem or crisis, these works move characters and audiences through the familiar four-stage dramatic model of conflict, tension, crisis and resolution. In this way, they offer kernels of utopian hope. They show how these anxieties and fears can be satisfactorily addressed by the existing social order (Jameson 1990: 30). Hence the audience is lulled into believing that the problems of the social order have in fact been successfully resolved.

The mystory occupies a similar ideological space, except it functions as critique. The mystory is also ideological and utopian; it begins from a progressive political position stressing the politics of hope. The mystory uses the methods of drama and personal narrative to present its critique and utopian vision. It presumes that the social order has to change if problems are to be resolved successfully in the long run. If the status quo is maintained, if only actors and not the social order change, then the systemic processes producing the problem remain in place. To provide an example, Troy Anthony LaRaviere (2001) began his mystory this way:[6]

> *My first memory is my mother's first memory of me.*
> *She's told me this story so many times that I feel like I'm telling the story from my own memory. As if I remember being in the delivery room …*
> 'Boy I remember that labour I had with you!
> Lord Jesus! You was the worst of all of 'em'.
> 'You came out weighing ten pounds and five ounces.'
> 'And once you came out, the doctors and the nurses just looked at you like they was in shock. Then they kept calling other doctors in to come and look at you'.
> 'But they wouldn't let me see you. My legs was propped up with sheet in the way. So I couldn't see nothin'...'
> Doctor: 'We never seen anything like this!'

'And they just kept calling more doctors in, and all the doctors kept saying the same thing ... But they still wouldn't let me see you'.
Finally I just started yelling: 'Let me see my child. What's wrong with my baby?!'
'The doctor finally looked at me and said: 'Ma'am, this is the cleanest baby I've ever seen.' They gave you to me and you didn't have fluid or blood on you. Not one drop.'
'Perhaps all the blood was used up from hundreds of years of doing nothing but bleeding'.
When the doctor cut the umbilical cord, cutting me off from the source of all that was life -giving; my mother
How different was that cut from the cut his great, great, great, great, great-grandfathers made when they cut us off from our African mother culture and all in it that was life-giving to us .... All that was life-giving to me?
But it wasn't at my birth that the cord was torn
It was severed from me long before I was born....
I remember the work I must do to insure my name is called.

Remembering his birth, as told to him by his mother, LaRaviere connects this birth memory to the struggles of all African-Americans to maintain a living connection to family and a mother culture. Ending on a utopian note, he bitterly criticizes the larger culture which has cut African-Americans off from their mother culture.

History and biography

Perhaps the myth of 'a total cinema' (Bazin 1967) extends to sociology and anthropology. When cinema was born, film makers believed that their cameras would faithfully and realistically capture and reproduce social life. They quickly abandoned this myth and turned to a narrower, narrative focus. Perhaps we cannot produce a sociology that realistically captures the postmodern world out there. It is simply too complex, too diverse, too heterogeneous. Our focus must become narrower.

Like the film maker, however, we can tell tiny stories, mystories or epiphanies, about the postmodern human condition. We can show how these histories we live, the freedoms we gain and lose, are constrained by larger cultural narratives which work their interpretive ways behind our backs. Mindful of the logics that structure our tales, we can turn to a personal, cinematic-ethnographic existential, interpretive interactionist sociology which begins always with our personal experiences and works outward and forward, attempting to discover a mode and style of representation that universalizes our experiences.

Our dilemma is this, as it always has been:

> By the time we understand the pattern we are in, the definitions we are making for ourselves, it is too late to break out of the box. We can only live in terms of the definitions, like the prisoner in the cage .... Yet, the definitions we have made of ourselves is ourselves .... To break out of it, we must make a new self. But how can the self make a new self when the self when the selfness which it is, is the only substance from which the self can be made?
> (Warren 1959: 351)

It is to be hoped that the postmodern pattern is by now more clear. It is, however, not too late to break out of the box. The self which emerges will itself be a tangled web of all that has come before.

By stressing the interrelationship between history and biography, interpretive interactionism also focuses on how the postmodern self is anchored in the shifting structures of postmodernism. These structures are filtered through and defined by the electronic and print media, by television, the new media and the cinematic apparatus itself. Postmodernism is defined by the following terms: a nostalgic, conservative longing for the past coupled with an erasure of the boundaries between the past and the present; an intense preoccupation with the real and its representations; a pornography of the visible; the commodification of sexuality and desire; a consumer culture which objectifies a set of masculine and feminine cultural ideals; intense emotional experiences shaped by anxiety, alienation, resentment and a detachment from others.

The cinema, the new media, television, YouTube, MySpace and blogs are the new postmodern reality. Members of the contemporary world are voyeurs adrift in a sea of symbols, images and personal stories. They know and see themselves through these visual apparatuses. An essential part of the contemporary postmodern global scene can be found in the images and meanings that flow from these mediated sites. Thus, the postmodern terrain is defined almost exclusively in visual terms, including the representations of the real seen through the camera's eye, captured in digital and videotape format, and given in the moving picture. In these traces of the visible, the figure of postmodern woman, man and child emerge, as if out of a misty fog. The search for the meaning of the postmodern moment is a study in looking. It can be no other way.

The ingredients of the postmodern self are given in three performances connected to race, class and gender. These cultural identities are filtered through the personal troubles and the emotional experiences that flow from the individual's interactions with postmodern everyday life. These existential troubles loop back into the dominant cultural themes of the postmodern era, including the cult of Eros and its idealized conceptions of love and intimacy.

The raw economic, racial and sexual edges of contemporary life produce anxiety, alienation, radical isolation from others, madness, violence and insanity. Large cultural groupings (young women, the elderly, queers, racial and ethnic minorities) are unable either to live out their ideological versions of the neo-liberal dream or to experience personal happiness. They are victims of anhedonia; they are unable to experience pleasure. They bear witness to an economy, a political ideology and a global popular culture which can never deliver the promised goods to their households. As a consequence, a 'ressentiment' (Scheler 1912/1961) based on the repeated inability to experience the pleasant emotions promoted by the popular culture takes hold. Self-hatred, anger, envy, false self-pride and a desire for revenge against the other are experienced. Sexism, racism, and homophobia are the undersides of ressentiment. From this springs the violence, prejudice and hatred that women, persons of colour, gays and lesbians confront on a daily basis.

Interpretive interactionism and late postmodern everyday life

'All classic social scientists have been concerned with the salient characteristics of their time' (Mills 1959: 165). This means they have been preoccupied with how history and human nature are being made within their historical moment. They have been concerned with the variety and types of men, women and children, who have prevailed in any given historical moment (Mills 1959: 165). At least four previous epochs have captured human history: Antiquity, the Middle Ages, the Modern Age and now the Fourth Epoch or 'the postmodern period' (Mills 1959: 166). The last two decades of the 20th century and the first decade of the 21st century find us in the middle of the late postmodern period, which began after the Second World War. This is the age of multinational corporations, of satellite communication systems, of an interdependent world economy, of racism and racial injustice, of single-parent families, day-care children, working mothers, the 'greying' of America, the threat of nuclear annihilation, environmental destruction, the increased domination of biomedical technologies, problems with drug and alcohol addiction, armed confrontations in the Middle East, Central America and Southern Africa, and so on.

The late postmodern period is one in which advertising, the mass media, especially television and the computer, have gained ever greater control over human lives and human experience. This is an age in which problematic experiences are given meaning in the media. Social objects have become commodities. Human experience and social relationships have also become commodities, as anyone who scans the travel sections of the Sunday newspapers, with their supplements on holiday tours, can quickly confirm. It is also an age marked by nostalgia for the past. Extreme self-interest and personal gain, coupled with the ostentatious display of material possessions, characterize the lifestyle of many today. At the same time massive anxieties at the level of the personal and the social are felt. According to some sources one in three American adults are now seeking psychotherapy and other forms of professional help for their individual problems. This is an age of personal unrest in which individual, family, sexual, leisure and work experiences are becoming more and more problematic (Lemert 1997: 159).

Interpretive interactionism in the late postmodern period is committed to understanding how this historical moment universalizes itself in the lives of interacting individuals. Each person and each relationship studied is assumed to be a universal singular, or a single instance of the universal themes that structure the late postmodern period. Each person is touched by the mass media, by alienation, by the economy, by the new family and child-care systems, by the increasing technologizing of the social world and by the threat of nuclear annihilation. Interpretive interactionism fits itself to the relation between the individual and society, to the nexus of biography and society. Interpretive interactionism attempts to show how individual troubles and problems become public issues. In the discovery of this nexus, it attempts to bring alive the existentially problematic, often hidden, and private experiences that give meaning to everyday life as it is lived in this moment in history.

To make the invisible more visible to others is, after all, a major goal of the interpreter (Merleau-Ponty 1968). This means that we want to capture the stories of everyday persons as they tell about the pains, the agonies, the emotional experiences, the small and the large victories, the traumas, the fears, the anxieties, the dreams, fantasies and hopes in their lives. We want to make those stories available to others. This is an ongoing interpretive project. Its challenge is clear: to represent and perform the many different ways in which humans make and inscribe history, but not under circumstances of their own choosing (see Willis and Trondman 2000: 6).

Ben Agger says we want a good sociology that is 'unashamed in its advocacy'. This is a public sociology that addresses 'social problems accessibly' (Agger 2000: 257) and does so with good writing. But there is more to good writing than just this. In 1972, Laurel Richardson was almost killed in an automobile accident. Two years later she returned to her writing table. Speaking of the centrality of writing in her life, she stated, 'Writing was the method through which I constituted the world and reconstituted myself' (Richardson 1999: 89). She learned that she was 'writing for her life' (Richardson 1999: 89). We are writing for our lives and for the lives of others as well, for our words matter. The sociologist's voice must speak to the terrible and magnificent world of human experience in the first years of the 21st century. And so, in the eighth moment, at the beginning of the 21st century, we confront the pressing demand to show

how the practices of critical, interpretive interactionist qualitative research can help change the world in positive ways. This is what this chapter has been all about.

Notes

1. I wish to thank Michael Hviid Jacobsen for his constructive comments on and many ideas for this chapter.
2. This chapter draws on and reworks materials from Denzin (1989, 1992, 1995, 1997, 2001, 2003, 2007).
3. Interpretive interactionism, as a perspective and method, has received considerable interest and attention in the social science community (see Schwandt 2000; Carspecken 1996; Creswell 2007; Coffey 1999; Charmaz 2000; Gubrium and Holstein 1997; Hollway and Jefferson 2000).
4. Denzin and Lincoln (2005:14–20) define eight moments of qualitative inquiry, all of which operate in the present, as follows: 'the traditional' (1900–1950), 'the modernist' (1950–1970), 'blurred genres' (1970–1986), 'the crisis of representation' (1986–1990) 'post-modern or experimental' (1990 to 1995), 'post-experimental' (1995–2000), the 'contested present' (2000–2005) and 'the future'.
5. The following section reworks Denzin (1997:115–20).
6. While this narrative could be divided into speaking parts, when first performed, Troy Anthony LaRaviere delivered it as a dramatic monologue.

Bibliography

Agger, Ben (2000) *Public Sociology: From Social Facts to Literary Acts*. New York: Rowman & Littlefield.

Allport, Gordon W. (1942) *The Use of Personal Documents in Psychological Research*. New York: Social Science Research Council.

Bazin, Andre (1967) *What Is Cinema?* Berkeley, CA: University of California Press.

Blumer, Herbert (1969) *Symbolic Interactionism*. Englewood Cliffs, NJ: Prentice-Hall.

Campuzano, Hugo (2001) 'In the name of tradition.' Unpublished mystory text, University of Illinois, Institute of Communications Research, Urbana.

Carspecken, Phil Frances (1996) *Critical Ethnography in Educational Research*. New York: Routledge.

Charmaz, Kathy (2000) 'Grounded theory: objectivist and constructivist methods', in Norman K. Denzin and Yvonna S. Lincoln (eds), *Handbook of Qualitative Research*, 2nd Edition. Thousand Oaks, CA: Sage.

Cho, Joo-Hyun (1987) *A Social Phenomenological Understanding of Family Violence: The Case of Korea*. Unpublished doctoral dissertation, Department of Sociology, University of Illinois, Urbana.

Cho, Joo-Hyun (1988) *Battered Wives: Violence and Ressentiment in the Korean Family*. New York: Aldine de Gruyter.

Coffey, Amanda (1999) *The Ethnographic Self*. London: Sage.

Creswell, John W. (2007) *Qualitative Inquiry and Research Design: Choosing Among Five Traditions*. Thousand Oaks, CA: Sage.

Denzin, Norman K. (1989) *Interpretive Biography*. Thousand Oaks, CA: Sage.
Denzin, Norman K. (1992) *Cultural Studies and Symbolic Interactionism*. Oxford: Blackwell.
Denzin, Norman K. (1993) *The Addiction Society*. New Brunswick, NJ: Transaction.
Denzin, Norman K. (1995) *The Cinematic Society*. London: Sage.
Denzin, Norman K. (1997) *Interpretive Ethnography*. Thousand Oaks, CA: Sage.
Denzin, Norman K. (2001) *Interpretive Interactionism*, 2nd edition. Thousand Oaks, CA: Sage.
Denzin, Norman K. (2003) *Performance Ethnography*. Thousand Oaks, CA: Sage.
Denzin, Norman K. (2007) *On Understanding Emotion* (with a new introduction by the author). New Brunswick, NJ: Transaction.
Denzin, Norman K. (2008) *Searching for Yellowstone: Race, Gender, Family and Memory in the Postmodern West*. Walnut Creek, CA: Left Coast Press.
Denzin, Norman K. and Yvonna S. Lincoln (2005) 'Introduction: the discipline and practice of qualitative research', in Norman K. Denzin and Yvonna S. Lincoln (eds), *Handbook of Qualitative Research*, 3rd edition. Thousand Oaks, CA: Sage.
Fontana, Andrea (2007) 'Short stories from the salt', in Joseph A. Kotarba and John M. Johnson (eds), *Postmodern Existential Sociology*. Walnut Creek, CA: AltaMira.
Foucault, Michel (2000) *Power: Essential Works of Foucault, 1954–1984*, Vol. 3. New York: New Press.
Freire, Paulo (1998) *Pedagogy of Freedom: Ethics, Democracy and Civic Courage*. Boulder, CO: Roman & Littlefield.
Garfinkel, Harold (1967) *Studies in Ethnomethodology*. Englewood Cliffs, NJ: Prentice-Hall.
Garfinkel, Harold, Michael Lynch and Eric Livingston (1981) 'The work of a discovering science construed with material from the optically discovered pulsar.' *Philosophy of the Social Sciences*, 11: 131–58.
Goffman, Erving (1959) *The Presentation of Self in Everyday Life*. New York: Doubleday.
Goffman, Erving (1961a) *Asylums*. New York: Doubleday.
Goffman, Erving (1961b) *Encounters*. Indianapolis: Bobbs-Merrill.
Goffman, Erving (1967) *Interaction Ritual*. New York: Doubleday.
Goffman, Erving (1971) *Relations in Public*. New York: Basic Books.
Goffman, Erving (1974) *Frame Analysis*. New York: Harper & Row.
Goffman, Erving (1981) *Forms of Talk*. Philadelphia: University of Pennsylvania Press.
Goffman, Erving (1983) 'The Interaction Order.' *American Sociological Review*, 48: 1–17.
Gubrium, Jaber F. and James A. Holstein (1997) *The New Language of Qualitative Method*. New York: Oxford University Press.
Hollway, Wendy and Tony Jefferson (2000) *Doing Qualitative Research Differently*. London: Sage.
Jameson, Fredric (1990) *Signatures of the Visible*. New York: Routledge.
Johnson, John M. and Joseph A. Kotarba (2007) 'Postmodern existentialism', in Joseph A. Kotarba and John M. Johnson (eds), *Postmodern Existential Sociology*. Walnut Creek, CA: AltaMira.
Joyce, James (1976) 'The Dubliners', in Harry Levin (ed.), *The Portable James Joyce*. New York: Penguin.
Kotarba, Joseph A. (2007) 'Preface', in Joseph A. Kotarba and John M. Johnson (eds), *Postmodern Existential Sociology*. Walnut Creek, CA: AltaMira.
LaRaviere, Troy Anthony (2001) 'Remembering me.' Unpublished mystory text, University of Illinois, Institute of Communications Research, Urbana.
Lemert, Charles (1997) *Postmodernism Is Not What You Think*. Oxford: Blackwell.
Levin, Harry (1976) 'Editor's preface', in *The Portable James Joyce*. New York: Penguin.

Merleau-Ponty, Maurice (1968) *The Visible and the Invisible*. Evanston, IL: Northwestern University Press.

Mills, Charles Wright (1959) *The Sociological Imagination*. New York: Oxford University Press.

Mills, Charles Wright (1963) *Power, Politics and People: The Collected Essays of C. Wright Mills* (edited with an Introduction by Irving Louis Horowitz). New York: Ballantine.

Olesen, Virgina (2005) 'Early millennial feminist qualitative research: challenges and contours', in Norman K. Denzin and Yvonna S. Lincoln (eds), *Handbook of Qualitative Research*, 3rd edition. Thousand Oaks, CA: Sage.

Ortner, Sherry B. (1997) 'Introduction.' *Representation*, 59: 1–13.

Pike, Kenneth (1954) *Language in Relation to an Unified Theory of the Structure of Human Behavior*, Vol. 1. Glendale, CA: Summer Institute of Linguistics.

Raines, Howell (1986) 'Review of *Bearing the Cross: Martin Luther King Jr. and the Southern Christian Leadership Conference* by David J. Garrow.' *New York Review of Books* (30 November): 133–4.

Richardson, Laurel (1999) 'Paradigms lost.' *Symbolic Interaction*, 22: 79–91.

Rosaldo, Renato (1984) 'Grief and a headhunter's rage: on the cultural force of emotions', in Edward M. Bruner (ed.), *Text, Play and Story: The Construction and Reconstruction of Self and Society*. Washington, DC: American Ethnological Society.

Sartre, Jean-Paul (1956) *Being and Nothingness*, trans.Hazel Bames. New York: Philosophical Library.

Sartre, Jean-Paul (1963) *Search for a Method*. New York: Alfred Knopf.

Sartre, Jean-Paul (1981) *The Family Idiot: Gustave Flaubert, 1821–1857, Vol. I.* Chicago, IL: University of Chicago Press.

Schwandt, Thomas A. (2000) 'Three epistemological stances for qualitative inquiry', in Norman K. Denzin and Yvonna S. Lincoln (eds), *Handbook of Qualitative Research*, 2nd edition. Thousand Oaks, CA: Sage.

Scheler, Max (1912/1961) *Ressentiment*. New York: Free Press.

Strauss, Anselm L. (1959) *Mirrors and Masks: The Search for Identity*. Glencoe, IL: Free Press.

Strauss, Anselm L. (1987) *Qualitative Analysis for Social Scientists*. New York: Cambridge University Press.

Turner, Victor W. (1986) 'Dewey, Dilthey, and drama: an essay in the anthropology of experience', in Victor W. Turner and Edward M. Bruner (eds), *The Anthropology of Experience*. Urbana, IL: University of Illinois Press.

Ulmer, Gregory (1989) *Teletheory*. New York: Routledge.

Ulmer, Gregory (1994) *Heuretics*. Baltimore: Johns Hopkins University Press.

Warren, Robert Penn (1959) *All the King's Men*. New York: Bantam.

Willis, P. and Trondman, M. (2000) 'Manifesto for ethnography.' *Ethnography* 1 (1): 5–16.

Index

T